Hideko S. Kunii   Sushil Jajodia
Arne Sølvberg (Eds.)

Conceptual Modeling – ER 2001

20th International Conference
on Conceptual Modeling
Yokohama, Japan, November 27-30, 2001
Proceedings

Springer

Series Editors

Gerhard Goos, Karlsruhe University, Germany
Juris Hartmanis, Cornell University, NY, USA
Jan van Leeuwen, Utrecht University, The Netherlands

Volume Editors

Hideko S. Kunii
Ricoh Company, Ltd., Software Research Center
1-1-17 Koishikawa, Bunkyo-ku, Tokyo 112-0002, Japan
E-mail: hkunii@src.ricoh.co.jp

Sushil Jajodia
George Mason University, Center for Secure Information Systems
Mail Stop 4A4, Fairfax, VA 22030-4444, USA
E-mail: jajodia@gmu.edu

Arne Sølvberg
The Norwegian University of Science and Technology
Department of Computer and Information Science
7491 Trondheim, Norway
E-mail: Arne.Soelvberg@idi.ntnu.no

Cataloging-in-Publication Data applied for

Die Deutsche Bibliothek - CIP-Einheitsaufnahme

Conceptual modeling : proceedings / ER 2001, 20th International Conference on Conceptual Modeling, Yokohama, Japan, November 27 - 30, 2001. Hideko S. Kunii ... (ed.). - Berlin ; Heidelberg ; New York ; Barcelona ; Hong Kong ; London ; Milan ; Paris ; Tokyo : Springer, 2001
 (Lecture notes in computer science ; Vol. 2224)
 ISBN 3-540-42866-6

CR Subject Classification (1998): H.2, H.4, F.4.1, I.2.4, H.1, J.1, D.2, C.2

ISSN 0302-9743
ISBN 3-540-42866-6 Springer-Verlag Berlin Heidelberg New York

This work is subject to copyright. All rights are reserved, whether the whole or part of the material is concerned, specifically the rights of translation, reprinting, re-use of illustrations, recitation, broadcasting, reproduction on microfilms or in any other way, and storage in data banks. Duplication of this publication or parts thereof is permitted only under the provisions of the German Copyright Law of September 9, 1965, in its current version, and permission for use must always be obtained from Springer-Verlag. Violations are liable for prosecution under the German Copyright Law.

Springer-Verlag Berlin Heidelberg New York
a member of BertelsmannSpringer Science+Business Media GmbH

http://www.springer.de

© Springer-Verlag Berlin Heidelberg 2001
Printed in Germany

Typesetting: Camera-ready by author, data conversion by Boller Mediendesign
Printed on acid-free paper   SPIN: 10840957   06/3142   5 4 3 2 1 0

Message from the Conference Chair

The 20th International Conference on Conceptual Modeling (ER 2001) was the first ER conference in the 21st Century as well as the first ER conference held in Japan. It was a great honor and pleasure to host such a memorable conference in Yokohama, an exotic and fashionable seafront city. We were particularly pleased with the high quality of the ER 2001 papers, which were gathered from all over the world.

The technical program of the conference was selected by the Program Committee. Co-chairs were Hideko S. Kunii, Arne Sølvberg, and Sushil Jajodia, and they all did an excellent job. Firstly, I would like to express my appreciation to these PC Co-chairs, and all the staff who worked for H. Kunii at Ricoh as well.

In addition to the research papers, industrial presentations and invited papers, the conference program included four workshops, three short tutorials, and one panel discussion. Workshop Co-chairs, Yahiko Kambayashi and Hiroshi Arisawa, Tutorial Chair, Katsumi Tanaka, and Panel Chair, Sudha Ram all deserve appreciation and recognition.

I would also like to express my special thanks to the other members of the ER 2001 organization team. Steering Committee member Stefano Spaccapietra was in charge of liaison. Hirotaka Sakai, Tok Wang Ling, David Embley, and Mokrane Bouzeghoub assisted us as coordinators. Ryosuke Hotaka made an important contribution to ER 2001 by obtaining support and cooperation from mainly Japanese corporations. Hiroshi Arisawa and Takashi Tomii (Local Arrangement Co-chairs), Kazumasa Yokota (Publicity Chair and Web Master), Michiko Kitagawa (Treasurer and Assistant to the PC Co-chair, H. Kunii), and Mana Nakayama (Registration Chair and Assistant to the Conference Chair, Y. Ishii) all worked hard and contributed to the success of the conference.

Finally, I would like to express my appreciation to Yokohama National University and its President, Dr. Hiroshi Itagaki, for the special support and cooperation.

November 2001   Yoshioki Ishii

Message from the Program Chairs

In this, the first year of the 21st century, the series of International Conferences on Conceptual Modeling (known in short as ER conferences) reached its 20th edition. Continuing a long tradition, the 20th International Conference on Conceptual Modeling (ER 2001) provided an international forum for presenting and discussing current research and applications with the common interest of conceptual modeling.

Our emphasis this year was on internet-based information modeling and systems. Remarkable progress in computers and networking has changed our way of doing business as well as our personal living environment. Business practices are being forced to dramatically evolve to face challenges from worldwide competition, where information and information services play a key role. Individuals are learning to move in a world of over-abundant information, where everything is available to everyone but difficult to find. In both cases conceptual modeling provides a path to semantically rich and meaningful information exchange and thus plays an essential role, particularly in supporting the internet-based information revolution.

ER 2001 covered a wide spectrum of conceptual modeling, from theoretical foundations to implementation. We invited researchers and practitioners from both computer sciences and management information systems to present and share their advances: new ideas and new approaches as well as fruitful experiences and informative experiments.

Acceptance into the conference proceedings was very competitive this year. We received 197 submissions all together. The program committee selected 39 regular papers out of 182 – an acceptance rate of approximately 21%, and 6 industrial presentations out of 15 – an acceptance rate of 40%.

In addition, we were indeed honored to include three very distinguished Keynote Speakers whose abstracts and papers present trends in emerging technologies. Dennis Tsichritzis, an outstanding leader in the field, spoke to us on "The Role of Research in the New Economy." Umeshwar Dayal, a distinguished researcher, presented "Conceptual Modeling for Collaborative E-Business Processes." Our third speaker was the father of i-mode, Kei-ichi Enoki, who jump-started the success of the mobile internet business.

The conference would not have been a success without the help of the many volunteers who worked hard to make this conference a success. First, we thank the members of the Technical Program Committee and the external reviewers for their countless hours reviewing the papers. Katsumi Tanaka and Sudha Ram organized a very interesting tutorial program, and timely panel, respectively. Yahiko Kambayashi and Hiroshi Arisawa did a wonderful job bringing together four outstanding workshops on emerging topics. The next debt of thanks goes to Kohki Ohhira and Ricoh Co., Ltd., for maintaining the online reviewing software and hosting the site that handled the submission, distribution, and review of the papers. The software was originally developed for ER 2000 at Salt Lake City by Stephen Liddle who also provided us with valuable advice. We extend very sincere thanks to the members of the Software Research Center of Ricoh

Co., Ltd., including Masumi Narita, Phyllis Anwyl, and Masayuki Kameda for their assistance with Program Committee activities. Finally, we are extremely indebted to Michiko Kitagawa for her devotion to the administrative support at all stages of the conference.

We hope that you found ER 2001 to be stimulating, interesting, and informative.

November 2001   Hideko S. Kunii, Sushil Jajodia, and Arne Sølvberg

Sponsorship

Sponsored by:

- Yokohama National University
- Information Processing Society of Japan (IPSJ)
- ER Institute (ER Steering Committee)

In cooperation with:

- ACM, ACM SIGMOD, and ACM SIGMOD Japan
- The Institute of Electronics, Information and Communication Engineers (IEICE)
- Consortium for Business Object Promotion (CBOP)
- IMS Promotion Center, Manufacturing Science and Technology Center
- DAMA International

Corporate Sponsors:

- Ascential Software K.K.
- Beacon IT Inc.
- Microsoft Company, Ltd.
- Oracle Corporation Japan
- Ricoh Company, Ltd.

ER 2001 Conference Organization

Conference Chair
Yoshioki Ishii (Beacon IT Inc.)

Program Co-chairs
Hideko S. Kunii (Ricoh Co., Ltd.)
Arne Sølvberg (Norwegian University of Science and Technology)
Sushil Jajodia (George Mason University)

Organization Supporters' Committee Chair
Ryosuke Hotaka (Tokyo University of Technology)

Steering Committee Liaison
Stefano Spaccapietra (Swiss Federal Institute of Technology, Lausanne)

Coordinators
Japan: Hirotaka Sakai (Chuo University)
Asia: Tok Wang Ling (National University of Singapore)
Europe: Mokrane Bouzeghoub (University of Versailles)
U.S.A.: David W. Embley (Brigham Young University)

Tutorial Chair
Katsumi Tanaka (Kyoto University)

Workshop Co-chairs
Yahiko Kambayashi (Kyoto University)
Hiroshi Arisawa (Yokohama National University)

Panel Chair
Sudha Ram (University of Arizona)

Publicity Chair/Web Master
Kazumasa Yokota (Okayama Prefectural University)

Local Arrangements Co-chairs
Hiroshi Arisawa (Yokohama National University)
Takashi Tomii (Yokohama National University)

Treasurer
Michiko Kitagawa (Ricoh Co., Ltd.)

Registration Chair
Mana Nakayama (Beacon IT Inc.)

Tutorials

Modeling B2B Integration
Christoph Bussler (Oracle Corporation, U.S.A.)

Knowledge Management for E-business
Larry Kerschberg (George Mason University, U.S.A.)

Workshops

HUMACS 2001
International Workshop on Conceptual Modeling of Human/Organizational/Social Aspects of Manufacturing Activities
General Chair: Hiroshi Arisawa

DASWIS 2001
International Workshop on Data Semantics in Web Information Systems
General Chair: Vijay Kumar

eCOMO 2001
Conceptual Modeling Approaches for E-business
General Chair: Heinrich C. Mayr

DAMA International Workshop
Global Data Modeling in the New Millennium
General Chair Committee: Michael Brackett and Ingrid Batiste Hunt

Program Committee

Gail-Joon Ahn, U.S.A.
Vijay Atluri, U.S.A.
Claudio Bettini, Italy
Terje Brasethvik, Norway
KJ Byeon, Korea
Sang K. Cha, Korea
Chin-Chen Chang, Taiwan
Arbee L.P. Chen, Taiwan
Roger Chiang, U.S.A.
Wesley Chu, U.S.A.
Panos Constantopoulos, Greece
Umeshwar Dayal, U.S.A.
Jan Dietz, The Netherlands
Johann Eder, Austria
Ramez Elmasri, U.S.A.
Tetsuya Furukawa, Japan
Joe Giordano, U.S.A.
Terry Halpin, U.S.A.
Shuji Harashima, Japan
Sumi Helal, U.S.A.
Teruhisa Hochin, Japan
Hiroshi Ishikawa, Japan
Matthias Jarke, Germany
Christian S. Jensen, Denmark
Manfred Jeusfeld, The Netherlands
Paul Johannesson, Sweden
Yahiko Kambayashi, Japan
Hannu Kangassalo, Finland
Hirofumi Katsuno, Japan
Hiroyuki Kitagawa, Japan
Yasushi Kiyoki, Japan
Michiharu Kudo, Japan
Takeo Kunishima, Japan
Alberto Laender, Brazil
Byung Suk Lee, U.S.A.
Chiang Lee, Taiwan
Dik Lun Lee, Hong Kong
Mong Li Lee, Singapore
Sukho Lee, Korea
Yoon-Joon Lee, Korea
Michel Leonard, Switzerland
Qing Li, China

Stephen Liddle, U.S.A
Tok Wang Ling, Singapore
Peng Liu, U.S.A.
Leszek A. Maciaszek, Australia
A. K. Majumdar, India
Luigi Mancini, Italy
Salvatore March, U.S.A.
Yoshifumi Masunaga, Japan
Peter McBrien, UK
Vojislav B Misic, Hong Kong
Rokia Missaoui, Canada
Renate Motschnig, Austria
Ravi Mukkamala, U.S.A.
John Mylopoulos, Canada
Antoni Olive, Spain
Maria E. Orlowska, Australia
Brajendra Panda, U.S.A.
Oscar Pastor, Spain
Barbara Pernici, Italy
Sudha Ram, U.S.A.
Collette Rolland, France
Pierangela Samarati, Italy
Sumit Sarkar, U.S.A.
Gunter Schlageter, Germany
Peretz Shoval, Israel
Keng Siau, U.S.A.
Ken Smith, U.S.A.
Il-Yeol Song, U.S.A.
Ju-Won Song, Korea
Veda Storey, U.S.A.
Wonhee Sull, Korea
Keishi Tajima, Japan
Bernhard Thalheim, Germany
Ramesh Venkataraman, U.S.A.
Yair Wand, Canada
X. Sean Wang, U.S.A.
Kyu-Young Whang, Korea
Roel Wieringa, The Netherlands
Alec Yasinsac, U.S.A.
Yelena Yesha, U.S.A.
Masatoshi Yoshikawa, Japan

External Referees

Toshiyuki Amagasa
Mordechai Ban-Menachem
Maria Bergholtz
Thomas Berkel
Anke Biedebach
Birgit Bomsdorf
Nicolo Cesa-Bianchi
Shermann Chan
Chao-Chun Chen
Sophie Chessa-Dupuy
Dickson K.W. Chiu
Vassilis Christophides
Cecil Chua
Ajantha Dahanayake
Pascal van Eck
Joerg Evermann
Leonidas Fegaras
Birgit Feldmann
C.W. Fung
Ehud Gudes
Jon Atle Gulla
Rakesh Gupta
Hyoil Han
Kenji Hatano
Bart-Jan Hommes
Jia-Lien Hsu
Eenjun Hwang
Atsushi Iizawa
Satosi Imago
Marta Indulska
Hiromu Ishii
Yoshiharu Ishikawa
Katsumi Kanasaki
Kaoru Katayama
Akinori Kawachi
Goshima Kazumasa
Chih-Horng Ke
Vijay Khatri
Hyoung Do Kim
Christian Koncilia
Yongsik Kwon
Frank Laskowski
Dongwon Lee
Guanling Lee
Jong-Hyun Lee
Ryong Lee
Huagang Li
Xiaobai Li
Edgar Chia-Han Lin
Youzhong Liu
Zhenyu Liu
Akira Maeda
Oscar Mangisengi
Inderjeet Mani
Wenlei Mao
Jie Meng
Bongki Moon
Atsuyuki Morishima
Ralf Muhlberger
Makoto Murata
Eng Koon Sze
Dorit Nevo
Selmin Nurcan
Ying-Lie O
Leo Obrst
Manabu Ohta
Chang Il Park
Jangho Park
Amir Parssian
Torben Bach Pedersen
Vicente Pelechano
Dieter Pfoser
Dimitris Plexousakis
Ivan S. Radev
Young Ryu
Shazia Sadiq
Karsten Schulz
Yipeng Shen
Michael E. Shin
Norihide Shinagawa
Altigran Soares da Silva
Paulo Pinheiro da Silva
Giedrius Slivinskas
Martin Steeg
Erlend Tosebro
Pit Koon Teo
Manos Theodorakis
Nectaria Tryfona

Yannis Tzitzikas
Naohiko Uramoto
Petko Valtchev
Sabrina De Capitani di Vimercati
Yi-Hung Wu
Jianliang Xu
Yohei Yamamoto

Michiko Yasukawa
Kuo-Her Yen
Manen Ying
Yusuke Yokota
Baihua Zheng
Xiaofang Zhou

Table of Contents

Keynote

Conceptual Modeling for Collaborative E-business Processes 1
Qiming Chen, Umeshwar Dayal, and Meichun Hsu

"i-mode", Now & Future 17
Kei-ichi Enoki

The Role of Research in the New Economy 19
Dennis Tsichritzis

Panel

Semantic B2B Integration: Is Modeling the Superior Approach over
Programming? 26
Christoph Bussler

Spatial Database

Modeling Topological Constraints in Spatial Part-Whole Relationships 27
Rosanne Price, Nectaria Tryfona, and Christian S. Jensen

Source Description-Based Approach for the Modeling of Spatial
Information Integration 41
Yoshiharu Ishikawa and Hiroyuki Kitagawa

Topological Relationships of Complex Points and Complex Regions 56
Thomas Behr and Markus Schneider

Spatial and Temporal Databases

DISTIL: A Design Support Environment for Conceptual Modeling of
Spatio-temporal Requirements 70
Sudha Ram, Richard T. Snodgrass, Vijay Khatri, and Yousub Hwang

Tripod: A Comprehensive Model for Spatial and Aspatial Historical
Objects 84
*Tony Griffiths, Alvaro A.A. Fernandes, Norman W. Paton,
Keith T. Mason, Bo Huang, and Michael Worboys*

A Design of Topological Predicates for Complex Crisp and Fuzzy
Regions 103
Markus Schneider

XML

A Semantic Approach to XML-based Data Integration 117
  Patricia Rodríguez-Gianolli and John Mylopoulos

A Rule-Based Conversion of a DTD to a Conceptual Schema 133
  Ronaldo dos Santos Mello and Carlos Alberto Heuser

Semantic Data Modeling Using XML Schemas 149
  Murali Mani, Dongwon Lee, and Richard. R. Muntz

Information Modeling

Modelling Strategic Actor Relationships to Support Intellectual Property
Management 164
  Eric Yu, Lin Liu, and Ying Li

SiteLang: Conceptual Modeling of Internet Sites 179
  Bernhard Thalheim and Antje Düsterhöft

A Frame Work for Modeling Electronic Contracts 193
  Kamalakar Karlapalem, Ajay R. Dani, and P. Radha Krishna

Database Design

CASE Tool Support for Temporal Database Design 208
  Virginie Detienne and Jean-Luc Hainaut

Domain-Specific Metadata a Key for Building Semantically-Rich Schema
Models 225
  Abdel-Rahman H. Tawil, Nicholas J. Fiddian, and William A. Gray

Coping with Inconsistent Constraint Specifications 241
  Sven Hartmann

Data Integration

Integration of Biological Data and Quality-Driven Source Negotiation 256
  Laure Berti-Equille

Accessing Data Integration Systems through Conceptual Schemas 270
  *Andrea Calì, Diego Calvanese, Giuseppe De Giacomo,
  and Maurizio Lenzerini*

Resolving Conflicts and Handling Replication during Integration of
Multiple Databases by Object Deputy Model 285
  Zhiyong Peng and Yahiko Kambayashi

Data Warehouse

Efficient Execution of Range-Aggregate Queries in Data Warehouse
Environments 299
Seokjin Hong, Byoungho Song, and Sukho Lee

A Pragmatic Approach to Conceptual Modeling of OLAP Security 311
Torsten Priebe and Günther Pernul

A Randomized Approach for the Incremental Design of an Evolving Data
Warehouse 325
*Dimitri Theodoratos, Theodore Dalamagas, Alkis Simitsis,
and Manos Stavropoulos*

UML

Semantics of Stereotypes for Type Specification in UML: Theory and
Practice 339
François Pinet and Ahmed Lbath

Towards Ontologically Based Semantics for UML Constructs 354
Joerg Evermann and Yair Wand

Developing Sequence Diagrams in UML 368
Il-Yeol Song

Conceptual Models

Translation of a High-Level Temporal Model into Lower Level Models:
Impact of Modelling at Different Description Levels 383
Peter Kraft and Jens Otto Sørensen

Relationship Type Refinement in Conceptual Models with Multiple
Classification 397
Dolors Costal, Antoni Olivé, and Ernest Teniente

A Metamodel for Part – Whole Relationships for Reasoning on Missing
Parts and Reconstruction 412
Martin Doerr, Dimitris Plexousakis, and Chryssoyla Bekiari

System Design

Developing XML Documents with Guaranteed "Good" Properties 426
David W. Embley and Wai Y. Mok

Dimension Hierarchies Design from UML Generalizations and
Aggregations 442
Jacky Akoka, Isabelle Comyn-Wattiau, and Nicolas Prat

Minimize Mark-Up ! Natural Writing Should Guide the Design of Textual
Modeling Frontends 456
   Markus Lepper, Baltasar Trancón y Widemann, and Jacob Wieland

Method Reengineering and Video Databases

An Approach for Method Reengineering 471
   Jolita Ralyté and Colette Rolland

Modeling and Structuring Multiple Perspective Video for Browsing 485
   Yoshihiro Nakanishi, Tatsuo Hirose, and Katsumi Tanaka

Modeling Dynamic Objects in Video Databases: A Logic Based
Approach 499
   Biswajit Acharya, Arun K. Majumdar, and Jayanta Mukherjee

Workflows

Pockets of Flexibility in Workflow Specification 513
   Shazia Sadiq, Wasim Sadiq, and Maria Orlowska

Agent-Oriented Enterprise Modeling Based on Business Rules 527
   Kuldar Taveter and Gerd Wagner

A Three-Layer Model for Workflow Semantic Recovery in an
Object-Oriented Environment 541
   Dickson K.W. Chiu

Web Information System

Recognizing Ontology-Applicable Multiple-Record Web Documents 555
   David W. Embley, Yiu-Kai Ng, and Li Xu

Querying Web Information Systems 571
   Klaus-Dieter Schewe

A Conceptual Modelling Framework for Standards-Driven Web-Based
Distance Learning.. 585
   Luis Anido, Martín Llamas, Manuel J. Fernández, Judith Rodríguez,
   Juan Santos, and Manuel Caeiro

Applications

XML-schema Dynamic Mapped Multimedia Content Description Tool 599
   Takayuki Kunieda and Yuki Wakita

Constructing a Data Map of Korea Telecom 602
   Eunsook Jin, Jungmin Seo, Kwangjoon Lee, and Ju-won Song

Competency of Set Analysis in CRM Closed Loop Marketing 604
Tatsuo Oba

Software Engineering

XML-based E2E Test Report Management 607
Ray Paul, Wei-Tek Tsai, Bing Li, and Xiaoying Bai

A Framework for Reusing Business Objects by Multilevel Object
Patterns 609
Hajime Horiuchi, Masaharu Obayashi, and Yoshihide Nagase

A Mediation System Based on Universal Relation Modeling 611
*Takashi Honishi, Gengo Suzuki, Nobuyuki Kobayashi,
and Kazuya Konishi*

Author Index 613

Conceptual Modeling for Collaborative E-business Processes

Qiming Chen, Umeshwar Dayal, Meichun Hsu [1]

Hewlett-Packard Laboratories
1501 Page Mill Road, Palo Alto, CA 94304, USA
dayal@hpl.hp.com

Abstract. As the Web evolves from providing information access into a platform for e-business, there is a need for modeling and automating inter-business interactions. Today, business-to-business interaction based on XML document exchange has been widely discussed. However, there is only limited technology for defining and automating these interactions at the business process level. In this paper, we introduce **Common Business Collaboration (CBC)** protocols based on common business objects, as well as **Inter-business Collaborative Processes (ICP)**. An ICP expresses process-level business interaction, while allowing complete autonomy of the internal processes at each participating party. The automation of these inter-business collaborative processes is based on a peer-to-peer implementation paradigm, rather than a single centralized process engine. An XML-based **CBC Description Language, CBCDL**, is introduced to model inter-business collaborative processes. The feasibility and practical value of this approach have been demonstrated through prototypes implemented at HP Laboratories.

1 Introduction

To support inter-business interaction among trading partners, agreement on common protocols at several levels is necessary. Such protocols must cover the vocabulary, the types of documents (or business objects) to be exchanged, the business rules of conversation, and the collaborative business processes between which the participating parties. Fig. 1 shows the layers of a technology stack to support these protocols, and example technologies available today for the different layers.

Most of the existing approaches cover limited layers of the above technology stack. For example, the vocabulary layer is covered by most of the distributed computing architectures such as CORBA [12], e-speak [15], Jini [19], etc. Consortial efforts such as the Common Business Library (CBL) [10,11] from CommerceNet cover the business object layer. BizTalk [3], SOAP [25], and the RosettaNet PIPs (Partner Interface Processes) [24], which address task–level interactions, belong to the conversation layer; ebXML [14], tpaML [26], and WSFL [29] specify business

---

[1] Current Address: Commerce One Laboratories, Cupertino, CA, USA; meichun.hsu@commerceone.com

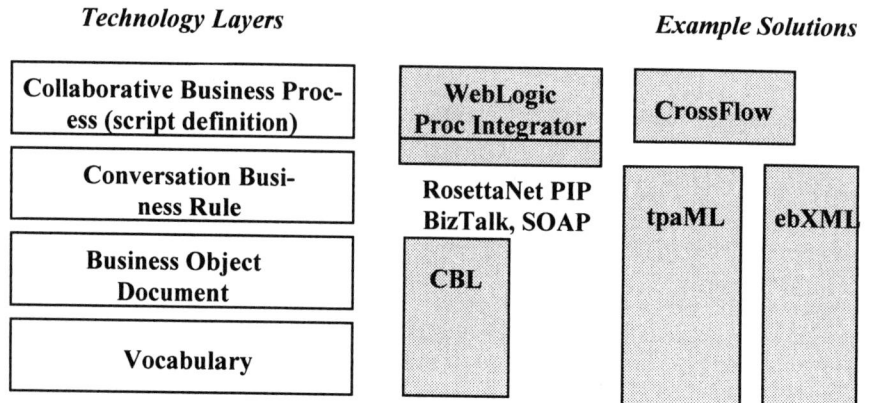

Fig. 1. Technology Stack for Inter-business Interaction

collaboration at the conversation layer as individual rules. CrossFlow [20] handles inter-process invocation at the process layer.

There is a need for an integrated approach that combines business object modeling and business process modeling, and that covers all the layers of the technology stack for business interaction. In addition to providing languages to specify bilateral business protocols, industry-wide standard templates for both business objects and business processes are necessary. Otherwise, if each pair of business partners defines its own interaction protocols, there will be too many protocols to follow, thereby making business interactions extremely complicated. We adopt the standard document templates of the Common Business Library (CBL), and introduce CBL document exchange based business processes. We extend the standard Process Definition Language, PDL, defined by the WFC (Workflow Coalition [28]).

There are two conceptually different approaches to managing inter-enterprise business processes. The first approach, typified by current products such as WebLogic Process Integrator and others, is based on the integration of different processes from the different participating enterprises, and requires the use of a single process manager as the integration point. In an inter-enterprise application, however, where each party desires to keep certain internal processing steps and data private, it is difficult to reach agreement on the use of a single process engine.

The second approach is based on reaching agreement on a common process between all participants, and synchronizing peer-executions of this common process based on commonly agreed protocols and process definitions, without relying on any centralized process manager. Toward this end, we introduce the notion of **Inter-business Collaborative Processes (ICP)**. An ICP is defined through the agreement of all the participating parties (or by standards bodies in a given industry). It is not executed on a centralized workflow engine. Instead, each execution of the ICP consists of a set of peer process instances executed collaboratively by the peer engines of the participating parties. These peer instances share the same process definition, but may have private process data and sub-processes. The peer engine of each party is used to schedule, dispatch and control the tasks that that party is responsible for, and the peer engines synchronize their progress in process execution through a messaging protocol. Further, document exchange is made through such process synchronization. In [6] we described collaborative process management from the agent cooperation point of view. In this paper we shall discuss the formal ICP protocol, and integrate it into a general inter-business collaboration framework.

Consider the following scenario, involving two parties: a buyer and a seller. The buyer-side engine, A, creates a logical instance of the purchasing process, and initiates a "buyer-side" peer instance; A then notifies the seller-side engine, B, to instantiate a "seller-side" peer instance of the purchase process. The peer process instances at both sides can be considered as autonomous, but they follow a purchasing protocol with which both the buyer and the seller are willing to comply. In the collaboration, each peer has a *role*, e.g. buyer-role or seller-role, and is responsible only for the tasks belong to its role. For example, A only manages the tasks for the buyer-role, and skips the other tasks; B only manages the tasks for the seller-role. When A finishes a task, it informs B of the task status, in order for B to proceed, and vice versa. The entire purchase process is not handled by any common server, but by the peer-to-peer cooperation of multiple servers. This scenario can be extended to include multiple parties, as illustrated in Fig. 2.

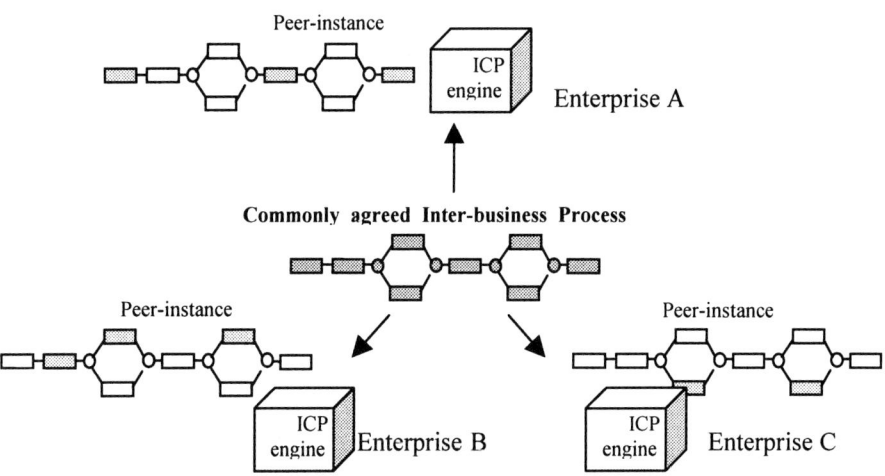

Fig. 2. Peer-to-peer inter-business collaborative process

Besides combining CBL-based object modeling and ICP-based process modeling, we also provide specifications at the conversation level, to form an integrated **Common Business Collaboration (CBC)** protocol framework. An XML [1] based

Common Business Collaboration Description Language (CBCDL) that incorporates and extends CBL and the process definition language, PDL, is developed.

Thus, our approach covers multiple layers of the technology stack for business interaction, supports business interactions by means of synchronized peer-executions of the commonly agreed process template, rather than integrating different processes at any single server. By combining CBL and ICP, we extend the goal of providing a *community standard* from business object modeling to inter-business process modeling. However, it should be understood that a CBC specification is not a complete description of the application but only a description of the interactions between the participating parties.

Section 2 describes inter-business interaction at the business object layer based on CBL document exchange. Section 3 discusses the P2P Inter-business Collaborative Process (ICP) model. Section 4 shows our CBC Description Language (CBCDL) with examples.

2 Business Interaction at the Business Object Layer

E-business interaction is based on a *document service architecture,* which takes documents as the basic business objects, and document exchange as the basic business interface. The document service architecture enables an enterprise to interact with other enterprises, while shielding it from changes in internal implementation, organization, and processes that might occur in the other enterprises. This elevates business-to-business integration from the system level (invoking applications through API function calls, as is the case with traditional distributed computing infrastructures such as CORBA) to the business level. Defining a *business interface* in terms of documents rather than APIs also allows for an incremental path to business automation, since applications can be initially handled manually through a Web browser interface, before migrating to fully automated processing.

Several XML languages, such as ebXML, e-speak, tpaML, provide the means to describe vocabulary, statements and documents. However, document based e-business interoperation requires not only standard specification tools, but also standard document templates. Otherwise, for instance, if two trading partners use different formats for purchase orders, then they cannot interoperate; if people "reinvent" business concepts for each new partnership, there will be too many types of documents; and if each pair of business partners use different bilaterally agreed document templates, it is difficult to support business interaction in a general way. This is the reason for us to support business interaction based on trading community standards, for example CBL or RosettaNet. In this paper, we will use CBL to illustrate our ideas, although a similar approach can be taken with any community standards.

The goal of CBL is to provide reusable semantic components common to many business domains. Such components can be understood by any business through their common elements (such as *address, date, part number, phone number,* etc.). CBL is made up of a set of XML building blocks and document templates commonly used in businesses. It provides vocabulary (syntax and semantics) for business concepts, as well as standard document templates for interchanging. The business concepts include

- business description primitives: *company, service, product*
- business forms: *catalog, purchase order, invoice*; and
- standard measurements: *data, time, location,* ...etc.

The document templates, for example, as published by Commerce-Net in xCBL 2.0, include PurchaseOrder, PurchaseOrderResponse, OrderStatusRequest, OrderStatusResult, Invoice, ProductCatalog, and so on. Each document has a *header*, several *core modules*, a *summary* and certain optional *attachments*. For example, PurchaseOrder has the following fields.

PurchaseOrder

Field	Content
Header	OrderHeader
Core Modules	ListOfOrderDetail
Summary	OrderSummary
Optional Attachment	Extensions

Thus, CBL has added to XML/DTD the notions of strong typing and inheritance. Furthermore, CBL documents currently are passive information objects. We extend this in the following ways.

First, associated with each type of CBL document (e.g. PurchaseOrder), an enterprise-internal business process for processing the CBL object can be specified. Accordingly, a CBL object can be used to instantiate the corresponding business process with the specific information contained in the CBL document.

Next, document level business rules can be defined based on CBL document exchange. For example, the following rule is defined based on the exchanges of three types of CBL documents in an application-specific context:

"If a *purchase order* is received, then an *invoice* and a *shipping notice* are to be sent back as reply."

Further, a legal sequence of such rules may be specified as a business process. We shall discuss later how inter-business interaction is handled as a peer-to-peer process.

Since CBL documents contain extensible attachments with changing content, it is unlikely that we can use fixed programs for document accessing and processing. Our solution is to provide tools for generating CBL-oriented data access and processing programs based on object Document Type Descriptors (DTDs). A DTD (like a schema) provides a grammar that specifies which data structures can occur, and in what sequence. Such schematic information is used to automatically generate programs for basic data access and processing, i.e. creating classes that recognize and process different data elements according to the specification of those elements. For example, from a document including tag SHIPPING_DESTINATION, it is easy to generate a Java method "getShippingDestination()", provided that the meanings of tags are understood. Automatic program generation allows tasks to be created on the fly for handling the possible extensions of document structures.

3 Inter-business Collaboration Processes (ICP)

The rule in the example given above describes a one-round conversation. Managing an inter-business application by means of individual rules offers a certain degree of flexibility, but it is difficult to scale. An inter-business application may involve concurrent, long-duration, nested tasks for document generation and processing, which are difficult to track through individual rules or single-round conversations. Rule enforcement is server-centric. While the order of rule firing can be controlled at the server site based on the logged operation states, the client is not bound by such state control. For example, a client may send the same purchase order repeatedly without a business reason.

For these reasons, we handle inter-business applications at the process level, and extend business process management from the single-server model to a multi-server peer-to-peer model. We introduce the notion and the implementation framework of Inter-business Collaborative Processes (ICP). An ICP is defined based on a commonly agreed protocol among the participating parties. The execution of an ICP is not based on a centralized workflow engine, but includes multiple individual peer process instances executed by the participating parties. The process definition is used as the common template shared by these peer process instances. The ICP engine at each peer site recognizes its own share of the tasks based on role matching. The synchronization of peer executions is made through messaging.

For example, consider two business partners, one buyer and one seller, each provided with an individual ICP engine. An ICP, such as one for on-line trading, is executed collaboratively by the two engines with each peer executing an individual instance of the common process. The server at the buyer side is responsible for scheduling and dispatching only the tasks to be executed by the buyer (e.g., preparing a purchase order, making a payment), and skips the tasks not matching the role of buyer; it simply waits for the seller side server to handle the tasks on the seller's side. The engines at both sites exchange task execution status messages for synchronization. The executions of peer process instances at both peers progresses in this way, towards their end steps.

Like any business process, an ICP is modeled as a DAG with nodes representing the steps (or tasks), and arcs representing dependencies among the steps. A *task-node* is associated with an activity to be executed either by a program (e.g. a software agent) or by a human worker. A *route-node* specifies the rules and conditions for flow control, process data update, etc. An ICP is associated with a *process data container*. When an activity is launched, a packet containing a subset of the process data, is passed to it; when it is completed, together with task status information, the data packet, possibly updated during the task execution, is sent back for reconciliation with the process data.

An ICP involves multiple parties, and explicitly specifies the *role* of each party. The process is defined based on a commonly agreed operational protocol, such as the protocol for on-line purchase or auction. Unlike a conventional process execution, which creates a single process instance, the execution of an ICP consists of a set of individual *peer process instances* run at the peer sites. These peer process instances are executed based on the same ICP definition, and synchronized through messages.

Each ICP is defined with a list of **process-roles**, indicating the logical participants. For example, a simple purchase process may have two roles, "buyer" and "seller".

Each task has a **task-role**, and that must match one of the process-roles. In the above example, tasks can have roles "buyer" and "seller".

The process data objects can be specified with sharing scopes, such as *public*, i.e. sharable by all process-roles (and thus by all peer process instances), or *process-role specific*. The role-specific data objects are accessible to the peer process instances of the given roles (one or more) only.

Let us assume that an ICP, say P, is *defined* with process-roles R_a, R_b, R_c ... . When a logical process instance of P is *created*, the players, A_a, A_b, A_c, ..., and their roles, R_a, R_b, R_c ...respectively, are specified. The player at the creating party obtains a key for this logical process, creates a peer process instance P_a for itself, and associates this key with its peer process instance. Through messaging, it also tells the participating players to create the peer process instances P_b, P_c, ..., corresponding to the roles they chose.

Assume that tasks T_i, T_j, T_k, ..., are to be executed in sequence by the players with roles R_a, R_b, R_c ... respectively.

Each *logical execution* of an ICP consists of a set of *peer process instances* run by the players (engines) of the participating parties. These peer instances observe the same process definition, but may have private process data and sub-processes. Each peer process instance has a role that must match one of the process-roles. An identifier is assigned to each logical execution of an ICP, to correlate and synchronize the peer executions of the same process; the unique identifier of that logical execution marks all the messages exchanged between the peer process instances.

Player A_a, representing the process-instance-role of R_a, dispatches and executes T_i, and upon receipt of the *task return message*, r_i, forwards it to *all* other players of the process. Then players A_a, A_b, A_c, ..., ..., all update their process states and schedule the possible next step of their own peer process instance based on that message.

When A_a, A_c, ..., proceed to activity T_j, since the roles represented by them do not match the role of T_j, they simply wait for the peer player, that is A_b in this example, to handle it at the peer site.

When A_b proceeds to activity T_j, since the role represented by A_b matches that of T_j, T_j will be handled by A_b.

The execution of peer process instances at all peers progresses in this way, towards their ends.

An important advantage gained from modeling inter-business interactions at the ICP level is the ability to preserve transactional properties. For each player, the documents exchanged, including those sent to and received from the peer players, are kept in the process data container, until all the process instances finish, and then made persistent (commit) or dropped (abort). Upon termination of the process execution, the peer engine initiating the process instance, can act as the coordinator for executing the 2-Phase Commit protocol for synchronizing peer commitment. Introducing a coordinator ensures the consistency of the commit/abort decision, without assuming the use of any global database.

A significant feature of ICP is the combination of document exchange and synchronization of peer process instances. Most of the existing approaches separate the information interface and the activity interface of inter-business collaboration. Under those approaches, such as BEA Process Integrator [2] or TPA [26], document exchanges are made at the action layer rather than at the process layer. We integrate the information and actions of a business interaction into a single ICP definition, making task flow naturally consistent with the document flow.

- o The document generation and exchange steps, e.g. preparing business documents according to appropriate business logic, are handled as process tasks.

- o The data container for document exchange is the process data container. Each peer process instance maintains an individual process data container. Each task is given a sub-set of the process data (e.g. documents) passed to or generated by the task.

o The messages for document exchange are combined with the task return messages.

An action for a task is dispatched to a software agent or a human user to perform, and upon its termination, a task return message is sent back and used to trigger the next step in process execution. Such a task return message contains not only the identification and status information, but also the subset of process data passed to or generated by the action.

When a task return message comes back to the local ICP engine, the subset of the process data passed to the action must be reconciled with the process data after returning. However, before such a message is forwarded to a peer player for synchronizing peer process execution, only the updated data elements that are shared with the player are retained (recall that the sharing scope of each data element is specified in the process definition). A forwarded task return message can carry the appropriate business documents to be delivered. This allows us to integrate document exchange with inter-enterprise collaborative process management.

4 Common Business Collaboration Description Language

To specify inter-business interaction, we have developed the Common Business Collaboration Description Language (CBCDL), which covers multiple layers of the technology stack for business collaboration.

CBC Context Specification

Collaborative business applications are grouped into Common Business Collaboration (CBC) contexts. The top-level XML structure of a CBC context is shown below.

```
<CBCcontext>
    <Header>
        ... <!-- name, create date, validated date, author, etc.-->
    </Header>
    <Roles>
        ... <!-- roles appear in the CBC of this context -->
    </Roles>
    <Docs>
        ... <!-- types of the documents that can be exchanged -->
        ... <!-- transition rules for document exchange -->
    </Docs>
    <DataTemplates>
        ... <!-- data containers to be used by the processes of this context -->
    </DataTemplates>
</CBCcontext>
```

For inter-business interaction, the role of each participating party must be distinguishable. For reusability, a CBC definition only specifies the roles rather than specific party names that can play the corresponding roles. The role definitions are included under the <Roles> tag. Each <Role> tag gives the information of a specific role, as shown in the following example.

```
<Roles>
    <Role>
        <RoleName>seller</RoleName>
        <RoleDesc> ... </RoleDesc>
    </Role>
    <Role>
        <RoleName>buyer</RoleName>
        <RoleDesc> ... </RoleDesc>
    </Role>
</Roles>
```

During business collaboration, such as executing an ICP, a party must be bound to a role to become a player of the process execution. A party may be bound to different roles in different process executions. Player specification is not part of the static ICP definition, but enclosed in the messages for initiating ICP executions. The XML structure of player specification is shown below.

```
<Players>
    <Player>
        <RoleName>seller</RoleName>
        <PlayerName>Retailer:OfficeDepot<PlayerName>
    </Player>
    ......
</Players>
```

Externally to CBC context specifications, information about the potential players, i.e., the enterprises such as Retailer:OfficeDepot, are given in a business registry, including address, email, URL and transport protocol (e.g. http), etc. It is worth noting that the binding of a player and a role is dynamic, allowing a player to play different roles in different ICP executions. In fact, a single ICP engine belonging to a party, can execute multiple ICPs concurrently, and play multiple roles simultaneously in these executions. This also makes CBCDL more flexible than tpaML.

The <docs> section specifies the legal document types allowed in this CBC context, as well as the typing rules for document exchange (conversation). Corresponding to each in-bound document for a request, there may be multiple possible out-bound documents as response. Other general properties of document exchange, such as digital signature, are optional. Conversation control is role-sensitive and context-specific, as illustrated in Fig. 3.

Conceptual Modeling for Collaborative E-business Processes   11

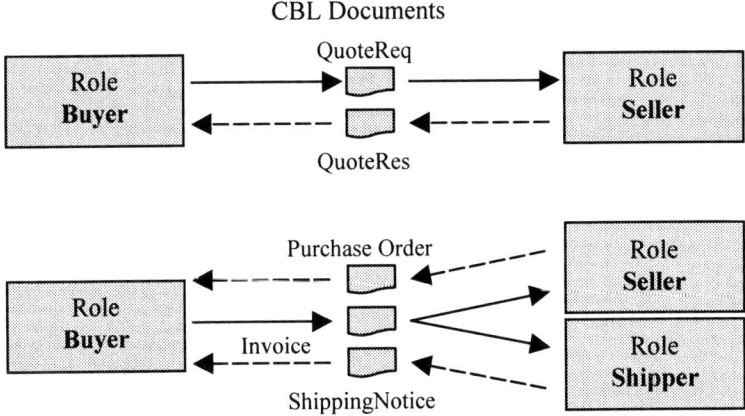

Fig. 3. Role and context based document exchange (conversation)

```
<Docs>
    <DocTypes> QuoteReq, QuoteRes, ... </DocTypes>
    <DocExchSeq>
        <Request> QuoteReq </Request>
        <Response> QuoteRes, Catolog, ... </Response>
    </DocExchSeq>
    <DocExchSeq>
        <Request Role=buyer> PurchaseOrder </Request>
        <Response Role=seller> Invoice </Response>
        <Response Role=shipper> ShippingNotice </Response>
    </DocExchSeq>
    ...
</Docs>
```

The following are also worth noting.

o   Document exchange is context sensitive, and therefore enclosed in <CBCcontext>.

o   Document exchange may be role-sensitive but optional.

o   A DataTemplate holds the definitions and initial values of process data objects, including CBL document templates. These data objects may be updated during ICP execution.

o   The process state transition as a result of document exchanging is encapsulated in ICP process definitions. The typing rules of document exchange are used to validate ICP definitions and will be enforced during process execution.

ICP Specification

In developing the ICP specification language, we start by extending the standard Process Definition Language, PDL, defined by the WFC (Workflow Coalition [28]). The ICP specification language is in XML format. When compiled, it is first translated into a DOM (Document Object Model) tree of Java objects, then into a Java class for cooperative process definition.

As an example, an ICP is specified with the following structure. Each ICP has a start point, i.e. the node with a in-bound arc with type "start"; and one or more termination points, i.e. the nodes without an out-bound arc.

```
<ICP name=... CBCcontext=...>
    <ROLES> Seller, Buyer </Roles>
    <Task name="T1">
        <Role> Buyer </Role>
        <Desc> ... </Desc>
        <Action> PurchaseOrderAction </Action>
    </Task>
    <Task name="T2">
        <Role> Seller </Role>
        <Desc> ... </Desc>
        <Action> PurchaseOrderResponseAction </Action>
    </Task>
    ...
    <RouteNode>
    ...
    </RouteNode>
    <Arc name="Arc0" type="Start"> <To>T1</To> </Arc>
    <Arc name="Arc1" type="Forward"> <From>T1</From> <To>T2</To> </Arc>
    ...
    <ProcData>
        <Role> Seller </Role>
        <Template> seller_tpl </Template>
    </ProcData>
    <ProcData>
        <Role> Buyer </Role>
        <Template> buyer_tpl </Template>
    </ProcData>
</ICP>
```

The process, tasks and process data are all role-sensitive. The list of **process-roles**, such as "buyer" and "seller", indicates the logical participants. The role of a task must match one of the process-roles. In this example, tasks can have roles "buyer" and "seller". In an inter-enterprise collaborative process execution, each party may want to keep some of the process data private. In the <ProcData> specification, a data **template** holding the definitions and initial values of process data objects (documents) can be specified with appropriate **sharing scopes**. A template or a data object specified in a template, may be *public*, i.e. sharable by all process-roles (and thus by all peer process instances) or *process-role specific*. A role-specific template is used by the peer process instances of the given roles (one or more) only, and such templates can be made different for different process-roles. Consider a collaborative process with roles "buyer", "seller" and "bank"; some data are private to "buyer"; some are sharable by "buyer" and "seller"; some are public to all three roles. A process data container can be updated or expanded at peer process run time.

Action Specification

Conceptually an action specification contains two parts: public interface and private interface.

Under the **public interface**, the *Name, Type, Version, Timeout*, etc, may be specified. The *Type* of an action can be "Regular" (default) or "Cancel" (compensate on failure). InBound and OutBound documents consistent with the typing rules of document exchange, are specified. Optionally, another action for canceling the effects of this action can be given.

Under the **private interface**, the enterprise internal dispatching information of an action is given, such as who will be the physical or logical actor for performing the action. The *Implementation* of an action can be "Automatic" (by a program), "Manual" (by a user through a Web interface), or "Process", meaning that an ICP or a private sub-process is to be invoked for that action. When an action represents a program, information about downloading that program is given.

```
            <Action>
                <Public>
                    <Name> PurchaseOrderResponseAction </Name>
                    <Type> "Regular" </Type>
                    <Desc> Process purchase order </Desc>
                    <InBound>PurchaseOrder, Catalog</InBound>
                    <OutBound>PurchaseOrderResult, Invoice, ShippingNotice
</OutBound>
                </Public>
                <Private>
                    <implementation> Automatic </Implementation>
                    <Method> PurchaseOrderProc </Method>
                    <Desc> Program for processing purchase order </Desc>
                    <Class> PurchaseOrderProc </Class>
                    <URL> file:cba.hp.com/ecarry/CBLclasses </URL>
                    <Args> ... </Args>
                </Private>
            </Action>
```

Process Nesting and Association

A task may represent a "private" sub-process. The sub-process binding is dynamic, that is, bound at run time, and this allows it to be designed separately from the host process. The process data of a private sub-process is entirely internal to the parties executing the sub-process.

A task may also represent an ICP to be executed by multiple parties collaboratively. For example, in the ICP "Payment" between a "Seller" and a "Bank", the task CheckCreditTask is executed by the peer playing the role of "Bank"; this task is performed as a sub-process, CheckCreditProcess, that is also an ICP between the "Bank" and the "Credit Bureau", without involving the peer playing the role of "Buyer". Data (documents) passed into or out from the ICP CheckCreditProcess are also specified.

```
<Task name="CheckCreditTask">
    <Role> Seller </Role>
    <Desc> Check buyer's credit for verifying payment </Desc>
    <Action> CheckCreditAction </Action>
    <OutBound> CheckCreditRequest, CheckCreditResult </OutBound>
</Task>

<Action>
    <Public>
        <Name> =" CheckCreditAction </Name>
        <Type> Regular </Type>
    </Public>
    <Private>
        <implementation> SubProc </Implementation>
        <Procss> CheckCreditProcess </Process>
    </Private>
</Action>
```

Conceptually, there is a symmetry in the sub-process relationship

- from the "purchase" process point of view, the "payment" process can be considered as a sub-process representing a necessary step of "purchase"; and
- from the "payment" process point of view, the "purchase" process can be considered as a sub-process representing a sufficient step of "payment".

In fact, in a multi-party collaboration environment, the ICPs associated in an application context actually form a *fabric*, and this is our basic view for modeling e-businesses built on one another's services. For instance, a multi-party e-business application is viewed as the composition of the following processes:

- the ICP "purchase" between the *buyer* and the *seller*,
- the ICP "payment" between the *seller* and the *bank*, and
- the ICP "credit checking" between the *bank* and the *credit bureau*.

These ICPs are associated with overlapping players. However, the parties participating in an ICP only agree on the process definition, but not necessarily on the association of that process with other processes. For example, besides the finally resulting document to be used in the process "purchase", the internal steps and data of process "CreditChecking" are invisible to the player *buyer* of the process "purchase".

5 Conclusion

We have presented the **Common Business Collaboration protocol framework**. In this work we address the combination of two key elements of inter-business interaction: common business objects and inter-enterprise process interaction. A prototype of this framework has been implemented at Hewlett-Packard Labs.

In summary this approach has the following advantages.

- o Instead of addressing business interaction at a specific layer, we integrate business object modeling and business process modeling to provide an integrated solution.

- o Instead of using individual rules for single-round conversational interactions, we elevate business interaction from the conversation level to the process level.

- o Instead of *integrating* different processes, we support inter-business interaction by peer-to-peer execution and synchronization of *common processes*.

- o In addition to providing tools for specifying bilateral business contracts, we focus on community standards for business collaboration.

- o Instead of introducing a new language from scratch, we extend the existing PDL and CBL to develop the XML-based CBCDL.

References

1. T. Bray, J. Paoli, C. M. Sperberg-McQueen, "Extensible Markup Language (XML) 1.0 Specification", February 1998, (http://www.w3.org/TR/REC-xml)
2. BEA WebLogic Process Integrator, http://www.bea.com/products/weblogic/integrator/
3. Biztalk, http://www.biztalk.org/
4. A. Chavez and P. Maes, Kasbah: An Agent Marketplace for Buying and Selling Goods, Proc. of PAAM96, 1996.

5. Qiming Chen, Meichun Hsu, Igor Kleyner, "How Agents from Different E-Commerce Enterprises Cooperate", Proc. of The Fifth International Symposium on Autonomous Decentralized Systems (ISADS'2001), 2001, USA.
6. Qiming Chen, Meichun Hsu, "Inter-Enterprise Collaborative Business Process Management", Proc. of 17th International Conference on Data Engineering (ICDE-2001), 2001, Germany.
7. Qiming Chen, Umeshwar Dayal, "Multi-Agent Cooperative Transactions for E-Commerce", Proc. Fifth IFCIS Conference on Cooperative Information Systems (CoopIS'2000), 2000, Israel.
8. Qiming Chen, Umesh Dayal, Meichun Hsu, Martin Griss, "Dynamic Agent, Workflow and XML for E-Commerce Automation", Proc. First International Conference on E-Commerce and Web-Technology, 2000, UK.
9. Qiming. Chen, P. Chundi, Umesh Dayal, M. Hsu, "Dynamic-Agents", International Journal on Cooperative Information Systems, 1999, USA.
10. Common Business Library, http://www.oasis-open.org/cover/cbl.html.
11. xCBL 2.0, http://www.commerceone.com/xml/cbl/.
12. CORBA, "CORBA Facilities Architecture Specification", OMG Doc 97-06-15, 1997.
13. Document Object Model, http://www.w3.org/DOM/
14. EbXML, http://www.ebXML.org/
15. E-Speak, http://www.e-speak.net/
16. R. S. Gray. Agent Tcl: A flexible and secure mobile-agent system. Dr. Dobbs Journal, 22(3):18-27, 1997.
17. Groove.net, www.groove.net/peer.gtml.
18. N. R. Jennings (1999) "Agent-based Computing: Promise and Perils" Proc. IJCAI-99, Sweeden. 1429-1436.
19. Jini, http://www.sun.com/jini/whitepapers/
20. M. Koetsier, P. Grefen, J. Vonk, "Contracts for Cross-Organizational Workflow Management", Proc. EC-Web'2000.
21. N.Krishnakumar and A.Sheth"Specification of workflows with heterogeneous tasks in meteor", Proc. VLDB'94, 1994.
22. A.G. Moukas, R. H. Guttman and P. Maes, "Agent Mediated Electronic Commerce: An MIT Media Laboratory Perspective", Proc. of International Conference on Electronic Commerce, 1998.
23. PeerMetrics, www.peermetrics.com.
24. Rosetta-net, www.rosettaNet.org.
25. Soap: Simple Object Access Protocol, http://msdn.Microsoft.com/xml/general/soapspec.asp, 2000
26. tpaML, http://www.research.ibm.com/journal/sj/401/dan.html
27. UDDI: A new Proposed Standard Delivers on Promise of Internet for Business of All Sizes, http://msdn.Microsoft.com/presspass/features/2000, 2000
28. Workflow Management Coalition, www.aiim.org/wfmc/mainframe.htm.
29. WSFL, http://www-4.ibm.com/software/solutions/webservices/pdf/WSFL.pdf

"i-mode", Now & Future

Kei-ichi Enoki

Managing Director, i-mode Business
NTT DoCoMo, Inc.
2-11-1 Nagatacho, Chiyoda-ku, Tokyo 100-6150, Japan

The number of cellular phone subscribers in Japan has now topped 60 million, which means that 50% of Japan's population own cellular phones. That number is greater than the subscribers of fixed-line telephones. In the midst of this mobile phone market much attention has been focused on "i-mode."

The "i-mode service", which DoCoMo launched on Feb. 22nd, 1999 had 26 million subscribers by July 2001.

"i-mode" services include voice calls, e-mail and Internet access. An "i-mode" cellular phone with an HTML browser connects to the Internet through a 9.6kbps packet switched network. This system enables users to receive information from Internet web sites.

We provide over 1,800 sites from 1,000 DoCoMo's application alliance partners. Under the concept of "My Concierge", we offer a full range of services, which include ticket booking (airline tickets and concert tickets), selling books and CDs, games, animated pictures, ringing tones, horoscopes, restaurant guides such as ZAGAT, and news including CNN, Bloomberg, and Dow Jones. Weather forecasts are also available. We also provide mobile banking by over 400 banks including CITIBANK, as well as mobile trading and on-line stock selling/buying.

We can directly access more than 46,000 independent web sites through over 100 search engines such as Yahoo, Infoseek, and LYCOS.

The cellular phone is a media that directly accesses individuals instead of accessing them through companies or families, and a great advantage is that users always carry their own terminals. "i-mode", which has the features of a conventional cellular phone, has captured the consumer market as its core market. Our range has been expanding to the business market, with such services as e-mail, individual scheduling, inventory control and market research.

The advent of i-mode" terminals has changed the cellular phone from being simply a tool for "talking" into an intelligent device for "data collection".

In January, 2001, we introduced JAVA technology and SSL functionality to "i-mode" so that we could target the game, Intranet and EC markets. On May 30th, 2001 the third generation IMT2000 mobile cellular phone, which is called FOMA, started service in Japan. FOMA enables high-speed data transmission over a network with 2Mbps. "i-mode" in FOMA provides contents of a richer and higher quality and can, for example, deliver news and concert promotion information with pictures.

The 21st century is the start of an era of multimedia. A huge volume of content will be available in whatever format the user wants, be it voice, the written word, music, picture, or maybe even some format we have not yet thought about. And we can be sure that the public will choose the most cost effective means of delivery from among the public network, CATV network, broadcast network, packaged media, and mobile multimedia. I am convinced that even in the future, "i-mode" will be spotlighted as the most significant media for "individuals" and "consumers in the business" market.

"i-mode" burst onto the scene at the end of 20th century. In this century, it will change our business style, not only in a mobile communication industry, but in just about every other industry, including some that have not yet been born. We believe "i-mode" will be providing the leading services in multimedia and will contribute to the affluent society way into the future.

The Role of Research in the New Economy

Dennis Tsichritzis

Fraunhofer Gesellschaft and University of Geneva
Dennis.Tsichritzis@gmd.de

1 What's "New" in the New Economy

It is increasingly becoming clear that there is no separate new Economy. The new Economy is an integral part of the old Economy. It does not operate with completely new rules. On the other hand, it is also widely accepted that there is another type of Economy which is taking shape. The same happened in Art at the beginning of the 20th century. The so called "Art nouveau" was a style of Art in objects and Architecture. Art Nouveau had clear characteristics that set it apart from other styles of Art. It is, therefore, pertinent to look for the new characteristics of the new Economy. In what way is the Economy of today different enough to warrant a new name?

A first characteristic of the new Economy is globalization. Capital is globally accessible and markets are global. As a result, goods and services are produced, traded and consumed in a global way. Whether one is a proponent or an opponent of globalization is irrelevant; the trend is clear. The new Economy is different in terms of its scope, i.e., it is global.

A second characteristic of the new Economy is the importance of immaterial products. As the world market for material goods matures, there is an increasingly important part of the Economy which is based on services and media content. As a result, quality of service and Intellectual Property Rights are becoming essential factors. In addition, there is no apparent limit on launching new services and creating new content. Human creativity is scarce, it is but renewable unlike other resources of our planet.

A third characteristic of the new Economy is the speed of development. New products achieve extraordinary sales volumes in almost no time. An existing product can go out of style or be substituted quickly. The same can be said for companies and whole industry sectors. The ups and downs are not only cyclic but they depend very much on the mood of the consumer. New products are important not only for better functionality, but also to retain the interest and the excitement of consumers and the financial markets.

A fourth characteristic of the new Economy is the rate of innovation. Most sales of even established companies are based on relatively new products. A good brand name standing for quality is not enough. A fast rate of innovation is essential to run ahead of the competition. It is important for companies to have a very dynamic pace of concepts that can be quickly turned into products.

In the rest of the paper we will concentrate exclusively on the innovation characteristic of the new Economy. How can we achieve maximum innovation at reasonable cost? The new Economy changes many aspects of the innovation process for a Company.

- There is a need for peripheral vision, since innovation is a competitive advantage.
- There is a constant fear of disruptive technologies which can completely change the picture.
- There is an aspect of "right-on-time delivery". The timing of innovation is essential.
- Innovation does not need to be provided in-house. Outsourcing of Research projects is increasingly more efficient and creates a vast Research Market.
- Protection is becoming critical. Intellectual Property Rights need to be safeguarded.
- New products and technologies can be obtained through mergers and acquisitions.

Research is the main vehicle for innovation. Companies, however, do not need Research. They need innovation. It is important, therefore, to ponder whether Research as it is traditionally practiced delivers the right innovation process for companies.

2 The Traditional Model of Research

Over the years a traditional model of Research has been developed. It is practiced in excellent Universities and the best Research Centers. This model is based on academic excellence and peer evaluation. The Research activity can be outlined by the following steps. Please notice the analogy to cooking.

1) Take excellent people on the basis of achievements or potential. (ingredients)
2) Give them the resources they need. (seasoning)
3) Provide a stimulating environment for scientific exchange. (heat)
4) Establish a minimum form of supportive management. (stir)
5) Wait patiently and without rushing for the results. (cook)

Like good cooking the basic steps are simple (ingredients + seasoning then heat, stir and cook). Nevertheless it is a real Art to set up a proper Research organization. The driving force in such an environment is peer pressure. The best people produce excellent results to achieve fame matching their peers. The main results are publications and prototypes demonstrating original ideas.

The transfer of the ideas into innovative products is considered a separate activity. It is organized through publications, people and prototypes. An idea picked up from a paper and successfully implemented in practice. People sometimes leave Research and transfer to development. They then carry their know-how into new products. A prototype is picked up as a first version and is reimplemented as a product.

This traditional model of Research is relevant both for theoretical and applied Research. Over the years it has produced the transistor, UNIX, the PC environment, Internet, the Web and most of the extraordinary advances in our discipline. In the last few years, however, the new Economy and its environment are putting a tremendous strain of this model. Many difficulties arise due to the changed economic environment.

The essence of scientific activity has not changed. Its relation to the Economy has, however, evolved.

In a perfect world without narrow corporate, regional or state interests the traditional model of Research is still valid. Our world, however, is not perfect. The model was primarily developed to support science. The benefits to the sponsors by this I mean those who pay were indirect, for example, fame, know-how, people. Today, however, there is a strong concept of the sponsor's value. The result of Research should mainly benefit the organization (company, region, state) that is financing the effort. Patents and not publications are important. Transfer should be carefully organized to the appropriate destinations. The Research activity should be only open to take advantage of other people's ideas. The Research effort should be orchestrated to maximize the sponsor's value.

The traditional Research effort is currently directed from the scientific domain's peers. In such an environment it is difficult to concentrate on a specific problem and it is difficult to redirect. It is easy to lose focus or direction. Innovation in the new Economy, however, has specific needs and specific time frames. There is often a mismatch between what the traditional Research effort delivers and the Innovation that the new Economy needs.

The traditional Research effort is heavily based on excellence. Excellent people working in a free and open environment produce excellent results. There are two difficulties with excellence. First, it does not scale in numbers. It is possible to get ten of the best people in a discipline. If you need one hundred or one thousand, it is impossible. You will probably end up with many mediocre people. Second, there is some sort of relaxation process. Most excellent people become mediocre over the years. There is a need to replenish or reshape. This means that people should either stay a short time and be often replaced, or they have to be shaken up from time to time to stay excellent. Both operations provide discontinuities which are inconsistent with the "right-on-time" requirements of the innovation process in the new Economy.

We argued that the traditional Research Model has to adapt to the new economic environment. In the next section we will outline a more appropriate Research model.

3 A New Model of Research

There is a new emerging Model of Research which provides better sponsor value. In addition, it is more flexible and responds better and faster to the needs of the Research Market. The basic elements remain the same as the traditional Model. But there are some differences in emphasis. The main discrepancies, however, are in the domain of technology transfer.

As in the traditional Research Model we need excellent people, or at least people who are as good as we can get. The new Model does not depend so much on extraordinary individual performance but in a well coordinated collective effort.

As in the traditional Research Model we have to provide the necessary resources. The new Model takes economic feasibility into consideration. We provide adequate labs but within reasonable economic constraints. The idea that in Research every wish is legitimate and honored cannot survive in an era of shareholders value.

As in the traditional Research Model we need a stimulating environment. This is based more on creativity and impact on the Research Market and less on peer evaluation and pressure. People compete to be more effective and not to become famous.

The main differences between the Research Models are in the way that the Research results are evaluated, promoted and used. In addition, there is an indirect influence on the career paths and perspectives of the researchers. The emphasis is on patents and not on publications. In this way sponsor value is maximized. The Research results are successfully promoted and sold in the Research Market. The effort is organized in Competence Centers according to the needs of the Research Market and not according to academic disciplines. There is a multipurpose link between Research and the Economy to maximize Innovation. This link has many channels, all of which should be exploited and each one should be operating based on financial benefits.

The first channel is contract Research. The sponsor and the research team together define a project and sign a contract. The results are delivered according to contractual arrangements. This implies much less flexibility for the researchers but a clear indication of sponsors value plus a financial envelope for the project.

The second channel is consulting. The researchers operate as technology consultants with clear contractual arrangements. This implies high availability of the researchers and an understanding of the clients problems. The researchers do not provide solutions looking for problems. They provide expertise to bear on specific problems that the client identifies. To properly organize this effort we need Knowledge Management within the Research organization. In addition, we need constant contact with the prospective clients, plus a high quality of service.

The third channel is corporate e-learning. The expertise stemming from the Research should be quickly targeted to the people in organizations which can best use it. With this activity we do not merely transfer Research results, but current know-how in a particular domain. This service should be organized in terms of presence and electronic media to provide the appropriate package to the client. It means explaining the Research results not to peers but to normal company development people. It implies the readiness of researchers to appropriate package and promote their expertise in courses for an enumeration.

The fourth channel is start-up companies. When appropriate and economically feasible the know-how should be transferred internally to a new start-up company. The researchers should be encouraged to form a new company. This implies an entrepreneurship mentality plus organized access to outside expertise in Marketing and Venture Capital. The company founders along with the Research team and the organization should all obtain benefits from this effort.

Finally, the fifth channel is the acquisition and marketing of patents. The research organization should actively scout for potential patents among its researchers. Emphasis should not be on the number of patents but on great potential value and immediate promotion of the appropriate patents. This implies a constant and trusted liaison between Research organizations and the operative divisions of Technology companies.

All of these Technology Transfer channels cannot be organized solely by researchers. We need professionals who will seriously undertake all these activities. The researchers, however, should be open and have a clear understanding that all these activities are essential. They are critical for the success of the Research organization and for the individual and collective benefit.

4 Restructuring a Research Organization

It is very seldom, that a Research Organization is created from scratch. In most cases it exists with its history, culture and people. The issue is not how to design a Research Organization according to a new Research Model. The issue is how to reorganize a Research Organization to move it towards a new Research Model. We propose three phases and several steps on how to evolve from a traditional Model to a new Research Model. We assume that we depart with an organization with some history, reasonable fame and a good financial situation. We further assume that its employees are a heterogeneous set of Researchers ranging from excellent and active to mediocre and passive. In short, a situation that does not warrant alarm but is not particularly successful.

Phase I

1) We need to identify a minimum set (less than 10%) of excellent groups. They are built around extraordinary individuals who are authorities, let us call them Research Fellows, on a subject. These groups should be encouraged to operate in the traditional model of research as long as they retain their excellence. The identification and the evaluation of these "Research islands" is not particularly difficult. An external commission can help. Excellence is easy to spot when it is there.
2) We need to create a relatively flat organization with Units that operate autonomously and independently. Each Unit can identify its proper research agenda and it is totally responsible as a cost center. It worries about the quality of its services and obtains the economic benefits from the Research Market. It should be led by leader with demonstrable management ability, not necessarily a Research Fellow. Each Unit should also have its own administration to make it flexible and independent.
3) All researchers (or at least all new appointments) should have an understanding that their careers are not solely within Research. People should be encouraged to pursue other careers in business or academia after a time period of say 5-10 years. Very few people less than 10% should be retained. Continuous education in technological and managerial subjects is important to help people exit and pursue their careers elsewhere. In short, the Research Center is a step phase and not a permanent destination for most people.

Phase II

In the second phase we need to move a major part of financing, for example, a target of 50% from base Institutional financing to dynamic financing in terms of internally administered funds. We propose at least three funds.

1) A matching FUND A for government sponsored projects. This fund provides extra financing for these groups that are successful in attracting extra government programs and projects.
2) A matching FUND B for industrially sponsored projects. This fund provides extra financing for the groups that are successful in attracting industrial projects from companies.
3) A reorganization FUND C for repositioning of groups and Units. This fund provides extra financing as seed money for positioning groups in new fields or creating new Units.

Phase III

In the third phase we concentrate on active promotion of the tangible Research results, and the generated know-how of the research effort. There are four directions.

1) Consulting services. Professional consulting services should be organized around the technological expertise of the Research effort. Most clients require a mix of expertise which is not solely available in a group. To put together the right package for the client we need to link to other parts of the organization and to amortize expertise over many clients. This implies proper Knowledge Management. Consulting should be a professional and lucrative activity for both the researchers and the units.
2) Corporate Education. Companies require a continuous update of expertise for their staff. This expertise is up-to-date and usually not available in normal educational programs. Active Researchers have such expertise and their know-how should be properly organized and marketed. Large Companies usually have their own in-house activity for such continuous technological education. Smaller companies and individuals need, however, a neutral and appropriate provider of technological know-how. Research organizations are in a position to provide it. It should be organized for lucrative purposes.
3) Start-ups. Technological advances are sometimes best promoted through start ups. The start up effort should again be properly organized. Entrepreneurship know-how should be transmitted to the researchers early on. The potential projects for start ups should be nurtured and followed closely. Marketing contacts and venture capital should be provided. This effort can potentially be lucrative for both the researchers as individuals and the organization. It needs, however, seed money to get started plus a very professional attitude.
4) Active promotion of patents. Patent acquisition and marketing should be organized in a professional way. Individual researchers and units should receive compensation and prospective benefits for patents. This effort requires a special investment to get it started before it is able to get financing from outside. It should be organized from the beginning for financial success.

5 Concluding Remarks

We have emphasized the role for Innovation in the new Economy. We argued that the traditional model of Research is no longer appropriate to provide such Innovation and deliver sponsor's value. We then outlined a new emerging model of Research which seems to be promising. Finally, we enumerated a series of steps to turn around a Research Organization and move it into this new environment.

There is always the question of whether such a restructuring is realistic and urgent. It is realistic since it is happening already at different speeds in many existing Research Organizations. It is also urgent. Sponsor value is not an abstract term. All companies and most government agencies question the role and the costs of their research organizations. Restructuring is painful and takes time. It should happen before cuts and closures create a negative environment. In that case substance and momentum is lost. It is then impossible to effect any constructive changes.

The last question involves quality. Is the new environment capable providing the scientific excellence in quality and the quantum departures in scientific knowledge. The answer is a clear no. The traditional model of Research is inefficient and ill adapted to the needs of the new Economy. It has, however, the potential to provide spectacular results. The new model is better adapted but it cannot produce miracles. The analogy to cooking is relevant.

Excellent ingredients plus high quality seasoning and great care in heating, stirring and cooking can produce excellent results. Adequate ingredients with appropriate seasoning and a fast process for cooking ready for consumption is much more efficient. We cannot expect, however, a gourmet meal.

Semantic B2B Integration: Is Modeling the Superior Approach over Programming?

Christoph Bussler

Oracle Corporation, Redwood Shores, CA 94065, U. S. A.
`Chris.Bussler@Oracle.com`

Abstract. Business-to-business (B2B) integration can be achieved by programming using a programming language or by modeling in a modeling and execution environment that provides semantic B2B integration concepts. This panel will discuss if semantic B2B integration by modeling is superior to integration by programming.

1 Panel Topic

Many technologies developed in recent times can be deployed to implement semantic B2B integration. Some of them are XML, XSLT, HTTP/S, Java, J2EE, persistent transactional queuing, workflow management, application servers, and legacy application system adapters. With enough "programming power" an enterprise can implement B2B protocols like RosettaNet or ebXML based on these technologies and establish an architecture for the electronic exchange of messages across networks like the Internet with their legacy application systems.

In contrast to this programming approach a modeling approach can be applied to semantic B2B integration. In this case B2B protocols, workflows or transformations can be modeled using graphical user interfaces and the model is interpreted by a semantic B2B integration server. No coding is required at all to define and to execute semantic B2B integration.

The panel will address these different approaches through the following questions:
- Is it possible to follow a 100% modeling approach for semantic B2B integration?
- Is current technology sufficiently expressive to support 100% modeling or do we miss specific functionality?
- What are the runtime challenges like throughput and performance in a modeling and model interpretation approach?
- Is there sufficient understanding of the semantic integration requirements to build a modeling environment?
- Why are so many programming projects started to implement rather than to model semantic B2B integration?

Modeling Topological Constraints in Spatial Part-Whole Relationships

Rosanne Price[1], Nectaria Tryfona[2], Christian S. Jensen[2]

[1]Department of Computer Science, RMIT University, GPO Box 2476V
Melbourne 3001, Australia
School of CSSE, Monash University, Caulfield East, Vic. 3145 Australia
rosanne@cs.rmit.edu.au
[2]Department of Computer Science, Aalborg University, Fredrik Bajers Vej 7E
DK-9220 Aalborg Øst, Denmark
{tryfona, csj}@cs.auc.dk

Abstract. To facilitate development of spatial applications, we investigate the problem of modeling topological constraints in part-whole relationships between spatial objects, where the related objects may themselves be composite. An example would be countries that belong to a supranational organization, where the countries are themselves composed of states. Current topological classification schemes are restricted to simple, bounded, regular, and/or 0-2D spatial data types; do not support the set-based topological constraints required to describe inter-part relationships such as those between members of a supranational organization; and focus primarily on query rather than design. We propose an approach to modeling topological relationships that allows specification of binary and set-based topological constraints on composite spatial objects. This approach does not depend on restricting the type of spatial objects, can be used to describe part-whole and inter-part relationships, and is at a level of detail suitable for use in conceptual modeling.

1 Introduction

Spatial applications must manage complex relationships between *spatial objects*, objects with associated spatial extents, where the individual spatial objects may be simple (connected) or composite (consisting of disjoint spatial components). Examples are a supranational organization formed from member countries, the division of an administrative region into voting districts, or the structures erected on a building site during construction. Such complex relationships typically involve an asymmetric relationship between spatial objects, where one object—the *whole*—can be used to represent a group of other objects—the *parts*. We refer to this as a *spatial part-whole* (PW) *relationship,* described in detail in [9]. The spatial relationships between the whole and all of its parts and between the individual parts are important for constraint specification during conceptual design as well as in later stages of database development. These characteristics include *orientation, metrics,* and *topology*. Of these, topology serves as a particularly useful descriptor in conceptual application modeling both because of its qualitative, thus more intuitive, nature and because—unlike orientation and metrics—it is preserved through many of the common distortions that can occur in representations of real world objects. The focus of this paper is to develop techniques for modeling topological constraints on spatial PW relationships during requirements analysis and conceptual design that are of general applicability in the context of composite spatial objects.

Classification schemes for binary topological relationships have been the subject of extensive study over the years [2,3,4,5,6,7,11]. The research focus is on the development of mathematical formalisms to precisely specify topological relationships. The majority of topological research to date is based on assumptions that are too restrictive for use as a general modeling technique, assuming objects with simple, bounded, and regular regions and lines embedded in 2D space. However, many spatial applications involve semantic entities having holes, discontinuities, and other irregularities. For example, the land mass of a country such as Indonesia or the spatial distribution of different soil types both involve discontinuous spatial extents. Furthermore, applications such as those measuring location in terms of latitude, longitude, and elevation require 3D spatial objects and embedding space.

Recently, researchers have tried to address the challenges of extending topological research to include a wider range of spatial objects, including regions with holes, lines with multiple end-points [5,6], and composite spatial extents [2,3,4,11]. In [5,6,11], topological relations between spatial objects are described based on boundary and interior intersections between object closures (to regularize spatial extents with holes or discontinuities) and object components or discontinuities (e.g. holes or gaps). The most comprehensive work, in terms of the range of spatial object types considered, is described in [4]; including bounded composite spatial objects formed exclusively from either lines (possibly with self-crossings or extra end-points beyond the usual two), points, or regions (possibly with holes). A mutually exclusive and complete set of binary topological relations—*touch, in, overlap, disjoint,* and *cross*—is defined based on boundary, interior, and object intersections and their dimensions. Separate definitions of boundary and interior are used for each type of composite spatial object. In [3], equivalent definitions for the binary topological relations between composite regions are given in terms of relations between their components, i.e. within any component pair composed of a component from each composite object.

A more comprehensive solution to describing topological relationships between composite objects at the component level is proposed in [2]. This is based on a complete set of adverbs that can be used to refine an existing binary classification scheme by extending it to the component level. The adverbs *never, occasionally* (or *partially* if unrelated pairs are disjoint), or *entirely* are used respectively to describe when *no* pair, *some* pair, or *every* pair of composite object components is related by a given binary topological relationship. The adverbs *mostly, mostly$_{rev}$,* or *completely* are used respectively to describe when a component from the other composite object can be found that is related by a given binary topological relationship to (1) each of the second composite object's components, (2) each of the first composite object's components, or (3) both, but using the inverse relationship in the second case. For example, the components of two countries such as Indonesia and the Philippines consisting of island archipelagos should ideally *never* overlap (i.e. no pair of components, one from each country, overlaps). However, if the reality of boundary disputes is considered, the two countries may *partially* overlap (i.e. there may be some component pairs with overlap where there are boundary disputes, but otherwise component pairs are disjoint). For formal definitions of these adverbs refer to [2].

In the context of modeling spatial PW relationships, existing topological research has limitations with respect to the range of spatial data types considered, the understandability of the models proposed, and support for modeling n-ary topological relationships (required to model constraints between spatial parts). To the authors' knowledge, none of the binary topological classification schemes to date explicitly consider spatial extents that are not closed; irregularities such as loops, punctures, and cuts; mixed-dimension composites (e.g. a single composite object consisting of regions, lines, and points); or 3D objects and embedding space. In addition, even when the work considers more complex spatial objects, it is fundamentally based on boundaries and interior intersections [3,4,5,6,11]. Although this allows a high degree of expressiveness in terms of being able to precisely describe a wide range of topological configurations, this comes at the price of increased complexity and reduced understandability. An example is the redefinition of boundary and interior required for each type of composite spatial object in [4] or the identification of topological classes by number [6] or complex conjunctions [11] instead of by name.

A further problem is that the definitions of boundary, interior, and dimension used vary depending on the underlying mathematical model assumed and may not match the intuitive understanding the user has of these concepts. For example, the definition of boundary and interior are formulated only in terms of the spatial object itself in algebraic topology; whereas, in point-set topology, they depend on the embedding space as well. This means that the boundary of a line is its end-points in algebraic topology and for a 1D embedding space in point-set topology, but it is the whole line for a 2D or 3D embedding space in point-set topology. Similarly, the concept of dimension is less intuitive if applied to mixed-dimension composites or their intersections.

In the context of analysis and design of spatial applications, we need a different modeling approach to address application developers' requirements. The level of complexity must be suitable for use in early application development phases and for integration with existing conceptual modeling languages. This potentially means sacrificing, to some degree, the expressiveness of the model (i.e. the level of detail that can be specified for a topological relationship) for the sake of generality (i.e. being able to model the range of different types of spatial objects in spatial applications) and clarity (i.e. based on highly intuitive concepts and classifications).

Furthermore, in order to model spatial PW relationships, we must be able to describe the n-ary topological relationships between the parts. Topological research to date has focussed on binary topological relationships suitable only for describing the relationship between the whole and the geometric union of its parts. In the context of multimedia databases, [8] defines an n-ary temporal relation consisting of an ordered, finite sequence of time intervals where any two adjacent intervals have an identical temporal relation. However, ordering is not suitable for describing topological relationships between a set of spatial objects since, in general (except in the special case of 1D space), there is no inherent linear order in space.

In this paper, a simple framework and modeling constructs intended to facilitate specification of general topological constraints between two or more spatial objects, in the context of spatial PW relationships, are proposed. In Section 2, we describe a simple approach to modeling binary topological relationships based fundamentally on intersection and difference of spatial extents. This is extended to describe n-ary topological relationships in the Section 3. Finally, in Section 4, we apply these methods to the spatial PW relationships discussed in [9], using the proposed binary and n-ary topological relationships to describe constraints on whole-part and part-part relationships respectively. Examples are given to show the applicability and ease of use of the approach adopted.

2 Modeling Binary Topological Relationships

A classification scheme that is both simple (i.e. easy to use) and flexible (i.e. applicable to a wide range of spatial applications) is required to model topological constraints between the whole and the geometric union of the parts in spatial PW relationships. Consider the building site example described in Section 1. It is essential that any structure erected on that site does not extend beyond the site boundary. In an analogous manner, when an administrative region is divided into voting districts, the combined spatial extents of the resulting voting districts must be exactly equal to that of the administrative region. To model these constraints, we require a formal yet simple method of describing binary topological constraints. In this section, we propose a method specifically designed to facilitate conceptual modeling of spatial PW relationships. We first review the assumptions and terminology relevant to the work presented here. For the purposes of this work, it is sufficient to assume an Euclidean model of space (1D, 2D, or 3D) with embedded spatial objects. The classification described here holds under either point-set or algebraic topology; therefore, either can be used as a theoretical basis for discussion. Since the proposed classification scheme is based fundamentally on the set-based concepts of intersection and difference, point-set topology is the more natural choice.

A *spatial extent* is then described as a subset of the points in the embedding space. The spatial extent is considered to be *connected* if any two of its points can be connected by a path consisting entirely of points within the spatial extent and considered to be *disconnected* otherwise. It is *weakly connected* if the same spatial extent becomes disconnected after removal of a finite number of points and *strongly connected* otherwise. A spatial extent that is disconnected is called a *composite* spatial extent consisting of a finite set of *components*, each of which is a connected (weakly or strongly) spatial extent. A *Geometric Union* (GU) of a finite number of spatial extents is the set consisting of all the points from each of the spatial extents including all of their components.

Point-set topology is built from the concept of *neighborhoods*, where there exists a neighborhood both for every point in space and inside the intersection of any two neighborhoods for that point. A *near point* for a spatial extent is one where each of its neighborhoods includes a point in the spatial extent. A spatial extent—whether *connected* or *composite*—forms an *open set* if every point has a neighborhood completely within the spatial extent and forms a *closed set* if it includes all its near points. A spatial extent is called *unbounded* if open, *bounded* if closed, and *partially bounded* otherwise. The largest *open set* in the spatial extent is usually called the *interior* and the rest the *boundary*; however, these terms are not always used consistently in the literature for the reasons discussed earlier. A spatial extent is called *simple* if it is connected and *regular* if it is bounded and contains no irregularities (e.g. no holes, crossings, isolated missing punctures or cuts, extra end-points).

Finally, we adopt the well-known concept of a minimum bounding box, used to approximate an object's location in the embedding space by the smallest rectilinear rectangle completely enclosing that spatial extent. More generally and without restricting the dimension or the type of figure used, the term minimum bounding figure is used here to refer to any simple, regular bounding figure.

With this foundation, the proposed two-level classification scheme for binary topological relationships (between two spatial extents) can be described. A given spatial extent can consist of a finite number of disconnected or weakly connected parts of the same or different dimensions (from 0D to 3D); can have irregularities such as holes, punctures, cuts, self-crossings, extra end-points and loops; and can be bounded, partially bounded, or unbounded.

The first level of classification is based only on whether the intersection (∩) and difference (-) of the two spatial extents is empty or non-empty, concepts that are easily understandable, intuitive, and not dependent on the dimension of the embedding space. The classification scheme is illustrated in Table 1. Colors are used to distinguish between the two spatial extents and a dotted line used to indicate a partially bounded or unbounded spatial extent. Only simple spatial extents are used in the table for understandability. Composite spatial extents are shown in Fig. 1-3.

After eliminating trivial cases where at least one of the two spatial extents is the empty set, we have the non-intersecting category (the intersection is the empty set) *disjoint* and the intersecting categories (the intersection is not empty) *equal(s)*, *contain(s)*, *inside*, and *connected* as shown in Table 1. So, for example, the equal and contain relationships can be used to model the voting district and building site examples respectively. This set of relationships is complete and mutually exclusive for two non-empty spatial extents, i.e. any topological relationship between two objects falls into exactly one of these categories. For any two non-empty spatial extents, their intersection and differences must be either empty or non-empty. Therefore, by considering exhaustively all the possible permutations (as in Table 1), the resulting categories must be both complete and mutually exclusive. The two non-symmetrical relationships, *contain* and *inside* (i.e. contained-by), can be combined through disjunction into one symmetric *nested* relationship where either the forward difference (A-B) or the reverse difference (B-A), but not both, is the empty set. The connected and disjoint categories have a further level of classification defined when more refinement of the model is required for a specific application.

Connected objects can be further classified based on whether they have a *boundary*, *interior*, or *mixed overlap*, i.e. whether their intersection includes only boundary, only interior, or both boundary and interior points. Since boundary and interior points often represent semantic differences in applications, it is useful to be able to specify whether the intersection involves object boundaries, interiors, or both. For example, in the case of voting districts for a given administrative region, interior points are used to represent administrative jurisdiction and boundary points are used to represent a change in jurisdiction. This example will be discussed further in Section 3, in the context of n-ary topological constraints between spatial parts.

Table 1. Binary Topological Relationships based on Intersection and Difference

Example(s)	∩	A-B	B-A	R Name (A R B)
	∅	∅	∅	no name (A,B =∅)
	∅	¬∅	∅	no name (B = ∅)
	∅	∅	¬∅	no name (A = ∅)
	∅	¬∅	¬∅	Disjoint
	¬∅	∅	∅	Equal
	¬∅	¬∅	∅	Contains (Nested)
	¬∅	∅	¬∅	Inside (Nested)
	¬∅	¬∅	¬∅	Connected

A crucial aspect of the connected sub-categories is that, in contrast to other proposed topological classifications, the only assumption is that every point in a spatial extent must be either a boundary or interior point, but not both. Further definition is left to the user as appropriate to specific application requirements. This approach supports the intuitive notion that boundary points differ semantically from interior points, but does not dictate further those aspects of the definition that may vary between applications.

To illustrate the sub-categories of *connected* in Fig. 1, we assume a 2D embedding space and point-set boundary and interior definitions dependent on the embedding dimension. Thus a 1D line embedded in 2D space or a single point consists only of boundary points. Note that if we were to assume that the embedding space was 3D instead of 2D, then all the examples shown as *Interior-Overlap* or *Mixed-Overlap* would also become *Boundary-Overlap*. This is because all the points in a 2D area embedded in 3D space are boundary points in point-set topology.

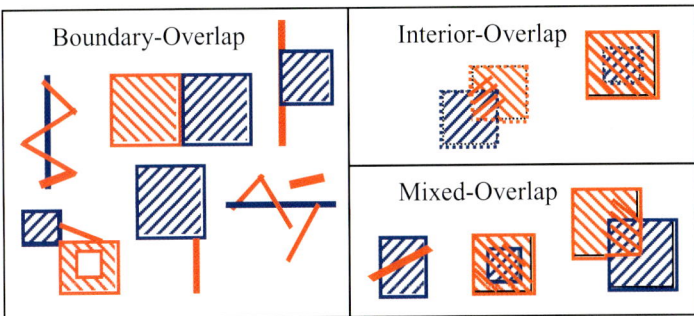

Fig. 1. Connected Sub-Categories

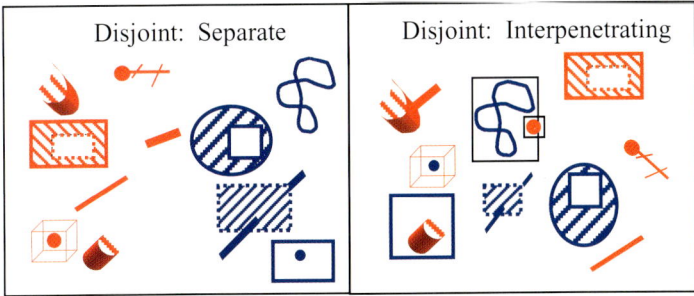

Fig. 2. Disjoint Sub-Categories

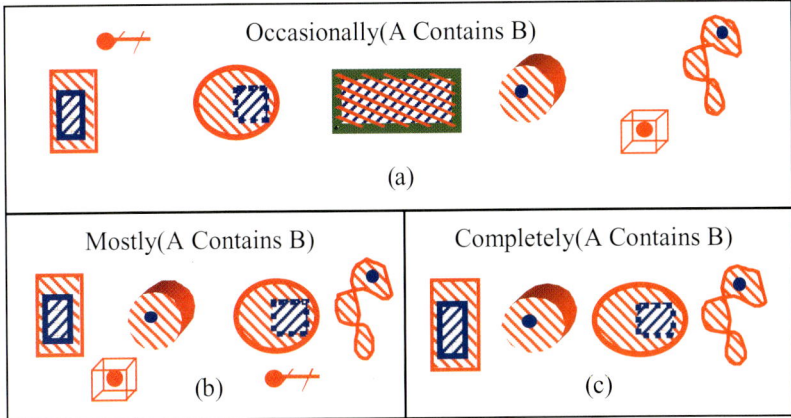

Fig. 3. Using Adverbs to Describe Component-Level Topological Constraints

A disjoint relationship between two spatial entities can be further distinguished based on whether their spatial extents inter-penetrate, i.e. whether the minimum bounding figures of the two objects intersect. The method used to calculate the minimum bounding figure is application dependent, e.g. with respect to the orientation of the axes and granularity. As with the definition of boundary and interior used for the sub-categories of *connected*, the decision as to exactly how to determine the minimum bounding figure is left to the user. *Separate* is a disjoint relationship where the minimum bounding figures of the two spatial extents do not intersect and *interpenetrating* is a disjoint relationship where they do intersect. This distinction is particularly relevant for the applications involving archipelagos, such as the distribution of soil types discussed in Section 1, where the spatial parts in a spatial PW relationship are widely dispersed. Fig. 2 shows examples of separate and interpenetrating disjoint relationships between two composite spatial extents, one colored red and the other blue. Even two simple spatial extents can have an interpenetrating relationship, as shown by the two minimum bounding boxes in black.

The second level of classification consists of complete and mutually exclusive sub-categories in the specific category. For example, every disjoint relationship is either separate or interpenetrating, but not both. That follows logically from the definition of the two categories based on whether the minimum bounding figures of the two spatial extents intersect. Similarly, mutual exclusivity of the *connected* subcategories follows logically from the assumption stated earlier that a spatial extent can be completely partitioned into mutually exclusive sets of boundary and interior points.

Thus the seven categories—separate, interpenetrating, equal, contain, inside, boundary-overlap, mixed-overlap, and interior-overlap—represent a complete and mutually exclusive set of binary topological relationships as shown in the preceding discussions. The more general categories—disjoint, nested, connected, and intersecting—can be derived from these seven relationships. Except for contain and inside, all of the relationships are symmetric.

Although the set of topological relationships is complete and mutually exclusive, there may be certain applications that require a model with greater degree of precision even at the requirements analysis and conceptual modeling phases of system development. For applications requiring a more detailed understanding of the topological relationships between components in pairs of composite objects, the adverbs of [2] can be employed with the binary topological relationships introduced in this section. For instance, Fig. 3 (a), (b), and (c) are all examples of the binary inclusion relationship *A Contains B*. The adverbs from [2] can be used to specify more restrictive constraints and differentiate between these three examples as shown in Fig. 3, with increasing restrictions from (a) to (c). When yet further precision in describing topological relationships is required, e.g. to distinguish between the different cases of boundary-overlap shown in Fig. 1; models involving a more limiting set of assumptions and more complex geometric concepts—such as those described in Section 1—are required.

3 Defining Topological Relationships between *n* Spatial Extents

The binary topological classification described in Section 2 is sufficient to describe topological constraints between a whole and the GU of its parts (i.e. between the *spatial extent* of the whole and the GU of the *spatial extents* of its parts, where the

Modeling Topological Constraints in Spatial Part-Whole Relationships 35

latter is called the part union). However, n-ary topological relationships are required to describe topological constraints between the parts. For example, the voting districts created for an administrative region cannot have overlapping interiors, as this would allow a single constituent to vote in more than one district. In this section, a general method of modeling n-ary topological relationships is described.

Given some binary topological relationship R defined for two spatial objects, how can we extend this to n spatial objects? For example, how can we extend the definition of boundary-overlap to describe the constraint on the set of voting districts, i.e. that none of the voting districts can share interior points? It follows logically that if a binary topological constraint R is extended to n spatial objects at least one of three following conditions is true:
1. R holds for every pair (i.e. *all*) of the n spatial objects.
2. R holds for at least one pair (i.e. *some*) of the n spatial objects.
3. R holds for no pair (i.e. *none*) of the n spatial objects.

Although it is clear that this set of three conditions is complete (i.e. given a binary relationship R and n spatial extents at least one of the three conditions holds), they are not minimal (since *none* can be modeled as $\neg$ *some*) or mutually exclusive (since condition 2 does not exclude condition 1). However, the conditions are formulated with reference to conceptual modeling with simplicity and ease of modeling as a priority. It is more intuitive to model *none* directly and *some* as *at least one* as evidenced by common usage in natural language. If required, the constraint *at least one but not all* can still be expressed as *some* $\wedge$ ($\neg$ *all*). This set of conditions is used as the basis for defining modeling constructs to describe n-ary topological relationships. These are defined formally after describing the notation used as follows.

Let $O \stackrel{def}{=} \{ o_1,...,o_i,...,o_j,...,o_n \} \stackrel{def}{=}$ a finite set of n spatial extents, where $n>=2$ and $i \diamond j$.

Let $R \stackrel{def}{=}$ a topological expression consisting of:
1. one, a disjunction, or conjunction of the binary relationships from Section 2, or
2. one of the adverbs *mostly, mostly$_{rev}$, completely, partially, occasionally, entirely*, or *never* from [2] with (1)
3. a disjunction and/or conjunction of (2).

Let $S \subseteq O$ (a non-empty subset of O) $\stackrel{def}{=} \{ s_1,...,s_k,...,s_p \} \stackrel{def}{=}$ a set of p spatial extents, where $p>=1$ and $p<=n-2$.

We then define the following four modeling constructs for describing n-ary topological relationships, assuming $i \diamond j$.

$$all(R, O) \stackrel{def}{=} \forall\, o_i, o_j \in O\ (o_i\,R\,o_j) \qquad (1)$$

$$some(R, O) \stackrel{def}{=} \exists\, o_i, o_j \in O\ (o_i\,R\,o_j) \qquad (2)$$

$$none(R, O) \stackrel{def}{=} \neg\exists\, o_i, o_j \in O\ (o_i\,R\,o_j) \qquad (3)$$

$$linked(R, O) \stackrel{def}{=} \forall\ o_i, o_j \in O \quad (4)$$

$$((o_i\ R\ o_j) \vee (\exists\ S, ((o_i\ R\ s_1) \wedge ... \wedge (s_{k-1}\ R\ s_k) \wedge ... \wedge (s_p\ R\ o_j))))$$

The first three constructs are based on the three conditions discussed earlier. The last construct, *linked*, describes a special case of *some* where any two spatial extents in the set can be related directly or indirectly by the given topological expression.

Note that the definition of O excludes sets of spatial extents having zero members or one member. If O is empty or has only one member, then *all*, *some*, *none*, and *linked* are defined to be true for all R. If O has two members, then *all* $\Leftrightarrow$ *some* $\Leftrightarrow$ *linked* for all symmetric R.

These modeling constructs allow specification of general topological relationships between the spatial extents—whether simple or composite—of n spatial objects. With the adverbs from [2], the same modeling constructs allow specification of topological relationships between components of pairs of n different composite spatial extents.

There may be some cases where we want to treat a set of composite spatial extents as a set of their individual components. This could be used to model topological constraints between all the individual components of a set of composite spatial extents without any reference to the original composite configurations. To do this, we need to define an additional modeling construct that decomposes a set of spatial extents into the set of all their individual components. That is, given a set O of m composite spatial extents $o_1,...,o_i,...,o_m$ with $n_1,...,n_i,...,n_m$ components respectively and where c_{ik} is the kth component of the ith composite spatial extent o_i, we have the following:

$$decompose(O) \stackrel{def}{=} \{...,c_{ik},...\} \text{ where } 1<=i<=m \text{ and } 1<=k<=n_i \quad (5)$$

We can then use any of the previously defined constructs for n-ary topological relationships, replacing O with *decompose(O)*. For example, consider the case of a national road network, with the entities being individual roads with spatial extents describing their location and geometry. Although a single road usually is a simple polyline, there may be cases where a road may consist of several disconnected segments. For instance, consider a long-distance road that is a freeway for most of the distance, but has a few segments inherited from local road networks that have different names, are not freeways, and may not even be administered by the same transport authority. When modeling the national road network, we want to enforce the constraint that the road network as a whole must be continuous. Since a road can have a composite spatial extent consisting of disconnected segments, this means that there must be some way to travel between every two segments of road in the network. In order to evaluate topological relationships between the set of road segments (rather than roads) in the network, the *decompose* operator is used to refer to individual road segments. The *connected* binary topological operator discussed earlier is used to compare pairs of road segments. The *linked* relation is then used to specify that it must be possible to find a finite sequence of connected pairs linking any two road segments. Assuming that we have the set of roads $r_1,...,r_n$ in the road network, this constraint would be formally specified as *linked(connected, decompose($\{r_1,...,r_n\}$))*.

4 Topological Constraints on Spatial PW Relationships

In [9], we classify spatial PW relationships based on whether the spatial extent of the whole object is *derived* from or *constraining* those of its parts, termed *spatial derivation* and *spatial constraint* and illustrated respectively by a supranational organization and a building site. Topological constraints between parts are listed as a secondary characteristic leading to further variants beyond the basic classification. The binary and n-ary topological relationships defined in Sections 2 and 3 respectively can now be used respectively to refine the spatial constraint category based on whole-part topology and to illustrate the definition of additional variants based on part-part topology. Formal definitions for spatial PW relationships are given in [9].

Only the inclusion relationship (part union *inside* or *equals* whole) was considered and defined as a sub-category (*spatial inclusion*) of spatial constraint in [9]. We can use the classification of binary topological relationships proposed in Section 2 to provide a more general method of defining topological relationships between a whole and its parts and to further refine the spatial constraint category. As in [9], the goal is to identify useful types of spatial PW relationships. Therefore, refinement is pragmatic (i.e. where we were aware of clear examples) rather than exhaustive. Following this rationale, three more spatial constraint types are identified: *spatial interior*, *spatial equal,* and *spatial cover;* where the relationship of the part union with the whole is respectively *inside*, *equals*, and *contains* or *equals*. The spatial inclusion and spatial interior constraints are transitive, since the topological constraint between the part union and the whole can be equivalently expressed as a constraint between each part and the whole individually. Therefore, any sub-components of a structure located on a building site are also located on that building site. The same is not true of spatial cover or equal, and so these categories are not transitive.

Spatial constraint sub-categories are illustrated in the top portion of Fig. 4, with the specific binary topological constraint between the *part union* and the *whole* indicated in bold type for each sub-category. *Spatial cover* is exemplified by a guaranteed phone service coverage area that must be completely covered by (i.e. inside or equal to) the GU of the phone service cells' spatial extents. A building site and the structures on that building site represent an example of *spatial inclusion*, since no structure can extend outside the building site. The stricter constraint of *spatial interior* applies to house furnishings (referring here to appliances and furniture), since the furnishings must be inside but cannot completely cover the area of the house in order to ensure walking room. Finally, the GU of taxi dispatch zones (the area over which a given taxi driver ranges) must be exactly equal to the metropolitan area covered by the taxi company, i.e. *spatial equal*. This ensures complete coverage of the metropolitan area without risking cases where the company insurance policy may not be applicable.

Variants of the basic spatial constraint sub-categories can be defined based on additional topological constraints between the parts using the n-ary topological relationships from Section 3, as illustrated by the examples in the bottom portion of Fig. 4. The n-ary topological constraint applicable to a specific example is indicated in bold type. The second argument of the n-ary topological constraint (the set of spatial extents) is omitted in the figure and following discussion for readability.

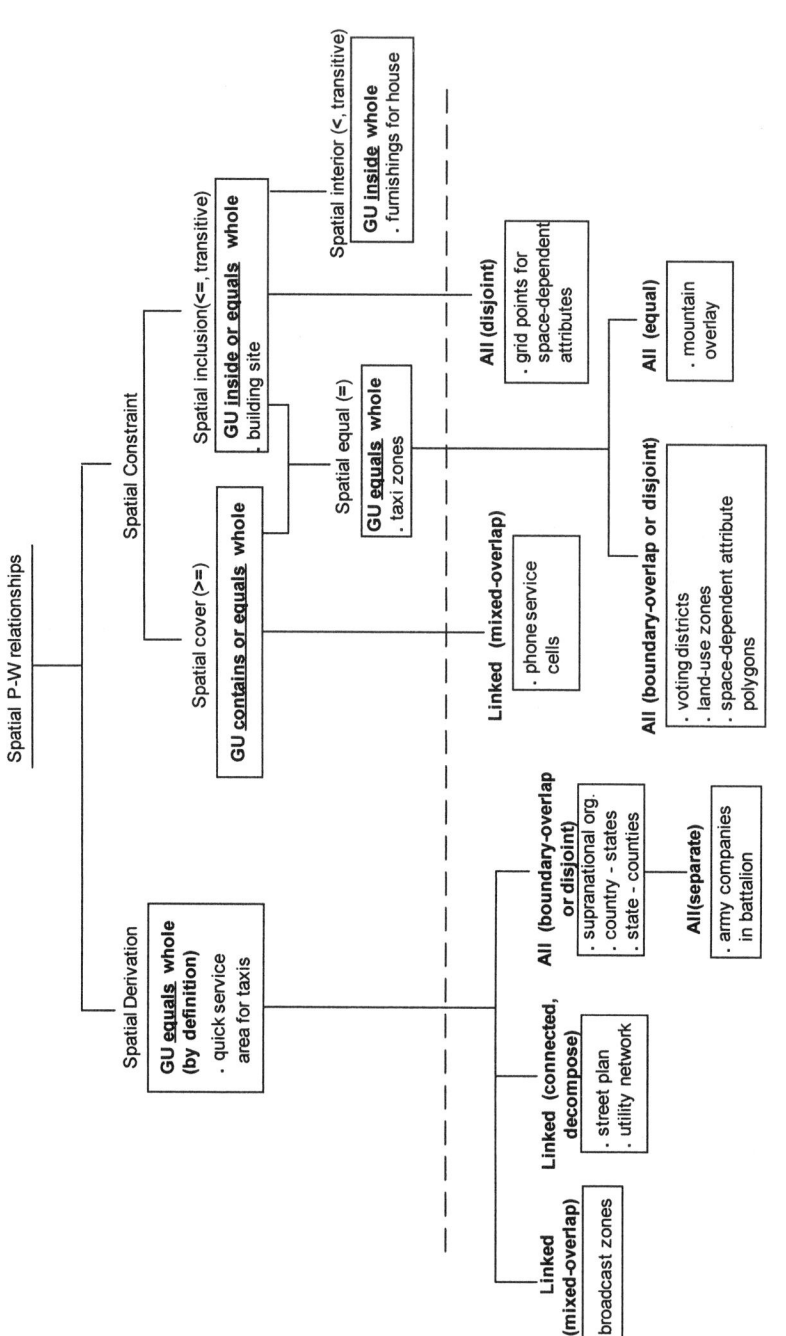

Fig. 4. Topological Constraints in Spatial Part-Whole Relationships

To ensure that the placement of a set of broadcasting transmitters results in continuous broadcasting coverage across the set of transmitters, the *linked(mixed-overlap)* constraint is used to specify that there is a sequence of overlapping broadcast zones—each a simple, bounded spatial extent. Constraints on a set of phone service cells are similar to those on broadcast zones, except with the additional constraint that every point in a given area has phone service—that is, is contained in some phone service cell. This is reflected in the use of a spatial constraint (*spatial cover*) modeling construct for phone cells instead of spatial derivation.

In the transport and utility application examples where a given street or utility component can have a composite spatial extent, *decompose* is used with the *linked(connected)* constraint to ensure a continuous transport and utility network (i.e. the *whole*) with no isolated components (i.e. the *parts*).

Since boundaries are used to uniquely partition administrative responsibility, there cannot be cases of overlapping interior points for member countries of a supranational organization, states in a country, counties in a state, or voting districts. Similarly, shared interior points would be inconsistent in the case of land-use zones and space-dependent attribute polygons, used to represent differences in permissible land usage or an observed attribute values respectively. The predicate *all(boundary-overlap or disjoint)* is used to specify the constraint that interior points cannot be shared between parts in a spatial PW relationship.

In the case of army companies, they must be disjoint and spread out (i.e. not interpenetrating so *all(separate)*) for strategic reasons and to reduce the risk of friendly fire. Sample points used to measure space-dependent attributes should be spread out to improve the sampling accuracy. In this case, disjoint points are necessarily separate, so there is no need to specify this constraint explicitly.

Finally, we have the case of overlays for different thematic attributes over a given region (e.g. mountain vegetation, hydrography, and elevation) in a geographic application. In this case, the constraint *all(equal)* is used to specify that the spatial extents of overlays must be equal.

5 Conclusions

In this paper, we discuss techniques for specifying topological constraints on spatial PW relationships during the analysis and conceptual design phases of spatial application development. A two-level classification scheme for describing binary topological relationships is proposed that is general enough to be suitable for a range of different applications yet is simple to use and understand. The final set of seven relationships—separate, interpenetrating, equal, contain, inside, boundary-overlap, mixed-overlap, and interior-overlap—is complete and mutually exclusive. The defined relationships include those between single and mixed-dimension composites, irregular (with cuts, punctures, holes, self-crossings, extra end-points, loops, etc.), partially bounded or unbounded, and 3D spatial objects. We then define modeling constructs for the specification of n-ary topological relationships. Finally, we show how the proposed techniques can be used to specify topological constraints—both between parts and between the whole and parts—in spatial PW relationships.

Existing conceptual modeling languages such as UML or spatiotemporal extensions based on UML [1,10] contain provisions for general constraint specification but no specific support for describing topological constraints on spatial composites. The techniques proposed here can be used in conjunction with such languages to add the necessary support. For example, to specify that the set of land-use zones associated with an administrative region must be overlapping, the n-ary topological constraint *all(boundary-overlap or disjoint)* can be included in curly braces (used to indicate a constraint in UML) on the association link between the administrative regions and land-use zone classes. The efficient implementation of the specified constraints in later development phases requires the use of representation-dependent algorithms to verify intersection and difference of spatial extents and their components (for composite spatial extents). An overview of the types of representations used for 0D-3D spatial objects and associated algorithms used for these operations are described in [12].

Future work includes the extension of set-based constraint specification to other spatial characteristics such as orientation or metrics and the incorporation of time restrictions in the topological modeling techniques proposed here to support spatiotemporal applications.

References

1. Brodeur, J., Y. Bedard, and M. Proulx. Modelling Geospatial Application Databases using UML-based Repositories Aligned with International Standards in Geomatics, Proc. 8th ACM GIS, 2000, 39-46.
2. Claramunt, C. Extending Ladkin's Algebra on Non-convex Intervals towards an Algebra on Union-of Regions, Proc. 8th ACM GIS, 2000, 9-14.
3. Clementini, E., P. Di Felice, and G. Califano. Composite Regions in Topological Queries, Information Systems, 20(7), 1995, 579-594.
4. Clementini, E. and P. Di Felice. A Model for Representing Topological Relationships between Complex Geometric Features in Spatial Databases, Info. Sciences, 1994, 1-17.
5. Egenhofer, M, E. Clementini, and P. Di Felice. Topological Relations between Regions with Holes, Intl. Journal of GIS, 8(2), 1994, 129-142.
6. Egenhofer, M. and J.R. Herring. Categorizing Binary Topological Relationships Between Regions, Lines, and Points in Geographic Databases, Technical Report, Dept. of Surveying Engineering, Univ. of Maine, Orono, ME, 1991, 1-33.
7. Hadzilacos, T. and N. Tryfona. A Model for Expressing Topological Integrity Constraints in Geographic Databases, Proc. of Intl. Conf. GIS—From Space to Territory: Theories and Methods of Spatiotemporal Reasoning, 1992, 252-268.
8. Little, T.D.C. and A. Ghafoor. Interval-Based Conceptual Models for Time-Dependent Multimedia Data, IEEE TKDE, 5(4), 1993, 551-563.
9. Price, R., N. Tryfona, and C.S. Jensen. Modeling Part-Whole Relationships for Spatial Data, Proc. 8th ACM GIS, 2000, 1-8.
10. Price, R., N. Tryfona, and C.S. Jensen. Extended Spatiotemporal UML: Motivations, Requirements, and Constructs, Journal of Database Management, 11(4), 2000, 14-27.
11. Tryfona, N. and M.J. Egenhofer. Consistency Among Parts and Aggregates: A Computational Model, Transactions in GIS, 1 (3), 1997, 189-206.
12. Worboys, M.F. GIS, A Computing Perspective, Taylor & Francis, London, 1995.

Source Description-Based Approach for the Modeling of Spatial Information Integration

Yoshiharu Ishikawa and Hiroyuki Kitagawa

Institute of Information Sciences and Electronics, University of Tsukuba
{ishikawa,kitagawa}@is.tsukuba.ac.jp

Abstract. Rapid development of information technology such as mobile terminals and GPS systems enabled information services that provide location-oriented information based on users' positions. In this paper, we propose an approach for the modeling of information integration applications that incorporate spatial information sources in addition to conventional information sources to provide appropriate location-oriented information to users. First, we present our approach to the modeling of spatial information sources based on the source description framework. It provides a way to represent the content and the query capability of a spatial information source in a descriptive manner. Then we show a query processing scheme that finds a combination of information sources to respond to given queries and to evaluate them efficiently.

1 Introduction

Recent development of technologies such as GPS (global positioning system), PDA (personal digital assistants), and mobile communication made it easy to obtain the positional information of mobile objects such as mobile users carrying PDAs and vehicles with car navigation systems. Along with this, the progress of digital cartography and Internet technologies enabled new types of services on the network—information sources that provide information within some specific geographic areas, retrieval services which allow map-oriented query interfaces, and so on. In this paper, we call such services *spatial information sources*. While some approaches to provide location-oriented information to mobile users have already been proposed, they do not consider existing other spatial information sources and their integration.

In this paper, we propose a modeling framework to integrate spatial information sources to provide location-oriented information to users. Our main focus is *heterogeneity* of spatial information sources. Since existing spatial information sources differ in their contents and query capabilities, integration of such sources requires an appropriate framework to describe the contents and capabilities of spatial information sources. In this paper, we introduce such a description framework and show query processing methodologies that efficiently utilize spatial information source descriptions. Another focus in this paper is the support of distance-based filtering queries because they are essential for the integration of spatial information sources.

For the interoperability of geographic information, there exist other many issues such as coordinate transformation, differences of resolution, and the handling of semantic mismatches and vagueness. While a lot of studies have been performed according to such interoperability problem for GISs [1], we can see little work on the integration of spatial information sources with consideration of their contents and query capabilities as discussed in this paper. Therefore, we mainly focus on the problem here.

This paper is organized as follows. In Section 2, we describe the background and related work of our research. In Section 3, we introduce a common data model, the relational model augmented with spatial data types, to describe spatial information sources. Section 4 provides examples of a user query and source descriptions and introduces some important notions. In Section 5, we show how source descriptions are used in generating query plans to access underlying spatial information sources and to generate query results. Finally, the conclusions and the future work are described in Section 5.

2 Background and Related Work

2.1 Integration of Heterogeneous Information Sources

There are an emerging number of information sources such as search engines, databases, and document archives are available today. To integrate such heterogeneous information sources and provide useful information to end users, information integration facilities, which select useful information sources based on the given queries and process them over the sources, are required. An approach often taken to tackle this problem is to use an information integration architecture, known as the *wrapper/mediator model*, which consists of wrappers and a mediator [2]. A *wrapper* encapsulates each information source and provides a database view that conforms to a common data model, and a *mediator* integrates information obtained from wrappers and provides an integrated view of the information sources. In this paper, we adopt this approach.

To select information sources to be accessed in processing given queries, a mediator requires a metadata description framework to represent the contents and the query facilities of the underlying information sources. Such a framework requires flexibility to represent heterogeneous information sources and conciseness to enable the generation of efficient query plans. The *source description* framework, proposed by the Information Manifold system [3], is one of such approaches of metadata description framework. The approach first defines a *global schema* over the underlying heterogeneous information sources to be integrated; an end user will describe his or her queries over this schema. A *source description* for each information source specifies the metadata information of the source and consists of two main parts—a *contents description* specifies to which part of the global schema the contents of the source corresponds, and a *capability description* describes the types of queries to which the source can produce the query results. Given a query from a user, the mediator utilizes the source descriptions in selecting available information sources for the query and in generating a query plan for the information integration.

2.2 Spatial Information Sources

Development of technologies and standards for digital documents, geographic information, and spatial databases [4], which are the foundations of spatial information source construction, is steadily in progress. For example, there are an activity of Open GIS consortium [5] and the proposals of POIX [6] (a language for location-oriented information exchange), G-XML [7] (a geographic information description language standardized in Japan), and RWML [8] (a road information description language).

We can find several spatial information sources on the Internet. In the United States, "Yahoo! map" service [9] provides location-oriented information such as local map, driving direction, and nearby businesses. "Digital City" [10] and "citysearch.com" [11] are other available location-oriented information services. In Japan, "Ekimae Tanken Club" [12] to search local information nearby a specified rail station, and MONET system for car navigation users [13] are major examples of available spatial information sources.

We can also find some research prototypes of location-oriented information services. SpaceTag system [14] enables location-based information display and location-aware communication and information exchange for mobile users. Mobile Info Search (MIS) system [15,16] is a kind of Web search engines, but it provides location-oriented information search facilities. It collects Web pages and extracts address information contained in them. If a user specifies a location, the MIS system presents a local map, business information obtained from Yellow Pages, and related Web pages that are supposed to contain local information.

3 Data Model for Spatial Information Integration

For the integration of spatial information sources, we use a common data model, the relational data model augmented with spatial data types. In this section, we first introduce the basic notions of our framework based on an illustrative example. Then we describe spatial data types used in this paper.

3.1 An Example of Spatial Information Integration Requirement

Source Description Framework In this research, we extend the idea of *source description* [3] to represent spatial information sources for their integration; some basic notions introduced here are similar to that of [3]. First, a *global schema* is defined over the information sources to be integrated. The global schema is constructed according to the integration requirement. Next, a wrapper on each information source is built. A *wrapper* encapsulates the details of the target information source and provides a source view conforming to the global schema.

It is important to use a flexible common data model in describing and integrating heterogeneous information sources. For example, the TSIMMIS system [17] is based on a *semistructured data model* called OEM. Information Manifold [3] uses the relational data model extended with object-oriented features (e.g., inheritance and object identity) to describe information sources and specify queries. In this paper, we use a data model based on the standard relational data model enhanced with *spatial data types* such as Point and Rectangle. The model is simple and clear, and has a power to express the contents and the query capabilities of spatial information sources.

Examples of Global Schema and User Query Let us consider that a mobile user wants to search a nearby restaurant with good reputation from information sources on the network. Assume that we have a global schema for restaurant information as shown in Fig. 1. The Restaurant relation contains information about restaurants. The category attribute represents the type of a restaurant (e.g., "Japanese"). The location attribute stores the location of a restaurant as a Point data value. The Evaluation relation stores evaluation scores for restaurants.

```
relation Restaurant {                relation Evaluation {
    name string;                         name string;      // restaurant name
    category string;                     score real;       // 0.0 ~ 3.0
    address string;                  };
    location point;
};
```

Fig. 1. An Example of a Global Schema

Figure 2 shows a query to select names and addresses of the nearest 20 restaurants which have scores more than 2.5 and their distances from the user's current position are smaller than 1,000 meters, where mypos is a Point value representing user's current position. In this example, some non-standard SQL constructs are used: the Distance predicate [18] calculates the distance between two points and STOP AFTER clause [19] specifies to retrieve top-N items.

```
SELECT r.name, r.address
FROM Restaurant as r, Evaluation as e
WHERE r.name = e.name, e.score >= 2.5,
      Distance(r.location, mypos) <= 1000
ORDER BY Distance(r.location, mypos)
STOP AFTER 20
```

Fig. 2. An Example Query

3.2 Spatial Data Types and Spatial Operators

In this paper, we utilize the relational data model enhanced with *spatial data types* such as Point and Polygon to describe the information structures of spatial information sources. The reason to adopt the data model is based on the requirement that we need a simple and clear data model with spatial information handling facility. According to spatial data types and spatial operations, the model is based on the OpenGIS proposal [5], a standardization effort for spatial data interoperability. In particular, we take into consideration the specification for accessing spatial information sources via ODBC API using SQL [18].

First, we briefly describe the spatial data types of OpenGIS framework considered in this paper. In the OpenGIS standard, Geometry class is defined as the top-level class for geometry objects. As the sub-classes of Geometry, there exist four classes: Point,

Curve, Surface, and GeometryCollection. Point class is defined for point objects, Curve class is for curve objects which are defined as collections of points, and Surface class is for surface objects which are also defined as collections of points. GeometryCollection class is used to represent collections of Geometry objects. We do not include, however, GeometryCollection class and its subclasses in the scope of the following discussion to simplify the problem.

As some of the classes shown above are in conceptual-level for representing geographic objects in computers, we have to use their representation-level OpenGIS subclasses that have more concrete representations. While we can still use Point class in representation-level, we have to use LineString class and Polygon class instead of Curve class and Surface class, respectively. LineString class is a subclass of Curve and represents curves by collections of line segments, and Polygon class is a subclass of Surface and also represents surface objects by collections of line segments. Therefore, the spatial data types considered in the following part of the paper result in Point, LineString, and Polygon.

For predicates used in queries to specify spatial relationships, we consider the following ones based on the OpenGIS specification for its SQL features [18]. In the following, g_1 and g_2 represent Geometry objects belonging to Point, LineString, or Polygon classes[1].

- $equals(g_1, g_2)$: true if the spatial extents of g_1 and g_2 are equal.
- $disjoint(g_1, g_2)$: true if g_1 and g_2 do not have any overlaps.
- $intersects(g_1, g_2)$: true when g_1 and g_2 have one or more intersections. Note that the condition $intersects(g_1, g_2) \Leftrightarrow \neg disjoint(g_1, g_2)$ holds.
- $touches(g_1, g_2)$: true if g_1 and g_2 touch at one or more points. This predicate is not applicable when both g_1 and g_2 are Point objects.
- $crosses(g_1, g_2)$: true if g_1 and g_2 have one or more intersections. The difference between $intersects$ and $crosses$ is that $crosses$ is applicable only when the arguments are (LineString, LineString) or (LineString, Polygon). In the former case, the predicate becomes true if two LineString objects have overlaps as Point objects. In the latter case, the predicate becomes true if the overlapped regions of two Polygon objects are Point or LineString objects.
- $within(g_1, g_2)$: true if g_1 is contained in g_2. When $equals(g_1, g_2)$ is true, $within(g_1, g_2)$ becomes false.
- $contains(g_1, g_2)$: true if g_1 contains g_2. This is equivalent to $within(g_2, g_1)$.
- $overlaps(g_1, g_2)$: true if g_1 and g_2 have one or more overlaps. This predicate is applicable only when the arguments are (LineString, LineString) or (Polygon, Polygon). In the former case, the predicate becomes true if two LineString objects share some of their line segments. In the latter case, the predicate becomes true if the overlapped regions of two Polygon objects are Polygon objects (not Point or LineString objects). Note that either of $equals(g_1, g_2)$, $within(g_1, g_2)$, and $contains(g_1, g_2)$ is satisfied, $overlaps(g_1, g_2)$ becomes false.

---

[1] Since we did not take GeometryCollection class into consideration, some of the semantics of predicates shown here are simplified ones than their original OpenGIS definitions.

Although the OpenGIS specification contains additional predicate *Relate* to specify spatial topological relationships using pattern matrices, we do not consider it to simplify the discussion.

In addition to spatial predicates, we assume the use of the following functions. They are also contained in the OpenGIS specification.

- *envelope*(g): returns a Polygon object that is the Minimum Bounding Box (MBB) of g.
- *distance*(g_1, g_2): returns the minimal distance between g_1 and g_2.
- *intersection*(g_1, g_2): returns the overlapped region(s) of g_1 and g_2.
- *union*(g_1, g_2): returns the unified region of g_1 and g_2.
- *isempty*(g): returns true if g is an empty region.

In the following discussion, we assume that the *distance* function can be used in the specification of a query: other functions are only used in the query processing.

4 Query Specification and Source Descriptions

In the following, we particularly focus on the following two problems in spatial information integration:

- how to select useful spatial information sources for the given query from various information sources.
- how to construct queries to retrieve required information from the selected information sources.

In heterogeneous information integration, we have to take limitations of each information source into consideration. For example, Information Manifold [3] have presented a query planning and processing scheme applicable even when all of the input attributes or the output attributes of an information source are not necessarily specifiable by the mediator. In this paper, however, we do not consider such input/output limitations; the limitations we mainly focus in this paper is that spatial query facilities provided by each spatial information source do not necessarily cover the full set of spatial predicates introduced in Section 3.2.

4.1 Description of Queries

In this paper, we describe queries as *conjunctive queries*. Since we have incorporated spatial predicates (e.g., *contains*), spatial functions *distance*, and numerical comparisons using inequality predicates in our framework, our queries have extended forms compared to the conventional conjunctive queries in the standard relational model. Consider the following query: this is a modification of the SQL query shown in Fig. 2.

$$ans(n, a) \leftarrow Restaurant(n, c, a, l), Evaluation(e, s),$$
$$n = e, s \geq 2.5, distance(l, \mathrm{p}) \leq 1000,$$

where l is a Point class variable and p is a constant value of Point class that represents the user's current position. The query specifies to select the names and the addresses of the restaurants that have high evaluation scores (≥ 2.5) and are located within 1,000 meters from the user's current position p. Although the SQL query in Fig. 2 specifies ranking and top-N selection, we omit them since the conjunctive queries do not have such expressive powers.

The general form a conjunctive query is as follows:

$$ans(u) \leftarrow \mathbf{R}_1(u_1), \ldots, \mathbf{R}_n(u_n), c_1, \ldots, c_m, \qquad (1)$$

where $\mathbf{R}_1, \ldots, \mathbf{R}_n$ ($n \geq 1$) are global relations, each of $u, u_1, \ldots, u_n$ is a sequence of variables, and $c_1, \ldots, c_m$ ($m \geq 0$) are conditions. As a condition, we assume that it has either of the following forms:

- simple comparison ($x \theta y$ or $x \theta c$): where x and y are variables bound to primitive attributes, c is a constant value, and $\theta \in \{=, \neg, <, >, \leq, \geq\}$ is a comparison predicate.
- spatial predicate-based condition: we allow the spatial predicates introduced in Section 3.2. For example, $contains(g_1, g_2)$, $contains(g, g)$, and $contains(g, g)$ are specifiable conditions, where g, g_1, g_2 are variables bound to Geometry class-valued attributes and g is a constant Geometry object.
- condition based on *distance* function: let g, g_1, g_2 be variables bound to Geometry class-valued attributes, g be a constant Geometry object, d be a real variable, d be a real constant, and $\theta \in \{=, \neq, <, >, \leq, \geq\}$ be a comparison operator. We allow the following four cases of conditions: $distance(g_1, g_2)\theta d$, $distance(g_1, g_2)\theta d$, $distance(g, g)\theta d$, $distance(g, g)\theta d$.

We assume that every variable appeared in a condition is bound to a constant value or some attribute of a global relation. As exceptional cases, for $distance(g_1, g_2)\theta d$ or $distance(g, g)\theta d$, we allow that d's are free variables.

4.2 Conditions with Spatial Range Restrictions

In this subsection, we introduce the notion of a condition with spatial range restriction. For example, consider the following query:

$$ans(n) \leftarrow Restaurant(n, c, a, l), contains(g, l).$$

This query retrieves all names of restaurants such that their locations are contained in the constant spatial region g. In this case, the positions which the variable l can take are restricted inside of the region g. In such a case, we call $contains(g, l)$ a *condition with spatial range restriction* and l is called a *variable with spatial range restriction*. Note that either of the cases that two arguments are variables (e.g., $contains(g_1, g_2)$) and the inclusion relationship is opposite (e.g., $constants(l, g)$) is not a condition with spatial range restriction. Considering the spatial predicates introduced in Section 3.2, the following three cases become the conditions with spatial range restrictions:

- *equals*(g, g) (also *equals*(g, g))
- *within*(g, g)
- *contains*(g, g)

Among three conditions shown above, the condition *equals*(g, g) is easily reduced by deleting variable *g* by replacing it with g, and the condition *within*(g, g) is also reducible since it is equivalent to *contains*(g, g). Therefore, we only consider the case of *contains*(g, g) in the following discussion.

Additionally, there exists another case of spatial range restriction. Since we have allowed conditions based on the *distance* function, we can construct queries such as

$$ans(n) \leftarrow Restaurants(n, c, a, l), distance(l, \text{p}) \leq 1000.$$

In this case, the spatial region which the location variable *l* can take is restricted by the Position class constant p. We also call '*distance*(*l*, p) ≤ 1000' a condition with spatial range restriction. In general, a predicate with *distance* function becomes a condition with spatial range restriction when it has the form

$$distance(g, g)\,\theta\,d, \qquad (2)$$

where *g* is a variable, g is a constant Geometry object, d is a real constant, and θ is < or ≤.

4.3 Examples of Source Descriptions

A *source description* is a kind of metadata described for each information source and consists of the following two descriptions:

– *contents description*: describes the contents of the source.
– *capability description*: represents the query processing capability of the source.

Figure 3 shows examples of source descriptions. There are two global relations *Restaurant* and *Evaluation*: their definitions have appeared in Section 3.1. As described in the figure, we assume that each source description is associated with exactly one global relation: sources A, B, and C correspond to the global relation *Restaurant* and source D corresponds to the global relation *Evaluation*. In the following, we denote the set of information sources associated with a global relation **R** as *sources*(**R**).

Contents Description We briefly describe the syntax and the semantics of the contents description part. This part specifies the contents of the information source in terms of the global schema. The **contents** part of source A, for instance, shows that the contents of the source, represented by a relation $S_A(n, c, a, l)$, is associated with the global (virtual) relation *Restaurant*. The notation '$S_A(n, c, a, l) \subseteq Restaurant(n, c, a, l), contains(\text{r}, l)$' means that for a relation *ans*(*n*, *c*, *a*, *l*) defined as

$$ans(n, c, a, l) \leftarrow Restaurant(n, c, a, l), contains(\text{r}, l),$$

the relationship

$$S_A(n, c, a, l) \subseteq ans(n, c, a, l)$$

holds. Namely, it means that the set of tuples provided by source A is a subset of the query result issued to the virtual global database. The symbol '⊆' means that the contents of the source do not necessarily contain all the query results for the virtual global

Source A: provides restaurant information within the area bounded by the polygon $\mathbf{r}$ and allows retrieval by restaurant name and address.   **contents**: $S_A(n, c, a, l) \subseteq Restaurant(n, c, a, l), contains(\mathbf{r}, l)$ **filters**: $\langle \mathbf{n}\text{: string} \rangle \Rightarrow n = \mathbf{n}, \langle \mathbf{a}\text{: string} \rangle \Rightarrow a = \mathbf{a}$
Source B: given a query point and a threshold value of distances, this source returns nearby restaurants within the distance threshold. It allows a category-based condition as an additional filter condition.   **contents**: $S_B(n, c, a, l) \subseteq Restaurant(n, c, a, l)$ **filters**: $\langle \mathbf{p}\text{: Point}, \mathbf{d}\text{: real} \rangle \Rightarrow distance(l, \mathbf{p}) \leq \mathbf{d}, \langle \mathbf{c}\text{: string} \rangle \Rightarrow c = \mathbf{c}$
Source C: given a restaurant name, this source returns restaurants that match the specified name. An optional polygon value is given, it only considers restaurants within the specified polygon region.   **contents**: $S_C(n, c, a, l) \subseteq Restaurant(n, c, a, l)$ **filters**: $\langle \mathbf{n}\text{: string} \rangle \Rightarrow n = \mathbf{n}, \langle \mathbf{g}\text{: Polygon} \rangle \Rightarrow contains(\mathbf{g}, l)$
Source D: provides restaurant evaluation scores and allows retrieval by restaurant name and/or evaluation score.   **contents**: $S_D(n, s) \subseteq Evaluation(n, s)$ **filters**: $\langle \mathbf{n}\text{: string} \rangle \Rightarrow n = \mathbf{n}, \langle \mathbf{s}\text{: real} \rangle \Rightarrow s\,\theta\,\mathbf{s}\;(\theta \in \{=, \neg, <, >, \leq, \geq\})$

Fig. 3. Examples of Source Description

database. Note that the contents description for source A contains a constant Polygon value $\mathbf{r}$ and a *contains* predicate. It represents that the restaurant information provided by source A is limited within the geographic region of $\mathbf{r}$.

The general form of a **contents** field is defined as

$$\textbf{contents}: S(u) \subseteq \mathbf{R}(u), c_1, \ldots, c_n, \qquad (3)$$

where u is a sequence of variables, $\mathbf{R}$ is a global relation name, and $c_1, \ldots, c_n$ ($n \geq 0$) are conditions. We allow the following two types of conditions in the specification:

- comparison conditions $x\,\theta\,c$: where x is a variable bound to a primitive value of $\mathbf{R}$, c is a primitive constant, and θ is a comparison operator.
- conditions with spatial range restriction: conditions $contains(g, g)$ and $distance(g, g)\,\theta\,d$ ($\theta \in \{<, \leq\}$) belong to this category, where g is a variable bound to a Geometry class attribute of $\mathbf{R}$.

According to the definition, the contents description

$$S(n, c, a, l) \subseteq Restaurant(n, c, a, l), contains(g, l), distance(l, p) \leq 5000$$

specifies an information source that contains tuples for the restaurants such that they are contained in the region g and within 5,000 meters from the point p. As an another example, the description

$$S(n, c, a, l) \subseteq Restaurant(n, c, a, l), c = \text{``Italian''}$$

specifies a source that provides information about Italian restaurants.

Capability Description In the **filters** part, we describe the query patterns specifiable in a query for the information source. In the notation '*pat* $\Rightarrow$ *out*', *pat* enumerates mandatory input arguments (input pattern) and *out* denotes the condition issued to the underlying source when the input arguments are given. For example, if we assign a value "Yokohama" to the input value a in the **filters** part of source A, the condition associated with a is activated then we get the result of the query

$$ans(n, c, a, l) \leftarrow S_A(n, c, a, l), a = \text{``Yokohama''}$$

from source A. When two or more arguments are given, multiple conditions are activated. In such cases, we assume that they are conjunctively connected to generate the query result.

5 Query Processing

In this section, we describe query processing steps to integrate spatial information sources for a given query. The main topics are selection of useful information sources for the query, generation of subqueries to retrieve information from the selected sources, and integration of the retrieved results.

5.1 Overview of Query Processing

Given a query from the user, the mediator constructs a query plan. The construction consists of the following steps:

1. First, the mediator checks the correctness of the given query according to the global schema. Then deletion of redundant variables and simplification of expressions are performed. For example, given an expression '$distance(p, q) \leq d$' for two constant variables p and q, we can transform it to a more simplified expression based on the actual distance between p and q such as '$100 \leq d$'. Then the query is decomposed into subqueries: a subquery exactly corresponds to one information source and aims to retrieve the required information from the source.
2. Next, selection of useful information sources is performed. For each subquery of the given query, we evaluate the possibility whether the subquery is satisfiable or not for each information source and exclude information sources that have no chance to retrieve tuples for the subquery. For this purpose, we utilize the contents description of each information source.
3. Third, we judge whether each condition of a subquery can be pushed into the underlying information source. In this step, we try to push as many conditions as possible. Since the pushed conditions work to decrease the size of the query results from the information sources, this step is considered to be a kind of query optimization.
4. Finally, we generate the query plan for the integration of partial results from the underlying information sources.

In the following, we mainly focus on Step 2 and 3 since these steps are essential for the integration of heterogeneous spatial information sources, the main topic of our paper.

5.2 Selection of Information Sources

In this subsection, the selection scheme of useful information sources is described. The scheme uses the information in contents descriptions to evaluate the satisfiability of a subquery.

Processing Conditions with Spatial Range Restriction We can judge the possibility that an information source has a chance to satisfy the given subquery by examining its contents description so that we can exclude information sources not useful for the subquery from the consideration. In the following, we focus on conditions with spatial range restrictions introduced before.

Example 1. Assume that a subquery over the global schema

$$ans(n) \leftarrow Restaurant(n, c, a, l), dist(l, \text{p}) \leq 1000$$

is given and assume that $E \in sources(Restauraunt)$; namely, source E corresponds to the global relation *Restaurant*. Suppose that the contents description of source E is

$$S_E(n, c, a, l) \subseteq Restaurant(n, c, a, l), c = \text{"Italian"}, contains(\text{r}, l).$$

In this case, we can say that source E has a possibility to satisfy the subquery when

$$\exists l (contains(\text{r}, l) \land dist(l, \text{p}) \leq 1000)$$

is true. The condition is equivalent to the case that the region r and the circle centered at p with the radius 1000 (we denote it by $circle(\text{p}, 1000)$) has an overlap, namely when

$$intersects(\text{r}, circle(\text{p}, 1000)) = true$$

holds. ∎

Based on the above consideration, we formally show our selection scheme. Let the given query be

$$ans(u) \leftarrow \mathbf{R}_1, \ldots, \mathbf{R}_n, c_1, \ldots, c_m, \quad (4)$$

where $\mathbf{R}_i$ ($1 \leq i \leq n$) are global relation names and c_i ($1 \leq i \leq m$) are conditions. Let the set of information sources which correspond to the global relation $\mathbf{R}_i$ be $sources(\mathbf{R}_i) = \{R_{i1}, \ldots, R_{il}\}$ and let the contents description of R_{ij} ($1 \leq j \leq l$) be

$$S_{R_{ij}}(v) \subseteq \mathbf{R}_i(v), e_1, \ldots, e_s. \quad (5)$$

Assume that $\mathbf{R}_i$ contains a spatial attribute a (such as "location" attribute in our example). Let $\{\tilde{c}_1, \ldots, \tilde{c}_{m'}\}$ ($m' \leq m$) be the largest subset of $\{c_1, \ldots, c_m\}$ such that $\tilde{c}_i$ ($1 \leq i \leq m'$) contains the same variable (say x) that is bound to the attribute a. Also, let $\{\tilde{e}_1, \ldots, \tilde{e}_{s'}\}$ ($s' \leq s$) be the largest subset of $\{e_1, \ldots, e_s\}$ such that $\tilde{e}_i$ ($1 \leq i \leq s'$) contains the same variable (say y) that is bound to the attribute a. Now assume that we replace every occurrence of the variable y in $\tilde{e}_i$ ($1 \leq i \leq s'$) to x. Then consider the formula

$$\exists x (\tilde{c}_1 \land \cdots \land \tilde{c}_{m'} \land \tilde{e}_1 \land \cdots \land \tilde{e}_{s'}). \quad (6)$$

When this formula is false, the source R_{ij} has no possibility to satisfy the query condition $\tilde{c}_1 \wedge \cdots \wedge \tilde{c}_{m'}$ so that we can exclude R_{ij} from the target of the query. The problem whether Eq. (6) is true or false can be determined by taking the intersection of the regions represented by $\tilde{c}_1, \ldots, \tilde{c}_{m'}$ and $\tilde{e}_1, \ldots, \tilde{e}_{s'}$ (by using the *intersection* function shown in Section 3.2) and by evaluating its emptiness (by using the *isempty* function). Such processing scheme of contents description is implementable if a SQL processing system conforming to the OpenGIS specification [18] is available.

It is not efficient, however, to compute intersections of Geometry objects having arbitrary shapes. To reduce the processing cost, we can use the *envelope* function to compute the MBB of each region and take their intersection to evaluate the possibility that the source R_{ij} satisfies a given query. In that case, however, we have a possibility that we should access unuseful information sources since the intersection of MBBs are not necessarily equivalent with the original intersection. This is a tradeoff between the query planning cost and the query processing cost.

So far, we have focused on the cases of spatial attributes. For an atomic attribute, we can also exclude unuseful information sources from a query evaluation process. For example, for the query

$$ans(n) \leftarrow Restaurant(n, c, a, l), c = \text{``Japanese''},$$

we can exclude the sources that only provide information of Italian restaurants. The detail of the query processing scheme for this case is omitted since it is not a scope of this paper.

Processing Join Conditions Based on Spatial Relationships For queries including join conditions with spatial relationships, we can omit redundant join processing by considering contents descriptions.

Example 2. Let $BusStop(m, p)$ be a global relation which holds bus stop names (m) and their positions (p). Consider the query

$$ans(n, m) \leftarrow Restaurant(n, c, a, l), BusStop(m, p), distance(l, p) \leq 200$$

for the global relation. Assume that sources F and G satisfy $F \in sources(Restaurant)$ and $G \in sources(BusStop)$ and that their contents descriptions are specified as shown below:

$$S_F(n, c, a, l) \subseteq Restaurant(n, c, a, l), contains(\mathtt{r}, l)$$
$$S_G(m, p) \subseteq BusStop(m, p), contains(\mathtt{s}, p)$$

When $distance(\mathtt{r}, \mathtt{s}) \leq 200$, there is a room that the spatial join condition is satisfied so that we have to issue queries to the sources F and G. When $distance(\mathtt{r}, \mathtt{s}) > 200$, however, there is no possibility that the join condition is satisfied: therefore, we do not have to consider to process this query. ∎

The detail our approach is given as follows. For a query

$$ans(u) \leftarrow \mathbf{R}, \mathbf{S}, c_1, \ldots, c_n, \tag{7}$$

assume that the contents descriptions of the sources $R_i \in source(\mathbf{R})$ and $S_j \in sources(\mathbf{S})$ are

$$S_{R_i}(v) \subseteq \mathbf{R}(v), e_1, \ldots, e_m \qquad (8)$$
$$S_{S_j}(w) \subseteq \mathbf{S}(w), f_1, \ldots, f_l. \qquad (9)$$

Let r and s be the variables bound to spatial attributes a_R and a_S of R_i and S_j, respectively. Then let $\{\tilde{e}_1, \ldots, \tilde{e}_{m'}\}$ ($m' \leq m$) be the largest subset of $\{e_1, \ldots, e_m\}$ such that $\tilde{e}_i$ ($1 \leq i \leq m'$) is bound to the attribute a_R and let $\{\tilde{f}_1, \ldots, \tilde{f}_{l'}\}$ ($l' \leq l$) be the largest subset of $\{f_1, \ldots, f_l\}$ such that $\tilde{f}_j$ ($1 \leq j \leq l'$) is bound to the attribute a_S. Also let e be the union of the regions corresponding to $\tilde{e}_1, \ldots, \tilde{e}_{m'}$ and let f be the union of the regions corresponding to $\tilde{f}_1, \ldots, \tilde{f}_{l'}$. Based on these definitions, we can use the following strategies:

- when a predicate $equals(r, s)$ is included in a query, the join result of R_i and S_j by the condition $equals(r, s)$ becomes empty if $intersects(\mathtt{e}, \mathtt{f}) = false$. Therefore, we do not have to the join between R_i and S_j according to $equals(r, s)$ if this condition is satisfied. Similarly, we can exclude unnecessary joins for the join predicates $intersects(r, s)$, $touches(r, s)$, $crosses(r, s)$, $within(r, s)$, and $contains(r, s)$ by using the predicate $intersects(\mathtt{e}, \mathtt{f})$ in the judgment.
- when a predicate $distance(r, s) \theta d$ ($\theta \in \{=, <, \leq\}$) is included in a query, we can reduce the judgment to the evaluation of the condition $distance(\mathtt{e}, \mathtt{f}) \leq d$.

Based on the approach shown above, we can omit unnecessary joins between information sources so that the query processing cost will be reduced.

5.3 Pushing Conditions Based on Capability Descriptions

To process given queries efficiently, we have to utilize filtering facilities provided by each information source. In this subsection, we discuss how to push query conditions to the underlying sources with the focus on the cases of spatial attributes.

Our approach is to push as many conditions as possible to reduce the size of retrieved query results. For example, when a query

$$ans(n) \leftarrow Restaurant(n, c, a, l), contains(\mathtt{r}, l)$$

is given, if we have a filtering condition in the capability description that matches to the query condition, such as

$$\langle \mathtt{g}: Geometry \rangle : contains(\mathtt{g}, p),$$

we can push the condition $contains(\mathtt{r}, l)$ to the source. Note that we do not require two predicates are exactly same ones: for instance, *within* and *contains* will match since they have exactly opposite roles.

Even if there is no filtering conditions that matches to the given query condition, we may have a room to find a more general condition as a filtering condition. For example, given the query condition $equals(g, g)$, we first try to find the predicate *equals* in the filtering conditions. If it is failed, we next try to find the filtering condition *intersects(h,* h). If the filtering condition is found, we can push *intersects(g,* g) to the underlying source, but note that we have to examine whether each retrieved tuple satisfies the condition *equals(g,* g) after the retrieval since we have used an weaker condition. For other predicates such as *equals, touches, crosses, within, contains*, and *overlaps*, the above strategy to use more general filtering conditions are also applicable when the filtering predicate *intersects* is available in the underlying information source. Also, a query containing the *distance* function such as

$$ans(n) \leftarrow Restaurant(n, c, a, l), distance(l, \text{p}) \leq 1000$$

can be reduced to the processing of an *intersects* predicate between the circle centered at p with the radius 1000 and restaurant locations l's.

Summarizing the above discussion, the query processing strategy in our framework is shown as follows:

1. Push as many query conditions as possible into the underlying information sources. Each wrapper has a role to efficiently process the pushed filtering conditions.
2. When pushing query conditions, we use the following strategies:
   (a) if an equivalent filtering condition to the given query condition is available in the information source, we directly push the query condition into the source.
   (b) Otherwise, if a more general condition is applicable, we push the general condition to the source. In this case, we need an additional step to check the retrieved results exactly satisfy the given query condition.

6 Conclusions and Future Work

In this paper, we have proposed a framework to integrate heterogeneous spatial information sources and provide location-oriented information services to users. It is based on the source description framework in which the contents and the query capabilities of the underlying information sources are declaratively described as source descriptions, and they are used by the mediator in selecting target information sources and generating query plans. The features of the proposed source description framework is as follows:

1. The ability to specify the contents of spatial information sources as queries (possibly include spatial predicates) over the sources.
2. Specification facility of the contents and filter conditions for spatial information sources: the mediator can use these specifications to select target information sources and generate efficient query plans.

We have shown with examples how the mediator selects appropriate information sources and generates query plans using source descriptions. Our future work includes further investigation of source selection and query planning strategies. Since there are various spatial data types and spatial predicates in real spatial information sources, we have to consider their relationships in source selection and plan generation steps.

Acknowledgments

This research was supported in part by the Grant-in-Aid for Scientific Research from the Ministry of Education, Science, Sports and Culture, Japan (#12780183 and #12480067).

References

1. A. Včkovski, K.E. Brassel, and H.-J. Schek (eds.). *Proc. of Second Intl. Conf. on Interoperating Geographic Information Systems (INTEROP'99)*, Zurich, Switzerland, Lecture Notes in Computer Science, Vol. 1580, Springer-Verlag, Mar. 1999.
2. H. Kitagawa, A. Morishima, and H. Mizuguchi. Integration of Heterogeneous Information Sources in InfoWeaver. in *Advances in Multimedia and Databases for the Next Century — A Swiss/Japanese Perspective —*, Y. Masunaga and S. Spaccapietra (eds.), World Scientific, 2000, pp. 124–137.
3. A.Y. Levy, A. Rajaraman, and J.J. Ordille. Querying Heterogeneous Information Sources Using Source Descriptions. In *Proc. of VLDB*, pp. 251–262, Mumbai, India, Sept. 1996.
4. P. Rigaux, M. Scholl, and A. Voisand. *Spatial Databases: With Application to GIS*. Morgan Kaufmann, San Francisco, CA, 2001.
5. Open GIS Consortium Home Page. http://www.opengis.org/
6. POIX: Point Of Interest eXchange Language. http://www.w3.org/TR/poix/
7. G-XML Home Page. http://gisclh.dpc.or.jp/gxml/contents/index.htm
8. Proposal of RWML. http://www2.ceri.go.jp/its-win/RWML.htm
9. Yahoo! Maps and Driving Directions. http://www.yahoo.com/r/mp/
10. Digital City: Home – Make It Your Own Town. http://www.digitalcity.com/
11. citysearch.com. http://www.citysearch.com/
12. Ekimae Tanken Club. http://ekimae.toshiba.co.jp/
13. MONET Information Service. http://www.tms.ne.jp/
14. H. Tarumi, K. Morishita, M. Nakao, and Y. Kambayashi. SpaceTag: An Overlaid Virtual System and its Applications. in *Proc. of IEEE Intl. Conf. on Multimedia Computing and Systems* (ICMCS'99), Volume I, pp. 207–212, Florence Italy, Jun. 1999.
15. K. Takahashi, N. Miura, S. Yokoji, and K. Shima. Mobile Info Search: Information Integration for Location-Aware Computing. *IPSJ Journal*, Vol. 41, No. 4, pp. 1192–1200, Apr. 2000.
16. MIS2: Mobile Info Search 2. http://www.kokono.net/
17. S. Chawathe, H. Garcia-Molina, J. Hammer, K. Ireland, Y. Papakonstantinou, J. Ullman, and J. Widom. The TSIMMIS Project: Integration of Heterogeneous Information Sources. *IPSJ Research Report*, 94-DBS-100, pp. 7–18, Oct. 1994.
18. Open GIS Consortium, Inc. Open GIS Simple Features Specification for SQL, Revision 1.1, May 1999. OpenGIS Project Document 99-049.
19. M.J. Carey and D. Kossmann. Processing Top N and Bottom N Queries. *IEEE Data Engineering Bulletin*, Vol. 20, No. 3, pp. 12–19, Sept. 1997.

Topological Relationships of Complex Points and Complex Regions

Thomas Behr and Markus Schneider

FernUniversität Hagen, Praktische Informatik IV
D-58084 Hagen, Germany
studium.da@thomas-behr.de, markus.schneider@fernuni-hagen.de

Abstract. Topological relationships between spatial objects have been a focus of research on spatial data handling and reasoning for a long time. Especially as predicates they support the design of suitable query languages for spatial data retrieval and analysis in databases. Unfortunately, they are so far only applicable to simplified abstractions of spatial objects like single points, continuous lines, and simple regions, as they occur in systems like current geographical information systems and spatial database systems. Since these abstractions are usually not sufficient to cope with the complexity of geographic reality, their generalization is needed which especially has influence on the nature, definition, and number of their topological relationships. This paper partially closes this gap and first introduces very general spatial data types for complex points and complex regions. It then defines the corresponding complete sets of mutually exclusive, topological relationships.

Keywords. Topological predicate, spatial data type, 9-intersection model

1 Introduction

For a long time topological relationships have been a focus of research in disciplines like spatial databases, geographical information systems, CAD/CAM systems, image databases, spatial analysis, computer vision, artificial intelligence, cognitive science, psychology, and linguistics. Topological relationships like *overlap*, *inside*, or *meet* describe purely qualitative properties that characterize the relative positions of spatial objects and that are preserved under continuous transformations such as translation, rotation, and scaling. They exclude any consideration of quantitative measures like distance or direction measures and are associated with notions like adjacency, coincidence, connectivity, inclusion, and continuity. In particular, they are needed for spatial reasoning and in spatial query languages where they are, for instance, employed as part of a filter condition in a query.

Some well known, formal models for the definition of topological relationships have already been proposed (see Section 2.2). But they are essentially tailored to the treatment of simple regions and lines. Simple regions are two-dimensional point sets topologically equivalent to a closed disc, and simple lines are one-dimensional features embedded in the plane with two end points. Points are not taken into account, since their interrelations are trivial. Unfortunately, the variety and complexity of geographic entities can be hardly modeled with these simple geometric structures. Due to a lack of space, we will confine ourselves to points and regions in this paper. With regard to points, we will allow finite collections of single points as point objects. With regard to regions, the two main extensions relate to separations of the exterior (holes) and to separations of the interior (multiple components). Both extensions ensure closure of geometric operations and are common in geographical applications. Countries, e.g., can be made up of multiple components (islands) and can have holes (enclaves).

The goals of this paper are twofold: first we introduce and formalize spatial data types for *complex points* and *complex regions*. Then all possible topological relationships between two complex points and between two complex regions, respectively, are derived from the well known 9-intersection model. For this purpose, we draw up collections of constraints specifying conditions for valid topological relationships and satisfying the properties of *completeness* and *exclusiveness*. The property of completeness ensures a full covering of all topological situations. The property of exclusiveness ensures that two different relationships cannot hold for the same two spatial objects.

The remainder of the paper is organized as follows: Section 2 discusses related work regarding spatial objects and topological relationships. Section 3 summarizes the spatial data model for which topological relationships will be investigated. Section 4 explains the strategy for deriving topological relationships from the 9-intersection model. In Section 5 all topological relationships between complex points are analyzed. Section 6 does the same for complex regions. Finally, Section 7 draws some conclusions and discusses future work.

2 Related Work

In this section we discuss some related work about spatial objects as the operands of topological relationships (respectively corresponding predicates) (Section 2.1) and about topological relationships themselves (Section 2.2).

2.1 Spatial Objects

In the past, numerous data models and query languages for spatial data have been proposed with the aim of formulating and processing spatial queries in databases (e.g., [8, 9]). *Spatial data types* (see [9] for a survey) like *point, line,* or *region* are the central concept of these approaches. They provide fundamental abstractions for modeling the structure of geometric entities, their relationships, properties, and operations. Topological predicates operate on instances of these data types, called *spatial objects*. So far, rather simple object structures (like *simple* points, lines, and regions) have been used as arguments of topological predicates. In this paper, we are interested in topological predicates on *complex* spatial objects for two reasons. First, from an application point of view, simple spatial structures are insufficient abstractions of spatial reality. For example,

Italy cannot be modeled by a simple region, since it has the Vatican as a hole and comprises islands in the Mediterranean Sea. Second, from a formal point of view, we have to require closure properties for the spatial data types. This means, e.g., that the geometric intersection, union, and difference of two point, two line, or two region objects, respectively, may not leave the corresponding type definition. Similar considerations lead to a generalization of point objects.

We will give formal definitions of these object structures in Section 3. For the definition of a point data type we use set theory. For the definition of a region data type and its topological predicates we employ the point set paradigm and *point set topology* [7]. Regions are modeled as infinite point sets in the Euclidean plane. Point set topology permits to distinguish different *parts* of the point set of a region. Given such a point set, say A, these parts identify its *boundary* ∂A, its *interior* $A°$, and its *exterior* A^-, which are pairwise disjoint. The union of $A°$ and ∂A corresponds to the *closure* $\overline{A}$ of A. The effect of applying the *interior* operation to a point set is to eliminate dangling points, dangling lines, and boundary parts. The effect of the *closure* operation is to eliminate cuts and punctures by appropriately supplementing points as well as adding the boundary. Hence, it makes sense only to consider point sets A for which $A = \overline{A°}$ holds. This concept of regularity avoids geometric anomalies in regions and leads to so-called *regular closed* point sets respectively regions without degeneracies [10].

2.2 Topological Relationships

An important approach for characterizing topological relationships rests on the so-called 9-*intersection model* [3, 4, 5]. This model allows one to derive a complete collection of mutually exclusive topological relationships for each combination of spatial types. The model is based on the nine possible intersections of boundary (∂A), interior ($A°$), and exterior (A^-) of a spatial object A with the corresponding components of another object B. Each intersection is tested with regard to the topologically invariant criteria of emptiness and non-emptiness.

$2^9 = 512$ different configurations are possible from which only a certain subset makes sense depending on the *definition* and combination of spatial objects just considered. For each combination of spatial types this means that each of its predicates can be associated with a unique intersection matrix (Table 1) so that all predicates are mutually exclusive and complete with regard to the topologically invariant criteria of emptiness and non-emptiness. Topological relationships that have been investigated so far are restricted in the sense that their argument objects are not allowed to have the most general, possible structure. It is just the objective of this paper to give the most general definitions of spatial objects and to identify the topological relationships between them.

Topological relationships have been first investigated for simple regions [2, 3, 4, 5]. For two simple regions eight meaningful configurations have been identified which lead to the well known eight predicates called *disjoint, meet, overlap, equal, inside, contains, covers,* and *coveredBy*. The 9-intersection model has been extended with further topological invariants (like the dimension of the intersec-

$$\begin{pmatrix} A^\circ \cap B^\circ \neq \varnothing & A^\circ \cap \partial B \neq \varnothing & A^\circ \cap B^- \neq \varnothing \\ \partial A \cap B^\circ \neq \varnothing & \partial A \cap \partial B \neq \varnothing & \partial A \cap B^- \neq \varnothing \\ A^- \cap B^\circ \neq \varnothing & A^- \cap \partial B \neq \varnothing & A^- \cap B^- \neq \varnothing \end{pmatrix}$$

Table 1. The 9-intersection matrix. Each matrix entry is a 1 (*true*) or 0 (*false*).

tion components, their types (touching, crossing), the number of components) to discover more details about topological relationships (e.g., [2]).

It is surprising that topological predicates on complex regions have so far not been defined. But the definition of these predicates is particularly important for spatial query languages that aim at integrating complex regions having holes and separations. Two works have so far contributed to a definition of topological relationships for more complex regions. In [1] the so-called TRCR (Topological Relationships for Composite Regions) model only allows sets of disjoint simple regions without holes. But topological relationships between composite regions are defined in an ad hoc manner and are not systematically derived from the underlying model. Moreover, the model is only related to but not directly based on the 9-intersection model. In [6] topological relationships of simple regions with holes are considered. Unfortunately, multi-part regions are not permitted. While the authors take the number of components (area without holes, holes) of two regions into account and consider the large number of topological relationships between all component pairs of both regions, we pursue a global approach that is independent of the number of components. Hence, a further goal of this paper is to provide an integrated treatment of holes and separations for regions and to define topological predicates on complex regions in a systematic way.

Topological predicates between simple points are trivial: either two simple points are *disjoint* or they are *equal*. We have a more general view of point objects and consider a complex point as a finite collection of single points. This leads to the necessity of investigating further topological relationships.

3 Spatial Data Model

In this section we strive for a very general definition of complex spatial objects in the Euclidean plane $\mathbb{R}^2$. The task is to identify those point sets that are admissible for complex point and region objects.

A value of type *point* is defined as a finite set of points in the plane. Thus a type for complex points can be specified as

$$point = \{P \subset \mathbb{R}^2 \mid P \text{ is finite}\}$$

We call a value of this type *complex point*. If $P \in point$ is a singleton set, i.e., $|P| = 1$, P is denoted as a *simple point*. For a simple point p we specify $\partial p = \varnothing$ and $p^\circ = p$, which is the commonly accepted definition. For a complex point $P = p_1, \ldots, p_n$ we then obviously obtain $\partial P = \varnothing$ and $P^\circ = \bigcup_{i=1}^n p_i^\circ$.

Since complex regions can be arbitrary points sets but without the geometric anomalies discussed in Section 2.1, we are now already able to give an appropriate definition of a type for *complex regions*:

$$region = \{R \subset \mathbb{R}^2 \mid R \text{ is bounded and regular closed}\}$$

This definition is conceptually somehow "structureless" in the sense that only "flat" point sets are considered and no structural information is revealed. The "structured" view of a regular closed set is that of a region possibly consisting of several area-disjoint components and possibly having area-disjoint holes (Figure 1). Boundary, interior, and exterior result from the corresponding operators on arbitrary point sets.

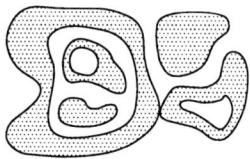

Fig. 1. A complex region.

4 Deriving Topological Relationships from the 9-Intersection Model

Our strategy for the analysis of topological relationships between two complex points or regions is quite simple and yet very general: instead of applying the 9-intersection model to point sets belonging to simple spatial objects, we extend it to point sets belonging to complex spatial objects. Due to the special features of the objects (point, areal properties), the embedding space (here: $\mathbb{R}^2$), the relation between the objects and the embedding space (e.g., it makes a difference whether we consider a point in $\mathbb{R}$ or in $\mathbb{R}^2$), and the employed spatial data model (e.g., discrete, continuous), a number of topological configurations cannot exist and have to be excluded.

Our goal is to determine for each pair of complex spatial data types the corresponding topological constraints or conditions that have to be satisfied; these serve as exclusion criteria for all other impossible configurations. The approach taken starts with the 512 possible matrices and is a two-step process:

(i) For each type combination we give the formalization of a collection of topological constraints for existing relationships in terms of the nine intersections. For each constraint we give reasons for its meaningfulness. The evaluation of each constraint gradually reduces the set of the currently valid matrices by all those matrices not fulfilling the constraint under consideration.

(ii) The existence of topological relationships given by the remaining matrices is verified by realizing prototypical spatial configurations in $\mathbb{R}^2$, i.e., these configurations can be drawn in the plane.

Still open issues relate to the evaluation order, completeness, and minimality of the collection of constraints. Each constraint is a predicate that is matched with all intersection matrices under consideration. All constraints must be satisfied together so that they represent a conjunction of predicates. To say it in other words, constraints are all formulated in conjunctive normal form. Since the conjunction (logical *and*) operator is commutative and associative, the order in which the constraints are evaluated is irrelevant; the final result is always the same. The completeness of the collection of constraints is directly ensured by the second step of the two-step process. The aspect of minimality addresses the possible redundancy of constraints. Redundancy can arise for two reasons. First, several constraints may be correlated in the sense that one of them is more general than the others, i.e., it eliminates at least the matrices excluded by all the other constraints. This can be easily checked by analyzing the constraints themselves and searching for the most non-restrictive and common constraint. Even then the same matrix can be excluded by several constraints simultaneously. Second, a constraint can be covered by some combination of other constraints. This can be checked by a comparison of the matrix collection fulfilling all n constraints with the matrix collection fulfilling $n-1$ constraints. If both collections are equal, then the omitted constraint was implied by the combination of the other constraints and is therefore redundant.

5 Topological Relationships between Complex Points

We now present the constraints for two complex point objects A and B. Each constraint is first formulated colloquially and afterwards formalized by employing the nine intersections. Then a rationale is given explaining why the constraint makes sense. We presuppose that A and B are not empty, because topological relationships for empty operands are not meaningful.

Constraint 1 *All intersections comprising an operand with a boundary operator yield the empty set, i.e.,*

$$\forall C \in \{A°, \partial A, A^-\} : C \cap \partial B = \varnothing \ \land \ \forall D \in \{B°, \partial B, B^-\} : \partial A \cap D = \varnothing$$

Rationale. According to the definition of a complex point $\partial A = \partial B = \varnothing$ holds. The intersection of the empty set with any other component yields the empty set. □

Constraint 2 *The exteriors of two complex point objects always intersect with each other, i.e.,*

$$A^- \cap B^- \neq \varnothing$$

Rationale. We know that $A \cup A^- = \mathbb{R}^2$ and $B \cup B^- = \mathbb{R}^2$. Hence, $A^- \cap B^-$ is only empty if either (i) $A = \mathbb{R}^2$, or (ii) $B = \mathbb{R}^2$, or (iii) $A \cup B = \mathbb{R}^2$. All three situations are impossible, since A, B, and $A \cup B$ are finite sets and $\mathbb{R}^2$ is an infinite set. Thus $A \subset \mathbb{R}^2$, $B \subset \mathbb{R}^2$, and $A \cup B \subset \mathbb{R}^2$ holds. □

Constraint 3 *Each non-empty part of a complex point intersects at least one non-empty part of the other complex point, i.e.,*

$(\forall C \in \{A^\circ, A^-\} : C \cap B^\circ \neq \emptyset \lor C \cap B^- \neq \emptyset) \land$
$(\forall D \in \{B^\circ, B^-\} : A^\circ \cap D \neq \emptyset \lor A^- \cap D \neq \emptyset)$

Rationale. We know that $A^\circ \cup A^- = \mathbb{R}^2$ and that $B^\circ \cup B^- = \mathbb{R}^2$. That is, the complex point A, respectively B, together with its exterior forms a complete partition of the Euclidean plane. Hence, and because only non-empty object parts are considered, the interior and the exterior of A, respectively B, must intersect at least either the interior or the exterior or both parts of B, respectively A. □

Since $\partial A = \partial B = \emptyset$, the second row and the second column of an intersection matrix only yield empty intersections, and we do not have to consider them any further. The remaining intersections are those in the four corners of a matrix. Hence, in the first and third row and in the first and third column of a matrix at least one "corner" intersection must yield true so that we find the value 1 in the matrix there.

It has been checked with a trivial test program that none of the three constraints can be omitted (otherwise we would obtain more matrices). As a result, we obtain five remaining topological relationships between complex points. The corresponding matrices and their geometric interpretations are given in Table 2.

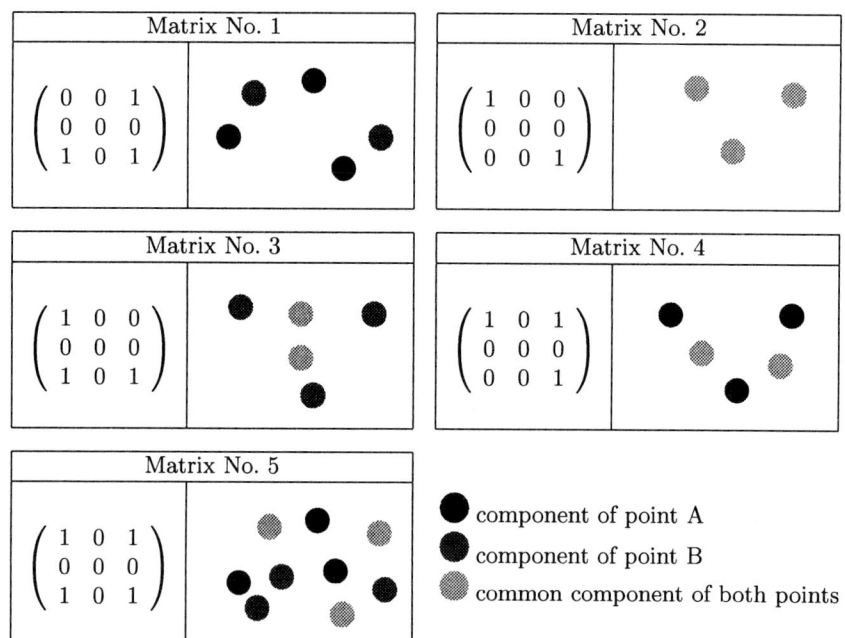

Table 2. The five topological relationship for complex points.

With each matrix we can associate a name for the corresponding topological predicate. Matrix 1 describes the relationship *disjoint*, matrix 2 the relationship *equal*, matrix 3 the relationship *inside*, matrix 4 the relationship *contains*, and matrix 5 the relationship *overlap*.

6 Topological Relationships between Complex Regions

In this section we identify those topological relationships that can be realized between two non-empty, complex regions A and B. We pursue the same strategy as for points and first present constraints that exclude non-existent topological configurations. Note that a *part* of a complex region denotes either its boundary, interior, or exterior and that all parts are non-empty.

Constraint 1 *Each part of a complex region intersects at least one part of the other complex region, i.e.,*

$$(\forall C \in \{A^\circ, \partial A, A^-\} : C \cap B^\circ \neq \emptyset \lor C \cap \partial B \neq \emptyset \lor C \cap B^- \neq \emptyset) \land$$
$$(\forall D \in \{B^\circ, \partial B, B^-\} : A^\circ \cap D \neq \emptyset \lor \partial A \cap D \neq \emptyset \lor A^- \cap D \neq \emptyset)$$

Rationale. We know that $A^\circ \cup \partial A \cup A^- = \mathbb{R}^2$ and that $B^\circ \cup \partial B \cup B^- = \mathbb{R}^2$. That is, the complex region A, respectively B, together with its exterior forms a complete partition of the Euclidean plane. Hence, each part of A, respectively B, must intersect at least one part of B, respectively A. □

Constraint 2 *Neither the interior nor the exterior of a complex region can be completely contained in or equal to the boundary of the other complex region, i.e.,*

$$A^\circ \not\subseteq \partial B \land A^- \not\subseteq \partial B \land B^\circ \not\subseteq \partial A \land B^- \not\subseteq \partial A$$
$$\Leftrightarrow (A^\circ \cap B^\circ \neq \emptyset \lor A^\circ \cap B^- \neq \emptyset) \land (A^- \cap B^\circ \neq \emptyset \lor A^- \cap B^- \neq \emptyset) \land$$
$$(A^\circ \cap B^\circ \neq \emptyset \lor A^- \cap B^\circ \neq \emptyset) \land (A^\circ \cap B^- \neq \emptyset \lor A^- \cap B^- \neq \emptyset)$$

Rationale. The obvious reason is that the dimension of a boundary with its linear structure is less than the dimensions of the interior and the exterior with their areal structures. The constraint definition shows that the formalization based on subset relationships can be transformed to an equivalent formalization based on the nine intersections. If the interior and the exterior, respectively, of a region is not completely contained in or equal to the boundary of the other region, it intersects either the interior or the exterior or both parts of the other region, and vice versa. □

Constraint 3 *The exteriors of two complex region objects always intersect with each other, i.e.,*

$$A^- \cap B^- \neq \emptyset$$

Rationale. We know that $\overline{A} \cup A^- = \mathbb{R}^2$ and $\overline{B} \cup B^- = \mathbb{R}^2$. Hence, $A^- \cap B^-$ is only empty if either (i) $\overline{A} = \mathbb{R}^2$, or (ii) $\overline{B} = \mathbb{R}^2$, or (iii) $\overline{A} \cup \overline{B} = \mathbb{R}^2$. The situations are all impossible, since A, B, and hence $A \cup B$ are bounded, but $\mathbb{R}^2$ is unbounded. □

Constraint 4 *The boundaries of two complex regions are equal if and only if the interiors and the exteriors, respectively, of both regions are equal, i.e.,*

$$(\partial A = \partial B \Leftrightarrow A^\circ = B^\circ \wedge A^- = B^-)$$
$$\Leftrightarrow (c \Leftrightarrow d) \Leftrightarrow ((c \wedge d) \vee (\neg c \wedge \neg d)) \text{ where}$$
$$c = A^\circ \cap \partial B = \varnothing \wedge \partial A \cap B^\circ = \varnothing \wedge \partial A \cap \partial B \neq \varnothing \wedge$$
$$\partial A \cap B^- = \varnothing \wedge A^- \cap \partial B = \varnothing \text{ and}$$
$$d = A^\circ \cap B^\circ \neq \varnothing \wedge A^\circ \cap \partial B = \varnothing \wedge A^\circ \cap B^- = \varnothing \wedge$$
$$\partial A \cap B^\circ = \varnothing \wedge A^- \cap B^\circ = \varnothing \wedge \partial A \cap B^- = \varnothing \wedge$$
$$A^- \cap \partial B = \varnothing \wedge A^- \cap B^- \neq \varnothing$$

Rationale. This very special constraint expresses that complex regions are uniquely characterized by their boundaries. This is ensured by the Jordan Curve Theorem [7]. □

Constraint 5 *If the boundary of a complex region intersects the interior of the other complex region, both its interior and its exterior intersect the interior of the other region, i.e.,*

$$((\partial A \cap B^\circ \neq \varnothing \Rightarrow (A^\circ \cap B^\circ \neq \varnothing \wedge A^- \cap B^\circ \neq \varnothing)) \wedge$$
$$(A^\circ \cap \partial B \neq \varnothing \Rightarrow (A^\circ \cap B^\circ \neq \varnothing \wedge A^\circ \cap B^- \neq \varnothing)))$$
$$\Leftrightarrow ((\partial A \cap B^\circ = \varnothing \vee (A^\circ \cap B^\circ \neq \varnothing \wedge A^- \cap B^\circ \neq \varnothing)) \wedge$$
$$(A^\circ \cap \partial B = \varnothing \vee (A^\circ \cap B^\circ \neq \varnothing \wedge A^\circ \cap B^- \neq \varnothing)))$$

Rationale. On each side of the boundary of a region there is either the region's interior or exterior (Jordan Curve Theorem). On both sides of a line intersecting the interior of this region, we find the interior of the region. If the line is part of the boundary of another region, we obtain the intersection of both regions' interiors and the intersection between the interior of the first region and the exterior of the other region. □

Constraint 6 *If the boundary of a complex region intersects the exterior of the other complex region, both its interior and its exterior intersect the exterior of the other region, i.e.,*

$$((\partial A \cap B^- \neq \varnothing \Rightarrow (A^\circ \cap B^- \neq \varnothing \wedge A^- \cap B^- \neq \varnothing)) \wedge$$
$$(A^- \cap \partial B \neq \varnothing \Rightarrow (A^- \cap B^\circ \neq \varnothing \wedge A^- \cap B^- \neq \varnothing)))$$
$$\Leftrightarrow ((\partial A \cap B^- = \varnothing \vee (A^\circ \cap B^- \neq \varnothing \wedge A^- \cap B^- \neq \varnothing)) \wedge$$
$$(A^- \cap \partial B = \varnothing \vee (A^- \cap B^\circ \neq \varnothing \wedge A^- \cap B^- \neq \varnothing)))$$

Rationale. The argumentation is similar as for the previous constraint. On each side of the boundary of a region there is either the region's interior or exterior. On both sides of a line intersecting the exterior of this region, we find the exterior of the region. If the line is part of the boundary of another region, we obtain the intersection of both regions' exteriors and the intersection between the interior of the first region and the exterior of the other region. □

Constraint 7 *The boundaries of two complex regions intersect, or the boundary of one region intersects the exterior of the other region, i.e.,*

$$\partial A \cap \partial B \neq \emptyset \ \lor \ \partial A \cap B^- \neq \emptyset \ \lor \ A^- \cap \partial B \neq \emptyset$$

Rationale. Assuming that the constraint is false. Then neither the boundaries of the two regions nor the boundary of one region and the exterior of the other region intersect. Consequently, according to Constraint 1, each boundary of one region intersects the interior of the other region. Without loss of generality, let us consider a point $p \in A° \cap \partial B$ and an infinite ray s emanating from p in an arbitrary direction. Since the component of A containing p is bounded, s encounters the boundary of A in a point, say, q. This boundary intersects the exterior, the boundary, or the interior of B. According to our assumption the first two cases cannot hold so that q must lie inside the interior of B. We obtain a similar situation as before, except for the fact that now A and B change their roles. We continue to observe the course of s: the ray over and over again alternately encounters a point of $A° \cap \partial B$ and then a point of $\partial A \cap B°$. Since the ray can be prolonged arbitrarily, A and B must be unbounded. But this is a contradiction to the definition of the *region* data type. □

Constraint 8 *If the interiors of two complex regions intersect, the interior of one region also intersects the boundary of the other region, or the regions' boundaries intersect, i.e.,*

$$(A° \cap B° \neq \emptyset \Rightarrow (A° \cap \partial B \neq \emptyset \ \lor \ \partial A \cap B° \neq \emptyset \ \lor \ \partial A \cap \partial B \neq \emptyset))$$
$$\Leftrightarrow (A° \cap B° = \emptyset \ \lor \ A° \cap \partial B \neq \emptyset \ \lor \ \partial A \cap B° \neq \emptyset \ \lor \ \partial A \cap \partial B \neq \emptyset)$$

Rationale. Let us consider a component of the first region and a component of the second region with intersecting interiors. We have to distinguish three situations. First, if the interiors of both components are equal, also their boundaries are equal and hence intersect. Consequently, also the regions' boundaries intersect. Second, if the interiors of both components but not their boundaries intersect, one component is contained in the other. Since this is a proper containment (otherwise the boundaries would intersect), the boundary of one component must be inside the interior of the other component. Consequently, the interior of one region intersects the boundary of the other region. Third, if the interiors and the boundaries of the two components intersect, both conclusions of the constraint hold. □

Constraint 9 *If the interior of a complex region intersects the exterior of the other region, either the interior of the first region intersects the boundary of the second region, or the boundary of the first region intersects the exterior of the second region, or both regions' boundaries intersect, i.e.,*

$$((A° \cap B^- \neq \emptyset \Rightarrow (A° \cap \partial B \neq \emptyset \ \lor \ \partial A \cap B^- \neq \emptyset \ \lor \ \partial A \cap \partial B \neq \emptyset)) \land$$
$$(A^- \cap B° \neq \emptyset \Rightarrow (\partial A \cap B° \neq \emptyset \ \lor \ A^- \cap \partial B \neq \emptyset \ \lor \ \partial A \cap \partial B \neq \emptyset)))$$
$$\Leftrightarrow ((A° \cap B^- = \emptyset \ \lor \ A° \cap \partial B \neq \emptyset \ \lor \ \partial A \cap B^- \neq \emptyset \ \lor \ \partial A \cap \partial B \neq \emptyset) \land$$
$$(A^- \cap B° = \emptyset \ \lor \ \partial A \cap B° \neq \emptyset \ \lor \ A^- \cap \partial B \neq \emptyset \ \lor \ \partial A \cap \partial B \neq \emptyset))$$

Rationale. If there is an intersection between the interior of a complex region and the exterior of the other complex region, a few different situations for each component causing the intersection can be distinguished. The first situation is that a component partially intersects the interior and the exterior of the other region. Then the boundary of the other region intersects the interior of the first region.

The second situation is that the interior of a component lies completely inside the exterior of the other region. Several cases can now be distinguished. The first case is that also the boundary (and thus the entire component) lies inside and consequently intersects the exterior of the other region. The second case is that the boundary of a component lies only partially inside the exterior of the other region. Again we obtain an intersection between boundary and exterior. The third case is that the boundary of a component intersects the boundary of the other region. Note that the boundary of the component cannot cross the interior of the other region, since then the interior of the component would not be entirely within the exterior of the other region. □

An investigation of the nine constraints with the aid of a trivial test program reveals that all of them are needed with one exception. Constraint 2 is redundant, since the matrices it removes are also eliminated by some combination of the other constraints. Hence it can be omitted. All remaining constraints exclude at least one matrix each. As a result, we obtain 33 topological relationships between complex regions. The corresponding matrices and their geometric interpretation are given in Table 3. The topological relationships between simple regions correspond to the intersection matrices with the numbers 1, 4, 5, 7, 9, 19, 24, and 33.

7 Conclusions and Future Work

In this paper we have defined very general spatial data types for complex points and complex regions in the two-dimensional Euclidean plane on the basis of point set theory and point set topology. The increasing complexity of spatial data types leads to a larger variety of topological relationships. The investigation and formalization of complete collections of mutually exclusive topological relationships between complex points and between complex regions, respectively, has been the main contribution of this paper. It has been done on the basis of the well-known 9-intersection model. We have identified 5 binary relationships between complex points and 33 binary relationships between complex regions.

For future work one could analyze possible topological relationships between complex lines. This first necessitates a formal definition of a corresponding type. Similarly, one could investigate the possible relationships between the three pairs of mixed types. Another problem of interest is the large number of relationships. Whereas the 5 relationships between complex points are manageable by the user, this is not the case for the 33 relationships between complex regions. Here one could think about clustering techniques in the sense of [2].

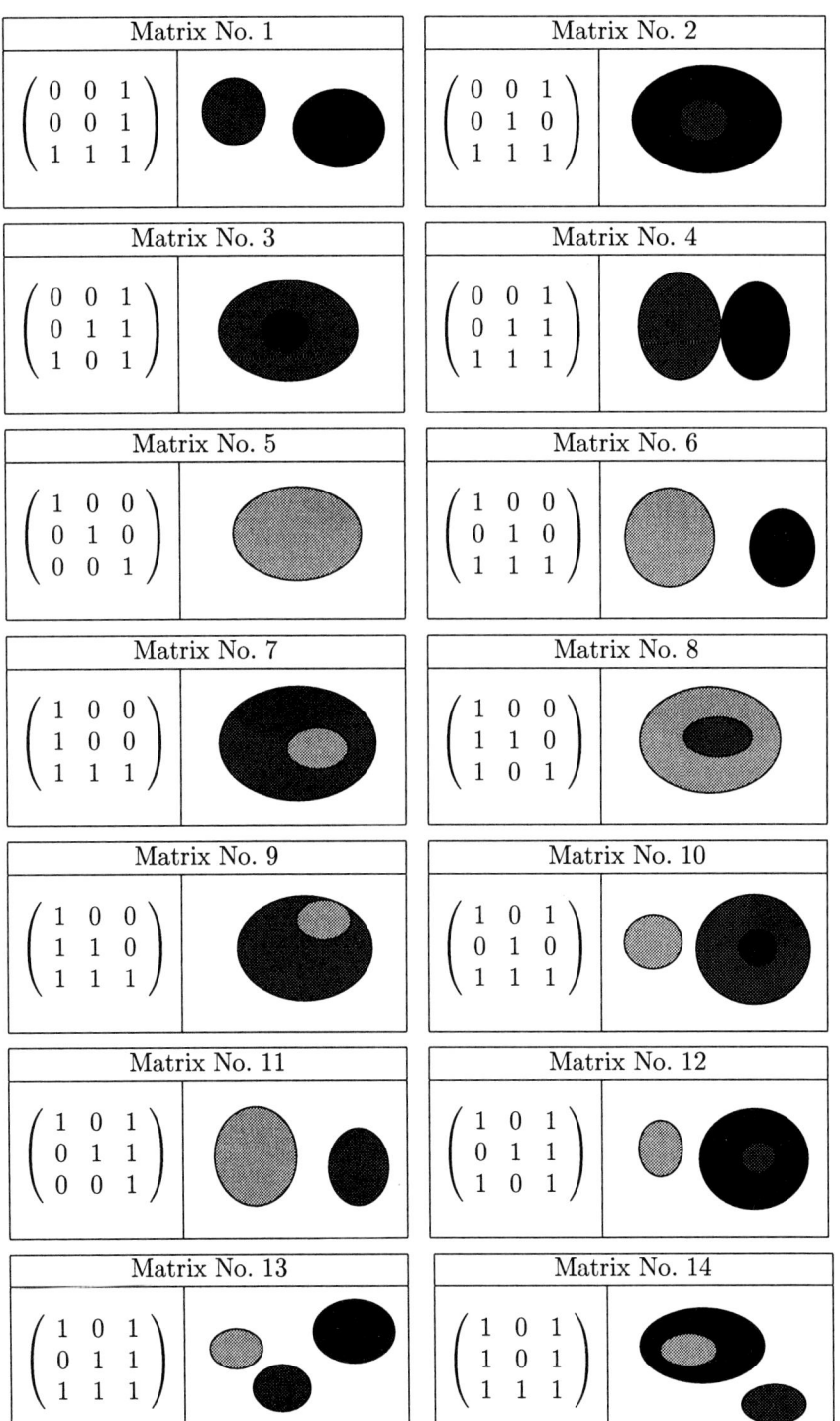

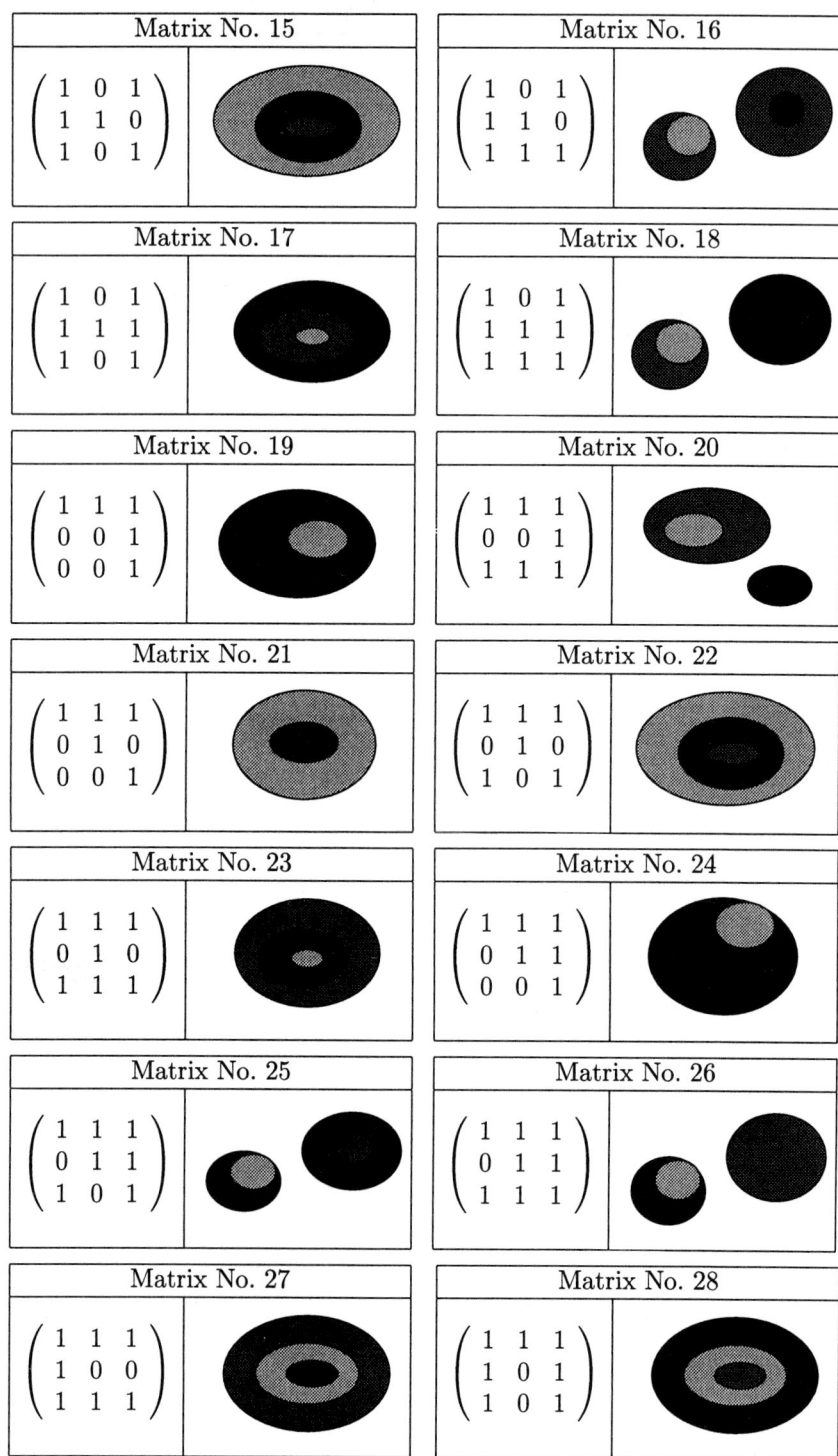

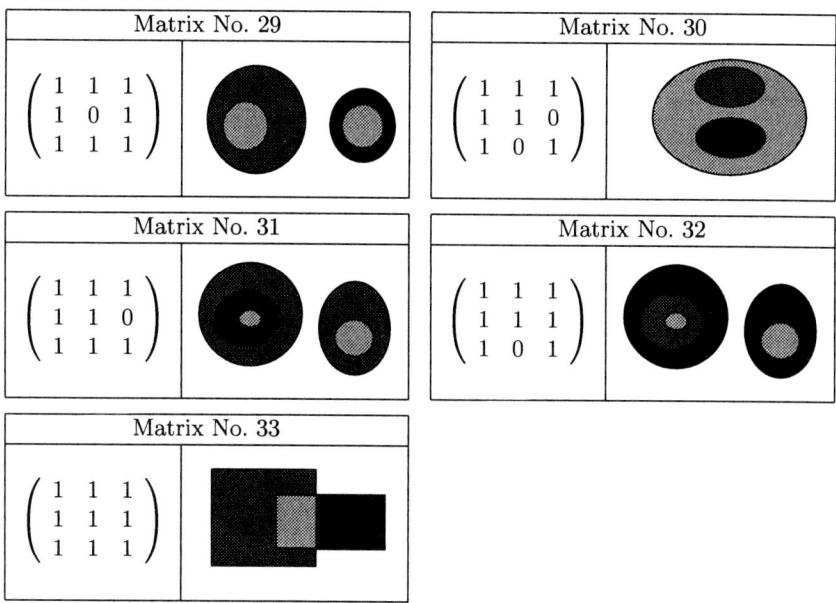

Table 3. The 33 topological relationships for complex regions.

References

[1] E. Clementini, P. Di Felice, and G. Califano. Composite Regions in Topological Queries. *Information Systems*, 20(7):579–594, 1995.
[2] E. Clementini, P. di Felice, and P. van Oosterom. A Small Set of Formal Topological Relationships Suitable for End-User Interaction. In *3rd Int. Symp. on Advances in Spatial Databases*, LNCS 692, pages 277–295, 1993.
[3] M. J. Egenhofer, A. Frank, and J. P. Jackson. A Topological Data Model for Spatial Databases. In *1st Int. Symp. on the Design and Implementation of Large Spatial Databases*, LNCS 409, pages 271–286. Springer-Verlag, 1989.
[4] M. J. Egenhofer and R. D. Franzosa. Point-Set Topological Spatial Relations. *Int. Journal of Geographical Information Systems*, 5(2):161–174, 1991.
[5] M. J. Egenhofer and J. Herring. A Mathematical Framework for the Definition of Topological Relationships. In *4th Int. Symp. on Spatial Data Handling*, pages 803–813, 1990.
[6] M.J. Egenhofer, E. Clementini, and P. Di Felice. Topological Relations between Regions with Holes. *Int. Journal of Geographical Information Systems*, 8(2):128–142, 1994.
[7] S. Gaal. *Point Set Topology*. Academic Press, 1964.
[8] R. H. Güting and M. Schneider. Realm-Based Spatial Data Types: The ROSE Algebra. *VLDB Journal*, 4:100–143, 1995.
[9] M. Schneider. *Spatial Data Types for Database Systems - Finite Resolution Geometry for Geographic Information Systems*, volume LNCS 1288. Springer-Verlag, Berlin Heidelberg, 1997.
[10] R. B. Tilove. Set Membership Classification: A Unified Approach to Geometric Intersection Problems. *IEEE Trans. on Computers*, C-29:874–883, 1980.

DISTIL: A Design Support Environment for Conceptual Modeling of Spatio-temporal Requirements

Sudha Ram, Richard T. Snodgrass, Vijay Khatri and Yousub Hwang

University of Arizona, USA
ram@bpa.arizona.edu, rts@cs.arizona.edu,
vkhatri@bpa.arizona.edu, yhwang@bpa.arizona.edu

Abstract. We describe DISTIL (DIstributed design of SpaTIo-temporaL data), a web-based conceptual modeling prototype system that can help capture the semantics of spatio-temporal data. Via DISTIL, we describe an annotation-based approach that divides spatio-temporal conceptual design into two steps: first capture the *current reality* of an application using a conventional conceptual model *without considering the spatial aspects*, and only then annotate the schema with the spatio-temporal semantics of the application. A database development team can use DISTIL to capture and validate their spatio-temporal data requirements. Using DISTIL we demonstrate that the annotation-based approach for capturing spatio-temporal requirements is straightforward to implement, satisfies ontology-based and cognition-based requirements, and integrates seamlessly into the existing database design methodologies.

1 Introduction

A design support environment automates many of the analysts' tasks in developing software; it helps reduce time and money spent on a project and can improve the quality of the end product. Lately, geographic information is increasingly employed for a wide array of applications—land information systems, environmental modeling, resource management, transportation planning, geo-marketing, geology and archaeology. As a result, there is a need for a mechanism to capture requirements for time-varying geographically referenced data, referred to as spatio-temporal requirements. In this paper, we describe a web-based spatio-temporal conceptual modeling environment called DISTIL (DIstributed design of SpaTIo-temporaL data).

Underlying the geographic applications described above is spatio-temporal data having a *theme*—the phenomenon or object being observed, and *location* and *time* associated with the phenomenon. Via DISTIL, we describe an annotation-based approach that divides spatio-temporal conceptual design into two steps: (i) capture the *current reality* of an application using a conventional conceptual model *without considering the spatial aspects*, and only then (ii) annotate the schema with spatial and temporal semantics of the application. Rather than creating any new constructs, DISTIL uses annotations to capture temporal and spatial aspects of the application.

Our work makes several contributions. First, DISTIL is based on an annotation-based approach, which integrates and extends prior research related to spatio-temporal conceptual modeling. We describe an intuitive ontology-based grammar (Appendix)

for annotation, which comprehensively captures semantics related to space and time. Our approach to spatio-temporal conceptual modeling includes a mechanism to capture spatio-temporal semantics comprehensively, e.g., *event* and *state, valid time, existence time* and *transaction time,* various types of geometries associated with spatiality, user-defined *granularities, indeterminacy,* and *topological relationships.* Second, DISTIL demonstrates a comprehensive methodology for spatio-temporal conceptual modeling that can be applied to any traditional conceptual model, thereby translating it to a spatio-temporal conceptual model. We show how our proposed approach integrates with conventional conceptual design methodologies. Third, via a spatio-temporal application we demonstrate that our approach to spatio-temporal database design using DISTIL is practical and is straightforward to use. Fourth, DISTIL provides an integrated modeling environment that can be used by a distributed team of users and data analysts; it takes advantage of interconnectivity made possible by the Internet. Fifth, our design tool environment parallels human perception for spatio-temporal data. Mennis et al. [10] cite that humans cognitively store *what, where* and *when* data in separate knowledge structures. DISTIL with its two-step approach that first focuses on facts (*what*) and then on the context (*where* and *when*) related to the facts corresponds to the human perception of spatio-temporal data.

In summary, we present a web-based spatio-temporal database design environment that is intuitive from users' point of view, is straightforward to implement from CASE (Computer-Aided Software/System Engineering) tool vendors' perspective, comprehensively captures semantics related to space and time in a way that parallels human cognition, and integrates into existing database design methodologies.

The rest of the paper is organized as follows. In section 2, we motivate the need for an automated spatio-temporal database design tool using a hydrogeologic application at the United States Geological Survey (USGS). We outline the spatio-temporal ontology in section 3, which is the basis for annotations in DISTIL. In section 4, we describe how DISTIL supports spatio-temporal modeling using the example of section 2. In section 5, we present the architecture of DISTIL that supports spatio-temporal design described in the previous section. Finally, comparison with related work and future directions of our research round out the paper.

2 Motivation

Conceptual database design is widely recognized as an important step in the development of database applications. As a result of conceptual design, a conceptual schema is developed that captures database requirements of the users. This schema is very useful in the event of technology upgrades and transfer, and acts as a communication vehicle between different groups of end-users and the data analyst.

We are designing a database for a group of researchers at USGS who are developing a ground-water flow model for Death Valley [4]. The objective of the ground-water flow model is to characterize regional 3D ground water flow paths so that policy makers can make decisions related to radio-nuclide contaminant transport and the impact of ground water pumping on national parks and local communities in the region. However, the predictions based on the model are dependent on the data that form an input to this model.

A large part of the input data for this model is geo-referenced and temporal in nature. For example, two key objects of interest for the application are spring-water sites and borehole sites, which are spatial in nature. A spring-water site is a spring represented as a point on the surface of the earth whose location is given by geographic x- and y-coordinates, with spatial granularity of degree. A borehole site refers to a part of the well whose 3D location is given by the x- and y-coordinates on the earth's surface with spatial granularity of degree, and depth below land surface with spatial granularity of foot; there can be different borehole sites at different depths at the same surface location. Other input data for the model includes discharge at the spring site and water level at the borehole site, both of which are collected by source agencies. Additionally, there are various hydraulic tests conducted at the borehole site. Borehole sites may include a pump that removes water from the borehole site; this can impact other data collected at the borehole site.

Capturing requirements related to spring-water sites, borehole sites, source agencies and pump lifts has many associated issues and a design tool developed to capture these user requirements should: (i) be based on a comprehensive methodology that adequately captures the semantics related to space and time; (ii) be easy to use from the data analysts' point of view, i.e., include a formalism that is intuitive and that provides spatio-temporal modeling support as an extension from their existing database design paradigm; (iii) incorporate a metaphor that bridges the conceptual gap between a computer system and how human beings perceive the real world; (iv) be straightforward to implement from the perspective of a CASE tool vendor; and (v) support geographically distributed users and data analysts. Having elucidated the spatio-temporal requirements, we briefly describe the spatio-temporal ontology that is the basis for spatio-temporal semantic concepts embedded in DISTIL.

3 Ontology

A *time domain* is denoted by the pair $(T, \leq)$, where T is a nonempty set of *time instants* and "$\leq$" is the total order on T; e.g., $(\mathbf{Z}, \leq)$ represents a discrete time domain, where the instants are isomorphic to integers. There are two kinds of facts associated with time, *events* and *states*. An event occurs at a point of time, i.e., an event has no duration. A state, on the other hand, has duration, e.g., a storm occurred from 5:07 PM to 5:46 PM. Facts can interact with time in two orthogonal ways [14] resulting in *transaction time* and *valid time*. Valid time denotes when the fact is true in the real world. On the other hand, transaction time links an object to the time it is current in the database. *Existence time*, which applies to objects, is the valid time when an object exists; it is also referred to as a *lifespan* of an entity. *Temporal granularity* is an integral part of temporal data [2] and refers to the measure of temporal datum. Temporal granularities in the same time domain can be related by *coarser than* and *finer than* relationships. For many applications, it is known only approximately when the event occurred and this is referred to as *valid-time indeterminacy* [6]. While the temporal granularity can be specified for existence time and valid time, that for transaction time is system-defined.

We can view the Earth as a spheroid in three-dimensional space; let us assume that Z^3 represents the space domain. A spatial object is associated with *geometry* and *position*. Geometry represents the shape and size of an object [5]. The position in space is based on co-ordinates in a mathematically defined reference system, e.g., latitude and longitude. Geometry of the spatial object may be 0-, 1- or 2- dimensional corresponding to a point, a line and a region. Like temporal granularity, spatial granularity can be defined for horizontal and vertical dimension [8]; e.g., the granularity of the *x*- and *y*-dimension can be in degree and that of the *z*-dimension may be foot.

Three types of interaction between an object and space-time are possible [12, 17]: (i) moving objects, i.e., position changes but the geometry does not (e.g., car moving on a road network); (ii) objects whose characteristics and position change with time, i.e., change of position by changing geometry (e.g., change of the position of land parcels in a cadastral application); (iii) integration of the above two behaviors, i.e., moving and changing phenomena (e.g., modeling a storm).

In the following sections, we describe how we have incorporated these ontological concepts into DISTIL.

4 Spatio-temporal Conceptual Design Using DISTIL

In this section, we illustrate how a typical data analyst interacts with DISTIL, using the example scenario described in section 2. We highlight how DISTIL applies the two-step annotation-based approach to capture the users' spatio-temporal requirements.

4.1 Developing a Core Schema

DISTIL uses USM [13], an extended ER Model [3], as the base model for conventional conceptual design; however, the spatio-temporal modeling methodology exemplified with DISTIL is not specific to USM and can be applied to any conventional conceptual model. As a first step to spatio-temporal design using DISTIL, a data analyst develops a conceptual schema without considering the spatial and temporal aspects of the application; we refer to this as the *core USM schema*. We summarize key terms and terminology related to conceptual modeling, specifically for USM. Next, we show how a core USM schema can be developed using DISTIL.

A real world object is referred to as an *entity*. A collection of entities for which common characteristics are to be modeled is called an *entity class* (or simply *class*). Characteristics or properties of an entity are referred to as *attributes* of the entity class. An *interaction relationship* refers members of one entity class to members of one or more entity classes. The reader is referred to [13] for details related to *weak entity class*, *superclass/subclass*, *composite class* and *grouping class*.

Fig. 1 shows an example of a core USM Schema developed by a data analyst. This schema includes entity classes like SPRING_SITE, BORE_HOLE_SITE, SOURCE_AGENCY, and PUMPLIFT and their various attributes.

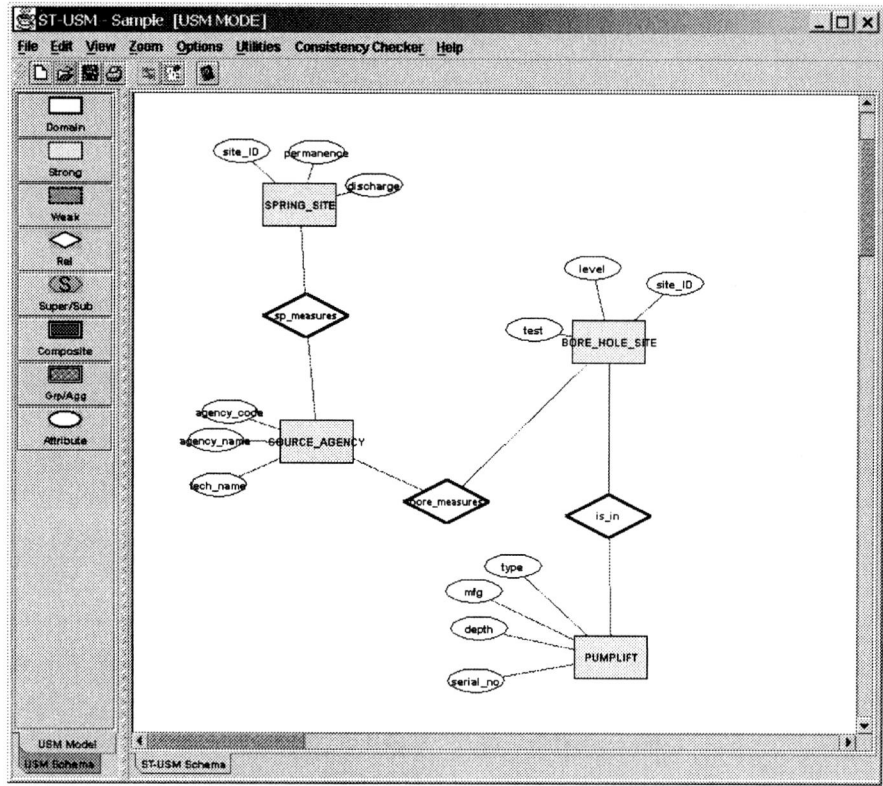

Fig. 1. Developing a schema using USM constructs

These entity classes are created by using the constructs on the "USM Model" panel on the left side. For example, the relationship sp_measures between SPRING_SITE and SOURCE_AGENCY relates an entity of SPRING_SITE with that of SOURCE_AGENCY. Each entity class has associated properties; e.g., PUMPLIFT has properties like type and manufacturer (mfg).

4.2 Annotating the Core Schema

After having developed a core USM schema without considering spatial and temporal aspects, the data analyst next annotates the spatial and temporal aspects of the application; we refer to the schema with annotations as an *Annotated Schema*, or an *ST-USM Schema*. Our annotation-based approach integrates the semantics related to space and time into a traditional conceptual model without adding any special constructs. Since various types of conceptual modeling abstractions (i.e., *entity class, attribute, relationship, subclass, composite* and *grouping*) are orthogonal to space and time, the annotations are generic and applicable to all types of conceptual modeling abstractions. We first describe the syntax for annotating spatial and temporal aspects of the application. Next, we show how DISTIL provides a convenient way of automatically producing these short annotation phrases, which are displayed in the ST-USM schema.

As shown in the Appendix, the overall structure of spatio-temporal annotation phrase is:

⟨temporal annotation⟩ // ⟨spatial annotation⟩ // ⟨spatiotemporal annotation⟩

The temporal, spatial, and spatiotemporal annotations are each separated by a double forward slash (//).

The temporal annotation first specifies the existence time (or valid time) followed by the transaction time. The temporal annotation for existence time and transaction time is segregated by a forward slash (/). Any of these aspects can be specified as not being relevant to the associated conceptual construct by using a "-". The valid time or existence time can be modeled as an event (E) or a state (S) and has an associated temporal granularity. For example, "S(day)/-//" succinctly denotes that entities in the entity class PUMPLIFT have an associated existence time with a temporal granularity of day (day) and the lifespan of entities is modeled as states (S); no transaction time is recorded for such entities. Similarly, "E (min)/T//" denotes that entities in the entity class exist in a bitemporal space. The temporal granularity of the event (E) is minute (min). Additionally, we also need to capture transaction time (T) associated with the entities. In this second example, the granularity associated with transaction time is not specified, as it is system-defined.

The spatial annotation includes geometry and position in x-, y- and z-dimension, each dimension segregated by a forward slash (/). For example, "//P(deg)/P(deg)/-" for SPRING_SITE describes a spatial entity with a geometry of points in the x-y plane. The associated spatial granularity is degree.

The interaction between an object and space-time can result in change in the shape and/or change in the position of an object. A spatiotemporal annotation can be specified only if spatial and temporal annotations have already been specified. For example, "E(sec)/-//P(deg)/P(deg)/-//Pos@xy" denotes that entities in the entity class have only time-varying position while the shape is time-invariant. The geometry of the entities is a point (P) in an x-y plane with a spatial granularity of degree. The position of the entity changes in the x-y plane (Pos@xy) over time and each geometry is valid for time granules (E) measured in second. Our annotation also includes a formalism to model indeterminacy [8]; e.g., an indeterminate state with a probability distribution function [6] is designated as S~. Many times the probability distribution may not be known and a user may make a simplified assumption of a uniform distribution and in that case an indeterminate state is represented as S+-.

Having described the annotations, we next describe how the data analyst can specify annotations in DISTIL.

For each construct in the core USM schema (e.g., Fig. 2) the data analyst together with the users consider whether temporality and spatiality is important for the application.

The data analyst asks questions like: Do you want to store the history or only the current value of this fact? Do you want to capture valid time or transaction time, or both? What is the associated temporal granularity? Is it important to store the geographical reference for the objects? What is the geographical shape of the objects? What is the associated spatial granularity? Can the spatial shape/position for these objects change over time? Accordingly, the data analyst enters the details using a pop-up box as shown in Fig. 2.

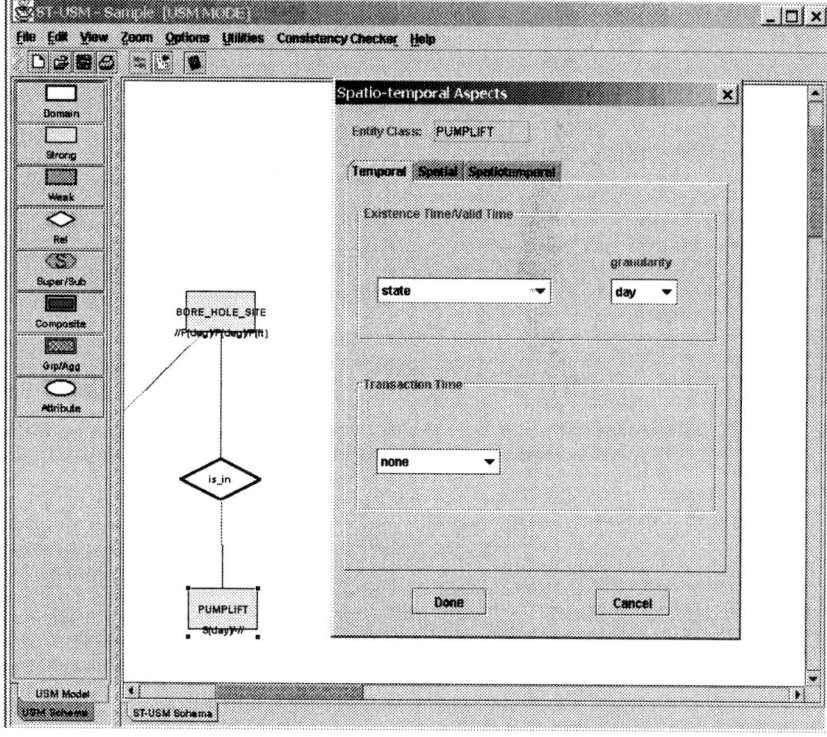

Fig. 2. Specifying the temporal aspects on the core USM schema

Fig. 2 shows that the data analyst enters temporal details which would result in an annotation "S(day)/-//" for PUMPLIFT. Similarly, the data analyst enters spatial details which would result in an annotation "//P(deg)/P(deg)/L(ft)" for BORE_HOLE_SITE. This implies that the BORE_HOLE_SITE needs to be represented as a point (P) on the x-y plane and a line (L) on the z-dimension. Additionally, the associated granularity in the x-y plane is degree (deg) and that in the z-dimension is foot (ft).

The data analyst also annotates SPRING_SITE resulting in the annotated schema shown in Fig. 3. The schema is automatically annotated depending on the information filled in the pop-up box. The data analyst can annotate each class, interaction relationship and attribute. Once the data analyst has made the annotated schema, the requirements so collected can be validated with other users. The distributed users may open the same project and make the necessary changes to the schema.

At this point, the data analyst can check if the Annotated Schema is consistent using "Consistency Checker". For example, if a spatial interaction relationship were specified between non-spatial entity classes, the "Consistency Checker" would give an error message.

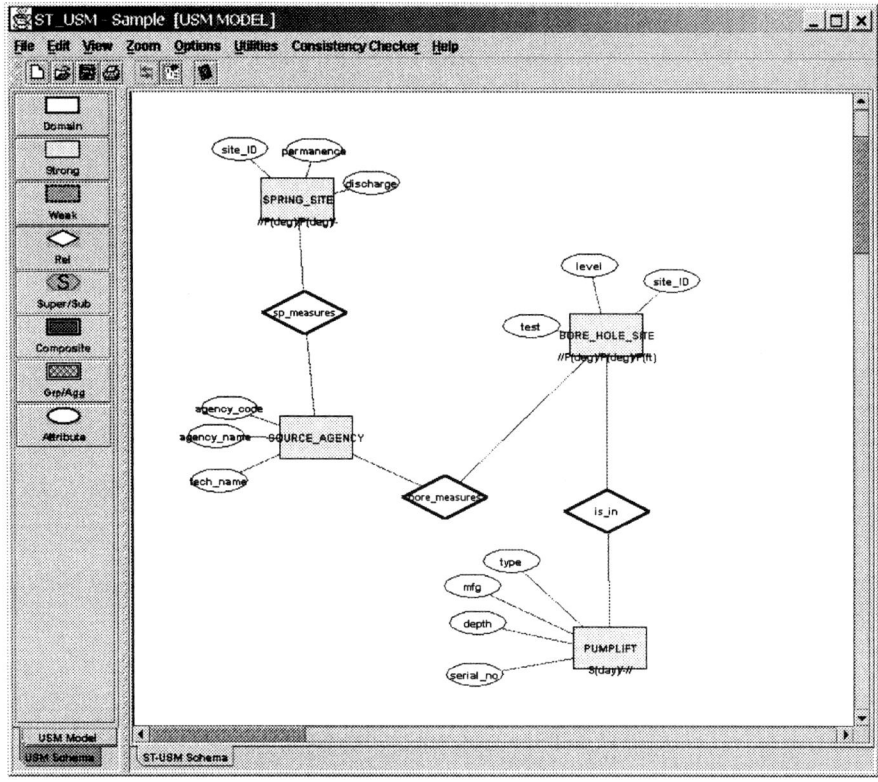

Fig. 3. Annotated schema (ST-USM Schema)

4.3 Semantics of the Annotated Schema

The Annotated Schema described in the previous sub-section can be used as communication vehicle between users and data analysts. We now explicate how data analysts can obtain explicit spatial and temporal semantics from the annotated schema; we refer to the schema so obtained as the *Translated USM Schema*. We use an example of a temporal entity class to briefly describe the semantics of an annotated ST-USM construct via a formal mapping to the USM schema. As USM constructs have been carefully defined, this mapping provides a comprehensive semantics for the richer ST-USM schema. We then show how these mapping rules have been embedded in DISTIL.

The existence time of a temporal entity class refers to the lifespan of the entity and defines the time when the facts associated with the entity can be true. Fig. 4 shows a temporal entity class for which we want to capture the existence time expressed as state (S) with $\langle g_{et} \rangle$ as the granularity name (e.g., day). Based on the users' requirements, the data analyst simply annotates ⟨ENTITY_CLASS⟩ as "S($\langle g_{et} \rangle$)/-//"

and does not need to contend with the complexity of the underlying semantics or the associated constraints.

Fig. 4 shows the semantics of a simple temporal entity class using USM constructs. In order to express the semantics of a temporal entity class, we need to specify a TEMPORAL_GRANULARITY in which the evolution of the temporal object is embedded. The relationship ⟨ENTITY_CLASS⟩_has_ET associates an entity with a corresponding TEMPORAL_GRANULARITY. Each TEMPORAL_GRANULARITY is uniquely identified by a granularity_name. The relationship anchor_gran helps create a granularity lattice, which can help a user choose the level of detail associated with facts.

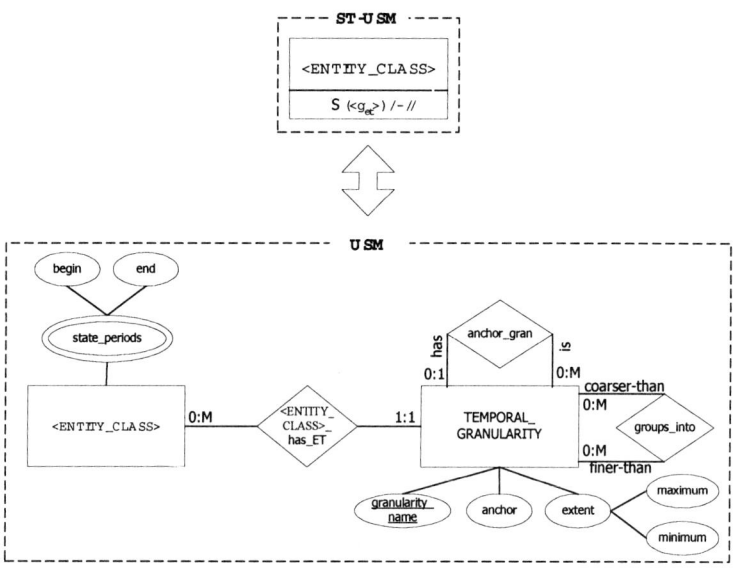

Fig. 4. Temporal Entity Class in ST-USM and its semantics in USM

Each anchor_gran is a recursive relationship (i.e., a relationship where an entity from the same entity set can play different roles) such that each participating granularity optionally has an anchor and each granularity is an anchor for 0-to-many (0:M) other granularities. A finer-than and a coarser-than relationship between granularities is denoted by a recursive relationship groups_into, where one entity plays the role of finer-than and the other the role of coarser-than. The translation from the ST-USM schema to the USM schema also includes constraints, which are implicit in the ST-USM schema but are explicit in the USM schema. An example of such a constraint is that a temporal element formed by the state_periods is well formed, i.e., it is a union of non-overlapping intervals. Details of the semantics for annotated constructs and the associated constraints are outside the scope of this paper and are defined formally elsewhere [7, 8].

We now describe how these semantic mapping rules have been embedded in DISTIL. To view detailed explicit semantics associated with the annotated schema, the data analyst clicks on the "USM Schema" tab to obtain a translated USM schema corresponding to the ST-USM schema (Fig. 5). We have embedded translation rules (e.g., Fig. 4) into DISTIL, which help translate the annotated constructs to an equivalent USM schema with explicit representation of the associated spatiality and temporality. For example, the semantics associated with a temporal entity class PUMPLIFT includes an entity class TEMPORAL_GRANULARITY, which specifies the temporal granularity in which PUMPLIFT is embedded. The relationship PUMPLIFT_has_ET relates an entity from PUMPLIFT with a corresponding temporal granularity. A multi-valued attribute state_periods (with components **begin** and **end**) is added to the entity PUMPLIFT because PUMPLIFT lifespan was modeled as state. A multi-valued attribute implies that each PUMPLIFT can have many associated state_periods. Similarly, other constructs of the annotated ST-USM schema are converted to a translated USM schema using the embedded rules in DISTIL.

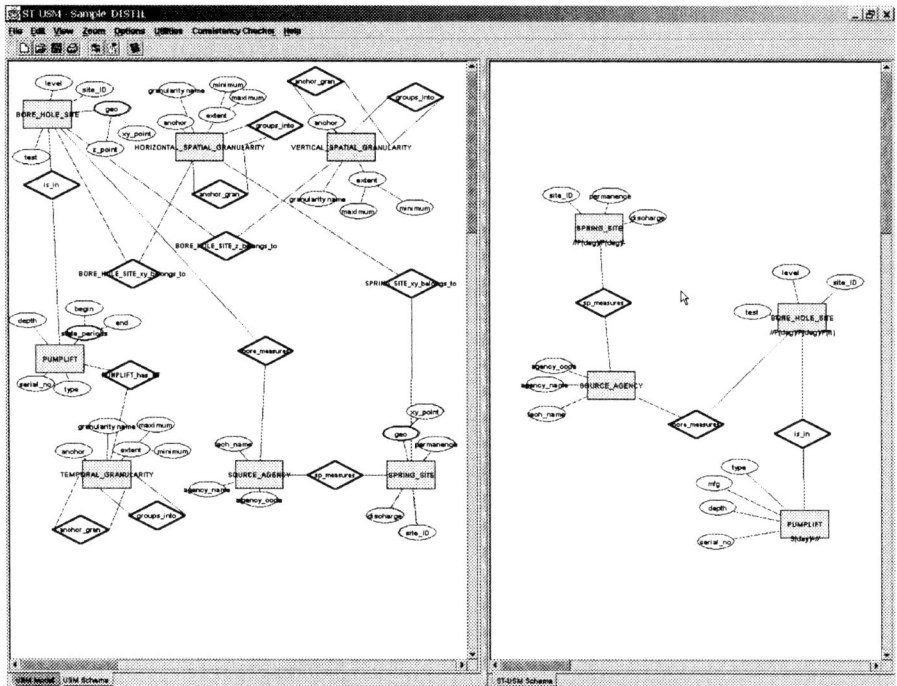

Fig. 5. Annotated Schema and its semantics using USM

In this section, we described a typical data analyst's interaction with DISTIL. The ST-USM schema can be used as communication vehicle. It can also be used to decide if all the spatio-temporal requirements of the user have been captured and whether the requirements are conflicting. On the other hand, the translated USM schema can be used by the data analyst to subsequently develop the logical schema.

5 Architecture

In this section, we describe the underlying architecture of DISTIL that enables the interaction described in section 4. DISTIL has been implemented using Java 2 (JDK 1.2) and Oracle 8.1.6. The prototype system is currently running on NT workstations. DISTIL can be accessed through a web-browser or be used as a stand-alone application.

As shown in Fig. 1, the data analyst first develops a *Core USM Schema* during *Conventional Conceptual Design* using *USM Schema Designer*. The USM Schema Designer allows the data analyst to develop a core conceptual schema (e.g., Fig. 1) that captures current reality without considering spatial aspects. Our *Spatio-temporal Conceptual Design* includes annotating the Core USM Schema via *Annotation Designer* (e.g., Fig. 2) resulting in the *ST-USM Schema* (e.g., Fig. 3), mapping the ST-USM Schema to a *Translated USM Schema* (e.g., Fig. 5) through the *Semantic Mapper* and checking the consistency (i.e., *Semantic Error Log*) in the ST-USM Schema via *Consistency Checker*.

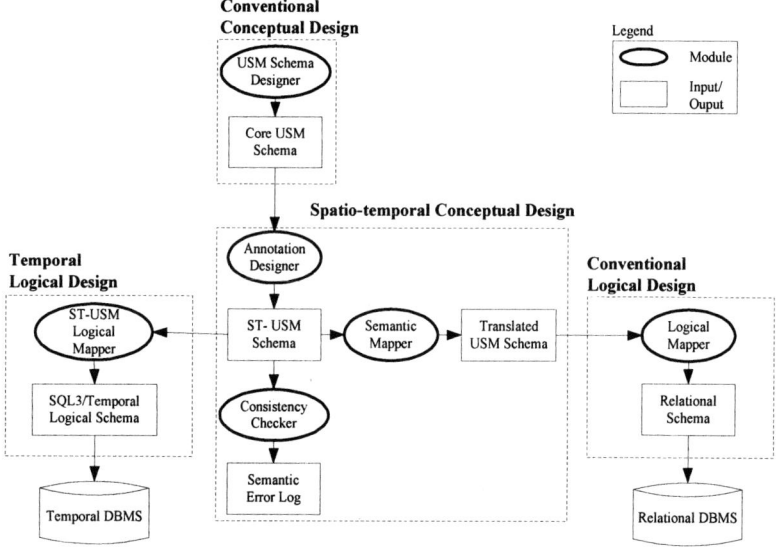

Fig. 6. DISTIL Architecture

As shown in Fig. 6, our proposed Spatio-temporal Conceptual Design implemented via DISTIL integrates with Conventional Conceptual Design and the translated USM Schema (including constraints) merges again with the *Conventional Logical Design*. The *Logical Mapper* in Conventional Logical Design includes rules to convert a Translated USM Schema to *Relational Schema* with spatial support that can be implemented in a relational DBMS (e.g., Oracle Spatial). We also envision incorporating *ST-USM Logical Mapper*, which would translate the ST-USM schema to an *SQL3/Temporal Logical Schema* [15, 16] that can be implemented in a temporal DBMS.

6 Related Work

With the growth of geographic applications, recently design tools [1, 9, 11] to support modeling of spatio-temporal databases have been proposed. Perceptory [1] and GeoOOA [9] focus on capturing the semantics associated with geometry of the spatial objects; spatiality of entities is defined by a relationship link with geometry, e.g., point, line and region. A visual schema editor based on MADS [11] helps capturing some spatio-temporal semantics. However, none of these tools provide a mechanism to capture semantics related to granularity and indeterminacy. Granularities related to facts needs to be captured during conceptual design because under-specifying granularities can restrict an application, affect relative ordering of events, and impact topological relationships. Indeterminacy, i.e., don't know *exactly* where/when information, is important for many geographic applications. Because these tools do not demonstrate a generic spatio-temporal database design methodology that integrates naturally with conventional conceptual design, methodologies proposed via these tools cannot be easily adopted by existing CASE tools that support conventional conceptual design.

Our approach to spatio-temporal conceptual modeling is comprehensive and captures various aspects related to temporality and spatiality, e.g., valid time, transaction time, events, states, position, geometry, shape, granularities and indeterminacy. Additionally, our proposed annotation-based approach used in DISTIL integrates into existing database design methodologies. Annotating the schema is intuitive from the perspective of data analysts and users as it corresponds to the way human beings perceive spatio-temporal objects. Moreover, incorporating annotation—via pop-up boxes—into an existing CASE tool is also straightforward to implement.

7 Summary and Future Directions

With advances in technologies like high-resolution satellite-borne imaging systems and global positioning systems, geographic data is finding its way into many traditional applications. In this paper, we described a design support environment for modeling the users' spatio-temporal requirements that integrates with conventional conceptual design.

We are working on completing various aspects of spatio-temporal conceptual design support provided by DISTIL. We are embedding translation rules associated with complex abstractions, e.g., grouping and composite, and constraints including topological relationships. In future, we plan to conduct more case studies in different application domains and evaluate the design support provided by DISTIL.

We believe that with our annotation-based approach implemented using DISTIL, we have achieved both comprehensiveness and simplicity in spatio-temporal conceptual modeling.

References

[1] Y. Bedard, "Visual Modeling of Spatial Databases: Towards Spatial PVL and UML," *Geomatica*, Vol. 53, No. 2, pp. 169-186, 1999.

[2] C. Bettini, C. E. Dyreson, W. S. Evans, R. T. Snodgrass, and X. S. Wang, "A Glossary of Time Granularity Concepts," in *Temporal Databases: Research and Practice*, O. Etzion, S. Jajodia, and S. Sripada, Eds.: Springer-Verlag, 1998, pp. 406-413.

[3] P. P. Chen, "The Entity-Relationship Model - Toward a Unified View of Data," *ACM Transactions of Database Systems*, Vol. 1, No. 1, pp. 9-36, 1976.

[4] F. A. D'Agnese, C. C. Faunt, A. K. Turner, and M. C. Hill, "Hydrogeologic evaluation and numerical simulation of the Death Valley Regional ground-water flow system, Nevada and California," U.S. Geological Survey Water Resources 96-4300, 1997.

[5] B. David, M. V. D. Herrewegen, and F. Salge, "Conceptual Models for Geometry and Quality of Geographic Information," in *Geographic Objects With Indeterminate Boundaries*, P. A. Burrough and A. Frank, Eds.: Taylor & Francis, 1996, pp. 352.

[6] C. E. Dyreson and R. T. Snodgrass, "Supporting Valid-Time Indeterminacy," *ACM Transactions on Database Systems*, Vol. 23, No. 1, pp. 1-57, 1998.

[7] V. Khatri, S. Ram, and R. T. Snodgrass, "ST-USM: Bridging the Semantic Gap with a Spatio-temporal Conceptual Model," TIMECENTER Technical Report TR-64 2001.

[8] V. Khatri, S. Ram, and R. T. Snodgrass, "Supporting User-defined Granularities and Indeterminacy in a Spatiotemporal Conceptual Model," *Annals of Mathematics and Artificial Intelligence* (Also available as TIMECENTER Technical Report TR-55), 36 pages, forthcoming.

[9] G. Kösters and B.-U. Pagel, "The GeoOOA-Tool and Its Interface to Open Software Development Environments for GIS," in Proceedings of the fourth ACM workshop on Advances on Advances in Geographic Information Systems, Rockville, Maryland, pp. 163-171, 1996.

[10] J. L. Mennis, D. J. Peuquet, and L. Qian, "A Conceptual Framework for Incorporating Cognitive Principles into Geographical Database Representation," *International Journal of Geographic Information Science*, Vol. 14, No. 6, pp. 501-520, 2000.

[11] C. Parent, S. Spaccapietra, and E. Zimanyi, "Spatio-temporal conceptual models: Data structures + space + time," in Proceedings of the 7th ACM Symposium on Advances in Geographic Information Systems, Kansas City, USA, pp. 1999.

[12] D. Pfoser and N. Tryfona, "Requirements, Definitions, and Notations for Spatiotemporal Application Environments," in Proceedings of the 6th International Symposium on Advances in Geographic Information Systems, Washington, United States, pp. 124-130, 1998.

[13] S. Ram, "Intelligent Database Design using the Unifying Semantic Model," *Information and Management*, Vol. 29, No. 4, pp. 191-206, 1995.

[14] R. T. Snodgrass and I. Ahn, "Temporal Databases," *IEEE Computer*, Vol. 19, No. 9, pp. 35-42, 1986.

[15] R. T. Snodgrass, M. H. Böhlen, C. S. Jensen, and A. Steiner, "Adding Transaction Time to SQL/Temporal," ISO-ANSI SQL/Temporal Change Proposal, ANSI X3H2-96-152r ISO/IEC JTC1/SC21/WG3 DBL MCI-143, 1996.

[16] R. T. Snodgrass, M. H. Böhlen, C. S. Jensen, and A. Steiner, "Adding Valid Time to SQL/Temporal," ISO-ANSI SQL/Temporal Change Proposal, ANSI X3H2-96-151r ISO/IEC JTC1/SC21/WG3 DBL MCI-142, 1996.

[17] N. Tryfona and C. S. Jensen, "Conceptual Data Modeling for Spatiotemporal Applications," *Geoinformatica*, Vol. 3, No. 3, pp. 245-268, 1999.

Appendix: Annotation Syntax Using BNF

⟨ST-USM annotation⟩	::= ε | ⟨temporal annotation⟩//⟨spatial annotation⟩ | ⟨temporal annotation⟩//⟨spatial annotation⟩//⟨spatiotemporal annotation⟩
⟨temporal annotation⟩	::= ε | ⟨valid time⟩ / ⟨transaction time⟩
⟨valid time⟩	::= ⟨state⟩ (⟨g_t⟩) | ⟨indeterminate state⟩ (⟨g_t⟩) | ⟨event⟩ (⟨g_t⟩) | ⟨indeterminate event⟩(⟨g_t⟩) | -
⟨transaction time⟩	::= T | -
⟨state⟩	::= S | State
⟨indeterminate state⟩	::= ⟨state⟩~ | ⟨state⟩+-
⟨event⟩	::= E | Event
⟨indeterminate event⟩	::= ⟨event⟩~ | ⟨event⟩+-
⟨spatial annotation⟩	::= ε | ⟨horizontal geometry⟩ / ⟨vertical geometry⟩
⟨horizontal geometry⟩	::= ⟨geometry⟩ (⟨g_{sxy}⟩) / ⟨geometry⟩ (⟨g_{sxy}⟩)
⟨vertical geometry⟩	::= ⟨geometry⟩ (⟨g_{sz}⟩) | -
⟨geometry⟩	::= ⟨point⟩ | ⟨indeterminate point⟩ | ⟨line⟩ | ⟨indeterminate line⟩ | ⟨region⟩ | ⟨indeterminate region⟩ | -
⟨point⟩	::= P | Point
⟨indeterminate point⟩	::= ⟨point⟩~ | ⟨point⟩+-
⟨line⟩	::= L | Line
⟨indeterminate line⟩	::= ⟨line⟩~ | ⟨line⟩+-
⟨region⟩	::= R | Region
⟨indeterminate region⟩	::= ⟨region⟩~ | ⟨region⟩+-
⟨spatiotemporal annotation⟩	::= ε | ⟨position varying⟩ / ⟨shape varying⟩
⟨position varying⟩	::= ⟨position⟩@⟨varying in dimension⟩ | -
⟨shape varying⟩	::= ⟨shape⟩@⟨varying in dimension⟩ | -
⟨position⟩	::= Pos | Position
⟨shape⟩	::= Sh | Shape
⟨varying in dimension⟩	::= x | y | z | xy | yz | xz | xyz
⟨g_t⟩	::= ⟨day⟩ | ⟨hour⟩ | ⟨minute⟩ | ⟨user defined⟩
⟨day⟩	::= day
⟨hour⟩	::= hr | hour
⟨minute⟩	::= min | minute
⟨g_{sxy}⟩	::= ⟨dms degree⟩ | ⟨dms minute⟩ | ⟨user defined⟩
⟨g_{sz}⟩	::= ⟨foot⟩ | ⟨user defined⟩
⟨dms degree⟩	::= deg | degree | dms-degree | dms-deg
⟨dms min⟩	::= dms-min | dms-minute
⟨foot⟩	::= ft | foot

Tripod: A Comprehensive Model for Spatial and Aspatial Historical Objects

Tony Griffiths[1], Alvaro A.A. Fernandes[1], Norman W. Paton[1],
Keith T. Mason[2], Bo Huang[3], and Michael Worboys[3]

[1] Department of Computer Science, University of Manchester
Manchester M13 9PL, UK
{griffitt|alvaro|norm}@cs.man.ac.uk
[2] School of Earth Sciences and Geography, University of Keele
Staffordshire ST5 5BG, UK
k.t.mason@esci.keele.ac.uk
[3] Department of Computer Science, University of Keele
Staffordshire ST5 5BG, UK
{b.huang|michael}@cs.keele.ac.uk

Abstract Spatio-temporal extensions to data models have been an active area of research for a number of years. To date, much of this work has focused on the relational data model, with object data models receiving far less consideration. This paper presents a spatio-historical object model that uses a specialized mechanism, called a *history*, to maintain knowledge about entities that change over time. Key features of the resulting proposal include: (i) consistent representations of primitive spatial and temporal types; (ii) a component-based design in which spatial, temporal and historical extensions are formalized incrementally, for subsequent use together or separately; (iii) a formally specified data model. The model can be used directly during the design of spatio-historical applications, but also forms the basis of an implementation activity developing a spatio-historical object database management system.

1 Introduction

Spatio-temporal databases have been an active area of research for a number of years. Central to this effort has been the development of models to facilitate the description of complex applications with spatial and/or temporal features. Few of these models, however, provide facilities to track both spatial and aspatial changes to data over time. The temporal aspects of conceptual modelling have been considered by several researchers (see [24] for a survey), with more recent proposals dealing with both temporal and spatial concerns (e.g. [4, 16]). There has also recently been considerable interest in models that characterize objects whose properties (spatial and aspatial) are continuously changing – the so-called *moving object* approaches (e.g. [17, 20]). However, there remain considerable challenges concerning the modelling of discretely changing objects (as exemplified by the running example in this paper). Also, any implementation of a data model requires a formally specified model, considering not only the structure of the model and its inherent constraints, but also the pragmatics of how to manipulate and query its entities.

The Tripod project, from which this paper emerges, is seeking to design and prototype a complete spatio-temporal database system. The activity is focusing on the extension of the ODMG standard for object databases [3] with facilities for managing vector spatial data, and for describing past states of both spatial and aspatial data. The key principles underpinning the Tripod project are *orthogonality* and *synergy*. By *orthogonality* is meant that the different extensions to the ODMG standard should be coherent in isolation, so that, for example, the Tripod system should be effective as a historical database in which no spatial data is stored, or as a spatial database in which no use is made of the ability to record historical data. By *synergy* is meant that the system should allow the combined use of spatial and temporal capabilities in a seamless and complementary manner, so that full spatio-temporal applications benefit from integrated facilities without mismatches in the way different features are supported.

Figure 1 illustrates the relationships between the different components in the Tripod design. At the core is the ODMG object model, which is a subset of the Tripod object model. The ODMG model is extended with two new sets of primitive types, viz., spatial and temporal types. The spatial types used in Tripod are those of the ROSE algebra [18], i.e., Points, Lines and Regions. The temporal types supported in Tripod are one dimensional versions of the ROSE algebra types Points and Lines, and are known as Instants and TimeIntervals, respectively. The close relationship between the spatial and the temporal types increases consistency in the representation of the different kinds of data. Past states of all ODMG types, including the spatial and temporal types, can be recorded using histories. A *history* is a collection of *timestamp-value* pairs, where the timestamp is of a temporal type and the value is of any of the types in the extended ODMG model. Figure 1, from Histories inwards, represents a spatio-historical object model. The layers in Figure 1 from Histories outwards denote the interfaces that exist to populate, maintain and query instances of a Tripod database. Since the ODMG model does not define an object manipulation language, developers must use a programming language binding to create, update and delete objects. When the state of a database needs to be queried, developers can either write native language application programs or can issue declarative OQL queries. Tripod's ODL and OQL extend the ODMG ODL and OQL with spatial, historical and spatio-historical constructs. Queries are mapped to

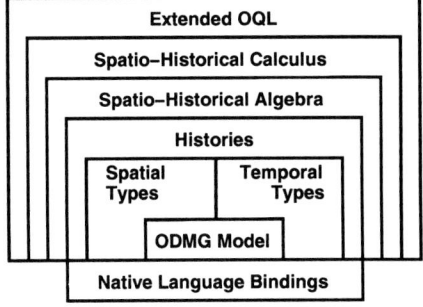

Fig. 1. Tripod Layered Architecture

a spatio-historical calculus and then to a spatio-historical algebra. These mappings provide several opportunities for optimization using rewrite rules that are extensions to the techniques used by Fegaras and Maier for optimizing object query languages [6]. Tripod's language bindings and its extended OQL use the services provided by the extended object model to access and manipulate historical, spatial and aspatial data.

This paper is structured to reflect Tripod's layered data model, concentrating in particular on the ways in which each layer builds upon the functionality provided by lower levels of the architecture, and how each successive layer conforms to the constraints stemming from these lower layers. The remainder of this paper is structured as follows. Section 2 presents a motivating case study. Section 3 describes the spatial and temporal literal types that Tripod uses to enhance the ODMG type system. Section 4 defines a history as an abstract data type (ADT) underpinned by these temporal types. Section 5 brings together the concepts described in this paper under the unifying framework of a spatio-historical extension to the ODMG object model. Section 6 discusses related work. Finally, some conclusions are drawn in Section 7. It is assumed that the reader is familiar with the ODMG object model.

2 A Motivating Example

The longitudinal study (LS) links census and vital events data (e.g., births, deaths, cancer registrations) for a one percent sample of the population of England and Wales — about 500,000 individuals at any one census point. The study was started in 1974 with a sample drawn from the residents of England and Wales born on one of four dates each year and enumerated at the 1971 Census. Selection into the LS is by birth date. The study was designed as a continuous, multi-cohort study, with subsequent samples being drawn at each census, using the same selection criteria,

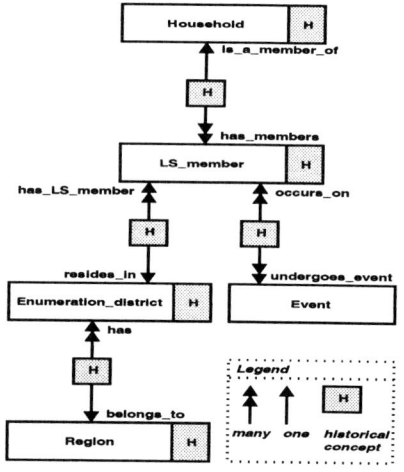

Fig. 2. Simplified LS Schema

and linked into the study. This study is of particular interest because of the spatial and aspatial changes that entities in the study can undergo. In particular, new members are included by virtue of birth on LS dates or by immigration (if born on LS dates) and excluded by death or emigration, and the enumeration districts in which members reside can change boundaries over time. A much simplified schema (adapting the notation in [3] with extensions to represent historical data) showing the main classes of interest in the LS is presented in Figure 2. Classes and relationships that can change over time are marked with a 'H' symbol (i.e., are historical). It should be noted that some of a member's attributes change over time (e.g., their marital status), whereas others (e.g., their place or date of birth) will not.

3 Spatial and Temporal Extensions to the Type System

This section shows how Tripod extends the ODMG type system with types to support the definition of spatial and temporal values. These extensions augment the set of ODMG structured literals, and support the definition of the mechanism by which Tripod maintains a history of changes in the state of modelled entities and relationships.

adjacent	: Regions × Regions	→ bool
area_disjoint	: Regions × Regions	→ bool
area_inside	: Regions × Regions	→ bool
border_in_common	: Regions × Lines	→ bool
common_border	: Regions × Lines	→ Lines
encloses	: Regions × Regions	→ bool
equal	: Regions × Regions	→ bool
intersects	: Regions × Lines	→ bool
length	: Lines	→ float
meets	: Regions × Lines	→ bool
not_equal	: Regions × Regions	→ bool
on_border_of	: Points × Lines	→ bool
on_border_of	: Points × Regions	→ bool

Fig. 3. Example Spatial Operations

Spatial Types Tripod extends the ODMG literal types with three new types for representing spatial data. These spatial data types (SDTs) are based on the ROSE (RObust Spatial Extensions) approach described in [18]. Underlying the ROSE approach is the notion of a *realm*. A realm is a finite set of points and non-intersecting line segments defined over a discrete grid that forms the ROSE algebra's underlying geometric domain. ROSE spatial values are represented in terms of points and line segments in a realm. A realm guarantees that all spatial operations over realm values are error bound and only take, and return, intersection-free spatial values. These properties lead to an algebra with an efficient implementation [19].

The ROSE approach defines an algebra over three SDTs, namely **Points**, **Lines** and **Regions**, and an extensive collection of spatial predicates and operations (including set operations) over these types. Figure 3 shows a small subset of the predicate operations. Every spatial value in the ROSE algebra is set-based, thus facilitating set-at-a-time processing. Roughly speaking, each element of a **Points** value is a pair of coordinates in the underlying geometry, each element of a **Lines** value is a set of connected line segments, and each element in a **Regions** value

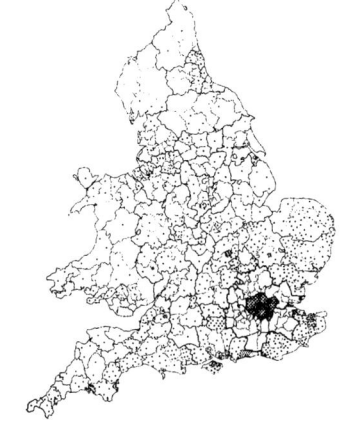

Fig. 4. Spatial Values over a Realm

is a polygon containing a (potentially empty) set of holes. Such collection-based SDTs are useful in modelling the LS, where areas need to be split. Figure 4 shows examples of spatial objects from the LS. Each LS Region is shown as a `Regions` value, and each LS Member is shown as a `Points` value. The figure illustrates migration destinations of a subset of the LS Members. At a finer scale, Figure 4 would also show LS Enumeration districts as `Regions` values contained within LS Regions.

Temporal Types Tripod extends the set of ODMG primitive types with two temporal types, called `Instants` and `TimeIntervals`. The underlying domain of interpretation is a structure which we refer to as a *temporal realm* because it is defined to be a one-dimensional specialization of two-dimensional (spatial) realms [18]. Roughly, a temporal realm is a finite set of integers (whereas a spatial realm is a finite integer grid). There are several reasons why we adopt this viewpoint and terminology. Realm values are collections, which we find more suitable than scalars for the kind of set-a-time strategies that are prevalent in query processing architectures. Also, realm operations are well-defined and have a rich set of predicates and constructors with nice closure properties. In addition, we find it useful (for users, developers and researchers) to have realms as a unifying notion for the interpretation of operations on spatial *and* temporal values. This unified interpretation propagates upwards in the sense that the predicates and operation on realms are defined once and used (possibly after renaming) over both spatial and temporal values. Finally, this allows the reuse of implemented software components, such as those described in [15].

In a temporal realm, we can view a time-point as an integer. Then, an `Instants` value is a collection of time-points and a `TimeIntervals` value is a collection of pairs of time-points, where the first element is the start, and the second the end, of a contiguous time-interval. A *timestamp* is either an `Instants` value or a `TimeIntervals` value. Figure 5 illustrates timestamps in graphical form. In Figure 5, ***A*** is a `TimeIntervals` value, and ***B*** and ***C*** are `Instants` values. Notice that ***B*** happens to be a singleton.

A temporal realm has an additional property to a spatial realm, namely a predefined ordering. In the ROSE algebra, there is no predefined notion of one `Points` value being ordered with respect to another `Points` value; any such notion of ordering must be defined within application programs that use the algebra. Temporal realms, however, must exhibit this property if they are to conform to our intuitions. The Tripod temporal algebra, therefore, extends the ROSE Algebra with ordering predicates based on the underlying order of the temporal realm's integer domain. In addition, the temporal realm uses a calendar that maps from the underlying integer domain to one more suited to human cognition.

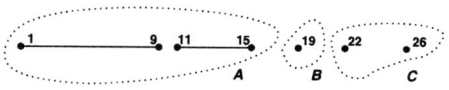

Fig. 5. Example Tripod Timestamps

Let $\mathbb{T}$ denote the set of all Tripod timestamps. Given $\tau \in \mathbb{T}$, representative predicates and operations defined on $\mathbb{T}$ are shown in Figure 6. It should be noted that predicates such as contains_ω are templates for a pair of signatures parameterized on an element of the set $\{\forall, \exists\}$,

equal : $\tau \times \tau$	$\rightarrow$ bool
before : $\tau \times \tau$	$\rightarrow$ bool
starts_before : $\tau \times \tau$	$\rightarrow$ bool
disjoint : $\tau \times \tau$	$\rightarrow$ bool
common_points : $\tau \times \tau$	$\rightarrow$ bool
meets_ω : TimeIntervals $\times$ TimeIntervals	$\rightarrow$ bool
contains_ω : TimeIntervals $\times$ TimeInstants	$\rightarrow$ bool
intersection : $\tau \times \tau$	$\rightarrow \tau$
plus : $\tau \times \tau$	$\rightarrow \tau$
minus : $\tau \times \tau$	$\rightarrow \tau$
vertices : TimeIntervals	$\rightarrow$ Instants

Fig. 6. Example Temporal Operations

representing the two possible semantics of the predicate. For example, must every element of a timestamp A be contained by an element from another timestamp B, or just one? The operation names should give readers an intuitive understanding of their meaning based on operations on sets of integers (and integer pairs) and on classical definitions for temporal predicates (such as Allen's [1], and those defined by Ladkin [13] on sets of intervals). For full details, see the formal semantics in [10, 11] (which follow [18] closely).

The discrete domain underlying the temporal realm is bounded by two integer values that correspond to the earliest and latest representable temporal values. These are given the special names beginning and forever, and can be referenced as Tripod temporal literals. Additionally, many applications require the formation of TimeIntervals values whose end instant is as yet undecided (i.e., is *pseudo-open* [22]). For example, a person's period of employment could be from 1/1/1990 until some as yet unspecified future date. Tripod uses the special temporal value until_changed to allow such TimeIntervals values to be declared. When evaluated during query-processing, any value that references until_changed is bound to a distinguished Instants value representing the current time now, thus having the effect of closing any pseudo-open TimeIntervals values. When used as a variable, now acts as a temporal placeholder which is filled with the current system time if and when it is evaluated in some expression.

The Complete Tripod Type System The complete set of Tripod types Tripod$\mathcal{T}$ can thus be seen to augment the set of ODMG Object Model types *ODMG*, as follows. Tripod$\mathcal{T}$ = *ODMG* $\cup$ *TripodLT*, where *TripodLT* = *TripodSLT* $\cup$ *TripodTLT*, *TripodSLT* ={Points, Lines, Regions, Point, Line, Region} is the set of Tripod spatial literal types and *TripodTLT* = {Instants, TimeIntervals, Instant, TimeInterval} is the set of Tripod temporal literal types. Note that for each collection-based spatial and temporal type there is a corresponding singular type. A collection value can be cast into a set of values of its corresponding singular type. This facilitates the derivation of new values from existing ones by application programmers. Although Tripod timestamps can be used by application designers to complement related primitive types in the ODMG standard (e.g., Interval or Time), their main purpose is to allow histories to be constructed and operated upon, as described below.

4 Histories

The Tripod history mechanism provides functionality to support the storage, management and querying of entities that change over time. A history models the changes that an entity (or its attributes, or the relationships it participates in) undergoes as the result of assignments made to it. In the Tripod object model, a request for a history to be maintained can be made for any construct to which a value can be assigned, i.e., a history is a history of changes in value and it records episodes of change by identifying these with a timestamp. Each such value is called a *snapshot*. As a consequence of the possible value assignments that are well defined in the ODMG object model, a history can be kept in the Tripod object model for object identifiers, attribute values, and relationship instances. Thus, a history associates timestamps and snapshots drawn from the domain of exactly one of object identifiers (if the history is of an object), or attribute values (whose type can be any valid Tripod, and hence ODMG, type), or relationship instances (of any ODMG-supported cardinality). In the remainder of this section, a history is defined as an ADT.

4.1 The Structure of Histories

A *history* is a quadruple $H = \langle V, \theta, \gamma, \Sigma \rangle$, where V denotes the domain of values whose changes H records, θ is either Instants or TimeIntervals, γ is the granularity of θ, and Σ is a collection of pairs, called *states*, of the form $\langle \tau, \sigma \rangle$, where τ is a timestamp and σ is a snapshot. In the rest of the paper, let $\mathbb{T}$ denote, as before, the set of all timestamps; $\mathbb{V}$, the set of all snapshots; $\mathbb{S}$, the set of all states; and $\mathbb{H}$, the set of all histories.

In a Tripod history, a collection Σ of states is constrained to be an injective function from the set $\mathbb{T}_H$ of all timestamps occurring in H to the set $\mathbb{V}_H$ of all snapshots occurring in H, i.e., for any history H, $states_H : \tau \in \mathbb{T}_H \to \sigma \in \mathbb{V}_H$. Therefore, the following invariants hold, for any history $H = \langle V, \theta, \gamma, \Sigma \rangle$:

1. Every timestamp occurring in Σ is of type $\theta \in \{\text{Instants, TimeIntervals}\}$ and has granularity γ.
2. For every snapshot σ occurring in Σ, $\sigma \in V$.
3. A particular timestamp is associated with at most one snapshot (note that snapshots can be collections), i.e., a history does not record different values as valid at the same time. For example, an LS member cannot be a member of more than one household at the same time.
4. A particular snapshot is associated with at most one timestamp, i.e., all value-equal snapshots within a history are merged together to form a single state with a collection-based timestamp. This process is called *coalescing*.

The notation used later in the paper is as follows. A TimeIntervals value is notated as $[t_1^s - t_1^e, \ldots, t_n^s - t_n^e]$, where each element is a *closed* interval (i.e., the delimiting instants are included). Simple integer values are used rather than calendar-based dates. Although all examples in this paper use the TimeIntervals

Tripod: A Comprehensive Model for Spatial and Aspatial Historical Objects   91

type, they are equally applicable to the Instants type. A single state is notated as $\langle [1-5, 6-9], \mathtt{r_1} \rangle$, where $\mathtt{r_1}$ is, e.g., a snapshot value from the domain of Regions that holds between the granules 1 to 5 and 6 to 9, inclusively. A history is notated as exemplified by $\{V, \theta, \gamma, \langle [1-3, 7-9], \{\mathtt{r_1}\}\rangle, \langle [4-5], \{\mathtt{r_1}, \mathtt{r_3}, \mathtt{r_4}\}\rangle, \langle [10-14], \{\mathtt{r_1}, \mathtt{r_4}\}\rangle\}$, with $V = \mathtt{bag}\langle\mathtt{Regions}\rangle$, $\theta = \mathtt{TimeIntervals}$, and $\gamma = \mathtt{DAY}$.

4.2 History Operations

The operations defined for the history ADT can be classified into *constructor*, *update*, *query*, *mutator*, and *merge* operations. A sample of each such group is given in Figure 7. It is exemplified below how they can be given a precise semantics.

In what follows, the dot notation is used to denote the individual elements of a particular state. For example, the timestamp of a particular state s is denoted by $s.\mathtt{t}$, and the corresponding snapshot by $s.\mathtt{v}$. Where reference is made to an operation defined on the underlying temporal structured literal types, the operation name is underlined. Let H (possibly primed or subscripted) range over $\mathbb{H}$. Given a history, let S^H denote its state set. Since the state set of a history is a function, its domain is the set of timestamps occurring in it, denoted by S_T^H, and its range the set of

create:		$\to$ H
create:	H	$\to$ H
DeleteTimestamp:	H $\times$ T	$\to$ H
DeleteSnapshot:	H $\times$ V	$\to$ H
DeleteState:	H $\times$ S	$\to$ H
DeleteAll:	H	$\to$ H
InsertState:	H $\times$ S	$\to$ H
UpdateTimestamp:	H $\times$ T $\times$ V	$\to$ H
UpdateSnapshot:	H $\times$ T $\times$ V	$\to$ H
IsEmpty:	H	$\to$ bool
ContainsTimestamp_ω:	H $\times$ T	$\to$ bool
ContainsSnapshot:	H $\times$ V	$\to$ bool
ContainsState_ω:	H $\times$ S	$\to$ bool
FilterByTimestamp_ω:	H $\times$ T	$\to$ H
FilterBySnapshot:	H $\times$ V	$\to$ H
FilterByState_ω:	H $\times$ S	$\to$ H
EarliestState:	H	$\to$ S
LatestState:	H	$\to$ S
GetLifespan:	H	$\to$ T
SubsetOf:	H $\times$ H	$\to$ bool
StrictSubsetOf:	H $\times$ H	$\to$ bool
Equals:	H $\times$ H	$\to$ bool
Brackets:	H $\times$ H	$\to$ bool
dissect^I:	H	$\to 2^{\mathtt{Instant} \times V}$
dissect^T:	H	$\to 2^{\mathtt{TimeInterval} \times V}$
⋓:	H $\times$ H	$\to$ H
⋒:	H $\times$ H	$\to$ H
\:	H $\times$ H	$\to$ H

Fig. 7. Operations on Histories

snapshots, denoted by by S_V^H. The semantics of an operation Ω is sometimes characterized by writing: $post(\Omega) \Rightarrow \{p_1, \ldots, p_n\}$, where each p_i is a predicate that evaluates to true after Ω is carried out. Alternatively, the semantics of Ω is sometimes characterized by a rewriting: $\Omega \equiv (\sigma)[\Omega_1, \ldots, \Omega_n]$, where each Ω_i is an operation (defined elsewhere) over elements generated in σ. [10, 11] give, in detail, the semantics of all operations on histories.

Constructor Operations A history is empty when created. It is also possible to create a history from the state information contained in another history. The signatures for the create operations are given in Figure 7. Their semantics are given by $post(H := \mathtt{create}()) \Rightarrow \{\mathtt{isEmpty}(H)\}$ for the empty constructor, and by $H := \mathtt{create}(H') \equiv H := \mathtt{create}() ⋓ (\forall s \in S^{H'})[\mathtt{InsertState}(\mathtt{create}(), s)]$, for the non-empty creator, where ⋓ and InsertState are defined below.

Update Operations The update operations in the history ADT provide the ability to insert, delete and update states of a history. These operations preserve the invariant properties previously described. Some examples are shown in Figure 7, and some of these are now described in detail.

InsertState takes a history $H = \langle V, \theta, \gamma, \Sigma \rangle$ and a state $\langle \tau', \sigma' \rangle$, where τ' is of type θ and $\sigma' \in V$, and yields a new history $H' = \langle V, \theta, \gamma, \Sigma' \rangle$. If σ' is equal to some σ occurring in Σ then the timestamp τ associated with it is recomputed into a timestamp τ_+ that includes τ', and $\Sigma' = \Sigma \setminus \{\langle \tau, \sigma \rangle\} \cup \{\langle \tau_+, \sigma \rangle\}$. If, on the other hand, σ' does not occur in Σ, then Σ is recomputed into a state set Σ_+ that is everywhere equal to Σ except that every state in Σ whose timestamp has common points with τ' has been recomputed so as to make that no longer the case in Σ_+, and $\Sigma' = \Sigma_+ \cup \{\langle \tau', \sigma' \rangle\}$. The InsertState operation can therefore be seen to be a *destructive*, and hence non-commutative, operation. For example, if $\langle \tau', \sigma' \rangle = \langle [5-8], o_2 \rangle$ and $\Sigma = \{\langle [1-6], o_1 \rangle\}$, then $\Sigma' = \{\langle [1-5], o_1 \rangle, \langle [5-8], o_2 \rangle\}$, and if $\langle \tau', \sigma' \rangle = \langle [5-8], o_1 \rangle$ and $\Sigma = \{\langle [1-6], o_1 \rangle\}$, then $\Sigma' = \{\langle [1-8], o_1 \rangle\}$.

DeleteTimestamp takes a history $H = \langle V, \theta, \gamma, \Sigma \rangle$ and a timestamp τ of type θ and yields a new history $H' = \langle V, \theta, \gamma, \Sigma' \rangle$. The operation maps Σ into a state set Σ' in which all states in Σ whose timestamp τ' is such that $\underline{\text{common\_points}}(\tau, \tau')$ is true, have been recomputed so that τ does not occur in Σ', otherwise Σ remains unchanged. For example, if $\tau = [2-3]$ and $\Sigma = \{\langle [1-6], o_1 \rangle\}$, then $\Sigma' = \{\langle [1-2, 3-6], o_1 \rangle\}$. More formally, $H' := \text{DeleteTimestamp}(H, \tau) \equiv H' :=$ create$() \uplus (\forall s \in S^H \mid \underline{\text{common\_points}}(s.t, \tau))[H \setminus\!\!\setminus_\tau \{s\} \uplus \text{InsertState}(\text{create}(),$ $\langle \underline{\text{minus}}(s.t, \tau), s.v \rangle)]$. It can be seen that if the input timestamp has common points with the timestamp of any existing state, then this state is initially deleted (using the specialized difference operator $\setminus\!\!\setminus_\tau$ on histories, defined below), and a new state is inserted whose timestamp is computed using $\underline{\text{minus}}$, and whose snapshot is the same as in the deleted state. This new state is merged with the history using the merge operator $\uplus$ on histories, defined below.

The DeleteSnapshot operation deletes all states within a given history whose snapshot is equal to the input operand.

The remaining update operations assign to existing states either a new timestamp value, τ, or a new snapshot value, σ. For example, the UpdateTimestamp operation updates all states whose timestamps have common points with the input timestamp. There can be several such states and each has its overlapping temporal components updated to the new value.

Query Operations Several operations can be used by the higher layers of the Tripod architecture to query a given history. Such operations can be classified into Boolean, retrieval and filtering operations. Signatures for some of these are shown in Figure 7.

Boolean operations leave the a history unchanged and return a Boolean value to indicate the truth or falsity of the predicate they denote. Filtering operations return a (possibly empty) history.

The ContainsTimestamp_ω and FilterBySnapshot operations are now defined to exemplify how query operations can be given a precise semantics. The former is defined as the template ContainsTimestamp_ω$(H, \tau) \equiv (\exists \tau' \in S_T^H)[\omega(\tau, \tau')]$. Note that ContainsTimestamp_ω is a template for a collection of signatures parameterized on any predicate operation on Tripod timestamps. Given that before and after are members of that set, they can instantiate the template. For example, if the state sets of two histories H_1 and H_2 both with $V =$ Regions, $\theta =$ TimeIntervals and identical γ, are $\Sigma_1 = \{\langle [1-6], r_1 \rangle, \langle [9-11], r_3 \rangle\}$ and $\Sigma_2 = \{\langle [5-10], r_2 \rangle, \langle [13-20], r_4 \rangle\}$ then ContainsTimestamp_before$(H_1, [9-10]) =$ true and Contains Timestamp_after$(H_2, [21-22]) =$ false.

In contrast to ContainsTimestamp_ω, which queries a history for a true/false reply, the FilterBySnapshot operation exemplifies operations that query histories for a reply that is itself a history. It is defined as $H :=$ FilterBySnapshot(H', v') $\equiv H :=$ create() $\uplus$ $(\forall s \in S^{H'} \mid s.v = v')$[InsertState(create(), $\langle s.t, v' \rangle)$]. For example, if H_1 and H_2 are as above, then to check whether H_1 and H_2 (perhaps recording the history of change to the boundaries of two enumeration districts) contain a particular value r_1, one can use FilterBySnapshot$(H_1, r_1) = H'_1 = \langle V, \gamma, \theta, \{\langle [1-6], r_1 \rangle\}\rangle$ and FilterBySnapshot$(H_2, r_1) = H'_2 = \langle V, \gamma, \theta, \{\}\rangle$.

The history ADT also provides several binary Boolean operations to test the relationship between two given histories. For example, it is possible to test if one history is a subset or a strict subset of another history, or whether one history is equal to another history using the SubsetOf, StrictSubsetOf and Equals Boolean operations. Finally, the Brackets operation takes two histories H_1 and H_2 (with identical θ, γ, and V) as arguments, and returns true if the lifespan of H_2 is contained within or equal to the lifespan of H_1. Formally, let $H_1^s :=$ EarliestStateH_1.t, $H_1^e :=$ LatestStateH_1.t, $H_2^s :=$ EarliestStateH_2.t, and $H_2^e :=$ LatestStateH_2.t, then Brackets$(H_1, H_2) \equiv$ (starts_before$(H_1^s, H_2^s) \vee$ equals$(H_1^s, H_2^s)) \wedge$ (starts_after$(H_1^e, H_2^e) \vee$ equals(H_1^e, H_2^e)). For example, if the state sets of two histories H_1 and H_2 are, respectively, $\{\langle [1-6], 12 \rangle, \langle [9-11], 14 \rangle\}$ and $\{\langle [2-11], 12 \rangle\}$ then Brackets$(H_1 H_2) =$ true.

Mutator Operations Tripod provides a collection of functions that transform a given history into another collection that represents a particular *view* over the history. Such views can be used (for example) by the Tripod query calculus [9] to provide different ways of iterating over a particular history. For example, while some users will want to view a history in its previously described canonical form, other users may want to view a history as a collection of states that are timestamped with individual temporal values. The collections returned by such operations may be ordered according to the semantics of the mutator function and the nature of the resultant collection.

For example, the dissect mutator function returns a set of snapshot/timestamp pairs, with the timestamp consisting of *individual* (i.e., Instant or TimeInterval) temporal elements. Given

```
R := {};
for each ⟨τ,σ⟩ in Σ do
    for each τ' in disassemble(τ)
        R := R ∪{⟨τ',σ⟩};
```

Fig. 8. The dissect Operation

$H = \langle V, \text{Instants}, \gamma, \Sigma \rangle$, $\text{dissect}^I(H)$ returns a set of pairs of the form $\langle \tau', \sigma \rangle$, where $\sigma \in V$ and the type of τ' is Instant, obtainable as shown in Figure 8. The views created by such mutator functions can be used by the Tripod spatio-historical calculus to provide different forms of iteration over a history. For example, expressions of the form $s \leftarrow H$ can be constructed, where $H : \mathbb{H}$ and $s : \mathbb{S}$, such that H is the *domain generator* from which bindings for s are drawn. However, if a calculus expression needs to range over states of the form $\langle s : \mathbb{V}, t : T \rangle$, where T is either Instant or TimeInterval, then dissect can be used, yielding generators like $s \leftarrow \text{dissect}(H)$.

Merge Operations The history ADT provides several binary operations that, based on different criteria, generate a new history from two others. The operations are shown in Figure 7.

Given $H_1 = \langle V, \theta, \gamma, \Sigma_1 \rangle$ and $H_2 = \langle V, \theta, \gamma, \Sigma_2 \rangle$, $H_1 \uplus H_2 = H_3 = \langle V, \theta, \gamma, \Sigma_3 \rangle$, where $\Sigma_3 = (state_{H_1} | (dom(state_{H_1}) \setminus dom(state_{H_2})) \cup state_{H_2})$, where, given a function $f(x)$, its *restriction to the set E*, denoted by $f|E$, is the set of pairs $\langle x, y \rangle$ such that $y = f(x)$ and $x \in E$. In other words, taking the union of two histories is equivalent to taking the union of their state sets but choosing the state in the second argument whenever there is a state in the first argument with the same timestamp but different snapshot. This is to satisfy the invariants that characterize histories. For example, if the state sets of two histories H_1 and H_2 are as exemplified above, then the state set of $H_3 = H_1 \uplus H_2$ is $\Sigma = \{\langle [1-5], \mathbf{r}_1 \rangle, \langle [5-10], \mathbf{r}_2 \rangle, \langle [10-11], \mathbf{r}_3 \rangle, \langle [13-20], \mathbf{r}_4 \rangle\}$.

The ⋒ operation is the history ADT's equivalent of the set intersection operation, in that, for two histories H_1 and H_2, its result contains the states that are members of both H_1 and H_2. This operation however has two variants: one, denoted by ⋒$_\tau$, tests for equality between states based on the timestamp values; the other, denoted by ⋒$_\sigma$, based on the snapshot value. Once again, any states from H_2 that are value equivalent take precedence in the result. For example, if the state sets of two histories H_1 and H_2 are as exemplified above, then the state set of $H_3 = H_1 ⋒_\tau H_2$ is $\Sigma = \{\langle [5-6, 9-10], \mathbf{r}_2 \rangle\}$, and the state set of $H_3' = H_1 ⋒_\sigma H_2$ is $\Sigma = \{\}$.

The \\ operation corresponds to set difference, in that, for two histories H_1 and H_2, its result contains all elements of H_1 that are not present in H_2. There are, again, two versions of this operation: one denoted by \\$_\tau$, based on equal timestamp values; the other, denoted by \\$_\sigma$, based on equal snapshot values. For example, if the state sets of two histories H_1 and H_2 are as exemplified above, then the state set of $H_3 = H_1 \setminus\!\!\setminus_\tau H_2$ is $\Sigma = \{\langle [1-5], \mathbf{r}_1 \rangle, \langle [10-11], \mathbf{r}_3 \rangle\}$, and the state set of $H_3' = H_1 \setminus\!\!\setminus_\sigma H_2$ is $\Sigma = \{\langle [1-6], \mathbf{r}_1 \rangle, \langle [9-11], \mathbf{r}_3 \rangle\}$.

5 A Spatio-historical ODMG Object Model

The Tripod Object Model (OM) provides the ability to record the history of change that entities and relationships undergo over time. It extend the ODMG model with the ability to track the changes caused by assignment operations on any assignable construct that is declared to be historical. In other words, any construct denoted by the left hand side of an assignment operation (i.e., an *l-value*) can have a record kept of the different values assigned to it over time. More specifically, the history ADT makes it possible to track the changes caused by the creation and deletion of objects, assignments to object attributes, assignments to object relationships, and assignment to named collections. For example, for the LS there is a need to track changes made to an LS member's marital status, the life events they undergo, and the districts they live in. For each ODMG Object Model concept that is value assignable (i.e., atomic object types, attributes, relationships and collection object types), the Tripod OM provides a *historical* counterpart.

Although histories can be thought of as collections, they are not denoted by a type constructor. Rather the keyword `historical`, as a modifier within the ODL, indicates that a history should be maintained of the modified concept. When such declarations are made, the OM internally creates an instance of the history ADT for each historicized concept. This approach has been taken because if the history mechanism were to appear as a type, then declarations such as `history<history<set<history<String>>>>`, would be syntactically valid, despite their semantics being unclear.

In addition to specifying that a database concept should have its history maintained, the designer can also specify certain defaulted properties of the history, viz., its *granularity* and its *temporal type*. Thus, if a history has granularity γ, then the changes maintained by the history cannot vary more than once for each granule of γ (the default is the CHRONON granularity [5]). Any attempt to specify a granularity finer than γ will cause the value to be converted to granularity γ. Also, each change is associated with either an `Instants` or a `TimeIntervals` timestamp. The default is `TimeIntervals`.

```
historical(TimeIntervals, DAY) class LS_member           // spatio-historical class
( extent LS_members )
{       attribute    enum {male, female} sex;            // aspatial and not historical
        attribute    TimeInstant         date_of_birth;  // temporal but not historical
    historical(TimeIntervals, DAY)                       // aspatial historical attribute
        attribute    enum {single,married,divorced,widowed} marital_status;
    historical(TimeIntervals, DAY)                       // spatio-historical relationship
        relationship Enumeration_district resides_in
        inverse      Enumeration_district :: has_LS_members;
};

historical(TimeIntervals, DAY) class Enumeration_district  // spatio-historical class
( extent Enumeration_districts )
{       attribute    string              name;            // aspatial and not historical
    historical(TimeIntervals, DAY)                        // spatio-historical attribute
        attribute    Regions             boundary;
    historical(TimeIntervals, DAY)                        // spatio-historical relationship
        relationship set<LS_member>      has_LS_members
        inverse      LS_member           :: resides_in;
};
```

Fig. 9. Historical Type Definitions

For example, Figure 9 shows how the model in Figure 2 can be declared (but some classes in the latter have been omitted). Note that the boundary attribute of an enumeration district implies a spatio-historical property for every LS member through the resides_in relationship.

Historical Atomic Object Types In the Tripod OM any user-defined type can be declared as historical. This causes an implicit historical attribute called lifespan to be maintained for each instance of that type. The lifespan attribute records whether the object is active or inactive at particular times in the modelled reality. This capability allows objects to be de-/reactivated within a particular database, as opposed to being simply inserted and deleted. For example, through the Tripod language bindings, an LS_member object ls_1 : T can be created (using an extended new operator) to exist during the time period $[10-20]$, and can be subsequently (logically) deleted (using an extended version of the delete operator) during the period $[12-15]$, where the lifespan attribute for T denotes a TimeIntervals history of snapshots drawn from a domain Status = {active, inactive}, thus giving ls_1 the history: o_1.lifespan =$\{\langle[10-12, 15-20], \texttt{active}\rangle, \langle[12-15], \texttt{inactive}\rangle\}$. With specific reference to the LS, this feature allows us to logically delete an LS_member when they undergo an *emigration* life event. If an object type is non-historical, then the type can still have historical properties, however its will not have a lifespan attribute and deletion will remove current and past states.

Historical Properties Any property (attribute or relationship) of an atomic object type can be declared as historical. For example, in Figure 9, boundary is a historical attribute and resides_in is a historical relationship. In the ODMG object model, the integrity of a relationship is automatically maintained by the ODBMS. This is also the case with historical relationships, although such maintenance is inherently more complex. For example, when a new state is added to the resides_in relationship, described above, the inverse history defined by the LS_member type must be maintained so that the constraints specified by the Tripod spatio-historical object model are satisfied (as defined in Section 5). Such maintenance is the responsibility of the Tripod kernel.

Collection Object Histories An instance of a collection object type is a named object whose component elements are of the same type. This type can be an atomic object type, another collection, or a literal type. A historical collection object type uses the history mechanism to allow the history of change of its composition to be recorded. For example, a named historical collection object called largest_Enumeration_districts could be created, where each state is a structure $\langle \tau, \sigma \rangle$, where $\sigma \in$ set$\langle$Enumeration_district$\rangle$ denotes the Enumeration_districts with area above a given limit at each timestamp τ.

Tripod: A Comprehensive Model for Spatial and Aspatial Historical Objects   97

Inheritance The ODMG object model supports inheritance-based type-subtype relationships, in which the subtype can specialize, and add to, the state and behaviour of the supertype. This ability gives rise to several important considerations in the Tripod OM regarding specializations of types with historical declarations. Since inheritance is defined to allow the *specialization* of a type, thus providing more specific information in the subtype, it follows that in the Tripod OM, a subtype may only have a more specialized historical nature than its supertype. Therefore, in the Tripod OM a historical type cannot be specialized into a non-historical type, but a non-historical type can be specialized into a historical one. The properties of a type may be added to by a subtype, or they may be refined according to some restrictions. For the same reasons as stated above, it is only possible for a non-historical property to be specialized to a historical property (on the same domain or a more specific one) in a subtype. The reverse is not possible since this will result in loss of information in the subtype. The substitutability property of the ODMG object model requires that any attribute refined in a subclass is viewable with respect to its superclass. Thus, in the Tripod OM, any non-historical property that is specialized in a subclass to become historical, is viewable as a non-historical property in its supertype. Since the value of a non-historical attribute is implicitly valid at the present time (now), the Tripod OM by default accesses a historical type/property snapshot at *now* in such circumstances. This function uses the history ADT's FilterByTimestamp_equals(now) operation to compute the current value of a historical property. Note that this value could be undefined if every value in the subtype history exists only in the past.

Containment Constraints The Tripod OM defines a set of containment constraints on historical objects and their properties. For example, the lifespan of a particular historical object instance must always contain the timestamps associated with each snapshot of its historical properties. If this were not the case then a database would contain historical information that is arguably incorrect. These constraints are defined as follows. For an instance o of an historical type, with a set of historical object-valued attributes $attrs$, the lifespan of o must bracket the lifespan of each of its attributes, i.e.: $\forall\ a \in attrs$, Brackets(o.lifespan, a.lifespan) = true. For an instance o of an historical type, with a set of historical relationships $rels$, the lifespan of o must bracket the lifespan of each of its relationships, i.e.: $\forall\ r \in rels$, Brackets(o.lifespan, r.lifespan) = true. For a historical relationship r, with state set $\Sigma = \{s_1, \ldots, s_n\}$, where the snapshot value of each s_i is an instance of an historical type, the timestamp associated with each state must be a subset of the lifespan of its corresponding historical object, i.e.: $\forall\ s_i \in \Sigma$, ContainsTimestamp_surrounds (s_i.v.lifespan, s_i.t) = true. For a historical collection object type O, with state set $\Sigma = \{s_1, \ldots, s_n\}$, the lifespan of O must bracket the timestamp in each state: $\forall\ s \in O$, ContainsTimestamp_surrounds (O.lifespan, s.t) = true. Note that the above containment constraints apply only when both concepts are historical. These constraints are invariant properties on historical objects.

An Example For the LS_member type declared in Section 5, each LS_member object will have a history for each of its historical properties. For example, the marital_status attribute is associated with a history with the structure $H_{\texttt{marital\_status}} = \langle V, \theta, \gamma, \Sigma \rangle$, where $V \subseteq \{\texttt{single},\texttt{married},\texttt{divorced},\texttt{widowed}\}$, $\theta = \texttt{TimeIntervals}$, $\gamma = \texttt{DAY}$, and Σ maps each different marital_status value to a TimeIntervals value.

---

ls_1: **A Historical Object** (*partial*)
$\Sigma_{\texttt{lifespan}} = \{\langle [5-40, 55-95], \texttt{active}\rangle, \langle [40-55], \texttt{inactive}\rangle\}$
sex = female
date_of_birth = $|1|$ // $|1|$ denotes a particular TimeInstant
$\Sigma_{\texttt{marital\_status}} = \{\langle [10-40, 55-60], \texttt{married}\rangle, \langle [60-75], \texttt{divorced}\rangle\}$
$\Sigma_{\texttt{resides\_in}} = \{\langle [5-40, 75-95], d_1\rangle, \langle [55-75], d_7\rangle\}$
A Historical Relationship at d_1
$\Sigma_{\texttt{has\_LS\_members}} = \{\langle [0-5], \{\texttt{ls}_3\}\rangle, \langle [5-15], \{\texttt{ls}_1, \texttt{ls}_3\}\rangle,$
$\langle [15-40], \{\texttt{ls}_1\}\rangle, \langle [40-55], \{\texttt{ls}_2\}\rangle,$
$\langle [75-95], \{\texttt{ls}_1\}\rangle\}$

Fig. 10. Historical, Aspatial Properties

Since LS_member is a historical type, each LS_member instance also has an implicit lifespan attribute which is a history of the form $H_{\texttt{lifespan}} = \langle \{\texttt{active}, \texttt{inactive}\}, \texttt{TimeIntervals}, \texttt{DAY}, \Sigma \rangle$. An LS member ls_1 could have value assignments as shown in Figure 10.

Note that ls_1 resided in enumeration district d_1, then emigrated (i.e., was logically deleted), then lived in enumeration district d_7, then returned to enumeration district d_1. The inverse of the resides_in relationship would be defined for each of the referenced objects. For example, for the object d_1, has_LS_members would be instantiated as shown in Figure 10.

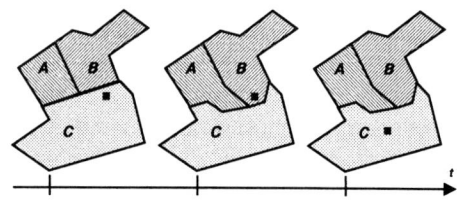

Fig. 11. A Historical, Spatial Property

Figure 11 illustrates the capabilities of the Tripod OM when considering spatial properties of LS objects as they change over time. It shows a single LS Region split into three enumeration districts whose boundaries change between the three states. In addition, the LS member object (associated with a Points value) can change location independently of changes that enumeration districts undergo.

ls_1 satisfies the containment constraints of Section 5. Note that the implicit lifespan attribute of this object indicates that ls_1 had been (logically) deleted from the database during the period $[40-55]$ (due to a life event that removed them from the LS). If subsequently the database were updated to reflect that ls_1 had a marital_status of widowed during $[42-53]$, then the stored data must still reflect the OM's containment constraints. It is an implementation issue as to whether this is achieved by either (a) rejecting this new information as inconsistent with the object's lifespan, or (b) accepting the new information, and updating the object's lifespan accordingly. Equally, if ls_1 were (logically) deleted during the period [20 − 30], then this operation can either be rejected or the object's properties can be modified according to the policy set down by the higher layers.

6 Related Work

The contributions reported in this paper build upon the large body of research in the general area of spatial and temporal databases, in both relational and object settings over the last three decades. Much of the recent work in this area has been surveyed in [7]. In general, there are two ways of providing support for spatio-temporal entities. The first of these is to provide tightly-coupled mechanisms for spatio-temporal support, the other is to provide a more general means of supporting the temporal aspects of data, of which spatial entities are just one type. The former of these approaches is exemplified by [25], where a spatio-temporal model and algebra are proposed whose entities are spatial objects (simplicial complexes) that have an integral temporal dimension. While such approaches provide highly specialized mechanisms for maintaining the history of purely spatial entities, these mechanisms have not been extended to aspatial entities. The remainder of this section focuses on data models that use more general mechanisms for storing changes not only to spatial but also to aspatial data, since that is the focus of this paper.

Current research into temporal object models stems from similar work in the relational setting during the 1980s. Such models typically used either tuple or attribute timestamping mechanisms to record the valid time of stored data. The property timestamping approach adopted in this paper can be seen to be an adaptation to an object-oriented setting of the methods employed by, e.g., Gadia [8], who modelled attribute values as functions from temporal elements onto the attribute's domain, where a temporal element is a union of disjoint time intervals. Such attribute timestamping methods have also been used in a purely spatial setting by researchers such as Langran [14], who proposed a spatial vector model in which stored line segments are used as primitives to produce stored polygons. Each of these polygons is then timestamped with its own attribute history using discrete semantics. These techniques however have not been extended to aspatial data. The operations defined over Tripod temporal types exploit constructs first proposed by Güting and Schneider in the early 1990s in a spatial setting. Our temporal predicate operations have their foundations in the interval algebra defined by Ladkin [13], which in turn extends that of Allen [1] to unions of convex intervals. There are many proposals of temporal relational models, however few have been implemented (see the excellent survey in [12] for details).

There are also relatively few proposals for temporal object models (see the survey in [21]). Of these, the historical object model proposed by Bertino et al. [2] most closely relates to our work. They propose a temporal extension to the ODMG object model, called *T_ODMG*, that uses property timestamping. The value for each *T_ODMG* object property is a function of time, using interval-based timestamps that closely resemble the primitive Tripod TimeInterval values. Particular attention is paid to modelling objects that migrate to another type during their lifetimes. While the structural component of *T_ODMG* is well documented, the behavioural aspects of temporal domains is less so. The details of such behaviour are a necessary precursor to the definition of a query language and corresponding optimizer, and without that it is difficult to compare the contributions of this paper with those of [2] in greater detail. There are even fewer proposals for spatio-temporal object models (see the survey in [23]). Of these the MADS model [16] reflects many of the concerns identified by the Tripod object model, including the orthogonal treatment of spatial and aspatial concerns. While the MADS model provides facilities to conceptually model spatio-temporal types and relationships, it does not consider the operations necessary for updating and querying.

Both our data model and that of [2] use a *discrete* model of time. Other proposals exist for data models that capture objects whose properties (spatial and aspatial) are continuously changing. These models are typified by the *moving object* approach adopted in [20] and [17]. Such models allow the state of each spatial and aspatial property to be expressed as a continuous function of time. Queries about the position of spatial data can then be inferred by the interpolation of spatial values between known bounds. This provides an expressive mechanism for the representation of moving points and polygons ([17] only considers points). Querying moving object databases is achieved by extending an existing database algebra through a process called *lifting*. This allows non-temporal kernel algebra operations to be applied to temporal types. It should be noted, however, that such models do not provide comprehensive support for temporally changing aspatial data and object model constructs such as relationships, which are supported in a uniform way by the Tripod data model. In contrast, the Tripod data model and calculus do not model continuous change, as we explicitly target the large body of applications in which objects change in discrete steps; for example cadastral, cartographic, and demographic applications.

7 Summary

The aim of the Tripod project is to design and prototype a complete spatio-temporal database system. This paper presents the core spatio-historical data model which forms the foundations of this work. In particular, this paper has presented a collection of primitive temporal types whose foundations lie in the existing spatial ROSE algebra [18]. The intrinsic relationship between these temporal and spatial types promotes consistent and complementary facilities for representing time and space. The paper has also described how these temporal types can be used to underpin the notion of a history, as a generalized mechanism through which both spatial and aspatial change can be recorded over time, and shown how Tripod's spatial and temporal types and the notion of a history can be used to orthogonally extend the ODMG object model to form a spatio-historical object model. Finally, through the use of an example application, the paper has illustrated how these core modelling concepts are used within a spatio-historical database architecture to provide a formal description of the data structures and operations that are necessary to underpin both a query calculus and native language bindings.

Acknowledgments: Discussions with John Stell and Chris Johnson helped shape the contributions of this paper. Support by the UK Engineering and Physical Sciences Research Council (EPSRC) is gratefully acknowledged. Figure 4 is Crown copyright material reproduced under Class Licence Number C01W0000487 with the permission of the Controller of HMSO and the Queen's Printer for Scotland.

References

[1] J. Allen. Maintaining knowledge about temporal intervals. *CACM*, 26(11):832–843, 1983.
[2] E. Bertino, E. Ferrari, G. Guerrini, and I. Merlo. Extending the ODMG Object Model with Time. *Proc. ECOOP'98*, pp. 41–66, 1998.
[3] R. G. G. Cattell, editor. *The Object Database Standard: ODMG 3.0*. Morgan Kaufmann, 2000.
[4] C. X. Chen and C. Zaniolo. SQL^{ST}: A spatio-temporal data model and query language. *Proc. ER 2000*, LNCS 1920, pp. 96–111, 2000.
[5] C. S. Jensen et al. The Consensus Glossary of Temporal Database Concepts. *Temporal Databases: Research and Practice*, LNCS 1399, pp. 367–405, 1998.
[6] L. Fegaras and D. Maier. Optimizing Object Queries Using an Effective Calculus. *ACM TODS*, 25(4):457–516, 2000.
[7] A. U. Frank et al. CHOROCHRONOS, A Research Network for Spatiotemporal Database Systems. *SIGMOD Record*, 28(3):12–21, 1999.
[8] S. K. Gadia. A Homogeneous Relational Model and Query Languages for Temporal Databases. *ACM TODS*, 13(4):418–448, 1988.
[9] T. Griffiths, A.A.A. Fernandes, N. Djafri, and N.W. Paton. A Query Calculus for Spatio-Temporal Object Databases. In *Proc. TIME'01*, pp. 101–110, 2001.
[10] T. Griffiths, N.W. Paton, and A.A.A. Fernandes. An ODMG-Compliant Spatio-Temporal Data Model. http://pevepc13.cs.man.ac.uk/PrePrints/index.htm.
[11] T. Griffiths, N.W. Paton, and A.A.A. Fernandes. Realm-Based Temporal Data Types. http://pevepc13.cs.man.ac.uk/PrePrints/index.htm.
[12] L. E. McKenzie Jr and R. T. Snodgrass. Evaluation of Relational Algebras Incorporating the Time Dimension in Databases. *ACM Computing Surveys*, 23(4):501–543, 1991.
[13] P. Ladkin. *The Logic of Time Representation*. PhD thesis, University of California at Berkeley, November 1987.
[14] G. Langran. *Time in Geographical Information Systems*. Taylor and Francis, 1992.
[15] V. Müller, N. W. Paton, A. A. Fernandes, A. Dinn, and M. H. Williams. Virtual Realms: An Efficient Implementation Strategy for Finite Resolution Spatial Data Types. *Proc. SDH'96*, pp. IIB.1 – IIB.13, 1996.

[16] C. Parent, S. Spaccapietra, and E. Zimányi. Spatio-temporal conceptual models: Data structures + space + time. *Proc. ACM-GIS '99*, pp. 26–33, 1999.
[17] D. Pfoser, C. S. Jensen, and Y. Theodoridis. Novel Approaches in Query Processing for Moving Object Trajectories. *Proc. VLDB 2000*, pp. 395–406, 2000.
[18] R. H. Güting and M. Schneider. Realm-Based Spatial Data Types: The ROSE Algebra. *VLDB Journal*, 4(2):243–286, 1995.
[19] R. H. Güting, T. de Ridder, and M. Schneider. Implementation of the ROSE Algebra: Efficient Algorithms for Realm-Based Spatial Data Types. *Proc. SSD'95*, LNCS 951, pp. 216–239, 1995.
[20] R. H. Güting, M. H. Böhlen, M. Erwig, C. S. Jensen, N. A. Lorentzos, M. Schneider, and M. Vazirgiannis. A Foundation for Representing and Querying Moving Objects. *ACM TODS*, 25(1):1–42, 1000.
[21] R. T. Snodgrass. Temporal Object-Oriented Databases: A Critical Comparison *Modern Database Systems: The Oobject Model, Interoperability and Beyond*, pp. 386–408. Addison-Wesley/ACM Press, 1995.
[22] R. Snodgrass. *Developing Time-Oriented Database Applications in SQL*. Morgan Kaufmann Publishers, 2000.
[23] A. Pavlopoulos and C.Theodoulidis. Review of Spatio-Temporal Data Models. Technical report, Department of Computation, UMIST, United Kingdom, October 1998. http://www.crim.org.uk/.
[24] C. Theodoulidis and P. Loucopoulos. The time dimension in conceptual modelling. *Information Systems*, 16(3):273–300, 1991.
[25] M. Warboys. A Unified Model for Spatial and Temporal Information. *The Computer Journal*, 37(1):25–34, 1994.

A Design of Topological Predicates for Complex Crisp and Fuzzy Regions

Markus Schneider

FernUniversität Hagen, Praktische Informatik IV
D-58084 Hagen, Germany
markus.schneider@fernuni-hagen.de

Abstract. For a long time topological predicates between spatial objects have been a main area of research on spatial data handling, reasoning, and query languages. But these predicates still suffer from two main restrictions: first, they are only applicable to simplified abstractions of spatial objects like single points, continuous lines, and simple regions, as they occur in systems like current geographical information systems and spatial database systems. Since these abstractions are usually not sufficient to cope with the complexity of geographic reality, their generalization is needed which especially has influence on the nature and definition of their topological relationships. This paper gives a formal definition of complex crisp regions, which may consist of several components and which may have holes, and it especially shows how topological predicates can be defined on them. Second, topological predicates so far only operate on crisp but not on fuzzy spatial objects which occur frequently in geographical reality. Based on complex crisp regions, this paper gives a definition of their fuzzy counterparts and shows how topological predicates can be defined on them.

1 Introduction

Representing, storing, quering, and manipulating spatial information is important for many non-standard database applications. Specialized systems like geographical information systems (GIS), spatial database systems, and image database systems to some extent provide the needed technology to support these applications. For these systems the development of formal models for spatial objects and for topological relationships between these objects is a topic of great importance and interest, since these models exert a great influence on the efficiency of spatial systems and on the expressiveness of spatial query languages.

In recent years, significant achievements have been made on the design of topological predicates for spatial objects with precisely defined boundaries, so-called *crisp* spatial objects. However, the structure of spatial objects upon which current topological predicates operate is restricted and not sufficient to cope with the complexity of geographic reality. For spatial regions this means that at most simple regions and topological predicates between them can be found in current GISs and spatial database systems. Only very few approaches exist for more complexly structured regions. General topological predicates on complex regions possibly consisting of several components and possibly having holes have so far not been designed. But in real applications complex regions are by far more common than simple ones. It is one of the goals of this paper to give a definition of complex crisp regions and to provide topological predicates for them.

Additionally, the current mapping of spatial phenomena of the real world to exclusively crisp spatial objects turns out to be an insufficient abstraction for many spatial applications, because the feature of *spatial vagueness* or *spatial fuzziness* is inherent to many geographic data [2]. Spatial fuzziness captures the property of many spatial objects in reality which do not have sharp boundaries or whose boundaries cannot be precisely determined. Examples are natural, social, or cultural phenomena like land features with continuously changing properties (such as population density, soil quality, vegetation, pollution, temperature, air pressure), oceans, deserts, English speaking areas, or mountains and valleys. We will designate this kind of entities as *fuzzy* spatial objects.

The definition of topological predicates on fuzzy spatial objects in general and fuzzy regions in particular is currently an open problem. For two fuzzy regions A and B we would like to be able to pose and answer queries like

- Do regions A and B overlap *a little bit*?
- Determine all pairs of regions that *nearly completely* overlap.
- Does region A *somewhat* contain region B?
- Which regions lie *quite* inside B?

Section 2 discusses related work. In Section 3, we present a formal model of complex crisp and fuzzy regions. For fuzzy regions we use a representation that reduces these objects to collections of so-called crisp α-level regions. This enables us to transfer our whole formal framework (and later all the well known implementation methods available) for crisp regions to fuzzy regions. In Section 4, based on well known topological relationships for *simple* crisp regions, in a bottom-up strategy we first define topological predicates for simple crisp regions with holes and afterwards for complex crisp regions with additional multiple components. Section 5 presents an approach for designing topological predicates for fuzzy regions. Finally, Section 6 draws some conclusions.

2 Related Work

This section summarizes some related work on the definition and representation of crisp and fuzzy regions (Section 2.1) and on the design and definition of binary topological predicates between regions (Section 2.2).

2.1 Crisp and Fuzzy Regions

In the past, a number of data models and query languages for *crisp* spatial data have been proposed with the aim of formulating and processing spatial queries in databases (see [12] for a survey). *Spatial data types* like *point*, *line*, or *region*, that are the central concept of these approaches, provide fundamental abstractions for modeling the structure of geometric entities, their relationships, properties, and operations. However, data models expressing spatial vagueness are rare. *Exact models* [4, 8, 11] transfer type systems for spatial objects with sharp boundaries to objects with unclear boundaries. The approaches in [4, 11] extend the indeterminate boundary of a region into a boundary zone, called *broad boundary*, which is situated around the region. The concept of *vague regions* [8] generalizes these approaches in the sense that such a region can be a pair of arbitrarily located, disjoint crisp regions. The *kernel region* describes the area which definitely belongs to the vague region. The *boundary region* describes the area for which it is not sure whether it or parts of it belong to the vague region or not. *Models based on rough sets* [16] work with lower and upper approximations of spatial objects. *Models based on fuzzy sets* [1, 13, 14] model the vagueness resulting from the imprecision of the meaning of a concept. A concept like 'ocean' or 'Southern England' cannot be modeled with crisp but with fuzzy means. *Fuzzy spatial data types* defined on an abstract (Euclidean space) and on a discrete (*grid partition*) geometric basis are introduced in [13, 14].

2.2 Crisp and Fuzzy Topological Predicates

Our definitions are based on the so-called 9-*intersection model* [6] from which a complete collection of mutually exclusive topological relationships can be derived for each combination of spatial types. The model is based on the nine possible intersections of boundary (∂A), interior (A°), and exterior (A^-) of a spatial object A with the corresponding components of another object. Each intersection is tested for the topologically invariant criteria of emptiness and non-emptiness. $2^9 = 512$ different configurations are possible from which only a certain subset makes sense depending on the combination of spatial objects just considered.

A restriction of the 9-intersection model with respect to regions is that regions must be homeomorphic to the closed disc, that is, they must be connected and are not allowed to have holes. These regions are usually called *simple regions*. For two simple regions, eight meaningful configurations have been identified which lead to the eight predicates of the set $T_{sr} = \{$ *disjoint, meet, overlap, equal, inside, contains, covers*, and *coveredBy* $\}$. Each predicate is uniquely determined so that all predicates are mutually exclusive and complete with regard to the topologically invariant criteria of emptiness and non-emptiness.

In this paper we aim at a formal definition of topological predicates for crisp and fuzzy complex regions with multiple parts and possibly with holes. It is surprising that topological predicates on crisp complex regions have so far not been defined. In [3] the so-called TRCR (Topological Relationships for Composite Regions) model only allows sets of disjoint simple regions without holes. In [7] only topological relationships of simple regions with holes are considered. Topological predicates on fuzzy spatial objects, let them be simple or complex, have so far not been defined.

3 A Model for Crisp and Fuzzy Complex Regions

In this paper we only consider topological predicates that operate on regions. Hence, in this section, we first clarify the structure and semantics of region objects. We begin with an abstract model for very general crisp complex regions, which results in a spatial data type *region*. Based on this specification, we define a data type *fregion* representing a fuzzy region as a collection of crisp regions with special properties. This representation is later used as operand of fuzzy topological predicates.

3.1 Modeling Crisp Regions

Our definition of regions is based on point set theory and point set topology [9]. Regions are embedded into the two-dimensional Euclidean space $\mathbb{R}^2$ and are thus point sets. Unfortunately, the use of pure point set theory for their definition causes problems. If regions are modeled as arbitrary point sets, they can suffer from undesired geometric anomalies. These degeneracies relate to isolated or dangling line and point features as well as missing lines and points in the form of cuts and punctures. A process called *regularization* [15] avoids these anomalies.

We briefly summarize some needed concepts from point set topology. Let X be a set and $T \subseteq 2^X$. The pair (X, T) is called a *topological space* if the following three axioms hold: (i) $U, V \in T \Rightarrow U \cap V \in T$, (ii) $S \subseteq T \Rightarrow \bigcup_{U \in S} U \in T$, and (iii) $X \in T$, $\emptyset \in T$. T is called a *topology* for X. The elements of T are called *open sets* and their complements in X are called *closed sets*. Several operations identify certain parts of a set. Let $S \subseteq X$. The *interior* of S is defined as the union of all open sets that are contained in S and is denoted by $S°$. The *closure* of S is defined as the intersection of all closed sets that contain S and is denoted by $\overline{S}$. The *exterior* of S is the union of all open sets that are not contained in S, that is, $S^- := (X - S)°$. The *boundary* of S is the intersection of the closure of S and the closure of the complement of S, that is, $\partial S := \overline{S} \cap \overline{X - S}$. Furthermore, we have $\overline{S} = S° \cup \partial S$.

In our case $X := \mathbb{R}^2$ holds. The concept of regularity defines a point set S as *regular closed* if $S = \overline{S°}$. We define a *regularization function* reg_c which associates a set S with its corresponding regular closed set as $reg_c(S) := \overline{S°}$. The effect of the *interior* operation is to eliminate dangling points, dangling lines, and boundary parts. The effect of the *closure* operation is to eliminate cuts and punctures by appropriately supplementing points and to add the boundary. We are now already able to give a general definition of a type for complex crisp regions:

$$region = \{R \subseteq \mathbb{R}^2 \mid R \text{ is bounded and regular closed}\}$$

In fact, this very "structureless" definition models complex crisp regions possibly consisting of several components and possibly having holes. But since the topological predicates of the 9-intersection model only work on simpler regions, we have to take a more fine-grained and structured view of regions.

A *simple region* is a bounded, regular closed set homeomorphic (that is, topologically equivalent) to a two-dimensional closed disc[1]. This, in particular, means that a simple region has a connected interior, a connected boundary, and a single connected exterior. Hence, it does not consist of several components, and it does not have holes.

The concept of a hole is topologically not inferable since point set topology does not distinguish between outer exterior and inner exteriors of a set. This requires an explicit and constructive definition of a region containing holes and a use of the topological predicates for simple regions. Let $\pi : \{1, \ldots, k\} \to \{1, \ldots, n\}, k, n \in \mathbb{N}, k \leq n$, be a total, injective mapping, and let $\{F_0, \ldots, F_n\}$ be a set of simple regions. The regular set $F = F_0 - \bigcup_{i=1}^{n} F_i^\circ$ is called a *simple region with holes* or a *face*, and $F_1, \ldots, F_n$ are called *holes* (Figure 1c) iff

(i) $\forall 1 \leq i \leq n : contains(F_0, F_i) \vee (covers(F_0, F_i) \wedge |F_0 \cap F_i| = 1)$
(ii) $\forall 1 \leq i < j \leq n : disjoint(F_i, F_j) \vee (meet(F_i, F_j) \wedge |F_i \cap F_j| = 1)$
(iii) $\not\exists \{\pi(1), \ldots, \pi(k)\} \subseteq \{1, \ldots, n\} : meet(F_0, F_{\pi(1)}) \wedge$
$meet(F_{\pi(1)}, F_{\pi(2)}) \wedge \cdots \wedge meet(F_{\pi(k-1)}, F_{\pi(k)}) \wedge meet(F_{\pi(k)}, F_0)$
(iv) $\not\exists \{\pi(1), \ldots, \pi(k)\} \subseteq \{1, \ldots, n\} : meet(F_{\pi(1)}, F_{\pi(2)}) \wedge$
$meet(F_{\pi(2)}, F_{\pi(3)}) \wedge \cdots \wedge meet(F_{\pi(k-1)}, F_{\pi(k)}) \wedge meet(F_{\pi(k)}, F_{\pi(1)})$

The first two conditions allow a hole within a face to touch the boundary of F_0 or of another hole in at most a single point. This is necessary in order to achieve closure under the geometric operations *union*, *intersection*, and *difference* (see also [10, 12]). For example, subtracting a face A from a face B may lead to such a hole in B. On the other hand, to allow two holes to have a partially common border makes no sense because then adjacent holes could be merged to a single hole by eliminating the common border (similarly for adjacency of a hole with the boundary of F_0). The third condition prevents the formation of "open hole chains" where any two subsequent holes meet and both the first and the last hole touch F_0. The fourth condition prevents the formation of "closed hole chains" within the face where any two subsequent holes meet and both the first and the last hole meet. All four conditions together ensure uniqueness of representation, that is, there are no two different interpretations of the point set describing a face. Hence, a face is atomic and cannot be decomposed into two or more faces. For example, the configuration shown in Figure 1a must be interpreted as two faces with two holes and not as a single face with four holes.

Let $F = F_0 - \bigcup_{i=1}^{n} F_i^\circ$ be a simple region with holes $F_1, \ldots, F_n$. Then the boundary and the interior of F are given as follows (Figures 1d and 1e):

(i) $\partial F = \bigcup_{i=0}^{n} \partial F_i$
(ii) $F^\circ = F_0^\circ - \bigcup_{i=1}^{n} F_i$

Let $\{F_1, \ldots, F_n\}$ be a set of simple regions with holes, that is, faces. The regular set $F = \bigcup_{i=1}^{n} F_i$ is called a *(complex) region* iff

---
[1] $D(x, \epsilon)$ denotes a two-dimensional closed disc with center x and radius ϵ iff $D(x, \epsilon) = \{y \in X \mid d(x, y) \leq \epsilon\}$ where d is a metric on X.

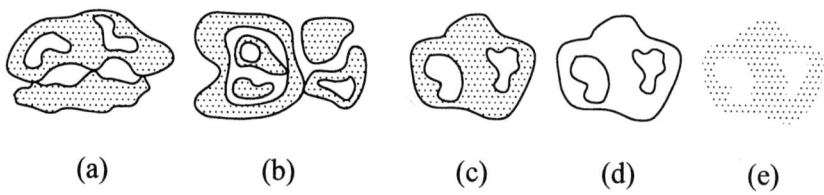

Fig. 1. Unique representation of a face (a), a complex region with five faces (b), a simple region with two holes (c), its boundary (d), and its interior (e).

(i) $\forall 1 \leq i < j \leq n : F_i^\circ \cap F_j^\circ = \emptyset$
(ii) $\forall 1 \leq i < j \leq n : \partial F_i \cap \partial F_j = \emptyset \ \vee \ |\partial F_i \cap \partial F_j|$ is finite)

Figure 1b shows an example of a region with five faces. The definition requires of a face to be disjoint to another face, or to meet another face in one or several single boundary points, or to lie within a hole of another face and possibly share one or several single boundary points with the boundary of the hole. Faces having common connected boundary parts with other faces or holes are disallowed. The argumentation is similar to that for the face definition.

Let $F = \bigcup_{i=1}^{n} F_i$ be a region with faces $\{F_1, \ldots, F_n\}$. Then the boundary of F is given as $\partial F = \bigcup_{i=1}^{n} \partial F_i$, and the interior of F is given as $F^\circ = \bigcup_{i=1}^{n} F_i^\circ = F - \partial F$.

3.2 Some Basic Concepts of Fuzzy Set Theory

Fuzzy set theory [17] is an extension and generalization of Boolean set theory. Let X be a classical (crisp) set of objects. Membership in a classical subset A of X can then be described by the *characteristic function* $\chi_A : X \to \{0, 1\}$ such that for all $x \in X$ holds $\chi_A(x) = 1$ if and only if $x \in A$ and $\chi_A(x) = 0$ otherwise. This function can be generalized such that all elements of X are mapped to the real interval [0,1] indicating the *degree of membership* of these elements in the set in question. We call $\mu_{\tilde{A}} : X \to [0, 1]$ the *membership function* of $\tilde{A}$, and the set $\tilde{A} = \{(x, \mu_{\tilde{A}}(x)) \, | \, x \in X\}$ is called a *fuzzy set* in X. Elements $x \in X$ that do (not) belong to $\tilde{A}$ get the membership value $\mu_{\tilde{A}}(x) = 1 \, (0)$.

A *[strict] α-cut* or *[strict] α-level set* of a fuzzy set $\tilde{A}$ for a specified value α is the crisp set $A_\alpha \, [A_\alpha^*] = \{x \in X \, | \, \mu_{\tilde{A}}(x) \geq [>] \alpha \ \wedge \ 0 \leq \alpha \leq [<] 1\}$. The strict α-cut for $\alpha = 0$ is called *support* of $\tilde{A}$, i.e., $supp(\tilde{A}) = A_0^*$. For a fuzzy set $\tilde{A}$ and $\alpha, \beta \in [0, 1]$ we obtain $X = A_0$ and $\alpha < \beta \Rightarrow A_\alpha \supseteq A_\beta$. The set of all levels $\alpha \in [0, 1]$ that represent distinct α-cuts of a given fuzzy set $\tilde{A}$ is called the *level set* $\Lambda_{\tilde{A}}$ of $\tilde{A}$: $\Lambda_{\tilde{A}} = \{\alpha \in [0, 1] \, | \, \exists \, x \in X : \mu_{\tilde{A}}(x) = \alpha\}$.

3.3 Modeling Fuzzy Regions

A "structureless" definition of fuzzy regions in the sense that only "flat" point sets are considered and no structural information is revealed has been given in

[13]. For our purposes we deploy a "semantically richer" characterization and approximation of fuzzy regions which describes them as *collections of crisp α-level regions*[2][13]. This view defines a fuzzy region in terms of regularized, nested α-cuts. Let $\tilde{F}$ be a fuzzy region. Then we represent a region F_α for an $\alpha \in [0,1]$ as

$$F_\alpha = reg_c(\{(x,y) \in \mathbb{R}^2 \,|\, \mu_{\tilde{F}}(x,y) \geq \alpha\})$$

We call F_α an *α-level region*. Clearly, F_α is a crisp complex region whose boundary is defined by all points with membership value α. In particular, F_α can have holes and consist of multiple parts. The kernel of $\tilde{F}$ is then equal to $F_{1.0}$. An essential property of the α-level regions of a fuzzy region is that they are nested, i.e., if we select membership values $1 = \alpha_1 > \alpha_2 > \cdots > \alpha_n > \alpha_{n+1} = 0$ for some $n \in \mathbb{N}$, then $F_{\alpha_1} \subseteq F_{\alpha_2} \subseteq \cdots \subseteq F_{\alpha_n} \subseteq F_{\alpha_{n+1}}$. We here describe the finite case. If $\Lambda_{\tilde{F}}$ is infinite, then there are obviously infinitely many α-level regions which can only be finitely represented within this view if we make a finite selection of α-values. In the finite case, if $|\Lambda_{\tilde{F}}| = n+1$ and if we take all these occurring membership values of a fuzzy region, we can even replace "$\subseteq$" by "$\subset$" in the inclusion relationships above. This follows from the fact that for any $p \in F_{\alpha_i} - F_{\alpha_{i-1}}$ with $i \in \{2,\ldots,n+1\}$, $\mu_{\tilde{F}}(p) = \alpha_i$. For the continuous case, we get $\mu_{\tilde{F}}(p) \in [\alpha_i, \alpha_{i-1})$. As a result, we obtain:

A *fuzzy region* is a (possibly infinite) set of α-level regions, i.e., $\tilde{F} = \{F_{\alpha_i} \,|\, 1 \leq i \leq |\Lambda_{\tilde{F}}|\}$ with $\alpha_i > \alpha_{i+1} \Rightarrow F_{\alpha_i} \subseteq F_{\alpha_{i+1}}$ for $1 \leq i \leq |\Lambda_{\tilde{F}}|-1$.

In Section 5 we will use this characterization for a definition of topological predicates on fuzzy regions. We can then reduce these predicates to topological predicates on collections of crisp regions. Unfortunately, the 9-intersection model only provides topological predicates for simple regions. Hence, we first need to generalize this concept to topological predicates for complex crisp regions. An essential requirement of such a collection is that any two predicates are mutually exclusive and that all predicates together cover all topological configurations.

4 Topological Predicates on Complex Crisp Regions

It is not an objective of this paper to find *all* possible topological relationships between two complex regions. We here confine ourselves to a straightforward generalization of the eight topological relationships for simple regions to complex regions. This procedure may be regarded as an ad hoc approach leading to too coarse predicates. But for many spatial applications this predicate collection is practicable enough, and a more fine-grained differentiation is even not desired.

In the following we use as a syntactical simplification the notation $(P_1|P_2|\ldots|P_n)(F,G)$ for the term $P_1(F,G) \lor P_2(F,G) \lor \ldots \lor P_n(F,G)$ where $P_i : region \times region \to \mathbb{B}$ is a topological predicate for each $1 \leq i \leq n$.

---
[2] Other structured characterizations given in [13] describe fuzzy regions as multi-component objects, as three-part crisp regions, and as α-partitions.

4.1 Topological Predicates on Simple Regions with Holes

As a first step to a general definition of topological predicates for complex crisp regions we consider such predicates for simple regions with holes and base their definition on the topological predicates for simple regions as they have been derived from the 9-intersection model (Section 2.2).

Let F and G be two simple regions with holes, that is, $F = F_0 - \bigcup_{i=1}^{n} F_i$ and $G = G_0 - \bigcup_{j=1}^{m} G_j$. We consider F and G to be disjoint if they have nothing in common, that is, either F_0 and G_0 are disjoint, and thus implicitly also their corresponding holes due to the definition of F and G, or F_0 (or G_0, respectively) and implicitly its holes are completely inside a hole G_j of G (F_i of F, respectively) (Figure 2a). Formally, we can then define the predicate $disjoint_{srh}$ as

$$\begin{aligned}
disjoint_{srh}(F, G) := \; & disjoint(F_0, G_0) \vee \\
& (\exists\, 1 \leq i \leq n : inside(G_0, F_i)) \vee \\
& (\exists\, 1 \leq j \leq m : inside(F_0, G_j))
\end{aligned}$$

The predicate $meet_{srh}$ is defined as follows (Figure 2b):

$$\begin{aligned}
meet_{srh}(F, G) := \; & meet(F_0, G_0) \vee \\
& (\exists\, 1 \leq i \leq n : coveredBy(G_0, F_i)) \vee \\
& (\exists\, 1 \leq j \leq m : coveredBy(F_0, G_j))
\end{aligned}$$

We consider F to be inside G if F_0 is inside G_0 and if each hole G_j of G is either disjoint from F_0 or inside a hole F_i of F. (Figure 3a). The definition for the predicate $inside_{srh}$ is:

$$\begin{aligned}
inside_{srh}(F, G) := \; & inside(F_0, G_0) \wedge \\
& (\forall\, 1 \leq j \leq m : disjoint(F_0, G_j) \vee \\
& \quad (inside(G_j, F_0) \wedge \exists\, 1 \leq i \leq n : inside(G_j, F_i)))
\end{aligned}$$

We do not have to take into account the topological relationships between the F_i's and G_0 in our definition, because $inside(F_0, G_0) \Rightarrow inside(F_i, G_0)$ due to $F_i \subset F_0$ for $1 \leq i \leq n$. The predicate $contains_{srh}$ is symmetric to the predicate $inside_{srh}$, that is, $contains_{srh}(F, G) := inside_{srh}(G, F)$.

We consider F and G to be equal if F_0 and G_0 are equal, if F and G have the same number of holes, and if each hole F_i of F coincides with a hole G_j of G and vice-versa, that is,

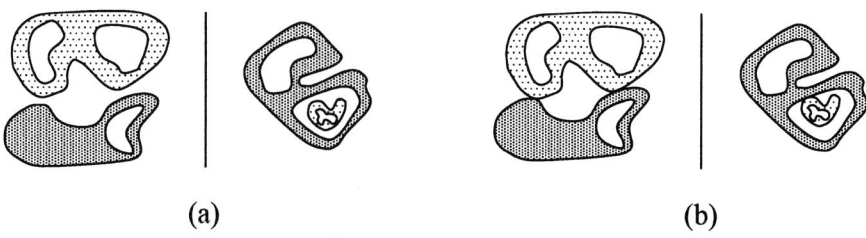

(a)   (b)

Fig. 2. Examples for the predicates $disjoint_{srh}(F, G)$ (a) and $meet_{srh}(F, G)$ (b).

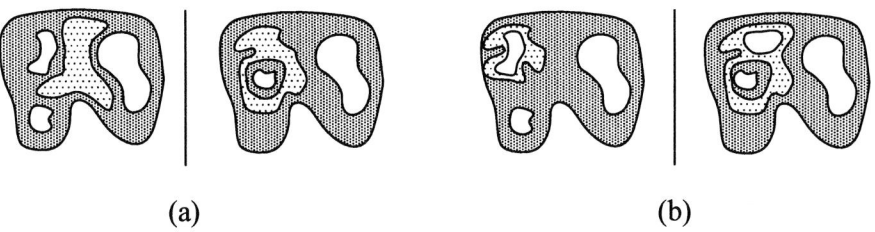

(a)   (b)

Fig. 3. Examples for the predicates $inside_{srh}(F,G)$ (a) and $coveredBy_{srh}(F,G)$ (b).

$$\begin{aligned}
equal_{srh}(F,G) := \quad & equal(F_0, G_0) \wedge n = m \wedge \\
& \exists \pi : \{1,\ldots,n\} \to \{1,\ldots,n\}, \pi \text{ bijective}, \\
& \forall 1 \leq i \leq n : equal(F_i, G_{\pi(i)})
\end{aligned}$$

F is considered to be covered by G if F is a proper subset of G and if F's boundary touches G's boundary (Figure 3b).

$$\begin{aligned}
coveredBy_{srh}(F,G) := \quad & \neg((inside_{srh}|equal_{srh})(F,G)) \wedge \\
& (inside|coveredBy|equal)(F_0, G_0) \wedge \\
& (\forall 1 \leq j \leq m : ((disjoint|meet)(F_0, G_j) \vee \\
& (\exists 1 \leq i \leq n : (inside|coveredBy|equal)(G_j, F_i))))
\end{aligned}$$

The predicate $covers_{srh}$ is symmetric to the predicate $coveredBy_{srh}$, that is, $covers_{srh}(F,G) := coveredBy_{srh}(G,F)$.

Finally, the predicate $overlap_{srh}$ (Figure 4) covers all remaining topological situations. This predicate can, of course, be defined directly in order to give an exact characterization of the remaining topological situations. But this makes the definition unnecessarily complicated and longish. We define instead:

$$\begin{aligned}
overlap_{srh}(F,G) := \quad & \neg((disjoint_{srh}|meet_{srh}|coveredBy_{srh}|covers_{srh}| \\
& inside_{srh}|contains_{srh}|equal_{srh})(F,G))
\end{aligned}$$

The set $T_{srh} = \{disjoint_{srh}, meet_{srh}, overlap_{srh}, coveredBy_{srh}, covers_{srh}, inside_{srh}, contains_{srh}, equal_{srh}\}$ provides a complete coverage of topological relationships for two simple regions with holes, and its elements are mutually exclusive. Completeness of T_{srh} follows immediately from the complementary

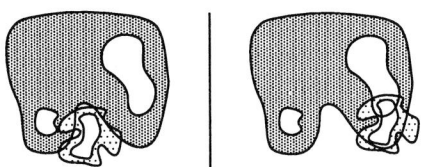

Fig. 4. Examples for the predicate $overlap_{srh}(F,G)$.

character of the definition of $overlap_{srh}$. Hence, at least one predicate must hold for any pair F, G of simple regions with holes. Mutual exclusion of each pair of different topological predicates P_1 and P_2 can be proved by showing that $\neg(P_1(F,G) \land P_2(F,G))$ holds for any pair F, G. Since we have $k = 8$ predicates, we have to check the diversity of $\frac{1}{2}(k^2 - k) = 28$ predicate pairs. We will not show the validity for the predicate pairs here in detail but only tell the strategy. First, we can use the mutual exclusion of the topological relationships for simple regions employed in the definition of some predicates. For instance, $disjoint_{srh}$ and $meet_{srh}$ exclude each other since $disjoint$ and $meet$ as well as $inside$ and $coveredBy$ are mutually exclusive in the 9-intersection model. Second, several predicates use the negation of other predicates on simple regions with holes for their definition. For instance, $overlap_{srh}$ excludes all other predicates. Similarly, $coveredBy_{srh}$ excludes both $inside_{srh}$ and $equal_{srh}$. Overall, at most one predicate is valid for any pair F, G.

The set T_{srh} of topological predicates on simple regions with holes is in two ways compatible with the set T of topological predicates on simple regions obtained by the 9-intersection model. First, if both F and G do not have holes, then T_{srh} and T coincide. Second, each of the eight topological predicates on simple regions with holes has the same boolean results for the nine intersections as the corresponding predicate on simple regions (see Section 2).

4.2 Topological Predicates on Complex Regions

With the aid of the topological predicates on simple regions with holes we are now able to define the corresponding predicates on complex regions. Let $F = \bigcup_{i=1}^{n} F_i$ and $G = \bigcup_{j=1}^{m} G_j$ be complex regions where the F_i and G_j are simple regions possibly with holes. We define the following predicates:

$$
\begin{aligned}
disjoint_{cr}(F, G) &:= \forall 1 \leq i \leq n \, \forall 1 \leq j \leq m : disjoint_{srh}(F_i, G_j) \\
meet_{cr}(F, G) &:= \neg disjoint_{cr}(F, G) \land \\
&\quad (\forall 1 \leq i \leq n \, \forall 1 \leq j \leq m : (disjoint_{srh}|meet_{srh})(F_i, G_j)) \\
inside_{cr}(F, G) &:= \forall 1 \leq i \leq n \, \exists 1 \leq j \leq m : inside_{srh}(F_i, G_j) \\
contains_{cr}(F, G) &:= inside_{cr}(G, F) \\
equal_{cr}(F, G) &:= n = m \land (\exists \pi : \{1, \ldots, n\} \to \{1, \ldots, n\}, \pi \text{ bijective}, \\
&\quad \forall 1 \leq i \leq n : equal_{srh}(F_i, G_{\pi(i)})) \\
coveredBy_{cr}(F, G) &:= \neg((inside_{cr}|equal_{cr})(F, G)) \land \\
&\quad (\forall 1 \leq i \leq n \, \exists 1 \leq j \leq m : \\
&\quad\quad (inside_{srh}|coveredBy_{srh}|equal_{srh})(F_i, G_j)) \\
covers_{cr}(F, G) &:= coveredBy_{cr}(G, F) \\
overlap_{cr}(F, G) &:= \neg((disjoint_{cr}|meet_{cr}|coveredBy_{cr}|covers_{cr}| \\
&\quad inside_{cr}|contains_{cr}|equal_{cr})(F, G))
\end{aligned}
$$

With similar arguments as in the last section we can recognize that two complex regions satisfy exactly one of these topological predicates. In other words, the topological predicates of the set $T_{cr} = \{disjoint_{cr}, meet_{cr}, inside_{cr}, contains_{cr}, equal_{cr}, coveredBy_{cr}, covers_{cr}, overlap_{cr}\}$ are mutually exclusive and complete. Note that the predicates $disjoint_{cr}$, $meet_{cr}$, $equal_{cr}$, and $overlap_{cr}$ are symmetric whereas the others are not.

One could possibly get the impression that in practice most topological configurations of two complex regions will be classified as overlapping. But this is a fallacy. In many geographic applications *spatial partitions* (maps) form the basic underlying structure. Their essential feature is a non-overlapping constraint imposed on the regions composing a partition.

5 Topological Predicates on Fuzzy Regions

In this section we introduce a concept of topological predicates for fuzzy regions. In a similar way as we can generalize the characteristic function $\chi_A : X \to \{0,1\}$ to the membership function $\mu_{\tilde{A}} : X \to [0,1]$ (Section 3.2)[3], we can generalize a (binary) predicate $p_c : X \times Y \to \{0,1\}$ to a (binary) *fuzzy predicate* $p_f : \tilde{X} \times \tilde{Y} \to [0,1]$. Hence, the value of a fuzzy predicate can be interpreted as the degree to which the predicate holds for its operand objects. In our case of topological predicates, $X = Y = region$, $\{0,1\} = bool$, and $\tilde{X} = \tilde{Y} = fregion$ hold. For the set $[0,1]$ we have to introduce a new type *fbool* for *fuzzy booleans*.

For the definition of fuzzy topological predicates, we take the view of a fuzzy region as a set of α-level regions (Section 3.3). We know that an α-level region is a crisp complex region (Section 3.1), and in the last section we have defined topological predicates on complex regions. This preparatory work now enables us to reduce topological predicates on fuzzy regions to topological predicates on collections of crisp regions[4].

The approach presented in this section is generic in the sense that any meaningful collection of topological predicates on complex crisp regions can be the basis for our definition of a collection of topological predicates on complex fuzzy regions. If the former collection additionally fulfils the properties of completeness and mutual exclusion (which is the case for T_{cr}), the latter collection automatically inherits these properties.

The open question now is how to compute the topological relationships of two collections of α-level regions, each collection describing a fuzzy region. We use the concept of basic probability assignment [5] for this purpose. A *basic probability assignment* $m(F_{\alpha_i})$ can be associated with each α-level region F_{α_i} and can be interpreted as the probability that F_{α_i} is the "true" representative of F. It is defined as

$$m(F_{\alpha_i}) = \alpha_i - \alpha_{i+1}$$

---

[3] Note that χ_A is a unary crisp predicate and that $\mu_{\tilde{A}}$ is a unary fuzzy predicate.
[4] Another great benefit of this approach is its easy implementability through well known concepts for crisp spatial objects and for crisp topological predicates.

for $1 \leq i \leq n$ for some $n \in \mathbb{N}$ with $\alpha_1 = 1$ and $\alpha_{n+1} = 0$. That is, m is built from the differences of successive α_i's. It is easy to see that the telescoping sum $\sum_{i=1}^{n} m(F_{\alpha_i}) = \alpha_1 - \alpha_{n+1} = 1 - 0 = 1$.

Let $\pi_f(F, G)$ be the value that represents a (binary) property π_f between two fuzzy regions F and G. Based on the work in [5] property π_f of F and G can be determined as the summation of weighted predicates by[5]

$$\pi_f(F, G) = \sum_{i=1}^{n} \sum_{j=1}^{n} m(F_{\alpha_i}) \cdot m(G_{\alpha_j}) \cdot \pi_{cr}(F_{\alpha_i}, G_{\alpha_j})$$

where $\pi_{cr}(F_{\alpha_i}, G_{\alpha_j})$ yields the value of the corresponding property π_{cr} for two crisp α-level regions F_{α_i} and G_{α_j}. This formula is equivalent to

$$\pi_f(F, G) = \sum_{i=1}^{n} \sum_{j=1}^{n} (\alpha_i - \alpha_{i+1}) \cdot (\alpha_j - \alpha_{j+1}) \cdot \pi_{cr}(F_{\alpha_i}, G_{\alpha_j})$$

If π_f is a topological predicate of $T_f = \{disjoint_f, meet_f, overlap_f, equal_f, inside_f, contains_f, covers_f, coveredBy_f\}$ between two fuzzy regions, we can compute the degree of the corresponding relationship with the aid of the pertaining crisp topological predicate $\pi_{cr} \in T_{cr}$. The value of $\pi_{cr}(F_{\alpha_i}, G_{\alpha_j})$ is either 1 (*true*) or 0 (*false*). Once this value has been determined for all combinations of α-level regions from F and G, the aggregated value of the topological predicate $\pi_f(F, G)$ can be computed as shown above. The more fine-grained the level set Λ for the fuzzy regions F and G is, the more precisely the fuzziness of topological predicates can be determined.

It remains to show that $0 \leq \pi_f(F, G) \leq 1$ holds, that is, π_f is really a fuzzy predicate. Since $\alpha_i - \alpha_{i+1} > 0$ for all $1 \leq i \leq n$ and since $\pi_{cr}(F_{\alpha_i}, G_{\alpha_j}) \geq 0$ for all $1 \leq i, j \leq n$, $\pi_f(F, G) \geq 0$ holds. We can show the other inequality by determining an upper bound for $\pi_f(F, G)$:

$$\begin{aligned}
\pi_f(F, G) &= \sum_{i=1}^{n} \sum_{j=1}^{n} (\alpha_i - \alpha_{i+1}) \cdot (\alpha_j - \alpha_{j+1}) \cdot \pi_{cr}(F_{\alpha_i}, G_{\alpha_j}) \\
&\leq \sum_{i=1}^{n} \sum_{j=1}^{n} (\alpha_i - \alpha_{i+1}) \cdot (\alpha_j - \alpha_{j+1}) \quad \text{(since } \pi_{cr}(F_{\alpha_i}, G_{\alpha_j}) \leq 1) \\
&= (\alpha_1 - \alpha_2)(\alpha_1 - \alpha_2) + \cdots + (\alpha_1 - \alpha_2)(\alpha_n - \alpha_{n+1}) + \cdots + \\
&\quad (\alpha_n - \alpha_{n+1})(\alpha_1 - \alpha_2) + \cdots + (\alpha_n - \alpha_{n+1})(\alpha_n - \alpha_{n+1}) \\
&= (\alpha_1 - \alpha_2)((\alpha_1 - \alpha_2) + \cdots + (\alpha_n - \alpha_{n+1})) + \cdots + \\
&\quad (\alpha_n - \alpha_{n+1})((\alpha_1 - \alpha_2) + \cdots + (\alpha_n - \alpha_{n+1})) \\
&= (\alpha_1 - \alpha_2) + \cdots + (\alpha_n - \alpha_{n+1}) \quad \text{(since } \sum_{i=1}^{n}(\alpha_i - \alpha_{i+1}) = 1) \\
&= 1
\end{aligned}$$

Hence, $\pi_f(F, G) \leq 1$ holds.

---

[5] For reasons of simplicity, we assume that $\Lambda_{\tilde{F}} = \Lambda_{\tilde{G}} =: \Lambda$. Otherwise, it is not difficult to "synchronize" $\Lambda_{\tilde{F}}$ and $\Lambda_{\tilde{G}}$ by forming their union and by reordering and renumbering all levels.

An alternative definition of fuzzy topological predicates, which pursues a similar strategy like the one discussed so far, is based on the topological predicates on simple regions possibly with holes, that is, on predicates $\pi_{srh} \in T_{srh}$. If F_{α_i} is an α-level region, let us denote its faces by $F_{\alpha_{i1}}, \ldots, F_{\alpha_{if_i}}$. Similarly, we denote the faces of an α-level region G_{α_j} by $G_{\alpha_{j1}}, \ldots, G_{\alpha_{jg_j}}$. We can then define a topological predicate π'_f as

$$\pi'_f(F,G) = \sum_{i=1}^{n} \sum_{k=1}^{f_i} \sum_{j=1}^{n} \sum_{l=1}^{g_j} \frac{(\alpha_i - \alpha_{i+1}) \cdot (\alpha_j - \alpha_{j+1}) \cdot \pi_{srh}(F_{\alpha_{ik}}, G_{\alpha_{jl}})}{f_i \cdot g_j}$$

It is obvious that $\pi'_f(F,G) \geq 0$ holds since all factors have a value greater than or equal to 0. We can also show that $\pi'_f(F,G) \leq 1$ by the following transformations:

$$\pi'_f(F,G) \leq \sum_{i=1}^{n} \sum_{k=1}^{f_i} \sum_{j=1}^{n} \sum_{l=1}^{g_j} \frac{(\alpha_i - \alpha_{i+1}) \cdot (\alpha_j - \alpha_{j+1})}{f_i \cdot g_j} \quad (\pi_{srh}(F_{\alpha_{ik}}, G_{\alpha_{jl}}) \leq 1)$$

$$= \sum_{i=1}^{n} \sum_{j=1}^{n} \frac{(\alpha_i - \alpha_{i+1}) \cdot (\alpha_j - \alpha_{j+1})}{f_i \cdot g_j} \cdot f_i \cdot g_j$$

$$= \sum_{i=1}^{n} \sum_{j=1}^{n} (\alpha_i - \alpha_{i+1}) \cdot (\alpha_j - \alpha_{j+1})$$

$$= 1$$

Hence, $\pi'_f(F,G) \leq 1$ holds. As a rule the predicates π_f and π'_f do not yield the same results. Assume that F_{α_i} and G_{α_j} fulfil a predicate $\pi_{cr} \in T_{cr}$. This fact contributes once to the summation process for π_f. But it does not take into account that possibly several faces $F_{\alpha_{ik}}$ (at least one) of F_{α_i} satisfy the corresponding predicate $\pi_{srh} \in T_{srh}$ with several faces $G_{\alpha_{jl}}$ (at least one) of G_{α_j}. This fact contributes several times (at most $f_i \cdot g_j$) to the summation process for π'_f. Hence, the evaluation process for π'_f is more fine-grained than for π_f.

Both generic predicate definitions reveal their quantitative character. If the predicate $\pi_{cr}(F_{\alpha_i}, G_{\alpha_j})$ and the predicate $\pi_{srh}(F_{\alpha_{ik}}, G_{\alpha_{jl}})$, respectively, is never fulfilled, the predicate $\pi_f(F,G)$ and $\pi'_f(F,G)$, respectively, yields *false*. The more α-level regions of F and G (simple regions with holes of F_{α_i} and G_{α_j}) fulfil the predicate $\pi_{cr}(F_{\alpha_i}, G_{\alpha_j})$ ($\pi_{srh}(F_{\alpha_{ik}}, G_{\alpha_{jl}})$), the more the validity of the predicate π_f (π'_f) increases. The optimum is reached if all topological predicates are satisfied.

6 Conclusions

In this paper we have developed a formal and coherent definition for simple regions with holes, crisp complex regions, fuzzy complex regions, and for corresponding topological predicates. Spatial query langages can now also be employed to pose queries using topological relationships on more complex regions. For fuzzy predicates their computationally determined quantification has to be additionally considered in a query language. A solution could be to embed adequate qualitative linguistic descriptions of topological relationships as appropriate interpretations of the membership values into spatial query languages. For instance, depending on the membership value yielded by the predicate $inside_f$, we could distinguish between *a little bit inside, somewhat inside, quite inside, nearly completely inside*, and *completely inside*. These linguistic terms could then be incorporated into spatial queries. Another subject of further investigation will be how these spatial data types and topological predicates can be implemented in an efficient, numerically robust, and topologically consistent manner.

References

[1] D. Altman. Fuzzy Set Theoretic Approaches for Handling Imprecision in Spatial Analysis. *Int. Journal of Geographical Information Systems*, 8(3):271–289, 1994.
[2] P. A. Burrough and A. U. Frank, editors. *Geographic Objects with Indeterminate Boundaries*. GISDATA Series, vol. 2. Taylor & Francis, 1996.
[3] E. Clementini, P. Di Felice, and G. Califano. Composite Regions in Topological Queries. *Information Systems*, 20(7):579–594, 1995.
[4] E. Clementini and P. Di Felice. *An Algebraic Model for Spatial Objects with Indeterminate Boundaries*, pages 153–169. In Burrough and Frank [2], 1996.
[5] D. Dubois and M.-C. Jaulent. A General Approach to Parameter Evaluation in Fuzzy Digital Pictures. *Pattern Recognition Letters*, pages 251–259, 1987.
[6] M. J. Egenhofer. A Formal Definition of Binary Topological Relationships. In *3rd Int. Conf. on Foundations of Data Organization and Algorithms*, LNCS 367, pages 457–472. Springer-Verlag, 1989.
[7] M.J. Egenhofer, E. Clementini, and P. Di Felice. Topological Relations between Regions with Holes. *Int. Journal of Geographical Information Systems*, 8(2):128–142, 1994.
[8] M. Erwig and M. Schneider. Vague Regions. In *5th Int. Symp. on Advances in Spatial Databases*, LNCS 1262, pages 298–320. Springer-Verlag, 1997.
[9] S. Gaal. *Point Set Topology*. Academic Press, 1964.
[10] R. H. Güting and M. Schneider. Realms: A Foundation for Spatial Data Types in Database Systems. In *3rd Int. Symp. on Advances in Spatial Databases*, LNCS 692, pages 14–35. Springer-Verlag, 1993.
[11] M. Schneider. *Modelling Spatial Objects with Undetermined Boundaries Using the Realm/ROSE Approach*, pages 141–152. In Burrough and Frank [2], 1996.
[12] M. Schneider. *Spatial Data Types for Database Systems - Finite Resolution Geometry for Geographic Information Systems*, volume LNCS 1288. Springer-Verlag, Berlin Heidelberg, 1997.
[13] M. Schneider. Uncertainty Management for Spatial Data in Databases: Fuzzy Spatial Data Types. In *6th Int. Symp. on Advances in Spatial Databases*, LNCS 1651, pages 330–351. Springer-Verlag, 1999.
[14] M. Schneider. Finite Resolution Crisp and Fuzzy Spatial Objects. In *Int. Symp. on Spatial Data Handling*, pages 5a.3-17, 2000.
[15] R. B. Tilove. Set Membership Classification: A Unified Approach to Geometric Intersection Problems. *IEEE Trans. on Computers*, C-29:874–883, 1980.
[16] M. Worboys. Imprecision in Finite Resolution Spatial Data. *GeoInformatica*, 2(3):257–279, 1998.
[17] L. A. Zadeh. Fuzzy Sets. *Information and Control*, 8:338–353, 1965.

A Semantic Approach to XML-based Data Integration

Patricia Rodríguez-Gianolli and John Mylopoulos

Department of Computer Science, University of Toronto,
6 King's College Road, Toronto, Canada M5S 3H5
{prg,jm}@cs.toronto.edu

Abstract. The paper describes a prototype tool, named DIXSE, which supports the integration of XML Document Type Definitions (DTDs) into a common conceptual schema. The mapping from each individual DTD into the common schema is used to automatically generate wrappers for XML documents, which conform to a given DTD. These wrappers are used to populate the common conceptual schema thereby achieving data integration for XML documents.

1 Introduction

Integrating data from multiple heterogeneous data sources has been a major focus of database research for more than two decades. Heterogeneity, in both conventional and semistructured databases, arises from the adoption of different data models and/or different schemas by two data sources. With the widespread acceptance of the Web as the primary vehicle for data interchange, interest in data integration has been renewed, with a focus on semistructured data. However, little has been proposed yet for data integration of XML documents. XML, as a standard for representing both structured text documents and data on the Web, facilitates data publishing and interchange. This is accomplished through a simple syntax which, unlike HTML, is intended for both human browsing and computer consumption. Among the many advantages of XML over HTML we note that XML separates cleanly information content from presentation details. Moreover, XML tags are user-defined and can therefore be used to describe what data mean as opposed to how they should look. Finally, XML documents can be validated against grammar-like specifications known as Document Type Definitions (DTDs). It must be emphasized, however, that XML is intended as a language for describing the syntactic structure of a document, not its meaning. This makes the data integration task a difficult one for XML data. As pointed out in [23], the key to successful data integration is the identification of interschema relationships. The more expressive the underlying data model(s), the higher the chance of identifying interschema relationships and hence the easier the task of data integration.

The DIXSE[1] system presented in this paper addresses in a semi-automatic fashion the integration problem for XML data. Unlike most approaches, we address the problem from a conceptual modeling perspective. DIXSE is capable of semi-

---

[1]DIXSE stands for "Data Integration for XML based on Schematic Knowledge".

automatically deriving a common semantic description (in the form of a conceptual schema) from a set of input DTDs and allows the user to enrich and fine-tune this description with additional domain expertise. Given the mapping from input DTDs to the common conceptual schema, DIXSE automatically generates wrappers for XML documents that conform to these DTDs and populates the conceptual schema. Full details about the DIXSE implementation and the case study that has been used to validate the approach can be found in [21].

Approaches to the problem of data integration have generally adopted a traditional schema integration approach for heterogeneous structured databases, or a (more recent) semistructured data integration approach.

In traditional schema integration research, the identification of interschema relationships can be done at different levels of abstraction. In their comprehensive schema integration survey, Ram and Ramesh [19] indicate that the abstraction level at which interschema relationship identification techniques operate defines the nature of available semantic knowledge. Approaches at the conceptual schema level can deduce relationships among objects [14,25,1]. Other approaches employ the semantics conveyed by integrity constraints [20] or data values [12] to support data integration. Regardless of the approach, the derived relationships can be modified or confirmed by human integrators. This external input can be viewed as adding domain knowledge that was not captured in the original data sources. The generation of the integrated schema is then driven by the expressiveness of the data model (relational, semantic, object-oriented or logic-based model) chosen to describe the input schemas. The DIXSE system we propose inherits and extends this approach.

Interschema relationship identification is done differently in data integration systems for semistructured data [5,16,4,13,6]. The lack of a schema in semistructured data sources makes the conceptual schema approach previously described inappropriate. The data integration approach, on the other hand, relies mostly on the query language provided by these systems. The query language supports special constructs for accessing and integrating data sources, such as query primitives for dealing with type or structure mismatches and data restructuring. A problem with semistructured data models is that they do assume a schema, but provide very few modeling abstractions (essentially, only labeled graphs) to capture semantics. Given that the main purpose of XML data is to facilitate data exchange with structure[2], we favor a semi-automatic schema integration approach rather than a data-centered one. The DIXSE system exploits the schematic information provided by XML DTDs to derive a conceptual schema of the information represented by XML data.

Related work with similar motivations has recently been presented in [15,2]. In [15], the authors also propose a semantic data model as the basis for integrating XML data sources; we differ from them by using a richer data model and a semi-automatic mechanism to derive the target schemas. In [2], pieces of information contained in XML fragments are mapped to domain specific ontologies. Unlike this work, DIXSE combines the conceptual schema definition and mapping creation into a single step. In addition, it supports the notions of user-defined keys and intradocument and interdocument links, which play a central role when performing object identification and object fusion during the data integration phase.

---

[2] The schema is mostly needed for interoperability.

DIXSE blends techniques from conventional and semistructured data integration systems into a framework specifically designed for XML data. A metamodeling language, Telos [17,18], is used to represent both the DIXSE data model and the derived conceptual schemas. Telos supports attribution, classification and generalization; it also offers a novel treatment of attributes, which can be exploited to define any conceptual model. Another research project that uses Telos as the target language for mapping DTDs is [7]. We differ from them by providing a user-customized mapping with an emphasis on data integration.

The rest of the paper is structured as follows. Section 2 presents a quick overview of XML and Telos. Section 3 describes the DIXSE framework for mapping DTDs to a Telos conceptual schema, while section 4 outlines the mapping language through which the user can define directives on how the mapping is to be done. Section 5 presents an overview of a case study that involves several XML documents and DTDs for SIGMOD Record publications. Section 6 describes the DIXSE architecture and implementation, while section 7 summarizes the contributions of the paper and suggests directions for further research.

2 XML and Telos

We provide a brief overview of XML and Telos. For more comprehensive information about XML and Telos, the reader is referred to [10] and [17,18], respectively.

XML is used to markup documents for purposes of presentation (like HTML) or further processing. Marked-up documents are called *XML documents*. The basic component of an XML document is the *element*, that is, a piece of text bounded by matching tags such as <article> and </article>. The content of an element can be raw text, other elements or a combination of the two. The term *subelement* is used to describe the relationship between an element and its component elements. In addition, elements may contain *attributes*. Attributes are "name-value" pairs specified in the start tag of an element. The structure of an XML document can be described by a *Document Type Definition* (DTD). A DTD provides a list of elements and attributes contained in a document and the relationships between them. *Element type declarations* describe the name of the tag being declared (e.g. article) and the allowed contents of that tag, usually referred to as *content specification*. Attributes are declared for specific element types using *attribute-list declarations*.

Telos provides facilities for constructing, querying and updating structured *knowledge bases*. A Telos knowledge base consists of structured objects built out of two kinds of primitive units: *individuals* and *attributes*. The first ones are intended to represent entities, while the second ones represent binary relationships between entities or other relationships. Individuals and attributes are treated uniformly by the mechanisms of structuring a knowledge base. The term *proposition* is used to denote either an *individual* or an *attribute*. Propositions are organized along three dimensions: *attribution*, *classification* and *generalization*. The first relates a proposition to the values of all its attributes (by default, attributes in Telos are multivalued). The classification dimension calls for each proposition to be an instance of one or more generic propositions or *classes*. Propositions (both individuals and attributes) are classified into *tokens* (propositions having no instances and representing concrete objects in the modeled domain), *simple classes* (propositions having tokens as instances; these represent generic concepts), *metaclasses* (propositions having simple classes as instances), *metametaclasses* and so on. In addition, *ω-classes* are propositions with instances from any level. Finally -- and orthogonal to the classification dimension -- class propositions can be organized in terms of generalization or ISA hierarchies. In general, there will be one such hierarchy for each classification level (i.e., for simple classes, metaclasses, etc.).

3 The DIXSE Framework

The DIXSE framework supports the derivation of a conceptual schema from several input DTDs. The data model used for the conceptual schema offers concepts such as entity, attribute, and mapping. Since Telos is a language for metamodeling, the data model can be extended with additional semantic primitives (e.g., activity, goal, agent) depending on the semantics of the information that is to be integrated. Figure 1 illustrates the structure of a Telos representation of the DIXSE XML model (at the MetaClass and ω levels), a DIXSE conceptual schema for an XML DTD (at the SimpleClass level) and some XML data (at the token or object level). Planes in the figure depict classification levels; gray links represent "instance-of" links between two consecutive classification levels or between a classification level and the ω-level.

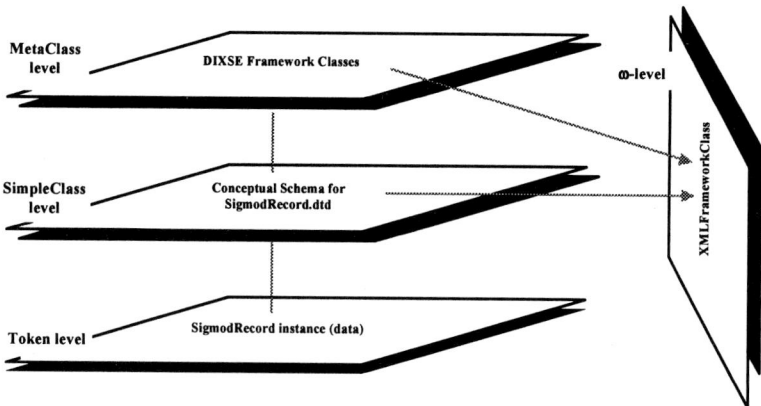

Fig. 1. Telos representation of the DIXSE data model

3.1 The Data Model

Conceptual schemas are represented in DIXSE as collections of entity types and their attributes. The model supports four main concepts: *entity class*, *entity attribute*, *mapping* and *document type*. An *entity class* represents types of objects or concepts found in the input DTDs. Figure 2 shows a DTD that describes the structure of a hypothetical XML-based SIGMOD Record database. In this schema, there are at least four XML elements that represent different types of entities: SigmodRecord, Issue, Article and Author. The rest of the elements and attributes (such as volume, title, contactAuthor, etc) may be thought as *attributes* of these entity types. *Mappings* describe particular conceptual schemas of the information represented by DTDs. A mapping may be thought as a wrapper for a collection of interrelated entity classes. Finally, *document types* describe DTDs and the collection of mappings attached to them.

```
<!ELEMENT SigmodRecord (issue)+>
<!ELEMENT issue (volume,number,articles)>
<!ELEMENT volume (#PCDATA)>
<!ELEMENT number (#PCDATA)>
<!ELEMENT articles (article)* >
<!ELEMENT article (title,numberOfPages,fullText,contact,authors)>
<!ATTLIST contact (EMPTY)>
<!ATTLIST contact contactAuthor IDREF #IMPLIED>
<!ELEMENT title (#PCDATA)>
<!ELEMENT numberOfPages (#PCDATA)>
<!ELEMENT fullText (size?)>
<!ATTLIST fullText xLink:type CDATA #FIXED 'simple'>
<!ATTLIST fullText xLink:href CDATA #IMPLIED>
<!ELEMENT size (#PCDATA)>
<!ELEMENT authors (author)*>
<!ELEMENT author (name,address)>
<!ATTLIST author organization CDATA #IMPLIED>
<!ATTLIST author degree (bachelor|master|phd) "phd">
<!ATTLIST author id ID #REQUIRED>
<!ELEMENT name (firstName?,lastName)>
<!ELEMENT firstName (#PCDATA)>
<!ELEMENT lastName (#PCDATA)>
<!ELEMENT address (home|office)>
<!ELEMENT home (#PCDATA)>
<!ELEMENT office (#PCDATA)>
```

Fig. 2. XML DTD SigmodRecord.dtd

Figure 3 offers a complete Telos description of the DIXSE data model in semantic network notation. The figure illustrates the different relationships among DIXSE concepts and how Telos has been used to model them. To improve readability, we have used several drawing conventions. Ellipses represent classes; gray links represent "instance-of" links while black links represent attributes.

In addition to the distinction between entity classes and attributes, the data model classifies attributes along two orthogonal dimensions. The first facility distinguishes three categories of attributes, namely **components**, **properties** and **links**. An attribute is a **component** when it represents one component (of the structure) of an entity (e.g. XML element name). An attribute is a **property** when it represents information about the content of an entity (e.g. organization CDATA attribute). Finally, a **link** attribute represents intradocument or interdocument information (e.g. contactAuthor IDREF and href XLINK attributes).

The distinction between components and properties in our data model is inspired by the difference between XML elements and attributes, according to the XML 1.0 Recommendation [10]. In addition, we have chosen to model IDREF and simple XLINK attributes as special **link** attributes because they represent special relationships among XML data. Through this distinction, the DIXSE model recognizes the different roles that each entity attribute plays at the time of data integration.

Attribute categories are represented in Telos using three attribute metaclasses: "hasComponents", "hasProperties" and "hasLinks". Instances of metaclass XmlPropertyClass (i.e. XmlCDATAProperty, XmlIDProperty and XmlENUMProperty) model different types of XML properties. Each of these attribute metaclasses contains as instances particular entity attributes (i.e. components, properties or links).

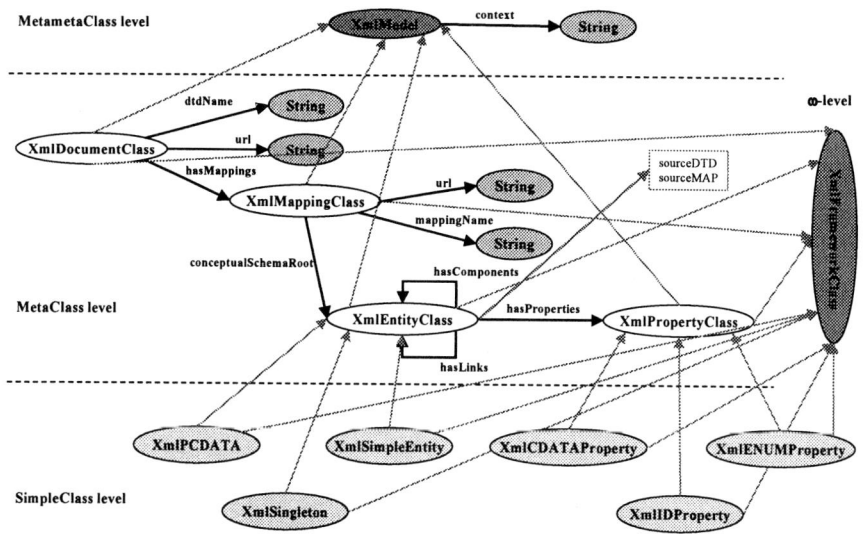

Fig. 3. Telos definition of the DIXSE data model

The second dimension for classifying attributes models frequently used constraints or characteristics of attribute values, regardless of their category. These constraints are inspired by the constraints that XML itself imposes on elements and attributes, namely: the occurrence and choice indicators for XML elements (i.e. "?", "*", "+" and "|") and the attribute modifiers for XML attributes (i.e. "#FIXED", "#REQUIRED" and "#IMPLIED").

Attribute constraints are modeled in Telos using nine attribute metaclasses at the ω-level. Attribute metaclasses "**exactlyOne**", "**atMostOne**", "**zeroOrMore**" and "**oneOrMore**" are used to model mandatory or optional single-valued attributes (the first two) or multi-valued attributes (the second two). The attribute metaclass "**union**" is used to restrict an attribute defined in a given class to be exclusive with respect to other "union" attributes (i.e. only one has a value). The attribute metaclass "**fixed**" is used to restrict an attribute to have a fixed (user-supplied) value. Attribute metaclasses "**idRef**" and "**xLink**" restrict an attribute to be the recipient of an intradocument or interdocument reference, respectively. Last, the attribute metaclass "**key**" restricts an attribute to have exactly one single and unique value. Instances of class XMLFrameworkClass can have a key composed of more than one attribute.

A *mapping* consists of a conceptual schema which models the information represented by a given DTD, typically authored for a given context. Mappings attempt to capture the meaning, interpretation or intended use of the data sources to be integrated. Different perspectives or views of the data may lead to different models of relationships among objects. The application context in which relationships are stated is fundamental for capturing the real-world semantics that will drive the data integration process (e.g. a bibliographical library context versus a scientific e-mail directory one).

Finally, a *document type* describes a given DTD and a collection of mappings (i.e. conceptual schemas) attached to it. *Contexts* are represented in the data model as distinguishing attributes (string names) of document types, mappings and entity classes. At a higher level, contexts may be thought of as partitions of the semantic model. Each partition clusters information about a specific application domain, and provides the appropriate framework for the creation of unique entity classes and their instances (that is, two conceptual schemas using entity class Author refer to the same concept if they belong to the same context).

Mappings and document types are represented in Telos using two metaclasses: XmlMappingClass and XmlDocumentClass, respectively. To record the origin of entity attributes, we define two attributes metaclasses (sourceMap and sourceDTD) using Telos' *"attributes on attributes"* feature.

3.2 Default Mapping

The DIXSE framework supports the derivation of a default conceptual schema for a given DTD. This mapping is based on heuristic rules on what DTD constructs usually represent, and thus captures only partially the semantics conveyed by the data. The main value of this mapping mechanism is that it offers a starting point for a user-defined mapping for a given DTD. Additional domain expertise or contextual knowledge can be added into the default mapping through specifications written in DIXml (see Section 4).

The conceptual schema derivation process takes a single DTD as input and generates a DIXSE conceptual schema as output. Basically, the process analyzes the schematic information provided by the DTD and mines a conceptual representation of it by applying a set of *heuristic rules*. These rules were discovered by manually trying out derivations, and analyzing the results. As a whole, they aim at identifying a correspondence between elements and attributes of DTDs and entity classes and attributes of the DIXSE model. Since mapping directly all elements with structure into entity classes is likely to lead to excessive fragmentation of the mapping, they also intend to reduce the number of entity classes. Only the most specific rule is applied. Below we describe two mapping rules that drive the derivation process and illustrate their use with examples from "SigmodRecord.dtd".

The first default mapping rule (DR1) maps an XML element with complex content model (i.e. excluding #PCDATA, ANY and EMPTY types) into a DIXSE *entity class*. In addition, it creates: a *component attribute* for each subelement, a *property attribute* for each XML CDATA, ID and ENUM attribute, and a *link attribute* for each XML IDREF or XLINK attribute. For example, this rule is applicable to the author element. The following Telos specification illustrates its mapping:

```
    SimpleClass Author in XmlEntityClass,
                          XmlFrameworkClass with
      hasComponents,exactlyOne
         name : Name;
         address : Address
    end
```
Another rule (DR3) maps the XML attributes of an EMPTY element into DIXSE *entity attributes*. The element's attributes are collapsed (or inlined) as either *property* or *link attributes* of immediate parent elements' entity classes. Each entity attribute is named with the result of concatenating the EMPTY element name, the string "_" and the proper XML attribute name. EMPTY elements without attributes are not mapped into DIXSE. This rule can be applied to the contact element; the following link attribute definition is included in the element article's entity class:

```
    SimpleClass Article in XmlEntityClass,
                           XmlFrameworkClass with
      hasLinks,atMostOne,idRef
         contact_contactAuthor : XmlSimpleEntity
    end
```

The complete set of default mapping rules can be summarized as follows. The first two (DR1 and DR2) are concerned with identifying XML elements that represent entities. For us, elements with structure or atomic elements with distinguishing characteristics (like an ID attribute) embody the notion of a concept or an entity. Therefore, such elements are considered good candidates for DIXSE entity classes. Rules DR3 and DR4 describe how the remaining elements can be mapped into entity attributes. Rules DR5 and DR6 indicate how constraints on element values can be translated into additional knowledge (DIXSE attribute constraints). Last, rule DR7 recognizes the fact that some elements in the DTD (in particular those representing "*" or "+" lists, like the articles element) function more as delimiters (non-terminals in the grammar) than as meaningful entities. This rule helps to reduce the number of entity classes in the derived schema.

Figure 4 shows the default conceptual schema derived for "SigmodRecord.dtd". Please note that only some "instance-of" links with respect to DIXSE metaclasses are shown to keep the figure relatively uncluttered. Unless otherwise specified, all entity attributes in the figure are instances of the "hasComponents" attribute category. According to this mapping, there are seven entity classes. Interestingly, users with specific domain expertise may indicate that the entity classes FullText, Address and Name do not represent objects in the underlying data sources. Moreover, they could argue that the derived mapping does not convey much of the implied semantics. To overcome these deficiencies, DIXSE offers the possibility of customizing the default mapping.

4 The Mapping Language

DIXml[3] is a declarative mapping language for specifying a DTD mapping to a conceptual schema. This specification annotates a DTD with simple instructions for generating entity classes from DTD element type declarations. In the same spirit of

---

[3] The acronym DIXml stands for "**D**ata **I**ntegration for **X**ML **m**apping language".

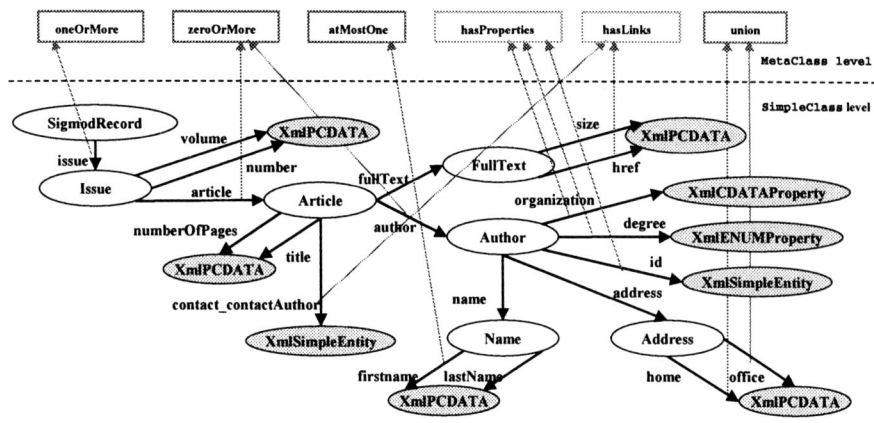

Fig. 4. Default Mapping for SigmodRecord.dtd

XSL stylesheets [11], DIXml specifications accompany DTDs to provide an extra level of information to XML data.

The DIXml specification model revolves around the idea of directive rules. A *directive rule*, hereinafter called directive, is the main mapping construct offered by the language. A DIXSE mapping can be defined by a collection of directives (at most one per DTD element declaration type). Each directive describes particular preferences for generating a conceptual representation of an XML element. These preferences are combined with the default mapping rules (presented in Section 3.2) to produce a conceptual schema.

There are five different *directive actions*, namely: **default**, **create-class**, **create-attribute**, **inline**, and **ignore**. The **default** directive indicates that the default mapping rules (DR1 to DR7) should be applied to the target element. Its inclusion or omission in the mapping specification does not affect the generated conceptual schema. The **create-class** directive says that the target element should be mapped into an entity class, while the **create-attribute** directive indicates that the target element should be mapped into a component attribute of immediate parent entity classes, without creating an entity class for it. On the other hand, the **inline** and **ignore** directives indicate that neither an entity class nor a component attribute should be created for the target element. In the first case, the meaning of the **inline** directive is to collapse the target element's content (both XML subelements and attributes) into entity attributes of immediate parent entity classes. This directive works as a grammar re-writing rule that can be applied to XML elements with content models made of atomic or empty subelements[4]. Last, the **ignore** directive indicates that neither the target element nor its content should be included in the derived mapping, unless otherwise specified (e.g. **keep** component directive for a particular subelement).

In addition, the user can provide supplementary information with each of these directives. For example: a different entity class name or attribute label (AS and

---

[4] This constraint prevents recursive collapsing of XML elements.

label clauses); classification or generalization relationships with respect to previously created entity classes (IN and ISA clauses); an indication for mapping XML attributes into entity properties (properties clause); explicit identification of interschema relationships (xLink clause); etc.

```
<?xml version="1.0" encoding="UTF-8"?>              <!ELEMENT component ( default
<!-- DTD File: DIXSEmapping.dtd  -->                                      | ignore
                                                                          | keep
<!-- DIXSE-MAPPING specification -->                                      | subclassing
                                                                          | union )>
<!ELEMENT DIXSEmapping (directive*)>                <!-- Attributes for component -->
<!-- Attributes for DIXSEmapping -->                <!ATTLIST component num CDATA #REQUIRED>
<!ATTLIST DIXSEmapping name CDATA #REQUIRED>        <!ATTLIST component label CDATA #IMPLIED>
<!ATTLIST DIXSEmapping dtd CDATA #REQUIRED>         <!ATTLIST component AT-class CDATA #IMPLIED>
<!ATTLIST DIXSEmapping context CDATA #IMPLIED>      <!ATTLIST component key (yes|no) 'no'>
                                                    <!ATTLIST component WITH-class CDATA #IMPLIED>
<!ELEMENT directive ( default
                    | create-class                  <!-- CREATE-ATTRIBUTE directive -->
                    | create-attr
                    | inline                        <!ELEMENT create-attr EMPTY>
                    | ignore ) >                    <!-- Attributes for create-attr element -->
<!-- Attributes for directive -->                   <!ATTLIST create-attr WITH-type CDATA #IMPLIED>
<!ATTLIST directive elem CDATA #REQUIRED>           <!ATTLIST create-attr properties (on|off) 'on'>
                                                    <!ATTLIST create-attr xlink CDATA #IMPLIED>
<!-- DEFAULT directive -->
                                                    <!-- INLINE directive -->
<!ELEMENT default EMPTY>
                                                    <!ELEMENT inline (component)*>
<!-- CREATE-CLASS directive -->                     <!-- List of attributes for inline -->
                                                    <!ATTLIST inline naming (on|off) 'off'>
<!ELEMENT create-class (component*)>                <!ATTLIST inline properties (on|off) 'on'>
<!-- Attributes for create-class -->                <!ATTLIST inline xlink CDATA #IMPLIED>
<!ATTLIST create-class AS CDATA #IMPLIED>
<!ATTLIST create-class IN CDATA #IMPLIED>           <!-- IGNORE directive -->
<!ATTLIST create-class ISA CDATA #IMPLIED>
<!ATTLIST create-class properties (on|off) 'on'>    <!ELEMENT ignore EMPTY>
<!ATTLIST create-class xlink CDATA #IMPLIED>
```

Fig. 5. DIXml syntax

A **create-class** or **inline** directive body can have zero or more component elements, where each one describes local mapping considerations for a subelement. For example, this allows choosing where the attribute definition should take place or indicating if the component should be part of the entity class key. The system supports a multivalued key per entity class. A component attribute can be part of the entity class key only if its value is single and mandatory. There are five possible component directives: *default, ignore, keep, subclassing* and *union*. The first one indicates that the default mapping rules should be applied to the component. The *ignore* and *keep* component directives allow us to explicitly discard or consider the element as a candidate component attribute. These directives serve to override any global directive stated for this particular XML element (i.e. **ignore** directive action). Last, the *subclassing* and *union* directives provide explicit instructions on how to map simple alternative components.

DIXml Specifications

Mapping specifications are written in XML. DIXml, as a markup language in its own right, provides a vocabulary to describe DIXSE mappings. The main two elements in this vocabulary are directive and DIXSEmapping. The first one represents a DIXml *directive rule*, while the second one represents the mapping itself by encompassing the collection of specified *directive rules*. Figure 5 shows the "end-user" syntax of DIXml, given as a DTD grammar.

5 The Case Study

We illustrate DIXSE's data integration approach through a case study. The case study we have adopted is based on the XML version of the ACM SIGMOD Record database [27]. The repository, built by the Araneus Group [3], contains a collection of approximately 1,000 XML documents. The documents are classified according to four different DTDs: HomePage.dtd, ProceedingsPage.dtd, OrdinaryIssuePage.dtd and IndexTermsPage.dtd. The HomePage DTD describes XML documents that represent the SIGMOD Record database as a collection of issues. Issues are firstly organized per year of edition, and then per number. Each issue contains some information about its volume, number and conference details. The ProceedingsPage and OrdinaryIssuePage DTDs describe two different types of issues: conference proceedings and ordinary issues, respectively. Regardless of whether an issue represents a conference proceedings or an ordinary issue, it is characterized by volume, number and date information, along with a collection of sections and articles. Each article has a title and a list of authors, among other relevant information. Last, the IndexTermsPage DTD describes specific indexing information for a SIGMOD Record article (such as its title, abstract, and a list of index terms).

Using the same application context, we process the four DTDs through the DIXSE system. The result of the process is an integrated conceptual schema in the DIXSE repository that encompasses four default mappings (one per each DTD). Figure 6 illustrates the configuration resulting from this schema integration process.

The integrated schema includes fourteen entities. The shared entity classes (i.e. classes whose name is used in more than one conceptual schema definition) represent the points where integration will occur when XML documents are uploaded. In particular, integration will occur for instances of SectionListTuple, ArticlesTuple, Author and FullText. For example, after loading several XML documents representing SIGMOD Record issues, the instances of the Author entity class will be all author objects described in these documents (that is, one object per XML element author). This would allow us to uniformly query the DIXSE repository and, for example, retrieve at the conceptual schema level all the author names that have written an article regardless of where the article was published (i.e. Proceedings or Ordinary issue).

In spite of the above results, the integrated schema does not capture much of the implied semantics of the data. First, it does not model the relationship between the HomePage DTD and the remaining three DTDs. As shown in Figure 6 (see block arrow number 1), the HomePage default conceptual schema is completely isolated from the rest. Moreover, the relationships between Proceedings and Ordinary issues, on one hand, and Proceedings and Index Terms, on the other, are only stated in terms of the sharing of entity classes (see block arrows number 2, 3 and 4). Second, the integrated schema does not provide information on how to uniquely identify objects

128   Patricia Rodríguez-Gianolli and John Mylopoulos

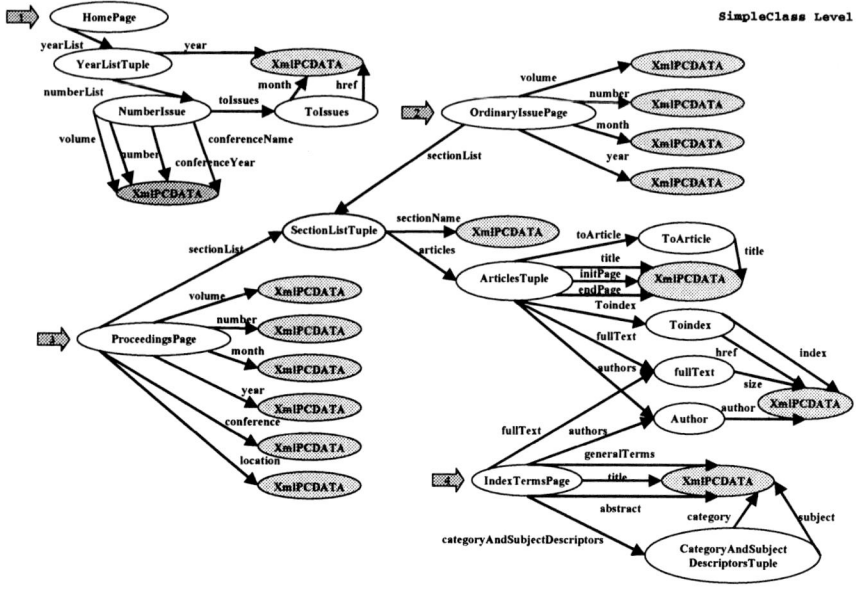

Fig. 6. Default Integrated Conceptual Schema

from the XML descriptions. Having the same author name in several XML documents will not be considered as the same object. Therefore, a new Author token will be created every time DIXSE uploads an XML document with an author element.

To overcome these deficiencies, we need to provide additional domain knowledge through DIXSE mapping specifications. Figure 7 depicts the integrated conceptual schema obtained after a series of improvements based on our understanding of the semantics of the SIGMOD data (numbered block arrows indicate the entry points for each separate conceptual schema).

The main difference between the two schemas is that the latter models the intended interpretation and usage of the information represented by the SIGMOD Record XML documents, and thus serves as a better guide for data integration. This is demonstrated by the following characteristics: use of meaningful entity class and attribute names (e.g. SigmodRecord instead of HomePage), distinction between two types of SIGMOD Record issues and their common and specialized information (illustrated by "isA" links in Figure 7), identification of key attributes (depicted by dashed-labeled attributes) and explicit assertion of interschema relationships (shown as thick-labeled attributes). As explained in Section 4, DIXSE seamlessly combines these additional knowledge sources with the schematic information provided by the DTDs.

6 System Architecture

The DIXSE system is based on a data warehouse approach to data integration. The storage mechanism employed is ConceptBase [8], an object base management system

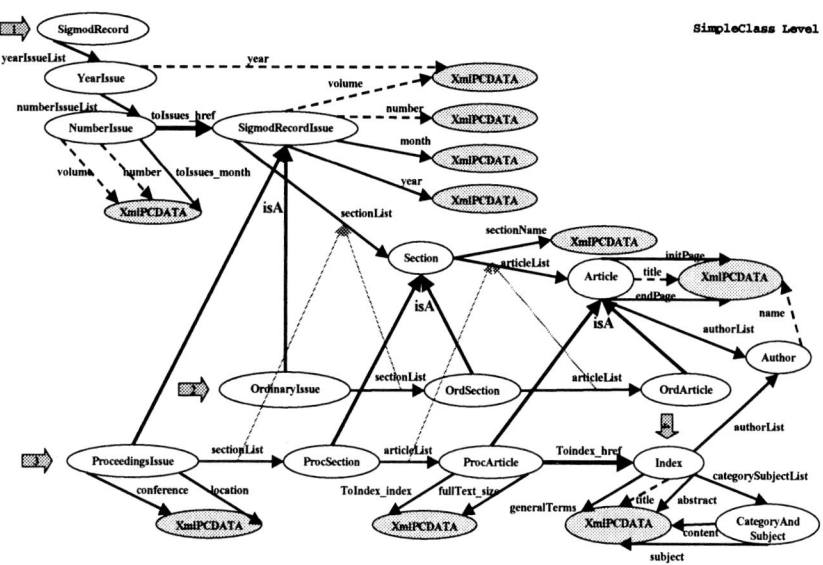

Fig. 7. User-customized Integrated Conceptual Schema

that implements a version of the Telos language. The system, implemented in Java 2, comprises two main subsystems: the `Schema Engine` and the `Document Loader`. The first one allows the user to register XML DTDs into the repository, while the second one allows populating the repository with a collection of XML documents conforming to registered DTDs.

Figure 8 depicts the system architecture and the various interactions among its components. The `Schema Engine` subsystem includes five components: the DTD parser, the XML parser, the Schema Derivator, the Schema Generator and the XSL Wrapper Generator. On the other side, the `Document Loader` consists of the XSL Processor and the Data Integrator. The communication between these two subsystems is accomplished through the Catalog Manager and the XSL Wrapper Repository.

We use the Xerces Java Parser and Xalan Java Processor as off-the-shelf components [24] (i.e. the *XML Parser* and the *XSL Processor*, respectively). Although Xerces is equipped with a *DTD Parser*, it doesn't provide external access to the grammar representation it builds. Thus, we have modified and extended the Xerces source code to provide both individual parsing of DTDs and access to their representations (DTD graphs).

The *Schema Derivator* applies a set of mapping directives to derive a conceptual schema from a DTD graph. These directives combine the knowledge embedded in the set of heuristic rules with any user-customized mapping information, provided in the form of a DIXSE mapping. The output conceptual schema is then used to generate the target schema definition and the corresponding wrapper (i.e. an XSL stylesheet), capable of converting XML documents that comply with the DTD into instances of the generated schema. Information about the generated database schema and wrapper is registered into the repository catalog.

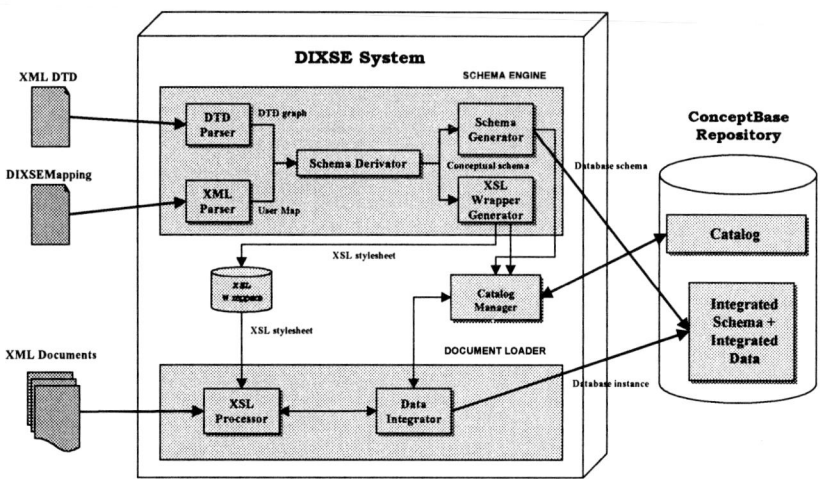

Fig. 8. System Architecture

At the time of loading an XML document into the ConceptBase repository, the loader retrieves the corresponding XSL stylesheet that will be used to transform the input document into a database instance. At several points, the *XSL Processor* interacts with the *Data Integrator*, which basically performs management of keys, object identification, and IDREF/XLINK value translation. These tasks are done using both conceptual schema and XML data information. The repository catalog is queried and updated during this process. Finally, the ConceptBase repository is populated with the newly created database instance.

7 Conclusions

This paper proposes a semantic framework for XML data integration. The framework, named DIXSE, has been implemented and evaluated with a case study. DIXSE offers a tool, which can be used semi-automatically to generate a conceptual schema from several DTDs. The tool can then parse XML documents to populate the conceptual schema.

Our approach differs from state-of-art data integration systems with respect to three main aspects. Firstly, and unlike [5,16,4,22,9], DIXSE employs conceptual modeling ideas to support data integration at a semantic level rather than at a logical level. Based on heuristics and user input, DIXSE extracts semantic details from DTDs to derive a conceptual schema. Secondly, the DIXSE approach is based on schema integration ideas like many conventional data integration systems [14,25,1]. But unlike them, DIXSE allows the user to enrich and fine-tune the default mapping derived from a set of DTDs. Finally, DIXSE employs a specialized object-based repository to store an integrated and semantically richer version of the data extracted from a collection of heterogeneous XML data sources. With the help of Telos, DIXSE provides a single framework for uniformly representing and querying conceptual schema information (metadata) and data. The paper includes elements of a detailed case study to illustrate the DIXSE approach.

We plan to try out DIXSE with another case study from the domain of knowledge management to illustrate its usefulness. We also propose to use XML Schema definitions [26] in place of DTDs, extend the implemented system so that it can produce an XML Schema definition from the derived conceptual schema, and generate a single XML document that integrates all the data included in the input XML documents. We expect that these extensions will be quite straightforward.

Acknowledgements

This research was partly funded by the Natural Sciences and Engineering Research Council (NSERC) of Canada.

References

1. Ahmed, R., De Smedt, P., Du, W., Kent, W., Ketbachi, M., Litwin, W., Raffi, A. and Shan, M.: The Pegasus heterogeneous multidatabase system. In IEEE Computer, 24(12):19-27 (1991)
2. Amann, B., Fundulaki, I., Scholl, M.: Mapping XML Fragments to Community Web Ontologies. In 4th WebDB Workshop (2001)
3. Atzeni, P., Mecca, G., Merialdo, P.: To Weave the Web. In 23rd VLDB Conference (1997)
4. Baru, C., Gupta, A., Ludäscher, B., Marciano, R., Papakonstantinou, Y., Velikhov, P., Chu, V.: *XML-Based Information Mediation with MIX*. In ACM SIGMOD International Conference (1999)
5. Chawathe, S., García-Molina, H., Hammer, J., Ireland, K., Papakonstantinou, Y., Ullman, J., Widom, J.: The TSIMMIS Project: Integration of heterogeneous information sources. In 16th Meeting of the IPSJ (1994)
6. Christophides, V., Cluet, S., Siméon, J.: On Wrapping Query Languages and Efficient XML Integration. In ACM SIGMOD International Conference (2000)
7. Christophides, V., Dörr, M., Fundulaki, I.: A Semantic Network Approach to Semi-Structured Documents Repositories. In 1st ECDL Conference (1997)
8. *ConceptBase.* www-i5.informatik.rwth-aachen.de/Cbdoc (1998)
9. Deutsch, A., Fernandez, M., Suciu, D.: Storing Semistructured Data with STORED. In ACM SIGMOD International Conference (1999)
10. Extensible Markup Language (XML) 1.0, W3C Recommendation. www.w3.org/TR/Rec-xml (2000)
11. Extensible Stylesheet Language (XSL) 1.0, W3C Recommendation. www.w3.org/TR/xsl (1999)
12. Holsheimer, M., Siebes, A.: Data Mining: The Search for Knowledge in Databases. Technical report CS-R9406, Amsterdam: CWI (1994)
13. Ives, Z., Florescu, D., Friedman, M., Levy, A., Weld, D.: An adaptive query execution system for data integration. In ACM SIGMOD International Conference (1999)
14. Larson, J., Navathe, S., El-Masri, R.: A theory for attribute equivalence and its applications to schema integration. In IEEE Transactions on Software Engineering, 15(4):449-463 (1989)

15. McBrien, P., Poulovassilis, A.: A Semantic Approach to Integrating XML and Structured Data Sources. In 13th CAiSE Conference (2001)
16. McHugh, J., Abiteboul, S., Goldman, R., Quass, D., Widom, J.: *Lore:* A database management system for semistructured data. In ACM SIGMOD Record, 26(3):54-66 (1997)
17. Mylopoulos, J., Borgida, A., Jarke, M., Koubarakis, M.: Telos: Representing Knowledge about Information Systems. In ACM Transactions on Information Systems, 8(4):325-362 (1990)
18. Mylopoulos, J.: Conceptual Modeling and Telos. In P. Loucopoulos and R. Zicari, editors, "Conceptual Modeling, Databases and Case", pages 49-68, Wiley (1992)
19. Ram, S., Ramesh, V.: Schema Integration: Past, Present and Future. In A. Emalgarmid, M. Rusinkiewicz, and A. Sheth, editors, "Management of Heterogeneous and Autonomous Database Systems", pages 119-155, Morgan Kaufmann (1999)
20. Ramesh, V., Ram, S.: Integrity constraint integration in heterogeneous databases: An enhanced methodology for schema integration. In Information Systems 22(8):423-446 (1997)
21. Rodríguez-Gianolli, P.: Data Integration for XML based on Schematic Knowledge. Master's Thesis, Department of Electrical and Computer Engineering, University of Toronto (2001)
22. Shanmugasundaram, J., Tufte, K., He, G., Zhang, C., DeWitt, D., Naughton, J.: Relational Databases for Querying XML Documents: Limitations and Opportunities. In 25th VLDB Conference (1999)
23. Sheth, A., Gala, S.: Attribute relationships: An impediment in automating schema integration. In NSF Workshop in Heterogeneous Databases (1989)
24. The Apache Software Foundation. www.apache.org (1999)
25. Thieme, C., Siebes, S.: Schema integration in object-oriented databases. In 5th CAiSE Conference (1993)
26. XML Schema, W3C Recommendation. www.w3.org/TR/xmlschema-0 (2001)
27. XML version of the ACM SIGMOD Record database. www.dia.uniroma3.it/Araneus/Sigmod (1999)

A Rule-Based Conversion of a DTD to a Conceptual Schema*

Ronaldo dos Santos Mello[1,2] and Carlos Alberto Heuser[1]

[1] Universidade Federal do Rio Grande do Sul - Instituto de Informatica
Cx. Postal 15064 - Porto Alegre - RS - Brasil. 91501-970
{ronaldo,heuser}@inf.ufrgs.br
[2] Universidade Federal de Santa Catarina - Depto. de Informatica e Estatistica
Cx. Postal 476 - Florianopolis - SC - Brasil. 88040-900
ronaldo@inf.ufsc.br

Abstract. XML is a common standard for semi-structured and structured data representation and exchange over the Web. This paper describes a *semi-automatic process* for converting an XML DTD to a schema in a *canonical conceptual model* based on ORM/NIAM and extended ER models. This process is part of a bottom-up approach for integration of XML sources that takes a set of DTDs and generates an ontology for query purposes. A conceptual schema for a DTD simplifies the integration activity because provides a semantically rich representation of an XML source. The core of the process is a set of *conversion rules* that consider the DTD structure and heuristics related to default semantic interpretations on such structure in order to generate the corresponding concepts in the canonical conceptual schema.

1 Introduction

XML (*eXtensible Markup Language*) is a W3C (*World Wide Web Consortium*) standard for semi-structured and structured data representation and exchange over the *Web* [17]. XML documents may be in accordance to a schematic representation described by a DTD (*Document Type Definition*). A DTD may be considered a logical model for XML because it describes a hierarchical structure for XML data representation.

Conceptual models provide a high-level abstraction for information concerning to an application domain, being a useful tool for tasks like database design, reverse engineering and semantic integration [1]. Semantic integration technics, in particular, aims at defining a mapping from a global schema to associated local heterogeneous schemas. Such global schema acts as a basis for an integrated service of data manipulation. The integration of conceptual schemas instead of logical schemas is preferable because conceptual models have a more clear semantics and are not bound to a specific data structure.

Considering the semantic integration of XML data, a conceptual representation to XML sources reduces the integration overhead, if compared to a DTD

---
* This work is partially supported by CAPES Foundation.

representation, because a DTD describes a grammar for semi-structured data description and not data semantics. There are recent proposals related to modeling of semi-structured data [9, 2, 4, 8, 3, 16, 10], but no one accomplishes conceptual abstraction of XML schemas considering heuristics for inferring some semantics about XML data.

We describe in this paper a *semi-automatic process* for converting a DTD to a conceptual schema in a *canonical conceptual model*. This canonical model mixes constructs from two common conceptual models to abstract XML schemas. The proposed process is part of an approach for semantic integration of XML sources, under development at the *Informatics Institute* of *Federal University of Rio Grande do Sul*, Brazil [11].

Our process is strongly based on a set of *conversion rules* that takes into account DTD elements and attributes, syntactical constructs (*sequences* and *choices*) and heuristics related to default semantic interpretations to generate the corresponding conceptual concepts. Final adjustments on a preliminary conceptual schema are accomplished by an *human analyst* (called *user*).

The remainder of this paper is organized as follows. Section 2 describes a terminology to a DTD, required to the definition of the conversion rules. Section 3 briefly comments the *Integration Layer* - a software component that applies the conversion process. Section 4, 5 and 6 present, respectively, the adopted canonical conceptual model, the conversion rules of a DTD to a conceptual schema, and the further expected manual adjustments on such conceptual schema. Section 7 comments related work and section 8 is dedicated to the conclusion.

2 DTD

The schema of an XML document may be defined by a DTD. A DTD describes a hierarchy of *elements*, rooted at the *root element*, and their optional *attributes*. Figure 1 (a) shows a DTD to the domain of *Conferences*.

An element content model in a DTD can hold: (i) no content (*EMPTY* type), free content (*ANY* type) or only character data (*#PCDATA* type) - a *simple element*; (ii) or only *component elements* or a mix of character data and component elements - a *composite element*. A composite element may be defined by two DTD syntactical constructs: *sequences* and *choices*. A sequence $(e_1, ..., e_n)$ defines n ordered component elements. A *choice* $(e_1 \mid .. \mid e_m)$ defines m alternatives of component elements. A component element may be: (i) another embedded *sequence* or *choice* definition - a *complex component element*; (ii) the name of an element - a *simple component element*; (iii) or a *#PCDATA* type - a *lexical component element*. A simple component element that occurs several times in a *sequence* is a *repeated simple component element*.

The *regular expression operators* '?', '*' and '+' denote allowed occurrences of component elements. An element content model or a component element followed by a regular expression operator '*' or '+' is a *repeatable element*.

Attributes can be associated to an element. Each attribute has a *name*, a *data type* and optional *constraints* that restrict its permitted values to an *enumeration*

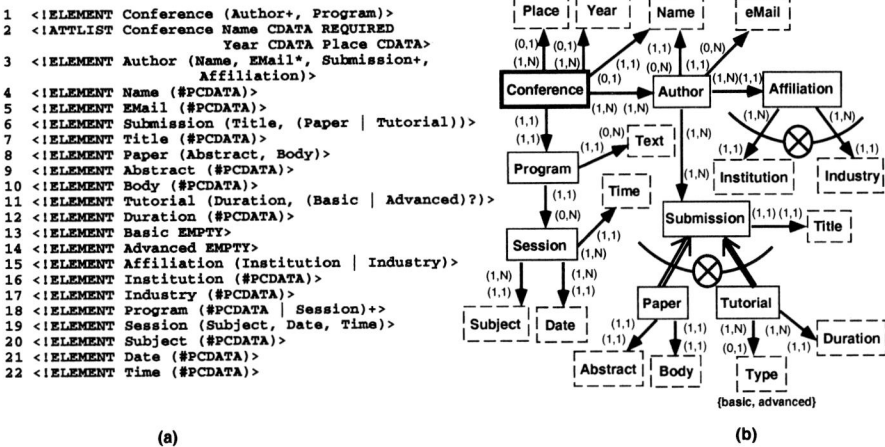

Fig. 1. An example of DTD (a) and a corresponding conceptual schema (b)

or a *fixed value*, or defines it as a *required* property. An element with attributes is also considered a *composite element*.

3 The Integration Layer

The *Integration Layer* is a component of a mediation framework for querying XML data from heterogeneous XML sources, being responsible to the semantic integration of XML schemas defined by DTDs [11]. It follows a *bottom-up integration approach* that takes as input a set of DTDs, converts each DTD to a *canonical conceptual schema*, and performs the semantic integration of these schemas, generating a *reference ontology* that acts as a front-end for querying XML sources [12]. This approach is supported by a *semi-automatic process* that considers user intervention to validate the canonical schemas as well as the ontology.

The focus of this paper is on the first task of the integration process, called *DTD Conversion*, that provides the conversion of a DTD to a conceptual schema. The *DTD Conversion* process has three phases: (i) *Conversion Rules Application*; (ii) *Analysis of XML Instances* and; (iii) *User Validation*. Phase (i) follows the DTD definition order, applying appropriated rules according to the syntax for element and attribute definition to generate a preliminary conceptual schema. Such rules are detailed in section 5, considering the conversion of the DTD of Figure 1 (a) as an example. The preliminary schema is further validated by the user in phase (iii) to generate the definitive conceptual schema. Section 6 comments this phase. The *Analysis of XML Instances* is optional, being set to be executed by the user. This phase takes a preliminary conceptual schema generated by phase (i) and tries to infer the cardinality of the relationship between a component element and its composite element, and a more precise data type to *#PCDATA* component elements. Such information is not available in a DTD but it is required to the semantic integration of conceptual schemas. Details about such analysis as well as the overall integration approach are available in [11].

4 The Canonical Conceptual Model

4.1 Overview

A *canonical conceptual model* is proposed to represent XML data. Despite of being applied to DTDs, it is able to abstract other semi-structured graph-based logical models, like *XML-schema* [18] and *OEM* [13]. This model is not a new formalism for conceptual modeling, but an adapted mix of the ORM/NIAM (*Object with Role Model/Natural language Information Analysis Method*) [7] and EER (*Extended Entity-Relationship*) [1] models to support semi-structured data representation.

The conceptual basis of the canonical model comes from ORM/NIAM, and most of the graphical notation comes from EER. Figure 1 (b) presents a corresponding schema in the canonical model to the DTD example. A *non-lexical concept* (solid rectangle) models information that is composed by other information, like *Author*. A *lexical concept* (dotted rectangle) models information that have a direct associated value, like *Year*. Lexical concepts can be specialized to *enumerated lexical concepts*, that additionally include a *value constraint*, like *Type*. A *value constraint* denotes an enumeration of permitted values. A *root concept* (thick rectangle) is provided as a type of non-lexical concept to represent the root object of a semi-structured object hierarchy, like *Conference*.

We introduce a *composition relationship* notation (an arrow from the composite to the component concept) to model the relationships in a hierarchy of a semi-structured object. The relationship between *Author* and its component *eMail* is an example: an *Author* may have zero or more *eMails*, and an *eMail* belongs to one and only one *Author*. Inheritance relationships are represented by double-line arrows, as illustrated to *Submission*, that can be specialized to a *Paper* or a *Tutorial*.

Exclusion constraints, borrowed from ORM/NIAM and represented by an "X" circled graphical notation, define disjoint relationships (suitable to support heterogeneous relationships of semi-structured objects). An example is *Affiliation*, that may be related to an *Institution* or an *Industry*.

4.2 Definitions

In order to define the conversion rules from a DTD to a conceptual schema, a tuple-based notation is introduced to the canonic conceptual model constructs.

A *conceptual schema* s is a 4-uple $s = <NL, L, R, EC>$ where NL is the set of non-lexical concepts, L is the set of lexical concepts, R is the set of binary relationships between concepts and EC is the set of exclusion constraints among relationships. A *non-lexical concept* $nl \in NL$ is a 2-uple $nl = <n, t>$, where n is the label of nl and t is the type of nl, with $t \in \{$"non-lexical", "root", "virtual"$\}$. A *root concept* **is a** non-lexical concept rt with $rt.t =$ "root". A *virtual concept* is a non-lexical concept vt with $vt.t =$ "virtual". A virtual concept is introduced to encapsulate a DTD *complex component element*. Let VL be the set of virtual concepts.

A *lexical concept* $l \in L$ is a 2-uple $l = <n, d>$, where n is the label of the l and d is the data type of l, with $d \in \{$string, integer, real, char, date, time$\}$.[1] An *enumerated lexical concept* el **is a** lexical concept with an additional property PV, where PV is the set of el permitted values. Let EL be the set of enumerated lexical concepts.

A *binary relationship* $r \in R$ is a 3-uple $r = <c1, c2, t>$, where $c1 \in NL$ and $c2 \in \{NL, L\}$ are references to the related concepts and t is the type of the relationship, with $t \in \{$"composition", "inheritance"$\}$.[2] An *inheritance relationship* **is a** binary relationship ir with $ir.t =$ "inheritance", being $c2$ an specialization of $c1$. A *composition relationship* **is a** binary relationship cr with $cr.t =$ "composition" and two additional properties $cp1$ and $cp2$, where $cp1$ and $cp2$ denote, respectively, the cardinality pairs of $c1$ and $c2$, and $c1$ and $c2$ denote, respectively, the source and the target concepts. A *named composition relationship* ncr **is a** composition relationship with an additional property nr, where nr is the label of the relationship. Let IR and CR be, respectively, the set of inheritance and composition relationships.

An *exclusion constraint* $ec \in EC$ is a 1-upla $ec = <ER>$, where ER is the set of mutual exclusive relationships $\{r_1, r_2, ..., r_n\}$, with $r_i \in R$. The following constraint holds to $ec.ER$: $r_1.c1 = r_2.c1 = ... = r_n.c1$, denoting that a exclusion constraint concerns to the relationships of a concept $c1$.

5 Conversion Rules

The conversion rules are the core of the *DTD Conversion* process. They consider the DTD syntax and heuristics concerning to semantic interpretations on the DTD - called *semantic heuristics* - with the purpose of generating a conceptual schema that does not require a lot of manual work to provide semantic adjustments. The conversion rules are organized in three classes:

1. **Transformation rules**: convert DTD elements and attributes to conceptual concepts. Such rules, in turn, are organized in two classes:
   - **Non-Lexical rules**: convert composite elements;
   - **Lexical rules**: convert simple elements and attributes.
2. **Restructuring rules**: generate *root concepts* and simplifies the conceptual schema generated by the application of the transformation rules;

---
[1] Currently supported data types. The default data type is *string*.
[2] Association relationships are also supported by the canonical model, but are not described here for sake of paper space.

3. **Cardinality rules**: determine the cardinality of source concepts. They are basic rules used by the two previous classes.

The conversion rules are defined and exemplified in the next sections, considering $\Delta_r(p_1, p_2, ..., p_n)$ the application of the rule r to the input parameters $p_1, p_2, ..., p_n$.

5.1 Transformation Rules

Non-lexical Rules This class of rules makes use of the semantic heuristics. One of them is defined in the following, being responsible to infer a specialization relationship between two elements.

Definition 1 (Inheritance Heuristics). *Given a pair of DTD element names (e_1, e_2), if a hypernymy relationship between them can be determined by a general or domain thesaurus (e_1 is broader than e_2), and e_1 and e_2 do not have inheritance conflict,[3] then e_2 is an specialization of e_1.*

The CE rule converts a composite element E to a non-lexical concept. The SCE, $RSCE$, CCE and LCE rules are related to the conversion of component elements. Table 1 shows the definition of these rules.

The followed reasoning to the conversion of a *sequence* of component elements of an element E, shown in Figure 2, concerns to the generation of default lexical concepts for each component element e, and composition relationships between E and each e. When e is a *lexical* or a *complex component element*, a special name is generated to their corresponding concepts. The source cardinality of a composition relationship is defined by the SCR, SC and RSC cardinality rules (see section 5.3). The target cardinality is set to (1,N) by default.

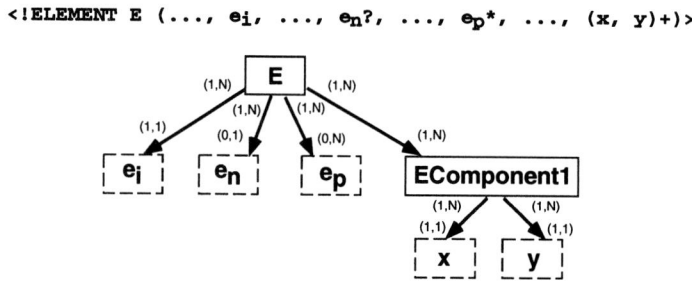

Fig. 2. Conversion of a DTD element defined by a *sequence*

---

[3] Inheritance conflict means that there is not a same element in the composition hierarchy rooted at e_1 but e_2, and the composition hierarchy rooted at e_2.

Table 1. Non-Lexical Rules (I)

Rule	Definition
CE (Composite Element)	Given a composite element E with name $EName$, generate $nl = <EName, "non-lexical"> \in NL$ if E is not defined as a non-lexical concept, and remove $l \in L$ if E is defined as a lexical concept.
SCE (Simple Component Element)	Given a simple component element e, with name $eName$, of a composite element E converted to a concept $nl \in NL$, generate $l = <eName, "string"> \in L$ if e is not defined as a lexical or non-lexical concept, and $r \in R$ where: $r = \begin{cases} <nl, l, "inheritance"> \in IR & \text{if } e \text{ definition is not followed by '+' or} \\ & \text{'*', and \textbf{inheritance heuristics} holds to} \\ & (EName, eName); \\ <nl, l, \Delta_{SC}(E,e) \text{ or } \Delta_{SCR}(E,e), & \\ (1,N), "composition"> \in CR & \text{otherwise.} \end{cases}$
RSCE (Repeated Simple Component Element)	Given a repeated simple component element e, with name $eName$, of a composite element E converted to a concept $nl \in NL$, generate $l = <eName, "string"> \in L$ if e is not defined as a lexical or non-lexical concept, and $r = <nl, l, \Delta_{RSC}(E,e), (1,N), "composition"> \in CR$.
CCE (Complex Component Element)	Given a complex component element e, with name $eName$, of a composite element E converted to a concept $nl \in NL$, generate $nl = <n, "virtual"> \in NL$, where $n = EName + "Component" + sequential$, and $r = <nl, l, \Delta_{SC}(E,e)$ or $\Delta_{SCR}(E,e), (1,N), "composition"> \in CR$.
LCE (Lexical Component Element)	Given a lexical component element e, with name $eName$, of a composite element E converted to a concept $nl \in NL$, generate $l = <n, "string"> \in L$, where $n = EName + "Text"$, and $r = <nl, l, \Delta_{SC}(E,e)$ or $\Delta_{SCR}(E,e), (1,N), "composition"> \in CR$.

The *SCE* rule makes use of the *inheritance heuristics* to check if a simple component e is a specialization of E. If so, an inheritance relationship is generated. A virtual concept vl is generated by the *CCE* rule. Once generated, vl is considered a composite element and the conversion rules are applied to its components.

Example 1 (DTD example - lines 3 and 6 (partial conversion)). Δ_{CE}**(Author)** $\Rightarrow nl_1 = <Author>$; Δ_{SCE}**(Author, EMail*)** $\Rightarrow l_1 = <EMail, "string">$, $cr_1 = <nl_1, l_1, (0,N), (1,N)>$; Δ_{CE}**(Submission)** $\Rightarrow nl_2 = <Submission>$; Δ_{CCE}**(Submission, (Paper | Tutorial))** $\Rightarrow nl_3 = <SubmissionComponent1, "virtual">$, $cr_2 = <nl_2, nl_3, (1,1), (1,N)>$;[4]

The **C** rule converts a composite element E defined by a *choice* and their component elements. Such conversion is ruled by the *enumeration* and *exclusion heuristics*, defined in the following.

Definition 2 (Enumeration Heuristics). *Given a component element e, with name $eName$, of a composite element E, if e is defined as an EMPTY type element without associated attributes, then e is a qualification of E with value $eName$.*

Definition 3 (Exclusion Heuristics). *Given a composite element E, with name $EName$, defined by a choice and their set Sc of component elements $e_1, e_2, ..., e_n$, where each element $e_i \in Sc$ has name e_iName, the relationship*

---
[4] For sake of paper space, the *type* attribute of non-lexical concepts and binary relationships are not shown in the examples.

between E and their components must match with one of the following *exclusion semantics*:

1. **Disjoint inheritance semantics:** *if the inheritance heuristics holds to (EName, e_iName), for all $e_i \in Sc$, then a disjoint set of inheritance relationships is generated;*
2. **Enumeration semantics:** *if the enumeration heuristics holds to all $e_i \in Sc$, then a concept $el \in EL$ is generated, with $el.PV$ being the set of e_i names. A composition relationship from the non-lexical concept corresponding to E to el is also generated;*
3. **Disjoint composition semantics:** *if the inheritance heuristics and enumeration heuristics do not apply to any $e_i \in Sc$, a disjoint set of composition relationships is generated;*
4. **Mixed semantics:** *a mix of the previous exclusion semantics.*

Figure 3 illustrates the exclusion semantics described by the *exclusion heuristics*. Items 1 to 4 of the *exclusion heuristics* correspond to the items (a) to (d) in Figure 3. To all exclusion semantics, except the *enumeration semantics*, an *exclusion constraint* is generated to denote that the component elements are disjoint.

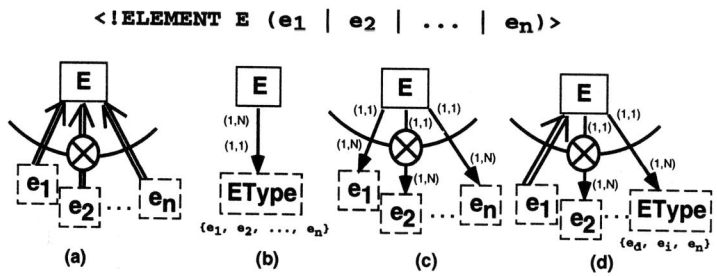

Fig. 3. Semantic interpretations of a DTD element defined by a *choice*

The RC rule deals with the conversion of *repeatable choices*. It does not generate inheritance relationships and exclusion constraints because one or more alternative component elements may be related to E several times. Table 2 shows the definition of the C and RC rules.

Example 2 (DTD example - lines 15 and 18). $\Delta_C(\textbf{Affiliation}) \Rightarrow nl_1 = <Affiliation>$, $l_1 = <Institution, "string">$, $l_2 = <Industry, "string">$, $cr_1 = <nl_1, l_1, (1,1), (1,N)>$, $cr_2 = <nl_1, l_2, (1,1), (1,N)>$, $ec = <\{cr_1, cr_2\}>$; $\Delta_{RC}(\textbf{Program}) \Rightarrow nl_2 = <Program>$, $l_3 = <Session, "string">$, $l_4 = <ProgramText, "string">$, $cr_3 = <nl_2, l_3, (0,N), (1,N)>$, $cr_4 = <nl_2, l_4, (0,N), (1,N)>$.

Table 2. Non-Lexical Rules (II)

Rule	Definition
C (Choice)	Given a composite element E, with name EName, defined as a choice and converted to a concept $nl \in NL$, with a set Se of component elements $e_1, e_2, ..., e_n$, where the name of an element $e_i \in Se$ is $e_i Name$: 1. Apply $\Delta_{CE}(E)$; 2. Generate $el = <n, "string", \{e'_1 Name, e'_2 Name, ..., e'_k Name\} > \in EL$, where $n = EName + "Type"$, and $r = <nl, el, \Delta_{UC}(\{\Delta_{SC}(E,e'_1), \Delta_{SC}(E,e'_2), ..., \Delta_{SC}(E,e'_k)\}), (1,N), "composition"> \in CR,^5$ if exists a subset $Se' = \{e'_1, e'_2, ..., e'_k\}$, $Se' \subseteq Se$, such that **enumeration heuristics** holds to (E, e'_i), for all $e'_i \in Se$; 3. For each $e_i \in Se - Se'$ apply $\Delta_{SCE}(E,e_i)$, $\Delta_{CCE}(E,e_i)$ or $\Delta_{LCE}(E,e_i)$ if e_i is, respectively, a simple, a complex or a lexical component; 4. Generate $ec = <ER> \in EC$, where ER is the set of relationships $r \in R$ generated by this rule, if SCE, CCE and LCE rules generate at least one relationship $r \in R$.
RC (Repeatable Choice)	Given a repeatable composite element E, with name EName, defined as a choice and converted to a concept $nl \in NL$, with a set Se of component elements $e_1, e_2, ..., e_n$, where the name of an element $e_i \in Se$ is $e_i Name$: 1. The same of item 1 of C rule; 2. The same of item 2 of C rule; 3. For each simple component $e_i \in Se - Se'$ generate $l = <e_i Name, "string"> \in L$ if e is not defined as a lexical or non-lexical concept, and $r = <nl, l, (O,N), (1,N), "composition"> \in CR$; 4. For each $e_i \in Se - Se'$ apply $\Delta_{CCE}(E,e_i)$ or $\Delta_{LCE}(E,e_i)$ if e_i is, respectively, a complex or a lexical component;

Lexical Rules The lexical rules convert simple elements (***SE*** rule) and attributes (***A*** rule), generating correspondent lexical concepts. The *A* rule can generate an enumerated lexical concept to an attribute if there is a *value constraint* associated to it. Attributes with the same name of elements in the conceptual schema receive special names because element names have precedence. Table 3 shows the definition of these rules.

Example 3 (DTD example - line 2). Δ_A (Conference, {Name CDATA REQUIRED, Year CDATA, Place CDATA}) $\Rightarrow nl = <Conference>, l_1 = <Name, "string">, l_2 = <Year, "string">, l_3 = <Place, "string">, cr_1 = <nl, l_1, (1,1), (1,N)>, cr_2 = <nl, l_2, (0,1), (1,N)>, cr_3 = <nl, l_3, (0,1), (1,N)>.

5.2 Restructuring Rules

Four rules comprises the restructuring rules, defined in Table 4. The ***RTC*** rule identifies non-lexical concepts that are *root concepts* and properly update them. A root concept is a concept that is not target of any binary relationship.

The other rules simplifies the conceptual schema, removing concepts that behave as additional connections among relevant concepts, like virtual concepts and concepts that may be converted to relationships. The ***NR*** rule states that a non-lexical concept nl (not root concept) that is composed by only one concept c is, in fact, an useless intermediate concept in the chain of composition relationships $nl' \rightarrow nl \rightarrow c$. Such chain is reduced to a relationship $r:nl' \rightarrow c$ where r is named with the nl label.

Table 3. Lexical Rules

Rule	Definition
SE (Simple Element)	Given a simple element e with name $eName$, generate $l = <eName, "string"> \in L$ if e is not defined as a lexical concept.

A (Attributes)	Given a set of attributes $a_1, a_2, ..., a_n$ defined to an element E with name $EName$:
	1. Apply $\Delta_{CE}(E)$;
	2. Generate $l = <n, "string"> \in L$, where $n = EName + "Context"$, and $r = <nl, l, (1,1), (1,N), "composition"> \in CR$, if E is #PCDATA or ANY type;
	3. For each $a_i \in a_1, a_2, ..., a_n$ with name $a_i Name$:
	  (a) Define $n := \begin{cases} EName + a_i Name & \text{if } a_i Name \text{ has name conflict;} \\ a_i Name & \text{otherwise;} \end{cases}$
	  (b) Generate $l = \begin{cases} <n, "string", PV> \in EL & \text{if } a_i \text{ has value constraint;} \\ <n, "string"> \in L & \text{otherwise;} \end{cases}$
	  and $r = <nl, l, cp1, (1,N), "composition"> \in CR$,
	  where $cp1 = \begin{cases} (1,1) & \text{if } a_i \text{ is a required attribute;} \\ (0,1) & \text{otherwise.} \end{cases}$

Example 4. Suppose that line 18 of the DTD example is $<!ELEMENT\ Program\ (Session)+>$ and the transformation rules generate: $nl_1 = <Conference>$, $nl_2 = <Program>$, $nl_3 = <Session>$, $cr_1 = <nl_1, nl_2, (1,1), (1,N)>$, $cr_2 = <nl_2, nl_3, (1,N), (1,N)>$. So, $\Delta_{RTC}(nl_1) \Rightarrow nl_1 = <Conference, "root">$; $\Delta_{NR}(nl_2) \Rightarrow ncr_1 = <nl_1, nl_3, (1,N), (1,N), "composition", "Program">$, remove cr_1, nl_2 and cr_2.

The **RG** rule considers inheritance relationships from a source non-lexical concept nl and a set C of specialized concepts $\{c_1, ..., c_n\}$, with $n > 1$. In this case, if all elements $c_i \in C$ are source concepts of a concept X in a composition relationship, then X becomes a direct component of nl (the composition relationships with target X are generalized).

The *VCR* rule states that a concept $vl \in VL$ that is a component of a concept $nl \in NL$, such that the *maximum source cardinality* of your composition relationship is 1, is an useless intermediate concept in the chain of composition relationships that connects nl to the set C of vl components. In this case, vl is removed and all C elements become direct nl components. Such simplification does not work only if the relationship from nl to vl is included in a *exclusion constraint* of nl, and vl encapsulates a *sequence* (called *exclusion-sequence constraint*).

Example 5. The (partial) application of the transformation rules on line 11 of the DTD example generates: $nl = <Tutorial>$, $vl = <TutorialComponent1, "virtual">$, $el = <TutorialComponent1Type, "string", \{basic, advanced\}>$, $cr_1 = <nl, vl, (0,1), (1,N)>$, $cr_2 = <vl, el, (1,1), (1,N)>$. So, $\Delta_{VCR}(vl) \Rightarrow cr_3 = <nl, el, (0,1), (1,N)>$, remove cr_2, vl and cr_1.

5.3 Cardinality Rules

The cardinality rules are basic rules used by the *transformation* and *restructuring* rules. Table 5 shows the definition of these rules. The *SC* and *SCR* rules

Table 4. Restructuring Rules

Rule	Definition
RTC (Root Concept)	Given a concept $nl \in NL$, do $nl.t :=$ "root" if does not exist $r \in R$ such that $r.c2 = nl$.

NR (Named Relationship)	Given a not root concept $nl \in NL$ such that exists only one relationship $r \in CR$ with $r.c1 = nl$, then:
	1. For each $nl' \in NL$ such that exists a relationship $r' \in CR$ with $r'.c1 = nl'$ and $r'.c2 = nl$:
	  (a) Generate $r'' = <r'.c1, r.c2, \Delta_{UC}(\{r.cp1, r'.cp1\}), r'.cp2,$ "composition", $nl.n> \in NCR$;
	  (b) $ec.ER := ec.ER \cup \{r''\} - \{r'\}$, if exists $ec \in EC$ such that $r' \in ec.ER$;
	  (c) Remove r';
	2. Remove nl and r.

RG (Relationship Generalization)	Given a concept $nl \in NL$, if for all relationship $r \in IR$ such that $r.c1 = nl$ there is a relationship $r' \in CR$ such that $r'.c1 = r.c2$ and $r'.c2 = X$, and does not exist $ec \in EC$ such that $r' \in ec.ER$, then: 1. Generate $r'' = <nl, X, \Delta_{UC}(\{r'_1.cp1, r'_2.cp1, ..., r'_n.cp1\}), (1,N),$ "composition"$> \in CR$, where $\{r'_1, r'_2, ..., r'_n\}$ is the set of all $r' \in CR$; 2. For each $r'_i \in \{r'_1, r'_2, ..., r'_n\}$ do remove r'_i.

VCR (Virtual Concept Removal)	Given a concept $vl \in VL$, component of a a concept $nl \in NL$, and $r \in CR$ with $r.cp1.c_{max} = 1$, where *exclusion-sequence constraint* does not hold:
	1. For each $r' \in CR$ such that $r'.c1 = vl$:
	  (a) Generate $r'' = <r.c1, r'.c2, \Delta_{UC}(\{r.cp1, r'.cp1\}), r'.cp2,$ "composition"$> \in CR$;
	  (b) If exists $r' \in ec.ER$, to an $ec \in EC$ defined to vl, then:
	  $\begin{cases} ec'.ER := ec'.ER \cup \{r''\} & \text{if exists } ec'' \in EC \text{ defined to } nl \\ & \text{and } r \in ec'.ER; \\ ec.ER := ec.ER \cup \{r''\} - \{r'\} & \text{otherwise}; \end{cases}$
	  (c) Remove r';
	2. Remove nl and r.

determine cardinalities of a composition relationship between concepts corresponding to a composite element E and a component element e, considering the case where E is a *repeatable element* or not.

The *RSC* rule defines the source cardinality of a *repeated component element* e, taking into account the number of occurrences of e into E definition. *UC* rule defines the *unified cardinality* to a set of cardinalities Sc. The unified cardinality is the broader cardinality for all Sc elements.

Example 6. Given the DTD element definitions <!ELEMENT E_1(e_1?, ..., e_x, ..., e_x+)> and <!ELEMENT E_2(..., e_i, ..., e_k?, ...)+>: $\Delta_{SC}(E_1, e_1) \Rightarrow (0,1)$; $\Delta_{RSC}(E_1, e_x) \Rightarrow (cp_{min} = 1+1, cp_{max} = N) = (2,N)$; $\Delta_{SCR}(E_2, e_i) \Rightarrow (1,N)$; $\Delta_{SCR}(E_2, e_k) \Rightarrow (0,N)$. Given three cardinalities $cp_1 = (0,1)$, $cp_2 = (1,1)$ and $cp_3 = (1,N)$: $\Delta_{UC}(\{cp_1, cp_2, cp_3\}) \Rightarrow (0,N)$.

Table 6 shows the application of the conversion rules to the DTD example. Resulting fragments of the conceptual schema are presented to each set of converted DTD lines.

Table 5. Cardinality Rules

Rule	Definition
SC (Source Cardinality)	The cardinality cp of a composite element E with regard to a component element e is: $$cp := \begin{cases} (0,1), & \text{if } e \text{ definition is followed by '?';} \\ (0,N), & \text{if } e \text{ definition is followed by '*';} \\ (1,N), & \text{if } e \text{ definition is followed by '+';} \\ (1,1), & \text{otherwise.} \end{cases}$$
SCR (Source Cardinality with Repetition)	The cardinality cp of a repeatable composite element E with regard to a component element e is: $$cp := \begin{cases} (0,N), & \begin{array}{l}\bullet \text{ if } E \text{ is defined as a choice;} \\ \bullet \text{ if } E \text{ is defined as a sequence followed by '*';} \\ \bullet \text{ if } E \text{ is defined as a sequence followed by '+' and } e \\ \quad \text{definition is followed by '?';}\end{array} \\ (1,N), & \text{otherwise.} \end{cases}$$
RSC (Repeated Source Cardinality Rule)	The cardinality pair (cp_{min}, cp_{max}) of a composite element E with regard to a n-repeated target component element e, being e_i the i-th occurrence of e in E, is defined as follows. 1. For each e_i: $cp_i := \Delta_{SC}(E, e_i)$ or $\Delta_{SCR}(E, e_i)$; 2. $cp_{min} := \Sigma_{i=1}^{n} cp_i.c_{min}$; 3. $cp_{max} := \begin{cases} N & \text{if exists } cp_i \in \{cp1_1, cp_2, ..., cp_n\} \text{ such} \\ & \text{that } cp_i.c_{max} = N; \\ \Sigma_{i=1}^{n} cp_i.c_{max} & \text{otherwise.} \end{cases}$
UC (Unified Cardinality)	Given a set of cardinalities Sc, where each $cp_i \in Sc$ has the form $cp_i = (c_{min}, c_{max})$, the unified cardinality $\overline{ucp}$ is defined as follows. – $\overline{ucp}.c_{min} := MIN(cp_1.c_{min}, cp_2.c_{min}, ..., cp_n.c_{min})$ – $\overline{ucp}.c_{max} := \begin{cases} N & \text{if exists } cp_i \in SC \text{ such that } cp_i.c_{max} = N; \\ MAX(cp_1.c_{min}, cp_2.c_{min}, ..., cp_n.c_{min}) & \text{otherwise.} \end{cases}$

6 User Validation

The *user validation* phase concerns to the user intervention with the purpose of validating the preliminary conceptual schema generated through the execution of the conversion rules. Such validation is required to obtain a conceptual schema semantically correct to the considered domain.

The most relevant manual adjustments are related to defaults assumed by the previous phases of the conversion process. Such adjustments are:

– *Target cardinalities of composition relationships*: the default target cardinality of a composition relationship may not be in accordance to the semantics of the domain, even after an analysis of XML instances;
– *Data types of lexical concepts*: the data type of a lexical concept may not match to the real domain of the correspondent element values, even after an analysis of XML instances;
– *Names of composition relationships*: names of elements that become relationships'names in a conceptual schema, according to *NR* rule, may not be suitable to the considered domain;
– *Generated names of concepts*: default names for virtual or lexical concepts must also be changed to much expressive names;
– *Merge of lexical concepts*: lexical concepts with the same semantics can be merged in a single representative lexical concept. It occurs when an element and attribute name conflict raises, and two lexical concepts are generated;

Table 6. Application of the Conversion Rules to the DTD Example

DTD Lines	Conversion Rules	Conceptual Schema
1 to 2	CE(Conference), SCE(Conference, Author+), SCE(Conference, Program), A(Conference, Name CDATA REQUIRED, Year CDATA, Place CDATA)	
3 to 5	CE(Author), SCE(Author, Name), SCE(Author, EMail*), SCE(Author, Affiliation), SCE(Author, Submission+), SE(Name), SE(EMail)	
6 to 14	CE(Submission), SCE(Submission, Title), CCE(Submission, (Paper | Tutorial)), C(*SubmissionComponent1*), SE(Title), CE(Paper), SCE(Paper, Abstract), SCE(Paper, Body), SE(Abstract), SE(Body), CE(Tutorial), SCE(Tutorial, Duration), CCE(Tutorial, (Basic | Advanced)?), C(*TutorialComponent1*), SCE(Tutorial, Duration)	
15 to 17	C(Affiliation), SCE(Affiliation, Institution), SCE(Affiliation, Industry), SE(Institution), SE(Industry)	
18 to 22	RC(Program), LCE(Program, #PCDATA), SCE(Program, Session), SE(Session), SCE(Session, Subjcet), SCE(Session, Date), SCE(Session, Time), SE(Subject), SE(Date), SE(Tutorial),	
Restructuring	VCR (*SubmissionComponent1*), VCR (*TutorialComponent1*)	

- *Exclusion semantics*: a default *exclusion semantics* can be updated by the user. The most usual case occurs when an implied specialization relationship is not inferred by the *inheritance heuristics* to all or some of the component elements.

Considering the preliminary conceptual schema shown at Table 6, four updates are supposed to be performed by the user:

- The lexical concepts *ConferenceName* and *Name* are merged in a lexical concept *Name*;
- *Adjustments on target cardinalities*: (0,1) to *Name-Conference* and (0,N) to *Name-Author* (a *Name* may belong to an *Author* or a *Conference*); (1,1) to *Program-Conference*; (1,1) to *EMail - Author*; (1,1) to *Abstract-Paper* and *Body-Paper*; (1,1) to *Text-Program* and *Session-Program*; and (1,1) to *Title-Submission*;
- The names of the concepts *TutorialComponent1Type* and *ProgramText* are reduced to the more readable names *Type* and *Text*, respectively;
- There is an implied *disjoint inheritance semantics* on the relationships from *Submission* to *Paper* and *Tutorial*. This update is manually provided.

On concluding this phase, the resulting conceptual schema is the one shown in Figure 1 (b).

7 Related Work

Several approaches define canonical representations of DTDs for integration purposes. The *MIX project* [9] and the works of [2] and [4] convert a DTD to a schema in a graph-based model that keeps a hierarchical organization of DTD elements. These schemas, however, are not conceptual schemas in sense that are strongly tied to the DTD structure and do not support semantic relationships. The *YAT model* [15], for semi-structured data representation, works on a similar way.

Other recent work deal with Web data modeling. One of them presents a conversion of HTML data to a conceptual model. This model follows an object-oriented formalism suitable for semi-structured data [8]. Compared to our canonic model, such a model has a lower abstraction level because it considers only constructs for composition relationships, and offers no support for XML schemas conversion. [3] and [5] propose, respectively, an ORM to *XML-Schema* and an UML to DTD mapping, for XML schemas design purposes; and [16] queries heterogeneous XML sources through a mediation-based system that uses a predefined domain ontology. All of them follow the opposite approach of the *DTD Conversion*, mapping a conceptual model to a logical model. Such conversion has a lower complexity level because does not need to infer semantics.

A close approach is followed by [10], that presents a semi-automatic conversion of a schema in XML to the ER model through intermediate mappings to a defined low-level graph-based model called *HDM*. However, the *DTD Conversion* does not consider an intermediate data model in the conversion process, and extracts inheritance relationships from XML schemas.

8 Conclusion

We present in this paper a rule-based process for converting a DTD to a conceptual schema suitable to the abstraction of semi-structured data. Such process is a contribution to problem of semantic integration of XML sources. The conversion rules generate conceptual schemas through the automatic inference of some semantics on a DTD, in order to reduce the user intervention. Compared to related work, our process produces a semantically more rich canonical representation of XML data for integration purposes.

The canonic model and the mapping information to a DTD are under definition in OIL (*Ontology Inference Language*), a language suitable to ontology and conceptual modeling specification [6]. We chose OIL because it allows a standard specification for canonic schemas and the reference ontology, making easy their mapping. OIL has a short and clear syntax and can be converted to the W3C recommended metadata standard RDF [14].

Future work concern to the study of new heuristics to improve the automated support of the conversion process and the conceptual abstraction of *XML-schema*. We consider first the DTD conversion because DTD is an early and widespread standard for XML logical modeling, whereas XML-Schema is a recent W3C standard. Anyway, the *XML-schema conversion* is supposed to be simpler than the *DTD conversion* because XML-schema constructs are much closer to conceptual constructs than the ones of DTDs.

Acknowledge. We thank Silvana Castano, from *Information Science Department* of *University of Milano*, by the suggestions given to the paper content and the co-operation in the development of the integration approach.

References

[1] C. Batini, S. Ceri, and S. B. Navathe. *Conceptual Database Design: An Entity-Relationship Approach.* Benjamin/Cummings Publishing Company, 1992.
[2] R. Behrens. A grammar based model for xml schema integration. In *XVII British National Conference on Databases (BCNOD)*, 2000.
[3] L. Bird, A. Goodchild, and T. Halpin. Object role modeling and xml-schema. In *19th International Conference on Conceptual Modeling (ER'2000)*, pages 309–322, October 2000.
[4] S. Castano, V. Antonellis, and S. C. Vimercati. An xml-based framework for information integration over the web. In *International Workshop on Information and Web-Based Application and Services (IIWAS 2000)*, Yogyakarta, Indonesia, September 2000.
[5] R. Conrad, D. Scheffner, and J. C. Freytag. Xml conceptual modeling using uml. In *19th International Conference on Conceptual Modeling (ER'2000)*, pages 558–571, October 2000.
[6] D. Fensel, I.Horrocks, F. V. Harmelen, S. Decker, M. Erdmann, and M. Klein. Oil in a nutshell. In *12th European Workshop on Knowledge Acquisition, Modeling, and Management (EKAW'00)*, 2000.

[7] T. Halphin. *Object-Role Modeling (ORM/NIAM), Handbook on Architectures of Information Systems*, chapter 4. Spring-Verlag Berlin/Heidelberg, 1998.
[8] M. Liu and T. W. Ling. A conceptual model for the web. In *19th International Conference on Conceptual Modeling (ER'2000)*, pages 225–238, October 2000.
[9] B. Ludäscher, Y. Papakonstantinou, P. Velikhov, and V. Vianu. View definition and dtd inference for xml. In *ICDT Workshop on Query Processing for Semistructured Data and Non-standard Data Formats*, 1999.
[10] P. McBrien and A. Poulovassilis. A semantic approach to integrating xml and structured data sources. In *13th Conference on Advanced Information Systems Engineering (to appear)*, June 2001.
[11] R. S. Mello. *An Integration Layer for Semantic Unification of XML sources*. PhD thesis, Informatics Institute - Federal University of Rio Grande do Sul, 2001.
[12] R. S. Mello and C. A. Heuser. A bottom-up approach for integration of xml sources. In *International Workshop on Information Integration on the Web*, apr 2001.
[13] Y. Papakonstantinou, H. Garcia-Molina, and J. Widow. Object exchange across heterogeneous information. In *International Conference on Data Engineering*, pages 251–260, 1995.
[14] W3C Resource Description Framework RDF. Available at: *http://www.w3.org/RDF*.
[15] S.Cluet, C. Delobel, J. Siméon, and K. Smaga. Your mediators need data conversion! In *SIGMOD Conference*, pages 177–188, June 1998.
[16] R. Vdovjak and Geert-Jan Houben. Rdf-based architecture for semantic integration of heterogeneous information sources. In *International Workshop on Information Integration on the Web*, apr 2001.
[17] W3C Extensible Markup Language XML. Available at: *http://www.w3.org/XML*.
[18] W3 XML-Schema. Available at: *http://www.w3.org/XML/Schema*.

Semantic Data Modeling Using XML Schemas

Murali Mani*, Dongwon Lee, and Richard R. Muntz

Department of Computer Science
University of California, Los Angeles
Los Angeles, CA 90095, USA
{mani,dongwon,muntz}@cs.ucla.edu

Abstract. Most research on XML has so far largely neglected the data modeling aspects of XML schemas. In this paper, we attempt to make a systematic approach to data modeling capabilities of XML schemas. We first formalize a core set of features among a dozen competing XML schema language proposals and introduce a new notion of *XGrammar*. The benefits of such formal description is that it is both concise and precise. We then compare the features of *XGrammar* with those of the Entity-Relationship (ER) model. We especially focus on three data modeling capabilities of *XGrammar*: (a) the ability to represent *ordered binary relationships*, (b) the ability to represent a set of semantically equivalent but structurally different types as "one" type using the closure properties, and (c) the ability to represent *recursive relationships*.

1 Introduction

With the growing popularity of XML (eXtensible Markup Language) [5] defined by W3C, XML schemas[1] expressed by schema languages (e.g., DTD [5], XML-Schema [14], RELAX [9]) are being widely used to describe data. Even though XML is largely used for transferring data at present, we envision that in the not-so-distant future, XML schemas will be used as the "external schema" for a large portion of the data. This makes the study of modeling capabilities of XML schemas very important. Furthermore, to bridge with other existing data models, it is becoming increasingly important to understand how to map features of XML schema to those of existing models and vice versa. In this paper, we attempt to make a systematic approach to data description using an XML schema and compare it to the widely-used conceptual model, the Entity-Relationship (ER) model [7]. Our contributions in this paper are as follows:

- We formalize a core set of features found in various XML schema languages into *XGrammar* – a grammar notation commonly found in formal language theory. The important building blocks of any XML schema language such

---

* This author is partially supported by NSF grants 0086116, 0085773, 9817773.
[1] We differentiate two terms – XML schema(s) and XML-Schema. The former refers to a general term for a schema for XML, while the latter [14] refers to one kind of XML schema language proposed by W3C.

Fig. 1. Cardinality representation in ER model.

as element-subelement relationships are well captured in *XGrammar* in a coherent and precise manner.
- We describe three features of *XGrammar* in detail and compare them with features of ER model: (a) representing *ordered binary relationships*, (b) representing a set of semantically equivalent but structurally different types as "one" type using the property that *XGrammar* is closed under the *union* boolean operation, and (c) representing *recursive relationships* using recursive type definitions. By doing so, we also identify features lacking in ER model to natively support the XML model and extend it to *EER model*.

Besides the new features present in *XGrammar*, they can also represent data modeling features such as n-ary relationships, composite attributes, generalization hierarchy etc. However, they are still in a development phase for schema language proposals such as RELAX, and we do not focus on them in this paper.

1.1 Background: ER Model and Our Extensions

Entity-Relationship model (ER model) and Entity-Relationship diagram (ER diagram) are defined by Chen in 1970s and has been widely used in data modeling ever since [7]. The basic features of the ER model are *entity* types and *relationship* types. An *entity* type is represented by a rectangular labeled box, and a *relationship* type is represented by a diamond labeled box in an ER diagram. For our purposes, we use ER diagram notations in [1]. Here a cardinality of an entity in a relationship is represented as a 2-tuple $(minC, maxC)$. We use this 2-tuple notation mainly to distinguish between the cardinalities: $(0, 1)$ and $(1, 1)$, and also $(0, *)$ and $(1, *)$, which are commonly found in XML schemas. Here $*$ means that there is no upper bound on the cardinality. For instance, the diagram in Fig. 1 illustrates "Dept can have one or many Employees while each Employee can belong to one and only one Dept". Note that our notations of cardinalities are exactly reverse of those used in [1].

In this paper, we are not concerned with the more advanced features of ER model such as the role of an entity in a relationship, n-ary relationships where $n > 2$, attributes of a relationship, and constraints. Instead, we focus only on the basic features of the ER model, and extend it with the following additional features:

- *Order in a binary relationship*: ER model is based on a notion of set, and thus does not have a construct for order. However, in XML model, order is important. For instance, the first and second authors of book are different in XML model. To express such ordering in an ER diagram, we denote

the in-between edge by a thick line. For instance, there is ordering among Employees in Fig. 1.
- *Element-subelement relationship*: One of the main constructs in XML model is the element-subelement (i.e., parent-child) relationship. We represent this relationship using a dummy "has" relationship in ER model (i.e., a diamond box with the label has). For instance, the relationship that Employee is a subelement of Dept is shown in Fig. 1.

For convenience, we denote *ordered* and *unordered* relationships, say X between two entities A and B, where the cardinality of A is (m_1, M_1), and the cardinality of B is (m_2, M_2) by $A(m_1, M_1) \stackrel{X}{\Longrightarrow} B(m_2, M_2)$ and $A(m_1, M_1) \stackrel{X}{\longrightarrow} B(m_2, M_2)$, respectively. ER model with our extensions will be referred to as "EER model" throughout the rest of the paper.

1.2 Related Work

Data modeling is an inherent part of database design, and deals with the structure, organization and effective use of data and the information they represent [15]. Such conceptual modeling of the data has been helped by data models such as ER model [7], which models an enterprise as a set of entities and relationships. However these data models cannot specify ordered relationships (i.e., cannot specify order between objects in a relationship). Ordered relationships exist commonly in practice such as the list of authors of a book. XML schemas, on the other hand, can specify such ordered relationships.

Semantic data modeling using XML schemas has been studied in the recent past. ERX [13] extends ER model so that one can represent a style sheet and a collection of documents conforming to one DTD in ERX model. But order is represented in ERX model by an additional order attribute. Other related work include a mapping from XML schema to an extended UML [4], and a mapping from Object-Role Modeling (ORM) to XML schema [2]. Our approach is different from these approaches; we focus on the new features provided by an XML Schema - element-subelement relationships, new datatypes such as ID or IDREF(S), recursive type definitions, and the property that *XGrammar* is closed under union, and how they are useful to data modeling.

1.3 Outline of the Paper

The remainder of this paper is organized as follows. In Sect. 2, we describe *XGrammar* that we propose as a formalization of XML schemas. In Sect. 3, we describe in detail the main features of *XGrammar* for data modeling. In Sect. 4, we show how to convert an *XGrammar* to EER model, and vice versa. In Sect. 5, an application scenario using the proposed *XGrammar* and EER model is given. Finally, some concluding remarks are followed in Sect. 6.

2 Notation for XML Schemas: *XGrammar*

Recently about a dozen XML schema languages have been proposed. Some proposals aim at full-fledged schema languages while others take a minimalistic approach. Therefore, they are not directly comparable with each other. Nevertheless, we believe it is meaningful to compare the main building blocks of each language. In [10] and [12], present authors analyzed various schema language proposals using comparative analysis and formal language theory and categorized them into different classes.

In this section, we propose a new notation called *XGrammar*. Instead of choosing one XML schema language as the basic data modeling language, we extract the most important features from the proposed XML schema languages and formalize them into *XGrammar*. This is an extension of the regular tree grammar definition in [12] (Def. 24), where we used a six tuple notation to precisely describe content models of XML schema languages. In this paper, we extend this 6-tuple notation with attribute definitions and data types.

Informally, *XGrammar* takes the structural specification feature from DTD and RELAX and the data typing feature from XML-Schema. Therefore, unlike DTD, *XGrammar* can specify the exact types of attributes. Furthermore, attributes of IDREF(S) type can specify which "target" types the current attributes refer to. *XGrammar* is thus our attempt to formalize some of the core ideas found in the various XML schema languages proposed recently. The benefits of a formal description is that it is both concise and precise. From RELAX, we borrow the notion of *tree* and *hedge* types: the values of a tree type are trees and the values of a hedge type are hedges – a sequence of trees (or an ordered list of trees) [11]. Both tree and hedge types are together called regular expression types in [8].

We use G to denote an *XGrammar* and $L(G)$ to denote the language that G generates. We assume the existence of a set $\widehat{N}$ of non-terminal names, a set $\widehat{T}$ of terminal names and a set $\widehat{\tau}$ of atomic data types defined in [3] (e.g., string, integer, etc), including ID and IDREF(S). We use the notations: ϵ denotes the empty string, "+" for the union, "," for the concatenation, "$a^?$" for zero or one occurrence, "a^*" for the Kleene closure, and "a^+" for "a, a^*". Now let us define *XGrammar* formally:

Definition 1 (*XGrammar*) An *XGrammar* is denoted by a 7-tuple $\mathbb{G} = (N_T, N_H, T, S, E, H, A)$, where:

- N_T is a set of non-terminal symbols that are tree types, where $N_T \subseteq \widehat{N}$.
- N_H is a set of non-terminal symbols that are hedge types, where $N_H \subseteq \widehat{N}$. We use N to denote $N_T \cup N_H$. Also, we place the constraint $N_T \cap N_H = \phi$.
- T is a set of terminal symbols, where $T \subseteq \widehat{T}$.
- S is a set of start symbols, where $S \subseteq N$.
- E is a set of element production rules of the form "$X \rightarrow a\ RE$", where $X \in N_T$, $a \in T$, and RE is:

$$RE ::= \epsilon \mid \tau \mid n \mid (RE) \mid RE + RE \mid RE, RE \mid RE^? \mid RE^* \mid RE^+$$

Table 1. An example XML-Schema `library.xsd`.

```
<schema xmlns:t='http://www.w3.org/namespace/'>
 <element name='Library'>
  <complexType>
   <sequence>
    <element ref='t:Book' minOccurs='0' maxOccurs='unbounded'/>
    <element ref='t:Magazine' minOccurs='0' maxOccurs='unbounded'/>
    <element ref='t:Person' minOccurs='0' maxOccurs='unbounded'/>
   </sequence>
  </complexType>
 </element>
 <element name='Book'>
  <complexType>
   <sequence>  <element ref='t:EMPTY'/>  </sequence>
   <attribute name='title' type='string' use='required'/>
   <attribute name='authors' type='IDREFS' use='required'/>
   <attribute name='publicationDate' type='date' use='required'/>
  </complexType>
 </element>
 <element name='Magazine'>
  <complexType>
   <sequence>  <element ref='t:EMPTY'/>  </sequence>
   <attribute name='title' type='string' use='required'/>
   <attribute name='editor' type='IDREF' use='optional'/>
   <attribute name='publicationDate' type='date' use='optional'/>
  </complexType>
 </element>
 <element name='Person'>
  <complexType>
   <sequence>
    <element ref='t:Spouse' minOccurs='0' maxOccurs='1'/>
    <element ref='t:Person' minOccurs='0' maxOccurs='unbounded'/>
   </sequence>
   <attribute name='personID' type='ID' use='required'/>
   <attribute name='name' type='string' use='optional'/>
  </complexType>
 </element>
 <element name='Spouse'> <complexType mixed='true'/> </element>
</schema>
```

where $\tau \in \hat{\tau}$ and $n \in N$. Note that RE is actually a hedge type, but it might not have a name associated with it. In other words, we can have anonymous hedge types not captured by N_H. Our examples will elaborate this point.
- H is a set of hedge production rules of the form "$X \rightarrow RE$", where $X \in N_H$, and RE is the same as the one for E.
- A is a set of attribute production rules of the form "$X \rightarrow a\ RE$", where $X \in N$, $a \in T$, and $RE ::= \epsilon \mid \alpha \mid (RE) \mid RE, RE$, where α is an attribute definition expression defined as:

$$\alpha ::= \begin{cases} \text{``@''}\ a\ [\ \text{``?''}\ ]\ \text{``::''}\ \tau & \text{if } \tau \notin \{\text{IDREF, IDREFS}\} \\ \text{``@''}\ a\ [\ \text{``?''}\ ]\ \text{``::''}\ \tau\ \text{``$\rightsquigarrow$''}\ RE_1 & \text{if } \tau = \text{IDREF} \\ \text{``@''}\ a\ [\ \text{``?''}\ ]\ \text{``::''}\ \tau\ \text{``$\rightsquigarrow$''}\ RE_2 & \text{if } \tau = \text{IDREFS} \end{cases}$$

$RE_1 ::= n \mid (RE_1) \mid RE_1 + RE_1$, where $n \in N_T$
$RE_2 ::= \epsilon \mid n \mid (RE_2) \mid RE_2 + RE_2 \mid RE_2, RE_2 \mid RE_2^? \mid RE_2^* \mid RE_2^+$,
  where $n \in N$

Table 2. An example DTD library.dtd equivalent to library.xsd in Table 1.

```
<!DOCTYPE Library [
  <!ELEMENT Library   (Book*,Magazine*,Person*)>
  <!ELEMENT Book      (EMPTY)>
  <!ATTLIST Book      title   CDATA   #REQUIRED    authors IDREFS  #REQUIRED
                      publicationDate CDATA   #REQUIRED>
  <!ELEMENT Magazine  (EMPTY)>
  <!ATTLIST Magazine  title   CDATA   #REQUIRED    editor  IDREF   #IMPLIED
                      publicationDate CDATA   #IMPLIED>
  <!ELEMENT Person    (Spouse?,Person*)>
  <!ATTLIST Person    personID   ID   #REQUIRED    name    CDATA   #IMPLIED>
  <!ELEMENT Spouse    (#PCDATA)>
]>
```

Table 3. An example XML Document library.xml conforming to schemas defined in Tables 1 and 2.

```
<library>
  <book title="Data Structures and Algorithms" authors="aho hopcroft ullman"
        publicationDate="January, 1983"/>
  <book title="Principles of Compiler Design" authors="aho ullman"
        publicationDate="1979"/>
  <book title="Introduction to Automata Theory" authors="hopcroft ullman"
        publicationDate="1979"/>
  <magazine title="Communication of ACM" editor="aho"/>
  <magazine title="IEEE Comp." editor="ullman" publicationDate="Sep,2000"/>
  <person personID="aho" name="Alfred. V. Aho">
    <spouse>WifeOfAho</spouse>
    <person personID="son1" name="Junior_1 Aho"/>
    <person personID="son2" name="Junior_2 Aho"/>
  </person>
  <person personID="ullman" name="Jeffrey. D. Ullman">
    <spouse>WifeOfUllman</spouse>
  </person>
  <person personID="hopcroft" name="John. E. Hopcroft"/>
</library>
```

For representation, we distinguish attributes from elements in the grammar using "@" as in [6] and specify the type τ of an attribute using "::". A specified attribute is considered mandatory unless qualified by "?". □

Example 1. Consider a scenario of "library" in the real world. Tables 1 and 2 show exemplar schema definitions to model the scenario. Note that not all constraints expressed in Table 1 are expressed in Table 2 due to the insufficient expressive power of DTD. Then, the schema definition can be encoded into XGrammar: $\mathbb{G}_1 = (N_T, \epsilon, T, S, E, \epsilon, A)$, where

$N_T = \{Library, Book, Magazine, Person, Spouse\}$

$T = \{library, book, magazine, person, spouse, title, authors, editor, publicationDate,$
$\quad\quad personID, name\}$

$S = \{Library\}$

$E = \{Library \rightarrow library\ (Book^*, Magazine^*, Person^*), Book \rightarrow book\ (\epsilon),$
$Magazine \rightarrow magazine\ (\epsilon), Person \rightarrow person\ (Spouse^?, Person^*), Spouse \rightarrow$
$spouse\ (string)\}$

$A = \{Library \rightarrow library(\epsilon), Book \rightarrow book\ (@title :: string, @authors :: \texttt{IDREFS} \leadsto$
$Person^+, @publicationDate :: date), Magazine \rightarrow magazine\ (@title :: string,$
$@editor^? :: \texttt{IDREF} \leadsto Person, @publicationDate^? :: date), Person \rightarrow$
$person\ (@personID :: \texttt{ID}, @name^? :: string), Spouse \rightarrow spouse(\epsilon)\}$

Observe that the IDREF(S) attributes identify the target types. For instance, an attribute @*editor* of type IDREF identifies the target type as *Person*. This means that in a document conforming to this schema, the value of the @*editor* attribute should be a valid ID value of an element of type *Person*. In addition, the target type of an IDREFS attribute is specified as a hedge type. For instance, the IDREFS attribute @*authors* of *Book* identifies its target type as $Person^+$, which is an anonymous hedge type. This means that the value of @*authors* should be a list of values that are ID values of *Person*. Table 3 shows an example XML document that conforms to $\mathbb{G}_1$. □

3 Semantic Data Modeling with *XGrammar*

Three main features of *XGrammar* that help to model XML data are as follows:

1. **Ordered binary relationships:** *XGrammar* can represent ordered binary relationships using element-subelement relationships and IDREF(S) attributes. Such relationships occur commonly in real world scenarios. For example, the authors of a book are typically ordered. The EER model can represent ordered binary relationships.
2. **Union types:** The closure properties of the different XML schema language proposals under boolean set operations are studied in [12]. Here, it was shown that (a) proposals such as DTD and XML-Schema are closed under *intersection*, but are not closed under *union* and *difference* operations, and (b) proposals such as RELAX, XDuce and TREX are closed under intersection, union and difference operations. Since *XGrammar* is equivalent to RELAX with respect to its structural expressiveness, *XGrammar* is also closed under all three boolean set operations. Therefore one can define union between any two tree types or hedge types. This is useful for several real-world data integration problems.
For example, we can define one type representing two semantically equivalent but structurally different types. Consider the types $Book1 \rightarrow book(Title, Author^+)$ and $Book2 \rightarrow book(Title, Author^+, Publisher)$. We can take union of these two types, and define the union type as $Book \rightarrow book(Title, Author^+, Publisher?)$. Similarly consider the types $Book \rightarrow book(Title, Author^+, Publisher?)$, and $Magazine(Name, Editor^+)$, we can define the union type as $ReadingMaterial \rightarrow (Book\ +\ Magazine)$.

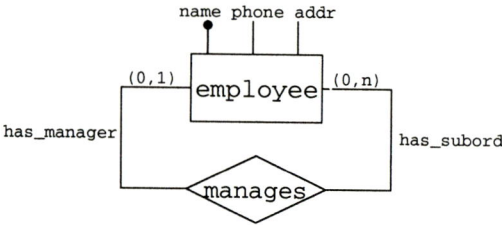

Fig. 2. An example of recursion in ER model.

3. **Recursive types:** *XGrammar* can represent recursive relationship types using recursive type definitions. In $\mathbb{G}_1$ of Example 1, we have a recursive type for *Person* in its element production rule; here the subelements of a *Person* represent the children of that *Person*. Unlike ER model, in general, XML model has two different notions of recursion: *structural* and *semantic* recursions. *XGrammar* can express both using element or attribute production rules, respectively. For instance, consider the classical "employee-manager-subordinate" relationships of ER model in Fig. 2. This model can be best represented by the two DTDs below. DTD (a) forms a recursion *semantically* if the subord attribute is assumed to point to some employee's name attributes, while DTD (b) forms a recursion *structurally* since employee element can contain subord subelement which can in turn contain employee element as child again.

```
// DTD (a)                                    // DTD (b)
<ELEMENT employee EMPTY>                      <ELEMENT employee (subord*)>
<ATTLIST employee                             <ATTLIST employee name  ID    #REQUIRED
         name    ID     #REQUIRED                              phone CDATA #IMPLIED
         phone   CDATA  #IMPLIED                               addr  CDATA #IMPLIED>
         addr    CDATA  #IMPLIED              <ELEMENT subord  (employee)>
         subord  IDREFS #IMPLIED>
```

The two DTDs (a) and (b) can be captured in *XGrammar* differently. Attribute production rule will capture the semantic recursion:

$$A = \{Employee \rightarrow employee\ (@subord^? :: \text{IDREFS} \rightsquigarrow Employee^+)\}$$

while element production rule will capture the structural recursion:

$$E = \{Employee \rightarrow employee\ (Subord^*), Subord \rightarrow subord\ (Employee)\}$$

4 *XGrammar* & EER Model

In this section, we discuss the relationships between *XGrammar* and EER model. Especially, we investigate issues of conversion between the two models.

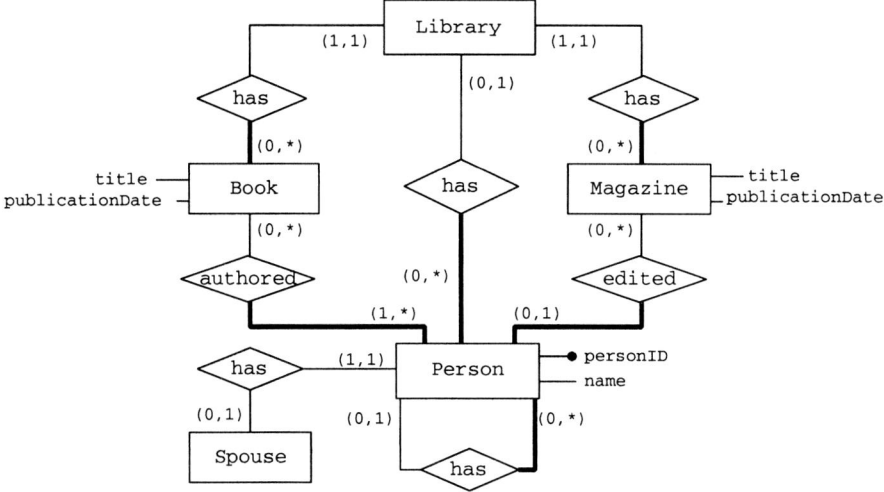

Fig. 3. An EER model representation of *XGrammar* $\mathbb{G}_1$ of Example 1.

4.1 Converting *XGrammar* to EER Model

XGrammar $\mathbb{G}_1$ of Example 1 can be, for instance, converted to EER model as shown in Fig. 3. The different types and production rules are converted as follows:

1. *Tree type:* Every tree type in N_T of *XGrammar* is represented as an entity type. For instance, in $\mathbb{G}_1$ of Example 1, there are five tree types and hence five entity types {*Library, Book, Magazine, Person, Spouse*}.
2. *Element production rule*: For every "child" tree type in the element production rule, a **has** *ordered* relationship is created. The cardinalities of the parent and child types are decided appropriately based on the regular expression operators such as ",", "+", "*", "?". For example, consider the element production rule *Library* → *library* (*Book**, *Magazine**, *Person**). There are three child tree types. Therefore in EER model, this element production rule will be represented as three ordered relationships, given by $Library(1,1) \stackrel{has}{\Longrightarrow} Book(0,*)$, $Library(1,1) \stackrel{has}{\Longrightarrow} Magazine(0,*)$, $Library(0,1) \stackrel{has}{\Longrightarrow} Person(0,*)$. Note that since *Book* and *Magazine* can occur in the document only as child of *Library*, the cardinality of *Library* in these relationships is (1, 1). However, *Person* can occur as child of either *Library* or *Person*. Therefore, the cardinality of *Library* in this relationship is (0, 1).
3. **IDREF** *attribute:* **IDREF** attribute is represented as an *unordered* binary relationship. The cardinality of the type that specifies the **IDREF** attribute in the relationship is (0, *). For identifying the cardinality of the target types, we consider three cases with examples:
   - *Case 1. The target type of an **IDREF** attribute is a union of at least two tree types*: For example, consider the attribute rule of type *X* to specify

@A :: IDREF $\leadsto$ ($B \mid C$). This is represented as two unordered relationships $X(0,*) \xrightarrow{A} B(0,1)$ and $X(0,*) \xrightarrow{A} C(0,1)$. This is irrespective of whether the attribute A is optional or not.
- *Case 2: The target type of an* IDREF *attribute is a single tree type, and this* IDREF *attribute is optional:* For example, consider the attribute @$editor^?$ :: IDREF $\leadsto$ $Person$ for the tree type $Magazine$ in $\mathbb{G}_1$ of Example 1. This is represented as an unordered relationship: $Magazine(0,*) \xrightarrow{edited} Person(0,1)$. Note that the name of the relationship is changed to a verb form (i.e., from "editor" to "edited") for clarity.
- *Case 3: The target type of an* IDREF *attribute is a single tree type, and this* IDREF *attribute is mandatory:* For example, consider the IDREF attribute for tree type X specified as @A :: IDREF $\leadsto$ (B). This is represented as one unordered relationship $X(0,*) \xrightarrow{A} B(1,1)$.

4. IDREFS *attribute:* IDREFS attribute is used to specify *ordered* relationships. As for IDREF attribute, the cardinality of the type that specifies the IDREFS attribute in the relationship is $(0,*)$. For identifying the cardinality of a target type in the relationship, we consider two cases:
   - *Case 1: The* IDREFS *attribute is optional:* For example, consider the attribute rule of type X to specify @$A^?$ :: IDREFS $\leadsto$ B^+. This is represented as $X(0,*) \xRightarrow{A} B(0,*)$. In other words, the minimum cardinality of a target type in the relationship is 0.
   - *Case 2: The* IDREFS *attribute is mandatory:* This is represented as an ordered binary relationship named with the attribute name just like in the previous case. However, the minimum cardinality of a target type need not be 0. For example, consider the attribute specification for the tree type $Book$ in $\mathbb{G}_1$ of Example 1 given by @$Authors$ :: IDREFS $\leadsto$ ($Person^+$). This is represented in the EER diagram as $Book(0,*) \xRightarrow{authored} Person(1,*)$.

The different relationships expressed in $\mathbb{G}_1$ of Example 1 are summarized in Table 4. The reader should observe that what we described above are binary relationships expressed in *XGrammar*. This represents only a subset of the relationships expressible in an *XGrammar*. For example, $\mathbb{G}_1$ of Example 1 specifies other relationships such as "the list of *Magazines* in *Library* occur after the list of *Books* in the *Library*". Such order specifications are outside the scope of this paper and not discussed further.

4.2 Converting EER Model to *XGrammar*

XML schema supports constraints such as key and foreign key constraints. Based on these constraints, we define *"joinable tree types"* – tree types that have a key-foreign key constraint. Joinable tree types are used to represent relationships, similar to key-foreign key constraints in the relational model. The translation of a given EER model to an *XGrammar* is done using the following steps. These steps are summarized in Table 5.

Table 4. The relationships specified by $\mathbb{G}_1$ of Example 1.

Type	Order	Relationships
1:1	-	$\{Spouse(0,1) \stackrel{has}{\Longrightarrow} Person(1,1)\}$
1:n	Ordered	$\{Library(1,1) \stackrel{has}{\Longrightarrow} Book(0,*), Library(1,1) \stackrel{has}{\Longrightarrow} Magazine(0,*),$ $Library(0,1) \stackrel{has}{\Longrightarrow} Person(0,*), Person(0,1) \stackrel{has}{\Longrightarrow} Person(0,*)\}$
n:1	Unordered	$\{Magazine(0,*) \stackrel{edited}{\Longrightarrow} Person(0,1)\}$
n:m	Ordered RHS	$\{Book(0,*) \stackrel{authored}{\Longrightarrow} Person(1,*)\}$

1. Each entity in EER model is translated to a tree type in *XGrammar*. For example, we will have a tree type corresponding to *Book*, a tree type corresponding to *Magazine* etc. Every simple attribute can be translated to an attribute for that tree type in *XGrammar*, a composite attribute can be translated to a subelement of the tree type. In our EER example, we have an entity *Book* with two attributes *name* and *publicationDate*. They are translated to a tree type *Book* with an attribute production rule as *Book* → *book*(@*title*, @*publicationDate*).

2. A 1 : 1 relationship is translated as follows. Consider a relationship: $A(m_1, M_1) \stackrel{R}{\Longrightarrow} B(m_2, M_2)$, where $M_1 = M_2 = 1$.
   - $m_1 = 0$ and $m_2 = 0$: This is represented using two different tree types with IDREF or with foreign key constraints (joinable tree types).
   - $m_1 = 1$ (or similarly $m_2 = 1$): This is represented using an element-subelement relationship, where B is a child of A (or vice versa). If $m_2 = 1$, then the content model of the element production rule for A will specify B, otherwise if $m_2 = 0$, then the content model will specify $B^?$. For example, Fig. 3 has the 1 : 1 relationship $Person(1,1) \stackrel{has}{\Longrightarrow} Spouse(0,1)$. This is represented in the *XGrammar* as an element-subelement relationship, where $Spouse^?$ is a subelement of *Person*. If both $m_1 = 1$ and $m_2 = 1$, then we can also represent this relationship using just one tree type as in the ER-relational conversion [1].

3. A 1 : n relationship is translated as follows.
   - The relationship is *ordered*: We can represent this as an element-subelement relationship, or using IDREFS attributes. The EER diagram of Fig. 3 has four ordered 1 : n relationships. We represent all of them as element-subelement relationships in the *XGrammar*. For example, $Library(1,1) \stackrel{has}{\Longrightarrow} Book(0,*)$ is represented by having $Book^*$ as a subelement of *Library*.
   - The relationship is *unordered*: We can represent this using IDREFS attribute or using joinable tree types. The EER diagram of Fig. 3 has one unordered 1 : n relationship $Magazine(0,*) \stackrel{edited}{\longrightarrow} Person(0,1)$, which is represented by having an IDREF attribute for Magazine as @$editor^?$ :: IDREF $\rightsquigarrow$ *Person*.

Table 5. Representing the different binary relationships in an *XGrammar* to satisfy the goodness criterion.

Relationship Type	Ordered/Unordered	How to represent them
$1:1$	-	{element-subelement, IDREF, joinable tree types}
$1:n$	Ordered	{element-subelement, IDREFS}
$1:n$	Unordered	{IDREF, joinable tree types}
$n:m$	Ordered	{IDREFS}
$n:m$	Unordered	{joinable tree types}

Table 6. The relationships specified by EER diagram of Fig. 4.

Type	Order	Relationships
$1:n$	Ordered	$\{Agency(1,1) \stackrel{funds}{\Longrightarrow} ResearchProject(1,*),$
		$ResearchProject(1,1) \stackrel{produces}{\Longrightarrow} ResearchReport(1,*),$
		$ResearchDB(1,1) \stackrel{has}{\Longrightarrow} ResearchTopic(0,*),$
		$ResearchDB(1,1) \stackrel{has}{\Longrightarrow} Employee(0,*),$
		$ResearchDB(1,1) \stackrel{has}{\Longrightarrow} Agency(0,*)\}$
$n:1$	Unordered	$\{ResearchReport(0,*) \stackrel{addresses}{\longrightarrow} ResearchTopic(0,1),$
		$Employee(0,*) \stackrel{isSupervised}{\longrightarrow} Employee(0,1),$
		$ResearchProject(0,*) \stackrel{IS\_PI}{\longrightarrow} Employee(1,1)\}$
$n:m$	Ordered RHS	$\{ResearchProject(0,*) \stackrel{hasEmployee}{\Longrightarrow} Employee(1,*)\}$

4. A $n:m$ relationship is translated as follows.
   - The relationship is *ordered*: We can represent this using IDREFS attribute. For example, consider the ordered $n:m$ relationship in the EER diagram of Fig. 3, $Book(0,*) \stackrel{authored}{\Longrightarrow} Person(0,*)$. This is represented in *XGrammar* using IDREFS attribute for *Book* as @authors? :: IDREFS $\leadsto Person^+$.
   - The relationship is *unordered*: This is represented using joinable tree types.
5. A recursive relationship is represented either using semantic recursion or structural recursion. The EER diagram has one recursive relationship, $Person(0,1) \stackrel{has}{\Longrightarrow} Person(0,*)$, which is represented using structural recursion in the *XGrammar* by having *Person** as a subelement of *Person*.

5 Application

In this section, we consider a real world example - that of a *Research Projects database*. This example is modified slightly from the one given in [1] (page 49). We illustrate how this is modeled using *XGrammar*. The EER diagram is shown in Fig. 4. To convert EER diagram to *XGrammar*, first introduce a root tree type for the *XGrammar* – ResearchDB. The child elements of the root are the entities

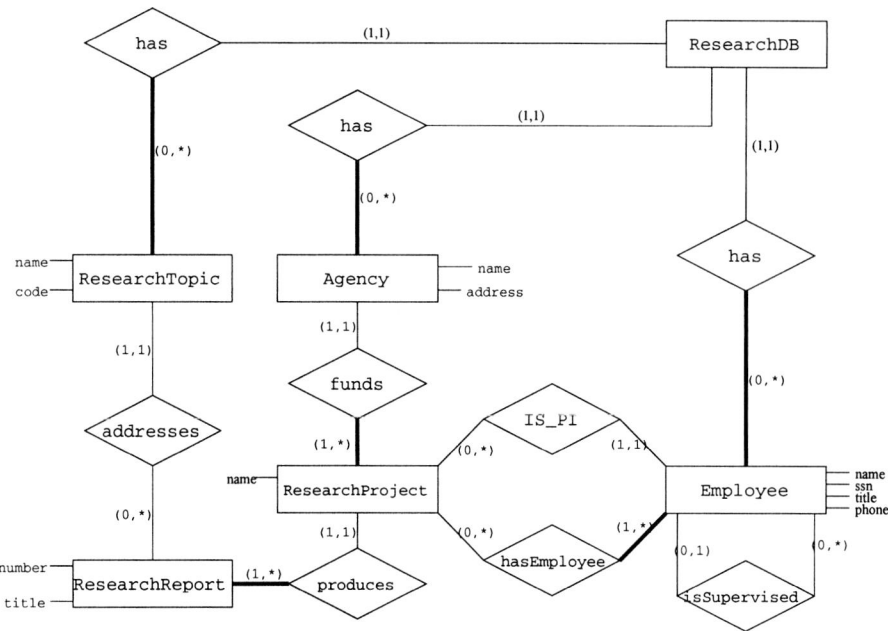

Fig. 4. Application scenario using *XGrammar* and EER model.

shown in EER diagram through **has** relationships from ResearchDB. There are six entities in this EER model - {ResearchDB, ResearchTopic, Agency, Employee, ResearchProject, ResearchReport}. The entity ResearchDB is mapped to the root tree type for *XGrammar*. The relationships in this EER diagram are shown in Table 6. For this example, we can represent all the ordered $1:n$ relationships using element-subelement relationships, the unordered $n:1$ relationships using **IDREF** attribute, and the ordered $n:m$ relationships using **IDREFS** attributes. The *XGrammar* is given by $\mathbb{G}_2 = (N_T, \epsilon, T, S, E, \epsilon, A)$, where

$N_T = \{ResearchDB, Agency, ResearchTopic, Employee, ResearchProject,$
$\quad\quad ResearchReport\}$

$T = \{researchDB, agency, researchTopic, employee, researchProject,$
$\quad\quad researchReport\}$

$S = \{ResearchDB\}$

$E = \{ResearchDB \rightarrow researchDB(Agency^*, ResearchTopic^*, Employee^*),$
$\quad\quad Agency \rightarrow agency(ResearchProject^+), ResearchProject \rightarrow researchProject$
$\quad\quad (ResearchReport^+), Employee \rightarrow employee(\epsilon), ResearchReport \rightarrow$
$\quad\quad researchReport(\epsilon), ResearchTopic \rightarrow researchTopic(\epsilon)\}$

$A = \{ResearchDB \rightarrow researchDB(\epsilon),$
$\quad\quad Agency \rightarrow agency(@name :: string, @address :: string),$
$\quad\quad ResearchTopic \rightarrow researchTopic(@name :: string, @code :: integer),$

$ResearchProject \rightarrow researchProject(@name :: string, @PI :: \text{IDREF} \leadsto$
$Employee, @members :: \text{IDREFS} \leadsto Employee^+),$
$ResearchReport \rightarrow researchReport(@number :: integer, @title :: string,$
$@topic :: \text{IDREF} \leadsto ResearchTopic)$
$Employee \rightarrow employee(@name :: string, @ssn :: integer, @title :: string,$
$@phone :: integer, @supervisor^? :: \text{IDREF} \leadsto Employee)\}$

6 Conclusions

In this paper, we examined several new features provided by XML schemas for data description. In particular, we examined how ordered binary relationships - $1 : n$ (through parent-child relationships and IDREFS attribute) as well as $n : m$ (through IDREFS attribute) can be represented using an XML schema. We also examined the other features provided by XML grammars - representing recursive relationships using recursive type definitions and union types. EER model, conceptualized in the logical design phase, can be mapped on to *XGrammar* (or its equivalent) and, in turn, mapped into other final data models, such as relational data model, or in some cases, the XML data model itself (i.e., data might be stored as XML documents themselves). We believe that work presented in this paper forms a useful contribution to such scenarios.

References

[1] C. Batini, S. Ceri, and S. B. Navathe. *"Conceptual Database Design: An Entity-Relationship Approach"*. The Benjamin/Cummings Pub., 1992.
[2] L. Bird, A. Goodchild, and T. Halpin. "Object Role Modeling and XML-Schema". In *Int'l Conf. on Conceptual Modeling (ER)*, Salt Lake City, UT, Oct. 2000.
[3] P. V. Biron and A. Malhotra (Eds). "XML Schema Part 2: Datatypes". W3C Recommendation, May 2001. http://www.w3.org/TR/xmlschema-2/.
[4] G. Booch, M. Christerson, M. Fuchs, and J. Koistinen. "UML for XML Schema Mapping Specification".
http://www.rational.com/media/uml/resources/media/uml_xmlschema33.pdf.
[5] T. Bray, J. Paoli, and C. M. Sperberg-McQueen (Eds). "Extensible Markup Language (XML) 1.0". W3C Recommendation, Feb. 1998.
http://www.w3.org/TR/1998/REC-xml-19980210.
[6] A. Brown, M. Fuchs, J. Robie, and P. Wadler. "MSL: A Model for W3C XML Schema". In *Int'l World Wide Web Conf. (WWW)*, Hong Kong, May 2001.
[7] P. P. Chen. "The Entity-Relationship Model". *ACM Trans. on Database Systems (TODS)*, 1:9–36, 1976.
[8] H. Hosoya and B. C. Pierce. "XDuce: A Typed XML Processing Language". In *Int'l Workshop on the Web and Databases (WebDB)*, Dallas, TX, May 2000.
[9] ISO/IEC. *"Information Technology – Text and Office Systems – Regular Language Description for XML (RELAX) – Part 1: RELAX Core"*, 2000. DTR 22250-1.
[10] D. Lee and W. W. Chu. "Comparative Analysis of Six XML Schema Languages". *ACM SIGMOD Record*, 29(3):76–87, Sep. 2000.

[11] M. Murata. "Hedge Automata: a Formal Model for XML Schemata". Web page, 2000. http://www.xml.gr.jp/relax/hedge_nice.html.
[12] M. Murata, D. Lee, and M. Mani. "Taxonomy of XML Schema Languages using Formal Language Theory". In *Extreme Markup Languages*, Montreal, Canada, Aug. 2001. http://www.cs.ucla.edu/~dongwon/paper/.
[13] G. Psaila. "ERX: A Data Model for Collections of XML Documents". In *ACM Symp. on Applied Computing (SAC)*, Villa Olmo, Italy, Mar. 2000.
[14] H. S. Thompson, D. Beech, M. Maloney, and N. Mendelsohn (Eds). "XML Schema Part 1: Structures". W3C Recommendation, May 2001. http://www.w3.org/TR/xmlschema-1/.
[15] D. C. Tsichritzis and F. H. Lochovsky. *"Data Models"*. Prentice-Hall, 1982.

Modelling Strategic Actor Relationships to Support Intellectual Property Management

Eric Yu, Lin Liu, Ying Li

Faculty of Information Studies, University of Toronto
{yu, liu, liy}@fis.utoronto.ca

Abstract. In today's increasingly knowledge-intensive economy, patents and other forms of intellectual property mechanisms are widely used to protect inventions, generate revenue, and build strategic alliances. Techniques from conceptual modelling can be used to analyze the structure of knowledge, highlighting crucial entities and relationships. However, to analyze the strategic significance of particular pieces or bodies of knowledge within an organizational and business context, we need an ontology that captures the social and intentional dimensions of knowledge management. In this paper, we outline the use of the *i** strategic actor relationships modelling framework to support IP management. In *i**, actors have goals, and know-how and resources for achieving goals. Patents restrict the use of know-how, thus prompting actors to reposition themselves within a network of dependency relationships. Examples from the e-commerce domain are used to illustrate.

1 Introduction

The value of knowledge is increasingly being recognized in today's knowledge economy and society. In the business arena, how specialized knowledge is created, managed, and used is becoming a crucial factor for success. Conceptual modelling techniques play an important role in managing knowledge in enterprise information systems. As organizations become more complex and dynamic, richer conceptual models are needed to help manage the wider range of enterprise knowledge. Conceptual modelling has focused in the past on static (entities, relationships, states, etc.) and dynamic (flows, transitions, etc.) ontologies. The management of knowledge in a social organizational context requires ontologies that incorporate the intentional and social dimensions [6], so that one can express and reason about motivations and rationales, and capabilities and vulnerabilities of social actors [19, 15].

The management of intellectual property (IP) is an important component of enterprise knowledge management. Patents and other forms of intellectual property mechanisms are used to protect inventions, generate revenue, and build strategic alliances. To manage IP effectively, one needs to understand a wide range of issues from technology innovations to product/service design to competitive strategies. For example:

- What innovative technologies are needed to sustain products and services in my business today and tomorrow?

- Which technologies do I have exclusive rights on, and which ones are owned by other players?
- How does the IP landscape constrain or enable my product and service strategies?
- What options are available to make the best use of IP in a given context, e.g., licensing, alliances, acquisitions, in-house R&D?

These and other issues related to IP management are evolving and expanding rapidly as technological advances continue at a rapid pace, and as various players constantly realign themselves in response. A systematic approach based on conceptual modelling can help manage the complex knowledge needed to support IP management.

This paper outlines an initial attempt to use strategic actor relationships modelling to express some key issues and relationships in IP management, and to illustrate how such models can support analysis and reasoning. We focus on the strategic context of patents. Patents restrict the use of know-how, thus putting constraints on the space of strategic actions that players can adopt. Strategic actors therefore need to assess their means and ends, as well as those of other actors, in seeking favorable positions for themselves within networks of inter-dependencies.

Section 2 briefly reviews the *i** framework, introducing its basic concepts using examples from the e-commerce domain. Section 3 presents a model of the relationships in a typical patent setting. Section 4 considers two examples of the strategic context for IP analysis – business expansion acknowledging patent protection, and the selection of patent-related partners. The impacts of IP on business decision making are explored through *i** modelling. Section 5 discusses our contributions, related work in various areas, as well as future research. The examples are intended for illustrating the modelling framework and are not necessarily accurate reflections of the domain.

2 Strategic Actor Relationships Modelling

Much of conceptual modelling has focused on information content and processes that are to be embedded in automated systems. Such models aim to be precise, detailed, and complete so that the behavior of the target system could be generated. Increasingly, it has been realized that it is equally important to model and analyze the surrounding context of systems so that the right system would be built, and that it would be able to respond to changing needs – the task of requirements engineering. Conceptual modelling techniques therefore need to be extended to encompass systems and world phenomena that are not fully controllable or knowable.

In an agent-oriented modelling approach [15], we treat systems and elements in the environment as only partially knowable and controllable. Agents are autonomous so that their specific actions are ultimately unpredictable. However, in a multi-agent world, the existences of mutual dependencies result in socially constrained behavior. By characterizing the relationships among agents at an intentional level – i.e., in terms of what each agent wants, and how those wants might be satisfied, possibly through other agents – one can express the different ways in which agents could associate with each other, without detailing specific actions and interactions.

This high level of abstraction is quite adequate for supporting the kind of strategic reasoning that is needed for exploring what system to build during the early stages of requirements engineering [16], and offers richer support for reasoning about business processes than conventional (non-intentional) process models [19]. As software agent technologies are beginning to come into the mainstream in network-centric and web-based computing, an agent-oriented modelling paradigm can potentially serve to link all stages of information and knowledge management, from enterprise conception to business process design to system requirements to implementation [7, 3, 20]. This would facilitate business analysis to take advantage of advanced systems technologies, and systems analysis to respond quickly to business level changes.

Intellectual property management is one specialized area of enterprise knowledge management in which the need for strategic modelling and reasoning is quite apparent. An agent-oriented modelling approach offers the potential for systematically relating technology decisions to business design to competitive strategy analysis. In this paper, we explore the use of the *i** strategic actor relationships modelling framework to model and reason about IP management issues.

The *i** framework consists of two kinds of models. The Strategic Dependency model describes the network of intentional relationships among actors. Actors depend on each other for goals to be achieved, tasks to be performed, and resources to be furnished. These dependencies are intentional in that they are based on underlying concepts such as goal, ability, commitment, belief, and so on [17]. The Strategic Rationale model describes and supports the reasoning that each actor has about its relationships with other actors, its alternative means to achieve goals, and how the qualitative expectations of actors are satisficed by these alternatives. Actors in *i** are strategic in that they evaluate their social relationships in terms of opportunities that they offer, and vulnerabilities that they may bring. Strategic actors seek to protect or further their interests.

2.1 The Strategic Dependency Model

Figure 1 shows an example of a Strategic Dependency (SD) model for a buyer-driven e-commerce system. In such a system, the customer depends on a middleman to find a service provider who is willing to accept a price set by the customer. The customer submits a priced request to a middleman. The middleman forwards the request to suppliers. If a supplier decides to accept the request, it makes an agreement with the middleman. The middleman expects the customer to pay for the purchase.

Note that while business processes are often described in terms of sequences of events and actions, what the SD model focuses on are the dependency relationships. In particular, some relationships do not have directly associated actions. In this example, the supplier depends on the middleman to attract more customers, which in turn relies on the customer for loyalty. The customer depends on the supplier for quality service (since the service is coming from the supplier, not from the middleman). Finally, the scheme works only if the prices set by customers are acceptable to suppliers.

A Strategic Dependency (SD) model consists of a set of nodes and links. Each node represents an actor, and each link between two actors indicates that one actor depends on the other for something in order that the former may attain some goal. We call the depending actor the depender, and the actor who is depended upon the dependee. The object around which the dependency relationship centers is called the dependum. By depending on another actor for a dependum, an actor (the depender) is able to achieve goals that it was not able to without the dependency, or not as easily or as well. At the same time, the depender becomes vulnerable. If the dependee fails to deliver the dependum, the depender would be adversely affected in its ability to achieve its goals.

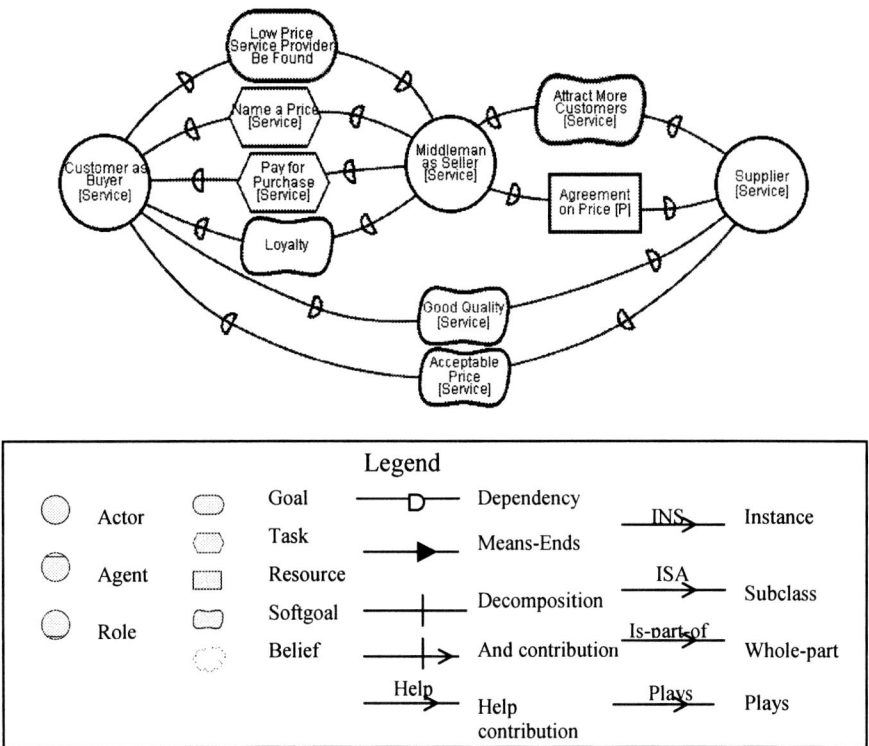

Fig. 1. Strategic Dependency model of a buyer-driven e-commerce system with middleman

The Strategic Dependency model distinguishes among several types of dependencies based on the ontological category of the dependum and the degree of freedom the dependee has when delivering the dependum to the depender. In a *goal dependency*, an actor depends on another to make a condition in the world come true. In Figure 1, the goal dependency **Low Price Service Provider Be Found** from the customer to the middleman means that it is up to the middleman to decide how to find the low price service provider.

In a *task dependency*, an actor depends on another to perform an activity. The activity description specifies a particular course of action. For example, the task dependency **Name A Price [Service]** expresses that the middleman depends on the customer to name his own price for the service in need by specifying the standard procedure for naming a price.

In a *resource dependency*, an actor depends on another for the availability of an entity. The depender takes the availability of the resource to be unproblematic. In Figure 1, the middleman's dependency on the supplier for Agreement on Price is modelled as a resource dependency.

The fourth type of dependency, *softgoal dependency*, is a variant of the first. It is different from a (hard) goal dependency in that there are no a priori, cut-and-dry criteria for what constitutes meeting the goal. The meaning of a softgoal is specified in terms of the methods that are chosen in the course of pursuing the goal. The dependee contributes to the identification of alternatives, but the depender makes the decision. The notion of softgoal allows the model to deal with many of the usually informal concepts. For example, the customer's dependency on the supplier for Good Quality [Service] can be achieved in different ways. The desired degree of how good the quality should be is ultimately decided by the depender.

2.2 The Strategic Rationale Model

The Strategic Rationale (SR) model provides a more detailed level of modelling by looking "inside" actors to model internal intentional relationships. Intentional elements (goals, tasks, resources, and softgoals) appear in SR models not only as external dependencies, but also as internal elements arranged into (mostly hierarchical) structures of means-ends, task-decompositions and contribution relationships.

Figure 2 is a SR model of the buyer-driven e-commerce system with middleman corresponding to Figure 1. In this model, the internal rationales of the customer and the middleman are elaborated. The customer's main goal is that Service Be Purchased [Service]. The goal is parameterized on Service so that the graph may be evaluated differently for different services.

One possible way to accomplish this goal is through the task Purchase By Naming My Own Price [Service]. It is connected to the goal with a *means-ends* link. This task has two sub-elements connected to it through *decomposition* links – the sub-task Name A Price [Service], and the sub-goal Low Price Service Provider Be Found. The purchase task is achievable only if all its sub-elements are achievable.

Naming one's own price contributes positively (Help) to the buyer's softgoal of Low Price, but negatively (Hurt) to Flexibility [Purchasing] because preferences about schedule, choice of airline, etc., could not be accommodated.

The buyer-driven system may be contrasted with the more familiar seller-driven system in Figure 3. Here, the Be Middleman goal is addressed by an alternate task Sell in Seller Driven Style. By doing this, the middleman is more profitable as he could earn more revenue by maximizing the margin. Though the higher price might impact Customer Attraction negatively (Hurt contribution from Sell at Supplier's Price [Service] to Customer Attraction), the middleman could regain some customer attraction by Provide Good Purchasing Environment. At the same time, the customer can enjoy more Flexibility [Purchasing] and is more likely to get Overall Satisfaction.

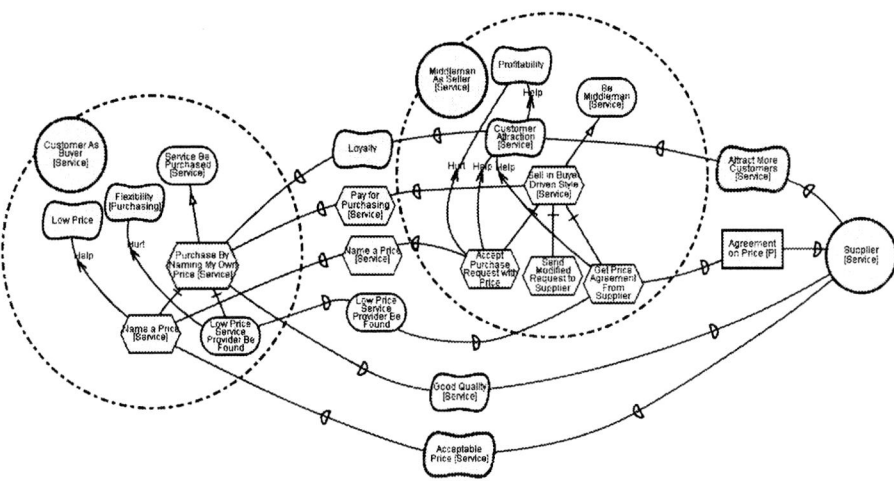

Fig. 2. Strategic Rationale model of a buyer-driven e-commerce system with middleman

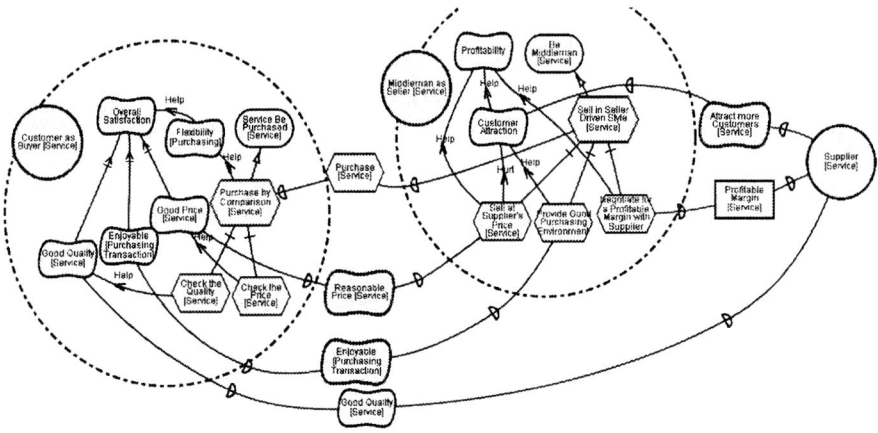

Fig. 3. Strategic Rationale model of a seller-driven e-commerce system with middleman

An interactive qualitative reasoning process [19] is used to evaluate whether an intentional element (goal, task, resource, or softgoal) is viable or not (e.g., whether a softgoal is sufficiently met). In the reasoning process, a semi-automated labeling algorithm propagates a series of labels through the graphs. The propagation depends on the type of link. For example, the positive contribution link types for softgoals are **Help** (positive but not by itself sufficient to meet the higher goal), **Make** (positive & sufficient) and **Some+** (positive in unknown degree). The corresponding negative types are **Hurt**, **Break** and **Some-**. **And** means if all subgoals are met, then the higher goal will be sufficiently met. **Or** means the higher goal will be sufficiently met if any of its subgoals are met.

In *i**, the term *actor* is used to refer generically to any unit to which intentional dependencies can be ascribed. An *agent* is an actor with concrete, physical manifestations, such as a human individual or an actual organization. A *role* is an abstract characterization of the behavior of a social actor within some specialized context or domain of endeavor.

3 Modelling for IP Management

Intellectual property includes patents, trademarks, copyrights and trade secrets. We will use patents to illustrate our modelling approach.

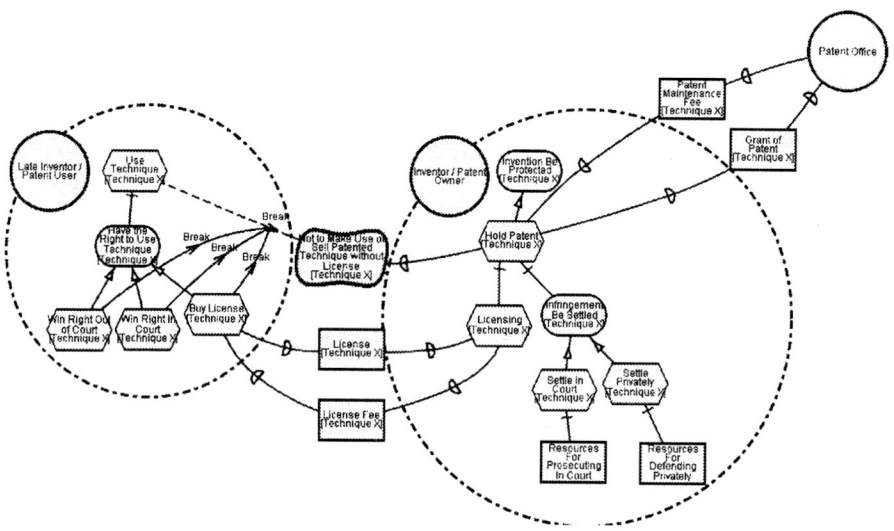

Fig. 4. A simplified generic IP management model

Figure 4 provides a model showing some key relationships surrounding a patent. The inventor of Technique X has the goal that the invention be protected. One way to achieve the goal is to hold a patent on the invention. The effect of the patent is represented as a softgoal dependency with the inventor/patent owner as depender. The patent owner depends on others **Not To Make, Use Or Sell The Patented Technique Without License**. Representing the patent as a softgoal reflects its disputable nature, requiring argumentation (possibly in court) to support its effectiveness. When someone other than the patent owner uses technique X (or a close resemblance), this dependency is violated. This is represented by the **Break** contribution link towards the softgoal. The dotted line notation indicates that this is a side effect arising from the "late inventor's" decision to use technique X. The task **Use Technique** now incurs a sub-goal **Have The Right To Use Technique**. This sub-goal can be met by any of three alternatives – **Buy License, Win Right in Court** or **Win Right Out of Court**. All of these are parameterized on [Technique X]. Each of these is sufficient to overcome the infringement conflict between the patent owner and the patent user – hence the **Break** contributions towards the dotted line **Break**.

This model illustrates the strategic nature of IP management reasoning and action. While there may be social constraints and even legal sanctions on agent behavior, opportunistic agents can choose to violate them and risk the consequences. The patent user may choose different actions depending on its assessments of its own strategic position and the patent owner's, e.g., requisite resources for prosecuting or defending an infringement.

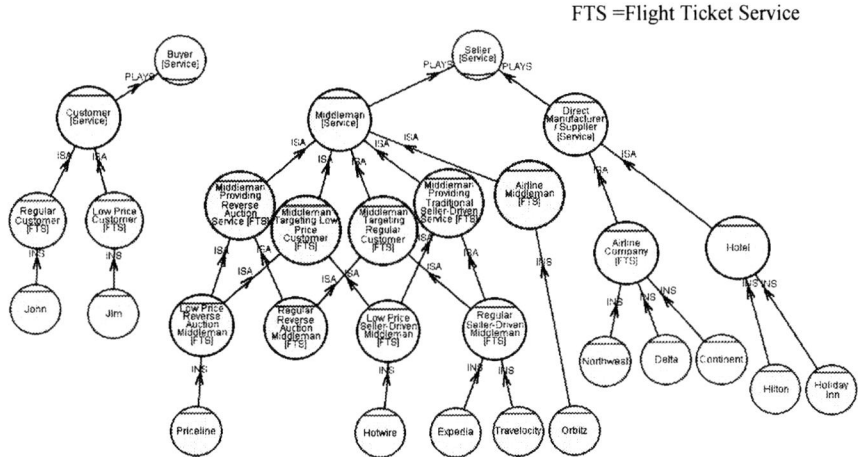

Fig. 5. Some classes of actors in the travel e-business domain

This basic pattern of relationships may appear in various contexts in which IP and potential infringements may occur. To place IP within its broader context (as in Figure 5), one needs to ask a wide range of questions such as:
- Who are the major players in the business domain?
- What kinds of relationships exist among them?
- What are the business objectives and criteria of success for these players?
- What are the alternative business processes/methods or technologies used in this industry? How are these alternatives serving the business objectives and the quality expectations of players? What are the essential sub-processes/components to implement these alternatives?
- What patents or other IP exist within the domain? Who owns them? Who depends on them?
- Are there any infringements on the IP rights? How are they likely to be settled?
- Should a new innovation be patented or kept as a trade secret? Is the innovation likely to be granted a patent?

The proposed modelling approach can help address these questions systematically. The next section considers two examples of modelling and reasoning in particular settings.

4 Strategic Issues for IP Management

In this section, we use the online travel booking industry to illustrate strategic issues for IP management. Major products and services provided in this industry are airline ticket sales, hotel reservations, and car rentals. The main players used in our examples are Expedia (www.expedia.com), Travelocity (www.travelocity.com), Hotwire (www.hotwire.com), Priceline (www.priceline.com) and Orbitz (www.orbitz.com). A summary of the major actors is shown in Figure 5.

4.1 Business Expansion Acknowledging Patent Protection

This section considers the strategic reasoning of a company wishing to adopt a new business method but is blocked by a patent.

Travelocity is an online travel booking service. It started with a seller-driven system targeted at regular customers. To expand its business, Travelocity would like to target low price customers as well. However, because Travelocity is aware that Priceline is holding an effective patent on its business method, that patent serves as a constraint on Travelocity's further expansion. The situation is depicted in Figure 6. The reasoning of Travelocity is shown as a Strategic Rationale model. Goals and their alternatives are shown on the left side whereas quality criteria are positioned on the right side of the SR model. The top part of the figure shows the major kinds of roles and agents in the online travel industry, and how Priceline and Travelocity might encroach on each other's territory.

In examining the SR model in Figure 6, we see that Travelocity has the main business goal of **Goods/Services Be Sold Online** (upper left side of the SR model). There are three means to this end: **Sell To Regular Customer; Sell To Low Price Customer; Sell To Both Regular And Low Price Customer**. To **Sell To Both Regular And Low Price Customer**, one of the subgoals is **Low Price Customer Be Attracted**. This goal can be met by **Develop New Technique In House** or by **Use Existing Technique To Attract Customers**. The subgoal of **Use Existing Technique** is **Existing Technique Be Available**. Three alternative ways to achieve this goal include **Buy License From Patent Owner, Form Alliance With Patent Owner**, and **Use Existing Technique Without License [Name Your Price]**.

As in Figure 4 of Section 3, the effect of holding a patent is represented as a softgoal dependency from patent owner to patent user **Not To Make, Use Or Sell Patented Technique Without License** (middle right side of the model). In this case, the fact that Priceline holds a patent on **Name Your Price** technique constrains the freedom of action that Travelocity has, because the alternative of **Use Existing Technique Without License [Name Your Price] Breaks** the dependency link from Priceline on others **Not To Make, Use Or Sell Without License [Name Your Price]**. Since Travelocity is aware that **Priceline Owns An Effective Patent [Name Your Price]** (expressed by a *belief* in the model), this belief of Travelocity confirms the **Break** link.

The alternative **Buy License** costs more and is not necessarily effective in competing with Expedia (Travelocity's major competitor). **Form Alliance** contributes negatively (**Some-**) to **Brand Dominance** of Travelocity, but **HELPs Low Cost** and aids in (Some+) Minimize Competitor Customer Base. Through alliance, Travelocity could also form more open and reciprocal relationships with Priceline [8]. Therefore, the alternative of Form Alliance is a better choice.

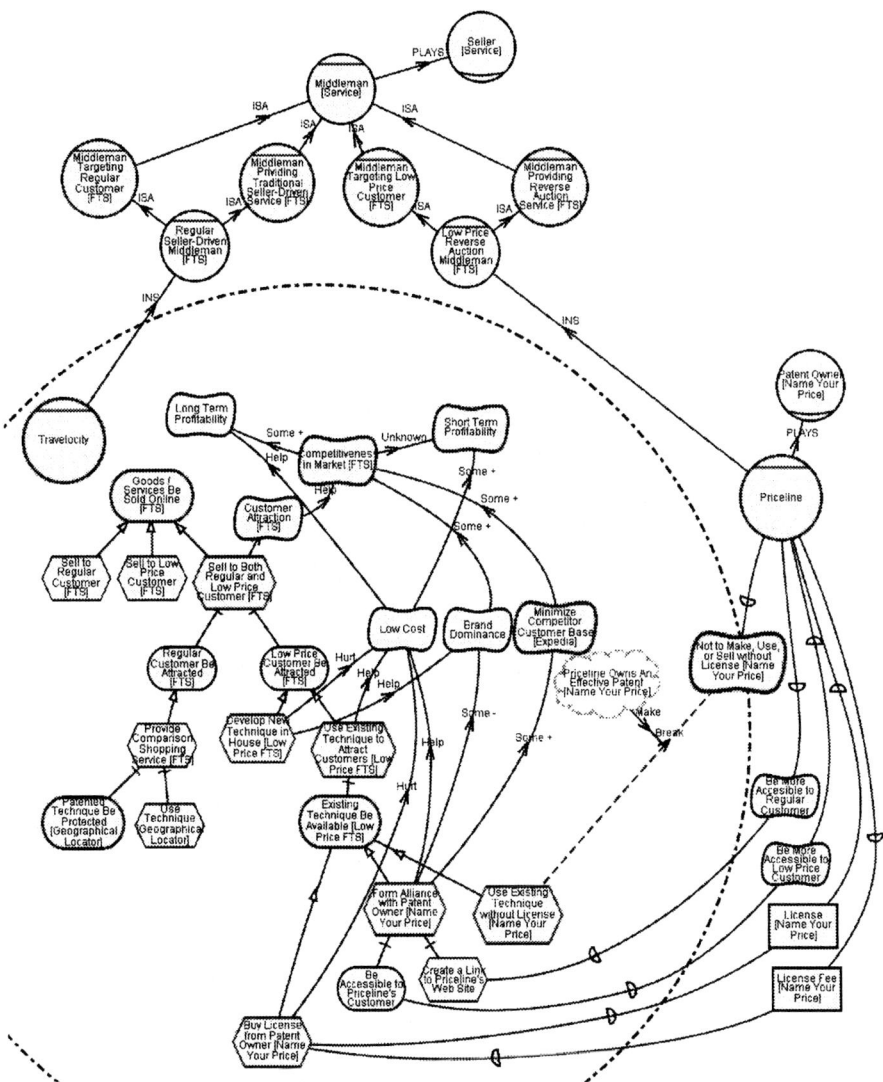

Fig. 6. Reasoning behind business expansion acknowledging patent protection

From this model we can see that *i** modelling technique enables methodical consideration of goals and how they can be met. Business objectives can be systematically refined into tasks which may contain further subgoals and subtasks. Evaluation of alternative ways to achieve a goal is realized through qualitative contributions to softgoals. Agent and role concepts are also beneficial in reflecting the actors' positions in the industry and in identifying potential relationships between the actors.

The picture would be different, if Travelocity takes a different route. For example, it could use Priceline's technique without license because of disbelief in the effectiveness of Priceline's patent. Conflict will arise from the actors' contradictory beliefs and there will be a need to resolve that conflict. **Settle In Court** or **Settle Privately** are two ways of resolving the conflict [14] (as in Figure 4). The two alternatives have different implications on each actor's goals, which need to be evaluated based on their respective contributions.

4.2 Patent Related Partnerships

Now we consider IP related decisions in the context of overall business objectives. The model in Figure 7 highlights the refinement of softgoals from higher level to lower level, and the reasoning for making choices among alternative options based on both strategic dependency relationships with other actors, and contributions to softgoals from alternative options.

Orbitz is an online travel middleman founded by five airline companies. Its major service is comparison shopping for airline tickets targeted towards regular customers. In order to expand the market, Orbitz could decide to provide low price flight ticket service to price sensitive customers. Figure 7 presents how i^* modelling can support Orbitz's decision making among alternative ways of providing low price ticket service.

The top part of the model shows the agents and roles of the actors at issue. Orbitz is an alliance founded by airline companies. It is categorized as a special middleman called airline middleman who depends on airline companies for investment and is depended upon by airline companies to **Attract More Customers**. In this case, it plays more of a seller's role than a supplier's role.

The model shows a SR for Orbitz and dependencies for Priceline and Hotwire. In the SR part for Orbitz, softgoals (positioned at the top of the SR) are developed in a systematic way to depict the progress from high level goals to low level goals. Only the most relevant softgoals in this example are presented to simplify the model. The highest level softgoal is **Profitability**. It is further developed into **Short-term Profitability** and **Long Term Profitability**. **Minimize Cost** and **Minimize Business Risk** are lower level softgoals to fulfill **Short-term Profitability**. **Competitiveness** is one lower level softgoal for **Long Term Profitability**. **Market Advantage** and **Brand Dominance** are softgoals to accomplish **Competitiveness** of the firm's business.

The model shows three alternative ways of providing low price ticket service (positioned at the bottom of the SR model for Orbitz): **Form Partnership with [Priceline]**, **Buy License [Name Your Price]** from Priceline, and **Form Partnership with [Hotwire]**. Partnership here implies a degree of ownership and usually means both parties invest in a new company and provides support for the new company.

In order to make decisions among the three alternatives, we need to evaluate their different contributions to softgoals as shown in the model as well as the opportunities or vulnerabilities arising from the dependency relationships with other actors. **Form Partnership with [Priceline]** contributes positively to **Minimize Cost** and **Market**

Advantage, but negatively to Minimize Business Risk and Brand Dominance. Buy License [Name Your Price] from Priceline contributes positively to Minimize Business Risk and Brand Dominance, but negatively to Minimize Cost. Form Partnership with [Hotwire] contributes positively to Minimize Cost, Minimize Business Risk and Market Advantage, but negatively to Brand Dominance.

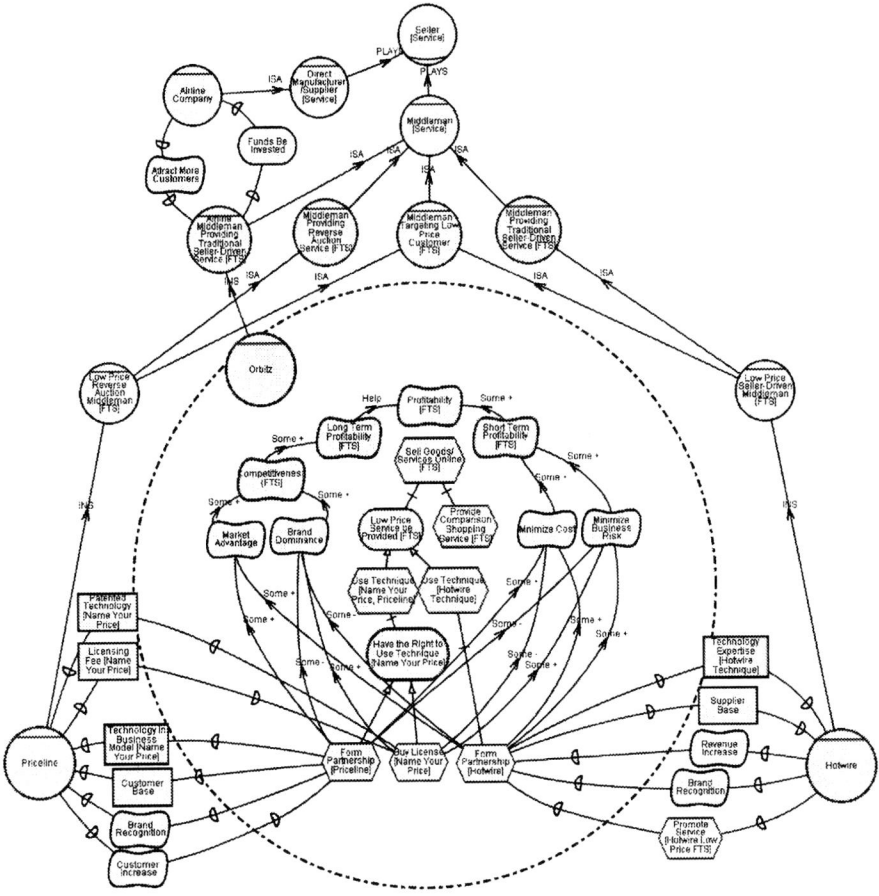

Fig. 7. Patent related partnerships and alliance

Comparing the dependency relationships (located on the lower left and right side of the model), we can see that Orbitz has more important dependencies on Priceline than the other way around through establishing partnership with Priceline. Therefore, it is difficult and uncertain for Orbitz to enforce the dependency relationships between Orbitz and Priceline. On the other hand, establishing partnership with Hotwire puts Orbitz at an advantage since Hotwire depends to a great extent on Orbitz for **Revenue Increase** and **Brand Recognition** while Orbitz's dependencies on Hotwire are not as important.

After evaluating the three alternatives based on their contributions to softgoals and strategic dependency relationships, one could conclude that establishing partnership with Hotwire is a better choice. This example illustrates the need to assess the viability of dependencies and how they contribute to meeting strategic goals.

5 Discussion and Conclusion

We have outlined an approach to modelling and analyzing IP management issues. The approach is based on an intentional and social ontology that is centered around strategic actor relationships. This ontology allows us to go beyond entity relationships and mechanistic behavior, to deal with the opportunistic behavior of strategic actors. Interdependencies among actors place constraints on their freedom of action. Nevertheless, constraints can be violated due to agent autonomy (unlike in mechanistic systems) as in patent infringement. Strategic actors seek to achieve goals (hard and soft) by exploring and evaluating alternatives, taking into account the opportunities and vulnerabilities arising from various dependency relationships, as illustrated in the patent licensing and alliance partnering examples.

Our approach is complementary to existing frameworks and techniques for IP management. Recent approaches have emphasized systematic IP management processes [12, 13] and analysis, particularly the quantification of economic value of intangible assets and intellectual property [11]. There is also increasing use of computational techniques, e.g., patent database search and retrieval, and cluster analysis to determine distribution of patents among subject areas [9]. Our approach emphasizes the systematic analysis of relationships among strategic actors by extending conceptual modelling techniques. It supports the exploration and management of structural alternatives, based on a qualitative style of reasoning, thus complementing the quantitative orientation of recent IP analysis techniques.

IP management is increasingly connected with other activities in enterprise management [9]. The strategic modelling approach provides a way of linking IP analysis to business strategy analysis and technology analysis. The recent trend towards the patenting of software and business processes and methods makes IP management a direct concern for information systems as well. A strategic conceptual modelling approach can thus provide a unifying framework for enterprise information systems, supporting decision making and the management of change across technical system development, business development, and IP management.

In information systems and software engineering research, enterprise modelling has been of interest, often in connection with requirements engineering. Goal-oriented approaches have been used in this context, and agents or actors are often part of the modelling ontology [4, 1, 10, 2, 5]. However, the *i** approach is distinctive in its treatment of agents/actors as being strategic [15], and thus readily adaptable to the IP analysis domain illustrated in this paper. A related technique was used earlier to model security and trust in a multi-agent context [18].

While this paper has outlined some basic modelling concepts, much remains to be done. Methodologies are needed to guide the development of the models, to help verification and validation, to discover constraints and side effects, and to provide criteria for completeness and adequacy. Other forms of analysis, e.g., scenario-based analysis, should also be explored. How the strategic analysis of roles leads to policies on roles (e.g. obligations, permissions, and prohibitions) and to behavioral specification (e.g. in UML) needs to be investigated.

There is much potential in the synergy between strategic modelling and the foundational principles in conceptual modelling. For example, in analyzing the content of intellectual properties, one would like to model the inter-relatedness (similarities and differences) among their subject matters. The interaction between intentional concepts and relationships (e.g., strategic actors, intentional dependencies) and non-intentional ones (e.g., specialization, instantiation, aggregation, time, etc.) need to be detailed. Libraries of reusable knowledge about classes of strategic agents and roles, and common patterns of relationships, would be very helpful during modelling and analysis. Knowledge-based techniques and tools are needed to support scalability. These are topics of ongoing research.

Acknowledgements

Financial support from the Bell University Labs, Communications and Information Technology Ontario, and the Natural Sciences and Engineering Research Council of Canada is gratefully acknowledged.

References

1. Bubenko, J. jr., Brash D. and Stirna J., EKD USER GUIDE. Institutionen för Data och Systemvetenskap, Stockholm Universitet, 1998. Also Available at: www.dsv.su.se/~js/ekd-user-guide.html.
2. Gans, G., M. Jarke, S. Kethers, G. Lakemayer, E. Ellrich, C. Funken. Requirements Modelling for Organization Networks: A (Dis-)Trust –Based Approach, in Int. Symp. Requirements Engineering, 2001.
3. Perini, A., P. Bresciani, F. Giunchiglia, P. Giorgini, J. Mylopoulos. A Knowledge Level Software Engineering Methodology for Agent Oriented Programming. Proceedings of the Fifth International Conference on Autonomous Agents, Montreal, Canada, 28 May - 1 June, 2001.
4. Kavakli,Vagelio and Pericles Loucopoulos. Goal-Driven Business Process Analysis Application in Electricity Deregulation. Information Systems, 24(3): 187-207, 1999.
5. Lamsweerde, Axel van. Requirements Engineering in Year 2000 – A Research Perspective, in Proceeding of 22nd International Conference on Software Engineering(ICSE 2000), Limerick, ACM Press, 2000. Also available at: //ftp.info.ucl.ac.be/pub/publi/2 000/icse2000-avl.pdf.
6. Mylopoulos, John. Information Modelling in the Time of the Revolution, Information Systems, 23(3/4): 127-155, 1998.
7. Mylopoulos, John and Jalson Castro. Tropos: A Framework for Requirements-Driven Software Development, In Information Systems Engineering: State of the Art and Research Themes, J. Brinkkemper and A. Solvberg (eds.), Lecture Notes in Computer Science, Springer-Verlag, pp. 261-273, June 2000.
8. Priceline.com Incorporated. Priceline.com, Travelocity.com Marketing Alliance Launches, Priceline.com News Release, April 10, 2000. Also available at: http://www.priceline.com/.

9. Rivette, K. G. and David Kline. Rembrandts in the Attic, Harvard Business School Press, Boston, Massachusetts, USA, 2000.
10. Rolland, Colette, C. Souveyet, and C.B. Achour. Guiding Goal Modelling Using Scenarios, IEEE Transactions on Software Engineering, 24(12): 1055 –1071, 1998.
11. Smith, Gordon V. and Russell L. Parr. Valuation of Intellectual Property and Intangible Assets, John Wiley & Sons Inc., New York, USA, 2000.
12. Sullivan, Patrick H. Profiting from intellectual capital: extracting value from innovation, John Wiley & Sons Inc., New York, USA, 1998.
13. Sullivan, Patrick H. Value Driven Intellectual Capital: How to Convert Intangible Corporate Assets Into Market Value. John Wiley & Sons, Inc., New York, USA, 2000.
14. Tessler, J. Expedia. Priceline settle suit. Mercury News, Jan. 9, 2001. Also available at: http://www0.mercurycenter.com/svtech/news/indepth/docs/price011001.htm.
15. Yu, Eric. Agent Orientation as a Modelling Paradigm, Wirtschaftsinformatik, 43(2): 123-132, April 2001.
16. Yu, Eric. Towards Modelling and Reasoning Support for Early-Phase Requirements Engineering, in *Proc. 3rd IEEE Int. Symp. On Requirements Engineering (RE'97)*, Annapolis, Maryland, USA, January 1997.
17. Yu, Eric. Modelling Strategic Relationships for Process Reengineering, Ph.D. thesis, also *Tech. Report DKBS-TR-94-6*, Dept. of Computer Science, University of Toronto, 1995.
18. Yu, Eric and Lin Liu. Modelling Trust in the i^* Strategic Actors Framework, in *Proceeding of 3rd Workshop on Deception, Fraud, and Trust in Agent Societies*, Barcelona, Catalonia, Spain, June 3-7, 2000, pp.137-147.
19. Yu, Eric and John Mylopoulos. From E-R to 'A-R' – Modelling Strategic Relationships for Business Process Reengineering, Int. Journal of Intelligent and Cooperative Information Systems, 4(2&3): 125-144, 1995. An earlier version appeared in *Proceedings of ER'94*.
20. Yu, Eric, John Mylopoulos and Yves. Lespérance. AI Models for Business Process Reengineering, IEEE Expert, 11(4): 16-23, 1996.

SiteLang: Conceptual Modeling of Internet Sites

Bernhard Thalheim and Antje Düsterhöft

Computer Science Institute, Brandenburg University of Technology at Cottbus,
03013 Cottbus, FRG
{thalheim|duest}@informatik.tu-cottbus.de

Abstract. Internet information services are developed everywhere. Such services include content generation and functionality support which has to be modeled in a consistent way. Within our projects we developed a methodology resulting in a language *SiteLang* which allows specification of information services based on the concepts of the story and interaction spaces as well as media objects.
The specification can be automatically mapped to implementations.

1 Introduction

Nowadays, 'internet' is one of the main buzzwords in journals and newspapers. However, to become a vital and fruitful source for information presentation, extraction, acquisition and maintenance, concepts have to be developed which allow flexible and adaptable services. Fundamental design concepts are required but still missing.

1.1 Variety of Internet Sites

Internet sites differ in their scopes, audiences, intentions, aims, themes and goals. There are six general categories of sites[ScT00] which usually are not separated but mixed within one site. We use the categorization pattern
  (from, what, to (2), whom, scenario type).

E-business sites ($B^{\mathcal{P}}2A^{buy}$, $B^{\mathcal{P}}2B^{buy}$, $B^{\mathcal{P}}2C^{buy}$, $A^{\mathcal{I}}2C^{buy}$, $C^{\mathcal{P}}2C^{buy}$)
support advertisement and sale of products ($^{\mathcal{P}}$) or information ($^{\mathcal{I}}$) by business or administration to business (B), administration (A) or customers(C) and are based on buying scenarios(^{buy});

Edutainment (learning) sites ($B^{\mathcal{K}}2C^{learn}$, $C^{\mathcal{K}}2C^{learn}$) support life-long learning of easy-to-grasp and edited knowledge ($^{\mathcal{K}}$) and are based on pedagogical scenarios (^{learn});

Information sites ($B^{\mathcal{I}}2V^{inform}$, $A^{\mathcal{I}}2V^{inform}$, $C^{\mathcal{I}}2V^{inform}$) provide all kinds of information, news or knowledge as a service to a certain community or just visitors (V) and are based on information supply scenarios (^{inform});

Community (group) sites ($G2G^{act}$, $G2V^{inform,act}$) support a well-defined group (G) of users with specific information depending on the scenarios which are specific for actions (^{act}) within this community;

Identity (personal) sites ($P^{\mathcal{I}}2V^{attend}$) present and advertise a virtual abstract person (P) (company, association, club or private person) in dependence on the mission or (corporate) identity and are based on presentation scenarios (^{attend});

Entertainment (fan) sites ($B^{\mathcal{F}}2V^{act}$, $V^{\mathcal{F}}2V^{act}$) such as games, game advices, hobbies, humor sites provide just fun ($^{\mathcal{F}}$) with associated information and are based on acting (^{act}) of users.

We are interested in **information-intensive sites which need a sophisticated database support** and which are based on a variety of various stories of their use. For instance, a city site can be based on $(A,G)^{\mathcal{I}}2(V,C,A,B)^{inform}$-scenarios.

1.2 Problems in Large Information-Intensive Sites

Internet information services have to cope with a broad variety of problems beside information presentation, information generation and graphics or multimedia design:

Personalization of services depending on user needs and semantics;
Adaptation to the environment currently in use (from WAP to browsers);
High usability also for large sites supporting a variety of use;
Various kinds of sites are mixed within one site;
Coping with change of underlying data in a consistent form.

At the same time we observe challenges which are hard to meet:

Full flexibility of site's scenarios;
Support of tracing for all users actions;
Push-up content just-in-time depending on actual requirements and demand;
Transactional semantics cannot be used for most of the actions of users.

1.3 Theoretical and Technical Approaches Used

Recent conference series such as CMWWW, Hypertext, SAC, WebDB, WebNet or WWWW have shown a lot of research in this area. The large research has let to a number of interesting approaches, e.g. [MMA99, CFP99, RSL00, GSV00]. These approaches have been summarized, extended and generalized in [ScT00].

There are some approaches which might be adopted to the development of internet sites. *Workflow* approaches try currently to cover the entire behavior of systems. Wegner's *interaction machines* [GST00] can be used for formal treatment of information services. Semantics of information services can be based on abstract state machines which enable in reasoning on reliability, consistency, liveness [Tha00']. This semantics neatly fits into the *statechart approach*. User interface and interaction modeling has achieved the maturity for utilization within information services [Lew00].

Internet site development can be based on a number of theories such as entity-relationship theory [Tha00], codesign of structuring, functionality and interaction [Tha00], abstract state machines [GuM97], theory of interaction and story spaces [Sri01], theory of media objects [FOS00], and abstraction layering of systems development [Tha00]

1.4 Overview on the Paper

This paper gives an introduction into our methodology of modeling internet applications resulting in the Cottbus internet site development language (*SiteLang*). The language has an operational semantics based on entity-relationship structuring and abstract state machines. It allows specification of entire websites, i.e. of structuring (structure, static integrity constraints), behavior (processes and dynamic semantics), information support (views, units and containers) and of the interaction and story space (scenes, media objects and dialogue steps). The methodology supports applications in different environments, e.g. internet websites, WAP technology, or TV channels. *SiteLang* has been developed in the cooperation of the Cottbus team (see acknowledgement) and based on components developed by the team members. The theoretical background of this work generalizes the approaches of [FOS00, Tha00].

2 Site Specification

The aim of specification of large, information-intensive websites is to develop websites which are generatable on the basis of the specification, which are error-prone and which are simple to change. Site specification might be rather complex. For this reason we prefer the following modeling concepts:

Stories are collected into the story space. The story space describes the set of all possible intended interactions of actors with the system.

Scenarios are used to describe a specific utilization of the website by an actor at a given moment of time. We might have a large variety of scenarios. For this reason, scenarios need to be integrated into the story space.

Scenes are macro-steps within a scenario. They involve a number of actors in various roles, rights and occasions. They are supported by media objects.

Dialogue steps describe specific actions of enabled actors which act in specific context. Dialogue steps are supporting different scenes. Any scene has a dialogue expression expressing the dialogue workflow.

Media objects describe the 'adornment' of a scene similar to the movie or drama production.

Each of the concepts has a specific representation formalism defined in the description language SiteLang and will be illustrated in the next parts.

2.1 Story and Scenario Specification

Interaction description can be based on notions developed in linguistics, in movie business or for the description of graphical animations. We use the aids, concepts and experiences for acquiring an adequate conceptual design. The *story* of interaction with the information system is the intrigue or plot of a narrative work or an account of events. Stories can be played in different *scenarios*. The term scenario in the context of information systems stands for the integrated behavioral contents of the interaction with the information system, i.e. what kind of events the information system will consume and what actions will be triggered as a results. Scenarios are separated into dialogues. A *dialogue* is - in its widest sense - the recorded conversation of two or more persons, especially as an element of drama or fiction. In a literary form, it is a carefully organized exposition, by means of intended conversation, of contrasting attitudes.

The story space can be modeled by many-dimensional (multi-layered) graphs [ScT00]:

Story-space(Site) = ({ scene } , E , λ, κ)
    transitions in $E \subseteq$ { scenes } × { scenes }
    λ : { scene } → sceneDescription
    κ : E → transitionDescription .

The function λ is described in detail in the next subsection. Each scene is marked by its identifier. It is associated with a media object, with a set of involved actors, the context of the scene, the applicable representation styles, and a dialogue step expression for the specification of the scene.

The function κ is used for the adornment of transitions by the events which allow to move from one scene to another by interacting of actors. A transition may be blocked until a certain post condition is valid for the acceptance of the completion of the corresponding scene. A transition may be used if a condition is valid for the states of the system. Thus, we define

transitionDescription $\subseteq$
    (events $\cup$ activities) × actors × preConds × postConds ×
    priorities × frequencies × repetition rates

Whenever a scenario is running a certain state of the systems may be associated with the scenario. This state might be changed during the scenario, e.g., on the basis of input information provided by the actor or by temporary information used for recording actions of the actor.

A *scenario* is a run through a system by a cooperating set of actors. A scenario may be cyclic or completely sequential as displayed in Figure 1. A scenario is composed of scenes which are discussed below. We model the order of scenes on scenarios by *event sequences*. Each scene belongs to a general activity. Each scenario has its history which can be accumulated and used for the representation of the *history* of the part of the scenario visited so far. This history is used for the *escort information* [FST98] attached to the media objects of the scenes of the scenario.

We distinguish between the *abstract scenario* and the *runtime scenario*. The later extends the specification of abstract scenarios by instantiation of parameters according to the concrete runtime history, according to the users acting currently in the scenario, and by the environment (channel, technical equipment) currently used.

main story (for example as a sequence)
scenario (run through story space) can or cannot use side paths

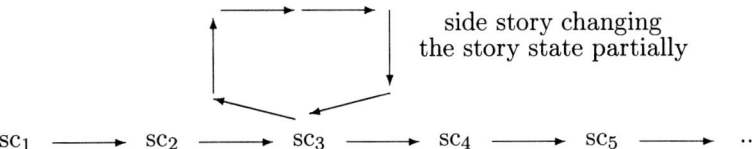
side story changing
the story state partially

Fig. 1. Story Space Specification Based on Scenarios

The abstract scenario specification consists of

1. dialogue scenes representing actions to be performed for a specific task and dialogue steps for representation of an episode,
2. actors with information need and interaction requirements,
3. media object satisfying interaction requirements and information need,
4. description of the intention of the dialogue scenes and steps which are consistent with the goals according the mission and outcome of the step and with the occasions depending on the aim,
5. context of the dialogue scenes and steps which are consistent with tasks and the history, with particular and environment according to the occasion.

The abstract scenarios are integrated into the story space. An example of the story space of city information systems is the following brief description of the www.cottbus.de story space:
Entry { Business { Portrait[1] | Technology Region | Real Estate
　　| Environment | Fairs, Exhibitions, Events[1] | Projects | Traffic[1] }
　| Culture & Tourism { Portrait | Tourist Service Center
　　| Calendar of Events | Eating & Dining
　　| Spare time, Relaxation, Entertainment | Sport | Traffic[2] }
　| Inhabitants { Political life | Town management | Guide for inhabitants
　　| Education | Social life and Associations | Traffic } }
For instance, we identified more than 30 scenarios for city information sites:
- *tourist content, e.g., inhabitants permanently living in the town, inhabitants temporarily living in the town, short-term tourist, business man on short term trip, vacationist planing a trip for more than 5 days, teenager with uncertain wishes, senior with profile of interest, visitor on week-end trip, visitor of highlights, festivals;*
- *official content, e.g., inhabitant on search through directory of public authority, inhabitant on search for emergency cases, inhabitant orienting before applying in public offices, inhabitant interested in problems of city management;*
- *business content, e.g., investor considering engagement in the area.*
In order to handle this variety we used the trick to interview the personnel currently providing the service outside the web area.

Due to this large variety of scenarios we integrate scenarios and stories to *story trees or graphs* for navigation, usage pattern, etc. We use approaches of case-based reasoning and decision theory. A composition of scenarios in information sites is displayed in Figure 2. We represent scenes by frame boxes and transitions with corresponding events by oval boxes.

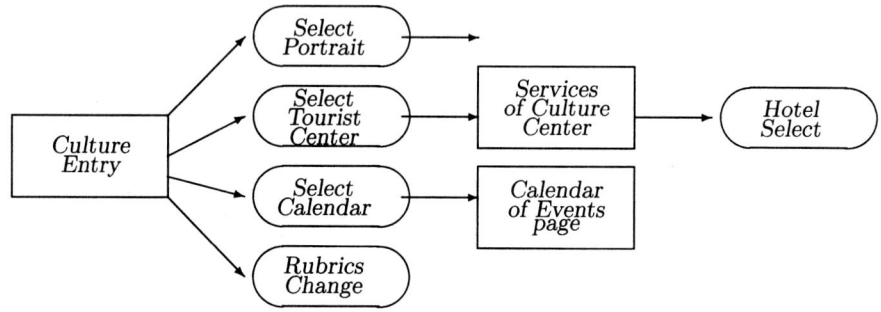

Fig. 2. Integration of some Tourist Scenarios into a Tourist Story

2.2 Scenes

Scenes are specified on the basis of the following specification frame:
    Scene = (Scene-ID
              DialogueStepExpression
              MediaObject
              Actors
                    ActorID
                    Right
                    Tasks
                        Assigned
                        Roles
            Representation (styles, defaults, emphasis, ...)
            Context (equipment, channel, particular))

The scene identification is the conceptual identification of the scene. It is extended by a runtime identification in order to distinguish scenes, to record the communication channel and specific communication restrictions.

The *scene* of an abstract scenario is associated with a consistent *expression of dialogue steps* which are considered in detail in the next subsection.

A scene is supported by *media objects* which are discussed in subsection 3.2. Media objects can be parameterized. Typical parameters are the representation style, the actor frame, and the context frame. Therefore we distinguish between media objects and *runtime media objects* which are send to the actor in a concrete runtime.

Furthermore, *involved actors* are specified in dependence on their profiles, tasks assigned to them , their access and manipulation rights, and their roles to be taken during visiting the scene. This specification is based on [Alt00] and similar to profiles of actors in information systems.

It is our aim to specify generic scenes. Thus, we add the *representation styles* which can be applied to the media object of the scene. Representation depends on the equipment of the actor. In the city site projects, we have experienced with different representation styles: internet display with high-speed channel, internet-display with medium speed display (default style), videotext and WAP display. For instance, for videotext any graphical information is cut out or replaced by textual information.

Finally, the *context of access* is specified. Access determines the display facilities. Channels can be of high or low speed. The particular of using a scene by an actor depends on the scenario history.

2.3 Dialogue Step Specification

Dialogue steps are the elementary units of internet sites. They are used to represent the basic state transformations triggered by actors. The distinction between dialogue scenes and dialogue steps is not strict but depends on the application. We use media objects for scenes. Dialogue steps use media objects or parts of them. In some applications we might use scenes consisting of one dialogue step. In this case we can integrate the dialogue step specification directly into the scene specification.

Dialogue steps can be represented by tables, *e.g. the dialogue steps of an actor A in a community service:*

step name	on event	precond	then with unit	using processes	let manipulation	by actor	accept on
registration	clickReg(A)	¬ member(A) ∧ permission(A)	member-ship_choices	collect-_Member_Data(A)	insert (member, A)	A	payment(A) = ok
with-drawal	clickWDraw(A)	member(A)	memberData(A)	collect-_reason(A)	delete(member,A)∧ send-_Message(A, Withdraw)	A	commit(A,Withdraw)

Based on the properties of the actions we conclude, for instance, that after withdrawal a previous member cannot participate in the discussions in the community.

The table frame we have used is called task property frame in [Pae98]. A task property frame is defined by a task name, reasons for task involvement, an aim, a postcondition (enabled next activities), the information from the database, the information for the database, the resources (actor, resources, partner), and a starting situation (precondition, activity, priority, frequency, repetition rate).

We have chosen the frames above instead of the ECA frame which is used for rule triggering systems because of the necessity to be as flexible as possible in the specification. The integration of post-conditions into the pre-conditions of the next dialogue steps is possible whenever the dialogue step has only one output or the post-conditions are identical for all incoming dialogue steps. Also, the trigger framework is too weak and contradictory [Tha00].

Dialogue scenes are represented by frame boxes. We represent dialogue steps by ellipses. The transitions among dialogue steps are represented by curves. Thus, we obtain the graphical representations displayed in Figure 3. The additional information attached to dialogue steps can be omitted whenever we want to have a schema surveyable.

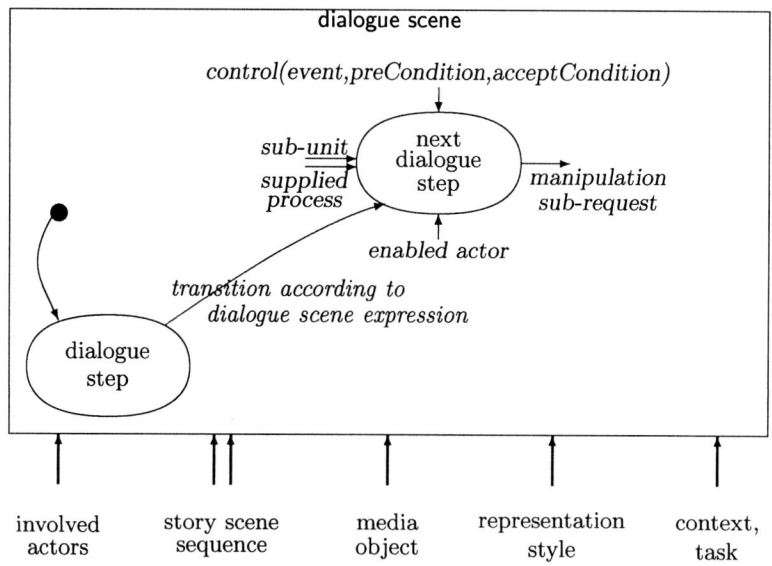

Fig. 3. Representation of Dialogue Steps within a Dialogue Scene

We adopt the graphical notation developed for statecharts, e.g., the default start step of a scene is denoted by a solid circle, the end state by a solid circle surrounded by an empty circle, the history entry into a scene is denoted by an 'H' surrounded by an empty circle. Furthermore, we can adopt refinement and clustering, concurrency, delays and time-outs, transient states, event priorities and parameterized states.

The preconditions can specified on the basis integrity constraint pattern [Tha00]: condition, localization (local restrictions, navigation, etc.), validity condition, exception condition, enforcement pattern, conditional operation (for example, synchronization conditions). Further, the precondition can extended by additional context restrictions. The postcondition is used for description of acceptance conditions. If those are invalid the entire dialogue step is not accepted.

Search is a very general functionality of a site. The search can be extended to booking. Thus, we obtain:

- Search patterns depending on information needs and actors, integration with browsing, search iterations;
- Search input: keywords, alternative terms, misspelling, multilingual, natural language searches, text entry support, spelling-reduced searches, fuzzy for-

mulation, modes of searching, clear search options, support for judgement, information retrieval techniques;
- Representation of search results: prioritizing, clustering, navigation support, feedback always or not;
- AI techniques: mining, discovery, concept hierarchies, information structuring, agents, uncertainty, incompleteness, heuristics;
- Search style: search without spelling, scoped searches, expression logics (and, or, NOT), buttons, search capabilities.

This frame is supported by the scene in Figure 4. The entry dialogue step enables in a number of choices such as search via categories (depending on the categories specified for events, restaurants, hotels) or properties (date, time, location, etc.), search via the map and locations, search via direct targeted input or search via full display. On the map several locations are noted. So the user can select those for targeted input. There are also points of interest which might be used for targeted search. If the actor however chooses the full display option then the clarification step allows to restrict the results of the search step by step. At each step the actor can leave the scene. Thus, each step might be the end step. By default, we assume this behavior. Defaults are not displayed. If the actor

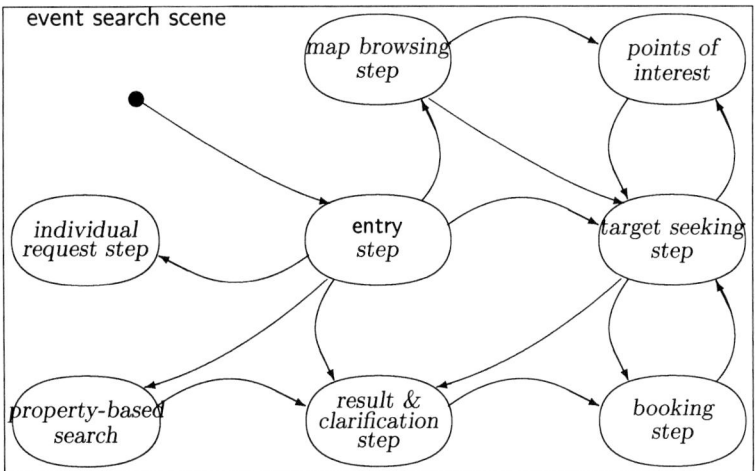

Fig. 4. Dialogue Steps for Event etc. Search

is coming from the area and made identifiable for the system then the booking dialogue step can be used after successful search. In this case, the actor is allowed to make a booking (with billing) or to ask for a ticket reservation (for example, for the theater). In some search scenes we allow also individual requests. For instance, actors accessing the hotel information scenario might be interested in specific offers such as long term conditions, group service, special tariffs etc. Therefore, we added the individual request dialogue step to the scene above.

The presentation of search results depends on the scene, the restrictions the actor made for the scope of the search. For instance, in the hotel search scene we used the following presentation structure:

```
hotelObject = (identification(name, hotelObjects's link,
    area (in raw map)), rooms (# per category),
    prices (range per category), equipment (icon-based))
hotelObject's link = additional (address, contact info, picture(s),
    video, map (with different travel details), travel info,
      location of closest places of interest, distance info)
    + reservation connection
```

3 Site Implementation

3.1 The Onion Approach

Layering of applications is one of the general approaches used in Computer Science. We observe that website functionality and content may be layered as well. On the outer layer, the presentation facilities may be introduced. Typical functions are style and context functions. Containers are used to ship the information and the functionality provided by the web engine. Their functionality is described in [FST98]. Containers contain information units which in general are views enriched by functions for operating on the views. Views may be provide information to the dialogue or may be used for updating the database. Further, views may be materialized. If they are materialized then the view handler provides an automatic refreshment support. Thus, we can use the onion system architecture displayed in Figure 5.

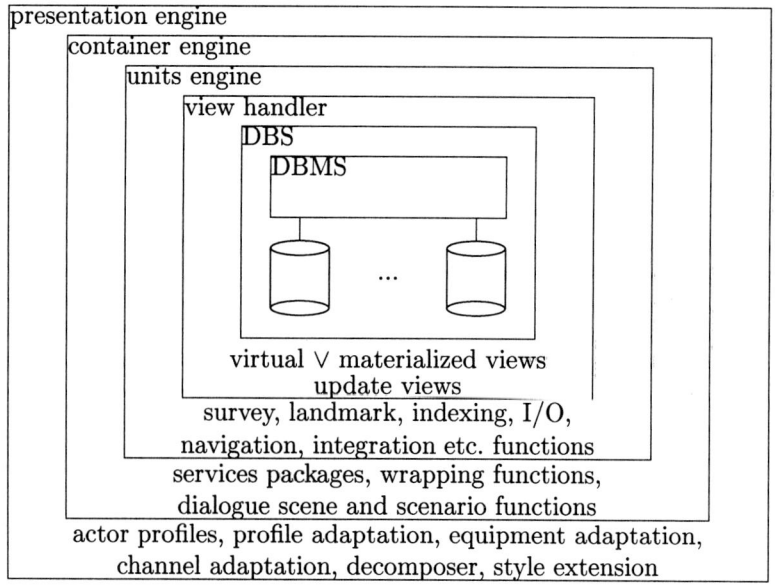

Fig. 5. The Onion Approach to Stepwise Generation of Sites

3.2 The DBS Functionality Behind

In [FST98] the codesign approach displayed in Figure 6 has been developed. This approach has been generalized to media objects. Media objects consist of *abstract containers, supplied DBMS processes* and *database manipulations requests*. Basic media objects [FOS00] are characterized by syntactic expressions, have a semantical meaning and are used within a certain pragmatical framework.

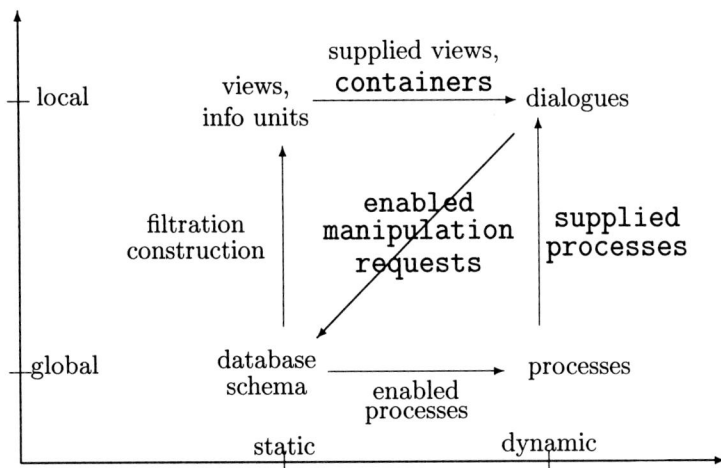

Fig. 6. Information Services Codesign: Data and Process Flow Perspective

During runtime, the media object is extended by specific *escort information* [FST98]. This escort information is represented for user support. It allows the user to see the history of steps performed before being in the current state. Escort information is further generated from the story space. In this case a user is informed on alternative paths which could be used to reach the given scene and which might be used for backtracking from the current scene.

For the generation of media objects and their composition on the basis of information units we extend the classical SQL frame to the frame

    generate MAPPING : VARS → STRUCTURE
        from VIEWS
        where SELECTION CONDITION
        represent using STYLE GUIDE
                & ABSTRACTION
        browsing definition CONDITION
                & NAVIGATION

Views and therefore the media object may have hidden parameters (for instance, EventID) which are not visible to the actor. They can be parameterized by variables (for instance, :Today). For media objects we reuse ideas developed for OLAP technology [Tha00]: *Views on ER schemata* (abstraction on schemata (aggregation, scoping, ...), versions), *variations of generation functions display with canonical functionality* (drill-down, roll-up, rotate, pivoting, push, pull, dimension, aggregation), *using generic evaluation functions and models, implicit incorporation of hierarchies* and *implicit incorporation of time, space,* ....

Scenes are dynamically adapted to the environment, to the specific profile of the actor and extended by the escort information.

The specific representation is selected among the possible representations of the media object. The context of the media object also depends on the scenario history at runtime. Thus, we extend the context of the container by the runtime history depending on the scenario chosen by the actor acting on the site. In order to handle the dynamic changes and the history we record the control information in the scene control component. Finally, the specific actor might obtain during the scenario an identity or other specific information such as products selected for later purchase. This information is stored in the component for scene actors.

For instance, given an internet channel with medium capacity. The entry page of a city information sites may be composed by a star graphics, extended by additional information such as town maps, imprint and contact information. For example, in this case the www.cottbus.de site has the following entry scene specification.

```
Add (Add (Add (ComposeGen ( genFrame, ComposeStar(t1, (t2, t3, t4), ov)),
    NavQuick (n1, n2, n3), style2 ), Text (entry), style1),
    NavQuick (townMaps) + imprint + cont1, derivStruct(site), style2)
```

The corresponding media object which is the central object of the entry page uses the following queries and navigation elements:

```
t1 = emblem(pyramid)          ....
t3 = RollNav( emblem(tourist), tourPage, repres1)
n1 = Sub( Query( calend (today), order1), repres2)
entry = "Known as the city ... <a> Energie Cottbus </a> ..."
cont1 = ComposeSub( email, guestsBook, seq1)
```

The event database is used by different parts of the website. Some of the events are accessed frequently. Thus, we use materialization of components of sites. Pages are
– either *static*, i.e. they have been developed once and stay for a longer period,
– *pseudo static*, i.e. generated and transformed to static pages whenever an update of the corresponding data is made, or are
– *fully-dynamic*, i.e. are generated during processing the request of an actor.

3.3 The XML-Perl Functionality Behind

The language Perl neatly support the onion approach since we can use Perl for conservative expansion of views to units, of units to containers, of containers to presentation objects. Further, the database connectivity is entirely supported. This onion generation mechanism is used too for the expansion of XML specifications to page objects.

4 Conclusion

In this paper we presented the Website specification language *Site Lang*. This language is based on a layering of website specification into the story space, dialogue scenes and dialogue steps. A scenario is in this case a run through the scenes and the story space.

We are concentrated on information-intensive and large websites. Small websites may not need any specification languages. Websites which are not information-intensive can be developed in a similar fashion. The *SiteLang* does support website specification for e-commerce sites, for information sites, for community sites and for learning (edutainment) sites. Identity sites are usually smaller if they do not include specifics of e-commerce or community sites. Also, entertainment sites are not within the scope of this paper since quality criteria to be applied to such sites [ScT00] are not oriented towards content but rather towards presentation and multimedia objects.

The aim of this paper has also been the brief discussion of the theoretical background of *SiteLang*. This language is based on an integration of five approaches:

- extended entity-relationship models [Tha00] with components enabling in integrated modeling of structuring, functionality and interaction;
- the theory of media objects [FOS00] specifically developed for website specification;
- investigations for developing a theory of interaction and story spaces [GST00];
- the codesign methodology for an integrated consistent specification of structuring, functionality and interaction of information-intensive applications [Tha00];
- the abstract state machines providing an operational semantics for *SiteLang* which can be executed and checked [Tha01] and which enables in proof and derivation of site properties.

Acknowledgement

The research presented and summarized in this paper is based on the work of the internet services Cottbusnet team at Cottbus Tech. The team has developed so far city information systems for 18 larger German towns (our main reference is the site www.cottbus.de), for 5 German regions, for 2 community sites, for one edutainment, B2C, B2B, B2A and A2C sites, respectively, with more than 35.000 pages overall. We are very thankful to PhD and Master students handling the implementations and developments within these projects, and furthermore to our commercial partners supporting and running the implementations. Furthermore, the research represented here is based on a tight collaboration with K.-D. Schewe [ScT00].

References

[ABS00] S. Abiteboul, P. Buneman, D. Suciu, Data on the web. Morgan Kaufmann Publs., San Francisco, 1998.

[Alt00] M. Altus, Decision support for conceptual database design based on the evidence theory - an intelligent dialogue interface for conceptual database design. PhD, BTU Cottbus, Cottbus, 2000.

[CFP99] S. Ceri, P. Fraternali, S. Paraboschi, Data-driven, one-to-one web site generation for data-intensive applications. VLDB 1999, 615-626.

[FeT99] T. Feyer, B. Thalheim, E/R based scenario modeling for rapid prototyping of web information services. Proc. Workshops on Advances in Conceptual Modeling, LNCS 1727, Springer, 1999, 243-263.

[FLe98] J. Fleming, Web navigation - Designing the user experience. O'Reilly, Sebastopol, 1998.

[FOS00] T. Feyer, K. Odey, K.-D. Schewe, B. Thalheim, Design of data-intensive webbased information services. Proc. 1st Intern. Conf. on Web Information Systems Engineering, WISE'2000, Hong Kong (China), June 19-21, 2000.

[FST98] T. Feyer, K.-D. Schewe, B. Thalheim, Conceptual design and development of information services. Proc. ER'98, LNCS 1507, Springer 1998, 7-20

[GST00] D. Goldin, S. Srinivasa, B. Thalheim, IS = DBS + interaction - towards principles of information systems. Proc. ER'2000, LNCS 1920, Springer, Berlin, 2000, 140-153.

[GSV00] N. Güell, D. Schwabe, P. Vilain, Modeling interactions and navigation in web applications. ER Workshops 2000, LNCS 1921, Springer, 2000, 115-127.

[GuM97] Gurevich, Y. May, 1997 Draft of the ASM Guide. Technical Report, Univ. of Michigan EECS Department, CSE-TR-336-97.

[Lew00] J. Lewerenz, Human-computer interaction in heterogeneous and dynamic environments: A framework for its conceptual modelling and automatic customization. PhD, BTU Cottbus, Cottbus, 2000.

[MMA99] G. Mecca, P. Merialdo, P. Atzeni, ARANEUS in the Era of XML. IEEE Data Engineering Bullettin, Special Issue on XML, September, 1999.

[Pae98] B. Paech, Aufgabenorientierte Softwareentwicklung. Springer, Berlin, 1998.

[RSL00] G. Rossi, D. Schwabe, F. Lyardet, User interface patterns for hypermedia application. Advanced Visual Interfaces 2000, 136-142.

[ScT00] K.-D. Schewe, B. Thalheim, Conceptual development of internet sites. Fullday tutorial, ER'2000, Salt Lake City, 2000, 470 slides, 10 demos.

[Sri01] S. Srinivasa, A calculus of fixpoints for characterizing interactive behavior of information systems. PhD, BTU Cottbus, Cottbus, 2001.

[Tha00] B. Thalheim, Entity-relationship modeling - Fundamentals of database technology. Springer, Berlin, 2000.

[Tha00'] B. Thalheim, Readings in fundamentals of interaction in information systems. Reprint, BTU-Cottbus (2000) (http://www.informatik.tu-cottbus.de/~thalheim).

[Tha01] B. Thalheim, ASM specification of internet information services. Proc. Eurocast2001, Las Palmas, 2001, 301-304.

A Frame Work for Modeling Electronic Contracts

Kamalakar Karlapalem[+], Ajay R. Dani[*], and P. Radha Krishna[*]

[+]IIIT, Hyderabad, India.
[*]Institute for Development and Research in Banking Technology, Hyderabad, India.
kamal@iiit.net, {ardani, prkrishna}@idrbt.ac.in

Abstract. A contract is an agreement between two or more parties to create business relations or legal obligations between them. A contract will define the set of activities to be performed by parties satisfying a set of terms and conditions (clauses). An e-contract is a contract modeled, specified executed, controlled and monitored by a software system. Typically, a workflow management system is used for e-contract management. E-contracts are complex inter related workflows that have to be specified carefully to satisfy the contract requirements. Most workflow models do not have the capabilities to handle the complexities of these interrelationships. That is, an e-contract does not adhere to activity/task oriented workflow process, thus generating a gap between a conceptual model of e-contract and workflow. Therefore, there is a need for a modeling framework to conceptualize e-contracts and model the complexity of interrelationships. In this paper, we present a framework for conceptually modeling e-contracts (using ER-R data model) and a methodology to translate an e-contract to a workflow that can be executed by a workflow management system.

1. Introduction

A contract is an agreement between two or more parties to create business relations or legal obligations between them. There are several stages involved in a contract such as exchange of information and negotiation, before the execution of the contract. A contract will define a set of activities to be performed by parties satisfying a set of terms and conditions (clauses). Thus, a contract consists of several entities such as parties, activities, and clauses. Each of the activities may involve a considerable period of time for its execution. The terminology of activities is according to the concept of activities as promoted by activity management system [KYH1995]. In rest of the paper, we mean an activity to be a workflow and an activity consists of set of tasks.

In recent years, the penetration of Information Technology into real-life applications has transformed the way business is being transacted. One such application is Electronic Contracts, which made business simple by effectively modeling and managing the processes/tasks involved. An electronic contract (e-contract) is a contract modeled, specified, executed, controlled and monitored by a software system. In e-contracts, all (or a number of) activities are carried out electronically and, thus, overcome the delays involved in the manual system and also personnel biases. In the literature, considerable work has been carried out on the legal aspects and negotiation stages of e-contracts [GSG2000][KS1998]. In this paper, our focus is to conceptualize and specify e-contracts.

A workflow is concerned with the automation of procedures where documents, information or tasks are passed between participants according to a defined set of rules to achieve, or contribute to, an overall business goal [WfMC1995]. The execution of an e-contract involves several processes/tasks and monitoring activities, which can be represented as workflows. However an e-contract involves the complex inter/intra relationships among workflows in a contract. An e-contract can be seen as a *global manifestation over a set of inter-related workflows*. Most workflow models do not have the capabilities to provide this global view of an e-contract arising out of these relationships. Due to this, the workflows for an e-contract must be carefully specified and related to meet the contract requirements. Therefore, in this paper, we present a framework for conceptually modeling e-contracts (using ER-R data model [TNCK1991]) and a methodology to translate an e-contract to a workflow that can be executed by a workflow management system. In our approach, the Entity-Relationship (ER) model is extended to model the e-contracts. We call the resulting model as the ER^{EC} model.

The rest of the paper is organized as follows. In section 2, we introduce e-contracts and Meta-Schemas for e-contracts and workflow. Section 3 presents an ER^{EC} Model for E-Contracts. In section 4, we describe a methodology to translate an e-contract to a workflow. Section 5 discusses related work, and section 6 concludes this paper.

2. E-contracts

In the present work, we consider a typical e-contract consisting of parties, activities and clauses. E-contract and contract are used synonymously in the rest of the paper.

Two or more parties are involved in performing activities of a contract. A contract has a set of clauses. Each party has a well-defined role in a contract, which is specified in the contract document. For example, in a purchase of goods contract, one party is a buyer and there can be many sellers. Even though a contract can have many entities involved, a contract in its simplest form can be characterized as an ordered list consisting of {P, A, CL}, where P = {P_1, P_2, . . ., P_n} is the set of parties, n ≥ 2; A is the set of activities to be performed by different parties; CL is the set of clauses.

A contract will specify how the contract will be executed, the restrictions on the parties involved, etc. Unless it is specified in the contract it can be assumed that

1. One or more parties involved in the contract can enter into a subcontract. A sub contract itself is a contract, thus may have its own parties, activities and clauses. Thus, contracts may be nested.
2. A clause can refer to another clause in the list of clauses of a contract.
3. A contract will have list of activities to be performed, some of the activities may be nested. That is, an activity is composed of other activities. Some activities may be carried out in parallel, and some sequentially.

The contract will be for a specified time period or duration, which will be defined in the contract. This duration will define the active life stage of the contract. It is expected to last till the contract is completed. A contract completion may not occur when some clauses beyond completion of activities need to be adhered to, for example, maintenance and warranty period. The activities will be linked with parties, and each party will have to carry out one or more activities. The clauses in the contract may list out the activities, however the activities may not be linked with clauses. For example, "70% of the payment is made after the systems received and the remaining amount will be paid in two installments after six months and one year respectively from the date of installation". In this example, the clauses are linked with payment activity, but not vice-versa. This helps us to have a library of common activities that cater to various clauses in the contracts.

2.1. E-contract Meta-schema

Figure 1 shows the meta-schema for a contract using the ER-R model. In addition to entities and relationships, and their attributes, it models exceptions as external rules using ER-R model. Exceptions in e-contracts will play a major role when a process/task deviates from a clause. The exceptions are represented as parallelograms (as rules). For the sake of simplicity, the attributes of entities and relationships are not shown in the ER-R diagram.

The meta-schema of e-contract allows us to capture the conceptual level details about the elements involved in a contract. The entities in the meta-schema are parties, activities, clauses, budget, roles and payments (see Figure 1). Note that this meta-schema also facilitates easier modeling of e-contracts by being a template (see Section 3.2) that can be instantiated for specific applications.

Subcontract is a weak entity of Contract. Though, a subcontract previously exists as a contract, it can also be a part of the main contract for an application. The entities parties, activities and clauses form a relationship with a contract. Activities have relationship with Synchronization, so that there is coordination among the activities during their process. **Clauses** in a contract are similar to constraints (or Conditions/Rules) in ER-R model. Since a clause can refer another clause, the Clause entity in the meta-schema is self-related. The relationship Lists between Clauses and Activities models the activities in a clause.

Each **party** plays some role in a contract. The many-to-many relationship between Parties and Roles in the meta-schema represents that one party can have many roles, and different parties can play the same role. **Payments** is an important entity in e-contracts. Payment transactions are always between the parties, and the payment is made to payee based on the clauses defined in the contract. The Payments in the meta-schema have a ternary relationship with Parties and Budget entities. The budget is continuously monitored during payments so that the expenditure is within the budget. If amount in a payment transaction exceeds the balance budget amount (i.e., budget exceeds), then an exception *budget over* is raised. **Exceptions** defined in the meta-schema are associated to entities in the form of Event-Condition-Action (ECA) rules. Specific ECA rules can then be bound to contract for versatile exception handling.

Contract events
The information about the contracts including parties, clauses and activities are stored in a database, and are linked with each other. The activities have attributes like Activity Identification, Starting-Date, Ending-Date, Name of Activity, Description, Requirements and Specifications. There may be Payment Schedule linked with the Activity, so that the payment may be done after successful completion of an activity.

Thus, when a contract is being executed, many events will occur and operations on different files (tables) will take place.

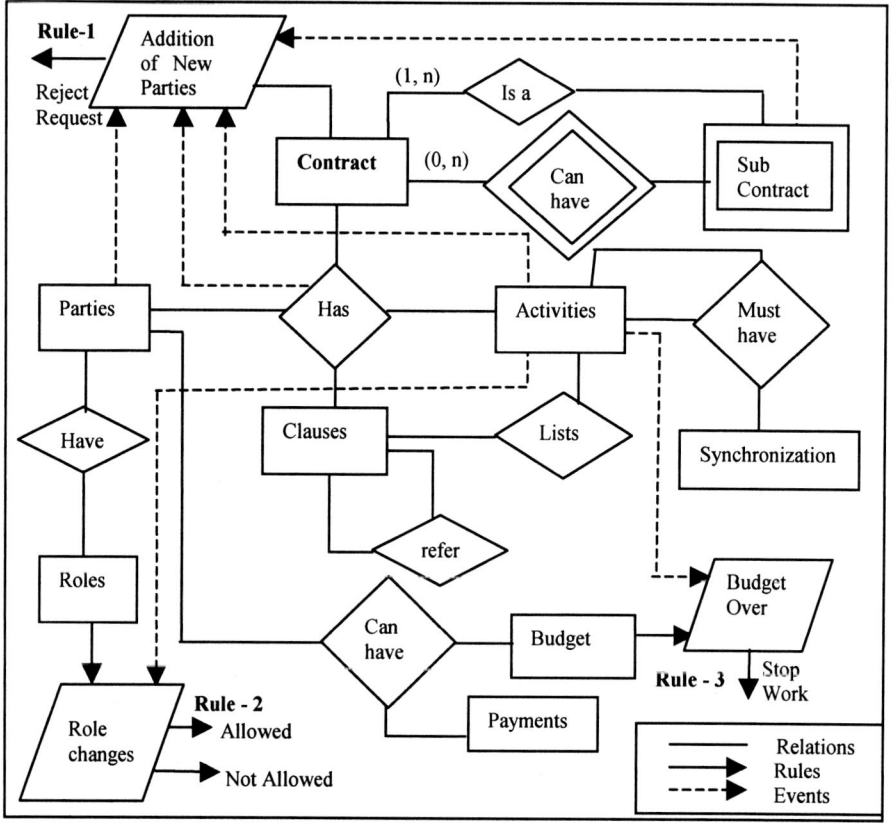

Fig. 1. A Meta-Schema for E-Contract

An event happens at any point of time and has no duration. At any particular time some action will cause an event to occur. The action like *"Change Status of Activity"* will cause the occurrence of an event like *"Status Updated"*. A Contract event such as adding of new party may trigger several database operations. Similarly, new activity may trigger several insertions or updates across the tables. The contract events will be caused by the actions in the execution of the contracts. A contract event may lead to several database events, however database event can occur independent of contract events. Suppose, when an address of a party in the contract is changed (a database event), it is not a contract event since it will not effect the execution of the contract. In the Figure 1, we use ER-R model to model an event.

Some of the contract events in the meta-schema are contract completed, subcontract made, subcontract over, new party joined, activity started, activity completed, party violates clauses, activity deviates from clauses, activity updated,

activity requires more budget, Payment initiated, payment made, role added and role updated, synchronization of activities not followed.
The event is defined as below:

```
<event>  ::=   <contract_event> | <database_event> |
               <temporal_event> | <external_event>

<composite-event> ::= <event> AND <event>
<contract Event>  ::= started <contract_object> attempted
                    | completed <contract_object> attempted
                    | deviates <CLAUSES> attempted
                    | <ACTIVITY> synchronization attempted
                    | update <contract_object> attempted.
```

The database events are associated with data objects (<data_object>), and <database_event> is defined as in [TNCK1991]. In the above definitions, <contract_object> and <data_object> can be an entity set or a relationship set, and <attribute> is an attribute of a <contract_object> or <data_object>. Further, both contract events and database events can have more events than those specified above. A temporal event is a time-based event, which could be relative (20 minutes after contract starts) or absolute (at 3.00 PM). An External event could be, for example, a document arrived.

Exceptions in a contract are mainly due to the deviations from the clauses defined in the contract. Some of the exceptions in the meta-schema are shown in the Table 1.

Table 1. Exceptions in the meta-schema for e-contract

(i) *Exception_name*:	Addition of new party
Event:	Insert a new party attempted
Condition:	New party can not be added during the execution of a contract
Action:	Reject the request
(ii) *Exception_name*:	Role Changes
Event:	Update the role of a party attempted
Condition:	Change of role violates the clauses.
Action:	Allowed (ROLE updated); Not Allowed
(iii) *Exception_name*:	Budget over
Event:	Total amount in the budget is over attempted
Condition:	Expenditure exceeds the budget
Action:	Stop work; allocate more budget (BUDGET updated)

2.2. ER^{EC} Meta-schema Template

The ER^{EC} meta-schema can be treated as a template of an ER^{EC} model for e-contracts. Because an e-contract has *a fixed set of relationships* that are commonly held over various entities within the conceptual model for an e-contract. For example, the *"has"* relationship among the entities *contract, parties, clauses* and *activities* will mostly exist in a conceptual model for an e-contract. That is:

    A. E-contracts are standardized with some parametric inputs required at specification time for a new e-contract.
    B. There are many fixed entities and relationships in an e-contract.

C. Additional flexibility is accommodated by customizing the e-contract instance with more relationships and entities specific to an e-contract being modeled.
D. There is a mix of entity types and entities (representing instances) co-existing in an ER^{EC} model. This is a special feature of this model that is used in translating an ER^{EC} model to a set of workflows.

2.3. Workflow Meta-schema

Workflow is automation of a business process. Workflow Management Systems (WFMS) have been extensively used in businesses to design, execute, and monitor processes [G+1995]. It provides an efficient environment for collaboration, coordination and communication among agents - people and software programs - to complete activities in a particular order and with certain rules, procedures and constraints.

Fig. 2 illustrates a typical workflow meta-schema [WfMC1995]. Note that workflow is same as an activity, and an activity of a workflow is same as a task as proposed in activity management system [KYH1995]. A reference to an activity should be clear based on whether it is a part of a workflow or an independent activity.

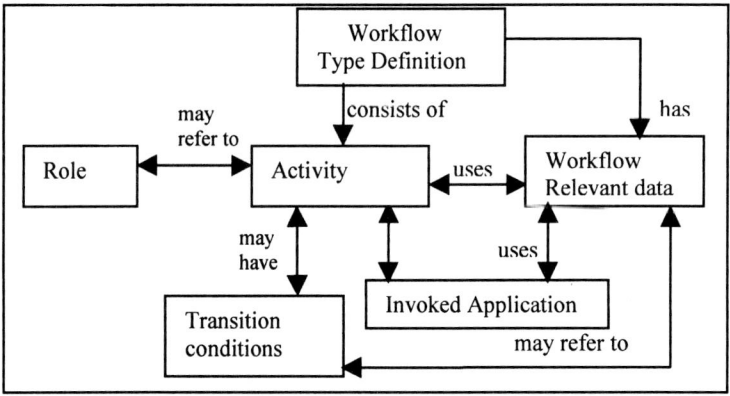

Fig. 2. A typical workflow meta-schema

2.4. Differences between the Meta-schemas for E-contract and Workflow

In sections 2.1 and 2.3, we presented the meta-schemas for e-contract and workflow. These two models combined together helps in the implementation of an e-contract, thus a mapping between the two models has to be performed. Unfortunately, the mapping may lose some semantics when transforming from a "semantically richer" ER^{EC} (explained in Section 3) model to a workflow. Therefore, the workflow model has to be augmented with a database for storing additional information about parties, clauses, contracts, and any other related data and business processes.

In general, a contract contains a number of clauses, and any deviation from a clause violates the contract. It is required that each clause should be monitored continuously during the entire contract process. Activities are the actual work elements in a contract. A contract consists of large number of activities, and each activity, in-turn, consists of multiple inter-dependent tasks that need to be coordinated, scheduled and executed. Also, there must be dependency checks among various activities.

The meta-schema of a contract shows exceptions, which occur frequently during the contract process due to the unanticipated possibilities, deviation from clauses, and a violation from contract law. Exceptions may occur asynchronously or occur in scattered places in a contract process (e.g., budget over), and these cannot be directly handled by explicit rule based processing such as IF-THEN-ELSE constructs. Thus, there is a requirement for extra constructs and semantics in a workflow meta-schema to address the exception modeling and management. In addition, the complexity arising due to large number of relationships among the entities shown in e-contract meta-schema cannot be handled with current commercially available WFMSs or research prototypes. Therefore, after mapping an ER^{EC} schema to a workflow, additional applications may need to be written to monitor and enforce e-contracts. Otherwise, workflow systems need to be enhanced to handle e-contracts. In this paper, our focus is on modeling e-contracts and developing a methodology for translating an e-contract conceptual model to an implementation level workflow or activity.

3. ER^{EC} Model

In our approach, we describe an ER^{EC} model as an extension of ER-R [TNCK91] model, to bridge the gap between the complexities in E-Contracts and Workflow process. The conceptual schema in the ER^{EC} model is represented by an ER^{EC} diagram (Figure 1.). An ER^{EC} model has the following constructs for modeling e-contracts:

1. Contracts – A contract is a legal agreement between multiple parties.
2. Clauses – A contract consists of many interdependent clauses that need to be fulfilled.
3. Activities – A clause is fulfilled by successfully executing one or more activities.
4. Parties – An activity is undertaken by one or more parties.
5. Exceptions – Exceptions model deviations from fulfillment of contracts.

The above five constructs form the core of ER^{EC} model. First, an e-contract is conceptualized from the requirements collected by the user. Once it is conceptualized, it is presented as a single ER^{EC} model. After that, the clauses within e-contract need to be fulfilled while executing one or more activities. Each activity is handled by one or more parties. Therefore, in an e-contract, the actual work done is modeled by activities. Many times, an activity fails triggering a violation of an important clause in a contract. This gives rise to an exception that needs to be handled by further augmenting activities with exception handling process. We illustrate an ER^{EC} model for an "Investment" example in the next subsection.

3.1. Investment E-contract - Example

Suppose, Financial Institution (FI) in a country has different types of investment schemes, and some of the schemes are opened for a short period, and other schemes for a longer period. The FIs periodically issue Bonds or Securities for fixed amount in which individual investors or the institutional investors can invest (i.e. Bond holders). The payment of interest, which is promised in advance, may be done electronically or through paper instruments.

When an individual/institution invests the amount with FI, they enter into a contract. The terms and conditions of the operation of Bond or security are defined by FI. It has to periodically pay the interest and must return the amount to the holder after the period defined in the contract is over. The investors will be making initial payments through bank. The FI will be periodically paying interest through banks.

Here, the contract and subcontracts involved are:
1. FI and Banks/agencies for accepting the Application Form and initial amount from Investors and sending the Application Forms to FI and collected amount to the account of FI (with FI's own bank).
2. FI and Banks (in some cases may be different from 1) for periodic payment of interest/warrant/dividend.
3. Among banks for inter bank funds transfer
4. Bank and investor – investor being the account holder of the bank
5. FI and Investors
6. Among the investors for the transfer of ownership
7. Agencies and banks for transfer of funds

In above case (5) is the main contract relevant to our example and others are sub contracts. However, the sub contracts listed in (3) and (4) can exist irrespective of main contract. The contract at (7) is required, if there is a contract between FI and agencies (i.e. not banks). In this case, there has to be another sub contract for the transfer of funds. The clauses in the main contracts will be as indicated by the FI at the time of notification. Table 2. and Table 3. shows some clauses and activities in the "investment" contract respectively. Table 4. shows some of the rules defined in the meta-schema for the present example.

Table 2. Some clauses in "investment" contract

CL-a. Who can invest (like say citizen of the country and or institutions), how they can invest (like say singly, jointly etc.)
CL-b. Minimum Amount, Maximum Amount and Other restrictions Maturity Period
CL-c. Promise of return, mode and periodicity of interest payment etc.
CL-d. Other conditions like whether Transfer of ownership allowed, Pre-mature withdrawal allowed or not, reinvestment in other schemes allowed or not etc. and penal clauses like payment of additional penal interest in case the interest is not paid in time.

Figure 3. shows the schema for the contract in our example. In the Figure 3, the "instance" level information is co-existing with conceptual level information. That is, in the case of Parties, FI is a particular instance of entity Party. But we show it as a specific entity (object) in the entity type "Parties". This feature is very much needed to model e-contracts, because the information captured at the instance level of an entity is different from other instances of the same entity type due to its specific behaviour in a contract. For example, the information captured for the Party instance FI is entirely different from the Party instance Investor. This feature is also a feasible solution because of small number of entities involved in each entity-type. In other words, the ER^{EC} meta-schema is a template for modeling e-contracts.

Table 3. Some Activities of FI, Investors and Banks in "Investment" contract

Activity FI	Activity Investors
1. Issuing notification for bonds/security	1. Submit the signed and completed application and pay the amount
2. Entering into an agreement with banks/agencies for acceptance of application forms and amount.	2. Get notification
	3. Hold the Bond/Security till maturity or carry out allowed operations like Transfer, pre mature withdrawal etc.
3. Receive Application forms and funds, scrutinize applications, pass accounting entries, allot bonds/ securities to investors, return the amounts for rejected applications and unallotted amount, issue bonds and certificates, send acceptance notifications to holding agencies and investors, periodically pay the promised interest, repay or reinvest in new scheme, etc.	4. Tally the periodic interest received
	Activity Bank
	1. Receive Application Form and Amount
	2. Send Applications to FI and collected Amount to FI's Bank
	3. FI's bank will credit the amount collected to FI's Account
	4. FI's Account will be debited for periodic interest and repayment, the amount to be transferred to different bank accounts.
	5. Transfer the interest and amount received to the investor's account.

Another interesting feature of ER^{EC} model is the relationships between the instances of entities. These relationships are in addition to the relationships between entities. That is, for example, consider the relationship between Activity instances "Submission" and "Fund-Receipt & Info. to FI" and Parties instance "FI" and "Investor". Here, the relationship is between the instances of entity types Activities and Parties. The investor submits an application for a bond through a bank/agency. The bank/agency receives the application and the required amount, and sends the information to FI. These low-level relationships among the instances of entity types will help to conceptualize the e-contract and facilitate translation of ER^{EC} model to workflow.

4. Mapping ER^{EC} to Workflow Specification

The mapping of ER^{EC} model to a workflow is done as follows:
    Step 1. All parties are mapped to agent types/roles.
    Step 2. Activities to workflows and activities in a workflow.
    Step 3. Contracts to events that occur.
    Step 4. Clauses to conditions that need to be satisfied.
    Step 5. Exception handling to additional activities in a workflow.
    Step 6. Payments and contracts to documents and additional input/output events.

The above steps for mapping an ER^{EC} model to a workflow needs to be carried out to facilitate an instantiation and execution of an e-contract. The steps are based on the relationship among various constructs in ER^{EC} model. Therefore, first, parties need to be mapped to agents that perform (are responsible for) various activities. Second, the activities themselves need to be mapped to a workflow. This may require additional

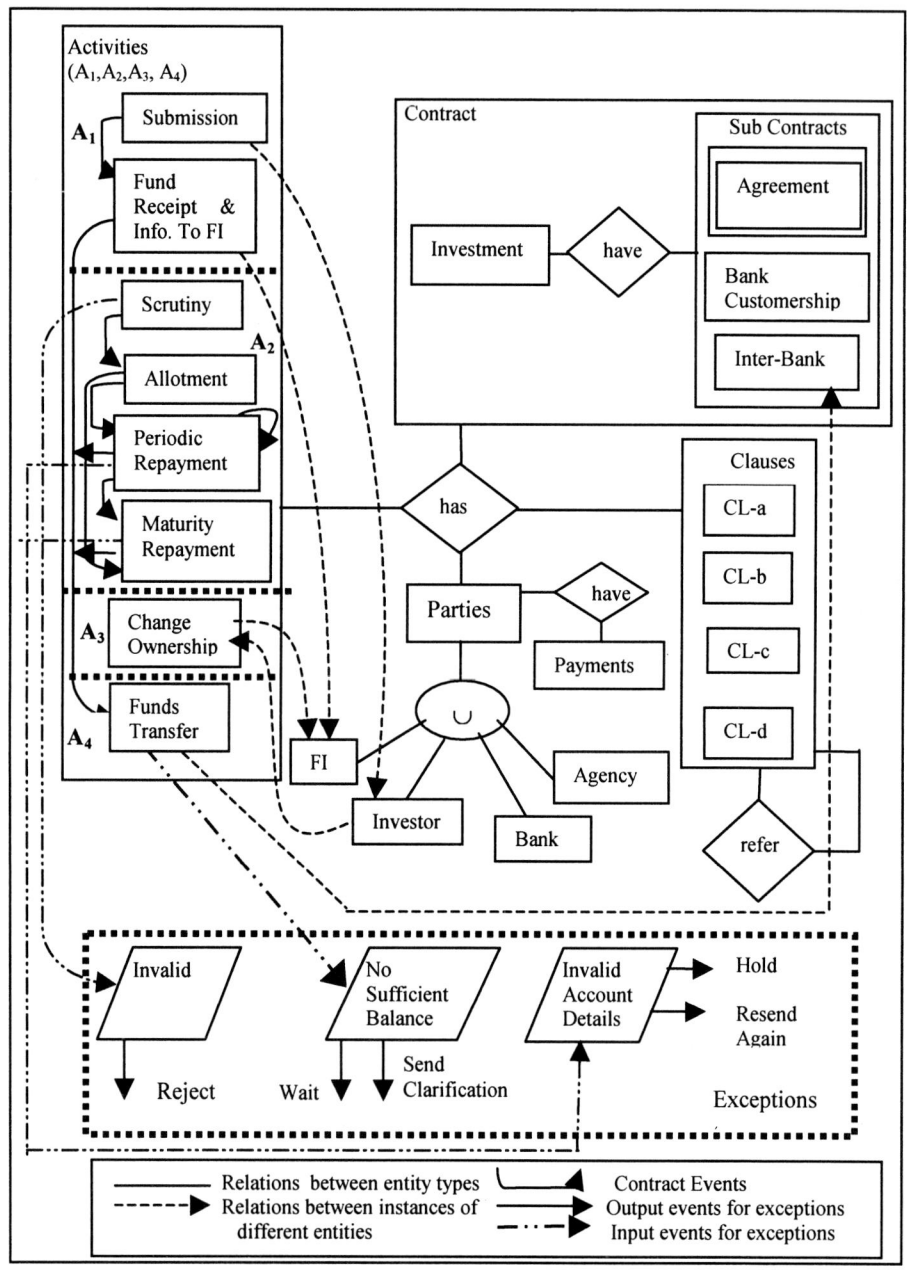

Fig. 3. A Meta-Schema for E-Contract

business processes to be specified. For example, the activity scrutiny may require a new business process in a FI to be specified. This Scrutiny workflow may require additional agents to be involved in the execution. Third, the contracts and clauses are mapped to events that need to occur to intimate the satisfaction of a clause or completion of a (sub-)contract. Note that these additional events need to be modeled and specified in the workflow. In case some of the clauses are not satisfied exception handling will take over the processing of a contract. This exception handling may require additional activities (depending on clauses) to be added to the workflow. Payments are also treated as clauses that need to be satisfied. It should be noted that this mapping only handles the "workflow support component" required to execute an e-contact. Additional databases and other "human-supported" activities and business processes need to be specified for the implementation support for e-contracts. Further, ER^{EC} model's main objective is to facilitate conceptual understanding of dependencies within an e-contract and their mapping to a workflow.

Table 4. Rules of "investment" contract for ER^{EC} model

Rule 1	Rule_Name :	Allot_Bonds_To_Investors
	Triggering_event :	Amount_Received and Application_Scrutiny_Successful
	Condition :	Decide upon the Bond Allocation policy.
	Action :	Return the remaining Amount if the Face_Value of Bonds allotted is less than paid amount.
	Resultant_Event :	{Allot Bonds, Return Amount, Inform_Depository}
	\multicolumn{2}{l}{Suppose that investor has applied for Bonds of face value say X and he has paid amount Y (>X) then the amount (Y-X) is returned. The information is sent to the depository.}
Rule 2	Rule_Name :	Pay_Interest
	Triggering_event :	Due_Date
	Condition :	There should not be any hold on interest payment
	Action :	Calculate the interest payable and credit it to the investor's Account
	Resultant Event :	{Calculate Interest Due, Amount_Transfer, Bank_Transfer}
	\multicolumn{2}{l}{The interest will be calculated and the amount will be transferred to the Account of the Customer}
	Exception :	Not able to credit – Incorrect_Account_Info, Interest cannot be paid
Rule 3	Rule_Name :	Transfer_Bond
	Triggering Event :	Transfer
	Condition :	There should not be any hold on transfer of ownership
	Action :	Update the Holder Database
	Resultant Event :	{Get_New_Act_Details, Change_Holder}
	\multicolumn{2}{l}{The bonds will be transferred to new holder. Transfer will change the ownership.}
	Exception :	Transfer not allowed
Rule 4	Rule_Name :	Repay_Bond
	Triggering Event :	Maturity_Period_Over
	Condition :	There should not be any hold on repayment
	Resultant Event :	{Calculate_Amount, Transfer_Funds}
	Exception :	Reinvest in new scheme, Not able to Repay, Incorrect Account details
Rule 5	Rule_Name :	Pre_Mature_Closure
	Triggering Event :	Holder_Request
	Condition :	There should not be any hold on pre-mature withdrawal
	Resultant Event :	{ Calculate_Amount, Transfer_Funds}
	Exception :	Premature withdrawal not allowed , Incorrect Account details

First, the parties are mapped to agents as described in Table 5. In Figure 4, we show how the activities A1, A2, A3, and A4 are mapped to workflows A, B, C, and D, respectively. In Figure 5, we augment workflows B and D with exception handling based on exceptions in Investment ER^{EC} model.

Table 5. Mapping of Parties to Agents

Workflow	Parties	Payments	(sub-)contracts
1	Investor, Bank, agency, FI	Investor -> Bank/Agency Bank/Agency -> FI	Bank Customership Inter-Bank
2	FI, Investor, Bank	FI -> Investor	Agreement, Bank Customership Inter-Bank
3.	Investor, FI	Investor -> Investor	Agreement
4	Bank	Bank -> Bank	Inter-bank

After specifying the workflows, they can be incorporated at various parties for supporting e-contracts. For example, workflow A enables an investor (say, Rama) to submit a requisition to buy some ICICI bonds from Citibank. At Citibank, the workflow A will enable relevant information, documents and payments (through his account in Citibank) to be provided by Rama. Further, workflow A will transmit the documents to ICICI and the payment is transferred from Citibank to ICICI. After that, workflow B is initiated at ICICI to scrutinize and allot the bonds to Rama. Once Rama is allotted the bonds, Workflow D is initiated at ICICI to transfer funds to Rama's account in Citibank, either periodically and/or at maturity time based on the contract. In case, Rama is interested to sell the bonds to another investor, (say, Sunil), the workflow C enables Rama to transfer the ownership of his bonds to Sunil. Here, the workflow C is initiated by Rama and the transfer takes place at ICICI.

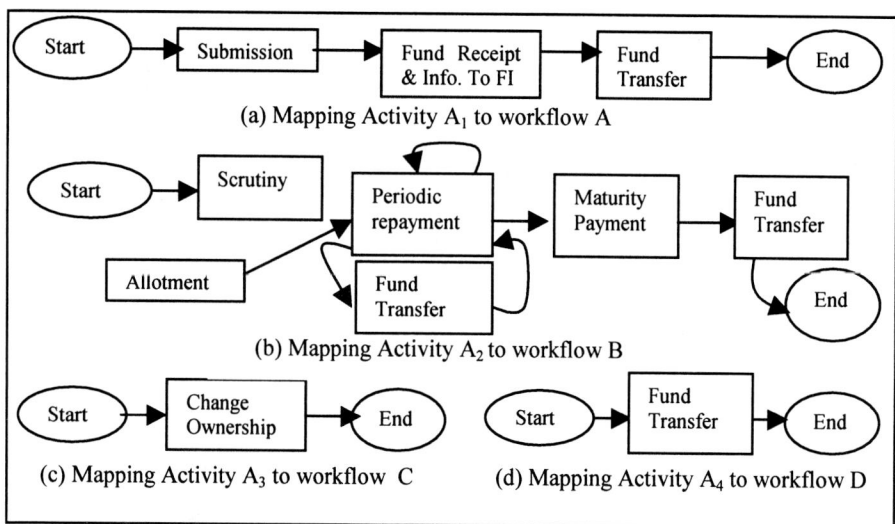

Fig. 4. Mapping Activities to workflow

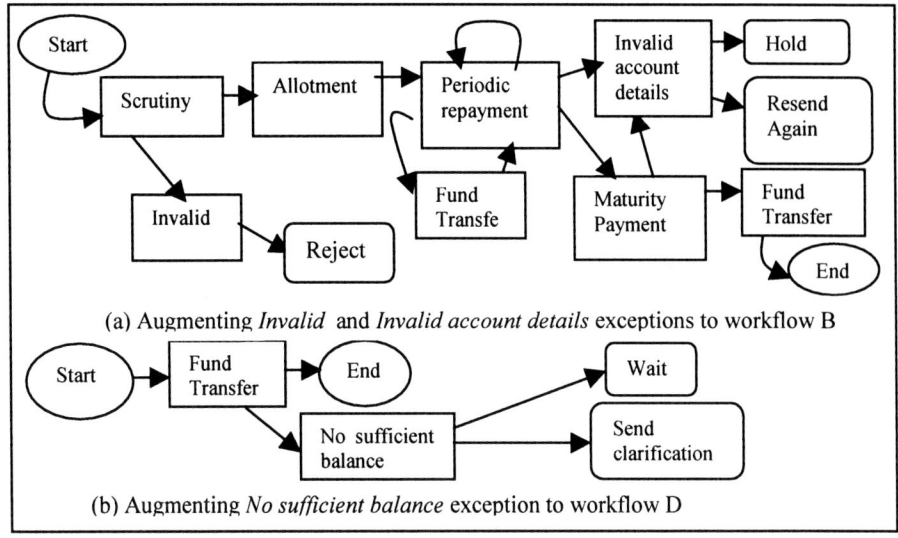

Fig. 5. Augmenting exceptions as additional activities to workflow

4.1. Discussion

E-contracts are complex and difficult to understand and facilitating an implementation of e-contracts is not straightforward. Therefore, we have developed a modeling framework for e-contracts, namely ER^{EC} data model and illustrated an investment ER^{EC} model and its mapping to a workflow. The points that need to be noted are:

1. The ER^{EC} model is a natural way for modeling e-contracts. The important aspects namely, clauses, activities and parties can be easily conceptualized and their relationships can be modeled.
2. Exceptions to clauses are integral part of e-contracts which needs to be modeled carefully. In ER^{EC} model, we provide facilities to link up contracts, activities and exceptions are modeled using rules.
3. A methodology is developed to map an e-contract to many workflows that need to be executed by various parties involved in the contract. Thus, ER^{EC} model is one of the first models to facilitate conceptual modeling of cross-organizational e-contracts that are implemented by cross-organizational workflows.
4. The meta-schema for e-contracts can be augmented to include additional e-contract requirements such as authorization and delegation.

5. Related Work

In the recent years, the research on E-Commerce and related areas made it a challenge to do business electronically. This is mainly due to the increase use of Internet and web driven business processes. The Domain Task Force established by OMG produced a working version of the electronic commerce reference model [O1997]. This model is largely based on the results of OSM (An Open Service Model for

Global Information Brokerage and Distribution) project [I1998], in which a framework was created for the electronic commerce. Jenny Hands et. al [H+2000] presented an architecture for electronic brokerage, and describes a reference model and functional architecture for value-added mediation in electronic commerce. A three level framework using Intelligent agents is presented in [LH2000] to support electronic trading.

In [GSG2000], a framework for legal e-contracts is developed, but a mechanism for modeling e-contracts is not provided. In [S1980], a contract net protocol is described for structuring contractor and subcontractor market places. A declarative approach to business rules in e-commerce contracts in [G1999] by combining CLP (Courteous Logic Program) and XML. Kersten and Szpakowicz presented modeling business negotiations for electronic commerce using software agents [KS1998]. In [LS1997], a detailed comparison of various workflow metamodels is discussed. But there has been no work on conceptually modeling e-contracts and developing a methodology for mapping an e-contract to workflow. In [TNCK1991] a modeling framework for rule processing and ECA triggers in active databases was developed. This work facilitated conceptual modeling of active databases. In this work, we build on it to develop a novel framework for conceptually modeling e-contracts. Further, in [CKL2000] a framework for e-services is developed as an application built on top of workflow systems. That is, it advocated the idea that the implementation vehicle for e-services is workflows. Along the same lines, we in this paper showed how conceptually modeled e-contracts are mapped to workflows.

6. Conclusion

In this paper, we focused on the framework for modeling an e-contract. The meta-schema for electronic contracts is presented and illustrated with a simple example. We proposed an extension to ER model called ER^{EC} model to represent the complex inter/intra relationships among entities in an electronic contract. We illustrated the utility of this ER^{EC} model through a detail example. The salient feature of the ER^{EC} model is the seamless conceptualization of "instances" and constructs, and relationships among them. This advocated the notion of an ER^{EC} model to be a template for a class of e-contracts to be supported by a set of parties. In this case, a particular e-contract may involve some of the parties to engage in fulfillment of the e-contract. For example, in the "Investment" ER^{EC} model, for a user Rama, the parties involved were Citibank and ICICI and the e-contract was among them. Thus, the notion of conceptual model as a template instantiated at run-time is proposed.

Further, we showed how an e-contract is mapped to a set of workflows that can be executed by different parties. A detailed methodology for this mapping has been provided along with an illustrative example. Overall, in this paper we focused on modeling e-contracts and mapping it to workflows. We are currently working on developing a toolkit for ER^{EC} data model and facilitate its mapping to workflows in commercially available workflow management systems.

References

[CKL2000] Dickson Chiu, Kamalakar Karlapalem, Qing Li. E-Adome: A framework for enacting e-services, Workshop on Technologies for E-Services (VLDB workshop), 2000.

[G1999] B. N. Grosof, A declarative approach to business rules in Contracts: Courteous Logic Programs in XML, Proceedings of the 1st ACM Conference on Electronic Commerce (EC99), Denver, Colorado, USA, Nov. 3-5, 1999.

[GHS1995] Dimitrios Georgakopoulos, Mark F. Hornick, Amit P. Sheth: An Overview of Workflow Management: From Process Modeling to Workflow Automation Infrastructure. Distributed and Parallel Databases 3(2): pages 119-153 (1995).

[GSG2000] M. Gisler, K. Stanoevska-Slabeva, and M. Greunz, Legal Aspects of Electronic Contracts, in CAiSE*00 Workshop of Infrastructures for Dynamic Business-to-Business Service Outsourcing (IDSO'00) Stockholm, 5 - 6 June 2000.

[H+2000] Jenny Hands, Mikhail Bessonov, Mike Blinov, Ahmed Patel and Ron Smith, An inclusive and extensible architecture for electronic brokerage, Decision Support Systems, **29**, 305-321, 2000.

[I1998] Infowin ACTS Project 1998, Information Brokerage, Deutshe Telekom Berkom, Berlin.

[KS1998] G. E. Kersten and S. Szpakowicz, Modelling business negotiations for electronic commerce, Proceedings of the 7th workshop on Intelligent Information Systems, Warsaw: IPI PAN, 1998, 17-28.

[KYH1995] Kamalakar Karlapalem, Helen P. Yeung, Patrick C. K. Hung: CapBasED-AMS - A Framework for Capability-Based and Event-Driven Activity Management System. CoopIS 1995: pages 205-219.

[LH2000] Ting-Peng Liang and Jin-Shiang Huang, A framework for applying intelligent agents to support electronic trading, Decision Support Systems, **28**, 305-317, 2000.

[LS1997] Yu Lei and Munindar P. Singh, A comparison of workflow metamodels, Proceedings of the ER'97 Workshop on Behavioral Models and Design Transformations: Issues and Opportunities in Conceptual Modeling, 6 - 7 November 1997, UCLA, Los Angeles, California.

[O1997] OMG/CommerceNet 1997, Joint Electronic Commerce Whitepaper. OMG Domain Technical Committee, Monreal (http://www.osm.net/upload/97-06-09.pdf)

[S1980] R. G. Simith, The contract net protocol: High Level Communication and Control in a Distributed Problem Solver, IEEE Transactions on Comp[uters (29;12), December 1980, 1104-1113.

[TNCK1991] A. K. Tanaka, S. B. Navathe, S. Chakravarthy and K. Karlapalem, ER-R: An enhanced ER model with situation-action rules to capture application semantics, in ER 1991: pages 59-75.

CASE Tool Support for Temporal Database Design

Virginie Detienne, Jean-Luc Hainaut

Institut d'Informatique, University of Namur
rue Grandgagnage, 21 - B-5000 Namur - Belgium
tel: +32 81 724985 - fax: +32 81 724967

Abstract. Current RDBMS technology provides little support for building temporal databases. The paper describes a methodology and a CASE tool that is to help practitioners develop correct and efficient relational data structures. The designer builds a temporal ERA schema that is validated by the tool, then converted into a temporal relational schema. This schema can be transformed into a pure relational schema according to various optimization strategies. Finally, the tool generates an active SQL-92 database that automatically maintain entity and relationship states. In addition, it generates a temporal ODBC driver that encapsulates complex temporal operators such as projection, join and aggregation through a small subset of TSQL2. This API allows programmers to develop complex temporal applications as easily as non temporal ones.

1 Introduction

A wide range of database applications manage time-varying data. Existing database technology currently provides little support for managing such data, and using conventional data models and query languages like SQL-92 to cope with such information is particularly difficult [12]. Developers of database applications can create only ad-hoc solutions that must be reinvented each time a new application is developed.

The scientific community has long been interested in this problem [9]. The research has focused on characterizing the semantics of temporal information and on providing expressive and efficient means to model, store and query temporal data.

A lot of those studies concerned temporal data models and query languages. Dozens of extended relational data models have been proposed [13], while about 40 temporal query languages have been defined, most with their own data model, the most complete certainly being TSQL2 [11]. However, it seems that neither standardization bodies nor DBMS editors are really willing to adopt these proposals, so that the problem of maintaining and querying temporal data in an easy and reliable way remains unsolved.

A handful of temporal DBMS prototypes have been proposed [1], [13]. Attention has been paid to performance issues because selection, join, aggregates and duplicates elimination (coalescing) require sophisticated and time consuming algorithms [2].

Several temporally enhanced Entity-Relationship (ER) models have been developed [6]. UML (Unified Modelling Language) also has been extended with temporal semantics and notation (TUML) [14].

Among those studies, few methodologies and tools support have been proposed for temporal database design.

About This Paper

Like for conventional databases, a temporal database design methodology must lead to correct and efficient databases. However, the design of even modest ones can be fairly complex, hence the need for CASE tools, specially for generating the code of the database. This paper describes a simple methodology and a CASE tool that is to help practitioners develop temporal applications based on SQL-92 technology.

These results are part of the TimeStamp project whose the goal is to provide practitioners with practical tools (models, methods, CASE tools and API) to design, manage and exploit temporal databases through standard technologies, such as C, ODBC and SQL-92. Though the models and the languages used are more simple than those available in the literature, the authors feel that they can help developers in mastering their temporal data.

Sections 2, 3 and 4 introduce the concepts of temporal conceptual, logical and physical models for relational temporal databases that are specific to the TimeStamp approach. Section 5 describes the methodology for temporal database design, and presents a CASE tool that automates the processes defined in the methodology.

2   A Temporal Conceptual Model

The database conceptual schema of an information system is the major document through which the user requirements about an application domain are translated into abstract information structures. When the evolution of the components of this application domain is a part of these requirements, this schema must include temporal aspects. This new dimension increases the complexity of the conceptual model, and makes it more difficult to use and to understand. To alleviate this drawback, we have chosen a simple and intuitive formalism that must improve the reliability of the analysis process. This model brings three advantages, which should be evaluated against its loss of expressive power. First, it has been considered easier to use by developers when the time dimension must be taken into account (for instance, temporal consistency through inheritance mechanism is far from trivial). Secondly, the distance between a conceptual schema and its relational expression is narrower, a quality that is appreciated by programmers. Thirdly, schema expressed in a richer model can be converted without loss into simpler structures through semantics-preserving transformations [8].

Though the concepts of temporal conceptual schemas have been specified for long in the literature, we will describe them very briefly [14], [6].

The conceptual model comprises three main constructs, namely entity types, single- valued atomic attributes and N-ary relationship types. Each construct can be non-temporal or temporal. In the first case, only the current states are of interest, while in the latter case, we want to record past, current and future states. In this presentation, we will address the modelling and processing of historical states, that is the past and current states only[1].

---

1   Though most of the principles described in this paper can be extended to future states as well, the latter induce some constraints that we do not want to discuss in this paper. For instance, not all data distribution patterns proposed in the physical model can accommodate future states.

The temporal dimension can be based on valid time (/v), on transaction time (/t) or on both (/b for bitemporal). The instances of a non-temporal *monotonic* entity type (/m) can be created but never deleted, so that the letter enjoys some properties of temporal entity types. A construct is non-temporal, unless it is marked with a temporal tag: /m, /v, /t or /b (Fig. 1). An entity type can have one primary identifier (or key) and some secondary identifiers. A relationship type has 2 or more roles, each of them being taken by an entity type. A role has a cardinality constraint defined by two numbers, the most common values being 0-1, 1-1, 0-N[2]. A non-temporal attribute can be declared *stable*, i.e., non-updatable. The temporal attributes of the time intervals of the states are implicit.

If an entity type is temporal, then, for each entity that existed or still exists, the birth and death instants (if any) are known (valid time), and/or the recording (in the database) and erasing instants (transaction time) are known. This information is implicit and is not part of the attributes of the entity type. If an attribute is temporal, then all the values associated with an entity are known, together with the instants at which each value was (is) active. The instants are from the valid and/or transaction time dimensions according to the time-tag of the attribute. If a relationship type is temporal, then the birth and death instants are known. The two time dimensions are allowed, according to the time-tag.

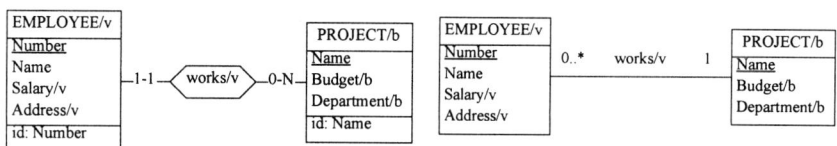

Fig. 1. A conceptual schema. Both ERA (left) and UML (right) notations are provided.

To ensure the consistency of the future temporal database, but also to limit its complexity and to make its physical implementation easier and more efficient, the model imposes some constraints of the valid schemas[3]. A conceptual schema is said to be *consistent* if:
1. the temporal attributes of an entity type have the same time-tag (mixing temporal and non-temporal attribute is allowed);
2. the time-tag of an entity type is the same as that of its temporal attributes; there is no constraints if it has no temporal attributes;
3. each temporal entity type has a primary identifier (or key) made up of mandatory, stable and unrecyclable[4] attributes; there is no constraints on the other identifiers;
4. the entity types that appear in a temporal N-ary relationship type are either temporal or monotonic;
5. the entity type that appears in the [i-1] role[5] of a *one-to-many* temporal relationship type R has the same time-tag as R; *one-to-one* relationship types are constrained as if they were one-to-many;

---
2   Though they have the same expressive power in binary relationship types, the ERA cardinality and UML multiplicity have different interpretations.
3   We leave this undemonstrated for space limit.
4   An attribute is unrecyclable if its values cannot be used more than once, even if its parent entity is dead.

6. the entity type that appears in the [0-N] role[6] of a *one-to-many* temporal relationship type R has a time-tag compatible (in a sense that translates into valid foreign keys as stated in Sec. 3.4) with that of R; *one-to-one* relationship types are constrained as if they were *one-to-many*;
7. the entity types that appear in the roles of a N-ary relationship type R have a time-tag that is *compatible* (same meaning as above) with that of R.

A conceptual schema that meets all these conditions can be translated into a *consistent relational* schema, as defined in Sec. 3.

3 A Temporal Relational Logical Model

This model defines the interface used by the programmer, that is, the data structures, the operators and the programming interface. We could have adopted a more general temporal relational model, such as that from [12]. However, the fact that the tables derive from a consistent conceptual schema induces specific properties that will simplify the implementation and (hopefully) the mental model of the programmer.

This model comprises tables, columns, primary keys, secondary (i.e., candidate, non-primary) keys and foreign keys. These constructs can be temporal (except for primary keys) or non-temporal, according to the same time-tag as those used in the conceptual model. A table that implements an entity type is called an *entity table*, while a table that translates a N-ary or *many-to-many* relationship type is called an *relationship table*[7]. Only entity tables can be monotonic.

The structure of temporal tables is as usual [12]:
1. valid-time tables have two additional timestamp columns, called Vstart and Vend, such that each row describes a fact (such as a state of an entity or relationship) that was (or is) valid in the application domain during the interval [Vstart,Vend);[8] these new columns can be explicitly updated by users according to limited rules;
2. any transaction-time table has two timestamp columns Tstart and Tend, that define the interval during which the fact was (is) recorded in the database; these columns cannot be updated by users;
3. in a bitemporal table, these four columns are present.

An entity table comprises three kinds of columns, namely the entity identifier, which forms the primary key of the set of current states of the entities, the timestamp columns Vstart, Vend, Tstart, Tend and the other columns, called attribute columns, that can be temporal or not. A *relationship table* is similarly structured: the relationship identifier, made up of the primary keys of the participating entity types, the timestamp columns and the attribute columns, if any. For simplicity, we ignore the latter in this paper.

---

5 i.e., the domain of the function that R expresses;
6 i.e., the range of the function that R expresses;
7 Though complex mapping rules can be used to translate entity types and relationship types, those that we adopt in the methodology are sufficiently simple to make these concept valid.
8 [i,j) is the standard temporal notation for a left-closed, right-open. Also noted [i,j[.

For each temporal dimension, the right bound of the interval of the current state is set to the infinite future, represented by a valid timestamp, far in the future (noted ∞ here).

The entity and relationship tables together form the set of *database tables*. However, other tables can be built and used, mainly by derivation from database tables. These tables may not enjoy the consistency properties that will be described, and therefore will require special care when used with database tables.

3.1 Temporal State Properties

The base tables of the database derive from the conceptual schema, so that not all data patterns are allowed. In this sense, the model is a subset of those proposed in the literature, e.g., in [12].

Let us first define their properties for temporal tables *with one dimension only*. The timestamp columns are simply called Start and End, since both kinds of time enjoy the same properties.

The granularity of the valid time clock is such that no two state changes can occur during the same clock tick for any given entity or relationship[9]. Similarly, no two states of the same entity/relationship can be recorded during the same transaction time clocktick. This gives a first property: for any state s, s.Start < s.End.

In a *temporal entity table*, be it transaction or valid time, all the rows related to the same entity form a *continuous history*, that is, each row, or state s1, but the last one, has a next state s2, such that s1.End = s2.Start. This property derives from the fact that, at each instant of its life, an entity is in one and only one state. Thirdly, any two states (s1,s2) such that s1.End = s2.Start (i.e., that are *consecutive*) must be different, that is, the values of at least one attribute column are distinct.

In a bitemporal entity table, each transaction time *snapshot*, i.e., the state of the table known as current at a given instant T, must be a valid time entity table that meets the properties described above.

In a *temporal relationship table*, a row tells that the participating entities were (are) linked during the interval [Start,End). For any two rows r1 and r2 defined on the same set of entities, either r1.End < r2.Start or r2.End < r1.Start hold.

3.2 Consistency State of a Table

The model defines four consistency states: a table can be corrupted, correct, normalized and fully normalized. In these definitions, two rows are said *value-equivalent* if they have the same values for all the columns (timestamp columns excluded).

A entity table is **corrupted** if, for some entity E and for some time point, it records at least two different states, i.e., states whose values differ for at least one attribute column. It is **correct** if, for any two states of the same entity that overlap, the values of the attribute columns are the same. It is **normalized** if, for any entity, its states do not overlap. It is **fully normalized** if any entity has a state for each instant of its life (continuous history). All entity tables must be fully normalized. Derived tables, i.e.,

---

[9] When this property is not ensured by the natural time(s), techniques based on an abstract time line can be used. This point is out of the scope of this paper.

tables resulting from the application of DML operators, that represent some part of the history of a database object must be at least correct.

A relationship table is **corrupted** if, for some value of the relationship identifier, there exist at least two non value-equivalent rows whose temporal interval overlap. Such a table is **correct** otherwise.

This classification is irrelevant for plain temporal table that are neither entity or relationship tables. In general, such tables will be said *non corrupted*.

3.3 Candidate Keys

If EI is the primary identifier of the entity/relationship type described by the valid time table T, then {EI,Vstart} is the primary key of T. {EI,Vend} is a secondary key, as well as {ESI,Vstart} and {ESI,Vend}, where ESI is any secondary identifier of the entity/ relationship type. For simplicity these candidate keys will not be represented in the logical schema, though they will be maintained in the database by the triggers of the physical schema. Similarly, the primary key of the transaction time table T is {EI,Tstart}. Its secondary keys are derived in the same way as in valid time tables. Finally, the primary key of bitemporal table T is conventionally {EI,Vstart,Tstart}. Note that these definitions are valid for database tables only and not necessarily for derived tables.

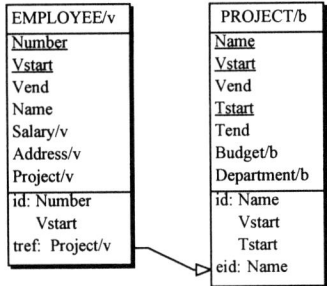

Fig. 2. A logical relational schema showing the transaction/valid timestamp columns. Tables and columns can have time-tags. EMPLOYEE.Project is a temporal foreign key to PROJECT, whose column Name is the entity identifier (eid).

3.4 Foreign Keys

Let us first define this concept for non bitemporal tables. A column or a set of columns FK of a source table S is a *foreign key* to the target table T, with the primary key (PK,Start), if, for each state s of S where FK is not null, and for each time point p in [s.Start,s.End), there exists at least one state t in T such that s.FK=t.PK and t.Start ≤ p < t.End. This property, which must be checked when tuples are inserted, updated and deleted, is complex and expensive to evaluate for temporal databases in which the target tables are only required to be normalized or even correct [12].

In this model, a foreign key belongs to an entity or relationship table, but the target table always is an entity table. Considering that entity tables are fully normalized by construction (*no gap, no overlap*), the definition degenerates into a property that is more straightforward and easier (i.e., *cheaper*) to check. Let us consider the source table S(..., Start, End, ..., FK) and the target table T(PK, Start, End, ...). S.FK is a temporal foreign key to S iff,

$\forall s \in S, \exists t1, t2 \in T:$
$t1.PK = t2.PK = s.FK \wedge t1.Start \leq s.Start < t1.End \wedge t2.Start < s.End \leq t2.End$

For bitemporal databases, this definition must be valid for each snapshot.

The foreign key, its source table and its target table need not have the same time-tag. For instance, a non temporal foreign key (in a temporal or non temporal source table) can reference a non temporal (including monotonic) or a temporal table; a valid time foreign key can reference monotonic, valid time and bitemporal target table. The allowed pairs of source and target time-tags define the compatibility rules, that will not be developed further in this paper.

3.5 Operators

The semantics of the usual relational operators have been extended to temporal tables, while new ones have been designed to cope with specific problems of temporal data [11]. This model includes four extraction operators, namely selection, projection, join, aggregation, and normalization transformations.

Temporal projection. This operator returns, for any correct source entity table S and for any subset A of its columns, a temporal table in which only the values of the columns in A are kept. If the set of the projection columns includes the entity identifier, the result is a normalized entity table. Conceptually, the temporal projection can be perceived as a standard projection followed by the merging (or *coalescing*) of the rows that have the same values of the non-temporal columns, and that either overlap or are consecutive.

Temporal selection. This operator returns the rows that meet some selection predicate in a correct source table. The selection can involve the temporal columns, the other columns, or both.

Temporal join. Considering two correct temporal source tables S1 and S2, and a predicate P, this operator returns, for each couple of rows (s1, s2) from S1xS2 such that P is true and the temporal interval i1 of s1 and i2 of s2 overlap, a row made up of the column values of both source rows and whose temporal interval is the intersection of i1 and i2. The result is a correct temporal table.

Temporal aggregation. Due to the great variety of aggregation queries, the process has been decomposed into four steps that are easy to encapsulate. Let us consider a correct entity table T with one time dimension (the reasoning is similar for other tables). The query class coped with has the general form : select A, f(B) from T group by A, where f is any aggregation function. First, a normalized state table minT is derived by collecting, for each value of A, the smallest intervals during which this value appears in T[10]. This table is joined with T to augment it with the value s of B, giving the correct table minTval. Then, the aggregation is computed through the query select select A, f(B) from T group by A. Finally the result is coalesced. In particular, this technique provides an easy way to compute temporal series (in this case, minT is a mere calendar).

---

10 If *T(E,Start,End,A,..)* has instances *{(e1,20,45,a1,..), (e2,30,50,a2,..), (e3,35,55,a1,..)}*, this step generates the states *{(a1,20, 35), (a1,35,45), (a1,45,55), (a2,30,50)}*.

Temporal normalization. This family of operators augment the consistency state (Sec. 3.2) of a correct table. By merging the value-equivalent overlapping or consecutive states, they produce normalized tables (no overlap), and by inserting the missing states of a non-fully normalized table, they produce a continuous history (no gap, no overlap).

3.6 The DML Interface

Though temporal operators can be expressed in pure SQL-92, their expression generally is complex and resource consuming [12], so that providing the programmer with a simple and efficient API to manipulate temporal data is more than a necessity. Developing a complete engine that translates temporal SQL queries would have been unrealistic, so that we chose to implement a (very) small subset of a variant of TSQL2 [11], called miniTSQL, through which the complex operators, such as project, join and aggregate can be specified in a natural way and executed[11]. Combining explicit SQL-92 queries with miniTSQL statements allows programmers to write complex scripts with reasonable effort. The API is a variant of ODBC, through which miniTSQL queries can be executed. The driver performs query analysis and interpretation based on a small repository that describes the database structures and their physical implementation (Sec. 4).

The following program fragment displays the name and salary of the employees of project BIOTECH as on valid time 35. The SQL query uses a temporal projection (including coalescing) and a temporal selection. It replaces about 100 lines of complex code that would have been necessary if operating directly on the tables of Fig. 2.

```
char name[50], salary [20], output[100];
sdword cbname, cbsalary ;
. . .; rc=SQLConnect(hdbc,...); ...
rc=TSQLExecDirect(hdbc,hstmt,"select snapshot Name, Salary
                        from    EMPLOYEE
                        where   valid(EMPLOYEE) contains
                                timepoint'35'
                        and     Project = 'BIOTECH'",type);
rc=SQLBindCol(hstmt,1,SQL_C_CHAR,name,50,cbname);
rc=SQLBindCol(hstmt,2,SQL_C_CHAR,salary,20,cbsalary);
do { rc = SQLFetch(hstmt);
    if(rc == SQL_NO_DATA)   break;
    strcpy(output,"Name: ")  ; strcat(output,name);
    strcat(output,"Salary: "); strcat(output,salary);
    MessageBox(output,"TUPLE",MB_OK);
  }while(rc!= SQL_NO_DATA);
...; rc=SQLDisconnect(hdbc); ...
```

To make the programmer's work easier and more reliable, the modification statements **insert, delete** and **update** apply on a view that hides the transaction temporal columns **Tstart** and **Tend**. More specifically, this view returns, respectively, (1) the current states of a transaction time table, (2) all the states of a valid time table and (3) the valid history of a bitemporal table.

---

11 miniTSQL and Temporal ODBC, as well as a procedural solution to bitemporal coalescing have been defined and prototyped by Olivier Ramlot (*Contribution à la mise au point d'un langage d'accès aux bases de données temporelles*, Mémoire présenté en vue de l'obtention du grade de Maître en Informatique, Université de Namur, Belgique, 2000).

4 A Temporal Relational Physical Model

The physical schema describes the data structures that actually are implemented in SQL-92. When compared with the logical schema, the physical schema introduces four implementation features.

Data distribution. The logical model represents the evolution of an entity/relationship set as a single table where each row represents a state of an entity/relationship. At the physical level, the states and the rows can be distributed, split and duplicated in order to gain better space occupation and/or improved performance. The first rule concern the distribution and duplication of states. A bitemporal historical table includes valid current states (**Tend**=∞ ∧ **Vend**=∞), valid past states (**Tend**=∞ ∧ **Vend**<∞) and invalid states (**Tend**<∞). This suggest various patterns of distribution, which each has advantages and drawbacks as far as performance and complexity are concerned: all the states in the same table, all the states in the same table + a copy of the valid current states in another table, the valid current states in a table + all the other states in another table, the valid states in a table + the invalid states in another table, to mention the most important. Tables with one dimension only can be organized in a similar way. Should future states be included, they would have to be stored in the same table as the current states.

A logical table comprises all the columns that implement the entity attributes and the one-to-many relationship types (as foreign keys), be they temporal or not. Storing rows in a single table may induce much redundancy[12,] so that distributing the columns into temporally homogeneous tables can decrease it dramatically. Three patterns are of particular importance: all the columns are collected in a single table (as in the logical schema), the non temporal columns form a table while a second table collects the temporal columns, the non temporal columns form a table while each temporal column forms a specific table. Other splitting patterns can be useful, that mainly pertain to the temporal normalization domain [16].

Indexing. As in conventional databases, indexes will be defined to improve the access time for the most frequent operations. Besides the primary keys, foreign keys, arguments of **group by** and **order by** clauses, frequent selection criteria, are candidate for indexing. Some temporal operators can be accelerated by using auxiliary structures. For instance, an entity table that stores the life span of each entity can be used to quickly check referential constraints in a bitemporal database. A *pre-join table TS*, that stores, for joinable tables T and S, the couples (s,t) of rows from T and S that overlap, can be use to replace the temporal join T*S by the standard join T*TS*S, which generally is faster.

Automatic data management. Managing a physical temporal database is particular complex, so that its automation must be pushed as far as possible. The approach we have chosen consists in implementing the logical database, as described in Sec. 3, as an *active database* whose active components are responsible for guaranteeing the consistency properties of the data and controlling the logical/physical mapping. Each logical table is given a set of triggers that control the **insert**, **delete** and **update**

---

12 The change of a single column in a row triggers the insertion of a new state, in which all the unchanged columns are merely copied.

operations by checking their validity and by propagating them among the physical tables.

For instance, the statement,
```
insert into EMPLOYEE(Number,Vstart,Salary,Address,Project)
values(:N,:VS,:SAL;ADD,:PRO);
```
triggers a procedure that performs the following operations, that can span several hundreds of lines of code for complex tables:
1. check: no current state where NUMBER=:N already exists (uniqueness); *2. check*: no past states, where NUMBER=:N already exist (non recyclability); *3. check*: Project=:PRO is a valid temporal foreign key (referential integrity); *4. check*: :VS is a past or current timepoint (pure history); *5. execute*: Vend is set to ∞ (current state); *6. execute*: the state is stored in the physical table(s) (logical/physical mapping); *7. execute*: the auxiliary structures are updated (logical/physical mapping).

5 Methodology and CASE Support for Temporal Databases

Despite the important research area of temporal databases, few methodologies for temporal databases design have been developed.

Some mappings from temporally extended ER models to relational model have been proposed [5], [7], [10], [15]. The models of [5], [7], [15] support only valid time, while the TempEER model [10] supports both valid time and transaction time of data. The TIMEER model [7] captures aspects such as the life span, valid time and transaction time of data too. A set of 31 constraints is defined to enforce the ER-specified time-related semantics in the relational context.

Those mappings allow to configure temporal data in only one way. However, we saw in Sec. 4 that it was possible to distribute data differently. Each data configuration has advantages and drawbacks, and designers must choose the distribution that corresponds best to the needs of their application. So, it would be interesting to allow different configurations, while hiding their complexity to the programmer.

Most often, the mappings are not supported by tools. However, the design of even modest temporal databases can prove very complex so that it cannot, most of the time, be carried out without the support of CASE tools. To mention one example only, a single *update trigger* controlling a bitemporal table with two foreign keys and referenced by another one, and that supports evolution and correction modifications, can be made up of *more than 500 lines of complex code.*

We will propose a solution to this problem in terms of the TimeStamp methodology for temporal databases design and of an extension of the CASE tool DB-Main that supports it. The products of the methodology are the temporal conceptual, logical and physical schemas, as well as the code necessary to manage and exploit the corresponding temporal relational database, as described in Sections 2, 3 and 4. The CASE tool allows to execute automatically all the processes of the methodology, including code generation, according to three different physical data configurations.

In this section, we first describe the conventional methodology, then we present its extension to temporal data together with the CASE tool DB-Main.

5.1 Conventional Methodology

Database design is usually carried out in three main phases: conceptual design (or analysis), logical design and physical design.

Conceptual design consists in expressing the concepts of the application domain into a high-level abstract model that is independent of the particular data model of the target DBMS. This expression is called the conceptual schema. The goal of logical design is to translate the conceptual schema into a structure adapted to the data model of the DBMS, namely the logical schema. In short, the logical schema is all the programmer have to know, and nothing more, in order to develop programs on the database. Physical design includes choosing technical implementation (e.g., indexes, data storage and clusters) and setting physical parameters.

These methodologies are now mastered and can be considered a integral part of the culture of developers.

5.2 Extension of the Methodology to Temporal Databases and CASE Tool DB-main

The methodology we propose is quite similar to the conventional one. Addressing the temporal dimension of data, merely adds new aspects to the standard processes (Fig. 3).

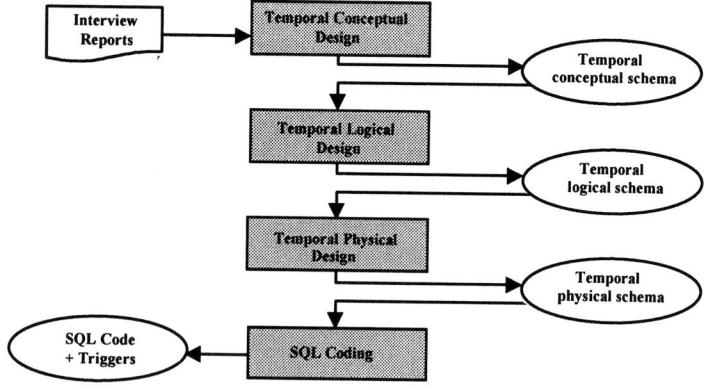

Fig. 3. Temporal Database Design Methodology. The information source is symbolically represented by *Interview reports*.

The tool that is being developed in the TimeStamp project is built as a plug-in of the DB-MAIN generic CASE platform [3]. It supports all the processes of the TimeStamp methodology, including code generation. In this section, we describe the different steps of the methodology and illustrate the main aspects of the tool through the processing of an example.

5.3 Conceptual Design

Temporal conceptual design is made up of three steps: non temporal analysis, temporal tagging and normalization.

Analysis and Temporal Tagging. In this first step, a non-temporal conceptual schema is built according to any standard methodology. Then, the schema objects that are to be temporally dimensioned are marked with the desire time-tag, namely transaction, valid, bitemporal or monotonic, as shown in Fig. 4.

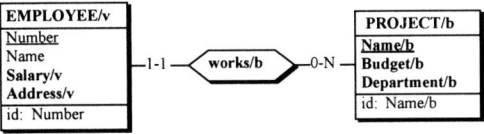

Fig. 4. Example of raw (un-normalized) temporal conceptual schema. An entity primary identifier is declared by the clause **id**. The tag /t, /v, /b, /m shows that the entity type, the relationship type or the attribute is timestamped with transaction time (t), valid time (v), both (b=bitemporal) or is monotonic (/m, for entity types only).

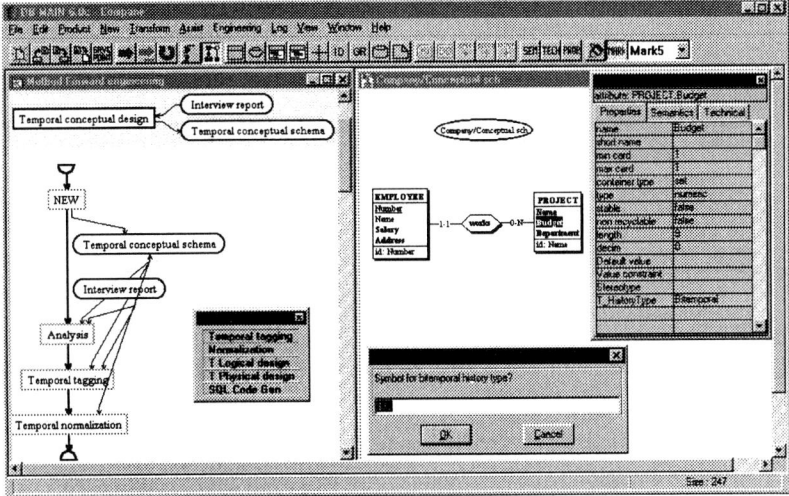

Fig. 5. *Temporal conceptual design*. The main window is that of DB-MAIN. The left hand side window shows the structure of the temporal conceptual design process. The toolbar located in this window is specific to temporal database design. It allows the automatically execution of the main four processes of the methodology. The designer draws the conceptual schema in the right side windows. The right side box shows the properties of the selected object *Budget*. The property *T_HistoryType* defines the type of time of the object (**Bitemporal**). The small box below permits to choose a suffix or a prefix to add automatically to the name of the temporal objects (represented by $). To tag objects, the designer selects a set of objects, then chooses the corresponding time- tag.

CASE support. DB-MAIN includes a graphical schema editor that allows designers to define their schemas according to various styles (UML, ERA, OO, etc.). A special property (T_HistoryType) is attached to each data structure to define its temporal characteristics. The designer chooses the way object names are tagged to show this property graphically (Fig. 4 and Fig. 5)

Normalization. Though the concept of normalized conceptual schema is well defined, introducing the time dimension induces new criteria of normalization. In short, a temporally normalized conceptual schema satisfies the consistency rules defined in Sec. 2.

As an example, the schema of Fig. 4 violates rule 5: the relationship type **works** is *bitemporal* while its 1-1 role is *valid-time* (this will introduce a temporal heterogeneity in the future relational table **EMPLOYEE**). To fix this problem, we can either mark *works* as valid time (Fig. 6).

The primary identifier of **PROJECT**, namely *Name*, is marked as temporal, violating rule 3. Therefore, we create a stable and non recyclable technical primary identifier **Code**, while *Name* becomes a secondary identifier (Fig. 6).This schema now meets all the normalization criteria.

CASE Support. The tool checks the properties that a conceptual schema must satisfy. The normalization rules that are violated are reported (Fig. 7).

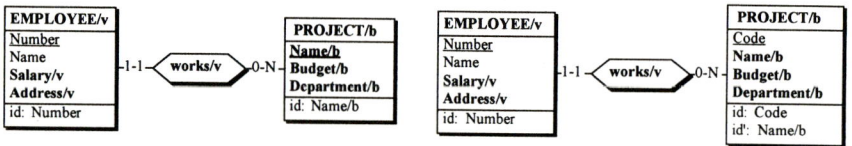

Fig. 6. Normalizing temporal relationship type *works* (left) and making entity primary identifiers non temporal, while preserving the origin uniqueness constraint (rigth).

Fig. 7. Temporal normalization tool. The checked schema is in the window. The box on the rigth cites the violated rules.

5.4 Logical Design

The temporal logical design phase consists in translating the conceptual constructs into relational structures and in adding the timestamp columns **Vstart**, **Vend**, **Tstart** and **Tend** as needed. Regarding the translation process, though sophisticated rules can be designed, we will adopt very simple mapping rules. According to them, an entity type is represented by a table, an attribute by a column, a many-to-many or N-ary relationship type into a table and foreign keys and a one-to-many relationship type by a mere foreign key.

The time tag of a relational construct is inherited from the conceptual object it derives from (Fig. 8). The temporal columns are then added: **Vstart** and **Vend** for the valid time and bitemporal tables, and **Tstart** and **Tend** for the transaction time and bitemporal tables. The primary keys are defined: (EI,Vstart), (EI,Tstart) and (EI,Vstart,Tstart) for respectively valid time, transaction time and bitemporal tables of entity tables. Similar rules applies for relationship tables. Where needed, the foreign keys are made temporal (Fig. 8).

As far as data management is concerned (through insert, delete, update statements), users can only manage current histories. They work then on a view that has the same configuration as the relational schema but that contains only the current histories, that is to say, all the states of a valid time table, the current states (**Tend**=∞) of a transaction time table, and the valid states (**Tend**=∞) of a bitemporal table.

CASE Support. The tool automatically transforms conceptual structures into relational constructions including inherited temporal tags. It adds the timestamp columns and defines the temporal foreign keys (Fig. 8).

5.5 Physical Design

During the temporal physical design, operational and performance issues are considered. Since no specialized technologies can be relied on, we have to stick to pure SQL- 92 data structures. Three optimization techniques are proposed.

1. *Table partitioning.* As briefly discussed in Sec. 4, states and columns can be distributed in different tables to improve the execution time of selected operations. The schema of Fig. 9 shows an example of physical schema in which the current states of each logical table have been duplicated into the specific tables **C_EMPLOYEE** and **C_PROJECT**.
2. *System index.* Standard index must be defined in order to support the most common temporal and non-temporal operations. They are described for monotemporal tables only, to simplify the discussion. A primary key index <EI,Start> supports (1) entity history and single state extraction, (2) projection and coalescing that include the entity primary identifier, (3) FK-to-PK temporal joins. An index on a temporal foreign key <FK,Start> supports PK-to-FK joins and FK selection. Extracting the current state of an entity can be improved by a <EI,End> index, though segregating current states in a specific table will generally be more efficient. Selecting the states that fall in a time interval will profit from an index on <Start,EI>.
3. *Auxiliary structures.* Besides standard index, additional technical tables can be built to accelerate such operations as temporal aggregation, temporal join or projections, as discussed in Sec. 4.

CASE Support. A state data distribution strategy must be chosen. At the present time, three predefined strategies are available, where temporal and non-temporal columns are all grouped in the same table:
1. all the states are in the same table;
2. a table contains the current states and another table the past and invalid states;

3. all the states are gouped in a same table and the current states are duplicated in a specific table (Fig. 9).

The temporal constraints known by the programmers at the logical level must be adapted for each of the three data configurations at the physical level. The expression of the constraints at the physical level remains hidden from the programmers, and those rules will be automatically managed by the triggers of the database.

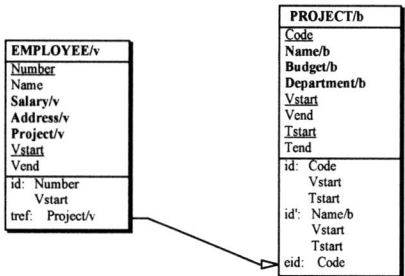

Fig. 8. Temporal logical design. The relationship types have been transformed into foreign keys and the temporal columns have been added. The clause **tref** symbolizes a temporal foreign key (*temporal reference*). The arc indicates the target candidate key, which is the entity identifier (**eid**).

SQL Code Generation. Managing and exploiting temporal data involves a high programming overhead. Therefore, it is important to relieve programmers from the burden of writing this code him/herself. The design of the database must include the writing all the technical procedures, particularly the *triggers*, that manage the tables and keep them in a consistent state.

CASE Support. A tool generates automatically the SQL code that implements the physical schema. This code can be processed by Oracle 8 and includes the definitions of the tables, views, indexes and triggers necessary to manage the temporal data, according to the physical parameters chosen by the developer. The generation of the temporal ODBC drivers, that implement the stratum architecture, still is under development.

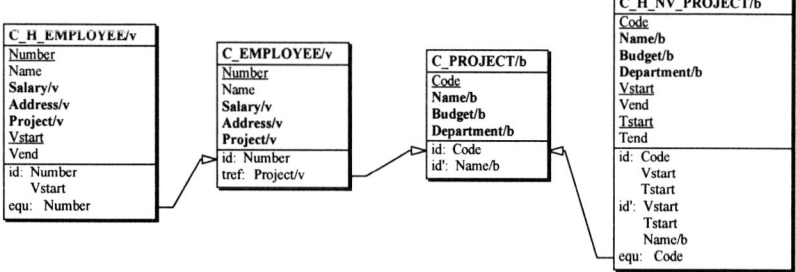

Fig. 9. Physical schema. The clause **equ** symbolizes an *equality* constraint, that combines a foreign key (ref) with an inverse inclusion constraint. For each logical table, a complete history table is maintained, together with a new table that includes the current states.

6 Conclusion

The goal of the TimeStamp project, which started in 1997, was to make, as much as possible, the research results in temporal databases available to practitioners, i.e., *standard* developers and programmers. Considering the richness and the complexity of the concepts of this domain, most of our effort was devoted to simplify them, while retaining enough power and flexibility for making them usable in practical situations.

The simplification has addressed two directions. First, the concepts have been reduced in order to make them easy to understand and to teach. The simplified temporal conceptual model induces a reduced temporal relational logical model, which in turn implies simple and efficient data management techniques. In addition, the methodology we propose is a slight extension of widespread approaches. Secondly, all the burden of developing temporal databases has been taken in charge by a CASE tool and an API has been defined and implemented to make the programming process easier and, more important, more reliable.

Despite this effort, mastering temporal database concepts still is a challenging task, as we experienced when teaching them to practitioners. In particular, understanding bitemporal databases and their dynamic behavior has proved very difficult, and often out of the competence of many ordinary programmers. Since the problem lies in the interpretation of bitemporal data, it cannot be completely solved by merely automating the development processes. Therefore, we consider that education is a major aspect of diffusing temporal database principles, at least as important as developing automated tools and API.

Several questions and points remain unsolved: optimized physical design in the context of the stratum architecture, migration of legacy data to temporal database and coping with schema evolution [4].

7 Credits

Jeff Wijsen kindly reviewed our results and made several important suggestions to improve the models. Babis Theodoulidis and his staff, hosted O. Ramlot during his stay in UMIST, Manchester. Their comments were essential for the definition of the temporal ODBC interface. Ramez Elmasri, who hosted one of our students too, helped him to understand and master physical implementation of temporal databases. Thanks to them.

8 References

1. BÖHLEN M., *Temporal Database System Implementations*, ACM SIGMOD Record, 24(4):53- 60, December, 1995.
2. BÖhlen M., Coalescing in Temporal Databases, Proc. of the 22nd VLDB Conference, Bombay, India, 1996.
3. DB-MAIN, http://www.db-main.be
4. ELMASRI R., WEI H., *Study and Comparison of Schema Versioning and Database Conversion Techniques for Bi-temporal Databases*, Proceedings of the Sixth International Workshop on Temporal Representation and Reasoning (TIME-99), Orlando, Florida, May 1999, IEEE Computer Society.

5. FERG S., *Modeling the Time Dimension in an Entity-Relationship Diagram*, Proceedings of the 4th International Confernce on the Entity-Relationship Approach, pages 280-286, Siver Spring, MD, 1985.
6. GREGERSEN H., JENSEN C. S., MARK L., *Evaluating Temporally Extended ER Models*, Proceedings of the Second CAISE/IFIP8.1 International Workshop on Evaluation of Modeling Methods in System Analysis and Design, 12p, K. Siau, Y. Wand, J. Parsons, editors, Barcelona, Spain, June 1997.
7. GREGERSEN H., MARK L., JENSEN C. S., *Mapping Temporal ER Diagrams to Relational Schemas*, Technical Report TR-39, Aalborg University, Department of Mathematics and Computer Science, December 1998.
8. HAINAUT, J.-L., ROLAND, D., HICK, J.-M., HENRARD, J., ENGLEBERT, V., Database Reverse Engineering: from Requirements to CARE tools, *Journal of Automated Software Engineering*, Vol. 3, No. 2, 1996
9. JENSEN C., SNODGRASS R., *Temporal Data Management*, Technical Report TR-17, TIMECENTER, 1997.
10. LAI V.S., KUILBOER J-P., GUYNES J. L., *Temporal Databases : Model Design and Commercialization Prospects*, DATA BASE, 25(3), 1994.
11. SNODGRASS R., *The TSQL2 Temporal Query Language*, Kluwer Academic Publishers, Massachussetts, USA, 1995.
12. SNODGRASS R., *Developing Time-Oriented Database Applications in SQL*, Morgan Kaufmann Publishers, USA, 2000.
13. STEINER A., *A Generalisation approach to Temporal Data Models and their Implementations*, Thesis of the Swiss Federal Institute of Technology for the degree of Doctor of Technical Sciences, Zürich, 1998.
14. SVINTERIKOU M., THEODOULIDIS C., *The Temporal Unified Modelling Language*, Department of Computation, UMIST, United Kingdom, October 1997.
15. THEODOULIDIS C.I., LOUCOPOULOS P., WANGLER B., *A Conceptual Modelling Formalism for Temporal Database Applications*, Information Systems, 16(4), 1991.
16. WIJSEN J., *Temporal FDs on Complex objects*, ACM Transactions on Database Systems, Vol 24., No.1,Pages 127-176, March 1999

Domain-Specific Metadata a Key for Building Semantically-Rich Schema Models

Abdel-Rahman H. Tawil, Nicholas J. Fiddian, and William A. Gray

Department of Computer Science, Cardiff University, U. K.
{Abdel-Rahman.Tawil, N.J.Fiddian, W.A.Gray}@cs.cf.ac.uk

Abstract. Providing integrated access to data from many diverse and heterogeneous Information Servers (ISs) requires deep knowledge, not only about the structure of the data represented at each server, but also about the commonly occurring differences in the intended semantics of this data. Unfortunately, very often there is a lack of such knowledge and the local schemas, being semantically weak as a consequence of the limited expressiveness of traditional data models, do not help the acquisition of this knowledge. In this paper we propose domain-specific metadata as a key for upgrading the semantic level of the local ISs to which an integration system requires access, and for building semantically-rich schema models. We provide a framework for enriching the individual IS schemas with semantic domain knowledge to make explicit the assumptions which may have been made by their designers, are of interest to the integrator (interpreter or user), and which may not be captured using the DDL language of their host servers. The enriched schema semantic knowledge is organised by levels of schematic granularity: database, schema, attribute and instance levels giving rise to semantically-rich schema models.

Keywords: Semantic interoperability, mediators, domain ontologies, schema enrichment.

1 Introduction

Recent advances in database and communication technologies have led to the wide-spread availability of a variety of Information Servers (ISs), and a corresponding demand for accessing and integrating data across these servers. Information servers include database systems, which may typically be relational or object-oriented, file systems, dedicated data servers for text and image databases.

Attempting to integrate data from many diverse and heterogeneous ISs can be problematic, not only because of the possible differences (heterogeneities) in the *structure* of the data represented in each server, but also because of the commonly occurring differences in the intended *semantics* or *the content* of this data. The same information could be represented in various incompatible structures, and the same structure could be used to represent information with many diverse and incompatible semantics. Unfortunately, current commercially available ISs generally provide very little support for higher level semantic (conceptual) modelling and do not offer a sufficiently rich set of constructs to adequately model the Real World (RW). As such, their data models are semantically weak in that they do not capture the full semantics of an application in a database nor can they expressively represent the Real World Semantics (RWSs) of its data in an explicit and natural manner. Consequently, databases hide much of the semantics about the objects they represent and may not contain sufficient RWS knowledge associated with these objects and known to the designer. Hence, the real challenge facing integration systems is how to identify semantically (conceptually) related data in different databases and to resolve the schematic (representational) conflicts among this data. This problem is traditionally referred to as the need for semantic interoperability among autonomous and heterogeneous systems [8].

Research into semantic interoperability includes techniques that attempt to provide an architecture, or an overall framework to support interoperability at the semantic level. A number of ideas concerning interoperable IS system approaches can be thought of as constructing answers to queries using views that represent the content and possibly the capabilities of several information servers. Prime examples of such approaches include the unified global schema approach [12] which describes a single integrated view, and the multiple integrated schema approach [6] which creates multiple federated views. Another emerging solution to this problem is the development of information mediators. An information mediator provides seamless access to a collection of related, but possibly heterogeneous and distributed ISs by constructing semantically-rich integrated views of the underlying information sources to which access is required. There are a variety of ways of building information mediators, illustrated by different approaches used in systems such as SIMS [1], COIN [8] and Information Manifold [11], to name but a few. However, one issue that is common to all of these approaches is how to provide semantically-rich integrated views over large numbers of information sources in a way that is both computationally tractable and natural to the developers of new applications.

As semantic interoperability is a process in which knowledge of the semantics of the data is required, it is no surprise that most of these integration ideas rely on a semantic data modelling approach (e.g. functional, object-oriented, frame-based). In particular the mediator approach advocates the use of Knowledge Representation Systems (KRSs), especially those descendent of the KL-One [16] family of Knowledge Representation Languages (KRLs), also known as concept languages or Description Logic (DL) languages. For example, the LOOM knowledge representation system was used in the SIMS project to describe an ontology of the transport domain; CARIN, a dialect of Classic description logic was used in the Information Manifold (IM) project for describing IM world-view concepts. However, description logic and KL-One style languages are not the only languages used for building ontologies. For example, in the context interchange project [8], F-Logic [10] is used to describe ontologies, while in [9], Prolog is used in a bottom-up approach to ontology construction. It is not clear to date which requirements a language for semantic modelling should satisfy.

In this paper we advocate the use of a Generic Knowledge Model (GKM) that is both DBMS Data Definition Language (DDL) and application-specific semantics independent. The MetaMed GKM (MGKM) is a 'logical' knowledge model in the sense that it uses a prefix version of first order predicate calculus (KIF) [7] as a way of representing knowledge (of the data being modelled) and as a language for expressing operations on these knowledge structures. At the same time it is an object-oriented model because it adopts the Open Knowledge Base Connectivity (OKBC) knowledge model [4] which assumes an 'object-centric' view of the world and supports many features (e.g. object-identity, type hierarchy, inheritance, subsumption, and overriding) commonly associated with object-orientation.

This paper is organised in the following way. In the next section we discuss how the MGKM is built. In section 3, we discuss the schema enrichment process and give an example of a semantically enriched schema model. Section 4 contains our conclusions.

2 The MetaMed Generic Knowledge Model

Providing integrated access to information dispersed across diverse ISs requires general familiarity with their *contents and structural representations*, with their *data models and query languages*, with their *location on existing networks*, and more. This, in turn, requires that the semantic model of the integration system provides the necessary '*vocabulary*' (*terms* or *concepts*) and language flexibility for describing such knowledge, and for reasoning about it. As a semantic model for a medical application domain the MGKM should accommodate the necessary body of knowledge required to transform a disparate collection of medical database schemas into semantically enriched schema models, and to provide integration information at the right level of abstraction for end-user applications. Considering that we are particularly interested in capturing the *structure* (representational details) and the *semantic content* (the domain about which information is stored) of the individual ISs, the MGKM should provide the necessary body of knowledge for capturing the semantic and structural details of these servers.

In the MGKM, this is achieved by means of an ODMG-93 based knowledge model accompanying the semantic knowledge model of the problem domain. We adopt *a subset* of the Object Definition Language (ODL) specification based on the ODMG standard [3], called ODL_{I^3} [1], as our GKM for addressing representational heterogeneity in the metadata of schema structures. We also advocate the use of a semantic model of the federation or application domain as our GKM

---

[1] Derived from the I^3 mediator language proposal, as described in [2].

for addressing the heterogeneity of metadata Real World Semantics (RWSs). Currently we are using a master notation of medical terminology and COding REference (CORE) model, called GALEN[2] (Generalised Architecture for Languages, Encyclopaedias and Nomenclatures), as the *semantic model* used to support the integration of medical ISs.

The Ontolingua OKBC internal Knowledge Representation Language (KRL) is the modelling formalism with which both the MetaMed ODL ($MODL_{I^3}$) and MetaMed GALEN (MGALEN) knowledge models are built. Both these models express conceptualisations which are specific to particular domains (the *ODL* and the *medical* domains) and hence are considered as domain ontologies.

2.1 A Shared Domain Model of Medical Concepts

The MGALEN domain model includes a hierarchical terminological knowledge base with nodes representing all objects, actions and states possible in the domain. In addition, it includes indications of all relationships possible between classes in the model. In MGALEN the primary breakdown is into:

- *Generalised-Structures* – abstract or physical things with parts independent of time;
  Generalised-Substances continuous abstract or physical things independent of time;
- *Generalised-Processes* – changes which occur over time; and
- *Modifiers* – a heterogeneous grouping of adjectives and qualifiers.

Entity	Example	Entity	Example
Generalised-Substance		**Generalised-Process**	
Energy	Radiation, SoundEnergy	Biological-Process	
Substance		Body-Process	Breathing, Clotting
Body-Substance	Urine, Bile, Sputum	Non-Biological-Process	
Chemical-Substance	Drug, Sodium, ...	Physical-Process	Irradiation
Generalised-Structure		**Modifier-Concept**	
Abstract-Structure		Aspect	
Solid-Structure		Feature	Sex, Chronicity, Shape, Malignancy
Microscopic-Structure	Cell, Micro-Organism	State	Male/Female, Acute/Chronic, Round/Square
Organic-Solid-Structure		Selector	Left-Selector/Right-Selector
Body-Structure		Status	Pathological/Physiological
Body-Part	Heart, Leg, Lung, Femur, ...	Modality	Family-History, Presence/Absence
Organism	Bacteria, Virus, Fungus, ...	Role	Drug-Role, Hormone-Role, Patient-Role

Table 1. A High-Level Taxonomy of Major Elementary Categories in MGALEN

MGALEN further divides structures, substances and processes into organic and inorganic or biological and non-biological categories, as shown in Table 1.

---

[2] GALEN is a EU-funded project as part of the Advanced Informatics in Medicine programme of the Commission of the European Union, AIM 2012 [13].

A taxonomy of *domain relations* is influenced by, and supports, the concept hierarchy (concept taxonomy) outlined in Table 1. It includes indications of all relationships possible between concepts in the model. Here, the primary distinction is between:

- *Constructive-Relations*, linking processes, structures, and substances together (e.g. Is-Suffering-From, Is-Suspected, Holds-Information-About, Has-Location, etc), and
- *Modifier-Relations*, linking processes, structures, and substances to modifiers (e.g. Has-Absolute-State, Has-Trend-In-State, Has-Pathological-Status, etc).

Domain relations (also referred to as *slots* or *roles*) are used to describe the *composition* (relationship) between two concepts or two concept values. A domain relation can be seen as a predicate with two arguments: the *domain* (the concept with which it is associated) and the *range* (the type of values that it can have). For example, there is an entity in the domain model representing the class (concept) of Lung and an entity representing the concept of Tumour. There is a *constructive anatomical-locative* relation has-location specified between the Tumour Concept (*the domain*) and the Lung Concept (*the range*) with a notation indicating that a disease (e.g. Tumour) is located in a body part (e.g the Lung). Thus the relationship (has-location Tumour Lung) can be composed. Similarly, *modifier* relations are specified between a disease and its chronicity, and take one of the following state values: acute, chronic or sub-acute. Thus the relation (has-chronicity Tumour Chronic) can also be composed.

The resulting concepts using this approach are called *composite concepts*. This allows for detailed description of complex concepts while preserving the structure provided by the individual basic concepts in the description. Compositional modelling provides a mechanism for representing descriptive knowledge using the defined vocabulary. For example, the Right-Lung-Pneumonia concept is a composite concept composed from both the Right-Lung and Pneumonia concepts. Moreover, Right-Lung is a composite concept composed from both the Lung concept and the Right selector concept, and Pneumonia is the name of an Infection located in the Lung. Hence, the KIF axioms shown in Figure 1 hold.

```
(=> (Patient ?X)                    (=> (and (Lung ?X)
    (Subclass-Of ?X Person)).                (Has-Laterality Lung Right))
                                        (Right-Lung ?X)).

(=> (Pneumonia ?X)                  (=> (and (Pneumonia ?X)
    (and (Infection ?X)                      (Has-Location ?X Right-Lung))
         (Has-Location ?X Lung))).      (Right-Lung-Pneumonia ?X)).
```

Fig. 1. A KIF Example of Compositional Modelling of Concepts

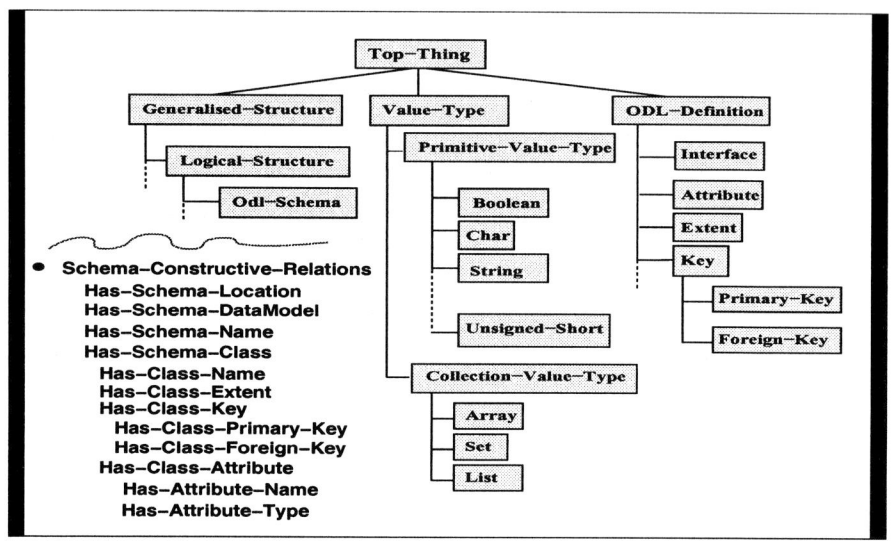

Fig. 2. A Fragment of the $MODL_{I3}$ Knowledge Model

2.2 A Shared $MODL_{I3}$ Model of Schema Structures

The MGALEN knowledge model provides shared terminology which can be used as a framework for expressing semantic domain knowledge about the content of the underlying ISs in a coherent and consistent manner. Another major problem to be faced in such an environment is related to representational heterogeneity. Representational conflict arises whenever parts of the same reality are represented in different ISs using different representational constructs. This is due, (i) to different perspectives and needs when modelling the same information, (ii) to the rich set of constructs in data models which result in variations in the conceptual database structures, and/or (iii) to different design specifications which lead to different schemas.

Acting as a schema specification language, $MODL_{I3}$ is capable of expressing the representational semantics of the schema structures of a variety of data models and Data Definition Languages (DDLs), (e.g. characteristics of relations including their attributes, primary keys and foreign key relationships). It is however unable and is not intended for capturing the actual semantics of the schema contents. The $MODL_{I3}$ knowledge model is much more restricted and confined compared with the MGALEN semantic model. The MetaMed prototype has so far been developed to handle relational data models, and is currently being extended to handle OO and semi-structured data models. The ODL_{I3} knowledge model offers a concept taxonomy with its primary break-down into *Logical-Structure*, *Value-Type* and *ODL-Definition*, see Figure 2.

Schema constructive relations (Figure 2) are used to link $MODL_{I3}$ schemas, classes, attributes and attribute types together. An $MODL_{I3}$ relationship can be seen as a predicate with two arguments: the *domain* —the ODL_{I3} concept with which it is associated; and the *range* —the type of ODL_{I3} values that it can have. Given a relational database B_{Rel}, the MetaMed ODL_{I3} logical model $B_{Rel-MODL}$ is specified in the order-category of $MODL_{I3}$ terms and relationships, which essentially defines an object logical view of the underlying relational database with the following sorts: a schema sort Sch, a table sort Tbl, an attribute sort Attr:

- a predicate Odl-Schema of sort Sch, where $B_{MODL} \vdash$ (Odl-Schema Sch) if Sch is an IS schema.
- a predicate Interface of sort Tbl, where $B_{MODL} \vdash$ (Interface Tbl) if Tbl is a primary relation.
- a predicate Attribute of sort Attr, where $B_{MODL} \vdash$ (Attribute Attr) if Attr is an attribute of an Odl-Schema.
- a predicate Has-Schema-Interface of sort Sch X Tbl (Has-Schema-Interface Sch Tbl) if Tbl is a table of the schema Sch.
- a predicate Has-Attribute-Type of sort Attr X Value-Type (Primitive-Value-Type: *Boolean, Char, String, .. etc*), where $B_{MODL} \vdash$ (Has-Attribute-Type Attr Value-Type).
- a predicate Subclass-Of of sort Tbl_x X Tbl_y, where $B_{MODL} \vdash$ (Subclass-Of Tbl_x Tbl_y) if there is an inclusion dependency between Tbl_x and Tbl_y in B_{rel}.

In the next section we present a framework for enriching the individual IS schemas with metadata descriptions formulated in terms of the MGKM vocabulary.

3 The Schema Enrichment Process

Our schema enrichment process relates the local schema elements to the MGKM concepts that they denote. Accordingly, the different local IS schemas are mapped to the MGKM structures in the component schemas. Thus an interpretation is provided, *in the form of descriptive knowledge* (metadata), for each local schema element, describing it to our system. Each MGKM schema view should provide a precise description of what information is stored in the local schema it represents.

In the following we discuss the relationship between the relational data model and the MGKM object knowledge model so that we can establish a mapping from the relational model to our object frame-based knowledge representation system. The choice of the relational data model is one of convenience rather than necessity, and is not to be construed as a constraint on the enrichment strategy being proposed.

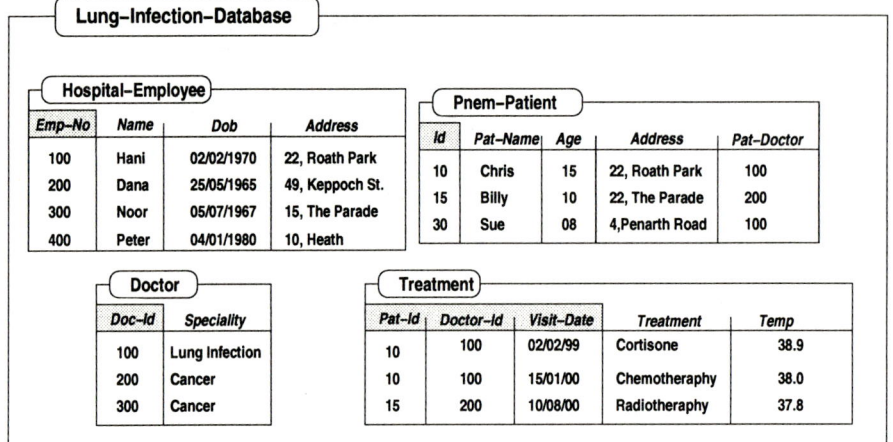

Fig. 3. The Lung-Infection-Database — example of a relational database

3.1 MODL$_{I^3}$ — Representing Data Structure

In the first step of our schema enrichment process, the MetaMed *schema extraction tool* extracts the metadata of the schema to be enriched and automatically builds an MODL$_{I^3}$ description of that schema. Consider the relational database example (Lung-Infection-Database) shown in Figure 3, which is deliberately kept simple for didactical reasons. The database stores information about patients suffering from *pneumonia*. The identification number Id, Pat-Name, Age, Address and Pat-Doctor for each patient are stored in the Pnem-Patient table. The treatments taken by each patient are stored in the Treatment table. A patient may undergo different types of treatments during his repeated visits. The Hospital-Employee table holds information about all the employees working in the hospital. The Doctor table identifies those employees of the hospital who are doctors and provides information about their Speciality. Boxed-in attributes are primary key attributes.

The following inclusion dependencies[3] hold in the Lung-Infection-Database:

```
Doctor.Doc-Id ⊆ Hospital-Employee.Emp-No
Treatment.Pat-Id ⊆ Pnem-Patient.Id
Treatment.Doctor-Id ⊆ Doctor.Id
```

Often there is a close correspondence between types in the MODL$_{I^3}$ object knowledge model and relations in the relational model, between *relations* and *interfaces*, and between *objects* and *tuples*. In reality there is no one-to-one correspondence between relational modelling constructs and the OO modelling con-

---

[3] An inclusion dependency R.x ⊆ S.y between a set of attributes x of relation R and a set of attributes y of relation S means that the values of x must also exist as values of y.

structs. There are always different ways to map between constructs in one of the data models to constructs in the other. In particular, there are some concepts in the object model for which there are no corresponding concepts in the relational data model. For example, complex objects are not supported by the relational data model — no multivalued or composite attributes are allowed; generalisation/specialisation has no correspondence in the relational data model. When subtype/supertype relationships exist between objects in the domain which is modelled, this is only represented implicitly in relational databases. Also, the concept of *object identity* is not present in the relational data model.

As an example, we will show how the relational database schemas Pnem-Patient and Doctor of the Lung-Infection-Database are mapped to an MODL$_{I^3}$ schema. The attributes Id, Pat-Name, Age, Address and Pat-Doctor in the Pnem-Patient relation each correspond to a slot defined on the Pnem-Patient type (Interface). A multivalued attribute is defined on the Pnem-Patient type corresponding to different *treatments* the patient is subjected to. Doctor is defined as a subclass of the Hospital-Employee relation:

```
(ODL-Schema Lung-Infection-Database).
(Interface Pnem-Patient).
(Interface Hospital-Employee).
(Interface Doctor).
(Interface Treatment).
(Is-Interface-Of-ODL-Schema Pnem-Patient
                    Lung-Infection-Database).
(Attribute Id).
(Attribute Pat-Name).
(Attribute Age).
(Attribute Address).
(Attribute Pat-Doctor).
(Has-Schema-Class   Lung-Infection-Database  Pnem-Patient).
(Has-Primary-Key    Pnem-Patient       Id).
(Has-Foreign-Key    Pnem-Patient       Pat-Doctor).
(Is-Foreign-Key-Of  Pat-Doctor     Doctor).
(and (Has-Class-Attribute Pnem-Patient Id)
     (Has-Attribute-Type  Id Integer)).
(and (Has-Class-Attribute Pnem-Patient Pat-Name)
     (Has-Attribute-Type Pat-Name String)).
(and (Has-Class-Attribute Pnem-Patient Pat-Doctor)
     (Has-Attribute-Type Pat-Doctor Doctor)).
...
(Subclass-Of Doctor Hospital-Employee).
(Attribute Doc-Id).
(Attribute Speciality).
(and (Has-Class-Attribute Doctor Doc-Id)
     (Has-Attribute-Type  Doc-Id String)).
....
```

If we examine the extension of the relational database, we will find that it stores information about *four* hospital employees and *three* patients. Three of the hospital employees are doctors, and two of the patients have undergone treatment, one of them *Chris* is treated twice. Informally the semantics of the mapping between *tuples* in the relational database and *objects* in the MODL$_{I^3}$ view is as follows. There is one object for each tuple in the employee table. A combination of the *table-name* and the *primary-key* is used to define the correspondence between tuples and objects. For example, the [Pnem-Patient:10] (*Oid* or *frame handle*) corresponds to the object patient *Chris* identified by identification number 10. If we ask the query (Select * from Pnem-Patient where Pat-Name = "Chris"), we will get the following answer:

```
(and (Id          [Pnem-Patient:10] 10)
     (Pat-Name    [Pnem-Patient:10] Chris)
     (Age         [Pnem-Patient:10] 15)
     (Address     [Pnem-Patient:10] 22, Roath Park)
     (Pat-Doctor  [Pnem-Patient:10] [Doctor:100])
     (Treatment   [Pnem-Patient:10] (Set-Of [Treatment:10:100:02/02/99]

[Treatment:10:200:15/01/00]))).
```

Note that the extension of the view is not physically stored anywhere. The values of the MODL$_{I^3}$ classes are computed every time the system is queried. However, to the user of the view, it behaves as if the extension had been physically stored.

3.2 MGALEN — Representing Data Semantics

A well-known problem with the relational data model is that it does not provide a rich type structure for values that occur in attributes and relations. Accordingly, the class graph of the generated MODL$_{I^3}$ KB (view) is trivial, in that it simply states the ontological commitments made by the relational model as it is mapped to an OO one.

In practice, relational databases have large hidden ontologies that are implicit in their schema design. For example, the database schema designer might have labelled a column Temp, but what was probably meant is '*temperature in degrees centigrade*'. A more sophisticated binding is required to represent the slot Temp not just as an *MODL$_{I^3}$ Integer*, but as a frame denoting '*temperature in degrees centigrade*'. Allowing for semantic values to be drawn from a rich set of types would considerably increase the modelling power (expressiveness) of the relational data model in representing data semantics. In the MetaMed system this is achieved by augmenting the MODL$_{I^3}$ view with semantic domain knowledge formulated in terms of the MGALEN semantic model.

The premise that data semantics are values drawn from semantic domains is key to our approach. Knowledge of data semantics is represented in the form of descriptions (composite concepts) formulated using terms drawn from a semantic domain model (ontology). For example, the assumptions regarding the temperature can be made explicit in the following way:

(and (Temperature Temp)
    (Has-Dimension Temp Temperature-Unit)
    (Has-Unit Temp Centigrade)).

The terms **Temperature**, **Centigrade** and the binary links (relationships) **Has-Dimension**, and **Has-Unit** are terms drawn from the MGALEN semantic model. Where **Temperature** is defined as a *physical substance feature*, **Centigrade** is defined as a *unit modifier concept*, and both **Has-Dimension** and **Has-Unit** are *quantity relations*. Given that the process of eliciting semantic domain knowledge is an expensive one, this knowledge should be represented in a form that is *sharable* and *reusable*. Also, knowledge of data semantics should be represented in a form from which relevant inferences can be made efficiently.

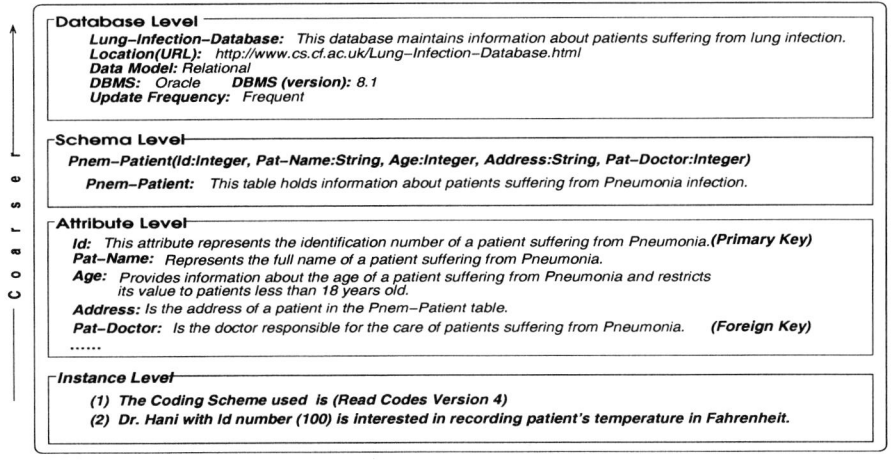

Fig. 4. A Partial Semantic View of the Pnem-Patient table

Figure 4 represents a *partial semantic view* of the **Pnem-Patient** table, used in the following discussion to illustrate the semantic enrichment process.

3.2.1 Eliciting Data Semantics

The viability of our approach for semantic interoperability is largely contingent on how knowledge of data semantics can be represented effectively. In this next step of our enrichment process, mapping from data sources to the MGALEN semantic model is enabled by a *semantic mapping* process, in which semantic domain knowledge of the stored information is gathered. The semantic domain knowledge (metadata) acquired is organised by levels of schematic granularity — *database, schema, attribute* and *instance* levels.

☐ The **database level** is general — it is knowledge that pertains to all levels of schematic granularity. It includes *direct-content metadata* about the domain and nature of the information stored in the database schema, as well as *content-independent metadata* necessary to access the extensions of the database. In our **Lung-Infection-Database** example, Figure 4, the direct-content metadata could simply be the knowledge that **Lung-Infection-Database** stores information about patients suffering from lung infection. Associated content metadata could be something like 'lung infection is an infection located in the lung' or 'lung infection is suspected from patients having a history of smoking'.

Hence, the **Odl-Schema** concept **Lung-Infection-Database** may be enriched by adding to it the following axiom (rule), described in the KIF formal specification language: *the Lung-Infection-Database maintains information about patients suffering from lung infection.*

```
(and (Holds-Information-About Lung-Infection-Database Patient)
     (Is-Suffering-From Patient Lung-Infection)).
```

Once this *domain knowledge* is asserted, the following *general associated knowledge* is automatically added to the knowledge base of the schema model: *Lung infection is an infection, which is located in the lung, and is suspected from patients having a history of smoking.*

```
(=> (and (Infection ?Inf) (Is-Located-In ?Inf Lung))
    (Lung-Infection ?Inf)).

(=> (Is-Suspected Lung-Infection ?Pat)
    (and (Patient ?Pat) (Has-History-Of ?Pat Smoking))).
```

Content-independent metadata at the *database level* includes information such as the *type, location, access rights, owner, creation date,* etc. In this respect, the **Lung-Infection-Database** may be enriched by adding the following knowledge:

```
(Has-Schema-DataModel  Lung-Infection-Database  Relational).
(Has-Schema-Location   Lung-Infection-Database
                       http://www.cs.cf.ac.uk/Lung-Infection-Database).
(and (Has-DBMS Lung-Infection-Database  Oracle)
     (Has-DBMS-Version Lung-Infection-Database  8.1)).
```

☐ The **schema level** includes an abstract (general) view of the cross-product of the domains of the attributes in a particular relational schema. Accordingly, the **Pnem-Patient** schema concept may be enriched by adding the *general domain knowledge* that **Pnem-Patient** holds information about patients suffering from pneumonia. Of course, the *general associated knowledge* that a *patient* is a *person* or that *pneumonia* is an *infection located* in the *lung* is automatically added to the schema model.

```
(and (Subclass-Of Pnem-Patient Patient) (Is-Suffering-From Pnem-Patient
    Pneumonia)).
```

The following knowledge is automatically added:

```
(=> (Patient ?X) (Person ?X))

(=> (Pneumonia ?X)
    (and (Infection ?X)
         (Has-Location ?X Lung))).
```

The *schema level* is considered to be one level in granularity below the *database level*. Knowledge captured at this level tends to be more specific and detailed in comparison to that captured at the database level. For example, we may be able to determine from the knowledge captured at the *database level* that the database stores information about patients suffering from lung infection. At the *schema level*, however, it may be possible to determine that one particular table of this database is storing information about *Pneumonia*, a particular type of lung infection.

□ The *attribute level* holds the semantic domain knowledge specific to each attribute in a particular schema, as well as additional constraint knowledge about the nature of the information corresponding to each attribute as represented in its respective schema. For example, the Age attribute of the Pnem-Patient schema represents the ages of patients suffering from pneumonia. Also, the ages stored are constrained to patients who are less than 18 years old (see Figure 4). To reflect this knowledge, we first define (Pnem-Patient.Age) as a *subrelation* of the Has-Person-Age relation of the MGALEN Person concept and then restrict its value to less than 18.

```
(Subrelation-Of Pnem-Patient.Pat-Name  Has-Person-Name).
(Subrelation-Of Pnem-Patient.Age  Has-Person-Age).

(=> (Pnem-Patient.Age ?Age-Value)
    (< (?Age-Value 18))).
```

Subrelation-Of is a binary relationship that maps schema attributes to MGALEN frames (slots). When a schema attribute is defined as subrelation-of an MGALEN frame it inherits all the properties associated with that frame. Accordingly, Pnem-Patient.Age inherits all the properties of the MGALEN Has-Person-Age frame it is a subrelation of (e.g. age must be greater than or equal to zero, a person can have only one age value at a particular point in time ...).

The semantics of the remaining attributes associated with the Pnem-Patient table are defined in the following way:

```
(Subrelation-Of Pnem-Patient.Id  Has-Patient-Identification-Number).
(Subrelation-Of Pnem-Patient.Pat-Doctor  Has-Patient-Doctor).
```

☐ Object identification techniques within a single database rely on the assumption that there is a one-to-one correspondence between RW objects and database objects. This assumption is no longer valid in interoperable IS systems. Accordingly, schema concepts which are intentionally similar at the *database, schema* or *attribute* levels may represent different RW objects at the *instance (extension)* level. Also, the same RW object may be identified, in different ISs, using different representations, primary keys or Oids.

MetaMed, as a schema integration tool, is responsible for defining rules associated with individual instances that assist in determining inter-object equivalences. Let us look at two different examples where *direct content metadata* plays an important role in determining inter-object relationships in the **Lung-Infection-Database**.

1. In the same hospital you may find some doctors recording the temperature in *Fahrenheit* while others do so in *Centigrade*. Hence, the temperature unit varies with respect to the individual (doctor) who is recording the data. This is possible because the unit used to measure a temperature is not an inherent property of the temperature whereas its dimension is (the dimension of all temperatures taken is **temperature-unit-degree**, but the magnitude of a temperature can be measured by any unit of the **temperature unit degrees** such as **Fahrenheit** or **Centigrade**). This is an example where *direct content metadata* is necessary when the data is to be considered for integration:

    ```
    (=> (and (Interface Treatment)
             (Has-Attribute-Value  Treatment.Doctor-Id  100))
        (Has-Temperature-Unit-Degree  Treatment.Temp  Fahrenheit)).
    ```

2. Coding and medical records have been closely linked, with coding being offered as a means to improve the ability of handling clinical information. Various medical information systems may use different coding schemes, or even different versions of the same coding scheme (see [5]). Integrating medical data from different ISs may require the mapping of entities to and from existing coding and classification schemes. Knowledge about the coding schemes used to record the data is essential. Such instance level semantic knowledge can be asserted by adding it to the concept representing the **Lung-Infection-Database**, as it affects the whole database.

    ```
    (and (Uses-Coding-Scheme Lung-Infection-Database Read-code)
         (has-Read-code-version Read-code 4)).
    ```

The accuracy of the system in discovering semantic relationships between the schema terms and the MGALEN semantic model increases as the level of schematic granularity becomes finer. The system uses the knowledge acquired at the previous (higher) levels to discover knowledge at the next level. MetaMed provides a graphical user environment to assist users during this phase of the enrichment process.

4 Conclusion

Clearly, it is not possible to completely define what an object denotes or means, no matter how expressive the modelling language is or how rich the semantic knowledge model can be. In this paper we have presented a formal framework for representing semantic domain knowledge of individual IS schemas. We endeavour to make explicit that knowledge which a human integrator uses implicitly to identify semantically similar schema concepts and to resolve semantic conflicts among schema elements that are to be integrated. The MGKM is an integral part of the MetaMed integration system which allows one to create semantically-rich descriptions of ISs by lifting the IS structural and semantic content into the MGKM vocabulary [14]. The MGKM is also used to reformulate global queries on the integrated schema as queries specific to the individual IS's query language and terminology [15].

References

[1] Y. Arens, C. Y. Chee, C. Hsu, and C. A. Knoblock. Retrieving and integrating data from multiple information sources. *International Journal of Intelligent and Cooperative Information Systems*, 2(2):127–158, 1993.

[2] P. Buneman, L. Raschid, and J. Ullman. Mediator languages - a proposal for a standard. Report of an I3/POB Working Group held at the University of Maryland, ftp://ftp.umiacs.umd.edu/pub/ONRrept/medmodel96.ps, April 1996.

[3] R.G. Cattel and Morgan Kufmann. *ODMG-93 The Object Database Standard Release 1.2.* Inc., San Francisco, California, 1996.

[4] Vinary K. Chaudhri, Adam Farquhar, Richard Fikes, Peter D. Karp, and James P. Rice. OKBC: A programmatic foundation for knowledge base interoperability. *AAAI-98*, pages 26–30, July 1998.

[5] J Chisholm. The read clinical classification. *British Medical Journal*, page 1092, 1990.

[6] Rehab M. Duwairi. *Views for Interoperability in a Heterogeneous Object-Oriented Multidatabase System*. PhD thesis, Department of Computer Science, University of Wales College of Cardiff, April 1997.

[7] M. Genesereth and R. Fikes. Knowledge Interchange Format. Technical report, Stanford University, June 1992.

[8] C. H. Goh, S. Bressan, S. Madnick, and M. Siegel. Context interchange: New features and formalisms for the intelligent integration of information. *ACM Transactions on Information Systems*, 17(3):270–293, July 1999.

[9] D. D. Karunaratna, W. A. Gray, and N. J. Fiddian. Establishing a knowledge base to assist integration of heterogeneous databases. In Suzanne M. Embury et al, editor, *Proceedings of 16th British National Conference on Databases (BNCOD16)*, LNCS 1405, Springer, pages 103–118, 1998.

[10] M. Kifer and G. Lauson. F-logic: A higher-order language for reasoning about objects, inheritance and scheme. *Proceedings of ACM SIGMOD Conference*, 1995.

[11] Alon Y. Levy, D. Srivastava, and T. Kirk. Data model and query evaluation in global information systems. *Journal of Intelligent Information Systems*, 5(2), 1995.

[12] Munib A. Qutaishat. *A Schema Meta-Integration System for a Logically Heterogeneous Distributed Object-Oriented Database Environment.* PhD thesis, Department of Computing Mathematics, University of Wales College of Cardiff, 1993.

[13] A. Rector, W. Solomon, W. Nowlan, and T. Rush. A terminology server for medical language and medical information systems. *Methods of Information in Medicine*, 34:147–157, 1995.

[14] A-R Tawil, W. A. Gray, and N. J. Fiddian. Discovering and representing interschema semantic knowledge in a cooperative multi-information server environment. *Proceedings of 11th International Conference and Workshop on Database and Expert Systems Applications (DEXA'2000), Greenwich, U.K.*, September 2000.

[15] A-R Tawil, W. A. Gray, and N. J. Fiddian. Integration operators for generating user-defined mediator views. *Proceedings of 5th World Multi-Conference on Systemics, Cybernetics and Informatics, (SCI'2001) Orlando, Florida, USA*, 2001.

[16] William A. Woods and James G. Schmolze. The KL-ONE family. *Computer Math. Applic.*, 23(2-5):133–177, August 1992.

Coping with Inconsistent Constraint Specifications

Sven Hartmann

FB Mathematik, Universität Rostock, 18051 Rostock, Germany

Abstract. Due to the complexity of modern database applications, semantic information is no longer a unified whole, but arises from multiple sources. Whatever the type of the sources, information fusion raises the crucial problem of inconsistent sets of integrity constraints. While earlier research mostly concentrated on consistency checking, less attention has been paid to the resolution of constraint conflicts in entity-relationship modeling. We suggest four strategies towards conflict resolution: (1) determination of superfluous object types, (2) incremental consistency checking, (3) detection of minimal inconsistent subsets, (4) constraint correction via feedback arc elimination, and apply them to constraint sets containing cardinality constraints and key dependencies.

1 Introduction

Designing a database starts with requirements engineering. A key activity during this process is the development of a conceptual schema. Conceptual schemas describe the properties that the desired information system must achieve, and serves as the basis for the following development phases. Though conceptual modeling represents only a small proportion of the overall development effort, it has a profound impact on the final result. Inadequacies in conceptual design are a major factor in information system failures.

In conceptual design, integrity constraints are used to specify the way by that the elements of a database are associated to each other, and thus describe which database instances are legal, that is, allowed to actually occur during the lifetime of the database.

The acquisition of integrity constraints is far from being trivial. Semantic information is often collected from a number of potentially conflicting perspectives or sources. These sources differ from each other in their viewpoint, precision, reliability or temporal appearance. As practice shows, information fusion may lead to inconsistent constraint sets. However, inconsistencies are not necessarily a problem as long as we know how to act in the presence of them. There are three major questions to be answered: (1) how to recognize inconsistencies, (2) how to report them to the designer, and (3) how to repair them.

Cardinality constraints are among the most popular classes of integrity constraints used in conceptual modeling. They impose restrictions on the number of relationships an object of a given type may be involved in. Generally, every set of cardinality constraints is satisfiable by the empty database. But even if other legal database instances exist, it may happen that some of the object sets are invariably empty in all of them. An object type is *superfluous* for a set of integrity constraints if its population is empty in every legal database instance. Usually, superfluous object types are considered to indicate errors in the conceptual schema. A constraint set is called *consistent* [19,23] if it does not force any object type to be superfluous, and *inconsistent* otherwise.

Consistent sets of cardinality constraints were characterized in [13,19,23]. A polynomial-time algorithm for consistency checking was presented in [12]. Moreover, [2] discusses the consistency of cardinality constraints in the presence of ISA-constraints, while [14] studies this question in the presence of key and functional dependencies. Despite several methods for consistency checking proposed in the literature, remarkably little has been said about the problem of resolving inconsistencies. Recognizing, that the collected information is inconsistent, is only half of the battle. Here trouble is just beginning for the responsible database designer: The indicated constraint conflicts have to be localized and fixed.

Due to the size of many conceptual schemas, this problem is difficult to cope with. Resolving inconsistency by arbitrarily removing some constraints can result in the loss of valuable information. This can include information which is actually correct and also information which is useful in managing the conflict. To handle inconsistency intelligently, we require good repair strategies.

Our objective is to present a number of strategies to repair inconsistent constraint sets in entity-relationship modeling. The techniques discussed within this paper are intended to help the designer to find the conflict and to support more appropriate decisions about how to proceed.

2 Integrity Constraints in Entity-Relationship Modeling

We shall assume that the conceptual schemas are defined on the basis of the entity-relationship model (cf. [3,23]), which represents data in the form of objects, that is, entities and relationships between them.

Throughout this paper, a *database schema* is a finite digraph $S = (V, L)$ without dicycles. Its vertices are the *object types* declared for some application, its arcs are said to be *links*. If $(\underline{r}, \underline{c})$ is a link in the schema, then $\underline{c}$ is called a *component* of $\underline{r}$. For every object type $\underline{r}$, let $Co(\underline{r})$ denote its component set.

Entity types do not posses components. Designing a database usually starts with specifying entity types to model the basic real-world objects in the target of the database. *Relationship types* have components. Roughly speaking, each relationship type $\underline{r}$ reflects real-world connections between objects of the types in $Co(\underline{r})$. Note that relationship types themselves may appear as components of other relationship types. Sometimes it is useful to allow an object type to occur several times as a component of the same relationship type. Then, the database schema contains parallel links, and *roles* are associated to them.

All objects modeled by an object type $\underline{v}$ form its *population* $\underline{v}^t$ at moment t. Its members are *instances of type* $\underline{v}$. Entities are instances of entity types, while relationships are instances of relationship types. Given a relationship type $\underline{r}$ with components $\underline{c}_1, \ldots, \underline{c}_n$, each of its instances may be considered as a tuple from the cartesian product $\underline{c}_1^t \times \ldots \times \underline{c}_n^t$. A *database instance* S^t contains a population $\underline{v}^t$ for each object type $\underline{v}$ in the database schema S.

Cardinality constraints are regarded as one of the basic constituents of the entity-relationship model. They are already present in Chen's seminal paper [3], and have been frequently used in conceptual design since then, see [20,23].

Let $\ell = (\underline{r}, \underline{c})$ be a link. For every object c in the population $\underline{c}^t$, let the *degree* $\deg(\underline{r}^t, c)$ denote the number of all those relationships r in $\underline{r}^t$ that the object c participates in. A *cardinality constraint* on $\underline{r}$ is a statement $card(\underline{r}, \underline{c}) = M$ where M is a set of non-negative integers. A population $\underline{r}^t$ satisfies this constraint if, for every object c in the population $\underline{c}^t$, the degree $\deg(\underline{r}^t, c)$ lies in M.

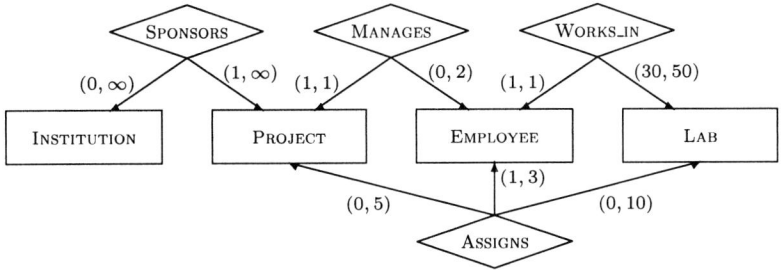

Fig. 1. A database schema with labels for the cardinality constraints.

For most applications, the sets M are intervals, i.e. of the form $(a, b) = \{a, a+1, \ldots, b\}$ or $(a, \infty) = \{a, a+1, \ldots\}$. Throughout, let $\operatorname{cmin}(\underline{r}, \underline{c})$ denote the minimum value in M, and $\operatorname{cmax}(\underline{r}, \underline{c})$ the maximum value in M. If M is infinite, we put $\operatorname{cmax}(\underline{r}, \underline{c}) = \infty$. If no cardinality constraint is specified for a link $(\underline{r}, \underline{c})$, we may assume the *trivial* cardinality constraint $card(\underline{r}, \underline{c}) = (0, \infty)$.

Within this paper, we almost exclusively use cardinality constraints to illustrate strategies towards conflict resolution. However, cardinality constraints are not the only constraints available in ER modeling. Key dependencies, for example, are of utmost importance as they are essential for the identification mechanism in databases. A *key dependency* on $\underline{r}$ is a statement $\underline{r} : X \to \underline{r}$, where X is a non-empty subset of $\operatorname{Co}(\underline{r})$. A population $\underline{r}^t$ satisfies the key dependency if the restrictions $r[X]$ are mutually distinct for all relationships r in $\underline{r}^t$. A key dependency is *unary* if X consists of a single component only.

Databases are used to store and manipulate data representing the target of the database. The typical situation in conceptual design is that we generate a database schema S together with an application-dependent constraint set Σ declared on it. A database instance S^t is only meaningful for the application if it satisfies all constraints in Σ. Such a database instance is *legal* for Σ.

Constraints are usually not independent. It is well-known that certain cardinality constraints can be used to express key dependencies, and vice versa. Generally, a key dependency $\underline{r} : \{\underline{c}\} \to \underline{r}$ is semantically equivalent to the cardinality constraint $card(\underline{r},\underline{c}) = (0,1)$. Thus, whenever a unary key dependency is gathered, we immediately have the corresponding cardinality constraint, too.

In [15] a complete list of seven implication rules is given that may be used to derive new cardinality constraints from given ones. A similar result is also presented for sets containing cardinality constraints, key dependencies and non-unary functional dependencies.

3 Constraint Acquisition

The formal specification of semantic constraints is among the most difficult tasks in conceptual design. It does not only demand high abstraction abilities but also tends to be very complex. For the correct utilization of semantic information a deep understanding of logics is required. Sometimes designers misunderstand integrity constraints and, consequently, interpret them badly. Some requirements are even too complicate to be modeled in a straightforward way. In addition, if different designers work together, it may be that they interpret the same constraints in different ways. Each of them has his own constraint acquisition skills, individual experience and knowledge. Mistakes may also occur when information is extracted from sample databases or via reverse engineering. In view of these problems it is desirable to have support for the acquisition of semantic constraints as suggested e.g. in [1].

Example. Let us look at the schema in Figure 1. The relationship type ASSIGNS associates employees and labs with certain projects. Suppose every lab wants to assign at most 10 employees to a single project. This requirement was erroneously modeled by the cardinality constraint card(ASSIGNS, LAB) = (0, 10), which causes an inconsistency as we shall see later on. Mistakes of this kind are often caused by differences between natural language and formal language specifications.

Constraint acquisition is even more difficult in the context of combining or interacting several pieces of information. Due to the size of modern database systems, relevant information has to be assembled from a variety of sources or perspectives. These perspectives usually intersect and give rise to potential conflicts. For example, two schemas modeling overlapping real world situations may possess very different constraint sets specified by their respective designers. Even if each source provides a consistent constraint set, it may happen in practice that the result of merging these sets will be inconsistent.

Ultimately, however, a single consistent perspective is desired. The process of deriving this single consistent perspective is known as information fusion [6]. The problem of information fusion appears frequently in conceptual design, as for example in viewpoint-oriented design or schema integration. While earlier research on schema integration mostly dealt with naming and type conflicts, less attention has been paid to constraint conflicts.

Lee and Ling [18] studied conflicts that arise when schemas represent different constraints on the same concept, such as different cardinality constraints specified for the same link. These conflicts are easy to detect by scanning the schema. Usually, the intention is to enforce the most precise constraint. If sample databases are available for the schemas to be combined, the integrated schema should enable the retrieval of all the data in the local databases.

On the other hand, inconsistencies may be caused by conflicting constraints which are specified for different links. Individually consistent parts of a schema can exhibit global inconsistency, due to distributed conflicting data. The combined information must be confirmed or corrected or removed by the designer responsible for the fusion of the gathered information.

4 Consistent Sets of Cardinality Constraints

Consistency checking is a ubiquitous problem in conceptual design. As pointed out in [13,19,23], methods from combinatorial optimization may be used to reason about cardinality constraints. Let us consider a database schema $S = (V, L)$. We obtain the *symmetric digraph* $D = (V, A)$ of the schema by adding the *reverse arc* $\ell^{-1} = (\underline{c}, \underline{r})$ for each link $\ell = (\underline{r}, \underline{c})$ in S. On the new arc set $A = L \cup L^{-1}$, we define a weight function $\omega : A \to \mathbb{Q} \cup \{\infty\}$ by

$$\omega(a) = \begin{cases} \frac{1}{\operatorname{cmin}(\underline{r},\underline{c})} & \text{if } a \text{ is a link } \ell = (\underline{r}, \underline{c}), \\ \operatorname{cmax}(\underline{r}, \underline{c}) & \text{if } a \text{ is the reverse arc } \ell^{-1} = (\underline{c}, \underline{r}) \text{ of a link } \ell. \end{cases}$$

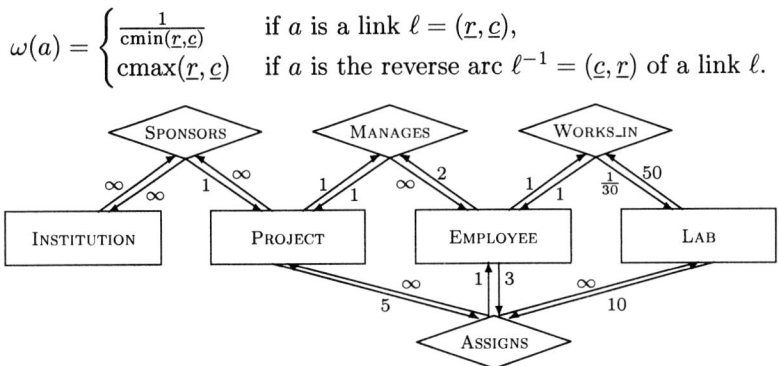

Fig. 2. The symmetric digraph of the database schema in Fig.1.

The weight function may easily be extended to walks in D. A *walk* P from a vertex v_0 to a vertex v_k is a sequence of arcs $(v_0, v_1), (v_1, v_2), \ldots, (v_{k-1}, v_k)$. Note that we do not claim the arcs in a walk to be pairwise distinct. The weight of a walk P is given by setting $\omega(P) = \prod_{i=1}^{k} \omega((v_{i-1}, v_i))$. A walk is a *dipath* if the vertices $v_0, v_1, \ldots, v_k$ are mutually distinct, whereas it is a *dicycle* if $v_0 = v_k$ holds and the vertices $v_1, \ldots, v_k$ are mutually distinct. A dicycle is said to be *critical* for a constraint set Σ if its weight is less than 1.

Characterizations of consistent sets of cardinality constraints were given in [12,13,19,23]. The impact of critical dicycles was first pointed out in [19]. For sets of key dependencies and cardinality constraints, the consistency problem was studied in [14]. We record the derived criterion for further reference.

Theorem 1 Σ *is consistent if and only if D contains neither critical dicycles nor arcs of weight 0.*

5 Superfluous Object Types

When the criterion in Theorem 1 fails, the constraint under discussion is inconsistent and we may conclude the existence of superfluous object types. Resolving inconsistencies usually means correcting or removing one or more constraints. If no additional information is available, any constraint is a candidate for this. But most constraints do not have any impact on the inconsistency. Thus we have to localize the conflict before we can fix it. The determination of superfluous object types is a helpful strategy to single out potentially incorrect constraints.

An object type $\underline{v}$ is said to be *superfluous* for a constraint set Σ if its population $\underline{v}^t$ is empty in every database instance S^t which is legal for Σ.

Lemma 2 *An entity type $\underline{c}$ is superfluous for Σ if and only if $\underline{c}$ is the component of some relationship type $\underline{r}$, such that Σ implies $\operatorname{card}(\underline{r},\underline{c}) = \emptyset$. A relationship type $\underline{r}$ is superfluous for Σ if and only if $\underline{r}$ has a component $\underline{c}$, such that Σ implies $\operatorname{card}(\underline{r},\underline{c}) = (0,0)$.*

Generally, we do not recommend to compute all implications of a constraint set to detect superfluous object types. It is just the other way round: Detecting superfluous object types enables us to derive further cardinality constraints.

In this section, we present an efficient method to find all superfluous object types for a set of cardinality constraints and key dependencies. Given a database instance S^t, let $g(\underline{v})$ denote the size of its population $\underline{v}^t$. If S^t is legal for a cardinality constraint $\operatorname{card}(\underline{r},\underline{c}) = M$ the inequality $g(\underline{c})\operatorname{cmin}(\underline{r},\underline{c}) \leq g(\underline{r}) \leq g(\underline{c})\operatorname{cmax}(\underline{r},\underline{c})$ is evidently valid. Due to the definition of the weight function above, we immediately derive $g(\underline{w}) \leq g(\underline{v})\omega(a)$ for every arc $a = (\underline{v},\underline{w})$ in the symmetric digraph D of the schema.

For any two object types $\underline{v}$ and $\underline{w}$, the *distance* from $\underline{v}$ to $\underline{w}$ is given by $\operatorname{dist}(\underline{v},\underline{w}) = \inf\{\omega(P) : P \text{ is a walk from } \underline{v} \text{ to } \underline{w} \text{ in } D\}$. By induction on the length of a walk, we may conclude $g(\underline{w}) \leq g(\underline{v})\operatorname{dist}(\underline{v},\underline{w})$ for any two object types $\underline{v}$ and $\underline{w}$, whenever the database instance under inspection is legal. This gives rise to the following observation:

Lemma 3 *An object type $\underline{w}$ is superfluous for a set Σ of cardinality constraints and key dependencies if there is some object type $\underline{v}$ with $\operatorname{dist}(\underline{v},\underline{w}) = 0$.*

Let V_0 denote the set of those object types which turn out to be superfluous due to this criterion. We may find all of them by a simple scanning procedure:

(S1) $V_0 \leftarrow \emptyset$;
    for $\underline{v} \in V$ do for $\underline{w} \in V$ do if $\operatorname{dist}(\underline{v},\underline{w}) = 0$ then add $\underline{w}$ to V_0; fi; od;

To apply this procedure, we need an efficient method to calculate the distances in the digraph D. This question is known as the all-pairs-shortest-distance problem. Efficient algorithms are given e.g. in [10]. Note, that we do not want to calculate the weight of a shortest dipath between any two vertices. The latter problem is essentially more difficult and known to be NP-complete in general.

Usually, the object types in V_0 are not the only superfluous ones. A relationship type with a superfluous component is superfluous itself. Further, suppose we are given a cardinality constraint for some link $(\underline{r}, \underline{c})$ where $\underline{r}$ is superfluous and $\mathrm{cmin}(\underline{r}, \underline{c})$ is positive. This claims every object of type $\underline{c}$ to participate in at least one relationship of type $\underline{r}$. But in legal database instances, there will never exist such a relationship. Thus the component $\underline{c}$ is superfluous, too.

Lemma 4 *Let $(\underline{r}, \underline{c})$ be a link in the schema. If $\underline{c}$ is superfluous for Σ, then $\underline{r}$ is superfluous, too. Conversely, if $\underline{r}$ is superfluous for Σ and $\mathrm{cmin}(\underline{r}, \underline{c}) \geq 1$, then $\underline{c}$ is superfluous, too.*

By constructing suitable example databases, we may prove that the criteria assembled so far are sufficient to describe all superfluous object types for a specified set of cardinality constraints and key dependencies. Note that this result may also be obtained as a consequence of the solution to the implication problem for cardinality constraints and key dependencies.

Theorem 5 *Consider a set Σ of cardinality constraints. An object type $\underline{v}$ is superfluous for Σ if and only if it is in V_0 or may be detected by applying Lemma 4.*

This result enables us to establish the set V_{su} of all superfluous object types for a given set of cardinality constraints and key dependencies. The idea is to start with V_0 and to gather all other superfluous object types iteratively by Lemma 4. This can be done efficiently if we maintain all arcs entering or leaving the set of superfluous object types recognized so far. Let A_{in} consist of all arcs which enter the set V_0, A_{out} consist of all arcs leaving this set, and A_{free} consist of all arcs whose vertices both are not in V_0. Clearly, these three sets can be determined in time $O(|A|)$.

We now check the criteria in Lemma 4 by studying all arcs entering or leaving the set V_{su} of those superfluous object types which have already been recognized. Whenever we find a new superfluous object type $\underline{w}$, we add it to the set V_{su} and update the sets A_{in}, A_{out} and A_{free} accordingly. For every vertex $\underline{w}$, let $A^-(\underline{w})$ be the set of all arcs with initial vertex $\underline{w}$ in D, and $A^+(\underline{w})$ be the set of all arcs with terminal vertex $\underline{w}$ in D.

(S2) $V_{\mathrm{su}} \leftarrow V_0$;
  while $A_{\mathrm{in}} \cup A_{\mathrm{out}} \neq \emptyset$ do
    choose $a \in A_{\mathrm{in}} \cup A_{\mathrm{out}}$;
    if $a \in A_{\mathrm{in}}$ then delete a from A_{in} else delete a from A_{out}; fi;
    if ($a \in A_{\mathrm{in}}$ is a link $(\underline{w}, \underline{c})$) or ($a \in A_{\mathrm{out}}$ is a link $(\underline{r}, \underline{w})$ with $\mathrm{cmin}(\underline{r}, \underline{w}) \geq 1$)
      then
        add $\underline{w}$ to V_{su};
        $A_{\mathrm{in}} \leftarrow A_{\mathrm{in}} \backslash (A^-(\underline{w}) \cap A_{\mathrm{in}}) \cup (A^+(\underline{w}) \cap A_{\mathrm{free}})$;
        $A_{\mathrm{out}} \leftarrow A_{\mathrm{out}} \cup (A^-(\underline{w}) \cap A_{\mathrm{free}}) \backslash (A^+(\underline{w}) \cap A_{\mathrm{out}})$;
        $A_{\mathrm{free}} \leftarrow A_{\mathrm{free}} \backslash (A^-(\underline{w}) \cup A^+(\underline{w}))$;
      fi;
  od;

In every run of the while-loop, the size of $A_{\text{in}} \cup A_{\text{out}} \cup A_{\text{free}}$ decreases by at least one. Hence, the step (S2) terminates after at most $|A| = 2|L|$ runs. By Theorem 5 the generated set V_{su} contains all superfluous object types.

Theorem 6 *Given all distances in D, the algorithm comprising steps (S1) and (S2) finds all superfluous object types in time $O(|V|^2 + |A|) = O(|V|^2 + |L|)$.*

Once we have found the superfluous object types, we may use this information to handle the constraint conflicts which are responsible for their occurrence. In order to resolve the inconsistency it suffices to study those constraints which are specified on superfluous relationship types. In practice, the superfluous object types will usually cover a small portion of the whole schema only.

Example. Consider the schema in Figures 1 and 2. The dicycle C from EMPLOYEE via WORKS_IN, LAB and ASSIGNS back to EMPLOYEE has weight $\omega(C) = 1/3$. On traversing this dicycle not only once but several times, we obtain walks of arbitrary small weight. This yields dist(EMPLOYEE, WORKS_IN) = 0. Consequently, EMPLOYEE is superfluous for Σ_C. On applying (S1) we derive the set V_0 containing the types EMPLOYEE, WORKS_IN, LAB, ASSIGNS, MANAGES and PROJECT. Afterwards, (S2) enables us to detect the set $V_{\text{su}} = V_0 \cup \{\text{SPONSORS}\}$ of all superfluous types.

6 Incremental Consistency Checking

A straightforward way to resolve the conflicts in an inconsistent constraint set is to delete all superfluous object types from the schema. However, this is usually not recommended. In general, the occurrence of superfluous object types points out a mistake made during the acquisition of constraints. If we do not fix this mistake, it will be a potential source for complications in future design steps or even failures during the lifetime of the database.

A simple strategy to avoid constraint conflicts is *incremental consistency checking*, see [24]. Whenever a new constraint is gathered and should be added to the schema, we first test whether it forces some object type to become superfluous. This enables us to decide whether the new constraint contributes to an inconsistency, and to react accordingly.

A constraint σ *competes* a consistent constraint set Σ if the union $\Sigma \cup \{\sigma\}$ is inconsistent. When doing incremental consistency checking, it is profitable to take into account the kind of the new constraint. For the constraints used during ER modeling, we make the following observations.

Theorem 7 *Let σ be a key dependency $\underline{r} : X \to \underline{r}$. Then σ competes Σ if and only if σ is unary and we have $\text{dist}(\underline{r}, \underline{c}) < 1$, where $X = \{\underline{c}\}$.*

If the key dependency to be added causes a conflict, it has to be refused. This ensures the constraint set to remain consistent. Note that non-unary key dependencies will never compete a given set of cardinality constraints and key dependencies. The same holds for non-unary functional dependencies, too. Conversely, unary functional dependencies sometimes cause non-trivial inconsistencies. Examples are given in [14]. A complete discussion, however, requires some deep results from discrete optimization and is out of the scope of the paper.

Theorem 8 *Let σ be a cardinality constraint* $\text{card}(\underline{r}, \underline{c}) = M$ *with* $M \neq \emptyset$. *Then σ competes Σ if and only if* $\text{dist}(\underline{c}, \underline{r}) < \text{cmin}_\sigma(\underline{r}, \underline{c})$ *or* $\text{cmax}_\sigma(\underline{r}, \underline{c}) < 1/\text{dist}(\underline{r}, \underline{c})$.

If the cardinality constraint to be added causes a conflict, it should be either refused or corrected. The previous result gives rise to an appropriate correction:

(C1) if $\text{dist}(\underline{c}, \underline{r}) < \text{cmin}(\underline{r}, \underline{c})$ then $\text{cmin}_{cor}(\underline{r}, \underline{c}) \leftarrow \lfloor \text{dist}(\underline{c}, \underline{r}) \rfloor$; fi;
(C2) if $\text{cmax}(\underline{r}, \underline{c}) < 1/\text{dist}(\underline{r}, \underline{c})$ then $\text{cmax}_{cor}(\underline{r}, \underline{c}) \leftarrow \lceil \frac{1}{\text{dist}(\underline{r}, \underline{c})} \rceil$; fi.

The discussion above gives us a possible strategy to avoid inconsistencies. We simply start with the empty constraint set, and successively add the constraints under inspection. Whenever a new constraint is competing, it has to be refused or corrected before it is added to the constraint set. With this, the generated constraint set always stays consistent.

Of course, the result of this procedure depends on the order in which the constraints are handled: Constraints added later are more likely to be corrected or refused. Often some constraints are more significant or reliable than others. These ones should be considered first.

Incremental consistency checking is useful when a small number of new constraints has to be added to a constraint set which is already known to be consistent. This happens when constraint sets have to be updated due to new requirements. Sometimes, integrity constraints change over time. To avoid undesired and expensive constraint violations by database operations, the specified semantics has to be revised, cf. [21]. Deleting constraints will never cause a new inconsistency, while adding a new constraint can be critical. In this case we should apply the strategy discussed above.

7 Minimal Inconsistent Constraint Sets

When a constraint set is recognized to be inconsistent, we are interested in extracting the conflicting kernels inside this set. We call an inconsistent constraint set Σ_0 *minimal* if every proper subset of Σ_0 is consistent. A good strategy towards conflict resolution is the following: For every minimal inconsistent subset Σ_0 of Σ we choose a constraint $\sigma \in \Sigma_0$ and remove it from Σ. However, we first need to detect the minimal inconsistent subsets.

We start with some preliminary results on minimal inconsistent subsets of cardinality constraints and key dependencies. If Σ_0 consists of a single constraint, say $\text{card}(\underline{r}, \underline{c}) = M$, then Σ_0 is minimal inconsistent if and only if $M = (0,0)$ or $\emptyset$. Clearly, this constraint has to be deleted first in order to avoid trivial conflicts. Usually constraints of this kind only occur as implications of the originally specified constraints. In this case, Σ_0 is not the reason for the inconsistency but only a symptom, while the real cause of the conflict still has to be found.

Next we are looking for minimal inconsistent subsets containing more than one constraint. Consider a dicycle C in the symmetric digraph D of the schema. Each arc in this dicycle carries a cardinality constraint. Let $\Sigma(C)$ consist of the constraints $\text{card}(\underline{r},\underline{c}) = M$ where either the link $\ell = (\underline{r},\underline{c})$ or its reverse arc $\ell^{-1} = (\underline{c},\underline{r})$ belongs to C. We say that $\Sigma(C)$ is *carried* by the dicycle C.

Theorem 9 *Let Σ_0 contain more than one constraint. Then Σ_0 is minimal inconsistent if and only if it is carried by a critical dicycle in D.*

The polynomial-time algorithm to decide the existence of a critical dicycle [12] uses single-root-shortest-path methods. This idea may be reused after some slight modification. Since there can be exponentially many minimal inconsistent subsets, we cannot expect a polynomial-time algorithm for their detection. Our goal is rather to obtain a method which determines these subsets quickly with respect to their number. In this section, we develop a method for this task which works fairly well in most situations.

First we add a new root vertex $\underline{s}$ to the symmetric digraph D and insert arcs $a = (\underline{s},\underline{v})$ connecting $\underline{s}$ to all object types $\underline{v}$. Moreover we put $\omega(a) = 1$ such that all the new arcs have weight 1. For every object type $\underline{v}$, we maintain its potential $\pi(\underline{v})$ and its parent $p(\underline{v})$. Initially we have $\pi(\underline{v}) = \infty$ and $p(\underline{v}) = nil$ for every $\underline{v}$. For the root $\underline{s}$ we declare $\pi(\underline{s}) = 1$ which stays constant during the whole procedure. At each step, the method selects an arc $a = (\underline{v},\underline{w})$ such that $\pi(\underline{v}) < \infty$ and $\pi(\underline{w}) > \pi(\underline{v})\omega(a)$ and puts $\pi(\underline{w}) = \pi(\underline{v})\omega(a)$ and $p(\underline{w}) = \underline{v}$. If no such arc exists, the algorithm terminates. Note that the resultant potentials $\pi(\underline{v})$ are positive rationals storing the minimum weight of a dipath from $\underline{s}$ to $\underline{v}$.

Efficient implementations of this idea such as the Bellman-Ford-Moore algorithm use priority queues to handle the order in which the arcs are inspected. For surveys on this topic, see [5,10].

At each step, the *parent digraph* D_P is the subgraph of D which contains the arcs $(p(\underline{w}),\underline{w})$ for all object types $\underline{w}$ with $p(\underline{w}) \neq nil$. The parent digraph has an important property which is profitable for our purposes here: We have $\pi(\underline{w}) \geq \pi(\underline{v})\omega(P)$ for every dipath P from a vertex $\underline{v}$ to a vertex $\underline{w}$ in the parent digraph D_P. In a certain step, let the algorithm described above select an arc $a = (\underline{v},\underline{w})$ with $\pi(\underline{v}) < \infty$ and $\pi(\underline{w}) > \pi(\underline{v})\omega(a)$. This arc will be inserted into the parent digraph. Suppose now, the arc a produces a dicycle $C = P \cup \{a\}$, where P is some dipath which has already been in D_P. We have $\pi(\underline{v}) \geq \pi(\underline{w})\omega(P)$, which implies $1 > \omega(a)\omega(P) = \omega(C)$, i.e. proves C to be a critical dicycle.

Theorem 10 *If a dicycle occurs in D_P, then it is critical. If Σ is inconsistent, then D_P will contain a critical dicycle after a finite number of steps.*

Thus we have to modify the algorithm as follows. After every step, when a new arc $a = (\underline{v},\underline{w})$ has been inserted into P, we look for a dicycle in D_P. This is fairly easy and can be done in linear time $O(|A|)$:

(M) while $(\underline{v} \neq \underline{s})$ and $(\underline{v} \neq \underline{w})$ do $\underline{v} \leftarrow p(\underline{v})$; od;
   if $\underline{v} = \underline{w}$ then Output("Critical dicycle in D_P detected"); fi;

The computational performance of classical shortest-path algorithms in the absence and presence of critical dicycles was studied in [4,5,17]. Heuristic improvements of the algorithms were presented in [9,22], some of which also analyze the parent digraph. The best-known time bound $O(|V||A|)$ is achieved by the Bellman-Ford-Moore algorithm as long as there are no critical dicycles.

Corollary 11 *If Σ is consistent, the algorithm proposed above stops in time $O(|V||L|)$. Otherwise it finds a minimal inconsistent subset of Σ in finite time.*

Whenever we find a critical dicycle C, it carries a constraint set $\Sigma(C)$ which is minimal inconsistent. At least one of the constraints in such a set has to be removed or revised in order to resolve the inconsistency. The selection of this constraint is due to the database designer. It suffices to correct the chosen constraint $\text{card}(\underline{r}, \underline{c}) = M$ as follows:

(M1) if $\ell = (\underline{r}, \underline{c})$ lies in C then $\text{cmin}_{cor}(\underline{r}, \underline{c}) \leftarrow \lfloor \omega(\ell)/\omega(C) \rfloor$; fi;
(M2) if $\ell^{-1} = (\underline{c}, \underline{r})$ lies in C then $\text{cmax}_{cor}(\underline{r}, \underline{c}) \leftarrow \lceil \omega(\ell^{-1})/\omega(C) \rceil$; fi.

In many situations, however, it is perhaps more appropriate to delete the bad constraint by setting $\text{cmin}_{cor}(\underline{r}, \underline{c}) = 0$ or $\text{cmax}(\underline{r}, \underline{c})_{cor} = \infty$, respectively. Afterwards, the algorithm has to be restarted with the modified constraint set. By iterated application of the algorithm we are able to find all critical dicycles.

Example. Recall the set Σ of cardinality constraints specified in Figure 1. The dicycle C from EMPLOYEE via WORKS_IN, LAB and ASSIGNS back to EMPLOYEE is critical and has weight $\omega(C) = 1/3$. The algorithm presented above finds this dicycle after a suitable number of steps. The set $\Sigma(C)$ of constraints carried by this dicycle is minimal inconsistent. We have to correct one of its constraints. An appropriate choice is to replace $\text{card}(\text{ASSIGNS}, \text{LAB}) = (0, 10)$ by $(0, 30)$ or $(0, \infty)$ which will fix the conflict under inspection. When the algorithm is started a second time it will stop without finding another critical dicycle. Consequently the symmetric digraph does no longer contain critical dicycles, and the corrected constraint set is consistent.

Note that the minimal inconsistent subsets are usually not disjoint: Thus the correction of a constraint could eliminate more than just a single minimal inconsistent subset. The essential factor determining the overall running time is the number of mutually disjoint critical dicycles. This number is unknown in advance, but expected to be reasonably small in most practical cases.

8 Feedback Arc Elimination

Detecting all minimal inconsistent subsets in Σ is without any doubt the most accurate way of resolving inconsistency. Unfortunately, it has two potential disadvantages: First, it is difficult to estimate its running time since we do not know how often the algorithm has to be restarted, i.e. how many conflicts actually have to be treated. But this problem is usually overcome by the processing power of modern computers.

Second, the detection of critical dicycles is a step-by-step process. We have to fix a recognized conflict before we can search for the next one. It is generally impossible to postpone a correction and to circumvent the respective conflict by then. Some designers will prefer methods that investigate all possible corrections in advance and then present the user a list of valid repair plans. Below, we use feedback arc sets to point out a strategy to develop candidate repair plans.

Consider some digraph G. A set F of arcs in G is said to be a *feedback arc set* if it intersects all dicycles in G. By deleting all the arcs in a feedback arc set we break every dicycle in G. The basic idea to derive a feedback arc set is to choose a linear ordering of the vertices in the digraph G, say $\underline{v}_1, \ldots, \underline{v}_n$. Then the backward arcs $(\underline{v}_j, \underline{v}_i)$, i.e. those with $j > i$, form a feedback arc set. Conversely, every feedback arc set corresponds to some linear ordering of the vertices in G.

Feedback arc sets give rise to the following strategy, which immediately resolves all inconsistencies in Σ: Suppose we have a feedback arc set F in the symmetric digraph D. Whenever a link $\ell = (\underline{r}, \underline{c})$ or its reverse arc occur in F, the corresponding cardinality constraint card$(\underline{r}, \underline{c}) = M$ has to be corrected:

(F1) if $\ell = (\underline{r}, \underline{c})$ belongs to F then cmin$_{cor}(\underline{r}, \underline{c}) \leftarrow 0$; fi;
(F2) if $\ell^{-1} = (\underline{c}, \underline{r})$ belongs to F then cmax$_{cor}(\underline{r}, \underline{c}) \leftarrow \infty$; fi.

This idea is unsatisfactory in two respects. First, we should not apply this procedure to an arbitrary feedback arc set, but to one which is 'well-chosen' for the underlying schema. In particular, it should be small to keep as many of the specified constraints as possible. Thus we ask for a feedback arc set of minimum size. The *feedback arc set problem (FAS)* is the problem of determining such a set. Unfortunately, this problem is well-known to be NP-hard.

Our second concern is the following: There is no need to break all dicycles in D but only those ones which are critical for the constraint set under inspection. In fact, we are interested in arc sets F which are feedback with respect to the collection of critical dicycles. But it is difficult to control this requirement, without explicitly determining the critical dicycles as done in the previous section. Just the very determination of all candidate arcs, i.e. all arcs lying on some critical dicycle, is computationally equivalent to the detection of all critical dicycles.

The good news, however, is that we are able to restrict the set of all vertices lying on some critical dicycle:

Lemma 12 *Let C be an critical dicycle. For any two vertices $\underline{v}$ and $\underline{w}$ on this dicycle we have* dist$(\underline{v}, \underline{w}) = 0$.

Thus all vertices on critical dicycles are superfluous and, in particular, belong to the set V_0 determined in Section 5. Trivially, the same holds for vertices on arcs of weight 0. Let use consider the *reduced digraph* D_R which is induced as a subgraph of D by the vertex set V_0.

Theorem 13 *The reduced digraph D_R contains all arcs of weight 0 and all critical dicycles from D.*

It is sufficient to find a feedback arc set F for D_R in order to fix all constraint conflicts. Applying (F1) and (F2) to all the arcs in F raises a valid repair plan. Of course, D_R can still contain some non-critical dicycles and thus some effort might be wasted. For real-world applications, however, one may expect that the reduced digraph D_R is considerably smaller than the whole schema.

In the literature, several algorithms have been proposed for the feedback arc set problem. In [8] an exact solution via branch-and-bound is presented together with a discussion of its computational performance. This method may be used to obtain all minimum size feedback arc sets in D_R. The acyclic subgraph polytope is studied in [11] which provides all minimum size feedback arc sets, too. Recent approximative solutions were given in [7,16]. The greedy heuristic in [7] finds small feedback arc sets and executes in time $O(|A|)$.

Every feedback arc set yields a candidate repair plan. But it is still the database designer who has to select the candidate which fits best. Due to restrictions imposed by time or manpower, we do not expect the database designer to consider the whole catalogue of possible repair plans. The system should present him a diversified list of repair plans among which the designer is asked to select. We adopted an idea from [16] and implemented a randomized algorithm to generate this list.

Though any feedback arc set may be used to resolve the inconsistency, not each of them is really a good choice in practice. In particular, a feedback arc set might suggest to delete a constraint which is well-known to be valid. To avoid this situation, we propose to remove in advance all those arcs from D_R which carry valid constraints. This speeds up the running time of the algorithm and prevents them from presenting repair plans which can be excluded due to the knowledge of the database designer.

9 Conclusion

In the present paper, we discussed strategies to handle inconsistent constraint sets. The current practice is often deficient in this area. Today, cardinality constraints are embedded in most design tools based on the ER model. While these tools include some basic reasoning methods, they neither offer intelligent consistency checking routines nor routines for semi-automatic conflict resolution.

Applying the strategies presented above, it is possible to give the designer further support in the process of constraint acquisition and conflict management. The strategies are intended to offer suggestions but the designer still controls the process of conflict resolution. In anything but the most trivial cases some intervention is required from the designer. The final selection of the constraint to be corrected must be at the discretion of the individual designer. Though this seems disappointing, we may not expect the system to decide this for us.

When all is going well, the consistency checking routines are invisible to the database designer. But when an inconsistency appears, the support system becomes visible to the designer. The recognized conflict must be reported to the designer, and the semantic information must be returned to a consistent state. In the present paper, we did not address the question how complex repairs are to be presented to designer. Nevertheless, the problem of reporting inconsistencies to the designer is equally important. If designers are to accept the introduction of new features to the design tools, they must be able to handle them. The success depends upon the readability of the language in which the conflicts are reported. Often, the person who must deal with the inconsistency is not responsible for it. It is important that the designer understands the nature of the detected conflict in order to give the most appropriate feedback. We propose using natural language descriptions, that can be displayed together with the formal description of the conflict. However this is out of the scope of the present paper, but suggested for future research.

References

1. M. Albrecht, E. Buchholz, A. Düsterhöft, and B. Thalheim. An informal and efficient approach for obtaining semantic constraints using sample data and natural language processing. *LNCS*, 1358:1–11, 1996.
2. D. Calvanese and M. Lenzerini. On the interaction between ISA and cardinality constraints. In *Proc. of Tenth Int. Conf. on Data Engin.*, pp. 204–213, 1994.
3. P.P. Chen. The entity-relationship model: towards a unified view of data. *ACM Trans. Database Syst.*, 1:9–36, 1976.
4. B.V. Cherkassy and A.V. Goldberg. Negative cycle detection algorithms. *Math. Programming*, 85:277–311, 1998.
5. B.V. Cherkassy, A.V. Goldberg, and T.Radzik. Shortest path algorithms: theory and experimental evaluation. *Math. Programming*, 73:129–174, 1996.
6. L. Cholvy and A. Hunter. Information fusion in logic: a brief survey. *LNAI*, 1244:86–95, 1997.
7. P. Eades, X. Lin, and W.F. Smyth. A fast and effective heuristic for the feedback arc set problem. *Inf. Process. Letters*, 47:319–323, 1993.
8. M.M. Flood. Exact and heuristic algorithms for the weighted feedback arc set problem. *Networks*, 20:1–23, 1990.
9. A.V. Goldberg and T.Radzik. A heuristic improvement of the Bellman-Ford algorithm. *Appl. Math. Letters*, 6:3–6, 1993.
10. M. Gondran and M. Minoux. *Graphs and algorithms*. Wiley, Chichecter, 1990.
11. M. Grötchel, M. Jünger, and G. Reichelt. On the acyclic subgraph polytope. *Math. Programming*, 33:28–42, 1985.
12. S. Hartmann. Graphtheoretic methods to construct entity-relationship databases. *LNCS*, 1017:131–145, 1995.
13. S. Hartmann. On the consistency of int-cardinality constraints. *LNCS*, 1507:150–163, 1998.
14. S. Hartmann. On interactions of cardinality constraints, key and functional dependencies. *LNCS*, 1762:136–155, 2000.
15. S. Hartmann. On the implication problem for cardinality constraints and functional dependencies. *Annals Math. Artificial Intell.*, 2001, to appear.
16. R. Hassin and S. Rubinstein. Approximations for the maximum acyclic subgraph problem. *Inf. Process. Letters*, 51:133–140, 1994.
17. S.G. Kolliopoulos and C. Stein. Finding real-valued single source shortest paths in $o(n^3)$ expected time. In *Proc. 5th Int. Prog. Combin. Opt. Conf.* 1996.

18. M.L Lee and T.W. Ling. Resolving constraint conflicts in the integration of entity-relationship schemas. *LNCS*, 1331:394–407, 1997.
19. M. Lenzerini and P. Nobili. On the satisfiability of dependency constraints in entity-relationship schemata. *Inform. Syst.*, 15:453–461, 1990.
20. S.W. Liddle, D.W. Embley, and S.N. Woodfield. Cardinality constraints in semantic data models. *Data Knowledge Eng.*, 11:235–270, 1993.
21. E. Di Nitto and L. Tanca. Dealing with deviations in DBMSs: an approach to revise consistency constraints. *Integrity in Databases, FMLDO96*, pp. 11–24. 1996.
22. R.E. Tarjan. *Data structures and network algorithms.* SIAM, Philadelphia, 1983.
23. B. Thalheim. *Entity-relationship modeling.* Springer, Berlin, 2000.
24. D. Theodorates. Deductive object oriented schemas. *LNCS*, 1157:58–72, 1996.

Integration of Biological Data and Quality-Driven Source Negotiation

Laure Berti-Equille

IRISA, Campus Universitaire de Beaulieu,
35042 Rennes cedex, France
berti@irisa.fr
http://www.irisa.fr

Abstract. Evaluation of data non-quality in database or datawarehouse systems is a preliminary stage before any data usage and analysis, moreover in the context of data integration where several sources provide more or less redundant or contradictory information items and whose quality is often unknown, imprecise and very heterogeneous. Our application domain is bioinformatics where more than five hundred of semi-structured databanks propose biological information without any quality information (i.e. metadata and statistics describing the production and the management of the biological data). In order to facilitate the multi-source data integration in the context of distributed biological databanks, we propose a technique based on the concepts of quality contract and data source negotiation for a standard wrapper-mediator architecture. A quality source contract allows to specify quality dimensions necessary to the mediator for data extraction among several distributed resources. The source selection is dynamically computed with the contract negotiation which we propose to include into the mediation and the global query processings before data acquisition. The integration of the multi-source biological data is differed for the restitution and combination of the results of the global user's query by techniques of data recommendation taking into account source quality requirements.

1 Introduction

Maintaining a certain level of quality of data and data sources is challenging in distributed multiple source environments. In practice, assessing data quality in database systems is mainly conducted by professional assessors with more and more cost-competitive auditing practices. Well-known approaches from industrial quality management and software quality assessment have been adapted for data quality and came up with an extension of metadata management [20, 13, 26, 27, 25]. Classically, the database literature refers to data quality management as ensuring : 1) syntactic correctness (e.g. constraints enforcement, that prevent "garbage data" from being entered into the database) and 2) semantic correctness (i.e. data in the database truthfully reflect the real world situation). This traditional approach of data quality management has lead to techniques such as integrity constraints, concurrency control and schema integration for distributed and heterogeneous systems. Techniques such as data tracking, data cleaning and data quality controlling are costly in practice and difficult to adapt efficiently for specific application domains. In the multi-source context, as recent studies show, applications built on top of data warehouses often experience several problems due to the reliability and the quality of integrated data [12]. The main reason is that the local databases participating in providing their data contain incorrect, inaccurate, outdated or poor quality data. The quality of integrated data then becomes even worse unless suitable methods and techniques are employed during the multi-source environment design. Despite the amount of work focuses on semantic heterogeneity among data and metadata [11], the quality of integrated data has been addressed by very few research projects focused on the issues of multi-source data quality control and on the management of enriched metadata [17, 4]. As a matter of fact, data quality mainly has been and still is an important research topic independent of database integration. In the biological databanks context, more than five hundreds of databanks store potentially redundant and erroneous information. Here, the question of data cleaning and data mediation is crucial but has not been addressed so far. The richness and the complexity of biological concepts make also very difficult the implementation of a classical mediation system based on a common semi-structured description model of the distributed resources. Moreover, biological databanks are intensively cross-referenced and dependent, they cover several common domains and adopt very close and inter-dependent description models.

2 Related Works

2.1 Mediation and Cleaning of Multi-source Data

We distinguish two main research approaches concerning mediation systems [30].

The first one is a query based approach relying on a common semi-structured data model which represents data coming from heterogeneous sources, and queries expressed in a common query language (TSIMMIS with the model OEM and the language LOREL [2, 19], Strudel [6], YAT [5]). To handle the structure and the semantic discrepancies of the resources, appropriate integration views are defined over the data sources with special logic-based object-oriented languages for wrapper and mediator specification.

The second approach is a domain-model based approach. It relies on a common domain model described in the mediator level. This domain model (or metadata schema) captures the basic vocabulary used for the description of information expressed in local databases (Information Manifold [18, 14], SIMS with the language LOOM [3], Context Interchange [8], Garlic [1]). Mediators are used to resolve semantic conflicts among independent information sources. Knowledge necessary for this resolution is stored in the form of shared ontologies. In the domain-model base approach, the condition of integration for a new information source is to provide an exhaustive description of its structure in terms of the domain model. The independence of resource-to-resource and mediator-to-resource description models is essential [11].

Data cleaning objectives are to detect matching records from several input extensional data structures (relational tables, object classes, DTDs), to find out and eliminate duplicate records in the integration process. As mentioned in [7], the main drawback of data cleaning methods is that, besides being a knowledge and time intensive task (since it implies several passes on the data), finding the suitable key for putting together similar records is very difficult. As another drawback, the support for cleaning rules offered in [16] allows matching rules to be applied only to pairs of neighbour records in the same file. Although, the problem of the possible conflict in data values was recognized, few specific solutions were offered [22]. Another problem arising from the proliferation of independent sources, some of them with overlapping information, is the inconsistency of information content, and hence there is a need for methods to resolve such inconsistencies in global answers. Inconsistencies result in multiple candidate answers ; the dual problem also exists, that is a global query might have no answer at all. Three usual approaches for reconciling the heterogeneities in data values are (1) to prefer the values from a more reliable database, (2) attach tags with data source identifications to data items and rely on the reputation of the data source [28], (3) store reliability measures of data sources from which a data item originated along with the data item itself [22]. These approaches also suffer from several drawbacks. First, it is not clear how to determine which of the sources is more reliable and how to measure reliability of a source. Second, even if the reliability of the data sources is somehow provided, it is implicitly assumed that the reliability remains the same for all data items from a particular data source. However, the reliability of the data items may be significantly different in the different parts of the source. And third, storing the reliability information or the data source tags along with the data items requires significant modifications in the conventional query processing mechanisms and increases data storage requirements.

2.2 Data Quality and Meta-data Management

There are a number of research investigating issues related to models and methodologies for data quality improvement [29, 27, 25], specifications and metrics for data quality dimensions [13]. Currently, data quality audits are the only practical means for determining quality of data in databases by using the appropriate statistical techniques. Since databases model a portion of the real world which constantly evolves, the data quality estimates become outdated as time passes. Therefore, the estimation process should be repeated periodically depending on the dynamics of the real world. The statistical aspects of data quality have been the primary focus with statistical methods of imputation (i.e., inferring missing data from statistical patterns of available data), predicting accuracy of the estimates based on the given data, data edits (automating detection and handling of outliers in data). The use of machine learning techniques for data validation and correction is considered in [23]. For example, [24] describes a prototype system for checking correctness of the existing data (called data validation and cleanup). Utilization of statistical techniques for improving correctness of databases and introduction of a new kind of integrity constraints were proposed in [10]. The constraints are derived from a database instance using the conventional statistical techniques (e.g., sampling and regression), and every update of the database is validated against these constraints. If an update does not comply with them, then a user is alerted and prompted to check correctness of the update. Despite the growing importance of data quality for end-users and that many techniques have been proposed to improve and maintain quality of local databases, very few projects try to use quality metadata for multivalued attributes in distributed and quality-heterogeneous environments (DWQ [4], HiQiQ [17]). The use of metadata for data quality evaluation and improvement was advocated in [21] where information producers are encouraged to perform Verification, Validation, and Certification (VV&C) of their data. The metadata help in the process of estimating and maintaining the quality of data. Across different applications domains (such as geographic information systems [9] or digital libraries), a great amount of effort has been invested in the development of metadata standard vocabularies for the exchange of information. For the biological data domain, we are not aware of any kind of project (even among the current standardization works) that tries to specify metadata and to control biological data quality.

3 Example of Biological Information Retrieval from Distributed Databanks

Searching across distributed, disparate biological databases is increasingly difficult and time-consuming for biomedical researchers. Bioinformatics is coming to the forefront to address the problem of drawing effectively and efficiently information from a growing collection of 511 multiple and distributed databanks [1]. For example, suppose a biological researcher working with a gene and wanting to know what gene it is and its DNA sequence, whether the rRNA sequence is known, how the gene is transcribed into mRNA, how the mRNA is translated into that protein, what the protein function is, its cellular location... With the currently available biological banks and tools the researcher has to search the relevant databases one by one and then to locate the information items of interest within the return results.

Our mediator is designed to provide information about genes. The mediator conceptual model is presented in Figure 1. The mediator of our example will query three existing sources S_1 (EMBL[2]), S_2 (GenBank[3]) and S_3 (SWISS-

---

[1] see the Public Catalog of Databases : DBcat,
  http://www.infobiogen.fr/services/dbcat
[2] EMBL (European Molecular Biology Laboratory), http://www.ebi.ac.uk/embl/
[3] GenBank, http://www.ncbi.nlm.nih.gov/

PROT[4]) for retrieving information on Gene HFE_Human (related to the hemochromatose, a gene hepatic pathology). The raw values are automatically extracted by scripts using the DTD of each source. Four records with their respective Accession Numbers (Acc. Nb.) are extracted for the same gene in EMBL and Genbank and one record is extracted from SWISS-PROT concerning the protein related to gene HFE_Human (see Table 1). The sequence types and sizes are different according to the sources. They correspond to different submitted records with more or less detailed or complete annotations and four different submission dates. Our objective is to systematically extract and aggregate the

Source	Acc. Nb	Seq. Type	Seq. Size	Links for Protein	Date	Annotation
EMBL (S_1)	Z92910	Complete	12146	Genbank CAB07442	Mar. 97	Complete annotation
GenBank (S_2)	AF204869	Partial	3043		Nov.99	No annotation but a relevant information item
GenBank	AF184234	Partial	772	Genbank AAF01222	Sept.99	Detailed but incomplete annotation
SWISS-PROT(S_3)	Q30201	Complete	348		Oct.2000	Complete annotation

Table 1. Example Results for biological information retrieval on gene HFE_Human

most exhaustive information on the expressed genes for instanciating and completing the gene sequence model of our mediator with considering the aspects of data and source quality for the integration process.

In order to define an appropriate data aggregation of all the available information items and rules for mapping the sources' records, obviously data conflicts have to be resolved due to the different values recorded for the same concept of gene HFE_Human. Traditional data integration approaches suggest a conflict resolution method that either chooses one value over the other (or that computes the average in case of the numerical values). A global query for the gene sequence would retrieve one data value from the source according to the specified data integration rule. For our example, the most complete sequence would be retrieved from S_1 skipping a relevant information item proposed by S_2 in the most recent record. Note that the same source (S_2) may propose several records for the same concept. Now assume the following scenarii :

Scenario 1 : S_1 updates their data every night, S_2 monthly and S_3 twice a month. In this case, the global query time may determine from which data source the most up-to-date data are retrieved.

Scenario 2 : S_3 is the server of an institute which does its own sequencing for human species. Sequence data are highly accurate for this species. S_2 data may have sometimes parsing errors and may come from other sites.

---
[4] SWISS-PROT, http://www.expasy.ch/sprot/sprot-top.html

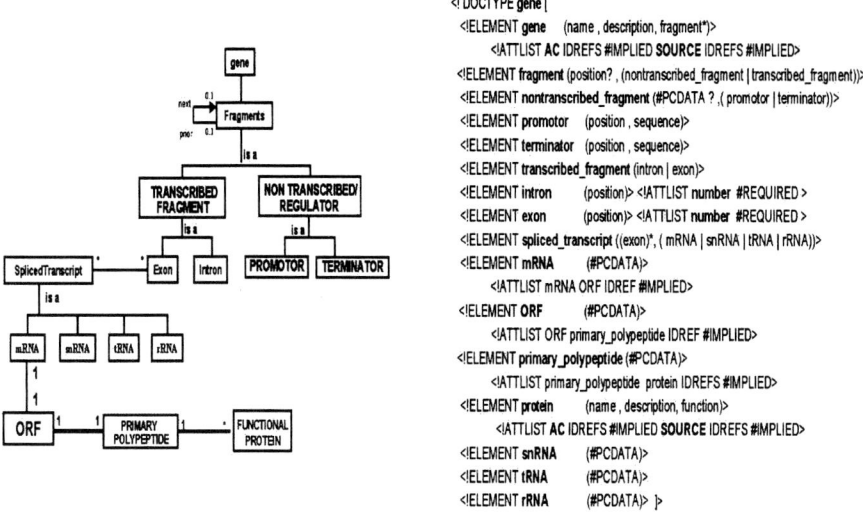

Fig. 1. The Gene Sequence Model and the corresponding DTD

Scenario 3 : S_1 and S_2 cover more biological domains than S_3. S_1 is one of the main genetic databanks and S_3 is one of the main databanks on proteins. Information items of S_2 are usually less complete and accurate than those of S_3 for the protein domain.

The above scenarii briefly show that the way of how and when data is populated into the local sources plays an important role for integrating local data for global queries. They also describe source dependencies and data quality dimensions such as freshness, accuracy, completeness or coverage. Up-to-date data does neither imply most accurate data nor most complete data. Actually, a global user might be interested in most complete data, and another one might be rather interested in most accurate data. In both cases, it should be possible for these users to specify tolerance thresholds for data and source quality (or, at least, to have technical means to estimate the quality of query results from the different sources). In this perspective, we propose the specification of quality contracts for the sources in order to use dynamically quality requirements in the query processing. This technique enables to differ data integration to end-user according to flexible quality criteria. Our approach is based on a standard mediator-wrapper architecture extending mediation with new functionalities such as the quality contract negotiation. A implicit assumption underlying this research is that we incorporate a set of controls on the top of data sources to enhance the global system's reliability and its integrated data quality ; the final aim is to maintain a high probability of preventing, detecting and eliminating data non-quality for data integration.

4   A Description of the Multi-source Architecture

We argue that database techniques such as having an expressive internal data model and query language, together with a meta-information repository and meta-information analysis techniques constitutes a necessary foundation for a mediator system. In order to alleviate the problem of information overload and confusion when results of a query are presented, the classical solution is to rank the results according to consistent relevance assessments. Our approach is to include quality specifications for sources and send them within the query. Such a functionality for retrieval and integration of information must be supported by an easily extensible, scalable and customizable architecture for addressing a wide range of specific applications such as the biological data domain. In this perspective, we propose a multi-source architecture (see Figure 2). From the application layer, the user can submit a global query to the mediator which conjointly sends the query and a quality contract type to the sources' wrappers. The wrappers send the corresponding local query to their respective source. Information sources may be cross-referenced, structured or not and with (or without) a meta-information repository. They respond to their wrapper with the query result and a quality contract instance. At the mediation layer, the mediator computes : 1) a conformance score for each source corresponding to the constraint satisfaction with respect to the contract specification, and 2) a conflict score for the queried integrated result which represent the importance of the data conflicts when distinct information items referring the same real-world concept are aggregated into a multi-source object structure. The mediator negotiates with the best sources and combines the query results, before sending it to the user.

5   Source Integration and Quality-Driven Negotiation

We considered the integration as a two-step process with 1) the schema integration and 2) the materialized data integration. As an input, we extract the different biological source schemata and their respective data sets in order to obtain as an output, a reconciled data view for a target schema. Our target schema is the DTD given in Figure 1.

- The first step of schema integration implies : comparing the sources' and mediator's schemata, detecting the structural analogies and correspondences, resolving the structural conflicts and transforming the source schemata into a canonical form (the target schema).
- The second step of data values integration implies : clustering and identifying the records that refer the same real object, expressing the criteria that define the conditions for the detection of matching records and eliminating data duplicates and inconsistencies.

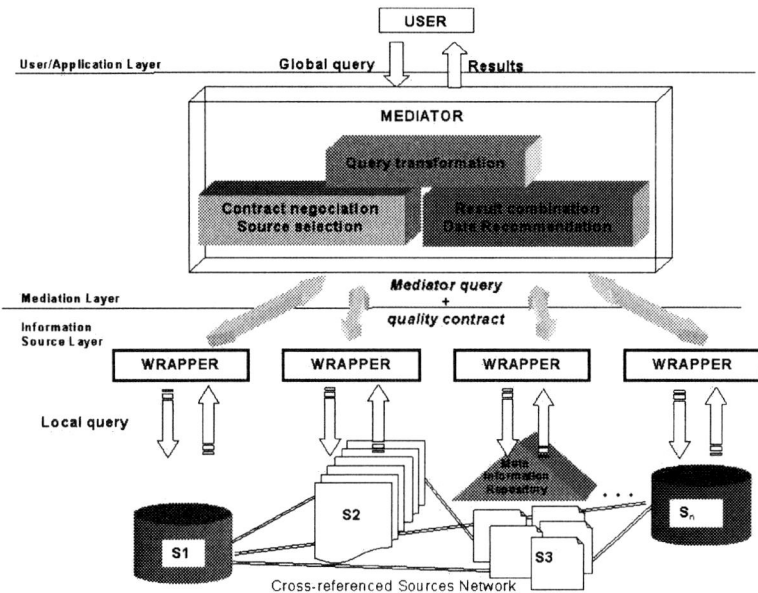

Fig. 2. The Multi-source Architecture including Quality Negotiation

5.1 Entity Identification

Anybody may submit biological information to public databanks with more or less formalized submission protocols which usually don't include names standardization or data quality controls. Erroneous data may be easily entered and cross-referenced. The available data sources have overlapping scopes with different levels of data quality. But the main problem of the biological databanks seems to be the entity identification. This problem arises when information from different information sources related to the same entity has to be merged. The databases may have inconsistent values in equivalent attributes of tuples referring to the same real-world object or may have mismatched attributes in them (i.e., attributes at the different level of abstraction), or have a combination of both. The identification problem appears as a biological description problem which requires a high-level expertise and the specialists' knowledge. Some tools (such as LocusLink [5]) propose clusters of records which identify the same biological concept accross different biological databanks : they are semantically related but biologists still must validate the correctness of the clusters and resolve interpretation differences among the records. As a starting point of our work, we considered that the biologist's expertise for entity identification is necessary. One of our objectives is to develop tools to assist the scientist in this task.

---

[5] LocusLink,http://www.ncbi.nlm.nih.gov/LocusLink/

5.2 Selective Structuration

In our example, each biological source propose a HTML document describing partially the gene HFE-Human identified by a particular record accession number. These documents are parsed and converted into the XML format and restructured according to our target schema (see Figure 3).

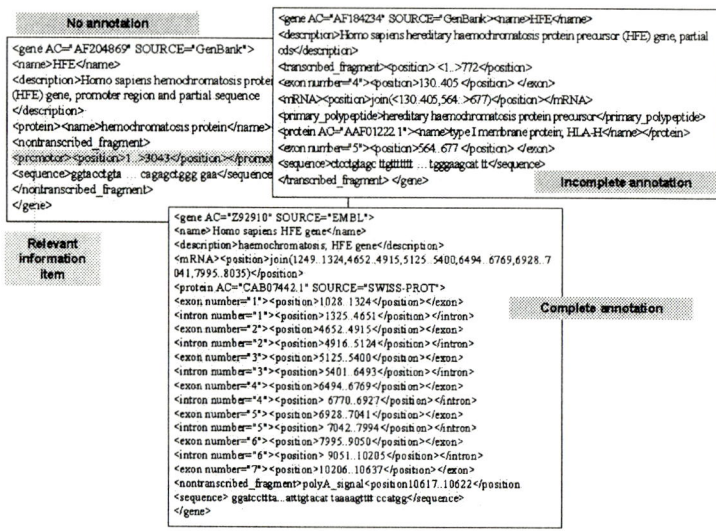

Fig. 3. Selective Structuration for Data Extraction

We use a set of mapping rules for identifying homologous structural elements (tags) based on biological shared ontologies which specifically help to determine the descriptive inclusions and the correspondances between the sources schemata and our target schema. Other rules are based 1) on the acquisition of biological expertise 2) on the results of statistical tools for sequence alignment (such as Blast[6]) 3) on format equivalence and conversion. In our example, the equivalence between exon positions elements can be automatically found out because the sequences respectively proposed by S_1 and S_2 have an alignment of 99% and the exons position proposed by S_2 is relative with an offset of 664 : exon.position(S_1.Z92910)= 6364 + exon.position(S_2.AF184234).

A multi-source data view is built by aggregating exhaustively all the information items available on gene HFE-Human proposed by the different sources if the following conditions are satisfied : i) the data refer to the same biological real-world concept ii) the data conflicts raised between more or less contradictory

---

[6] BLAST, http://www.ncbi.nlm.nih.gov/BLAST/

values are negligible (i.e. under a given threshold) and still allow data aggregation into a multi-source element which can be validated by the biologist. The sources' identification is mentioned for each value of the multi-source element. We obtain the following multi-source record for the HFE_Human in Figure 4.


```
<GENE AC="AF184234" source="GENBANK"
      AC="AF204869" source="GENBANK"
      AC="Z92910" source="EMBL">
<NAME>
<name AC="AF184234">HFE</name>
<name AC="AF204869">HFE</name>
<name AC="Z92910">Homo sapiens HFE gene</name>
</NAME>
<DESCRIPTION>
<description AC="AF184234">Homo sapiens hereditary haemochromatosis protein precursor(HFE) gene, partial
cds</description>
<description AC="AF204869">Homo sapiens hemochromatosis protein (HFE) gene, promoter region and partial
sequence</description>
<description AC="Z92910">haemochromatosis; HFE gene</description>
</DESCRIPTION>
<SEQUENCE>
<sequence AC="AF184234" >ctoctgtagc ttgtttttt ... tgggaagcat tt </sequence>
<sequence AC="AF204869">ggtacctgta atcccagctg... cagagctggg gaa</sequence>
<sequence AC="Z92910"> ggatccttta accgaggaga... taaaagtttt ccatgg </sequence>
</SEQUENCE>
<mRNA>
<mRNA AC="AF184234" ><position>join(<130..405,584..>677)</position></mRNA>
<mRNA AC="Z92910" ><position>join(1249..1324,4852..4915,5125..5400,6494..6769,6928..7041,
7995..8036)</position>
</mRNA>
<PRIMARY_POLYPEPTIDE>
<primary_polypeptide AC="AF184234">hereditary haemochromatosis protein precursor</primary_polypeptide>
</PRIMARY_POLYPEPTIDE>
<PROTEIN>
<protein AC="AAF01222.1" AC="AF184234"><name>type I membrane protein; HLA-H</name></protein>
<protein AC="AF204869"><name>hemochromatosis protein</name></protein>
<protein AC="CAB07442.1">
</PROTEIN>
<PROMOTOR>
<promotor AC="AF204869"><position>1..>3043</position></promotor>
</PROMOTOR>
<EXON>
<exon number="1" AC="Z92910"><position>1028..1324</position></exon>
<exon number="2" AC="Z92910"><position>4852..4915</position></exon>
<exon number="3" AC="Z92910"><position>5125..5400</position></exon>
<exon number="4" AC="AF184234" ><position>130..405 </position> </exon>
<exon number="4" AC="Z92910"><position>6494..6769</position></exon>
<exon number="5" AC="AF184234"><position>584..677</position> </exon>
<exon number="5" AC="Z92910"><position>6928..7041</position></exon>
<exon number="6" AC="Z92910"><position>7995..9050</position></exon>
<exon number="7" AC="Z92910"><position>10206..10637</position></exon>
</EXON>
<INTRON>
<intron number="1" AC="Z92910"><position>1325..4851</position></intron>
<intron number="2" AC="Z92910"><position>4916..5124</position></intron>
<intron number="3" AC="Z92910"><position>5401..6493</position></intron>
<intron number="4" AC="Z92910"><position> 6770..6927</position></intron>
<intron number="5" AC="Z92910"><position> 7042..7994</position></intron>
<intron number="6" AC="Z92910"><position> 9051..10205</position></intron>
</INTRON>
</GENE>
```


Fig. 4. Multi-source record aggregating available information on gene HFE_Human

5.3 Source Quality Negotiation

In order to provide adequate level of quality, the mediator needs to include capabilities such as negotiation, monitoring and adaptation. These capabilities all require the expected and the provided quality levels to be explicitly specified. Quality dimensions can be specified statically at the time of source integration or dynamically at deployment or runtime. We characterize quality of data and quality of source along named dimensions (mentioned non-exhaustively in Table 2). Specifying abstractly quality dimensions with a name and a domain value gives a flexible approach for deciding which dimension should be provided and implemented for a given application. The transparency of user's global query processing is weakened by the fact that the user can specify quality contracts for the query results. Based on the matching of user's quality requirements and the quality for each local source, source negotiation and data conciliation are generated dynamically by the global query processor of the mediator to ensure the retrieval of high quality data from the multiple local sources.

Quality Contract Type	Description
Availability	Time and way the source is accessible based on technical equipment and statistics (example of dimension : serverFailure)
Freshness	How up-to-date the information is (e.g. dataAge, lastUpdate, updateFrequency)
Accessibility	Estimation of waiting time for user seaching time and for request/response processing (including the time consumption per-query of the wrapper for translating, negotiating ...)
Security	Estimation of the number of corrupted data
Coverage	Estimation of the number of data for a specific information domain
Accuracy	Estimation of the number of data free-of-error
Completeness	Estimation of the number of missing data or null values (e.g. NbOfNullValue per object)
User satisfaction	User grade based on presentation of data results and ease of understanding and using

Table 2. Quality Contract Types

For our particular application, these quality dimensions may be specified in a contract type which represents quality dimensions, specifies the name, the domain and possibly user-defined ordering for each dimension. We can specify examples of source contract types such as : Availability, Freshness and Completeness. A contract is an instance of a contract type that represents a set of quality dimensions specifications for the source. A contract aggregates a number of constraints. Figure 5 presents three contract types and their instances.
Contract Conformance corresponds to constraint satisfaction for each dimension of each contract type.

Definition 1
We define a conformance score for each source S_j as a weighted function F on the i specified contract types and their k dimensions.
$\forall S_j, contractType_i, dimensionName_k,$
$\quad Conformance(S_j) = F(w_i, w_k, ContractType_i, dimensionName_k, S_j)$

Each contract type may have particular weights w_i indicating the relative importance of the ith contract type for computing the conformance score of each source S_j (e.g. the contract type on Freshness is more important than the one on Completeness). Each dimension of a contract type may have particular weights w_k indicating the relative importance of the kth dimension of the contract (e.g. dataAge is more important than updateFrequency). The conformance scores range from 0 to 1. A multi-source object is built for each element of the mediator conceptual model. The next step is to select among the multi-source values those that best match the query and whose source best conforms the quality contract. Given a global query Q, the mediator computes the conformance score $Conformance(S, Q, o)$ of each source S. Source S responds with the objects that

```
type Availability = contract {                  S1_Availability = Availability contract {
serverFailure :enum{halt,initState,rolledBack};  serverFailure == initState;
numberOfFailures :decreasing number fail./month; numberOfFailures <= 0.2 fail./month;
reliability : increasing number;};              reliability == 0.999; };

type Freshness = contract {                     S1_ Freshness = Freshness contract {
dataAge : number year,month,day;                dataAge == 8 years, 11 months, 3 days;
lastUpdate : number day(s);                     lastUpdate == 52 days;
UpdateFrequency : number updates/month;};       updateFrequency == 25 updates/day;};

type Completeness = contract {                  S1_Completeness = Completeness contract {
NbOfNullValue : increasing number/Object;};     NbOfNullValue : 3/Object;}
```

Fig. 5. Example of quality source contract types and their instances

best match the query values. The query results contain the values for $o_i, \ldots, o$ for every object returned.

5.4 Source Conformance and Query Results Scoring

Each object o in the result for query Q is ranked according to a conformance score $Conformance(S, Q, o)$ of the source S and a conflict score $Conflict(S, Q, o)$. The values of conflict score range from 0 to 1.

Definition 2
The conflict score $Conflict(S, Q, o)$ of source S for query Q corresponds to the distance between the object o of S and q the queried object of Q. The distance $Dis(o, q)$ is the sum of data conflict importances :
$Dis(o, q) = \sum_{j=1}^{n} I_j$ *with I_j the jth data conflict importance such as :*

$$I_j = \begin{cases} 0 & \text{if there is no data conflict} \\ 0.1 & \text{if the conflict is weak} \\ 1 & \text{if the conflict is strong} \end{cases} \quad (1)$$

6 Conclusion

In order to facilitate the multi-source data integration in the context of distributed biological databanks, we propose a technique based on the notions of quality contract and source negotiation. Our approach is based on a standard wrapper-mediator architecture. A quality contract with a source allows to specify quality dimensions necessary to the mediator for data selection between several distributed applications. The selectivity of data sources is dynamically computed during contract negotiation we propose to associate within the global query processing and before data acquisition. The importance of semi-structured data conflicts is evaluated and the quality conformance of sources is scored : the integration of the data is carried out according to the quality of the data required by users. The originality of our approach with respect to data mediation and conciliation is to include specifications quality of source into the query processing. From the biological application point-of-view, we first introduce the notion of biological integrated data quality and data recommendation for biologists. The complete toolkit for biological data cleaning and biologists' assistance for expressing mapping rules are under current development. Our final objective is to orientate the current standardization efforts to take into account the quality of biological data and to promote operational techniques and tools to evaluate and improve it.

References

[1] M. Carey, L. Haas, and P. Schwarz et al. Towards heterogeneous multimedia information systems: The GARLIC approach. In *RIDE-DOM*, pages 124–131, March 1995.
[2] S. Chawathe, H. Garcia-Molina, and J. Hammer et al. The TSIMMIS project: Integration of heterogeneous information sources. *IPSJ*, pages 7–18, October 1994.
[3] C. Chee, Y. Arens, C. Knoblock, and C. Hsu. Retrieving and integrating data from multiple information sources. *Intl. J. of Intelligent and Cooperative Information Systems*, 2(2):127–158, 1993.
[4] D. Clavanese, G. De Giacomo, and M. Lenzerini et al. Data integration in datawarehousing. Tech. Rep., 1997.
[5] S. Cluet, C. Delobel, J. Siméon, and K. Smaga. Your mediators need data conversion ! In *ACM SIGMOD Conf. on Management of Data*, pp. 177–188, 1998.
[6] M. Fernandez, D. Florescu, and J. Kang et al. Catching the boat with STRUDEL: Experiences with a web-site management system. In *ACM SIGMOD Conf. on Management of Data*, pp. 414–425, 1998.
[7] H. Galhardas, D. Florescu, D. Shasha, E. Simon, and C. Saita. Declarative data cleaning : Language, model, and algorithms. Tech. Rep. RR-4149, INRIA, 2001.
[8] C. Goh, S. Madnick, and M. Siegel. Context Interchange : overcoming the challenges of the large-scale interoperable database systems in a dynamic environment. In *Proc. of CIKM'94*, pp. 337–346, 1994.
[9] M. Goodchild and R. Jeansoulin. *Data quality in geographic information : from error to uncertainty*. Hermès, 1998.
[10] W. Hou, Z. Zhang. Enhancing database correctness : a statistical approach. In *Proc. of ACM SIGMOD Conf. on Management of Data*, 1995.
[11] R. Hull. Managing semantic heterogeneity in databases: a theoretical prospective. In *Proc. of PODS'97*, pp. 51–61, 1997.
[12] M. Jarke, M. Lenzerini, Y. Vassiliou, and P. Vassiliadis. *Fundamentals of Data Warehouses*. Springer, 1998.
[13] S. H. Kan. *Metrics and models in software quality engineering*. Addison-Wesley, 1995.
[14] A. Y. Levy, D. Srivastava, and T. Kirk. Data model and query evaluation in global information system. *J. of Intelligent Information Systems*, 5(2):121–143, 1995.
[15] E.P. Lim, J. Srivastava, and S. Shekhar. Resolving attribute incompatibility in database integration : An evidential reasoning approach. In *Proc. of the 10th Intl. Conference on Data Engineering (ICDE'94)*, 1994.
[16] A. Monge, C. Elkan. An efficient domain-independent algorithm for detecting approximately duplicate database records. In *Workshop on Research Issues on Data Mining and Knowledge Discovery*, 1997.

[17] F. Naumann, U. Leser. Quality-driven integration of heterogeneous information systems. In *Proc. of VLDB'99*, pp. 447–458, 1999.
[18] J. Ordille, A. Levy, and A. Rajaraman. Querying heterogeneous information sources using source descriptions. In *Proc. of VLDB'96*, pp. 251–262, 1996.
[19] Y. Papakonstantinou, H. Garcia-Molina, and J. Widom. Object exchange across heterogeneous information source. In *Proc. of ICDE'95*, pp. 251–260, 1995.
[20] T.C. Redman. *Data quality for the information age*. Artech House, 1996.
[21] J. Rothenberg. Metadata to support data quality and longevity. In *Proc. of IEEE Metadata Conf.*, 1996.
[22] F. Sadri. Reliability of answers to queries in relational databases. *IEEE TKDE*, 3(2):245–252, 1991.
[23] J. Schlimmer. Learning determinations and checking databases. In *Proc. of the AAAI-91 Workshop on KDD*, 1991.
[24] A. Sheth, C. Wood, and V. Kashyap. Q-data : Using deductive database technology to improve data quality. In *Proc. of ILPS'93*, pp. 23–56, 1993.
[25] D. Strong, Y. Lee, and R. Wang. Data quality in context. *Com. of the ACM*, 40(5):103–110, 1997.
[26] G. Tayi, D. Ballou. Examining data quality. *Com. of the ACM*, 41(2):54–57, 1998.
[27] R. Wang. A product perspective on Total Data Quality Management. *Com. of the ACM*, 41(2):58–65, 1998.
[28] R. Wang, S. Madnick. A polygen model for heterogeneous database systems : the source tagging perspective. In *Proc. of VLDB'90*, pp. 519–538, 1990.
[29] R. Wang, V. Storey, and C. Firth. A framework for analysis of data quality research. *IEEE TKDE*, 7(4):623–638, 1995.
[30] G. Wiederhold. Mediation in information systems. *ACM Computing Surveys*, 27(2):265–267, 1995.

Accessing Data Integration Systems through Conceptual Schemas

Andrea Calì, Diego Calvanese, Giuseppe De Giacomo, and Maurizio Lenzerini

Dipartimento di Informatica e Sistemistica
Università di Roma "La Sapienza"
Via Salaria 113, I-00198 Roma, Italy
lastname@dis.uniroma1.it,
http://www.dis.uniroma1.it/~*lastname*

Abstract. Data integration systems provide access to a set of heterogeneous, autonomous data sources through a so-called global, or mediated view. There is a general consensus that the best way to describe the global view is through a conceptual data model, and that there are basically two approaches for designing a data integration system. In the global-as-view approach, one defines the concepts in the global schema as views over the sources, whereas in the local-as-view approach, one characterizes the sources as views over the global schema. It is well known that processing queries in the latter approach is similar to query answering with incomplete information, and, therefore, is a complex task. On the other hand, it is a common opinion that query processing is much easier in the former approach. In this paper we show the surprising result that, when the global schema is expressed in terms of a conceptual data model, even a very simple one, query processing becomes difficult in the global-as-view approach also. We demonstrate that the problem of incomplete information arises in this case too, and we illustrate some basic techniques for effectively answering queries posed to the global schema of the data integration system.

1 Introduction

Data integration is the problem of combining the data residing at different sources, and providing the user with a unified view of these data, called global (or, mediated) schema [15, 16]. The global schema is therefore a reconciled view of the information, which can be queried by the user. It is the task of the data integration system to free the user from the knowledge on where data are, how data are structured at the sources, and how data are to be merged and reconciled to fit into the global schema.

The interest in this kind of systems has been continuously growing in the last years. Many organizations face the problem of integrating data residing in several sources. Companies that build a Data Warehouse, a Data Mining, or an Enterprise Resource Planning system must address this problem. Also, integrating data in the World Wide Web is the subject of several investigations and projects nowadays. Finally, applications requiring accessing or re-engineering legacy systems must deal with the problem of integrating data stored in different sources.

The design of a data integration system is a very complex task, which comprises several different issues. Here, we concentrate on the following issues: *(i)* dealing with heterogeneity of the sources, *(ii)* specifying the mapping between the global schema and the sources, *(iii)* processing queries expressed on the global schema.

Issue *(i)* refers to the fact that typically sources adopt different ontologies, models, and systems for storing data. This poses challenging problems in specifying the global schema. The goal is to design such a schema so as to provide an appropriate abstraction of all the data residing at the sources. One aspect deserving special attention is the choice of the language used to express the global schema. Since such a schema should mediate among different representations of overlapping worlds, the language should provide flexible and powerful representation mechanisms. This is the reason why many authors advocate the use of a conceptual data model for expressing the global schema [5, 21, 22, 3]. In this paper we follow this idea, and investigate the problem of query answering in data integration systems where the global schema is expressed in terms of an extended Entity-Relationship Model.

With regard to issue *(ii)*, two basic approaches have been used to specify the mapping between the sources and the global schema [15, 17, 18]. The first approach, called *global-as-view* (also global-schema centric, or simply global-centric), requires that the global schema is expressed in terms of the data sources. More precisely, to every concept of the global schema, a view over the data sources is associated, so that its meaning is specified in terms of the data residing at the sources. The second approach, called *local-as-view* (or source-centric), requires the global schema to be specified independently from the sources. In turn, the sources are defined as views over the global schema. A comparison of the approaches is reported in [24]. In this paper, we concentrate on the latter approach, which is generally considered sufficiently simple and effective for practical purposes.

Finally, issue *(iii)* is concerned with one of the most important problems in the design of a data integration system, namely, the choice of the method for computing the answer to queries posed in terms of the global schema. For this purpose, the system should be able to re-express the query in terms of a suitable set of queries posed to the sources. In this reformulation process, the crucial step is deciding how to decompose the query on the global schema into a set of subqueries on the sources, based on the meaning of the mapping. The computed subqueries are then shipped to the sources, and the results are assembled into the final answer. It is well known that processing queries in the local-as-view approach is a difficult task [23, 24, 14, 1, 13, 7, 8]. Indeed, in this approach the only knowledge we have about the data in the global schema is through the views representing the sources, and such views provide only partial information about the data. Therefore, extracting information from the data integration system is similar to query answering with incomplete information, which is a complex task [25]. On the other hand, query processing looks much easier in the global-as-view approach, where in general it is assumed that answering a query basically means unfolding its atoms according to their definitions in terms of the sources [15].

While this is a common opinion in the literature, we show that our framework poses new challenges, specially related to the need of taking the semantics of the conceptual global schema into account during query processing. Indeed, the first contribution in this paper is to show that the idea of adopting a conceptual data model for expressing the global schema, makes query processing more involved than in the simplified framework usually considered in the literature. In particular, we present the surprising result that the semantics of a data integration system is best described in terms of a set of databases, rather than a single one, and this implies that, even in the global-as-view approach, query processing is intimately connected to the notion of querying *incomplete databases*.

The second contribution of the paper is the formalization of the notion of correct answer in a data integration system with a conceptual global schema, and the presentation of a query processing strategy that is able to provide all correct answers to a query posed to the system.

The paper is organized as follows. In Section 2 we describe the conceptual data model we use in our approach. Section 3 illustrates a formal framework for data integration, by describing the main components of a data integration system, namely, the global schema, the sources, and the mapping between the two, and by specifying the precise semantics of the system. In Section 4 we present our query processing algorithm. By reasoning on both the query and the conceptual global schema, the algorithm is able to compute all correct answers to a query posed to the global schema. Section 5 concludes the paper.

2 The Conceptual Data Model

We present the conceptual model which is at the basis of the integration framework introduced in the next section. The model incorporates the basic features of the *Entity-Relationship* (ER) model [10], extended with subset (or is-a) constraints on both entities and relationships. Other characteristics that are not considered in this paper for the sake of simplicity (e.g., domain of attributes, identification constraints, etc.), can also be added without affecting the results in the next sections.

An *ER schema* is a collection of entity, relationship, and attribute definitions over an *alphabet $\mathcal{A}$ of symbols*. The alphabet $\mathcal{A}$ is partitioned into a set of entity symbols (denoted by E), a set of relationship symbols (denoted by R), and a set of attribute symbols (denoted by A).

An *entity definition* has the form

    define entity E
        isa: $E_1, \ldots, E_h$
        participates in: $R_1 : c_1, \ldots, R_\ell : c_\ell$
    end.

where E is the entity to be defined, the **isa** clause specifies a set of entities to which E is related via is-a (i.e., the set of entities that are supersets of E), and the **participates in** clause specifies those relationships, with respective components, to which an instance of E must necessarily participate. A *relationship definition* has the form

define relationship R **among** $E_1, \ldots, E_n$
isa: $R_1, \ldots, R_h$
end.

where R is the relationship to be defined, the entities listed in the **among** clause are those among which the relationship is defined (i.e., component i of R is an instance of entity E_i), and the **isa** clause specifies a set of relationships to which R is related via is-a. The number of entities in the **among** clause is the *arity* of R. An *attribute definition* has the form

define attribute A **for** X
qualification
end.

where A is the attribute to be defined, X is the entity or relationship to which the attribute is associated, and *qualification* consists of none, one, or both of the keywords **functional** and **mandatory**, specifying respectively that each instance of X has a unique value for attribute A, and that each instance of X must have a value for attribute A. If the **functional** keyword is missing, the attribute is multivalued, and if the **mandatory** keyword is missing, the attribute is optional.

In the definition of an entity or a relationship, the **isa** clause may be missing. Similarly, in an entity definition, the **participates in** clause may be missing. On the contrary, the **among** clause in a relationship definition must be present.

Notice that in our model each attribute is associated to a unique entity or relationship, i.e., different entities and relationships have disjoint sets of attributes. Also, for the sake of simplicity, we do not consider the specification of the domains of attributes in our model, and we simply assume that attributes have atomic values.

The semantics of an ER schema is defined by specifying when a database satisfies all constraints imposed by the schema. Formally, a database $\mathcal{B}$ is defined over a fixed (infinite) alphabet Γ of symbols, each one denoting a semantic value. $\mathcal{B}$ assigns to each entity a subset of Γ, to each attribute A of an entity a binary relation over Γ, to each relationship R of arity n, a set of n-tuples of elements of Γ, and to each attribute A of a relationship of arity n an $(n+1)$-ary relation over Γ. The set of objects assigned by $\mathcal{B}$ to an entity, attribute, or relationship is called the set of its *instances* in $\mathcal{B}$. We say that $\mathcal{B}$ is *legal* with respect to an ER schema $\mathcal{G}$ if the following conditions are satisfied:

- For each entity definition as the one above, the set of instances of E is a subset of the sets of instances of $E_1, \ldots, E_h$, and for each pair $R_i : c_i$ in the **participates in** clause of the definition, we have that each instance of E appears as c_i-th component is some instance of R_i.

- For each attribute specification as the one above, where X is an entity, we have that for each instance of A the first component is an instance of X. Moreover, if the *qualification* contains the keyword **mandatory**, then each instance of X must appear as the first component in some instance of A, and if it contains the keyword **functional**, then there may be no two instances of A coinciding on the first component (and differing on the second component). Similar conditions hold for the case where X is a relationship.
- For each relationship specification as the one above, for each instance $(o_1, \ldots, o_n)$ of R we have that o_i is an instance of E_i. Moreover, the set of instances of R is a subset of the sets of instances of $R_1, \ldots, R_h$.

The language we use to express queries over a global schema expressed in our conceptual model is that of conjunctive queries. Formally, a *conjunctive query* (CQ) Q of arity n is written in the form

$$Q(x_1, \ldots, x_n) \leftarrow conj(x_1, \ldots, x_n, y_1, \ldots, y_m)$$

where $conj(x_1, \ldots, x_n, y_1, \ldots, y_m)$ is a conjunction of atoms involving constants of Γ and variables $x_1, \ldots, x_n, y_1, \ldots, y_m$ from an alphabet of variables. The predicates in the atoms are the so-called *concepts* of the conceptual schema, i.e., its entities, relationships and attributes:

- Each entity E in $\mathcal{G}$ has an associated predicate E of arity 1. Intuitively, $E(c)$ asserts that c is an instance of entity E.
- Each attribute A for an entity E has an associated predicate A of arity 2. Intuitively, $A(c, d)$ asserts that c is an instance of entity E and d is the value of attribute A associated to c.
- Each relationship R among the entities $E_1, \ldots, E_n$ has an associated predicate R of arity n.
- Each attribute A for a relationship R among the entities $E_1, \ldots, E_n$ has an associated predicate A of arity $n+1$. Intuitively, $A(c_1, \ldots, c_n, d)$ asserts that $(c_1, \ldots, c_n)$ is an instance of relationship R and d is the value of attribute A associated to $(c_1, \ldots, c_n)$.

From a semantic point of view, the extension of a predicate P in a database $\mathcal{B}$ coincides with the set of instances that the concept associated to P has in $\mathcal{B}$. With this consideration, we can turn our attention to the semantics of queries, and simply observe that the semantics of conjunctive queries is the usual one, where the variables in the body are existentially quantified [2]. Thus, the *answer set* $Q^\mathcal{B}$ of Q over a database $\mathcal{B}$ is the set of tuples $(c_1, \ldots, c_n)$ of $\mathcal{B}$ for which there are $d_1, \ldots, d_m$ in $\mathcal{B}$, such that for each atom $e(b_1, \ldots, b_k)$ in $conj(c_1, \ldots, c_n, d_1, \ldots, d_m)$, where each b_i is one of $c_1, \ldots, c_n, d_1, \ldots, d_m$, we have that $(b_1, \ldots, b_k) \in e^\mathcal{B}$.

Example 1. Consider the ER schema shown in Figure 1, depicted in the usual graphical notation for the ER model. The elements of such a schema are Person/1, Employee/1, City/1, Lives_In/2, pname/2, salary/2, cname/2, since/2.

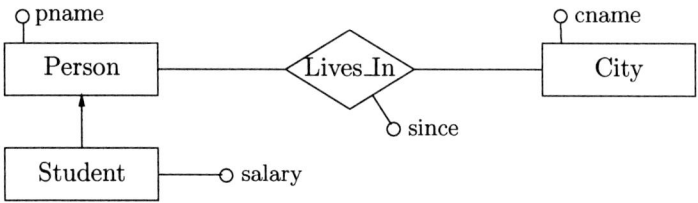

Fig. 1. ER schema of Example 1

Suppose we want to know the names of the employees who live in Rome since 1997. The corresponding CQ is

$$q(y) \leftarrow \mathsf{Employee}(x), \mathsf{pname}(x,y), \mathsf{Lives\_In}(x,z), \mathsf{since}(x,z,1997),$$
$$\mathsf{cname}(z, \text{``Rome''})$$

The answer of q over the database shown in Figure 2, is *Ann*.

3 The Formal Framework for Data Integration

In this section we set up a formal framework for data integration. In particular, we describe the main components of a data integration system, namely, the global schema, the sources, and the mapping between the two. Finally, we provide the semantics both of the system, and of query answering.

Definition 1. *A* data integration system $\mathcal{I}$ *is a triple* $\langle \mathcal{G}, \mathcal{S}, \mathcal{M}_{\mathcal{G},\mathcal{S}} \rangle$, *where* $\mathcal{G}$ *is the global schema,* $\mathcal{S}$ *is the source schema, and* $\mathcal{M}_{\mathcal{G},\mathcal{S}}$ *is the mapping between* $\mathcal{G}$ *and* $\mathcal{S}$.

We describe the characteristics of the various components of a data integration system in our approach:

- The *global schema* $\mathcal{G}$ is expressed in the conceptual data model described in the previous section.
- The *source schema* $\mathcal{S}$ is constituted by the schemas of the source relations. Note that we assume that the sources are expressed as relational data bases.

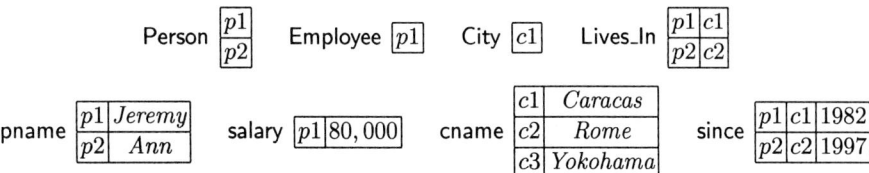

Fig. 2. Extension of relations of Example 1

This is not a strong limitation, since, in case of sources of different type, we can assume that suitable wrappers present the data at the source in relational form. Moreover, we observe that all considerations presented in this paper still hold in the case of other types of sources (e.g., semistructured sources).
- The *mapping* $\mathcal{M}_{\mathcal{G},\mathcal{S}}$ between $\mathcal{G}$ and $\mathcal{S}$ is given by associating to each concept C (either entity, relationship, or attribute) in the global schema a query $\mathcal{V}_C$ over the sources. We do not pose any constraint on the language used to express the queries in the mapping. Since sources are relational databases, we simply assume that the language is able to express computations over relational databases. Note that the *elements* that are assigned a query over the sources by the mapping coincide with the concepts of the global schema.

More precisely, the mapping associates queries to the elements of $\mathcal{G}$ as follows:

- The mapping associates a query of arity 1 to each entity of $\mathcal{G}$.
- The mapping associates a query of arity 2 to each attribute A defined for an entity in $\mathcal{G}$. Intuitively, if the query retrieves (c, d) from the sources, this means that d is a value of the attribute A of the entity instance c.
- The mapping associates a query of arity n to each relationship R of arity n in $\mathcal{G}$. Intuitively, if the query retrieves the tuple $(c_1, \ldots, c_n)$ from the sources, this means that $(c_1, \ldots, c_n)$ is an instance of R.
- The mapping associates a query of arity $n+1$ to each attribute A defined for a relationship R of arity n in $\mathcal{G}$. Intuitively, if the query retrieves $(c_1, \ldots, c_n, d)$ from the sources, this means that d is a value of the attribute A of the relationship instance $(c_1, \ldots, c_n)$.

As specified above, the intended meaning of the query $\mathcal{V}_C$ associated to the concept C is that it specifies how to retrieve the data corresponding to C in the global schema starting from the data at the sources. This confirms that we are following the global-as-views approach: the concepts in the global schema are defined as views over the source data.

Notice that all considerations reported in this paper still hold if we choose a different set of elements for specifying the mapping. For example, we could associate a single query of arity $m+1$ to each entity with m attributes (similarly for the relationships).

In order to specify the semantics of a data integration system, we have to characterize, given the set of tuples satisfying the various source relations, which are the data satisfying the global schema. In principle, given a set of data at the sources, one would like to have a corresponding single database for the global schema. Indeed, this is the case for most of the data integration systems described in the literature. However, we will show in the following the surprising result that, due to the presence of the semantic conditions that are implicit in the conceptual schema $\mathcal{G}$, in general, we will have to account for a set of databases.

We remind the reader that we assume that the databases involved in our framework (both global databases, and source databases) are defined over a fixed (infinite) alphabet Γ of symbols. In order to assign semantics to a data integration system $\mathcal{I} = \langle \mathcal{G}, \mathcal{S}, \mathcal{M}_{\mathcal{G},\mathcal{S}} \rangle$, we start by considering a *source database*

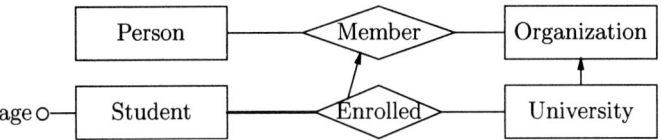

Fig. 3. Global schema of Example 2

for $\mathcal{I}$, i.e., a database $\mathcal{D}$ for the source schema $\mathcal{S}$. Based on $\mathcal{D}$, we now specify which is the information content of the global schema $\mathcal{G}$. We call *global database* for $\mathcal{I}$ any database for $\mathcal{G}$. A global database $\mathcal{B}$ for $\mathcal{I}$ is said to be *legal* with respect to $\mathcal{D}$, or, simply, *legal for $\mathcal{I}$ with respect to $\mathcal{D}$*, if:

- $\mathcal{B}$ is legal with respect to $\mathcal{G}$,
- for each element e of $\mathcal{G}$, the set of tuples $e^{\mathcal{B}}$ that $\mathcal{B}$ assigns to e is coherent with set of tuples computed by the associated query $\mathcal{V}_e$ over $\mathcal{D}$, i.e., $\mathcal{V}_e^{\mathcal{D}} \subseteq e^{\mathcal{B}}$.

The above definition implies that sources are considered *sound*: the data they provide to the integration system satisfy the global schema, but are not necessarily complete [13]. Another possibility would be to consider them *exact*. When sources are exact, the mapping between the global schema and the sources is defined in such a way that, for every source database $\mathcal{D}$, and every element e of $\mathcal{G}$, it holds that $\mathcal{V}_e^{\mathcal{D}} = e^{\mathcal{B}}$.

Example 2. Figure 3 shows the global schema $\mathcal{G}_1$ of a data integration system $\mathcal{I}_1 = \langle \mathcal{G}_1, \mathcal{S}_1, \mathcal{M}_1 \rangle$, where *age* is a functional attribute, Student has a mandatory participation in the relationship Enrolled, Enrolled is-a Member, and University is-a Organization. The schema models persons who can be members of one or more organizations, and students who are enrolled in universities. Suppose that $\mathcal{S}_1$ is constituted by $s_1, s_2, s_3, s_4, s_5, s_6, s_7, s_8$, and that the mapping $\mathcal{M}_1$ is as follows:

Person(x) ← $s_1(x)$
Organization(x) ← $s_2(x)$
Member(x,y) ← $s_7(x,z), s_8(z,y)$

Student(x) ← $s_3(x,y) \vee s_4(x,z)$
University(x) ← $s_5(x)$
Enrolled(x,y) ← $s_4(x,y)$
age(x,y) ← $s_3(x,y) \vee s_6(x,y,z)$

We are now ready to provide the definition of the semantics of a data integration system in our formalization.

Definition 2. *Let $\mathcal{I} = \langle \mathcal{G}, \mathcal{S}, \mathcal{M}_{\mathcal{G},\mathcal{S}} \rangle$ be a data integration system, and let $\mathcal{D}$ be a source database for $\mathcal{I}$. The semantics of $\mathcal{I}$ with respect to $\mathcal{D}$, denoted sem($\mathcal{I},\mathcal{D}$), is the set of global databases that are legal for $\mathcal{I}$ with respect to $\mathcal{D}$.*

From the above definition it is easy to see that, in our framework, given a source database $\mathcal{D}$, different situations are possible:

1. No legal global database exists. This happens, in particular, when the data at the sources retrieved by the queries associated to the elements of the global schema do not satisfy the functional attribute constraints.

Example 3. Referring to Example 2, consider a source database $\mathcal{D}_1$, where s_3 stores the tuple (t_1, a_1), and s_6 stores the tuple (t_1, a_2, v_1). The query associated to age by the mapping $\mathcal{M}_1$ specifies that, in every legal database of $\mathcal{I}_1$ both tuples should belong to the extension of age. However, age is a functional attribute in $\mathcal{G}_1$, and therefore no legal database exists for the data integration system $\mathcal{I}_1$.

2. Several legal global databases exist. This happens, for example, when the data at the sources retrieved by the queries associated to the global relations do not satisfy the is-a relationships of the global schema. In this case, it may happen that several ways exist to add suitable objects to the elements of $\mathcal{G}$ in order to satisfy the constraints. Each such ways yields a legal global database.

Example 4. Referring again to Example 2, consider a source database $\mathcal{D}_2$, where s_1 stores p_1 and p_2, s_2 stores o_1, s_5 stores u_1, and s_4 stores t_1, and the pairs (p_1, o_1) and (p_2, u_1) are in the join between s_7 and s_8. By the mapping $\mathcal{M}_1$, it follows that in every legal database of $\mathcal{I}_1$, $p_1, p_2 \in$ Person, $(p_1, o_1), (p_2, u_1) \in$ Member, $o_1 \in$ Organization, $t_1 \in$ Student, $u_1 \in$ University. Moreover, since $\mathcal{G}_1$ specifies that Student has a mandatory participation in the relationship Enrolled, in every legal database for $\mathcal{I}_1$, t_1 *must* be enrolled in a certain university. The key point is that nothing is said in $\mathcal{D}_2$ about *which* university, and therefore we have to accept as legal all databases for $\mathcal{I}_1$ that differ in the university in which t_1 is enrolled.

In our framework, we assume that the first problem is solved by the queries extracting data at the sources. In other words, we assume that, for any functional attribute A, the corresponding query implements a suitable data cleaning strategy that ensures that, for every source database $\mathcal{D}$ and every x, at most one tuple (x, y) belongs to $\mathcal{V}_A^{\mathcal{D}}$ (similar condition holds for functional attributes of relationships). The interested reader is referred to [12] for more details of data cleaning techniques.

The second problem shows that the issue of query answering with incomplete information arises even in the global-as-view approach to data integration. Indeed, the existence of multiple global databases for the data integration system implies that query processing cannot simply reduce to evaluating the query over a single database. Rather, we should in principles take *all* possible legal global databases into account when answering a query.

It is interesting to observe that there are at least two different strategies to simplify the setting, and overcome this problem:

1. Data integration systems usually adopt a simpler data model (often, a plain relational data model) for expressing the global schema. In this case, the data retrieved from the sources trivially fits into the schema, and can be directly considered as the unique database to be processed during query answering.
2. The queries associated to the elements of the global schema are often considered as exact. In this case, analogously to the previous one, it is easy

to see that the only global database to be considered is the one formed by the data retrieved by the source. However, when data at the sources do not obey all semantic conditions that are implicit in the conceptual global schema, this single database is not coherent with the global schema, and the data integration system is inconsistent. This implies that query answering is meaningless. We argue that, in the usual case of autonomous, heterogeneous sources, it is very unlikely that data fit in the global schema, and therefore, this approach is too restrictive, in the sense that the data integration system would be often inconsistent.

The fact that the problem of incomplete information is overlooked in current approaches can be explained by observing that traditional data integration systems follow one of the above mentioned simplifying strategies: they either express the global schema as a set of plain relations, or consider the sources as exact (see, for instance, [9, 19, 4]). On the contrary, the goal of our work is to study the more general setting where the global schema is expressed in terms of a conceptual model, and sources are considered sound (but not necessarily complete). The above result demonstrates that, in this case, we have to account for multiple global databases, and the results described in Section 4 show how to process queries in this setting.

We conclude the section by defining the notion of query posed to the data integration system. A query Q to a data integration system $\mathcal{I} = \langle \mathcal{G}, \mathcal{S}, \mathcal{M}_{\mathcal{G},\mathcal{S}} \rangle$ is a conjunctive query, whose atoms have symbols in $\mathcal{G}$ as predicates, as illustrated in Section 2. Our goal here is to specify which are the tuples that form the answer to a query posed to a data integration system $\mathcal{I}$. The fact that, given a source database $\mathcal{D}$, several global databases may exist that are legal for $\mathcal{I}$ with respect to $\mathcal{D}$ complicates this task. In order to address this problem, we follow a first-order logic approach: a tuple $(c_1, \ldots, c_n)$ is considered an answer to the query only if it is a *certain* answer, i.e., it satisfies the query in *every* database that belongs to the semantics of the data integration system.

Definition 3. *Let $\mathcal{I} = \langle \mathcal{G}, \mathcal{S}, \mathcal{M}_{\mathcal{G},\mathcal{S}} \rangle$ be a data integration system, let $\mathcal{D}$ be a source database for $\mathcal{I}$, and let Q be a query of arity n to $\mathcal{I}$. The set of certain answers $Q^{\mathcal{I},\mathcal{D}}$ to Q with respect to $\mathcal{I}$ and $\mathcal{D}$ is the set of tuples $(c_1, \ldots, c_n)$ such that $(c_1, \ldots, c_n) \in Q^{\mathcal{B}}$, for each $\mathcal{B} \in sem(\mathcal{I}, \mathcal{D})$.*

Example 5. Referring to Example 4, consider the query Q_1 to $\mathcal{I}_1$:

$$Q_1(x) \leftarrow \mathsf{Member}(x,y), \mathsf{University}(y)$$

It is easy to see that $\{p_2, t_1\}$ is the set of certain answers to Q_1 with respect to $\mathcal{I}_1$ and $\mathcal{D}_2$. Thus, although $\mathcal{D}_2$ does not indicate which university t_1 is enrolled in, the semantics of $\mathcal{I}_1$ specifies that t_1 is enrolled in *a* university in all legal database for $\mathcal{I}_1$. Since Member is a generalization of Enrolled, this implies that t_1 is in the set of certain answers to Q_1 with respect to $\mathcal{I}_1$ and $\mathcal{D}_2$.

4 Answering Queries over the Global Schema

In this section we present an algorithm for computing the set of certain answers to queries posed to a data integration system. The key feature of the algorithm is to reason about both the query and the conceptual global schema in order to infer which tuples satisfy the query in all legal databases of the data integration system. Thus, the algorithm does not simply unfold the query on the basis of the mapping, as usually done in data integration systems based on the global-as-view approach. Indeed, we now show that a simple unfolding strategy does not work in our setting.

Example 6. Consider again Example 5, and suppose we simply unfold the query Q_1 in the standard way, by substituting each atom with the query that $\mathcal{M}_1$ associates to the element in the atom. Then we get the query

$$q(x) \leftarrow s_7(x,z), s_8(z,y), s_5(y)$$

If we evaluate this query over $\mathcal{D}_2$, we get $\{p_2\}$ as result, thus missing the certain answer t_1.

Next we illustrate our algorithm for computing all certain answers. The algorithm is able to add more answers to those directly extracted from the sources, by exploiting the semantic conditions expressed in the conceptual global schema.

Let $\mathcal{I} = \langle \mathcal{G}, \mathcal{S}, \mathcal{M}_{\mathcal{G},\mathcal{S}} \rangle$ be an integration system, let $\mathcal{D}$ be a source database, and let Q be a query over the global schema $\mathcal{G}$. The algorithm is constituted by three major steps.

1. From the query Q, obtain a new query $exp_{\mathcal{G}}(Q)$ over the elements of the global schema G in which the knowledge in $\mathcal{G}$ that is relevant for Q has been compiled in.
2. From $exp_{\mathcal{G}}(Q)$, compute the query $unf_{\mathcal{M}_{\mathcal{G},\mathcal{S}}}(exp_{\mathcal{G}}(Q))$, by unfolding $exp_{\mathcal{G}}(Q)$ on the basis of the mapping $\mathcal{M}_{\mathcal{G},\mathcal{S}}$. The unfolding simply substitutes each atom of $exp_{\mathcal{G}}(Q)$ with the query associated by $\mathcal{M}_{\mathcal{G},\mathcal{S}}$ to the element in the atom. The resulting $unf_{\mathcal{M}_{\mathcal{G},\mathcal{S}}}(exp_{\mathcal{G}}(Q))$ is a query over the source relations.
3. Evaluate the query $unf_{\mathcal{M}_{\mathcal{G},\mathcal{S}}}(exp_{\mathcal{G}}(Q))$ over the source database $\mathcal{D}$.

The last two steps are quite obvious. Instead, the first one requires to find a way to compile into the query the semantic relations holding among the concepts of the global schema $\mathcal{G}$. Such semantic relations can indeed be crucial for inferring the complete set of certain answers.

The basic idea to do so is that the relations among the elements in $\mathcal{G}$ can be captured by a suitable *rule base* $\mathcal{R}_{\mathcal{G}}$. To build $\mathcal{R}_{\mathcal{G}}$, we introduce a new predicate P' (called primed predicate) for each predicate P associated to an element P of $\mathcal{G}$. Then, from the semantics of the ER schema we devise the following rules (expressed in Logic Programming notation [20]):

– for each entity E, attribute A and relationship R in $\mathcal{G}$, we have:

$$E'(x) \leftarrow E(x)$$
$$A'(x,y) \leftarrow A(x,y)$$
$$R'(x_1,\ldots,x_n) \leftarrow R(x_1,\ldots,x_n)$$

- for each is-a relation between E and E_i, or between R and R_i in an entity or relationship definition of $\mathcal{G}$, we have:

$$E'_i(x) \leftarrow E'(x)$$
$$R'_i(x_1,\ldots,x_n) \leftarrow R'(x_1,\ldots,x_n)$$

- for each attribute A for an entity E or a relationship R in an attribute definition in $\mathcal{G}$, we have:

$$E'(x) \leftarrow A'(x,y)$$
$$R'(x_1,\ldots,x_n) \leftarrow A'(x_1,\ldots,x_n,y)$$

- for each relationship R involving an entity E_i as i-th component according to the corresponding relationship definition in $\mathcal{G}$, we have:

$$E'_i(x_i) \leftarrow R'(x_1,\ldots,x_i,\ldots,x_n)$$

- for each mandatory participation of an entity E in a relationship R_j in an entity definition of $\mathcal{G}$, we have:

$$R'_j(f_1(x),\ldots,x,\ldots,f_n(x)) \leftarrow E'(x)$$

where f_i are fresh Skolem functions [20].
- for each mandatory attribute A for an entity E or a relationship R in an attribute definition of $\mathcal{G}$, we have:

$$A'(x,f(x)) \leftarrow E'(x)$$
$$A'(x_1,\ldots,x_n,f(x)) \leftarrow R'(x_1,\ldots,x_n)$$

where f is a fresh Skolem function.

Once we have defined such a rule base $\mathcal{R}_\mathcal{G}$, we can use it to generate the query $exp_\mathcal{G}(Q)$ associated to the original query Q. This is done as follows:

1. First, we rewrite Q by substituting each predicate P in the body $body(Q)$ of Q with P'. We denote by Q' the resulting query. In the following we call "primed atom" every atom whose predicate is primed.
2. Then we build a *partial resolution tree* for Q', i.e., a tree having each node labeled by a conjunctive query q, with one of the atoms in $body(q)$ marked as *"selected"*, obtained as follows.
   (a) The root is labeled by Q', and has marked as selected any (primed) atom in $body(Q')$ (for example the first in left-to-right order).
   (b) Except if condition (2c) below is satisfied, a node, labeled by a query q having a "selected" atom α, has one child for each rule r in $\mathcal{R}_\mathcal{G}$ such that there exists a most general unifier[1] $mgu(\alpha, head(r))$ between the atom α and the head $head(r)$ of the rule r. Each of such children has the following properties:

---

[1] We recall that given two atoms α and β the most general unifier $mgu(\alpha,\beta)$ is a most general substitution for the variables in α and β that makes α and β equal [20].

- it is labeled by the query obtained from q by replacing the atom α with $body(r)$ and by substituting the variables with $mgu(\alpha, head(r))$;
    - it has as marked "selected" one of the primed atoms (for example the first in left-to-right order).
  (c) If a node d that is labeled by a query q and there exists a predecessor d' of d labeled by a query q' and a substitution θ of the variables of q' that makes q' equal to q, then d has a single child, which is labeled by the empty query (a query whose body is false).
3. Finally we return as result the query $exp_{\mathcal{G}}(Q)$ formed as the union of all non-empty queries in the leaves of the partial resolution tree.

The following three observations are crucial for characterizing both the termination and the correctness of our algorithm:

- The termination of the construction of the tree, and thus of the entire algorithm, is guaranteed by the condition (2c) and by the observation that all the rules in $\mathcal{R}_{\mathcal{G}}$ have a single atom in the body.
- By exploiting results on partial evaluation of logic programs (see [11]), it can be shown that $exp_{\mathcal{G}}(Q)$ is equivalent to the original query Q with respect to the global schema $\mathcal{G}$, that is, for each database $\mathcal{B}$ that is legal for $\mathcal{G}$, the evaluation of Q yields the same result as $exp_{\mathcal{G}}(Q)$, i.e., $Q^{\mathcal{B}} = (exp_{\mathcal{G}}(Q))^{\mathcal{B}}$.
- The query $exp_{\mathcal{G}}(Q)$ returned by the algorithm is a union of conjunctive queries. Each disjunct of $exp_{\mathcal{G}}(Q)$ is a conjunctive query over the predicates of the global schema, i.e., the elements that have an associated query over the sources by virtue of the mapping.

The above observations imply that, if we evaluate $unf_{\mathcal{M}_{\mathcal{G},\mathcal{S}}}(exp_{\mathcal{G}}(Q))$ over the source database $\mathcal{D}$, we get exactly the set of certain answers $q^{\mathcal{I},\mathcal{D}}$ of Q with respect to $\mathcal{I}$ and $\mathcal{D}$.

With regard to the characterization of the computational complexity of the algorithm, we observe that the number of disjuncts in $exp_{\mathcal{G}}(Q)$ can be exponential in the number of rules in the rule base $\mathcal{R}_{\mathcal{G}}$ (and therefore in the size of the global schema $\mathcal{G}$), and in the number of variables in the original query Q. Note, however, that this bound is independent of the size of $\mathcal{D}$, i.e., the size of data at the sources. We remind the reader that the evaluation of a union of conjunctive queries can be done in time polynomial with respect to the size of the data. Since $exp_{\mathcal{G}}(Q)$ is a union of conjunctive queries, we can conclude that, if the queries associated by $\mathcal{M}_{\mathcal{G},\mathcal{S}}$ to the elements of $\mathcal{G}$ can be evaluated in polynomial time in the size of the data at the sources, then evaluating $unf_{\mathcal{M}_{\mathcal{G},\mathcal{S}}}(exp_{\mathcal{G}}(Q))$ over $\mathcal{D}$ is also polynomial in the size of the data at the sources. It follows that our query answering algorithm is polynomial with respect to data complexity.

Example 7. Referring again to Example 5, it is possible to see that, by evaluating the unfolding of the query returned by the algorithm, the whole set of certain answers to Q_1 with respect to $\mathcal{I}_1$ and $\mathcal{D}_2$ is obtained. In particular, t_1 is obtained by processing the rule Member$'(x,y) \leftarrow$ Enrolled$'(x,y)$, which takes into account that Member is a generalization of Enrolled and the rule Enrolled$'(x, f(x)) \leftarrow$ Student$'(x)$, which expresses the mandatory participation of Student in Enrolled.

5 Conclusions

While it is a common opinion that query processing is an easy task in the global-as-view approach to data integration, we have shown the surprising result that, when the global schema is expressed in terms of a conceptual data model, even a very simple one, query processing becomes difficult. The difficulties basically arise because of the need of dealing with incomplete information, similarly to the case of the local-as-view approach to data integration.

After a logic-based characterization of the data integration system, we have presented a novel query processing algorithm that is able to compute all correct answers to a query posed to the global schema, by reasoning on both the query and the conceptual global schema. We have also shown that query processing, although exponential with respect to the size of the query and the global schema, remains of polynomial data complexity.

We have implemented a first prototype of data integration system based on the presented algorithm. In addition to specifying the global schema in terms of a conceptual data model, the system allows several types of constraints to be expressed on the sources. Although we did not address this issue here, these constraints are used for carrying out several optimizations in accessing the sources. Overall, the first experiments about the performance of the system are extremely encouraging.

In this paper, we used a simple conceptual data model for expressing the global schema, and we used the language of conjunctive queries for expressing queries over the global schema. We observe, however, that all the results presented in the paper can be straightforwardly extended to the class of unions of conjunctive queries. As future work, we aim at enriching the conceptual model with more advanced features, such as disjointness assertions, and cardinality constraints on attributes and relationships. With these features, query answering becomes even more complex, due to the need of performing more sophisticated forms of data cleaning and reconciliation [6, 12]. Our goal is to modify the algorithm described in this paper so as to adapt to the new class of semantic conditions represented in the global schema.

References

[1] S. Abiteboul and O. Duschka. Complexity of answering queries using materialized views. In *Proc. of PODS'98*, pages 254–265, 1998.

[2] S. Abiteboul, R. Hull, and V. Vianu. *Foundations of Databases*. Addison Wesley Publ. Co., Reading, Massachussetts, 1995.

[3] S. Bergamaschi, S. Castano, M. Vincini, and D. Beneventano. Intelligent techniques for the extraction and integration of heterogeneous information. In *Proc. of the IJCAI'99 Workshop on Intelligent Information Integration*, 1999.

[4] M. Bouzeghoub and M. Lenzerini. Special issue on data extraction, cleaning, and reconciliation. *Information Systems*, 2001. To appear.

[5] D. Calvanese, G. De Giacomo, M. Lenzerini, D. Nardi, and R. Rosati. Information integration: Conceptual modeling and reasoning support. In *Proc. of CoopIS'98*, pages 280–291, 1998.

[6] D. Calvanese, G. De Giacomo, M. Lenzerini, D. Nardi, and R. Rosati. Data integration in data warehousing. *Int. J. of Cooperative Information Systems*, 2001. To appear.

[7] D. Calvanese, G. De Giacomo, M. Lenzerini, and M. Y. Vardi. Answering regular path queries using views. In *Proc. of ICDE 2000*, pages 389–398, 2000.

[8] D. Calvanese, G. De Giacomo, M. Lenzerini, and M. Y. Vardi. View-based query processing and constraint satisfaction. In *Proc. of LICS 2000*, pages 361–371, 2000.

[9] M. J. Carey, L. M. Haas, P. M. Schwarz, M. Arya, W. F. Cody, R. Fagin, M. Flickner, A. Luniewski, W. Niblack, D. Petkovic, J. Thomas, J. H. Williams, and E. L. Wimmers. Towards heterogeneous multimedia information systems: The Garlic approach. In *RIDE-DOM*, pages 124–131, 1995.

[10] P. P. Chen. The Entity-Relationship model: Toward a unified view of data. *ACM Trans. on Database Systems*, 1(1):9–36, Mar. 1976.

[11] G. De Giacomo. Intensional query answering by partial evaluation. *J. of Intelligent Information Systems*, 7(3):205–233, 1996.

[12] H. Galhardas, D. Florescu, D. Shasha, and E. Simon. An extensible framework for data cleaning. Technical Report 3742, INRIA, Rocquencourt, 1999.

[13] G. Grahne and A. O. Mendelzon. Tableau techniques for querying information sources through global schemas. In *Proc. of ICDT'99*, volume 1540 of *LNCS*, pages 332–347. Springer-Verlag, 1999.

[14] J. Gryz. Query folding with inclusion dependencies. In *Proc. of ICDE'98*, pages 126–133, 1998.

[15] A. Y. Halevy. Theory of answering queries using views. *SIGMOD Record*, 29(4):40–47, 2000.

[16] R. Hull. Managing semantic heterogeneity in databases: A theoretical perspective. In *Proc. of PODS'97*, 1997.

[17] A. Y. Levy. Logic-based techniques in data integration. In J. Minker, editor, *Logic Based Artificial Intelligence*. Kluwer Publishers, 2000.

[18] C. Li and E. Chang. Query planning with limited source capabilities. In *Proc. of ICDE 2000*, pages 401–412, 2000.

[19] C. Li, R. Yerneni, V. Vassalos, H. Garcia-Molina, Y. Papakonstantinou, J. D. Ullman, and M. Valiveti. Capability based mediation in TSIMMIS. In *Proc. of ACM SIGMOD*, pages 564–566, 1998.

[20] J. W. Lloyd. *Foundations of Logic Programming (Second, Extended Edition)*. Springer-Verlag, Berlin, Heidelberg, 1987.

[21] B. Ludascher, A. Gupta, and M. E. Martone. Model-based mediation with domain maps. In *Proc. of ICDE 2001*, pages 81–90, 2001.

[22] L. Palopoli, L. Pontieri, G. Terracina, and D. Ursino. Intensional and extensional integration and abstraction of heterogeneous databases. *Data and Knowledge Engineering*, 35(3):201–237, 2000.

[23] X. Qian. Query folding. In *Proc. of ICDE'96*, pages 48–55, 1996.

[24] J. D. Ullman. Information integration using logical views. In *Proc. of ICDT'97*, volume 1186 of *LNCS*, pages 19–40. Springer-Verlag, 1997.

[25] R. van der Meyden. Logical approaches to incomplete information. In J. Chomicki and G. Saake, editors, *Logics for Databases and Information Systems*, pages 307–356. Kluwer Academic Publisher, 1998.

Resolving Conflicts and Handling Replication during Integration of Multiple Databases by Object Deputy Model

Zhiyong Peng[1] and Yahiko Kambayashi[2]

[1] State Key Lab of Software Engineering, Wuhan University, Wuhan 430072 China
[2] Graduate School of Informatics, Kyoto University, Kyoto 606-8501 Japan

Abstract. During integration of multiple databases, there are a lot of methods to resolve various syntactical and semantic conflicts. However, the replication problem has less been taken into consideration. The replication means that the same entity or attributes may appear in multiple databases. Once they are integrated, the replication should be eliminated from the integrated views and an update occurring at one database should be propagated into the others. In this paper, we will discuss integration of multiple databases by the object deputy model. The model can easily resolve conflicts using switching operations and an object deputy algebra. The replication can also be handled by the object deputy model.

1 Introduction

Along with widespread use of internet, there are more and more information sources on the web. It becomes very important to provide an integrated access to them. Various techniques [3,4,5,7,12] have been developed to create a multidatabase system which is a confederation of preexisting, autonomous, and possibly heterogeneous, database systems. When an information source participates in a multidatabase system, its data model is mapped to a data model that is the same for all participating systems, called the common data model. Many researchers have advocated the use of an object-oriented data model as the common data model because it is semantically rich and can provide a variety of abstraction mechanisms for data integration. Furthermore, the object-oriented data model can define methods that enable arbitrary combinations of information stored in local databases and makes it possible to integrate nontraditional databases through behavioral mapping.

However, the object-oriented model is not enough to provide database interoperability because it has two serious problems. Firstly, it can only provide subclass constructor and support inheritance from superclass to subclass. Data integration needs not only specialization but also aggregation and generalization. Aggregation can be used to integrate component objects distributed in different databases. The attributes and methods of the component objects are inherited by the complex object in the global schema. The generalization can be used to integrate specific objects into general ones. Thus, the object-oriented model should be extended with superclass constructor and can define inheritance from a subclass to a superclass and from the component objects to the complex object. Secondly, the view mechanism is very difficult to be implemented. In order to integrate databases, their schemas should be dynamically defined and modified. The view mechanism plays an important role in restructuring the schema resulting from the merging of component schemas.

In this paper, we propose an object deputy approach to integrate multiple databases under a distributed environment. The object deputy model[9] introduced by authors is the extension of the conventional object-oriented data model with the concepts of deputy objects and deputy classes. A deputy object is used to extend and customize its source object(s). Its schema is defined by a deputy class which can be derived by an object deputy algebra. The major features of deputy objects are summarized as follows.

1. A deputy object has its own persistent identifier, and may have additional attributes and methods that are not derived from its source object(s).
2. The attributes and methods of an object can be inherited by its deputy objects. The inheritance is realized through switching operations that can change the names and types of the inherited attributes and methods.
3. There is a bilateral link between an object and one of its deputy objects, which allows not only inheritance but also update propagation between them.

The object deputy model is more flexible than the traditional object-oriented model. It can provide inheritance for specialization, generalization and aggregation. In addition, as we discussed in the paper[8], the view mechanism is easy to be implemented by the object deputy model. The use of the object deputy model as the common data model can facilitate the creation of the federated schema. Due to heterogeneity, the various conflicts will arise during integration. The object deputy model can resolve these conflicts by switching operations and an object deputy algebra. If there are replications, they can be eliminated from the integrated view and their consistency among the local information sources can be maintained through update propagation.

The paper is organized as follows. Section 2 introduces an object deputy approach for database integration. Resolving conflicts and handling replication are discussed in Section 3 and Section 4, respectively. Section 5 will give a conclusion.

2 An Object Deputy Approach

There are usually two ways to provide an integrated access to multiple, distributed, heterogeneous information sources. One is based on view mechanisms that are realized by computation methods. That is, the user query is divided into several sub-queries that are executed by information sources. The results of the sub-queries are integrated and returned to the user. The other way is through data warehousing that is based on materialized view mechanisms. At data warehouses, the data of interest are extracted from information source, and integrated in advance. When a user query is issued, the query is evaluated directly at the data warehouse, without accessing the underlying information sources.

In this paper, we will provide an object deputy approach which can combine the above two ways. The basic idea is (1) to select the objects of interest from information sources, (2) create their materialized deputy objects to avoid communication delays, and (3) form an integrated and application-specific view by properly selecting combination of computed and materialized deputy objects, considering the trade-off problems between storage cost and computation overhead.

In order to reduce storage overhead, deputy objects derived for integration are usually not materialized. If the integration requires time-consumption type convertion, some of them will be materialized. For example, converting images from a format into another may take too much time. Therefore, the deputy objects of those image objects with formats different from the uniform one should be materialized, and the others need not. Thus, an integrated view is realized by the computed/materialized deputy objects or their mixtures (Even in the same deputy object, some of its inherited attributes can be defined to be materialized, and the others to be unmateralized).

The concept of deputy objects was at first introduced by authors for the unified realization of object views, roles and migration. In order to illustrate that it is also useful for database integration, we will review its definition.

The object-oriented data model represents real-world entities in term of **objects**. Objects are identified by system-defined identifiers which are independent of objects' states. An object has attributes which represent properties of a corresponding real-world entity. The state of an object is represented by its attribute values, which are read and written by basic methods. In addition, there are general methods that represent behavior of objects. Objects having the same attributes and methods are clustered into **classes** which make it possible to avoid specification and storage of redundant information. A formal definition of objects and classes is given as follows.

Definition 1. *Each object has an identifier, attributes and methods. Schema of objects with the same attributes and methods is defined by a class which consists of a name, an extent and a type. The extent of a class is a set of objects belonging to it, called its instances. The type of a class is definitions of its attributes and methods. A class named as C is represented as*

$$C = \langle \{o\}, \{T_a : a\}, \{m : \{T_p : p\}\} \rangle$$

1. *$\{o\}$ is the extent of C, where o is one of instances of C.*
2. *$\{T_a : a\}$ is the set of attribute definitions of C, where a and T_a represent name and type of an attribute, respectively. The value of attribute a of object o is expressed by $o.a$. For each attribute $T_a : a$, there are two basic method: $read(o, a)$ for reading $o.a$ and $write(o, a, v)$ for writing $o.a$ with the new value v, expressed as follows.*

$$read(o, a) \Rightarrow\uparrow o.a, \quad write(o, a, v) \Rightarrow o.a := v$$

Here, $\Rightarrow$, $\uparrow$ and $:=$ stand for operation invoking, result returning and assignment, respectively.

3. $\{m : \{T_p : p\}\}$ is the set of method definitions of C, where m and $\{T_p : p\}$ are method name and a set of parameters, p and T_p represent parameter name and type, respectively. Applying method m to object o with parameters $\{p\}$ is expressed as follows.

$$apply(o, m, \{p\})$$

Deputy objects are defined as extension and customization of objects. An object can have many deputy objects that are used to customize objects for different applications or represent its many facet nature. The schemas of deputy objects are defined by deputy classes that are derived by creating deputy objects as their instances, generating switching operations for inheritance of attributes and methods, and adding definitions for their additional attributes and methods. A formal definition of deputy objects and deputy classes is given as follows.

Definition 2. *A deputy object is generated from object(s) or other deputy object(s). The latter is called source object(s) of the former. A deputy object must inherit some attributes/methods from its source object. The schema of deputy objects with the same properties is defined by a deputy class, which includes a name, extent and type. Deputy classes are derived from classes of source objects, called source classes. In general, let $C^s = \langle \{o^s\}, \{T_{a^s} : a^s\}, \{m^s : \{T_{p^s} : p^s\}\}\rangle$ be a source class. Its deputy class C^d is defined as*

$$C^d = \langle \{o^d \,|\, (o^d \to o^s) \vee (o^d \to ... \times o^s \times ...) \vee (o^d \to \{o^s\}),$$
$$sp(o^s) \vee cp(... \times o^s \times ...) \vee gp(\{o^s\}) == true\},$$
$$\{T_{a^d} : a^d\} \cup \{T_{a^d_+} : a^d_+\}, \{m^d : \{T_{p^d} : p^d\}\} \cup \{m^d_+ : \{T_{p^d_+} : p^d_+\}\}\rangle$$

1. $\{o^d\,|(o^d \to o^s) \vee (o^d \to ... \times o^s \times ...) \vee (o^d \to \{o^s\}), sp(o^s) \vee cp(... \times o^s \times ...) \vee gp(\{o^s\}) == true\}$ is the extent of C^d, where $(o^d \to o^s) \vee (o^d \to ... \times o^s \times ...) \vee (o^d \to \{o^s\})$ represents that o^d is the deputy object of o^s, $... \times o^s \times ...$, or $\{o^s\}$; sp, cp and gp represent selection, combination and grouping predicate, respectively.
2. $\{T_{a^d} : a^d\} \cup \{T_{a^d_+} : a^d_+\}$ is the set of attribute definitions of C^d.
   (a) $\{T_{a^d} : a^d\}$ is the set of the attributes inherited from $\{T_{a^s} : a^s\}$ of C^s, of which switching operations are defined as

   $$read(o^d, a^d) \Rightarrow\uparrow f_{T_{a^s} \mapsto T_{a^d}}(read(o^s, a^s)),$$
   $$write(o^d, a^d, v^d) \Rightarrow write(o^s, a^s, f_{T_{a^d} \mapsto T_{a^s}}(v^d))$$

   (b) $\{T_{a^d_+} : a^d_+\}$ is the set of the additional attributes of C^d, of which basic methods are defined as

   $$read(o^d, a^d_+) \Rightarrow\uparrow o^d.a^d_+,$$
   $$write(o^d, a^d_+, v^d_+) \Rightarrow o^d.a^d_+ := v^d_+$$

3. $\{m^d : \{T_{p^d} : p^d\}\} \cup \{m^d_+ : \{T_{p^d_+} : p^d_+\}\}$ is the set of method definitions of C^d.

   (a) $\{m^d : \{T_{p^d} : p^d\}\}$ is the set of the methods inherited from $\{m^s : \{T_{p^s} : p^s\}\}$ of C^s, of which are applied through switching operations as
   $$apply(o^d, m^d, \{p^d\}) \Rightarrow \uparrow apply(o^s, m^s, \{f_{T_{p^d} \mapsto T_{p^s}}(p^d)\})$$

   (b) $\{m^d_+ : \{T_{p^d_+} : p^d_+\}\}$ is the set of the additional methods of C^d, which are applied as
   $$apply(o^d, m^d_+, \{p^d_+\})$$

According to the above definition, deputy objects have persistent identifiers but their attribute values inherited from source objects are still computed through switching operations that need communicate with the underlying information sources. In order to improve performance, queries are required to be evaluated locally since information sources may be remote or unavailable for some time. For this reason, we extend deputy mechanisms to allow deputy objects to materialize their inherited attribute values. The definitions of basic methods for the inherited attribute of which value is materialized are changed as follows.

$$read(o^d, a^d) \Rightarrow \uparrow o^d.a^d,$$
$$write(o^d, a^d, v^d) \Rightarrow o^d.a^d := v^d \wedge write(o^s, a^s, f_{T_{a^d} \mapsto T_{a^s}}(v^d)),$$
$$update(o^d, a^d) \Rightarrow o^d.a^d := f_{T_{a^s} \mapsto T_{a^d}}(read(o^s, a^s))$$

That is, the inherited attribute values are precomputed and can be directly read from the deputy object. Thus, queries on the integrated views need not interfere with objects at remote sources. The update of the inherited attribute value of a deputy object need to be reflected in its source object(s). Therefore, the writing method is first to update the precomputed value and then propagate the change into the original one through the switching operation. On the other hand, the update of the original attribute value requires to recompute the inherited attribute value of the deputy object. This operation is realized by introducing another basic method for each inherited attribute. The basic update method updates the inherited attribute value according to its dependence relationship defined by the switching operation. It is triggered when the original attribute value is updated.

After the objects of interest are extracted from multiple heterogeneous information sources by creating their materialized deputy objects, their integration will be realized by an object deputy algebra, which consists of the six algebraic operations: Select, Project, Extend, Union, Join, Grouping.

In order to offer an integrated view, the schema mismatch of objects must be overcome at first. Since the inheritance by switching operations allows the names and types of attributes between objects and their deputy objects to be different, the synonym, homonym and type mismatch problems can be solved by defining appropriate switching operations. After the schema mismatch of objects has been solved, object integration can be realized by applying the object deputy algebra, of which the selection operation is mainly used to select objects of interest for integration. The same kind of real-world entities may be defined in multiple sources with attributes and methods more or less than what need be included in the integrated view. The project operation can be used to hide unnecessary ones, and the extend operation to add necessary ones (with default values). The objects with the same attributes and methods from different sources can be integrated into a single class by the union operation. If attributes and methods of a real-world entity are distributed in different sources, the conceptually related components can be combined by the join operation. In addition, the same objects replicately defined in different sources can be grouped by the grouping operation.

3 Resolving Conflicts

We firstly build object-oriented interfaces on top of non object-oriented information sources. The interface consists of a set of classes, which defines the properties and messages for a set of objects. Each definitional property has a name followed by its domain. The domain of a definitional property can be a basic type (for example, integer, boolean, string) or a class. The basic operations for messages are implemented in terms of primitives provided by the local information source. That means each local information source is converted into a uniform view. It mainly solves conflicts due to syntactical heterogeneity and different data models.

The next step is how to integrate semantically heterogeneous schemas in an integrated view. There may be various conflicts during integration. They can be resolved through homogenizing, specialization, generalization and aggregation.

3.1 Homogenizing Objects

When integrating several heterogeneous information sources, there are the problems of having different names for equivalent entities or attributes, or having the same name for different entities or attributes. In addition, different expressions, units or level of precision may be used to denote similar information. These conflicts can be resolved by defining deputy objects with switching operations which can rename attributes/methods and change their expressions, units or level of precision. For example, an employee's monthly income in one database is expressed as salary in another. Suppose that they have different units, Japanese yuan for the monthly income and USA dollar for salary. If they need be homogenized into salary with USA dollar as unit, we can define the deputy object with the following switching operation.

$Read(d, salary) \rightarrow Read(o, monthly\_salary) * ju\_rate;$
$Write(d, salary, v) \rightarrow Write(o, monthly\_salary, v/ju\_rate)$

Here ju_rate represents exchange rate from Japanese yuan to USA dollar.

Conflicts involving "missing attributes " arise when the numbers of attributes are different in semantically equivalent entities across several information sources. There are two ways to resolve this type of conflict. One way is to hide the extra attributes from the entities which have more attributes than other entities. This can be realized by deriving a deputy class using the algebraic operation: Project.

Resolving Conflicts and Handling Replication   291

The **Project** operation is used to derive a deputy class which only inherits part of attributes and methods of a source class. Its formal definition is as follows.

Definition 3. Let $C^s = \langle \{o^s\}, \{T_{a^s} : a^s\}, \{m^s : \{T_{p^s} : p^s\}\} \rangle$ be a source class, $\{T_{a^s_-} : a^s_-\}$ and $\{m^s_- : \{T_{p^s_-} : p^s_-\}\}$ be subsets of attributes and methods of C^s which are allowed to be inherited. A deputy class derived by the **Project** operation is represented as $C^d = \textbf{Project}(C^s, \{T_{a^s_-} : a^s_-\}, \{m^s_- : \{T_{p^s_-} : p^s_-\}\})$.

1. The extent of C^d is the set of deputy objects of instances of C^s, which is expressed as

$$\{o^d | o^d \to o^s\}$$

2. The set of attributes of C^d is defined as $\{T_{a^d} : a^d_-\}$, which are inherited from the attributes $\{T_{a^s} : a^s_-\}$ of C^s. The switching operations for inheriting $T_{a^s} : a^s_-$ in form of $T_{a^d} : a^d_-$ are realized in the following way.

$$read(o^d, a^d_-) \Rightarrow \uparrow f_{T_{a^s} \mapsto T_{a^d}}(read(o^s, a^s_-)),$$
$$write(o^d, a^d_-, v^d_-) \Rightarrow write(o^s, a^s_-, f_{T_{a^d} \mapsto T_{a^s}}(v^d_-))$$

3. The set of methods of C^d is defined as $\{m^d_- : \{T_{p^d} : p^d_-\}\}$, which are inherited from the methods $\{m^s_- : \{T_{p^s_-} : p^s_-\}\}$ of C^s. The switching operation for inheriting $m^s_- : \{T_{p^s_-} : p^s_-\}$ in form of $m^d_- : \{T_{p^d} : p^d_-\}$ is realized in the following way.

$$apply(o^d, m^d_-, \{p^d_-\}) \Rightarrow \uparrow apply(o^s, m^s_-, \{f_{T_{p^d} \mapsto T_{p^s}}(p^d_-)\})$$

The other way is to add the extra attributes to the entities which have less attributes than other entities. This can be realized by deriving a deputy class using the algebraic operation: Extend. The **Extend** operation is used to derive a deputy class of which instances are extended with additional attributes and methods that can not be derived from a source class. Its formal definition is as follows.

Definition 4. Let $C^s = \langle \{o^s\}, \{T_{a^s} : a^s\}, \{m^s : \{T_{p^s} : p^s\}\} \rangle$ be a source class, $\{T_{a^d_+} : a^d_+\}$ and $\{m^d_+ : \{T_{p^d_+} : p^d_+\}\}$ be sets of additional attributes and methods. A deputy class derived by the **Extend** operation is represented as $C^d = \textbf{Extend}(C^s, \{T_{a^d_+} : a^d_+\}, \{m^d_+ : \{T_{p^d_+} : p^d_+\}\})$.

1. The extent of C^d is the set of deputy objects of instances of C^s, which is expressed as

$$\{o^d | o^d \to o^s\}$$

2. The set of attributes of C^d is defined as union of attributes $\{T_{a^d} : a^d\}$ inherited from the attributes $\{T_{a^s} : a^s\}$ of C^s and its additional attributes $\{T_{a^d_+} : a^d_+\}$, expressed as $\{T_{a^d} : a^d\} \cup \{T_{a^d_+} : a^d_+\}$.

(a) The switching operations for inheriting $T_{a^s} : a^s$ in form of $T_{a^d} : a^d$ are realized in the following way.
$$read(o^d, a^d) \Rightarrow \uparrow f_{T_{a^s} \mapsto T_{a^d}}(read(o^s, a^s)),$$
$$write(o^d, a^d, v^d) \Rightarrow write(o^s, a^s, f_{T_{a^d} \mapsto T_{a^s}}(v^d))$$

(b) For each additional attribute $T_{a_+^d} : a_+^d$, the following two basic methods are realized, which are operated independently of the source object.
$$read(o^d, a_+^d) \Rightarrow \uparrow o^d.a_+^d,$$
$$write(o^d, a_+^d, v_+^d) \Rightarrow o^d.a_+^d := v_+^d$$

3. The set of methods of C^d is defined as union of methods $\{m^d : \{T_{p^d} : p^d\}\}$ inherited from the methods $\{m^s : \{T_{p^s} : p^s\}\}$ of C^s and its additional methods $\{m_+^d : \{T_{p_+^d} : p_+^d\}\}$, expressed as $\{m^d : \{T_{p^d} : p^d\}\} \cup \{m_+^d : \{T_{p_+^d} : p_+^d\}\}$.

(a) The switching operation for inheriting $m^s : \{T_{p^s} : p^s\}$ in form of $m^d : \{T_{p^d} : p^d\}$ is realized in the following way.
$$apply(o^d, m^d, \{p^d\}) \Rightarrow \uparrow apply(o^s, m^s, f_{T_{p^d} \mapsto T_{p^s}}\{p^d\})$$

(b) For each additional method $m_+^d : \{T_{p_+^d} : p_+^d\}$, the following switching operation is realized, which is applied independently of the source object.
$$apply(o^d, m_+^d, \{p_+^d\})$$

3.2 Specialization

Each application may have its own integrated views which select their needed objects from local information sources. The specialization abstract mechanism can be used to achieve such an objective. For example, an application wants to access all of undergraduates. There is a student class including both the graduates and the undergraduates in one information source and an undergraduate class in the other. In order to integrate the student class and the undergraduate class for the application, the student class should be specialized so that it can be integrated with the undergraduate class. We can define a deputy class as the specialization of the student class. The deputy class only contains deputy objects of student objects which are undergraduates.

The formal definition of the **Select** operation is as follows. It is used to derive a deputy class of which instances are the deputy objects of the instances of a source class selected according to a selection predicate.

Definition 5. Let $C^s = \langle \{o^s\}, \{T_{a^s} : a^s\}, \{m^s : \{T_{p^s} : p^s\}\}\rangle$ be a source class. A deputy class derived by the **Select** operation is represented as $C^d = $ Select(C^s, sp), where sp is a selection predicate.

1. The extent of C^d is the set of deputy objects of instances of C^s which satisfy the selection predicate sp, expressed as
$$\{o^d | o^d \to o^s, sp(o^s) == true\}$$

2. The set of attributes of C^d is defined as $\{T_{a^d} : a^d\}$, which are inherited from the attributes $\{T_{a^s} : a^s\}$ of C^s. The switching operations for inheriting $T_{a^s} : a^s$ in form of $T_{a^d} : a^d$ are realized in the following way.

$$read(o^d, a^d) \Rightarrow \uparrow f_{T_{a^s} \mapsto T_{a^d}}(read(o^s, a^s)),$$
$$write(o^d, a^d, v^d) \Rightarrow write(o^s, a^s, f_{T_{a^d} \mapsto T_{a^s}}(v^d))$$

3. *The set of methods of C^d is defined as $\{m^d : \{T_{p^d} : p^d\}\}$, which are inherited from the methods $\{m^s : \{T_{p^s} : p^s\}\}$ of C^s. The switching operation for inheriting $m^s : \{T_{p^s} : p^s\}$ in form of $m^d : \{T_{p^d} : p^d\}$ is realized in the following way.*

$$apply(o^d, m^d, \{p^d\}) \Rightarrow \uparrow apply(o^s, m^s, \{f_{T_{p^d} \mapsto T_{p^s}}(p^d)\})$$

3.3 Generalization

Data with the same attributes and methods may be distributed in different databases. For example, research reports are usually produced by researchers and stored in their private databases. They are treated as instances of several different data classes defined by interfaces for their respective databases. When these data items are requested to be used in the same application, they need to be included in a single class in order to offer an integrated view. We can define their deputy objects by a single deputy class which can be automatically derived by using the **Union** operation on the existing data classes. The deputy class can be treated as union of the existing data classes.

The formal definition of the **Union** operation is as follows. It is used to derive a deputy class of which extent consists of deputy objects of instances of more than one source class.

Definition 6. *Let $C_1^s = \langle \{o_1^s\}, \{T_{a_1^s} : a_1^s\}, \{m_1^s : \{T_{p_1^s} : p_1^s\}\}\rangle, ..., C_m^s = \langle \{o_m^s\}, \{T_{a_m^s} : a_m^s\}, \{m_m^s : \{T_{p_m^s} : p_m^s\}\}\rangle$ be source classes, $\{T_{a^s} : a^s\} = \{T_{a_1^s} : a_1^s\} \cap ... \cap \{T_{a_m^s} : a_m^s\}$ and $\{m^s : \{T_{p^s} : p^s\}\} = \{m_1^s : \{T_{p_1^s} : p_1^s\}\} \cap ... \cap \{m_m^s : \{T_{p_m^s} : p_m^s\}\}$ be common sets of attributes and methods of $C_1^s, ..., C_m^s$. A deputy class derived by the **Union** operation is represented as $C^d = \textbf{Union}(C_1^s, ..., C_m^s)$.*

1. *The extent of C^d is union of sets of deputy objects of instances of $C_1^s, ..., C_m^s$, which is expressed as*

$$\{o_1^d | o_1^d \to o_1^s\} \cup ... \cup \{o_m^d | o_m^d \to o_m^s\}$$

2. *The set of attributes of C^d is defined as $\{T_{a^d} : a^d\}$, which are inherited from the common attributes $\{T_{a^s} : a^s\}$ of $C_1^s, ..., C_m^s$. The switching operations for inheriting $T_{a^s} : a^s$ in form of $T_{a^d} : a^d$ are realized in the following way.*

$$read(o_1^d, a^d) \Rightarrow \uparrow f_{T_{a^s} \mapsto T_{a^d}}(read(o_1^s, a^s)),$$
$$write(o_1^d, a^d, v^d) \Rightarrow write(o_1^s, a^s, f_{T_{a^d} \mapsto T_{a^s}}(v^d))$$
$$;...;$$
$$read(o_m^d, a^d) \Rightarrow \uparrow f_{T_{a^s} \mapsto T_{a^d}}(read(o_m^s, a^s)),$$
$$write(o_m^d, a^d, v^d) \Rightarrow write(o_m^s, a^s, f_{T_{a^d} \mapsto T_{a^s}}(v^d))$$

3. *The set of methods of C^d is defined as $\{m^d : \{T_{p^d} : p^d\}\}$, which are inherited from the common methods $\{m^s : \{T_{p^s} : p^s\}\}$ of $C_1^s, ..., C_m^s$. The switching operations for inheriting $m^s : \{T_{p^s} : p^s\}$ in form of $m^d : \{T_{p^d} : p^d\}$ are realized in the following way.*

$$apply(o_1^d, m^d, \{p^d\}) \Rightarrow \uparrow apply(o_1^s, m^s, \{f_{T_{p^d} \mapsto T_{p^s}}(p^d)\})$$
$$;...;$$
$$apply(o_m^d, m^d, \{p^d\}) \Rightarrow \uparrow apply(o_m^s, m^s, \{f_{T_{p^d} \mapsto T_{p^s}}(p^d)\})$$

3.4 Aggregation

Attributes of a complex entity of real world may be distributed in different databases. Suppose each research report is requested to be reviewed by another researcher and the review result is stored in the reviewer's private database. In order to offer an integrated view, these two conceptually related components need be combined. A complex deputy object, namely a deputy object having several source component objects, is useful for such a purpose. The algebraic operation:Join provided by object deputy model can be used to derive automatically a complex deputy class.

The formal definition of the **Join** operation is as follows. It is used to derive a deputy class of which instances are deputy objects for aggregating instances of source classes according to a combination predicate.

Definition 7. Let $C_1^s = \langle \{o_1^s\}, \{T_{a_1^s} : a_1^s\}, \{m_1^s : \{T_{p_1^s} : p_1^s\}\}\rangle$,..., $C_n^s = \langle \{o_n^s\}, \{T_{a_n^s} : a_n^s\}, \{m_n^s : \{T_{p_n^s} : p_n^s\}\}\rangle$ be source classes. A deputy class derived by the **Join** operation is represented as $C^d = \mathbf{Join}(C_1^s, ..., C_n^s, cp)$, where cp is a combination predicate.

1. The extent of C^d is the set of deputy objects of aggregations of instances of $C_1^s, ..., C_n^s$ satisfying the combination predicate cp, which is expressed as

$$\{o^d | o^d \to o_1^s \times ... \times o_n^s, cp(o_1^s \times ... \times o_n^s) == true\}$$

2. The set of attributes of C^d is defined as the union of attribute sets $\{T_{a_1^d} : a_1^d\}, ..., \{T_{a_n^d} : a_n^d\}$ respectively inherited from $C_1^s, ..., C_n^s$, expressed as $\{T_{a_1^d} : a_1^d\} \cup ... \cup \{T_{a_n^d} : a_n^d\}$. The switching operations for attributes $\{T_{a_1^d} : a_1^d\}, ..., \{T_{a_n^d} : a_n^d\}$ respectively inherited from the attributes $\{T_{a_1^s} : a_1^s\}$ of C_1^s ,..., $\{T_{a_n^s} : a_n^s\}$ of C_n^s are realized in the following way.

$$read(o^d, a_1^d) \Rightarrow \uparrow f_{T_{a_1^s} \mapsto T_{a_1^d}}(read(o_1^s, a_1^s)),$$
$$write(o^d, a_1^d, v_1^d) \Rightarrow write(o_1^s, a_1^s, f_{T_{a_1^d} \mapsto T_{a_1^s}}(v_1^d))$$
$$;...;$$
$$read(o^d, a_n^d) \Rightarrow \uparrow f_{T_{a_n^s} \mapsto T_{a_n^d}}(read(o_n^s, a_n^s)),$$
$$write(o^d, a_n^d, v_n^d) \Rightarrow write(o_n^s, a_n^s, f_{T_{a_n^d} \mapsto T_{a_n^s}}(v_n^d))$$

3. The set of methods of C^d is defined as the union of method sets $\{m_1^d : \{T_{p_1^d} : p_1^d\}\}, ..., \{m_n^d : \{T_{p_n^d} : p_n^d\}\}$ respectively inherited from $C_1^s, ..., C_n^s$, expressed as $\{m_1^d : \{T_{p_1^d} : p_1^d\}\} \cup ... \cup \{m_n^d : \{T_{p_n^d} : p_n^d\}\}$. The switching operations for methods $\{m_1^d : \{T_{p_1^d} : p_1^d\}\}, ..., \{m_n^d : \{T_{p_n^d} : p_n^d\}\}$ respectively inherited from the methods $\{m_1^s : \{T_{p_1^s} : p_1^s\}\}$ of C_1^s ,..., $\{m_n^s : \{T_{p_n^s} : p_n^s\}\}$ of C_n^s are realized in the following way.

$$apply(o^d, m_1^d, \{p_1^d\}) \Rightarrow\uparrow apply(o_1^s, m_1^s, \{f_{T_{p_1^d} \mapsto T_{p_1^s}}(p_1^d)\})$$
$$,...,$$
$$apply(o^d, m_n^d, \{p_n^d\}) \Rightarrow\uparrow apply(o_n^s, m_n^s, \{f_{T_{p_n^d} \mapsto T_{p_n^s}}(p_n^d)\})$$

It should be noted that the complex deputy object is different from the usual complex object. It can restrict usage of attributes and methods of its components by switching operations while the usual complex object can use attributes of its component objects without any limitation through navigation. In addition, the semantic constraints on the component source objects of a complex deputy object can be defined by the combination predicate, which can be enforced through update propagation (since a complex deputy object and its source component objects are linked bilaterally, the update on any component source object can be propagated to the complex deputy object.)

4 Handling Replication

When integrating several databases, there exist replications. Replications means that the same entities or attributes may appear at different databases. In the integrated views, the replications need be eliminated. The integrated system is usually used both to access the data and to update the stored information. When an object is modified in the integrated view, all of replications at the local information sources should be updated at the same time. In addition, any modification on one of the replications should be propagated into the others. Therefore, we need a mechanism to handle replications in the integrated views.

The attribute replication may arise when several objects are combined into a complex deputy object. In this case, all of the replicated attributes are inherited as a single attribute by the complex deputy object. For example, a student has two records in different databases. One record has attributes including name and age while the other has attributes including name and address. When two records are integrated, the name attribute will be replicated. The attributes of the student are inherited by the deputy object in the following way.

$d \rightarrow r1 \times r2;$
$read(d, name) \rightarrow read(r1, name) \vee read(r2, name);$
$write(d, name, v) \rightarrow write(r1, name, v) \wedge write(r2, name, v)$
$read(d, age) \rightarrow read(r1, age);$
$write(d, age, v) \rightarrow write(r1, age, v)$
$read(d, address) \rightarrow read(r2, address);$
$write(d, address, v) \rightarrow write(r2, address, v)$

Here, r1 and r2 represent the two records of the student. d is a deputy object used to integrate r1 and r2. That means any one of the replicated attributes can be read but all of them should be written with the new value at the same time.

The entity replication may arise when a deputy class is defined as the union of several classes. The replication can be handled by deriving a deputy class of the deputy class through the algebraic operation: Grouping. The **Grouping** operation is used to derive a deputy class of which instances are deputy objects for grouping instances of a source class according to a grouping predicate. That is, the replicated objects are grouped by a single deputy object. The formal definition of the **Grouping** operation is as follows.

Definition 8. Let $C^s = \langle\{o^s\}, \{T_{a^s} : a^s\}, \{m^s : \{T_{p^s} : p^s\}\}\rangle$ be a source class. A deputy class derived by the **Grouping** operation is represented as $C^d = $ **Grouping** (C^s, gp), where gp is a grouping predicate.

1. The extent of C^d is the set of deputy objects for grouping instances of C^s according to the grouping predicate gp, which is expressed as

$$\{o^d | o^d \to \{o^s\}, gp(\{o^s\}) == true\}$$

2. The set of attributes of C^d is defined as $\{T_{a^d} : a^d\}$ which are inherited from the attributes $\{T_{a^s} : a^s\}$ of C^s. The switching operations for inheriting $T_{a^s} : a^s$ in form of $T_{a^d} : a^d$ are realized in the following way.

$$read(o^d, a^d) \Rightarrow \uparrow f_{\{T_{a^s}\} \mapsto T_{a^d}}(\{read(o^s, a^s)\}),$$
$$write(o^d, a^d, v^d) \Rightarrow \{write(o^s, a^s, f_{T_{a^d} \mapsto T_{a^s}}(v^d))\}$$

3. The set of methods of C^d is defined as $\{m^d : \{T_{p^d} : p^d\}\}$ which are inherited from the methods $\{m^s : \{T_{p^s} : p^s\}\}$ of C^s. The switching operation for inheriting $m^s : \{T_{p^s} : p^s\}$ in form of $m^d : \{T_{p^d} : p^d\}$ is realized in the following way.

$$apply(o^d, m^d, \{p^d\}) \Rightarrow \{\uparrow apply(o^s, m^s, \{f_{T_{p^d} \mapsto T_{p^s}}(p^d)\})\}$$

Suppose o1, o2 and o3 with attribute a1 and a2 are the replicated objects which are grouped by the deputy object d. d inherits attributes a1 and a2 of o1, o2 and o3 in the following way.

$d \to \{o1, o2, o3\}$
$read(d, a1) \to read(o1, a1) \vee read(o2, a1) \vee read(o3, a1)$
$write(d, a1, v1) \to write(o1, a1, v1) \wedge write(o2, a1, v1) \wedge write(o3, a1, v1)$
$read(d, a2) \to read(o1, a2) \vee read(o2, a2) \vee read(o3, a2)$
$write(d, a2, v2) \to write(o1, a2, v2) \wedge write(o2, a2, v2) \wedge write(o3, a2, v2)$

The above way can guarantee that any modification on the integrated view can be reflected in all of the replicated attributes and entities. Because the integrated view can be used as the bridge among the autonomous information sources, any update on the object in an information source can be propagated into another information source.

Consider the first example again. If the record r1 is modified with a new name, the deputy object d will be notified with the update because there exists a pointer from r1 to d. d can read the new name and then write the new name to r2. Thus, r2 is also updated with the new name.

In the similar way, the second example can deal with updates occurring in the local information sources. Suppose the attribute a1 of the object o2 is modified with a new value v1. The deputy object d will be notified with the update. Because the update is from the object o2, the new value can be read from o2. Using the writing operation, the new value can be writen into all of the replicated objects o1, o2 and o3. Because the attribute a1 of the object o2 has been modified before the update broadcasting, it does not need to be updated once again. It can be detected by comparing the new value with the current attribute value of the object o2. This method can avoid a lot of unnecessary modification.

Suppose o1 and o2 have the replicated attribute a and they are combined by the deputy object d1. Furthermore, d1 and d2 represent the replicated entities. They are grouped by a deputy object d. If the attribute a of the object o2 is modified, the attribute a of the object o1 will be updated using the deputy object d1 as the bridge. Once the attribute a of both o1 and o2 has been updated, it shows that attribute a of the deputy object d1 is updated. The update will be propapgrated to the deputy object d2 through the deputy object d. By comparing d1.a with the new value, the d1.a does not need to be updated once again. Thus, rewriting o1.a and o2.a can be avoided.

If there are attribute value conflicts, they can be resolved through update propagation. It means that the latest updated one is preferable. For example, the stock information is usually updated with the latest one. If the update does not occur, the conflict can be found by comparing the replicated attribute values when they are read. The latest updated one is always used to replace the other different values. In this way, the consistency among the replicated attributes can be maintained.

5 Conclusion

A lot of research efforts [3,4,5,7,12] have been made to integrate heterogenous information sources under the distributed environment. Object-oriented approach is thought as a good solution to the problem of the heterogeneous system interoperability because the object-oriented model is semantically rich and can define complex mapping even for information sources without database schema. In addition, methods can be used to resolve various syntactic and semantic conflicts. Especially, the inheritance mechanism can incrementally refine class for sepcialization and factor out the commonalities from several different class descriptions as a more general superclass. The object-oriented view mechanism is a major way to achieve such an objective.

However, the traditional object-oriented data model is not enough flexible so that its view mechanism is difficult to be implemented. Although a lot of view mechanisms [1,2,6,7,10] were published, to our knowledge, almost no commercial object-oriented databases provide true view supports. We know that flexibility of relational databases is due to their data independence that enables data to be divided and combined very easily. Similarly, a flexible object-oriented database should also allow objects to be restructured. Without this feature, view mechanisms are difficult to be incorporated into object-oriented databases.

We extended the traditional object-oriented data model with deputy objects. An object can have many deputy objects and a single deputy object can share multiple objects. Thus, although the encapsulation feature of object-oriented database limits capability of object restructuring, dividing and combining objects can still be done indirectly through their deputy objects. That is, the object deputy model enables object views to be easily realized. Thus, an object deputy approach is a better way to realize database integration.

References

1. Serge Abiteboul, Anthony Bonner, Objects and Views. Proc. of the Int. Conf. on Management of Data, pp.238-247 (1991)
2. E.Bertino, A View Mechanism for Object-Oriented Databases, 3rd International Conference on Extending Database Technology, LNCS 580, pp.136-151 (1992)
3. E.Bertino, Application of Object-Oriented Technology to the Integration of Heterogeneous Database Systems, Journal of Distributed and Parallel Databases, 2, pp.343-370 (1994)
4. Diego Calvanese, Giuseppe De Giacomo, Maurizio Lenzerini, Daniele Nardi, and Riccardo Rosati, Information Integration: Conceptual Modeling and Reasoning Support, Proc. of the 6th Int. Conf. on Cooperative Information Systems, pp. 280-291, 1998.
5. Czejdo, B., and Taylor, M.C., Integration of Database Systems Using an Object-Oriented Approach, Proc. of IEEE The First Workshop on Research Issues in Data Engineering - Interoperability among Multidatabase Systems, pp.30-37 (1991)
6. S. Heiler and S. Zdonick, Object Views: Extending the Vision, Proc. of IEEE 6th Int. Conf. on Data Engineering, pp.86-93 (1990)
7. M. Kaul, K. Drosten and EJ. Neuhold, ViewSystem:Integrating Heterogeneous Information Bases by Object-Oriented Views, Proc. of IEEE 6th Int. Conf. on Data Engineering, pp. 2-10 (1990)
8. Z. Peng, Y. Kambayashi, Deputy Mechanisms for Object-Oriented Databases, Proc. of IEEE 11th Int. Conf. on Data Engineering, pp.333-40 (1995)
9. Y. Kambayashi, Z. Peng, An Object Deputy Model for Realization of Flexible and Powerful Objectbases, Journal of System Integration, 6, pp.329-362 (1996)
10. Elke A. Rundensteiner, MultiView: A Methodology for Supporting Multiple Views in Object-Oriented Databases, Proc. of the 18th VLDB Conference, pp.187-198 (1992)
11. Cassio Souza dos Santos, Design and Implementation of Object-Oriented Views, Proc. of DEXA95, pp. 91-102 (1995)
12. Won Kim, Injun Choi, Sunit Gala, and Mark Scheevel, On Resolving Schematic Heterogeneity in Multidatabase Systems, Journal of Distributed and Parallel Databases 1, pp.251-279 (1993)

Efficient Execution of Range-Aggregate Queries in Data Warehouse Environments*

Seokjin Hong[1], Byoungho Song[2], and Sukho Lee[1]

[1] School of Electrical Engineering and Computer Science,
Seoul National University, Korea
jinny@db.snu.ac.kr, shlee@cse.snu.ac.kr
[2] Dept. of Software Science, Sangmyung University, Korea
bhsong@pine.sangmyung.ac.kr

Abstract. Range-aggregate queries on the data cube are powerful tools for analysis in data warehouse environments. Cubetree is a technique materializing a data cube through an R-tree. It provides efficient data accessibility, but involves some drawbacks to traverse all the internal and leaf nodes within given query ranges to compute range-aggregate queries. In this paper, we propose a novel index structure for materializing a data cube, called aggregate cubetree. Each record in all internal nodes of an aggregate cubetree stores the aggregate value of all child nodes of it. Therefore, range-aggregate queries on an aggregate cubetree can be processed without visiting child nodes whose parent node is fully included in the query range, by using the aggregate values in the records of each internal node. The aggregate cubetree is superior to the original cubetree because it can execute queries with a smaller number of node accesses, and shows even better performance than the original cubetree as the query range becomes larger.

1 Introduction

Data warehouse[1] is a database system for analysis, which extracts, integrates, and transforms data from an OLTP database, and stores them in efficient structures for analysis. Relational databases use star schemas[2] for representing analysis data. The fact table is the center of the star schema, and it consists of dimension attributes related to the dimension tables and measure attributes that are numeric values. The queries executed on the fact table are made up of group operations on measure attributes and aggregate operations[14] on measure attributes. In data warehouse environments, generally, the size of the fact table is so large, and the number of the dimension attributes is also abundant, that the query processing can be time consuming.

Various methods have been proposed to solve this problem. The scheme maintaining materialized views[3][9][10] for the fact table through the data cube[4][11][12] is one of those. The data cube is an operation that computes aggregate

---

* This work was supported by the Brain Korea 21 Project

functions over all possible groups in the fact table. By keeping the result of the data cube operation as a materialized view, fast query execution can be possible through the summary information of the fact table.

This materialized view is stored as a relation, and the size can be large. Therefore, there is an overhead for creating an additional index on the materialized view in order to execute queries through it efficiently. [7][8] worked out this problem by organizing this materialized view into an R-tree-like[5][13] cubetree, but there are some drawbacks to traverse all internal and leaf nodes in the query range to compute range-aggregate queries[6].

In this paper, we propose the aggregate cubetree. Each record in the internal nodes of the aggregate cubetree stores aggregate values of all child nodes of it; thus it is possible to process range-aggregate query efficiently, because not all the child nodes need to be accessed, when their parent records are included in the query range.

The rest of this paper is organized as follows. Section 2 explains the range-aggregate query and presents the cubetrees proposed in [7][8]. In section 3, we introduce the aggregate cubetree that is enhanced against the original cubetree, and present the structure and algorithms of it. In section 4, we summarize our experiment results, and section 5 concludes the paper.

2 Related Work

2.1 Range-Aggregate Query

An example of a range-aggregate query over a relation $F(D_1, D_2, ..., D_n, M)$ is as follows

```
SELECT  Aggregate-Function(M)
FROM    F
WHERE   l₁<= D₁ <= h₁
and     l₂<= D₂ <= h₂
and     ...
and     lₖ<= Dₖ <= hₖ
```

F is a fact table that a range-aggregate query is executed on. $D_1, D_2, ...$, and D_n are dimension attributes, and M is a measure attribute. In order to determine the query range, k of n dimension attributes $(D_1, D_2, ..., D_k, k <= n)$ are used. Generally, aggregate functions are COUNT, SUM, AVG, MIN, and MAX, and a range-aggregate query is classified as a range-COUNT query, a range-SUM query, and etc., according to the aggregate function used in the query.

In order to execute this range-aggregate query on a fact table, we must scan the entire records in the table, and apply an aggregate function to the tuples that satisfy given query range. If there is any materialized view organized of data cube, the query can be executed over k-dimensional hyper-plane $(D_1, D_2, ..., D_k)$

of it. In general, the size of a fact table is very large. Thus it is too expensive to scan all records in the fact table. However, it is relatively less expensive to scan all records in the hyper-plane of the data cube, which have already been aggregated. If the cubetree proposed in [7][8] is used as the structure of the data cube, it is unnecessary to access all records of the hyper-plane within the query range from the R-tree to process query. But it is still expensive to access all leaf nodes of the cubetree within the query range.

2.2 Cubetree

The Cubetree is a tree structure for storing a data cube. If the data cube is built on the fact table that has n dimension attributes, it is composed of hyper-planes from n-dimension to 0-dimension. The basic idea of [7][8] is mapping these n to 0-dimensional hyper-planes into n-dimensional space, constructing n-dimensional data, and storing them in an R-tree. The data cube organized as n-1 to 0-dimensional data except for the original n-dimensional data is called dataless cubetree, and the cubetrees made up of several n-1 dimensional R-trees from dataless cubetree is called reduced cubetree. When the data cube is composed as the reduced cubetree, the size of data cube can be reduced and the clustering effects can be improved. Other techniques such as sorting and bulk loading can also be applied to improve the clustering effects.

However, the original cubetree proposed in [7][8] requires accessing all the leaf nodes within the query range to process a range-aggregate query. That is a primary factor that reduces the query performance as the size of a query range gets larger. In data warehouse environments, aggregate queries are frequently requested on a large range, and the queries that have to access almost parts of leaf nodes are often requested. In this case, the original cubetree can show worse performance than scanning the entire table.

We proposed a technique that does not have to access all the leaf nodes within a query range, called the *aggregate cubetree*. In section 3, we will explain the structure and algorithms of the aggregate cubetree.

3 Aggregate Cubetree

3.1 The Structure

The basic structure of the aggregate cubetree is similar to that of the original cubetree based on R-tree. Each node in the tree is composed of a number of records. Leaf node records are made up of dimension attributes and aggregate value of measure attribute which are components of data cube records, and internal node records are composed of MBR, child node pointer, and the aggregate value. We define an *aggregate value* as the value of an aggregate function of all leaf node records in the MBR. This aggregate value can be calculated from the aggregate values in all its child node records, and each aggregate value of all these child nodes can be obtained in the same way. By using these aggregate values stored in each internal node record, it is possible to execute range-aggregate queries without accessing all the leaf nodes in the query range.

With the original cubetree, range-aggregate queries are executed as range queries applied to R-tree. The range queries on R-tree are performed recursively by searching nodes overlapping the query range and executing range queries on the child nodes. In case of the range query, the data in the selected leaf nodes are final results. In case of the range-aggregate query, however, the result of aggregate function on the data in the selected leaf node is the output. So, in order to execute range-aggregate queries on the original cubetree, all the leaf nodes within the query range must be accessed.

Aggregate cubetree processes a range-aggregate query as follows. For the records in the nodes overlapping the query range, range-aggregate query is executed recursively as an original cubetree. However, for the records in the nodes fully included in the query range, the query processor uses the aggregate values in each record.

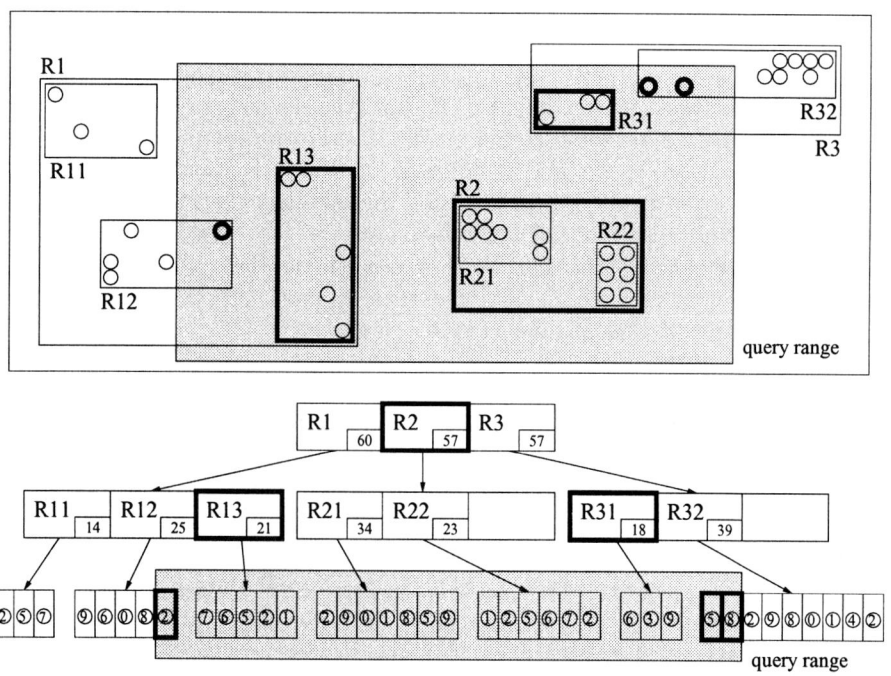

Fig. 1. Aggregate Cubetree

Thus, range-aggregate queries on the aggregate cubetree can be performed without visiting child nodes whose parent node is fully included in the query range, by using the aggregate values in the records of each internal node.

Fig.1 shows the example of the aggregate cubetree. Each internal node consists of three records. The root node contains record R_1, R_2, and R_3. Each record stores the MBR, the child node pointer, and the aggregate value. Record R_1 stores the aggregate value of records R_{11}, R_{12}, and R_{13} that are in the child node of it, and R_{11}, R_{12}, and R_{13} also store the aggregate values of the records in each leaf node that is the child nodes of them. So when the range-SUM query of fig.1 is requested, the query can be performed without accessing all the leaf nodes in query range. By using the aggregate values of the records R_2, R_{13}, and R_{31} that are exactly included in the query range, the nodes below R_2, R_{13}, and R_{31} don't need to be accessed. The leaf nodes that have to be accessed are the some rest leaf nodes in the query range that are below R_{12} and R_{32}. Therefore, the number of node accesses can be reduced compared with the cubetree, and it is self-evident.

3.2 The Algorithms

Insert Algorithm Algorithm.1 is the insert algorithm of aggregate cubetree. It is similar to that of R-tree, but the aggregate value of a parent node is updated through AdjustTree, and the MBR is recalculated when it is needed.

Algorithm 1: Insert Algorithm of Aggregate Cubetree

Procedure Insert(*record*)
Input: *record* : tuple to be inserted
begin

1:     $leafNode \leftarrow chooseLeaf(record)$;
2:     **if** $leafNode.Addrecord(record) == SUCCESS$ **then**
3:        $leafNode.UpdateMBR()$;
4:        $AdjustTree(leafNode)$;
    else
5:        $SplitNode(leafNode, record)$;
    end
end

Range-Aggregate Query Algorithm Algorithm.2 is the range-SUM query algorithm, and it is executed recursively. If the MBR in each record is fully included in the query range, the aggregate value, SUM in each record is added to the result, and if the MBR is overlapped with the query range, the range-SUM query is executed on the records of child node recursively.

Other range-aggregate queries like range-COUNT, range-AVG, range-MIN, and range-MAX can be executed by the similar way.

In case of range-COUNT query, the number of leaf records are stored as the aggregate values. Like range-SUM query algorithm, the aggregate values are added to the result for records within the query range.

In order to execute range-AVG queries, both the SUM and COUNT values are maintained as aggregate values. By the algorithms for range-SUM and range-COUNT queries, the SUM and COUNT values are computed, and the AVG value is calculated from them.

In case of range-MIN and range-MAX, the minimum(maximum) values of leaf nodes are used as the aggregate values. The range-MIN(range-MAX) queries are performed in a similar way. The minimum(maximum) value is picked up with traversing nodes in the query range. When the MBR is included in the query range, the minimum(maximum) value of the MBR is used instead of visiting the child nodes.

Algorithm 2: Range-SUM Algorithm of Aggregate Cubetree

Procedure RangeSUM(*rect*, *node*)
Input: *rect* : query range
        node : initial node of the query
Output: *result* : sum of all records of the leaf node within the query range
begin

1:    $result \leftarrow 0$;
2:    **foreach** *record in node* **do**
3:        **if** $rect.Inclusion(record.mbr) == TRUE$ **then**
4:           $result \leftarrow result + record.SUM$;
5:        **else if** $rect.Overlap(record.mbr) == TRUE$ **then**
6:           $result \leftarrow result + RangeSUM(rect, record.node)$;
       end
   end
7:    **return** *result*;
end

3.3 Overlapped MBRs

MBRs in the R-tree can be overlapped, and physical coordinates of low level MBR can be included in the several higher level MBRs. Fig.2 shows this situation. In Fig.2, although physical coordinates of MBR M_{1a} are included in the k overlapped MBRs $M_1, M_2, ..., M_k$, only one MBR M_1 can be the parent of it, and the aggregate value of MBR M_{1a} is reflected in the aggregate value of the parent MBR M_1.

When a range-aggregate query including MBR M_{1a} is requested, if the parent MBR M_1 is fully included in the query range, the query is executed using the aggregate value of M_1 reflecting the aggregate value of the child MBR M_1a, and if the parent MBR M_1 just overlap with the query range, the query is performed through the aggregate value of the child MBR M_{1a}.

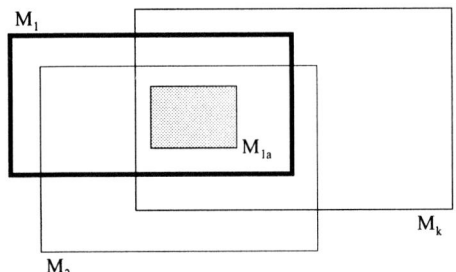

Fig. 2. Overlapped MBRs

3.4 The Aggregate Values

The aggregate values of the aggregate cubetree that are stored with MBRs are determined by the aggregate function used for composing the data cube. In case of COUNT, SUM, MIN, and MAX, the aggregate value is the result of each function, and for the AVG function, both COUNT and SUM value are used together. If several aggregate functions are used together for the data cube, the aggregate values are composed of each value of all appropriate aggregate functions. For example, if the data cube is constructed with SUM and MAX function, the aggregate value in each MBR stores the SUM and MAX value of the MBR.

4 Experiments

We constructed original cubetrees and aggregate cubetrees from data cubes, executed range-aggregate queries on each tree, and measured the numbers of node accesses. The data we used are synthetic data from 2-dimension to 5-dimension, and the size is 10,000, 100,000, and 1,000,000. We generated datasets following uniform distribution and zipf-distribution. The size of tree node is 4 kbytes, and the maximum number of records in a node depends on the dimension of the tree. In case of 2-dimensional data, the maximum number of records in a node is 340, and 169 for 5-dimensional data. The machine used for these experiments is Ultra Sparc II 333 MHz, and the OS is Solaris 7.

4.1 Size of the Query Range

We executed range-aggregate queries on each tree with varying query range size, and measured the number of node accesses. The query range size is the ratio of the length of query range to domain size of each dimension, and it is between 0 and 1. We executed each query 100 times, and used the average number of node accesses. Fig.3 is the result of the experiments that measure the number of node accesses and execution time for query ranges from 0.1 to 0.9 on a million dataset.

It shows that the aggregate cubetree needs smaller number of node accesses than the original cubetree. In case of the original cubetree, the number of node accesses is increasing rapidly as the query size grows, but the aggregate cubetree shows linear increment of node accesses because it don't have to access all the leaf nodes within the query range. It is remarkable that the difference of performance becomes prominent, as the query range is larger. This is because the proportion of MBRs fully included in the query range becomes bigger as the query range is larger. Generally, the MBRs located in the center of the query range are the parts fully included in the query range, and the MBRs around the query range are the parts whose leaf nodes need to be accessed. Thus, the larger query range becomes, the smaller the ratio of the leaf nodes accesses is.

4.2 Number of Records in the Data Cube

We observed the number of node accesses with changing the number of records in the data cube. The size of query range is 0.5, and 100 queries are executed on each data set. We used the average value of node accesses. Fig.4 shows the ratio of the average node accesses on the aggregate cubetree, when the average value of node accesses on the original cubetree is set to 1.

As the number of records is larger, the number of nodes to be accessed is reduced compared with the original R-tree, and practically, the query can be performed with 60% node accesses of the original cubetree in case of the million data set.

4.3 Dimension of the Data Cube

We examined the number of node accesses as the dimension of data varies. The size of data is 1,000,000 and the size of query range is 0.5. We used the average number of node accesses. Fig.5 is the ratio of the average node accesses on the aggregate cubetree, when the average value of node accesses on the original cubetree is set to 1.

When the dimension is high, the node access ratio of the aggregate cubetree is higher than that of low dimension. It is not only because the number of overlap between each MBR increases, but also because the data become sparse and the size of each MBR enlarges, as the dimension gets higher. If the size of MBR gets larger, the probability that the MBR is fully included in the query range decreases, thus the case of accessing leaf nodes became frequent. And it is also

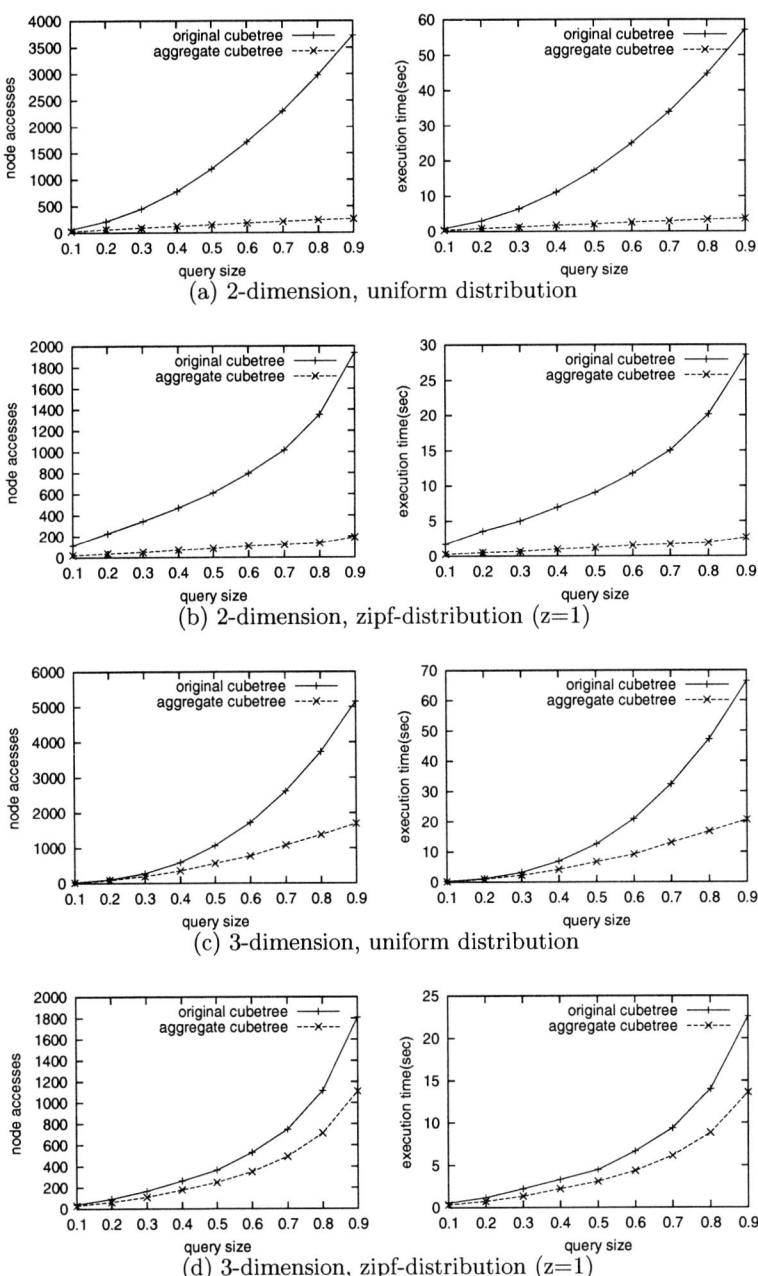

Fig. 3. Node accesses and execution time as the query range size varies

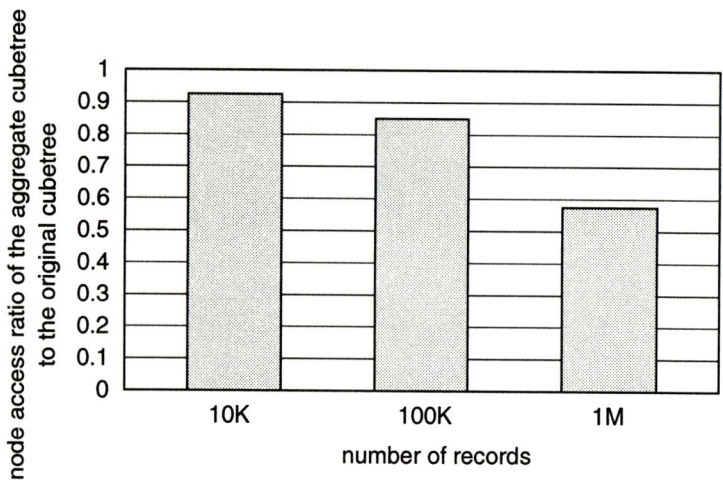

Fig. 4. Node access ratio as the number of records varies

because the proportion of the number of data to the entire space decreases, as the dimension gets higher. As the result of section 4.2, the performance of the aggregate cubetree increases with large data.

However, It is always possible to execute the range-aggregate query on the aggregate cubetree with a smaller number of node accesses than on the original cubetree. (The ratio is always below 1.)

4.4 Distribution of Data

The last experiments are for examining the effect of the distribution of data. The size of data is 1,000,000, the dimension of the data is 2, and the size of query range is 0.5. We used the average number of node accesses. Fig.6 is the ratio of the average node accesses on the aggregate cubetree, when the average value of node accesses on the original cubetree is set to 1.

As the level of data skew gets higher, the benefit of the aggregate cubetree decreases a little. However, the number of node accesses is always small compared with the original cubetree.

5 Conclusions

Range-aggregate queries are very time-consuming processing in data warehouse environments. Therefore, efficient materializing technique of data cube is needed. Previous method presents the cubetree that materializing the data cube into a tree structure, but it has a drawback to access too many leaf nodes.

In this paper, we proposed aggregate cubetree, method for materializing data cube. Aggregate cubetree stores the aggregate values in each MBR of all internal

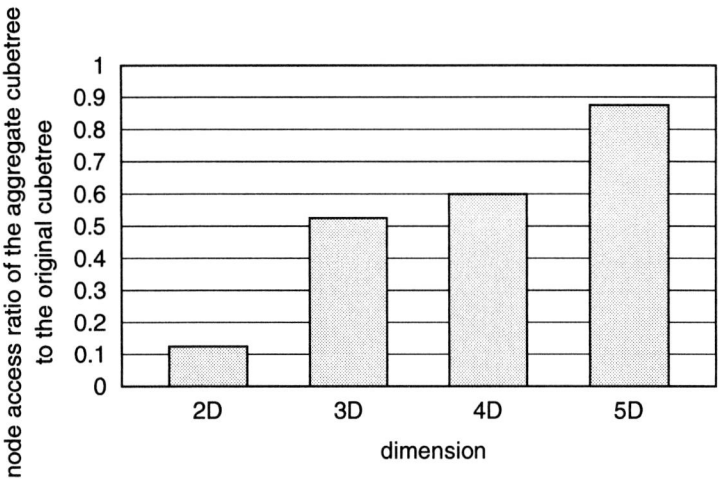

Fig. 5. Node access ratio as the dimension of data varies

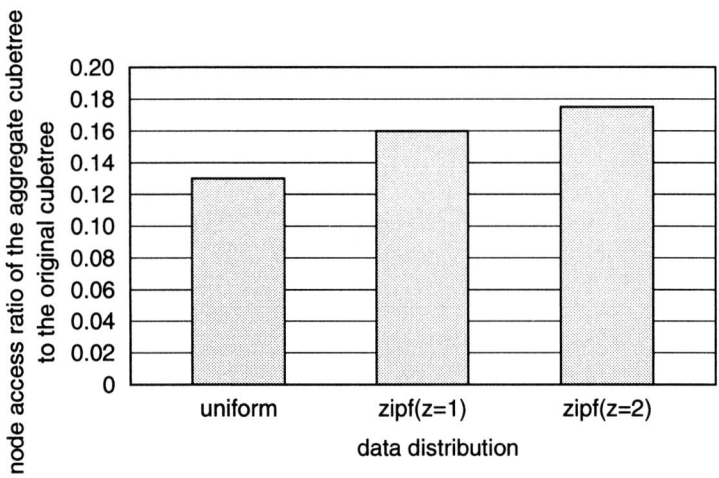

Fig. 6. Node access ratio as the distribution of data varies

nodes, thus efficient execution of the range-aggregate query is possible without accessing all leaf nodes within the query range. Experiments show that the aggregate cubetree is superior to the original cubetree because it can always execute queries with a small number of node accesses, and as query range is larger, it shows better performance relatively.

In the future we will generalize this idea, and apply it to existing tree structures.

Acknowledgements We would like to thank Bongki Moon for their helpful advice and assistance.

References

1. S. Chaudhuri and U. Dayal, "An overview of data warehousing and OLAP technology", ACM SIGMOD Record 26(1), pages 65-74, 1997
2. R. Kimball, "The Data Warehouse Toolkit", John Wiley & Sons, 1996
3. N. Roussopoulos, "Materialized Views and Data Warehouses", SIGMOD Record, 27(1), pages 21-26, March 1998.
4. J. Gray, A. Bosworth, A. Layman, and H.Piramish, "Data Cube: A Relational Aggregation Operator Generalizing, Group-By, Crosstab, and Sub-Totals", Int. Conference on Data Engineering, pages 152-159, 1996
5. A. Guttman. "R-Trees: A Dynamic Index Structure for Spatial Searching", In Proceedings of ACM SIGMOD, pages 47-57, 1984
6. C.Ho, R.Agrawal, N.Megiddo, R.Srikant. "Range Queries in OLAP Data Cubes", In Proceedings of ACM SIGMOD, pages 73-88, 1997
7. Nick Roussopoulos, Yannis Kotdis, Mena Roussopoulos, "Cubetree: Organization of and Bulk Incremental Update on the Data Cube", In Proceedings of ACM SIGMOD, pages 89-99, 1997
8. Yannis Kotdis, Nick Roussopoulos, "An Alternative Storage Organization for ROLAP Aggregate Views Based on Cubetrees", In Proceedings of ACM SIGMOD, pages 249-258, 1998
9. H. Gupta. "Selections of Views to Materialize in a Data Warehouse", In Proceedings of ICDT, pages 98-112, Delphi, January 1997
10. I. S. Mumick, D. Quass, and B. S. Mumick. "Maintenance of Data Cubes and Summary Tables in a Warehouse", In Proceedings of the ACM SIGMOD International Conference on Management of Data, pages 100-111, Tucson, Arizona, May 1997.
11. V. Harinarayan, A. Rajaraman, J. D. Ullman, "Implementing data cubes efficiently", In Proceedings of the ACM SIGMOD Conference, pages 205-216, 1996
12. S.Sarawagi, R. Agrawal, A. Gupta, "On the computing the data cube", Research Report, IBM Almaden Research Center, Sanjose, Ca, 1996
13. N. Beckmann, H. P. Kriegel, R. Schneider, and B. Seeger, "The R*-tree: an efficient and robust access method for points and rectangles", In Proceedings of the ACM SIGMOD Conference on Management of Data, pages 322-331, Atlantic City, NJ, May 1990.
14. S. Agrawal, R. Agrawal, P. Deshpande, A. Gupta, J. Naughton, R. Ramakrishnan, and S. Sarawagi. "On the Computation of Multidimensional Aggregates", In Proceedings of VLDB, pages 506-521, August 1996.

A Pragmatic Approach to Conceptual Modeling of OLAP Security [1]

Torsten Priebe, Günther Pernul

Department of Information Systems, University of Essen, Universitätsstr. 9,
D-45141 Essen, Germany
{priebe,pernul}@wi-inf.uni-essen.de

Abstract. Traditionally data warehouses were queried by high level users (executive management, business analysts) only. As the range of potential users with data warehouse access is steadily growing, this assumption is no longer appropriate and the necessity of proper access control mechanisms arises. The security capabilities of available commercial OLAP systems are highly proprietary and the syntax of their security constraints is not suitable for design and documentation purposes. Also, approaches trying to derive the access control policies from the operational data sources have not been very successful, as the relational model is predominate in operational systems while OLAP systems make use of the non-traditional multidimensional model. Access control schemes do not map easily. We approach the issue from the application side by introducing a methodology and a language for conceptual OLAP security design.

1 Introduction

With the use of data warehousing and online analytical processing (OLAP) for decision support applications new security issues arise. Data warehouses by their very nature create a security conflict [7]. On the one hand, the goal is to make all necessary data accessible as easy as possible. Especially exploratory ad-hoc OLAP analysis requires this open nature. On the other hand, the data is usually very valuable and sensitive. Traditionally data warehouses were queried by high level users (executive management, business analysts) only, which was used as an excuse for OLAP vendors not to provide support for fine grained access control. This assumption is, however, no longer appropriate. The range of potential users of analysis tools querying a data warehouse is steadily growing, up to customers and partners. Protecting the sensitive data from unauthorized access more and more becomes an issue, which leads to the necessity of proper access control policies for end-user access to the data warehouse. Not every user should be able to access all data.

Deriving the access control policies from the operational data sources is very difficult although some research efforts are made in this area [15]. Data from different systems (with different policies) is consolidated. Also, the users of the operational

---

[1] This work is supported in part by the European Union through INCO COPERNICUS grant no. 977091 (project GOAL – Geographic Information Online Analysis).

systems are not the same as the users of the data warehouse. However, the main problem is, that the relational model is predominate in operational systems while OLAP systems make use of the non-traditional multidimensional model. Access control schemes do not map easily. Protection is not defined in terms of tables, but dimensions, hierarchical paths, granularity levels.

The need for proper OLAP security design arises. However, the tools' security capabilities are highly proprietary and the syntax of their security constraints is not suitable for design and documentation purposes. In order to approach the topic from the application side, the classical database design methodology (requirement analysis, conceptual, logical, and physical design) should be applied to OLAP security as well. Such a multiphase methodology (adapted from [4]) is discussed in [13]. The main scope of this paper is the conceptual design phase.

We explore these issues in the context of the GOAL project which aims at studying the integration of geographical information systems (GIS) and data warehouse technology. In this project we are responsible for data integrity and security. Two pilot applications (A1 and A2) have been defined for the project. Application A1 is concerned about visitor admissions to the castles and other monuments in Southern Bohemia, Czech Republic. Application A2 deals with the drinking water distribution and consumption in the Western Bohemian region close to the city Sokolov, CZ. Throughout this paper we use application A1 as a case study. It turns out to be quite suitable for discussing security questions. The castle management is organized in a hierarchical way. All but two of the castles are managed by a regional institute, but still keep a certain degree of independence. They are only willing to provide their data for integration in a central data warehouse if they trust the installed security measures. Different user groups with only restricted access to the data warehouse have been defined. However, the developed concepts should be applicable for most other OLAP applications as well.

The rest of this paper is organized as follows: Section 2 covers the principles of multidimensional modeling using our ADAPTed UML notation [14]. Section 3 introduces our conceptual security model and a multidimensional security constraint language (MDSCL). Finally, section 4 concludes the paper and presents possible future work.

2 Multidimensional Modeling

In the introduction we already mentioned the multidimensional alignment of OLAP data. The multidimensional model differs from the relational one mainly by explicitly distinguishing qualitative (i.e. dimension) entities and quantitative entities (i.e. analytical measures). Another typical characteristic of OLAP models is the hierarchical structure of the dimension entities (hence called dimension levels).

2.1 Conceptual Model and ADAPTed UML

A conceptual (or semantic) model is a system independent "image" of reality, i.e. it is not relevant which database (or OLAP) software will finally be used. Various requirements for conceptual data models have been discussed in the literature (e.g. [5]). Among these the minimalism criteria leads to the conclusion to include only as many model elements as necessary. Thus, constructs like explicit dimensions and hierarchies are not considered part of the conceptual level as they are not real world objects but only pre-thought navigation paths for the OLAP application.

Several multidimensional models (e.g. [3]) and graphical design notations (e.g. M/ER [16]) have been proposed but there is no standard in sight. The Unified Modeling Language (UML) [11] has emerged as a de-facto standard for modeling complex software systems. In the data warehouse and OLAP area, however, UML based notations do not yet find too much acceptance in practice, either. If an explicit conceptual modeling is done at all, usually an intuitive ER like notation is used. The ADAPT[2] notation [1, 2] seems to be one of the few exceptions. It is for example mentioned at different ORACLE Express user group conferences. However, ADAPT lacks a proper formalization and sometimes a clear definition of its semantics.

In order to have a proper foundation for our security modeling approach, we tried to eliminate these disadvantages by creating a UML based notation named "ADAPTed UML" (which uses ADAPT symbols as stereotypes) [14]. The conceptual (meta) model that has been developed for conceptual OLAP models (see figure 1) introduces the elements *cube*, *measure*, *dimension level*, and *dimension attribute* (sometimes also referred to as a level property). The dimension levels are organized in partial orders (implicit dimensions). The granularity of a cube is defined through a set of base dimension levels.

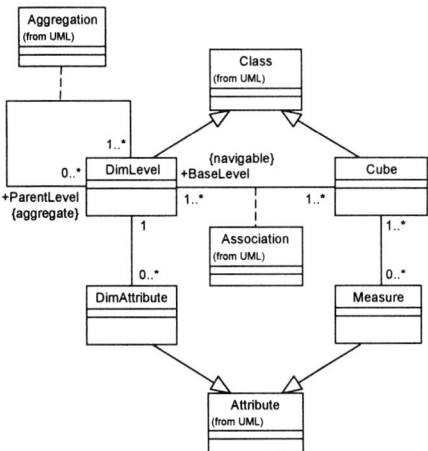

Fig 1. Meta model for conceptual OLAP models with ADAPTed UML notation elements

---

[2] ADAPT is a trademark of Symmetry Corporation, San Rafael, CA, U.S.A.

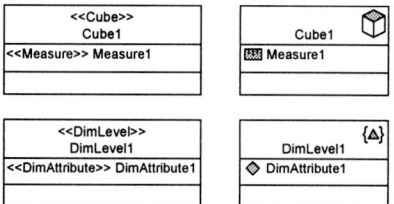

Fig. 2. ADAPT symbols as stereotypes in ADAPTed UML

Besides the mentioned model elements the meta model also contains references to core UML elements for their graphical representation in ADAPTed UML. The dependencies between cube and measure are drawn as associations with a defined navigability, the dimension hierarchies are represented by aggregations. ADAPT symbols are used as graphical stereotypes as shown in figure 2 [14].

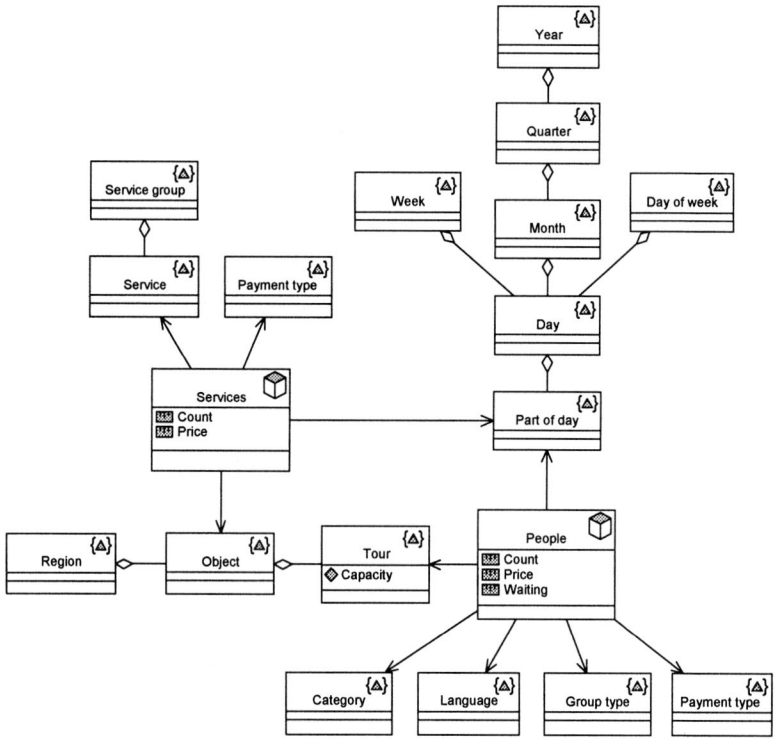

Fig. 3. Conceptual model of the scenario

Figure 3 shows the scenario data model, GOAL application A1 [8], in ADAPTed UML notation. There are two separate cubes (*People* and *Services*) with different sets of measures. *People* facts store the data containing the visitor admissions to the historical monuments. *Services* contains the data concerning the services consumed by the visitors within a monument visit. Four dimensions exist in total, two of them (*Time* and *Geography*) are shared by both cubes. Facts of the *People* cube are on a *Tour* granularity level, while facts of the *Services* cube are of less detail (*Object* granularity level). You should note that as mentioned above no explicit (i.e. named) dimensions and hierarchies are included in the diagram; they exist only implicitly through the chained dimension levels.

In classical database design usually only the schema level is considered. However, in the OLAP world it makes sense to look at the instances of more or less static (so called "slow-changing") dimensions already at design time in order to verify the aggregation paths. For this purpose dimension tree diagrams are introduced in ADAPTed UML. On the conceptual level dimension trees originate from a dimension level with maximum granularity, i.e. a "leaf" in the conceptual OLAP model. As the root of a dimension tree a virtual "All" dimension element is presented as the "super aggregate" of the model. Figure 4 shows a (slightly modified) excerpt of the geographic hierarchy of GOAL application A1.

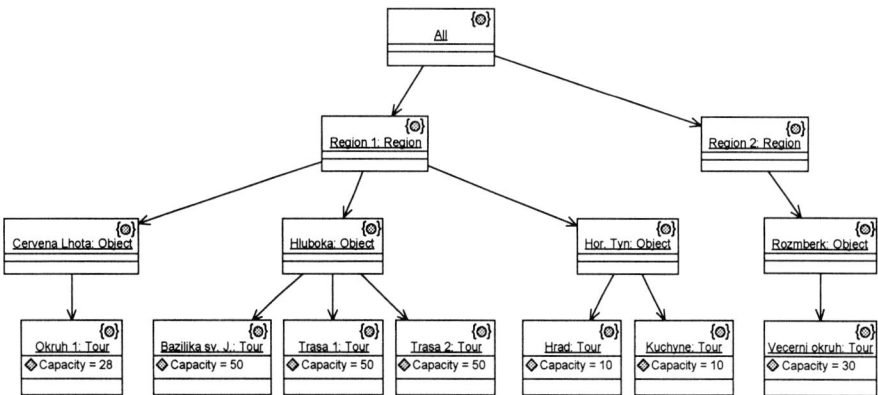

Fig. 4. Example of a dimension tree

2.2 Logical Model and MDX

As part of the logical design the system-independent conceptual model is transformed into a logical (system-dependent) "implementation model". Restrictions of the chosen system (i.e. DBMS or OLAP software) have to be taken into account. In the case of relational databases there is a unique (i.e. the one and only) relational model. However, in the multidimensional case of OLAP systems, the logical models of different products differ significantly. We use a logical OLAP model that is based on the Microsoft Analysis Services (shipped with SQL Server 2000 [10]). Additionally to the above model elements dimensions and hierarchies are introduced [14]. Some problems that might arise when translating a conceptual OLAP model into a specific logical one are also elaborated in [6].

As part of the OLEDB for OLAP specification Microsoft proposes a CREATE CUBE statement as part of the DDL capabilities of the MDX (multidimensional expressions) query language. It shares much of the SQL-92 syntax and semantics of the CREATE TABLE statement. Although it is originally only intended for creating local cubes (stored in a local data file) the syntax is well suited as a general means for describing logical Analysis Services OLAP models. The BNF for the CREATE CUBE statement can be found in the Microsoft SQL Server documentation [10]. As an example, a logical model of the scenario's *People* cube (see figure 3) would be specified with a CREATE CUBE statement like the following one:

```
CREATE CUBE People                DIMENSION Visitors,
(                                   HIERARCHY Category,
DIMENSION Time,                       LEVEL Category,
  HIERARCHY Week,                   HIERARCHY Language,
    LEVEL [All Time]                  LEVEL Language,
      TYPE ALL,                     HIERARCHY [Group type],
    LEVEL Week,                       LEVEL [Group type],
    LEVEL Day,                      HIERARCHY
    LEVEL [Part of day],              [Payment type],
  HIERARCHY Calendar,                 LEVEL [Payment type],
    LEVEL [All Time]                DIMENSION Geography,
      TYPE ALL,                       LEVEL Region,
    LEVEL Year,                       LEVEL Object,
    LEVEL Quarter,                    LEVEL Tour,
    LEVEL Month,                    MEASURE Count
    LEVEL Day,                        FUNCTION SUM,
    LEVEL [Part of day],            MEASURE Price
  HIERARCHY [Day of week],            FUNCTION SUM
    LEVEL [All Time]                  FORMAT "Currency",
      TYPE ALL,                     MEASURE Waiting
    LEVEL [Day of week],              FUNCTION SUM
    LEVEL Day,                    )
    LEVEL [Part of day],
```

3 Modeling OLAP Security

Especially the conceptual security design phase requires an in depth reflection. A first approach for conceptual modeling of security semantics can be found in [12]. Security semantics are defined as the security-relevant knowledge about the application domain. They are mainly concerned with the secrecy and privacy of information.

Our security model for OLAP is based on the assumption of a central (administrator based) security policy. The access restrictions are defined as authorization constraints making the identification of security objects and subjects necessary. At this point we assume the notion of (non-overlapping, non-hierarchical) roles as security subjects [17]. Therefore, in addition to the above elements (cubes, dimensions, etc.) the element *role* is introduced. Authorization constraints can either be positive (explicit grants) or negative (explicit denials). We base the security model on an *open world policy* (i.e. access to data is allowed unless explicitly denied) with negative authorization constraints. This corresponds to the open nature of OLAP systems. Additionally, we limit our security model to read access. The typical queries in OLAP systems are read-only. There are some systems that support write-back mechanisms (e.g. for future plan data), but these will not be considered in our model.

In [13] an analysis of OLAP security requirements is presented. As different applications lead to very different requirements (with different complexities), basic and advanced (high-level) requirements are distinguished. In the following section we propose a security constraint language to express OLAP security policies in a way that is suitable for subsequent design phases.

3.1 Specifying OLAP Security Constraints with MDSCL

The requirements have to be concretized and to some degree formalized in order to support the subsequent (conceptual and logical) design phases. In this section we present a multidimensional security constraint language (MDSCL) that is based on MDX with a syntax similar to the one of the CREATE CUBE statement presented in [10]. We use this approach rather than e.g. a formal tuple-based notation in order to make the language readable by system administrators and designers, or end-users.

Even though our language definition is linked to the MDX representation of the logical OLAP model used by Microsoft, we kept it as system independent as possible. It should thus be usable to define security restrictions for any target system. MDSCL is, however, dependent on our conceptual OLAP and security model described above. In order to express the (negative) authorization constraints, we propose a set of HIDE statements. The following BNF representation contains some restrictions that limit the (intuitively) possible number of HIDE statements in several ways. This is done for simplification reasons; bear in mind that we are acting on a conceptual abstraction level:

```
<hide cube statement> ::= HIDE CUBE <cube name>
   FOR ROLE <role name>
<hide measure statement> ::= HIDE MEASURE
   <measure name> [ WHERE <slicing constraint> ]
   FOR ROLE <role name>
<hide slice statement> ::= HIDE SLICE WHERE
   <slicing constraint> { AND <slicing constraint> }
   FOR ROLE <role name>
<hide level statement> ::= HIDE LEVEL <string>
   [ WHERE <slicing constraint> ] FOR ROLE <role name>
<slicing constraint> ::= <level name>
   <compare operator> <member name>
<role name> ::= <legal name>
<cube name> ::= <legal name>
<measure name> ::= [ <cube name> "." ] <legal name>
<level name> ::= <legal name>
<member name> ::= """ <string> """
<compare operator> ::= "=" | "!="
<legal name> ::= <unquoted name> | <quoted name>
```

```
<unquoted name> ::= <alpha> { <alpha> |
   <alphanumeric> }
<quoted name> ::= "[" <string> "]"
<string> ::= { <alpha> | <alphanumeric> | <space> }
```

3.2 Graphical Representation

We explicitly model the access by different roles (security subjects). This fact raises the question whether one single diagram should be used to present the policy for all roles or whether a distinct diagram should be used for each individual role. The right decision depends on the number of roles and the complexity of the security policy.

The design of the security semantics is based on the conceptual OLAP model represented as an ADAPTed UML diagram. This diagram can be extended by MDSCL expressions using the UML notation for constraints. Constraints can be drawn as UML notes bound to the model element that they concern. This fits perfectly for MDSCL as each constraint controls the access to a certain model element (cube, measure, dimension level). Figure 5 shows the scenario model with some sample MDSCL constraints.

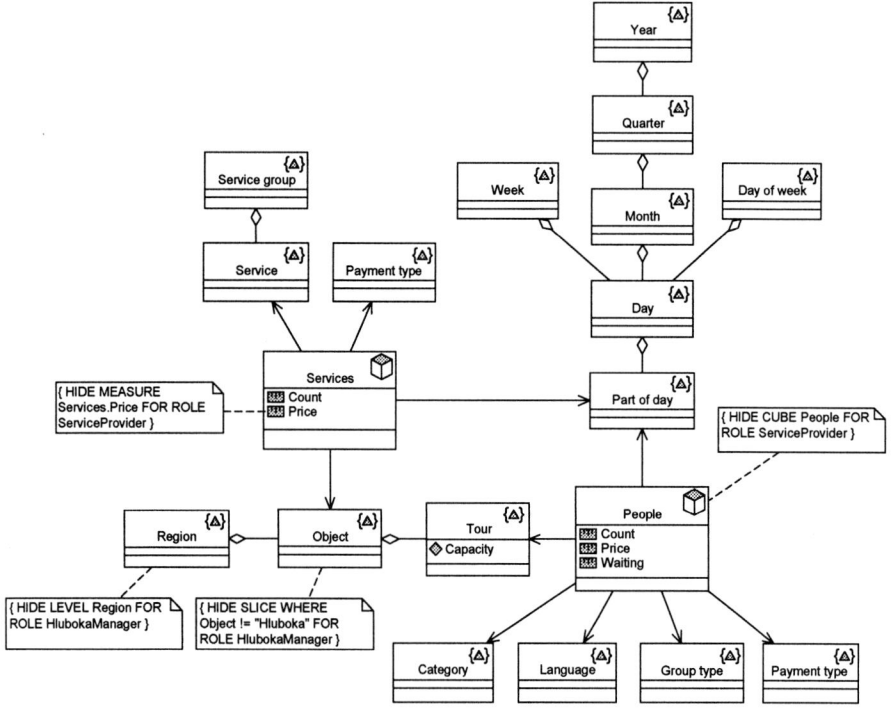

Fig. 5. Scenario model with sample MDSCL constraints

Besides this administrator or designer view it is possible to create graphical representations of restricted end-user views as well (e.g. for documentation purposes). Depending on the complexity of the constraints they result in hidden model elements (cubes, measures, dimension levels) or in hidden dimension members, which can be expressed by hidden (or somehow marked or labeled) elements in the ADAPTed UML model or dimension tree diagrams.

3.3 Examples and Constraint Types

In the following we will give some concrete examples for the supported security constraint types by using the GOAL application A1 data model as a scenario.

HIDE CUBE. The following HIDE CUBE statement hides the *People* cube from a *ServiceProvider* role's view, users with that role will not be able to access any measure of that cube:

```
HIDE CUBE People FOR ROLE ServiceProvider
```

HIDE MEASURE. In order to hide the *Price* measure of the *Services* cube for a *ServiceProvider* role, the following HIDE MEASURE statement would be used:

```
HIDE MEASURE Services.Price FOR ROLE ServiceProvider
```

Note the dot-notation for distinguishing measures of different cubes with the same measure name. The graphical representation would be similar to the one in the previous example.

HIDE SLICE. The HIDE SLICE statement specifies a cube slice to be hidden from a role's view. At this point only equal ("=") and not equal ("!=") are supported as compare operators, as others would require a proper ordering of the dimension members.

The following example hides all but the *Hluboka* object from the view of Hluboka's object manager. In order to prevent falsified or unclear data on a *Region* level, that dimension level should usually also be hidden with a HIDE LEVEL statement (see below).

```
HIDE SLICE WHERE Object != "Hluboka"
    FOR ROLE HlubokaManager
```

If multidimensional slices (dices) should be hidden, the HIDE SLICE statement can include multiple constraints connected with an AND keyword. The following example allows access to current (year 2001) data only for the Hluboka object:

```
HIDE SLICE WHERE Object != "Hluboka" AND Year = "2001"
    FOR ROLE HlubokaManager
```

HIDE LEVEL. A HIDE LEVEL statement is used to remove certain detail levels from a role's view. This usually makes only sense for the finest (leaf) granularity levels (in order to hide detail data, while access to aggregate data is allowed). Or, if certain cube slices are hidden (see above), a HIDE LEVEL statement could be used to make sure levels with filtered (and thus falsified) values cannot be queried.

The following example hides the *Tour* granularity level of the geographical hierarchy for a certain restricted role:

```
HIDE LEVEL Tour FOR ROLE RestrictedRole
```

A special case of hiding levels of detail is hiding a whole hierarchy (i.e. all levels in a hierarchy). When this is done, the user can only query aggregates over all members of that dimension.

HIDE LEVEL WHERE. We already presented simple HIDE SLICE and HIDE LEVEL constraints. For more complex policies it might be necessary to combine such two restrictions into a single constraint. Consider an object manager who can drill down to the *Tour* level for his own object but only to an *Object* level for the others. Such a constraint can be expressed by the following extended HIDE LEVEL statement:

```
HIDE LEVEL Tour WHERE Object != "Hluboka"
    FOR ROLE HlubokaManager
```

In the example only one dimension hierarchy is affected (*Tour* and *Object* belong to the same dimension), i.e. we are hiding levels of detail in slices of the same dimension (rather than a different dimension). This distinction is more important on a logical than on a conceptual level as the possibilities to implement the constraints differ significantly. The example creates data on different granularity levels in one dimension (some data exists on a *Tour* level, some only on an *Object* level). This is sometimes referred to as a frayed dimension (see figure 6).

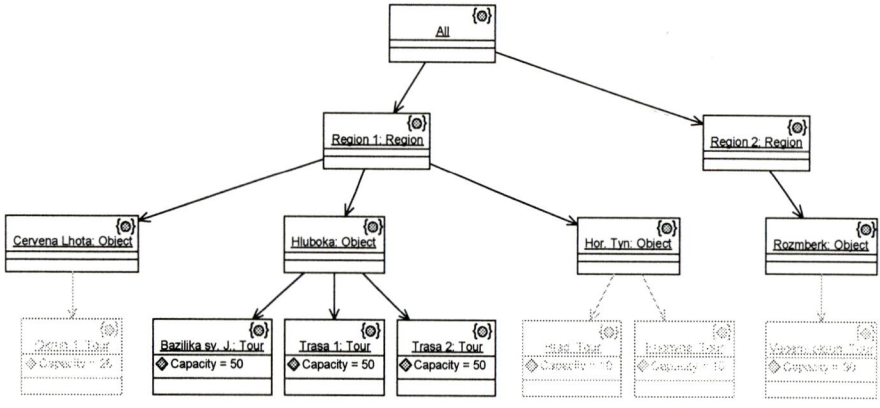

Fig. 6. Frayed dimension due to member filtering

Finally, if levels of detail should be hidden in certain slices of a different dimension, the HIDE LEVEL statement can be used in a similar way as above. However, the implementation is more challenging if two different dimensions are involved. The following statements make sure data on the *Day* and *Part of day* detail levels is only accessible for the *Hluboka* object:

```
HIDE LEVEL [Part of day] WHERE Object != "Hluboka"
    FOR ROLE HlubokaManager
HIDE LEVEL Day WHERE Object != "Hluboka"
    FOR ROLE HlubokaManager
```

HIDE MEASURE WHERE. Similar to the previous case a HIDE MEASURE statement can be extended to include a slicing constraint limiting the restriction to certain cube slices. For example the following statement only hides the *Price* measure only for objects other than *Hluboka*:

```
HIDE MEASURE Price WHERE Object != "Hluboka"
    FOR ROLE HlubokaManager
```

3.4 Evaluation and Possible Extensions

In this subsection we will evaluate the presented approach and outline possible extensions. Considering the OLAP security requirements presented in [13] we have addressed all but two of them. This restriction as well as other aspects will be discussed as follows:

- *Dynamic or data driven policies*, in which the sensitivity of certain cube cells depends not only on structural information (metadata, dimension members) but on the actual measure values themselves, are not supported. They are only applicable in very specific contexts and it is hardly possible to find a suitable and yet simple notation for them. However, we have addressed even quite complex dependencies within dimension data (e.g. if the sensitivity of dimension A depends on the content of dimension B) by means of the HIDE SLICE, HIDE LEVEL WHERE, and HIDE MEASURE WHERE constraint types.

- *Inference control.* In our model we have only considered direct access to sensitive data. Controlling indirect access by means of so called tracker queries has not been addressed. An example is the existence of a parallel classification in addition the regular navigation paths of the OLAP model [18]. Inference control measures are not available "out of the box" by any common OLAP system and the required efforts are probably not feasibly for most "real life" projects.

- *Hiding the existence.* In security critical applications it may be necessary to hide the existence of sensitive data, i.e. it is not sufficient to provide unauthorized users with null values of certain facts. This is not only a matter of security, end-user transparency and user-friendliness are also effected. In general, OLAP security can be implemented on metadata, dimension member, or fact data level (see next section). However, the mechanisms of the different systems differ significantly, also in their capabilities of hiding the existence of sensitive data. This hence becomes an implementation issue rather than a conceptual design issue.

- *Non-conflicting constraint set.* For large applications it might be necessary that a large set of security constraints needs to be expressed at the conceptual level. Checking for consistency of the specified constraints is one of the more difficult tasks of the design. At this point we have avoided most sources for conflicts through model simplifications (only negative authorizations, no role hierarchies). Possible extension to MDSCL, however, might make conflict resolution measures necessary.

- *Security subjects.* We have limited our model to very simple security subjects (non-hierarchical, non-overlapping roles). Role based access control models usually provide the possibility of role hierarchies [17]. A role can usually have a number of more specific sub-roles and one superior role. A role hierarchy is interpreted in such way that the authorizations or constraints of a superior role are inherited to subordinate roles. For positive authorizations this approach produces intuitively useful results. For the utilized negative authorization approach this would mean that a more specialized role would inherit the negative authorizations (i.e. denials) resulting in even more restricted access. On the other hand, also an inversion of the inheritance direction would not necessarily make more sense, either.

- *Positive and negative authorizations.* Additionally, due to the difficulty to keep the constraint set consistent we have limited our security model to negative authorizations. In principle a combination of negative and positive authorizations would be possible (i.e. HIDE and SHOW statements). Nevertheless, a combination with role hierarchies would make a conflict resolution strategy even more difficult.

4 Conclusions and Future Work

We have presented a methodology and language for conceptual modeling of OLAP security. Even though we used a rather pragmatic approach (limiting our model in several ways), it should be applicable not only for the GOAL prototype applications, but also for most other real-life projects. The aim was not to create an exhaustive model that would be able to cover all special requirements that might come up in rare occasions, but rather to present an approach that would be applicable in practice. Also throughout the design of the methodology we had the idea of a possible tool support in mind.

The Microsoft Analysis Services are capable of storing their metadata (i.e. the physical data model) in the Microsoft Repository. The data model used (the Metadata Coalition Open Information Model [9]) is published and open.[3] Other vendors will possibly follow that example, as the same data model is used by the OLE DB for

---

[3] By now the Meta Metadata Coalition (MDC) and the OMG have announced that their competitive meta models, the OIM and the CWM will be merged into a single one. The MDC will become a part of the OMG, details are, however, not yet available.

OLAP standard. On the other side, many modeling tools provide the possibility to store UML models in the repository as well. The UML model is also part of the OIM. It would thus make sense to use the repository as a central media to synchronize the conceptual and logical models (e.g. in for of ADAPTed UML diagrams) with the physical model of the OLAP tool. Such an architecture is already promising without the security aspect, but if the security constraints are also stored in the repository, a security implementation tool can make use of that as well.

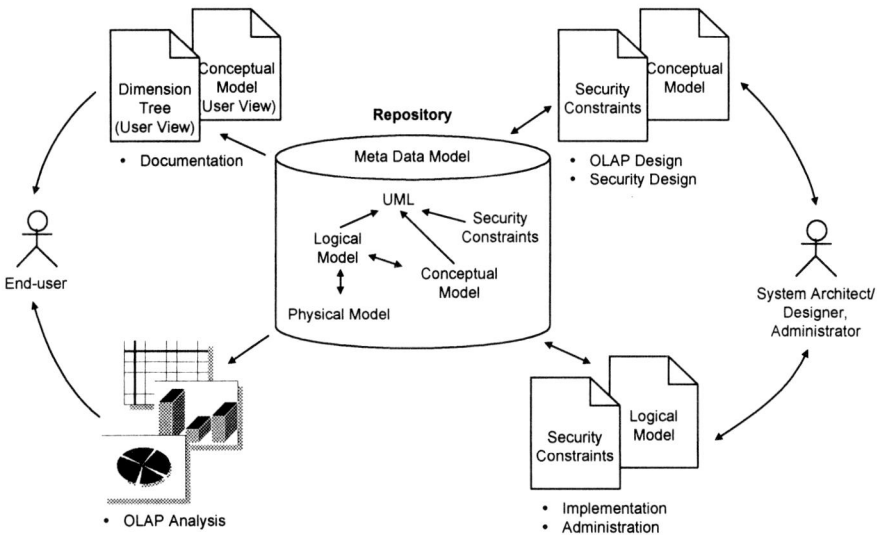

Fig. 7. Metadata flow and access using MDSCL and ADAPTed UML

Figure 7 shows a coarse architecture for integrating the different aspects of the proposed methodology. The ADAPTed UML diagrams are being used to support modeling and design. MDSCL constraints are utilized to define the security semantics. Through the diagrams, the validation of different user views becomes possible already at an early design stage, i.e. before the implementation of the system. This implementation process can then be supported by tools that make use of the models in the repository. The evaluation of this architecture idea and a possible realization are, however, subject to future work.

5 Acknowledgements

The GOAL project is carried out in an international research group within the INCO COPERNICUS program of the European Union. The partners involved in the project are Vienna University of Technology (A), Czech Technical University in Prague (CZ), University of Essen (D), Technical University Košice (SK), and CertiCon a.s. and ASP Systems s.r.o. companies (both CZ). We would like to thank our project partners for helpful comments and stimulating discussions.

References

1. Bulos, D.: A New Dimension. In Database Programming & Design; 6/1996; reprinted in Chamoni, P, Gluchowski, P. (Eds.): Analytische Informationssysteme. Springer; Berlin et al., 1998.
2. Bulos, D., Forsman, S.: Getting Started with ADAPT. Whitepaper, Symmetry Corp.; San Rafael, 1998.
3. Cabibbo, L., Torlone, R.: Querying Multidimensional Databases. Proc. 6th International Workshop on Database Programming Languages (DBPL), Estes Park, CO, USA, August 18-20, 1997.
4. Castano, S., Fugini, M., Martella, G., Samarati P.: Database Security. ACM Press; 1994.
5. Elmasri, R.; Navathe, S.B.: Fundamentals of Database Systems; Addison-Wesley Longman, Inc.; 3rd edition; 2000.
6. Hahn, K., Sapia, C., Blaschka, M.: Automatically Generating OLAP Schemata from Conceptual Graphical Models. Proc. Third ACM International Workshop on Data Warehousing and OLAP (DOLAP 2000), McLean, VA, USA, November 2000.
7. Kimball, R.: Hackers, Crackers, and Spooks; Ensuring that your data warehouse is secure. In DBMS Magazine; April 1997.
8. Mikšovský, P., Matoušek, K., Zach, P.: Application A1 Specification. GOAL Technical Report TR8, INCO-Copernicus project no. 977091, March 1999.
9. Meta Data Coalition: Open Information Model, Version 1.1 (Proposal); August, 1999.
10. Microsoft Corp.: Microsoft SQL Server 2000, Building Applications. Product documentation; Microsoft Corp., 1999.
11. Object Management Group: OMG Unified Modeling Language Specification. Version 1.3; March 2000.
12. Pernul, G., Winiwarter, W., Tjoa A M.: The Entity-Relationship Model for Multilevel Security. In Proc. 12th International Conference on the Entity-Relationship Approach (ER'93); Arlington, Texas, USA, December 15-17, 1993.
13. Priebe, T., Pernul, G.: Towards OLAP Security Design – Survey and Research Issues. Proc. Third ACM International Workshop on Data Warehousing and OLAP (DOLAP 2000), McLean, VA, USA, November 2000.
14. Priebe, T., Pernul, G.: Metadaten-gestützer Data-Warehouse-Entwurf mit ADAPTed UML. To appear in Proc. 5. Internationale Tagung Wirtschaftsinformatik (WI 2001); Augsburg, Germany, September 2001.
15. Rosenthal, A., Sciore, E.: View Security as the Basis for Data Warehouse Security. Proc. of the International Workshop on Design and Management of Data Warehouses (DMDW 2000); Stockholm, Sweden, June 5-6, 2000.
16. Sapia, C., Blaschka, M., Höfling, G., Dinter, B.: Extending the E/R Model for the Multidimensional Paradigm. In Kambayashi, Y. et. al. (Eds.), Advances in Database Technologies; LNCS Vol. 1552; Springer, 1999.
17. Sandhu, R.S., Coyne, E. J., Feinstein, H.L., Youman, C.E.: Role-Based Access Control Models. IEEE Computer, Vol. 29, Number 2; February 1996.
18. Steger, J., Günzel, H.: Identifying Security Holes in OLAP Applications. Proc. Fourteenth Annual IFIP WG 11.3 Working Conference on Database Security; Schoorl (near Amsterdam), The Netherlands, August 21-23, 2000.

A Randomized Approach for the Incremental Design of an Evolving Data Warehouse

Dimitri Theodoratos, Theodore Dalamagas, Alkis Simitsis, and Manos Stavropoulos

National Technical University of Athens
Department of Electrical and Computer Engineering
Zographou 157 73, Athens, Greece
{dth, dalamag, asimi, estavro}@dblab.ece.ntua.gr

Abstract. A Data Warehouse (DW) can be used to integrate data from multiple distributed data sources. A DW can be seen as a set of materialized views that determine its schema and its content in terms of the schema and the content of the data sources. DW applications require high query performance. For this reason, the design of a typical DW consists of selecting views to materialize that are able to answer a set of input user queries. However, the cost of answering the queries has to be balanced against the cost of maintaining the materialized views. In an evolving DW application, new queries need to be answered by the DW. An incremental selection of materialized views uses the materialized views already in the DW to answer parts of the new queries, and avoids the re-implementation of the DW from scratch. This incremental design is complex and an exhaustive approach is not feasible. We have developed a randomized approach for incrementally selecting a set of views that are able to answer a set of input user queries locally while minimizing a combination of the query evaluation and view maintenance cost. In this process we exploit "common sub-expressions" among new queries and between new queries and old views. Our approach is implemented and we report on its experimental evaluation.

1 Introduction

A Data Warehouse (DW) is a repository of information integrated from multiple data sources. A DW is devoted to On-Line Analytical Processing (OLAP) and Decision Support System (DSS) applications [30,15,11,2]. Current DWs accumulate enormous quantities of data. OLAP queries are complex data intensive queries involving grouping/aggregation and sequential scans. Therefore, query evaluation in the DW has to be efficient in order to guarantee fast answers to the analysts. The data stored in a DW need to be eventually updated in response to updates of the source data.

A DW is usually seen as a set of materialized views defined over the relations of the data sources. These views determine its schema and content in terms of the schema and the content of the data sources. In order to achieve high query performance, the queries are evaluated using exclusively the materialized views. The query evaluation cost of a set of queries is the cost of evaluating these queries rewritten completely [18,7,4,3] over the materialized views. The materialized views are usually maintained incrementally. In an incremental strategy, only the changes that must be applied to the views are computed from the changes of the source relations [8,6,19]. The DW view maintenance cost is the cost of propagating the source relation changes to the materialized views that are affected by these changes.

A central problem in the design of a DW is the selection of views to materialize given a set of input queries that the DW has to satisfy. When designing a DW, one of the most significant challenges is the minimization of the query evaluation cost. However, maintaining the materialized views is a particularly time consuming process that makes part of the data unavailable for querying. Therefore, in order to ensure sufficient availability of the stored data and satisfactory query response time, a reduction in the query evaluation cost must be balanced against an increase in the view maintenance cost. Many approaches attempt to appropriately select views for materialization that exploit common sub-expressions between the input queries and minimize a combination of the query evaluation and the view maintenance cost [9,27,1,31,28,26]. This last solution, though more complex, achieves a balance between query performance and availability of the data.

The problem. DWs are dynamic and evolve over time. As the needs of the analysts expand, new queries need to be satisfied by the DW. Some of these new queries can be answered by the views that are already materialized in the DW. In general though, new materialized views need to be added to the DW either for answering the new queries or for improving the evaluation performance of the new queries. The new queries are then answered through rewritings over the old views, or over the new views, or partially over the new and partially over the old views. Re-implementing the whole DW from scratch for dealing with the new queries is complex and implies the unavailability of the data for a long period of time. In [29] we avoid re-implementation and present an incremental approach that selects new views for materialization that minimizes the combined cost of evaluating the new queries and maintaining the new materialized views. We also provide transformation rules that generate alterative view selections for materialization and query evaluation plans for the queries from the views in the form of AND/OR dags. Each view in a view selection is used for evaluating at least one new query. The transformation rules are shown to be sound and complete. In this sense, by exhaustively applying the rules, the view selection that minimizes the combined cost can be found. Nevertheless, for a large number of complex queries, the search space can be very big. In real cases, it is unfeasible to use an exhaustive algorithm for exploring it.

Contribution. In this paper, we present a randomized approach for the incremental design of a DW that is, for the selection of new views to materialize in the DW. The approach is based on the Simulated Annealing process. Since its first appearance [16], Simulated Annealing has been used in a variety of optimization problems. In the Database area, it has been used for query optimization [14,24,23,13]. Even though it has been studied in research works, it has not been adopted in commercial products. The reason is that randomized algorithms such as Simulated Annealing, although they return far better results than heuristic or greedy algorithms, they require a longer running time [22]. In the incremental design of a DW, the time restrictions are not so crucial. Further, Simulated Annealing is especially well suited to optimization problems with large search spaces and with cost functions that manifest a large number of local minima [14] as is the case here. Thus, Simulated Annealing is a good candidate for incrementally designing a DW.

Some parameters of the simulated annealing algorithm depend on the problem addressed while others are implementation-dependent. For the problem in hand, we use multiquery AND/OR dags (AO dags) and transformations rules to define a search space suitable for applying the Simulated Annealing. The search space is a graph of states. The states of the search space (nodes of the graph) are multiquery AO dags. A move from one state to another in the search space (an edge of the graph) roughly corresponds to application of a transformation rule. The cost of each state is the combined cost of evaluating the new queries according to the evaluation plans represented in a state and maintaining new materialized views. Note that our approach does not depend on the way these costs are assessed.

We have implemented the Simulated Annealing approach for incrementally designing a DW. We have first run a number of experiments to choose the implementation dependent parameters. The approach is then applied for selecting views defined over a real-world star schema [15] comprising one fact table and three dimension tables with three to four hierarchy levels. The number of dimensions and hierarchy levels of this schema and the number of types of views are intentionally kept small so that the solution returned by our approach can be compared with that of the exhaustive algorithm when a number of the parameters of the problem vary.

Outline. The rest of the paper is organized as follows. The next section reviews related work. Section 3 introduces multiquery AO dags, states formally the incremental design problem in terms of multiquery AO dags, and describes the transformation rules. In Section 4 we briefly present the Simulated Annealing algorithm, and we show how the problem-dependent and implementation dependent parameters are defined for the incremental design problem. Section 5 deals with implementation issues and presents experimental results. We conclude in Section 6 and provide directions for further work.

2 Related Work

Although many works deal with the design of a DW, only few of them address dynamic issues. The works dealing with the design of a DW can be classified according to the class of queries and views considered, the cost function they attempt to minimize, the constraints that impose to the problem, and the approach adopted for solving it. [12] aims at minimizing the query evaluation cost in the context of aggregations and multidimensional analysis under a space constraint. In the same context, [1] proposes techniques that consider only the relevant elements in the search space of the problem.Given a materialized SQL view, [21] presents an exhaustive approach as well as heuristics for selecting auxiliary views that minimize the total view maintenance cost. Given an SPJ view, [20] derives, using key and referential integrity constraints, a set of auxiliary views, other than the base relations, that eliminate the need to access the base relations when maintaining both the initial and the auxiliary views (i.e. that makes the views altogether self-maintainable). In [9] greedy algorithms are provided for selecting views to materialize that minimize the query evaluation cost under a space constraint. A integer programming solution for selecting views that minimize the combined cost is given in [31]. A variation of the DW design problem endeavoring to select a set of views that minimizes the query evaluation cost under a total maintenance cost constraint is adopted in [10]. None of the previous approaches requires the queries to be answerable exclusively from the materialized views in a non-trivial manner (that is, without considering that the source relations and the materialized views reside in the same site, and without replicating all the source relation at the DW). This requirement is taken into account in [27] where the problem of configuring a DW without space restrictions is addressed for a class of select-join queries. This work is extended in [28] in order to take into account space restrictions, multiquery optimization over the maintenance expressions, and the use of auxiliary views when maintaining other views. [26] deals with the same problem for a class of PSJ queries under space restrictions.

The approaches adopted by the previous papers are tailored for the static DW design problem. An incremental version of the DW design problem (dynamic DW design) is addressed in [29]. [17] presents a system that dynamically materializes information at multiple levels of granularity. However, this approach is not based on a given set of queries for selecting view materializations but it cashes the results of incoming queries in order to match the workload and maintenance restrictions. [25] deals with a problem that is somehow complementary to the incremental design problem: detect materialized views that become redundant in an evolving DW. We are not aware of any work using the Simulated Annealing process for the design of a DW. Papers using Simulated Annealing for optimizing queries are cited in the introduction.

3 Problem Formulation and Transformation Rules

We present in this section an AO dag representation for multiple queries and views. We then formulate the problem in terms of AO dags and describe informally the AO dag transformation rules introduced in [29].

3.1 Problem Formulation

Multiquery AO dags [5,21] provide a convenient, compact, representation of alternative ways of evaluating multiple queries from source relations and views and of subexpression sharing between relations and views. This representation is quite general to allow for complex queries including grouping/aggregation queries that are extensively used in DWing applications. It distinguishes between AND nodes that correspond to views (henceforth *view nodes*) and OR nodes that correspond to operations (henceforth *operation nodes*). An extension of these dags with *marked view nodes* [29] allows the representation of views already materialized in the DW (old views).

Consider the following source relations that form a star schema:

Location(<u>Store</u>, City, Country, Continent) abbreviated as L
Product(<u>Item</u>, Type, Category) abbreviated as P
Time(<u>Date</u>, Month, Quarter, Year) abbreviated as T
Sales(<u>Store</u>, <u>Item</u>, <u>Date</u>, Amount) abbreviated as S

S is a fact table comprising one measure attribute Amount and foreign key attributes to the dimension tables L, P, and T. The dimension tables comprise different hierarchy attributes. We have used this schema for applying our approach in the experiments.

As an example, a small multiquery AO dag representing alternative ways of evaluating three queries Q_1, Q_2, and Q_3 from the source relations is shown in Figure 1(a). These queries join the fact and the dimension tables and aggregate the resulting table at different aggregation levels. For simplicity only the fact table S and the dimension tables L and P are involved. In Figure 1(a), small circles

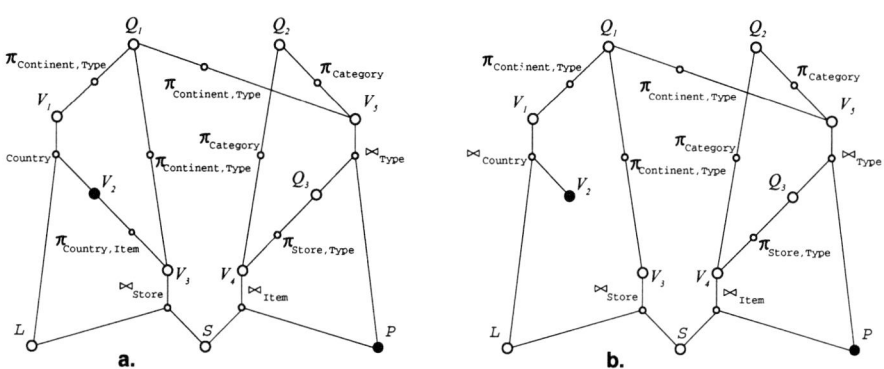

Fig. 1. (a) A multiquery AO dag for the queries Q_1, Q_2, and Q_3, (b) Initial multiquery AO dag.

represent operation nodes while bigger ones represent view nodes. An operation node is labeled by the corresponding operation, and a view node by a view name. Some view nodes correspond to the queries Q_1, Q_2 and Q_3. These view nodes are labeled by the names of the queries and are called *query nodes*. Marked view nodes (old materialized views) are shown by filled black circles (view nodes V_2 and P in Figure 1(a)). Only two types of operations are involved: (a) a binary one, the natural join operation, $\bowtie_A$, where A denotes the attribute on which the join is performed, and (b) a unary one, the generalized projection operation [7], $\pi_{X,\text{sum}(A)}$, where X is a set of grouping attributes from the dimension relations and A is a measure attribute aggregated by the aggregate function sum. For concreteness the aggregated measure sum(A) is omitted in the figures. Three different alternative plans for query Q_1, two for query Q_2, and one for query Q_3 are depicted in the multiquery AO dag of Figure 1(a). Note that some views (expressions) are shared between the plans of different queries. For instance, view V_5 is shared between a plan of query Q_1 and a plan of query Q_2, while query Q_3 is a view node in an evaluation plan of query Q_2.

Some other AO dags for the queries Q_1, Q_2 and Q_3 are shown in Figures 1(b), 2(a), and 2(b). These multiquery AO dags are subdags of the multiquery AO dag of Figure 1(a). In contrast to the multiquery AO dag of Figure 1(a), in the multiquery AO dags of Figures 1(b), 2(a), and 2(b) the sink nodes are not necessarily source relations. In a multiquery AO dag for a set of queries, all the query nodes are present, and the same holds for the marked nodes. All the root nodes are query nodes (but a query node is not necessarily a root node). The sink nodes are view nodes and *represent materialized views*. Those of the sink nodes that are not marked are the *new views to materialize in the DW*. For instance in the multiquery AO dag of Figure 2(b), the materialized views are the views (or relations) L, S, P, V_2, and V_5, of which L, S, and V_5 are new views to materialize in the DW, and P, V_2 are views already materialized in the DW (old views). For each query node, *at least one evaluation plan from the sink nodes is represented*. Note that since the sink nodes represent (old and new) materialized views, *every query can be evaluated using the materialized views*. Every sink node that is not a marked node occurs in at least one query evaluation plan.

The incremental design problem that we address in this paper can now be formulated as follows. Consider a multiquery AO dag **G**, for a set **Q** of new queries and a set **V**$_0$ of old views, which represents alternative evaluation plans for the queries in **Q** over the source relations. **G** is given as input to the problem. The goal is to find a multiquery AO dag **G**$'$ for **Q** and **V**$_0$, subdag of **G**, such that the combined cost of evaluating the queries in **Q** according to the query evaluation plans represented in **G**$'$, and maintaining the new materialized views represented in **G**$'$ is minimal. In our simplified example we let the multiquery AO dag of Figure 1(a) be the input to the problem.

3.2 An Example of Application of the Rules

In order to deal with the problem we first construct a multiquery AO dag **G**$_0$ from **G** as follows: Remove from **G** all the nodes and edges that appear solely in evaluation plans of the marked nodes (and not in those of any other query). **G**$_0$ is called *initial multiquery AO dag*. All the marked nodes in **G**$_0$ are sink nodes. In our example, the initial multiquery AO dag is shown in Figure 1(b). The intuition behind the construction of the initial multiquery AO dag is the following: since the marked nodes represent views that are materialized and thus are available, their evaluation need not be represented in the multiquery AO dag.

The initial multiquery AO dag is the starting point from which we can apply two transformation rules for multiquery AO dags. Consider a multiquery AO dag **G**. The first transformation rule (called here *New Materialized View Creation*)

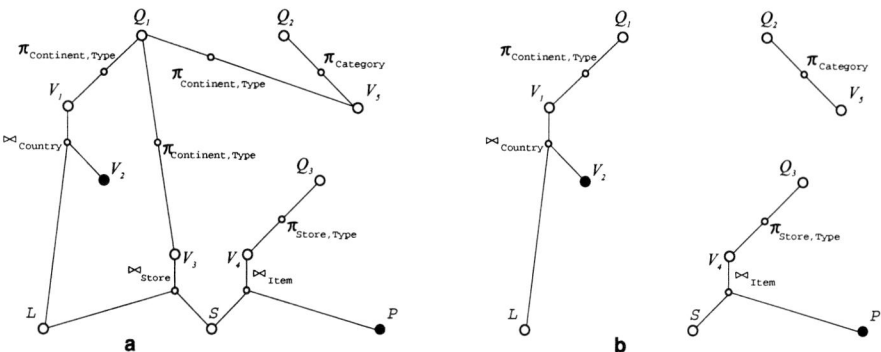

Fig. 2. A multiquery AO dag for Q_1, Q_2, and Q_3 after an application of (a) the first rule, and (b) the second rule.

can be applied to a view node V in **G** that is not a sink node and to a query node Q in **G** that can be evaluated in **G** using V. Nodes V and Q can coincide. New Materialized View Creation rule makes node V a sink node (new materialized view) and forces query Q to be evaluated using V. In order to do so, first, it removes from **G** all the nodes and the edges that are solely used for evaluating V (and not any other query). Then, it removes from **G** all the nodes and edges that are solely used for evaluating Q without using V. Figure 2(a) shows the result of applying the New Materialized View Creation rule to the view node V_5 and the query node Q_2 of the multiquery AO dag of Figure 1(b). Note that view node V_5 is now a sink node and query Q_2 can be evaluated only using V_5. The evaluation plans of the other queries are not affected.

The second transformation rule (called here *Evaluation Plan Elimination*) can be applied to a view node V in **G** that is a sink or query node and to a query node Q in **G** that can be evaluated in **G** using V but also without using V. Evaluation Plan Elimination rule forces Q to be evaluated using V. Thus, it removes from **G** all the nodes and edges that are solely used for evaluating Q without using V. Figure 2(b) shows the result of applying the Evaluation Plan Elimination rule to the view node V_2 and the query node Q_1 of the multiquery AO dag of Figure 2(a). Note that query Q_2 can now be evaluated only using V_2. The evaluation plans of the other queries are not affected.

If we assume that a new materialized view is used in at least one optimal query evaluation plan of a new query (that is, views are not materialized in the DW exclusively for supporting the view maintenance process) the previous two rules are sound and complete [29]. This means that an optimal solution to the problem (a multiquery AO dag, subdag of the initial multiquery AO dag, that yields the minimal combined cost) can be obtained by finitely applying in sequence the two transformation rules to the initial multiquery AO dag.

4 The Randomized Approach

Each solution to an optimization problem can be seen as a *state* in a *search space*. Each state has a *cost* associated with it which is given by a *cost function*. The states are connected by directed edges that are defined by moves. A *move set* is the set of moves available to go from one state to another. A move that reduce the cost of a state is called *downhill move*, while one that increases the cost of a state is called *uphill* move. Two states are called *adjacent* if one can go from one to the other by one move. A *local minimum* is a state that has the lowest cost among all its adjacent states. A *global minimum* is a state that has the lowest cost among all the states. In a search space there can be more than one local and global minimum. The optimal solution to the problem corresponds to a global minimum. Randomized algorithms perform a "random" walk through a solution space along the edges defined by the moves. Simulated Annealing is a randomized algorithm that has been successfully applied to a great number of different optimization problems. It has theoretical foundations and simplicity. We show in this section how the Simulated Annealing process can be adapted to the incremental DW design problem.

4.1 Simulated Annealing

The Simulated Annealing algorithm [16] tries to simulate the annealing process of crystals. In this process the temperature of a fluid is slowly decreased until the system reaches a state of minimum energy. The slower the temperature reduction, the lower the energy of the final state. The cost function of a state plays the role of the energy in the annealing process of crystals. As in other optimization techniques, the Simulated Annealing algorithm always accepts downhill moves but also uphill moves with some probability that depends on a number of parameters.

Figure 3 illustrates the behavior of Simulated Annealing. Two nested loops can be seen in this algorithm. In the inner loop the temperature is kept constant. A downhill move is always allowed. An uphill move is allowed with some probability that depends on the temperature and the difference between the actual state's cost and the new state's cost. The inner loop is finished when an equilibrium condition is met. Then the temperature is reduced and the inner loop is started again. The outer loop is finished when a freezing condition is met.

A number of parameters need to be determined for applying the algorithm to the incremental DW design problem. States, moves and cost function are problem dependent parameters. The parameters: initial state, initial temperature, temperature reduction, equilibrium condition, and freezing condition depend on the implementation of the process.

Input: *initial_state, initial_temperature;*
Output: *minstate;*

```
begin
  minstate := initial_state; cost := Cost(initial_state); mincost := cost;
  temp := initial_temperature;
  repeat
    repeat
      newstate :=state after random move; newcost := Cost(newstate);
      if newcost ≤ cost then
        state := newstate; cost := newcost
      else with probability e^(newcost-cost / temp)
        state := newstate; cost := newcost
      end;
      if cost < mincost then
        minstate := state; mincost := cost
      end
    until equilibrium not reached;
    reduce temperature
  until not frozen;
  return minstate
end
```

Fig. 3. Simulated Annealing Algorithm

4.2 Problem-Dependent Parameters

Consider a multiquery AO dag **G**, for a set **Q** of new queries and a set V_0 of old views, which represents alternative evaluation plans for the queries in **Q** over the source relations.

States. A state is a multiquery AO dag **G'** for **Q** and V_0 such that (a) **G'** is a subdag of **G**, and (b) all the marked view nodes in **G'** are sink nodes. Thus, the search space is a graph of multiquery AO dags.

Moves. There is a move (edge) from a state s to a state s' if s' can be obtained from s by applying any of the two transformation rules presented in the previous section. Each of these rules removes at least one edge from the multiquery AO dag to which it is applied. Thus, the search space defined this way is an acyclic directed graph. The Simulated Annealing process requires the search space to be a strongly connected graph i.e. for any two states s and s', there is path in the search space from s to s' and from s' to s. In the implementation of the algorithm, when a random move leading to a state s is performed, the adjacent to s state is kept available. Therefore, the moves are reversible. This way the previous requirement is satisfied.

Cost function. Given a state **G'**, the evaluation cost $E(\mathbf{Q})$ of the queries in **Q** is the (possibly) weighted sum of the cost of the optimal evaluation plan of each query in **Q** among the plans represented in **G'**. The weights in $E(\mathbf{Q})$ reflect the frequency (or importance) of the corresponding queries. Let **V** be the set of new materialized views in **G'** (that is, the set of sink nodes that are not in V_0).

The view maintenance cost $M(\mathbf{V})$ of the new views in $\mathbf{V}$ is the weighted sum of propagating the changes of the source relations to the views that are affected by these changes. The weights in $M(\mathbf{V})$ reflect the frequencies of propagating the changes of the corresponding source relations. The cost of the state $\mathbf{G}'$ is the combined sum $E(\mathbf{Q})+c*M(\mathbf{V})$. The parameter c indicates the importance of the query evaluation vs. the view maintenance cost and is set by the DW designer. A typical value of c is 1. $c < 1$ privileges the query evaluation cost, while $c > 1$ privileges the view maintenance cost in the incremental design of the DW. If the query evaluation cost is more important, the DW designer has the choice to give c a value much smaller than 1 in order to determine a view selection that has good query performance, and conversely. Low query evaluation cost can be obtained by materializing all the new queries (in general view nodes close to the root nodes of the graph). Low view maintenance cost can be obtained by materializing all the base relations that are not already materialized (non-marked sink nodes in the initial multiquery AO dag).

4.3 Implementation Dependent Parameters

Initial state. A theoretical analysis of the simulated annealing but also multiple experimental studies show that the effectiveness of the algorithm in finding the global minimum state is independent of the choice of the initial state [14]. Therefore we select as an initial state the initial multiquery AO dag $\mathbf{G}_0$.

Initial temperature. The initial temperature has to be sufficiently low to allow many uphill moves to be performed in the beginning. After a series of experiments we found that an initial temperature of twice the cost of the initial state shows a good performance. An increase of the multiplicative factor beyond 2 does not improve significantly the quality of the solution returned while importantly increasing the execution time of the algorithm.

Temperature reduction. Different previous works [24,13] have successfully experimented with a temperature reduction process where the new temperature is a percentage α of the old temperature and this percentage remains constant during the whole process. A typical value for α is in the range 0.9 to 0.95. Our experimental results indicated that 0.9 shows a good trade off between quality of the solution returned and execution time.

Equilibrium condition. This condition determines the number of times the inner loop of the algorithm is executed. This number can be dependent on the current temperature. Here it is assumed to be constant throughout the annealing and is experimentally set to be equal to 6.

Freezing condition. This condition determines when the annealing process terminates. The temperature is so low that accepted moves (either uphill or downhill) are negligible. A typical condition that is also adopted here consists of two tests: whether the temperature is below 1 and whether the final state does not change for four consecutive iterations through the outer loop of the algorithm.

Finally, each possible move from a state has equal probability to be chosen.

5 Experimental Results

We have performed a number of experiments to evaluate the Simulated Annealing process for incrementally designing a DW. We have chosen an input multiquery AO dag where the source relations are the dimension tables and the fact table presented in Section 3. The multiquery AO dag comprises both unary (generalized projection) and binary (natural join) operation nodes. It is reasonably sized so that an exhaustive algorithm can also be executed on it. We have adopted a simple cost model for evaluating the queries and maintaining the views. We consider that each view is maintained separately, and the materialized views are maintained by recomputation. The weights in the cost formulas are equal to 1. We have measured the time needed to execute the Simulated Annealing algorithm, and the quality of the solution returned when different factors of the problem vary. The quality of the solution is expressed as a percentage of the cost of the solution returned by the Simulated Annealing approach divided by the cost of the solution returned by the exhaustive algorithm. The varying factors are the size of the multiquery AO dag, the number of new queries, the number of marked nodes, and the parameter c in the cost function.

Experiment 1: The size of the Multiquery AO dag varies. This size is expressed as the number of view nodes in the Multiquery AO dag. Figures 4(a) and (b) plot the solution quality and the execution time against the number of view nodes in the multiquery AO dag. Each point in these and in the subsequent plots is averaged over four executions of the algorithm. The solution quality degrades as the number of view nodes increases but does not drop below 70%.

Experiment 2: The number of queries varies. Figures 4(c) and (d) plot the solution quality and the execution time against the number of query nodes in the multiquery AO dag. The solution quality increases and the execution time degrades as the number of query nodes increases. This is due to the fact that in contrast to the other view nodes, the query nodes are not removed from a multiquery AO dag by an application of the rules. Therefore, an increase in the number of the query nodes reduces the size of the search space.

Experiment 3: The number of marked nodes varies. Figures 4(e) and (f) plot the solution quality and the execution time against the number of marked nodes in the multiquery AO dag. The solution quality increases and the execution time degrades as the number of marked nodes increases. This is due to the facts that (a) the marked nodes are not removed from a multiquery AO dag by an application of the rules, and (b) their evaluation plans are removed from the multiquery AO dag. Therefore, as with the query nodes, an increase in the number of the marked nodes, reduces the size of the search space.

Experiment 4: The parameter c varies. Figures 4(g) and (h) plot the solution quality and the execution time against parameter c of the cost function. The solution quality increases and the execution time degrades as parameter c increases. This is due to the fact that when $c > 1$, the cost of a state is determined primarily by the materialized view maintenance cost. Low view maintenance cost

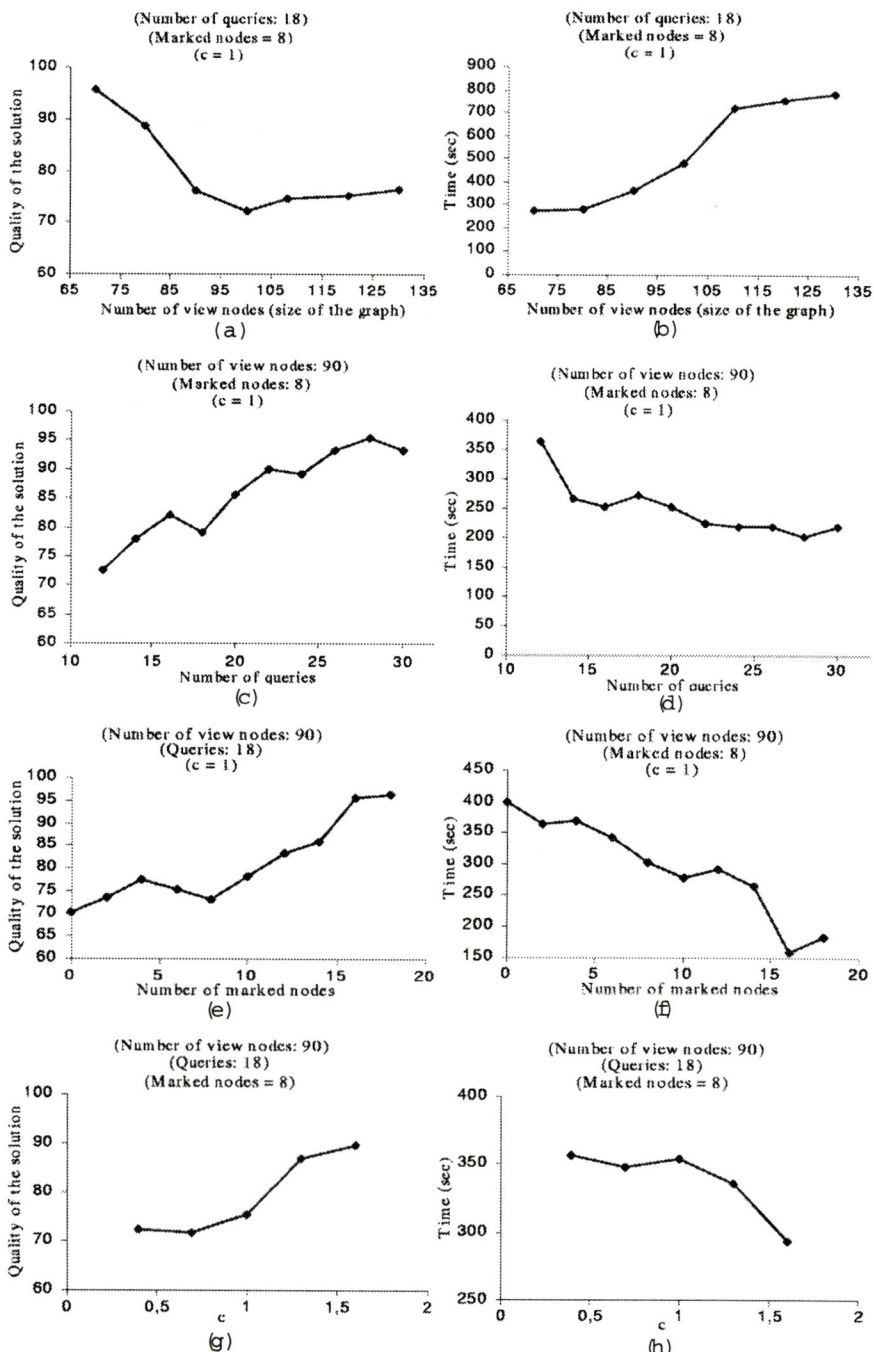

Fig. 4. Quality and time vs. number of view nodes, number of queries, number of marked view nodes and parameter c.

can be obtained by the states that are close to the initial state (that is, can be reached by few moves). In fact, if the cost of a state is determined uniquely by the view maintenance cost, the initial state has the minimal cost. The opposite happens when $c < 1$ where the cost of a state is determined primarily by the query evaluation cost.

6 Conclusion

Data Warehouses are dynamic entities that evolve over time. As the needs of the analysts grow new queries need to be satisfied. In general, new views need to be materialized either for satisfying the new queries or for performance reasons. Re-implementing the DW from scratch is complex and time consuming. A better solution is the incremental design of a DW where new views are materialized in order to minimize the combined evaluation cost of the new queries and the maintenance cost of the new views. A previous work on this problem provided theoretical foundations for a solution and an exhaustive algorithm. However, due to the size of the problem an exhaustive algorithm cannot be of practical interest in real cases.

We have presented a randomized approach based on the Simulated Annealing process for incrementally designing a DW. Simulated Annealing is an algorithm good for optimization problems with a large search space. The definition of the search space has been based on an AND/OR dag representation for multiple queries and views that is able to represent alternative evaluation plans of the queries from the materialized views and subexpression sharing among queries and between queries and views. Our approach has been implemented. The experimental results are encouraging and show the feasibility of the approach.

In this work we impose a constraint on a materialized view selection: the new views and the old views together must be able to answer all the new queries. An interesting extension of this work concerns the design of efficient approaches for the incremental design of a DW when additional constraints are imposed, as for instance, space or view maintenance cost constraints and integrity constraints.

References

1. E. Baralis, S. Paraboshi, and E. Teniente. Materialized view selection in a multidimensional database. In *Proc. of the 23rd VLDB Conf.*, pages 156–165, 1997.
2. S. Chaudhuri and U. Dayal. An Overview of Data Warehousing and OLAP Technology. *SIGMOD Record*, 26(1):65–74, 1997.
3. S. Cohen, W. Nutt, and A. Serebrenik. Rewriting aggregate queries using views. In *Proc. of the 18th ACM PODS Symp.*, pages 155–166, 1999.
4. S. Dar, H. V. Jagadish, A. Y. Levy, and D. Srivastava. Answering SQL Queries with Aggregation using Views. In *Proc. of the VLDB Conf.*, pages 318–329, 1996.
5. G. Graefe and W. J. McKenna. The Volcano Optimizer Generator: Extensibility and Efficient Search. In *Proc. of the 9th ICDE Conf.*, pages 209–217, 1993.
6. T. Griffin and L. Libkin. Incremental Maintenance of Views with Duplicates. In *Proc. of the ACM SIGMOD Conf.*, pages 328–339, 1995.

7. A. Gupta, V. Harinarayan, and D. Quass. Aggregate-Query Processing in Data Warehousing Environments. In *Proc. of the VLDB Conf.*, pages 358–369, 1995.
8. A. Gupta and I. S. Mumick. Maintenance of materialized views: Problems, techniques and applications. *Data Engineering*, 18(2):3–18, 1995.
9. H. Gupta. Selection of Views to Materialize in a Data Warehouse. In *Proc. of the 6th Intl. Conf. on Database Theory*, pages 98–112, 1997.
10. H. Gupta and I. S. Mumick. Selection of Views to Materialize Under a Maintenance Cost Constraint. In *Proc. of the 7th ICDT Conf.*, pages 453–470, 1999.
11. J. Hammer, H. Garcia-Molina, J. Widom, W. Labio, and Y. Zhuge. The Stanford Data Warehousing Project. *Data Engineering*, 18(2):41–48, 1995.
12. V. Harinarayan, A. Rajaraman, and J. D. Ullman. Implementing Data Cubes Efficiently. In *Proc. of the ACM SIGMOD Conf.*, 1996.
13. Y. Ioannidis and Y. Kang. Randomized algorithms for optimizing large join queries. In *Proc. of the ACM SIGMOD Conf.*, pages 9–22, 1990.
14. Y. Ioannidis and E. Wong. Query optimization by simulated annealing. In *Proc. of the ACM SIGMOD Intl. Conf. on Management of Data*, pages 9–22, 1987.
15. R. Kimball. *The Data Warehouse Toolkit*. John Wiley & Sons, 1996.
16. S. Kirkpatrick, C. D. Gelatt, and M. P. Vecchi. Optimization by simulated annealing. *Science*, 220(4598):671–680, 1983.
17. Y. Kotidis and N. Roussopoulos. DynaMat: A Dynamic View Management System for Data Warehouses. In *Proc. of the ACM SIGMOD Conf.*, pages 371–382, 1999.
18. A. Levy, A. O. Mendelson, Y. Sagiv, and D. Srivastava. Answering Queries using Views. In *Proc. of the ACM PODS Symp.*, pages 95–104, 1995.
19. D. Quass. Maintenance Expressions for Views with Aggregation. In *Workshop on Materialized Views: Techniques and Applications*, pages 110–118, 1996.
20. D. Quass, A. Gupta, I. S. Mumick, and J. Widom. Making Views Self Maintainable for Data Warehousing. In *Proc. of the 4th PDIS Conf.*, pages 158–169, 1996.
21. K. A. Ross, D. Srivastava, and S. Sudarshan. Materialized View Maintenance and Integrity Constraint Checking: Trading Space for Time. In *Proc. of the ACM SIGMOD Conf.*, pages 447–458, 1996.
22. M. Steinbrunn, G. Moerkotte, and A. Kemper. Heuristic and randomized optimization for the join ordering problem. *VLDB Journal*, 6:191–208, 1997.
23. A. Swami. Optimization of Large Join Queries: Combining Heuristics and Combinatorial Techniques. In *Proc. of the ACM SIGMOD Conf.*, pages 367–376, 1989.
24. A. Swami and A. Gupta. Optimization of Large Join Queries. In *Proc. of the ACM SIGMOD Intl. Conf. on Management of Data*, pages 8–17, 1988.
25. D. Theodoratos. Detecting Redundant Materialized Views in Data Warehouse Evolution. *Information Systems*, 26(5), 2001.
26. D. Theodoratos, S. Ligoudistianos, and T. Sellis. View Selection for Designing the Global Data Warehouse. To appear in *Data and Knowledge Engineering*.
27. D. Theodoratos and T. Sellis. Data Warehouse Configuration. In *Proc. of the 23rd Intl. Conf. on Very Large Data Bases*, pages 126–135, 1997.
28. D. Theodoratos and T. Sellis. Designing Data Warehouses. *Data and Knowledge Engineering, Elsevier*, 31(3):279–301, Oct. 1999.
29. D. Theodoratos and T. Sellis. Incremental Design of a Data Warehouse. *Journal of Intelligent Information Systems, Kluwer Academic Publishers*, 15(1):7–27, 2000.
30. J. Widom. Research Problems in Data Warehousing. In *Proc. of the 4th Intl. Conf. on Information and Knowledge Management*, pages 25–30, Nov. 1995.
31. J. Yang, K. Karlapalem, and Q. Li. Algorithms for Materialized View Design in Data Warehousing Environment. In *Proc. of the VLDB Conf.*, pages 136–145, 1997.

Semantics of Stereotypes for Type Specification in UML: Theory and Practice

François Pinet and Ahmed Lbath

Laboratory of Information System Engineering, INSA Lyon,
69621 Villeurbanne Cedex, France, and CIRIL SA, 69100 Villeurbanne, France
{fpinet, lbath}@lisi.insa-lyon.fr

Abstract. In the context of object-oriented formalism, stereotypes are presented as a new means for user-defined extensions of the Unified Modeling Language (UML). Unfortunately, the stereotypes syntax and semantics vary depending on the proposed extensions and it is not easy to propose a complete formalization of this mechanism. This is the reason why this paper tries to identify and formalize a pertinent set of stereotypes called stereotypes for type specification. This category of stereotypes was intuitively or implicitly presented in several works and has been experimented in different modeling methods, especially in the field of Geographic Information System (GIS). This paper proposes a complete study of this class of stereotypes and discusses the interest of their applications. Numerous examples will be presented in the field of GIS.

1 Introduction

Stereotypes provide a mechanism for extending the vocabulary of the Unified Modeling Language (UML). Indeed, the main goal of stereotypes is to adapt UML to specific fields such as real-time system, Geographic Information System (GIS), etc [1,2][4]. Since the introduction of the concept by Rebecca Wirfs-Brock [16], stereotypes have been used in numerous ways. In UML class diagrams, stereotypes usually define a secondary classification for objects which is independent of the classification by classes. In other words, it is possible to think of a stereotype as a type associated to class. In its simplest representation, a stereotype is rendered as a textual string enclosed by quotation marks; but stereotypes often have an associated iconic representation.

For example in most of GIS modeling methods, the proposed stereotypes focus on the geometry of the real-world entities [3,4][5-8][11,12]. Both a class Building and a class Lake can be associated to a stereotype <<Polygon>> (figure 1.a) that can also be represented by an icon (figure 1.b). In practice, stereotypes are often used as an alternative representation of inheritance. For example, classes of figures 1.a and 1.b can be viewed as classes that inherit from an implicit class Polygon. In the majority of cases, a class having a stereotype <<Polygon>> can be also rewritten as a class having an attribute of type Polygon (see figure 1.c). In this case, the type of this special attribute (named stereotyped attribute) directly corresponds to the type (i.e. the stereotype) of the class. This paper focuses on the category of stereotypes described in this example i.e. stereotypes that correspond to an implicit declaration of stereotyped attributes in class diagrams. These stereotypes are designed for class diagrams and will be called stereotypes for type specification.

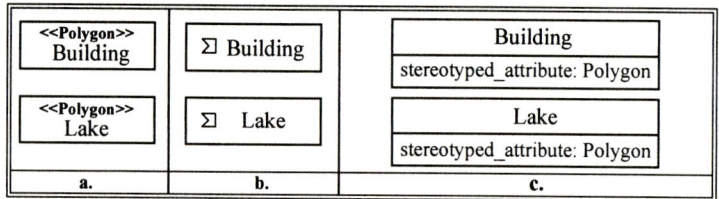

Fig. 1. Use of stereotypes for type specification: alternative representations

In several domain-specific modeling methods (for example in methods for GIS design), stereotypes can be combined in order to produce other stereotypes that correspond to complex types. For example, a class Waterway can be associated to a stereotype resulting from the combination of a stereotype <<Polyline>> and a stereotype <<Polygon>>. Indeed, the geometry of waterways is usually composed of a polyline (a river) and a polygon (a lake). Thus, this class implicitly contains a stereotyped attribute having a value domain constructed by the combination of polyline objects and polygon objects. Indeed, a value of the considered stereotyped attribute is a combination of objects having the type Polyline and objects having the type Polygon. The work of [4] introduces three combination operations for stereotypes: disjunction, conjunction, multiplicity operations. In the context of stereotyped attributes, these operations have the following semantics:

- disjunction operation between A and B; the value of the stereotyped attribute is either a value having the type A or a value having the type B (but not both).
- conjunction operation between A and B; the value of the stereotyped attribute is the combination of a value having the type A and a value having the type B.
- multiplicity operation between A and a multiplicity m; the value of the stereotyped attribute is composed of m values having the type A.

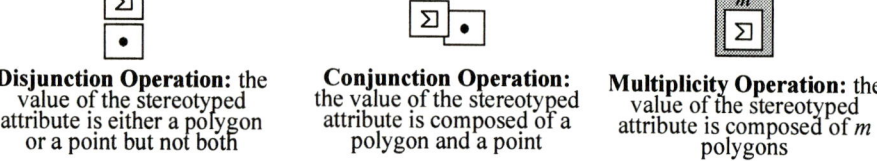

Disjunction Operation: the value of the stereotyped attribute is either a polygon or a point but not both

Conjunction Operation: the value of the stereotyped attribute is composed of a polygon and a point

Multiplicity Operation: the value of the stereotyped attribute is composed of m polygons

Fig. 2. Iconic representation of combination operations

Figure 2 presents an example of iconic representation of these operations in the context of GIS modeling. These three combination operations have not been arbitrarily chosen. Indeed, they are especially interesting because they allow the specification of all stereotypes resulting from the aggregation operation. The aggregation is one of the most important associations in object-oriented modeling [2]. For example, in class diagram of figure 3, an aggregation association is defined between a whole and its parts. In this example, a country (the whole) is composed of a frontier (a polygon), zero, one or many rivers (polylines), and a capital town (represented by either a point or a polygon but not both); according to the UML notation, a xor relation can link two aggregation associations. The type of the stereotyped attribute associated to the class Country (the whole class) is represented by a stereotype. This stereotype uses the new formalism presented in this paper, and corresponds to the aggregation of the types related to part stereotyped attributes. The multiplicity [0..*] is also introduced in the polyline stereotype of the whole; it means that the whole contains from zero to +∞ polylines.

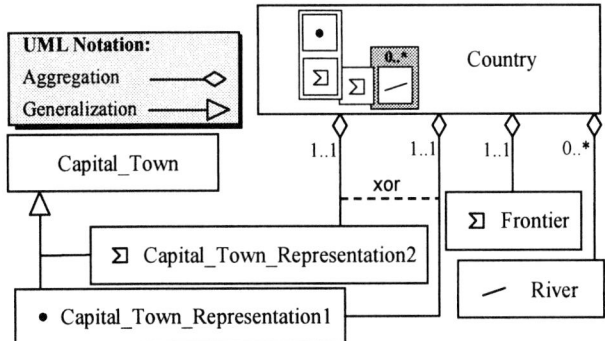

Fig. 3. Example of a class Country

As illustrated in the field of GIS, stereotypes for type specification provide a powerful tool that helps designers to adapt UML to a specific domain. The main contribution of this paper is to define the syntax and semantics of stereotypes for type specification in order to know exactly what it is possible to express in using this mechanism. The theoretic foundation presented in this paper can have several applications concerning:

- the implementation of an algorithm checking if two stereotypes have exactly the same semantics;
- concerning the aggregation, a process that generates a stereotype associated to a whole class from stereotypes associated to part classes.

Definitions presented in this paper will be exemplified in the field of GIS modeling but they can be applied in numerous other domains. Also, the work presented in this paper is part of the industrial AIGLE project. AIGLE is a CASE-Tool that supports the OMEGA method (Object-oriented Modeling for End-User Applications) [8]. AIGLE is marketed by the French Company CIRIL SA [9,10], and OMEGA is a UML-based method for the design of centralized [7,8] or distributed GIS [11][14]. The final goal is to integrate the presented work into OMEGA and AIGLE.

The rest of the paper is organized as follows. Section 2 describes syntax and semantics of stereotypes for type specification independently of the textual or iconic representation defined for combination operations. Section 3 establishes the semantics of stereotypes in the context of the aggregation, and presents the link existing between the stereotype of a whole class and stereotypes of its parts. Section 4 deals with the expressiveness of the stereotypes, and discusses the possibility to know if two stereotypes have the same semantics. Section 5 concludes and draws some perspectives for future work.

2 Syntax and Semantics of Stereotypes for Type Specification

2.1 Notation

The presented formalism uses two types of unordered collections: the set and the bag. The set doesn't contain duplicate elements; any element can be represented only once. A set is denoted by $\{element_1, \ldots, element_n\}$. Let S be a set, 2^S is the set of all subsets of S. The size of a set is its number of elements denoted by $|S|$. A bag is similar to a set, but it can contain duplicate elements; that is, the same element can occur in a bag more than once. A bag is denoted by $Bag\{element_1, \ldots, element_n\}$. The empty bag is $Bag\{\}$. The combination of bags is allowed by using the union operator. For example, $Bag\{a,b\} \cup Bag\{b,c\} \cup Bag\{\} = Bag\{a,b,b,c\}$. The cross-product (denoted by ×) provides the capability for combining sets of bags. Let S_1 and S_2 be two sets of bags, $S_1 \times S_2 = \{ Bag_i \cup Bag_j \mid Bag_i \in S_1 \text{ and } Bag_j \in S_2 \}$. For example, $\{ Bag\{a,b\}, Bag\{c\} \} \times \{ Bag\{c\} \} = \{ Bag\{a,b,c\}, Bag\{c,c\} \}$. The cross-product is associative. Also, because the bag is an unordered collection, the cross-product on sets of bags is commutative. S^n is the cross-product of S with itself n times; if applied to cross-product on a set of bags, $S^0 = \{Bag\{\}\}$; $S^1 = S$; $S^2 = S \times S$; $S^3 = S \times S \times S$; ... A multiplicity is denoted by $[min..max]$ with $min, max \in [0..+\infty[$ and $min \leq max$. Also, $+\infty$ is denoted by *.

2.2 Definition of Simple and Complex Stereotypes

In fact, stereotypes for type specification correspond to types of implicit stereotyped attributes. Consequently, the semantics of stereotypes can be represented by the value domains of these attributes. This subsection defines the concept of simple type. The domain of values of a simple type t is a set of bags that contain only one element. Let $Dom(\text{t})$ be the domain of values related to a type t. The value of a stereotyped attribute having a type t must match with one and only one bag in $Dom(\text{t})$. For example, in class diagrams of object-oriented methods for GIS, each class has one (and only one) implicit stereotyped attribute and a stereotype that represents the geographic type of this attribute. The value of a stereotyped attribute is an unordered collection (more precisely a bag) of geographic objects. In the following, geographic types will be called geoTypes. The simple geoTypes considered in this paper are: point, polyline, polygon, circle. Their domains of values are sets composed of bags that contain respectively one object point, polyline, polygon, or circle. For example, $Dom(\text{circle})$ is the infinite set of bags that contain one object circle, $Dom(\text{circle}) = \{ Bag\{circle_1\}, \ldots, Bag\{circle_i\}, \ldots \}$.

Semantics of Stereotypes for Type Specification in UML: Theory and Practice 343

Stereotype syntax. Each simple type can be visually represented in class diagrams by a stereotype. For that, a function *ToType* can be defined in order to associate a type t to a visual representation. The function *ToType* takes a visual representation as parameter and returns its associated simple type. The function that takes a type as parameter and returns its visual representation is called *ToVisu*. For example, figure 4 presents a correspondence between simple geoTypes and iconic stereotypes in using a specific definition of *ToType* and *ToVisu*. As described in definition 1, the set of all stereotypes related to a set T of simple types is $SType_{Simple}(T)$.

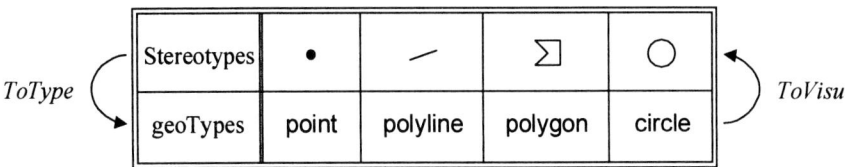

Fig. 4. Example of correspondence between simple geoTypes and iconic stereotypes

DEFINITION 1. *Let ToVisu be a function that takes a simple type as parameter and returns its associated visual representation. Let T be a set of simple types,*

$$STypes_{Simple}(T) = \{\ ToVisu(t_i) \mid t_i \in T\ \}$$

Let ToType be a function such as $\forall t \in T,\ ToType(ToVisu(t)) = t$

Conjunction, disjunction and multiplicity operations can be introduced in order to specify complex types. A complex type is composed by conjunction and disjunction between simple types. Let /4 and 01 be respectively visual operators related to the conjunction operation and the disjunction operation. Let ⊕ be a visual operator that associates a stereotype to a multiplicity. For example, a definition of these visual operators for geoTypes was described in figure 2. The use of these visual operators on stereotypes returns new stereotypes related to complex types (see definition 2).

DEFINITION 2. *Let Mult be the infinite set of multiplicities. The infinite set called $SType_{Complex}$ of all complex stereotypes is constructed by the following two rules. T is a set of simple types,*

$$x, y \in SType_{Simple}(T)\ \lor\ x, y \in SType_{Complex}(T)\ \rightarrow$$
$$(x\ /4\ y) \in SType_{Complex}(T)\ \land\ (x\ 01\ y) \in SType_{Complex}(T)$$
$$(\ x \in SType_{Simple}(T)\ \lor\ x \in SType_{Complex}(T)\ )\ \land\ m \in Mult\ \rightarrow\ (x \oplus m) \in SType_{Complex}(T)$$

The infinite set of all stereotypes related to T is SType,

$$SType(T) = SType_{Simple}(T) \cup SType_{Complex}(T)$$

Stereotype semantics. Another step is to define the function Dom_{SType} that associates a value domain to an element of $SType(T)$.

DEFINITION 3. *Let Dom_{Mult} be a function that applies a multiplicity $[min..max]$ on a value domain d. The result is a value domain.*

$$Dom_{Mult}(d, [min..max]) = d^{min} \cup ... \cup d^k \cup ... \cup d^{max} \quad \text{with } min \leq k \leq max$$

Let T be a set of simple types. The definition of Dom_{SType} is given by

d1. $Dom_{SType}(x) = Dom(ToType(x))$ *if* $x \in SType_{Simple}(T)$
d2. $Dom_{SType}(x\ /4\ y) = Dom_{SType}(x) \times Dom_{SType}(y)$
d3. $Dom_{SType}(x\ 01\ y) = Dom_{SType}(x) \cup Dom_{SType}(y)$
d4. $Dom_{SType}(x \oplus m) = Dom_{Mult}(Dom_{SType}(x), m)$

Dom_{SType} provides the exact semantics of stereotypes. Let $x, y \in SType(T)$; the stereotypes x and y have the same semantics iff $Dom_{SType}(x) = Dom_{SType}(y)$.

In fact, Dom_{Mult} applies the multiplicity effect to a value domain. For example,

$Dom_{Mult}(Dom(\texttt{circle}), [0..2]) = Dom(\texttt{circle})^0 \cup Dom(\texttt{circle})^1 \cup Dom(\texttt{circle})^2$
$= \{Bag\{\}\} \cup \{\ Bag\{circle_i\}, ... , Bag\{circle_i\}, ...\ \}$
$\cup (\ \{\ Bag\{circle_i\}, ... , Bag\{circle_i\}, ...\ \} \times \{\ Bag\{circle_i\}, ... , Bag\{circle_j\}, ...\ \}\ )$
$= \{\ Bag\{\}, Bag\{circle_i\}, ... , Bag\{circle_i\}, ... , Bag\{circle_i, circle_i\}, ... ,$
$Bag\{circle_i, circle_j\}, ...\ \}$

Intuitively, the application of the multiplicity $[0..2]$ on $Dom(\texttt{circle})$ returns the value domain composed of bags that contain from 0 to 2 circles.

The function Dom_{SType} decomposes the value domain of a stereotype into cross-products and unions of simple type domains. While the cross-product corresponds to a conjunction between value domains, the union is a disjunction between value domains. Remember that because a bag is an unordered collection, the cross-product on sets of bags is associative and commutative. Thus, all theoretic evaluations of Dom_{SType} with a specific input provide the same result. Figure 5 exemplifies an evaluation of Dom_{SType} with the visual operators defined in figure 2.

The next small examples briefly illustrate the fact that two distinct combinations of stereotypes can lead to the same semantics, even if combined stereotypes are syntactically different. Let t_1, t_2, t_3, t_4 be four distinct simple types having four distinct visual representations. Also, all simple types considered in this first example have distinct semantics.

$Dom(t_1) = \{\ Bag\{a\}, Bag\{b\}\ \}$ $\quad$ $Dom(t_2) = \{\ Bag\{c\}, Bag\{d\}\ \}$
$Dom(t_3) = \{\ Bag\{a\}, Bag\{c\}\ \}$ $\quad$ $Dom(t_4) = \{\ Bag\{b\}, Bag\{d\}\ \}$

Let x, y be two stereotypes such as

$$x = ToVisu(t_1) \text{ 01 } ToVisu(t_2) \quad \text{and} \quad y = ToVisu(t_3) \text{ 01 } ToVisu(t_4)$$

In this case, $Dom_{SType}(x) = Dom_{SType}(y) = \{ Bag\{a\}, Bag\{b\}, Bag\{c\}, Bag\{d\} \}$.
x and y are syntactically different but they have exactly the same semantics.
In the same way, let t_1, t_2 be other distinct simple types,

$$Dom(t_1) = \{ Bag\{a\} \} \quad \text{and} \quad Dom(t_2) = \{ Bag\{b\} \}$$

Let x, y be two new stereotypes such as

$$x = (ToVisu(t_1) \oplus [0..1]) / 4 ((ToVisu(t_2) \text{ 01 } ToVisu(t_1)) \oplus [0..1])$$
$$y = ((ToVisu(t_1) \oplus [0..1]) / 4 (ToVisu(t_2) \oplus [0..1])) \text{ 01 } (ToVisu(t_1) \oplus [0..2])$$

In this case, $Dom_{SType}(x) = Dom_{SType}(y) = \{ Bag\{\}, Bag\{a\}, Bag\{b\}, Bag\{a,a\}, Bag\{a,b\} \}$. Once again, x and y have exactly the same semantics.

3 Aggregation

In UML class diagrams, most of classes collaborate with others in a number of different ways. This collaboration can be formulated by associations (also called relationships). Aggregation is a special form of association between instances, where one of them (the whole) is assembled from others (the parts). In this section, a function will be defined in order to determine the domain related to the stereotype of the whole class from domains of stereotypes associated to the part classes. This definition gives the behavior of the stereotypes when aggregation is used.
Formal structure. The first step is to describe a formal structure for aggregation associations and xor relations existing between them.

DEFINITION 4. Let $P(C') = \{ R_1(C_1, min_1, max_1), \ldots, R_n(C_n, min_n, max_n) \}$. $P(C')$ is the set of relationships aggregating a class C'. For each relationships R_i, the part class is C_i and min_i, max_i are the multiplicity implied in R_i.

Let $X(C') = \{ \{R_i, R_j\}, \ldots, \{R_u, R_v\} \}$. $X(C')$ is the set of all binary relations xor between distinct elements of $P(C')$.

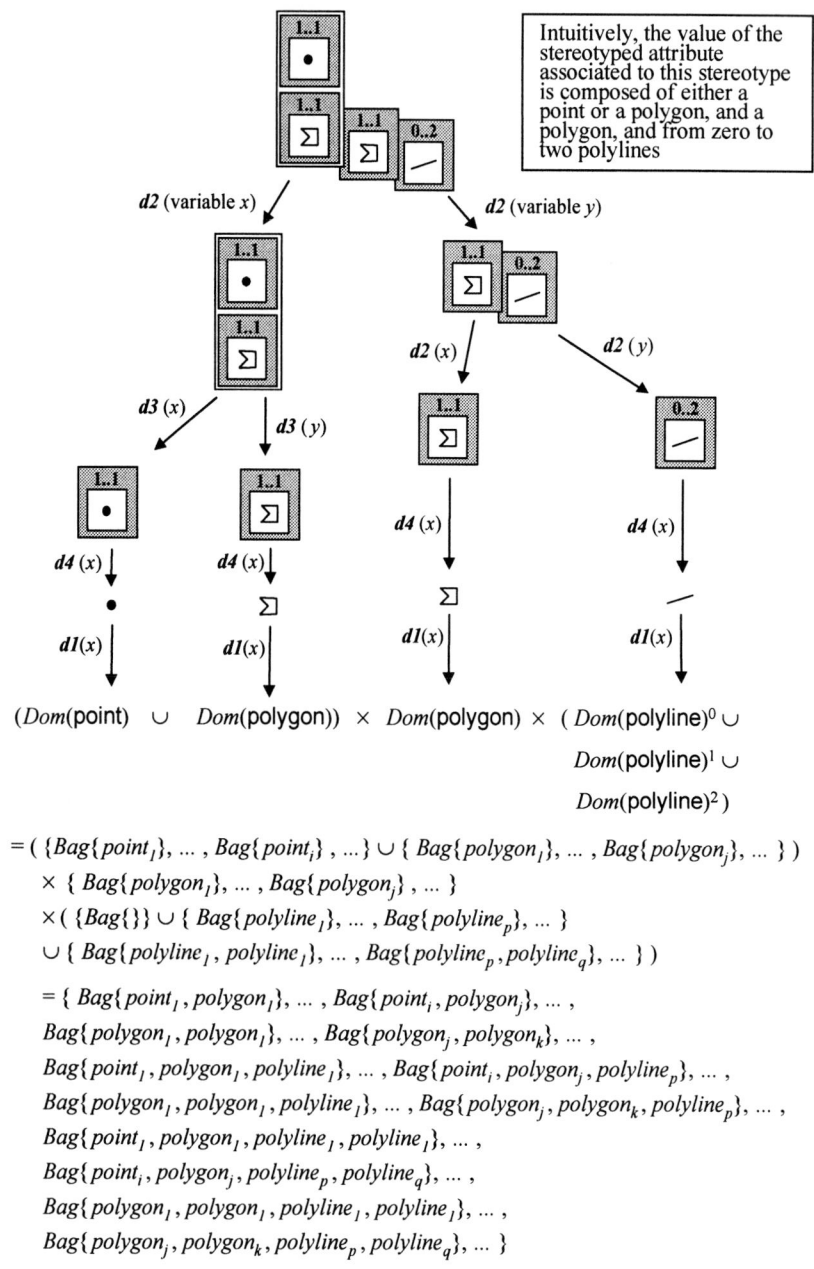

$$= (\{Bag\{point_1\}, ... , Bag\{point_i\}, ... \} \cup \{ Bag\{polygon_1\}, ... , Bag\{polygon_j\}, ... \})$$
$$\times \{ Bag\{polygon_1\}, ... , Bag\{polygon_j\}, ... \}$$
$$\times (\{Bag\{\}\} \cup \{ Bag\{polyline_1\}, ... , Bag\{polyline_p\}, ... \}$$
$$\cup \{ Bag\{polyline_1, polyline_1\}, ... , Bag\{polyline_p, polyline_q\}, ... \})$$

$$= \{ Bag\{point_1, polygon_1\}, ... , Bag\{point_i, polygon_j\}, ... ,$$
$$Bag\{polygon_1, polygon_1\}, ... , Bag\{polygon_j, polygon_k\}, ... ,$$
$$Bag\{point_1, polygon_1, polyline_1\}, ... , Bag\{point_i, polygon_j, polyline_p\}, ... ,$$
$$Bag\{polygon_1, polygon_1, polyline_1\}, ... , Bag\{polygon_j, polygon_k, polyline_p\}, ... ,$$
$$Bag\{point_1, polygon_1, polyline_1, polyline_1\}, ... ,$$
$$Bag\{point_i, polygon_j, polyline_p, polyline_q\}, ... ,$$
$$Bag\{polygon_1, polygon_1, polyline_1, polyline_1\}, ... ,$$
$$Bag\{polygon_j, polygon_k, polyline_p, polyline_q\}, ... \}$$

Fig. 5. Example of Dom_{SType} evaluation

Because binary xor relations are symmetric and irreflexive, elements of $X(C')$ are sets having a size equal to 2. In the example of figure 3,

$P(Country) = \{$ $R_1(Capital\_Town\_Representation1, 1, 1)$,
$R_2(Capital\_Town\_Representation2, 1, 1)$,
$R_3(Frontier, 1, 1)$, $R_4(River, 0, +\infty)$ $\}$
$X(Country) = \{ \{R_1, R_2\} \}$

DEFINITION 5. *Let ToSType be a function that takes as parameter an element R_i of $P(C')$, and returns the stereotype of the class C_i associated to R_i.*

DEFINITION 6. *Let $Dom_{Class} = ToSType \bullet Dom_{SType}$; the composition of ToSType followed by Dom_{SType}.*

For $R_4 \in P(Country)$, $Dom_{Class}(R_4) = Dom_{SType}(ToSType(R_4)) = Dom(\texttt{polyline})$.

Multiplicity effect. The second step is to study the effect of the multiplicity on a domain of a type. This is given by the function Dom_{MultR}.

DEFINITION 7. *Let $R(C, min, max)$ be an element of $P(C')$,*

$$Dom_{MultR}(R) = Dom_{Mult}(Dom_{Class}(R), [min..max])$$

For $R_4 \in P(Country)$,
$$Dom_{MultR}(R_4) =$$
$Dom(\texttt{polyline})^0 \cup Dom(\texttt{polyline})^1 \cup Dom(\texttt{polyline})^2 \cup Dom(\texttt{polyline})^3 \cup$
...

For example, the application of the multiplicity [0..*] on $Dom(\texttt{polyline})$ (which is the part value domain) returns the infinite set of all bags that contain only polylines (which is the whole value domain).

Link between the whole and its parts. The last step is to precisely define the link between the value domain of the whole and the value domain of its parts.

DEFINITION 8. *Let $Q_{\neg xor}(C')$ and $Q_{xor}(C')$ be two sets of sets. Each element of $Q_{\neg xor}(C')$ is composed of an association not implied in a xor relation.*

$$Q_{\neg xor}(C') = \{ \{R_i\} \mid R_i \in P(C') \text{ and } \forall S \in X(C'), R_i \notin S \}$$

Each element of $Q_{xor}(C')$ is composed of associations implied in a xor relation. $Q_{xor}(C') \subseteq 2^{P(C')}$. Let $S \in 2^{P(C')}$, $S \in Q_{xor}(C')$ iff
$(\forall R_i, R_j \in S \text{ such as } R_i \neq R_j, \{R_i, R_j\} \in X(C'))$ *and*
$(\forall R_i \in P(C') \text{ such as } R_i \notin S, \exists R_j \in S \text{ such as } \{R_i, R_j\} \notin X(C'))$ *and* $|S| \geq 2$

Let $Q(C') = Q_{\neg xor}(C') \cup Q_{xor}(C')$.

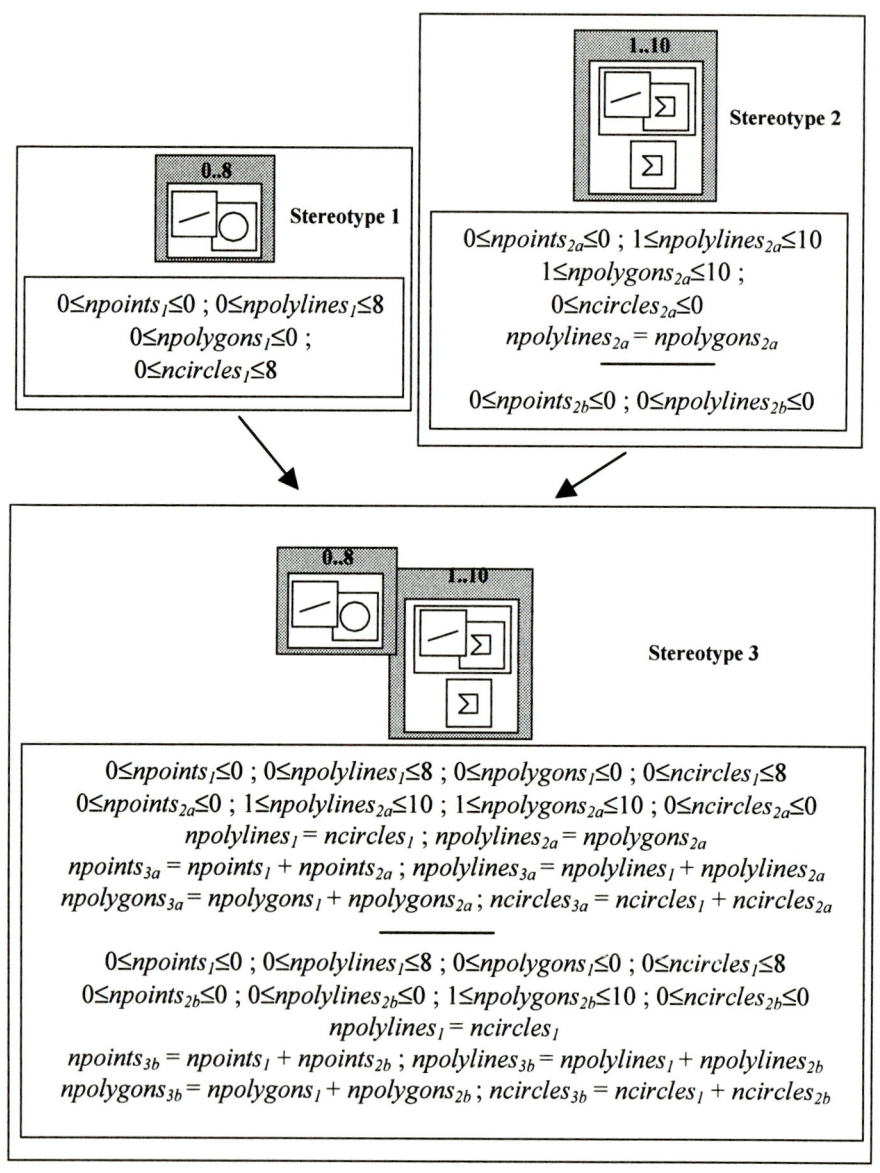

Fig. 6. Finite representation for stereotypes: sets of numeric constraints

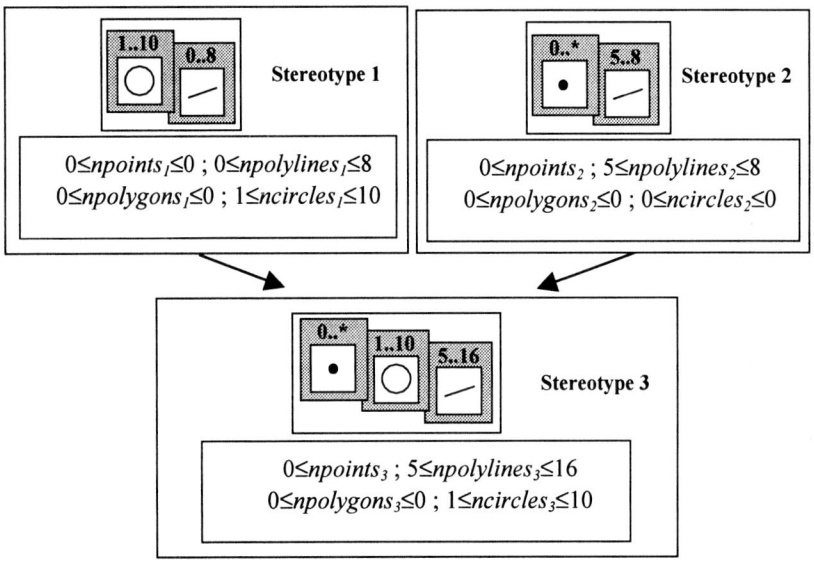

Fig. 7. Syntax simplification and sets of constraints

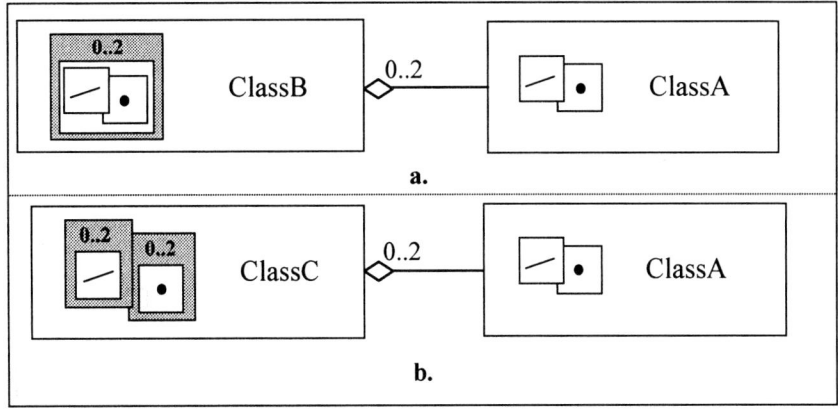

Fig. 8. Example using syntax simplification

Thus, $Q_{xor}(C')$ assembles binary xor relations in order to compose sets of n-arity xor relations. For example, if $X(C') = \{\{R_a, R_b\}, \{R_a, R_c\}, \{R_b, R_c\}\}$ then $Q_{xor}(C') = \{\{R_a, R_b, R_c\}\}$. In the previous example, $Q_{\neg xor}(Country) = \{\{R_3\}, \{R_4\}\}$; $Q_{xor}(Country) = \{\{R_1, R_2\}\}$; $Q(Country) = \{\{R_3\}, \{R_4\}, \{R_1, R_2\}\}$. Finally, the value domain of the stereotype associated to a whole class can be defined from its parts by the function Dom_{Whole}. This function is defined below and takes as parameter $Q(C')$.

DEFINITION 9. Let $Q(C') = \{\{R_{11}, \ldots, R_{1m}\}, \ldots, \{R_{np}, \ldots, R_{nq}\}\}$. $Dom_{Whole}(Q(C')) = (Dom_{MultR}(R_{11}) \cup \ldots \cup Dom_{MultR}(R_{1m})) \times \ldots \times (Dom_{MultR}(R_{np}) \cup \ldots \cup Dom_{MultR}(R_{nq}))$

More intuitively, $Q(C')$ can be viewed as a conjunctive normal form of associations. Indeed, conjunction operations link the elements of $Q(C')$ and disjunction operations link elements of each set that is included in $Q(C')$. In the previous example, the value related to the stereotyped attribute of a Country instance is composed of a polygon issued from R_3 and polylines issued from R_4 and (a point issued from R_1 (exclusive) or a polygon issued from R_2). Also, the function Dom_{Whole} applies the multiplicity on the value domain associated to the stereotype of each part class by using the function Dom_{MultR}. For example,

$Dom_{Whole}(Q(Country)) = Dom_{MultR}(R_3) \times Dom_{MultR}(R_4) \times (Dom_{MultR}(R_1) \cup Dom_{MultR}(R_2))$
$= Dom(\texttt{polygon}) \times Dom_{MultR}(R_4) \times (Dom(\texttt{point}) \cup Dom(\texttt{polygon}))$

The result of $Dom_{MultR}(R_4)$ was previously presented. To summarise this subsection, $P(C')$ and $X(C')$ are the formal structures of an aggregation. C' is the whole class. Dom_{Whole} is a function that determines the value domain (i.e. the semantics) of the stereotype associated to C'. Dom_{Whole} uses both the function Dom_{MultR} and the set $Q(C')$ constructed from $P(C')$ and $X(C')$.

4 Computation of Stereotype Semantics

4.1 Semantic Equivalence

It can be very interesting to know if two stereotypes have exactly the same semantics i.e. if they are associated with the same value domain. Unfortunately, it is often impossible or not reasonable to compute directly cross-products and unions of value domains in order to compare value domains of two stereotypes; in other words, it is often impossible or not reasonable to use Dom_{SType} and Dom_{Whole} to determine if two stereotypes are equivalent. Thus, this subsection presents intuitively a finite form of value domains related to stereotypes. This finite form is suitable for the semantic equivalence checking. Indeed, as presented in figure 6, each stereotype can be represented by a set of numeric constraints. The constraints of a stereotype x "decorated" by a multiplicity are related to the number of elements in bags included in the value domain associated to x. The first part of these constraints consists of inequalities that give absolute boundaries for each simple type. The general form of these inequalities is $min \leq n(t) \leq max$ where $n(t)$ is number of elements having the simple type t in a bag of the considered value domain. *min* and *max* are the boundaries of $n(t)$. For example, in numeric constraints of stereotype 1 presented in figure 6, the inequalities show that each bag of the considered value domain contains from 0 to 8 polylines, and from 0 to 8 circles. In the same way, the numeric constraints of stereotype 2 in figure 6 show that each bag of the considered value domain contains (2a) from 1 to 10 polylines and from 1 to 10 polygons, or (2b) only from 1 to 10 polygons.

The second part of numeric constraints is composed of equalities that underline the dependencies existing between element numbers of each bag. For example, a dependency exists between the number of polylines and the number of circles in each bag included in the value domain of the stereotype 1 (figure 6). This is due to the fact that a multiplicity is applied on a conjunction between a type Polyline and a type Circle. This leads to an equality between the number of polylines and the number of circles. In other words, the number of polylines and the number of circles are the same in each bag of the considered value domain.

The stereotype 3 in figure 6 corresponds to the conjunction of stereotypes 1 and 2 that are both "decorated" with a multiplicity. The constraints of the stereotype 3 consist of the union between the constraints of stereotype 1 and the constraints of stereotype 2. It becomes possible to know if two stereotypes have the same semantics by comparing their numeric constraints. It is important to notice that this method cannot be directly applied in the case of dependent simple types i.e. if it exists two distinct types which are dependent. Two simple types t_1 and t_2 are dependent iff $Dom(t_1) \cap Dom(t_2) \neq \emptyset$.

4.2 Expressiveness Vs Simplicity

The UML-based method described in [4] use multiplicity operator only on simple stereotypes. This constraint simplifies the syntax of stereotypes and increases the readability of stereotypes in preventing complex combinations of multiplicities. This new syntax of complex stereotypes is presented in definition 10.

DEFINITION 10. *Let Mult be the infinite set of multiplicities. The infinite set of all complex stereotypes is constructed by the following rules. T is a set of simple types,*

$$x, y \in SType_{Simple}(T) \lor x, y \in SType_{Complex}(T) \rightarrow$$
$$(x / 4 y) \in SType_{Complex}(T) \land (x \; 01 \; y) \in SType_{Complex}(T)$$
$$x \in SType_{Simple}(T) \land m \in Mult \rightarrow (x \oplus m) \in SType_{Complex}(T)$$

The semantic definition of this new stereotype set is left unchanged. Each element of this new stereotype set can be represented by inequalities. Equalities representing dependencies existing between element numbers of each bag are unnecessary. Figure 7 exemplifies the representation of these stereotypes by constraints. The union of constraints associated to these stereotypes becomes trivial.

Unfortunately, this new set of stereotypes cannot represent all stereotypes issued from aggregations. For example, the figure 8.a describes an aggregation using the stereotype definition 2. No stereotype issued from the definition 10 can have the semantics of the whole stereotype of this aggregation. Indeed, it is not possible to express the dependencies existing between the number of points and the number of polylines in using stereotypes presented in definition 10. As described in figure 8.b, the semantics can only be approximate. Let x be the whole stereotype of figure 8.a (issued from definition 2), and y be its approximation presented in figure 8.b (issued from definition 10), $Dom_{SType}(x) \subset Dom_{SType}(y)$. Thus, $Dom_{SType}(x) \neq Dom_{SType}(y)$. Indeed,

$$Dom_{SType}(x) = (Dom(\texttt{polyline}) \times Dom(\texttt{point}))^0 \cup$$
$$(Dom(\texttt{polyline}) \times Dom(\texttt{point}))^1 \cup$$
$$(Dom(\texttt{polyline}) \times Dom(\texttt{point}))^2$$
$$Dom_{SType}(y) = (Dom(\texttt{polyline})^0 \cup Dom(\texttt{polyline})^1 \cup Dom(\texttt{polyline})^2) \times$$
$$(Dom(\texttt{point})^0 \cup Dom(\texttt{point})^1 \cup Dom(\texttt{point})^2)$$

Let $B = Bag\{ polyline_i, polyline_j, point_k \}$. $B \in Dom_{SType}(y)$ but $B \notin Dom_{SType}(x)$.

Nevertheless, in the context of visual representation and in many other cases this approximation can be acceptable. The work of [13] presents an algorithm for semantic equivalence checking adapted to stereotypes using this syntactic simplification.

5 Perspectives

From a broad variety of common stereotype uses [1], this paper identifies a pertinent category of stereotypes (called stereotypes for type specification). This particular form of stereotypes has already proven its effectiveness in domain-specific applications design (for example in the field of GIS). This paper proposes theoretic syntax and semantics for this class of stereotypes (section 1-3), and studies its practical interest (section 4). The expressiveness of stereotypes introduced in [13] was also discussed in section 4.2. The presented formalism can be reused for other stereotype specifications. Also, as specified in introduction, the two major applications of the presented work concern:
- the definition of an algorithm for semantic equivalence checking (see section 4),
- the definition of an algorithm for automatic generation of stereotypes resulting from aggregations (see work presented in section 3 and [13]).

In the context of the AIGLE project, these two types of algorithms are being investigated [15]. At the conceptual level, it is very interesting for users of the CASE Tool AIGLE to exactly know the geographic type resulting from an aggregation and the corresponding stereotype. Indeed, this functionality can help designers to avoid conceptual errors in OMEGA class diagrams. In the same way, an algorithm for semantic equivalence checking can provide the capability to know if two versions of a class diagram are equivalent. AIGLE will support these new functionalities soon.

References

1. Berner, S., Glinz, M., Joos, S.: A Classification of Stereotypes for Object-Oriented Modeling Languages. In: Proc. of Int. Conference on the Unified Modeling Language. Springer-Verlag. Germany (1999) 249-264
2. Booch, G., Rumbaugh, J., Jacobson, I.: The Unified Modeling Language User Guide. Addison-Wesley (1999)
3. Borges, K., Laender, A., Clodoveu, D.: Spatial Data Integrity Constraints in Object Oriented Geographic Data Modeling. In: Proc. of the Int. Symposium on Geographic Information System. ACM Press. USA (1999) 1-6
4. Brodeur, J., Bedard, Y., Proulx, M.: Modelling Geospatial Databases using UML-based Repositories Aligned with International Standards in Geomatics. In: Proc. of the Int. Symposium on Geographic Information System. ACM Press. USA (2000) 39-46
5. Jugurta, L.F., Cirano, L.: Specifying Analysis Patterns for Geographic Databases on the Basis of a Conceptual Framework. In: Proc. of the Int. Symposium on Geographic Information System. ACM Press. USA (1999) 7-13
6. Kösters, G., Pagel, B., Six, H.: GIS-Application Development with GeoOOA. Int. Journal of Geographical Information Science, Vol.11(4). Taylor & Francis (1997) 307-335
7. Laurini, R.: Information Systems for Urban Planning. Taylor & Francis (2001)
8. Lbath, A.: AIGLE: a Visual Environment for Design and Automatic Generation of Geographic Applications. Phd Thesis. INSA Lyon. France (1997)
9. Lbath, A., Pinet, F.: The Development and Customization of GIS-Based Applications and Web-Based GIS Applications with the CASE Tool AIGLE. In: Proc. of the Int. Symposium on Geographic Information System (Industrial Track). ACM Press. USA (2000) 194-196
10. Lbath, A., Pinet, F.: Automatic Generation of Geographic Urban Applications for the Web with the CASE Tool AIGLE. In: Proc. of the Int. Symposium on Urban and Regional Data Management. Netherlands (2000) 6p
11. Lbath, A., Pinet, F.: Towards Conceptual Modelling of TeleGeoProcessing Applications. In: Proc. of the Int. Symposium on TeleGeoProcessing. France (2000) 25-39
12. Parent, C., Spaccapietra, S., Zimanyia, E.: Spatio-Temporal Conceptual Models: Data Structures + Space + Time. In: Proc. of the Int. Symposium on Geographic Information System. ACM Press. USA (1999) 26-33
13. Pinet, F., Lbath, A.: An Algorithm for Stereotype Deduction in UML-Based Formalism and its Application in Geographic Information Systems. In: Proc. of the Int. Symposium on Human-Centric Computing Languages and Environments (Visual/Multimedia Approaches to Programming and Software Engineering). IEEE Press. Italy (2001) 8p
14. Pinet, F., Lbath, A.: A Visual Modelling Language for Distributed Geographic Information Systems. In: Proc. of the Int. Symposium on Visual Languages. IEEE Press. USA (2000) 75-76
15. Pinet, F., Lbath, A.: Stereotypes in UML-Based Formalism. Technical Report. LISI INSA Lyon. France (2001)
16. Wirfs-Brock, R., Wilkerson, B., Wiener, L.: Responsibility-Driven Design: Adding to your Conceptual Toolkit. ROAD, Vol.1(2). (1994) 27-34

Towards Ontologically Based Semantics for UML Constructs

Joerg Evermann and Yair Wand

The University of British Columbia
Faculty of Commerce and Business Administration
evermann@interchange.ubc.ca, yair.wand@ubc.ca

Abstract. Conceptual models are formal descriptions of application domains that are used in early stages of system development to support requirements analysis.

The Unified Modeling Language was formed by integrating several diagramming techniques for the purpose of software specification, design, construction and maintenance. It would be advantageous to use the same modeling method throughout the development process of an information system, namely, to extend the use of UML to conceptual modeling. This would require assigning well-defined, real-world meaning to UML constructs.

In order to model the real-world, we need to specify what might exist in the world, namely, an ontology. We suggest that by mapping UML constructs to well-defined ontological concepts, we can form clear semantics for UML diagrams. Furthermore, based on the mapping we can suggest ontologically-based intra- and inter-diagram integrity rules to guide the construction of conceptual models.

In this paper we describe the results we obtained by mapping UML constructs to a specific well-formalized ontological model. In particular, we discuss the ontological meaning of objects, classes, and of interactions.

1 Introduction

This paper is concerned with conceptual modeling: "Conceptual modeling is the activity of formally describing some aspects of the physical and social world around us for purposes of understanding and communication" (Mylopoulos, 1992). Understanding and describing the real world system is the first step in the information system analysis and design (ISAD) process. The result is the *conceptual* or *enterprise model* that is used as an input to the design phase dealing with the information system to be constructed.

In order to describe the real world system in a model, we must specify what exists in this world. Ontology is the branch of philosophy that deals with what exists, or is assumed to exist. An ontological model makes specific assumptions about what exists and how things behave.

The description of an information system that is developed in the design phase differs from the initial description of the real world in the analysis phase because the context is increasingly shaped by technical considerations as we progress along the development process.

The transition from analysis to design in the system development process introduces two problems for developers. First, the object of modeling changes (from a real world domain to the information system artifact). Second, the description language changes as well.

Clearly, using the same modeling language for analysis and design has the potential advantage of eliminating confusion and translation problems.

The Unified Modeling Language (UML) (Bezivin and Muller, 1999; OMG, 1999) has become widely used as a way to describe elements of an information system during the design phase. There presently exist no generally-accepted guidelines how to use UML for modeling a real world system. In this work, we propose to examine the usability of UML as a language for describing the real world by mapping its constructs to a set of real-world concepts, that is, to an *ontology*. This mapping will provide real-world semantics to UML constructs originally intended to model software elements. [1]

If the ontology chosen includes specific assumptions about concepts in the worlds, the ontological mapping can lead to modeling rules and guidelines on *how* to use UML to model real-world systems. Such rules and guidelines can serve to reduce semantic ambiguity in conceptual modeling (Wand et al., 1999), but might not be obvious or applicable when UML is used for design purposes only. It is important that such rules do not necessarily guide us how to perceive the world. Thus, we might suggest rules how to model things and classes, but not how to identify them. Furthermore, since various UML constructs might map into related ontological constructs, we can generate ontologically-based intra- and inter-diagram integrity rules to test the correctness and guide the construction of conceptual models.

Due to space limitations, we cannot examine all UML constructs here. Rather, the paper attempts to show the feasibility of the approach and present some useful results. Specifically, we focus here on the ontological meaning of objects and classes, of state dynamics and of interactions.

Method of This Study

This paper follows the notion of *ontological expressiveness* of modeling languages (Wand and Weber, 1993). The mapping from the constructs of a modeling language into ontological concepts is called *interpretation mapping*. Analysis of this mapping can identify language elements that have no ontological counterpart (construct excess) or have multiple ontological interpretations (construct

---

[1] There have been other works on assigning semantics to UML constructs (Evans et al., 1999; Knapp, 1999; Lano and Bicarregui, 1999; Lilius and Paltor, 1999; Övergaard, 1999; Övergaard and Palmkvist, 1999). The OMG itself is also concerned with UML semantics (OMG, 2000). However, all of these works relate to internal consistency and the formalization of UML, not to its relationship to the real world.

overload). Use of a construct without ontological meaning may lead to an ontologically meaningless model. Construct overload may lead to ambiguous models which might cause false interpretations during the analysis and design process and result in a faulty information system.

The specific ontology we chose for our purposes is based on Bunge's work (Bunge, 1977, 1979) as applied in a number of studies related to modeling in information systems analysis (Wand and Weber, 1989, 1990, 1993; Wand et al., 1999). We will refer to this ontology as the BWW-ontology. We chose Bunge's ontology as the basis for our work for a number of reasons:

- It is well formalized in terms of set theory and has not been developed specifically for use in information systems analysis and design.
- It has been successfully adapted to information systems modeling and shown to provide a good benchmark for the evaluation of modeling languages and methods (Green and Rosemann, 2000; Opdahl and Sindre, 1993; Opdahl and Henderson-Sellers, 1999; Opdahl et al., 1999; Parsons and Wand, 1997; Wand and Weber, 1989, 1993; Wand et al., 1999).
- It has been used to suggest an ontological meaning to object concepts (Wand, 1989).
- It has been empirically shown to lead to useful outcomes by Bodart and Weber (1996); Gemino (1999); Weber and Zhang (1996).

The next section introduces the main concepts of the BWW ontology. Sec. 3 examines some UML constructs and diagrams from an ontological point of view. Sec. 4 provides an evaluation of the results and directions for future research.

2 Basic Concepts of the BWW-ontology

The world is made up of *substantial things* that posses *properties*. [2] A property can be either *intrinsic*— possessed by the thing itself (e.g. color), or *mutual*— possessed jointly by two or more things (e.g. distance).

Things can combine to form a *composite* thing. There exist basic things that cannot be decomposed. Composite things possess *emergent* properties that are not possessed by any component. For example, a computer possesses processing power, not possessed by any individual component.

Things change by acquiring or losing properties. Things are not destroyed or created. Rather, they come into being (or disappear) through acquisition or loss of properties, or via composition or decomposition.

---

[2] To avoid confusion between things in the ontological model and objects in UML, we will use generically the term *entity* for everything that exists in the world. When things or objects are mentioned, the context is assumed to be the ontology or UML respectively. When the intention might not be clear from the context, we will use prefixes, e.g. BWW-thing or UML-class. Similarly, we will generically refer to a property of an entity as a *feature* as the terms 'property' and 'attribute' have specific meanings in either or both UML and the ontology.

A law is a relationship between properties. In particular, a law can be specified in terms of *precedence of properties*: Property A *precedes* property B iff whenever a thing possesses B, it possesses A.

A BWW-*class* is the set of things that have one common property, a *kind* is the set of things that have two or more common properties and a *natural kind* is a kind where some of the properties are related by laws. Examples are respectively the set of red things, the set of red and heavy things and the set of things that are red and heavy whose color and weight are related by a law.

It is important to note that in our ontology, classes, kinds and natural kinds are defined over an existing set of things. In this sense, the things are the *primary* construct, not the class or natural kind. It follows that there can be no classes without members.

Attributes are representations of the properties of a thing as perceived by an observer. They can be thought of as functions of time (and other conditions of observation), e.g. specifying the color of thing x at time t. Such functions are called *state functions*. A set of attributes used to describe a set of things with common properties is called a *functional schema*. Depending on which aspects one is interested in, there can be different schemas describing the same thing. The *state* of a thing is a *complete* assignment of values to all state functions in the functional schema. A change of state is termed an *event*.

A thing is always in a *lawful* state, one that is allowed by the laws by which it abides. A state may be *stable* or *unstable*. If a thing is in an unstable state, it will spontaneously undergo a transition to another state until it reaches a stable state.

Two things are said to *interact* if the presence of one of them affects the states the other traverses. Interactions are manifested by mutual properties. For example, if one thing hits another, this will change the combined speed of the pair.

While the BWW-ontology appears oriented towards the physical world, it has sufficient descriptive power to give interpretation to what might be called 'conceptual constructs', i.e. constructs that do not refer to things that exist physically in the world. We demonstrate this with several examples. First, consider a customer's order of a product from a supplier. The order is an indication that the customer and supplier have interacted, and both their states have changed. Thus, it reflects an event. Note, the details of the event might be recorded physically, on an order form (or in an order record). However, this would be a record of the actual order, not the order itself. Next, consider the notion of a job. It reflects interaction between a person and a company. This interaction might be manifested by mutual properties, but in itself will not be viewed as a thing. Finally, consider an address. It is a reflection of some properties of a physical location. This location might have a mutual property with a person.

3 UML from an Ontological Perspective

Our world consists of things, changes in things and interactions of things. In what follows, we begin our discussion with the things that exist in the world, described in UML-class diagrams. We proceed to look at changes and dynamics of single entities, described by state charts. We conclude with a look at the interaction between entities, described in UML-collaboration and sequence diagrams. Each section first describes briefly the relevant UML constructs. This is followed by a discussion of the proposed ontological interpretation which in turn serves as the basis for the derivation of modeling rules. The UML reference manual (OMG, 1999) served as the basis for our analysis.

3.1 Class Diagrams

Class diagrams describe the static building blocks of any real world system. These include Objects, Classes, Attributes and Associations. For brevity, we do not discuss here other class diagram constructs, in particular, methods.

Objects Because every BWW-thing is an entity in the world, we propose that a BWW-thing be represented as a UML-object. Usually, not every UML-object is equivalent to a BWW-thing. For example, entities such as "order", "location" and "job" are not things in the ontological sense but are still often modeled by UML-objects for design purposes. To assign an unambiguous ontological semantic to a UML-object, we propose the following rule 1:

Rule 1 *Only substantial entities in the world are modeled as objects.*

If we use this rule, we must find an alternative description for conceptual entities such as "Job", "Order", etc. We return to this problem later in this section.

Object creation and destruction have no immediate equivalents in the BWW-ontology. Instead we relate these notions to Bunge's *principle of nominal invariance*: A thing keeps its name until it changes its natural-kind (Bunge, 1977). Such a change occurs through acquisition of properties. By analogy, object destruction occurs when an object loses a property which is necessary for membership in a certain class or kind.

We identify two common cases of property acquisition (loss):

1. Via interaction between things.
2. Via composition (decomposition) of things. The composite acquires (loses) emergent properties.

Consider the following examples: (1) A car might lose (e.g. due to an accident) some properties that make it able to move. It has now become something else (e.g. scrap metal). (2) A set of bricks combined into a house 'creates' the new thing 'house' with the emergent property of 'NumberOfBedrooms'. (3) Altering the way the bricks are combined makes the house into an office building. It undergoes a qualitative change, losing the property 'NumberOfBedrooms' and acquiring the property 'NumberOfOffices'. (4) A broken machine is fixed so that its parts start interacting again. It then acquires the emergent properties that enables it to generate products.

Using the house example: Assume the 'house' but not the 'bricks' are part of our world view, then it would appear to us that a house had been created. Similarly, assume the 'house' but not 'office building' is part of our description, then it would appear as a 'house' had been destroyed.

The above discussion motivates the following rule:

Rule 2 *Object creation represents an event when an entity acquires a property so it becomes a member of a class that is part of the description of the real world domain being modeled. (Object destruction analogous)*

For example, in the real world, a customer is not created, rather a person becomes a customer by acquiring the property of having bought an item. Note, this is reflected in the information system by creating a new customer record.

Classes Classes in UML serve as templates: objects cannot exist without classes. The reverse holds for our ontology: objects are primary and can exist without classes. Classes, kinds, and natural kinds play the role of descriptions and cannot exist without things possessing the relevant properties. A number of consequences follow.

UML-classes are defined as sets of attributes and methods and serve as templates for the objects that are their instances (OMG, 1999). In contrast, BWW-natural kinds are defined based on their extensions, i.e. on sets of things. Hence we cannot map a UML-class to a BWW-natural kind. Instead we propose that a UML-class is equivalent to a functional schema is used for modeling entities that form the corresponding BWW-natural kind. Note, since UML-types specify only behavior, not attributes, we do not compare them to BWW-kinds.

Recall, in our ontology things cannot be created, only become members of a natural kind by changing properties, or by being assembled by composition. Hence, the second important aspect of UML-classes, of object creators, has no ontological equivalent. Furthermore, in ontology there are no empty classes. As well, all things have properties. Hence, we suggest the following two modeling rules:

Rule 3 *No class can be abstract.*

Rule 4 *All classes must possess at least on attribute.*

If we want to apply these rules to UML-classes, we face a difficulty because classes in UML can be abstract, namely, possess no instances, and potentially no defining properties. We demonstrate this using the example shown in Figure 1.

The UML-class 'Vehicle' is an abstract class, i.e. it contains no members, because no vehicle is assumed to be able to fly and drive on tracks at the same time.

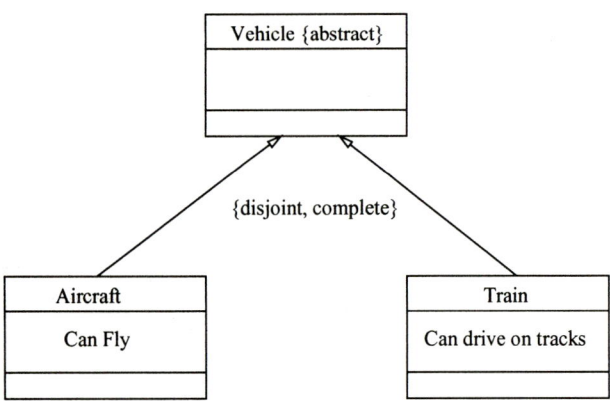

Fig. 1. Generalization in UML

To see how this difficulty can be overcome, consider that in UML generalization describes a relationship between two classes where a subclass has all the features of a more general superclass and may possess additional features. This means additional attributes and/or specialized methods. In what follows, we limit our analysis to 'static' properties (attributes) only.

In the BWW-ontology, we distinguish two types of generalization:

- Through inheritance of properties. This is equivalent to the UML semantics of attribute inheritance.
- Through specialization of properties. That is, when a subclass possesses a property preceded by a property of the superclass. This has no equivalent in UML.

In the real world, what defines a vehicle is that it 'can move'. In ontology, we model this by indicating that both 'can fly' and 'can drive on tracks' are *preceded by* the more general property 'can move'. Thus, the class of vehicles is non-empty, and has (at least) one defining property. This specialization cannot be expressed with the inheritance semantics of UML diagrams. Had we modeled 'can move' as an attribute of class 'vehicle', these semantics would have caused it to be an attribute of both 'Aircraft' and 'Train', in addition to the specialized attributes 'can fly' and 'can drive on tracks'. It follows that we need to distinguish two types of inheritance when dealing with generalization, only one of which can be modeled graphically in UML. This motivates the following two rules:

Rule 5 *If class B is subclass of class A, the attributes shown for class B are either specialized attributes of class A or additional attributes of class B.*

Rule 6 *Attribute specialization must be stated explicitly to distinguish specialized from additional attributes.*

Associations We propose that associations be mapped to mutual properties of two objects. For example, the property "time required to completion" is mutual between a machine and a slab of metal to be formed on that machine. Note, since in ontology properties cannot possess properties, we proscribe modeling mutual properties as attributes of an association. Furthermore, the analysis above indicates that associations should represent properties, not classes. Hence rule 7:

Rule 7 *If instances in two classes possess a property that cannot be possessed by instances of either alone, this mutual property must be modeled as an association. Associations should not be modeled as classes.*

Attributes We propose that attributes of a UML-class represent the functions that comprise the BWW-functional schema corresponding to the UML-class.

The BWW-ontology distinguishes clearly between BWW-properties and substantial BWW-things (see also Wand et al., 1999). For example, a thing of kind "person" can be "employed by" a thing of kind company. The specific person and the specific company have a mutual property, but the company itself is not a property of the person. We therefore propose the following modeling rule:

Rule 8 *Attributes in a UML-description of the real world cannot refer to substantial entities.*

Recall also rule 1 stating that only substantial entities be modeled as objects. Hence:

Rule 9 *Properties must be modeled as attributes or associations, depending on whether they represent intrinsic or mutual properties.*

Consider for example a person that has a language skill. Because a skill is a conceptual entity, i.e. it is not substantial, Rule 1 proscribes that it be modeled as an object. Hence, having a skill must be represented by an attribute of the person, not by an association. Note, in information system design, a skill is often modeled as an object or an entity. However, this is a design view, namely, a model of the IS, not of the real world.

UML also defines class attributes. A class attribute is an attribute of a UML-class, not of its instances. Ontologically, a class is not a substantial entity. Therefore, it should not possess properties. However, ontologically the composite made of the things comprising the extension of the class is a thing, and hence can possess properties. Thus, we suggest that for modeling the real-world, UML-class attributes such as "Number of Instances" be interpreted as properties of the composite thing made of the class extension. This interpretation would require that this composite be considered part of the model.

Rule 10 *Class attributes in UML can only represent (emergent) properties of the composite made of the instances of the class. This composite must be modeled explicitly (with its properties).*

3.2 State Charts

UML employs states and the semantics of state machines to specify discrete dynamic behavior. Here we only refer to states of things, represented by objects (UML allows the association of a state machine and states with other classifiers such as use cases). A UML-state of an object is defined by an invariant condition i.e. a condition that holds while the object is in that state. State semantics are based on Harel state charts (Harel, 1988; Harel and Gery, 1996).

In the BWW-ontology, the state of a thing is the set of values of state (attribute) functions in a functional schema used for modeling the thing. There is no notion of state independent of attributes. In contrast, UML provides no mechanism with which to specify the connection between the notion of state and the values of attributes.[3] To ensure inter-diagram consistency between class diagrams and state charts, we propose the following rule:

Rule 11 *A UML-state represents a specific assignment of values to the attributes of the object for which the state is defined. A UML-transition must change the value of at least one of these attributes.*

It is possible in UML to define a hierarchy of states. A composite state may be described by a state machine comprising (sub)states and transitions. A state may be described by one or more concurrently operating state machines. A substate is a partial assignment of values to a subset of state variables. Specifically, orthogonal subsets are partial assignments defined on disjoint subsets of state variables. These subsets do not need to conform to state descriptions of components (Harel and Gery, 1996).

An example of a UML state chart is provided in Fig. 2. It depicts a state in terms of an initial pseudostate and four substates (numbered 1-4). The pseudostate designates the substate the system is in when the superstate is entered. It is a purely syntactic construct. Hence we will not interpret it ontologically. The diagram implies that while the system (or object) under consideration can be in composite state s, it can be in four different substates, of which two are concurrent.

Because states in the BWW-ontology are defined as *complete* assignments to state variables, we cannot define substates in the way UML does. From our discussion in Sect. 2 we know that a thing can be described by multiple, different models or functional schemata, depending on which properties are of interest. Using the example of Fig. 2, we will show how functional schemata can be used

---

[3] Previous authors have noted the connection between attributes and states (Booch, 1994; Coad and Yourdon, 1990; Jacobson et al., 1992; Rumbaugh and Blaha, 1991). However, these authors do not provide explicit rules or constructs for specifying this connection and the UML description does *not* mention it.

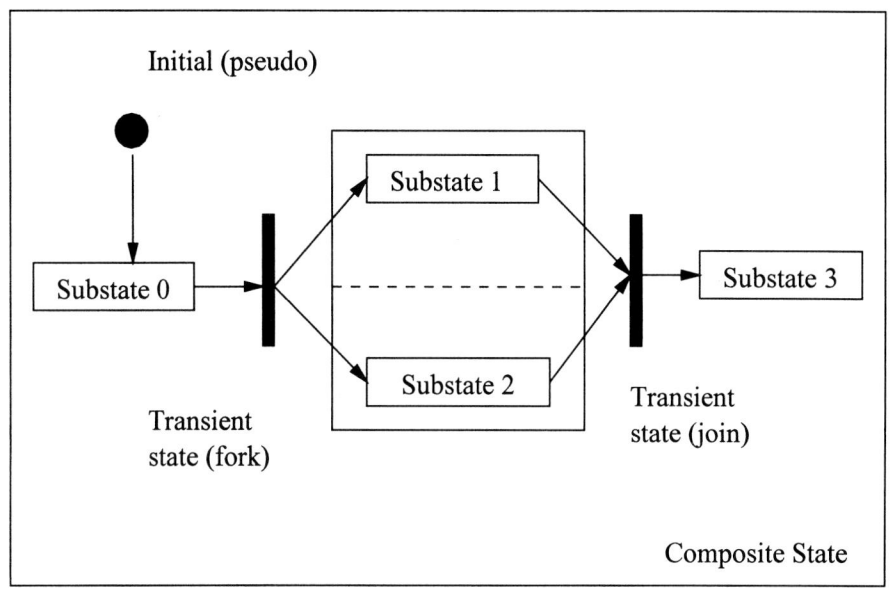

Fig. 2. Composite states and substates in UML

to provide the same level of detail found in UML state charts. To do this, we make two observations: (1) Whenever a thing changes from one state to another, at least one state variable must change its value; and (2) a thing can be modeled at the same time by different state vectors. Observation (2) enables us to model concurrent states. For example, consider the functional schema of a person. The person can be viewed as an employee by adding some state variables, and as a customer by adding other state variables. These views can coexist.

Assume that state s is described by assignment of values to the set of state functions F_s comprising of a vector of state variables U and an additional state variable v, $F_s := (U, v)$. The vector U is assigned a (vector of) values, a, for all substates of s. Substates 0 and 3 and the (unnamed) substate composed of two concurrent states 1 and 2 differ in the value of state variable v as follows: Substate 0: $< U = a, v = b_0 >$; substate 3: $< U = a, v = b_1 >$; the state composed of concurrent substates 1 and 2: $< U = a, v = b_2 >$. We still need to distinguish between the concurrent substates 1 and 2 that are at the same level of abstraction. We do this by adding to the schema two different state variables, to obtain two new schemata. State 1 will be described by $< U = a, v = b_2, w = d >$; state 2 will be described by $< U = a, v = b_2, y = e >$. In general, v, w, and y, can be replaced by vectors.

We can generalize the example using the following three rules:

Rule 12 *For all immediate substates of a superstate, the values assigned to attributes describing the superstate are invariant.*

Rule 13 *For every level of refinement of a state, there must be an additional set of attributes in the class description that change as the object transitions among the substates.*

Rule 14 *Concurrent substates require mutually disjunct sets of additional attributes in the class description.*

In conclusion, we have shown that we can link the static structure description of a system to the dynamic concept of states without compromising the level of detail that UML state charts provide.

Action States Action states are states during which the object undergoes a change. This is incompatible with the ontological idea that a state is an assignment of values to attributes at a specific instance in time. Using the idea of substates and the following rule allows us to express action states ontologically, using UML constructs:

Rule 15 *Action states are superstates of a set of substates. The object transitions among these while in the action state. State charts must reflect this fact.*

For example, an item that is in the action state of "being shipped" undergoes state transitions while being in that state, e.g. from state "on truck" to a new state "on loading dock" etc.

Since action states often appear in activity diagrams, this rule can be used to ensure inter-diagram consistency between state charts and activity diagrams.

3.3 Collaboration and Sequence Diagrams

Sequence diagrams describe time-ordered communication among objects, and collaboration diagrams describes the communication among objects to achieve a goal. Both employ the same constructs. Communication is accomplished through stimuli. In UML, a message is a specification of a stimulus, i.e. a stimulus is the instance of a message.

In our discussion in Sect. 2 we have seen that interaction can be described in the BWW-ontology using mutual properties and their changes. Adding rule 7 indicating that mutual properties must be modeled as associations, we suggest rules 16 and 17:

Rule 16 *The classes involved in an interaction must possess mutual attributes.*

Rule 17 *The classes involved in an interaction must have associations with one another.*

4 Conclusions and Future Research

Our goal is to assign real-world semantics to UML diagrams so they can be used for conceptual modeling. We have done this by suggesting a mapping from UML constructs to a specific ontological model. Our ontological model describes a world consisting of things, changes in things and interactions of things. Hence, we have examined UML constructs beginning with the class diagram concepts of objects, classes and attributes. We then looked at changes and dynamics of single entities, described in state charts. We concluded with a brief analysis of interaction between entities, described in UML-collaboration and sequence diagrams.

Based on the ontologically derived semantics, we have identified rules that we suggest should be followed when applying UML to conceptual modeling of real world domains. These rules can guide the use of UML constructs in specific situations and can help ensure that UML models will have a meaningful ontological interpretation. Since often the same ontological concept can be represented by different UML constructs in different diagrams, the proposed modeling rules can help ensure that UML-based conceptual models will be consistent across diagrams or that at least inconsistencies can be identified. We have given examples of inter-diagram consistency rules that arise out of these semantics.

While we feel this first ontological analysis of UML is encouraging, we recognize this is an initial effort. Much research remains to be undertaken. In particular:

- A broader look at UML encompassing more of its constructs should attempt to provide a more complete view and identify additional rules for using UML in conceptual modeling. We are currently studying in more detail the semantics of associations and of static and dynamic aspects of composite objects.
- Given that in practice modeling situations can be complex, it is of interest to examine how the rules can be incorporated in a CASE tool to enforce inter-diagram consistency.
- The results we have obtained depend on the adoption of a specific ontological model. Whether this model is an appropriate one can only be determined empirically. The application of the rules will have to be tested by experiment in order to see if they provide useful results.
- Even if the rules seem useful in simple, experimental cases, their usefulness if practical situations will have to be tested. Such tests are quite difficult to conduct.

The last two points are important steps towards empirical validation of this work and the proposed rules. The final verdict on this research must be based on empirical observations.

Acknowledgment

This research was supported by a grant from the Natural Sciences and Engineering Research Council of Canada. We would like to thank the three anonymous reviewers for insightful and helpful comments.

References

Bezivin, J. and Muller, P. (1999). UML: The Birth and Rise of a Standard Modeling Notation. In *The Unified Modeling Language UML'98: Beyond the notation, First International Workshop, Mulhouse, France, June 1998*.

Bodart, F. and Weber, R. (1996). Optional Properties Versus Subtyping in Conceptual Modeling: A Theory and Empirical Test. In *Proceedings of the International Conference on Information Systems, Dec. 16-18, 1996*, page 450.

Booch, G. (1994). *Object Oriented Analysis and Design with Applications*. Benjamin/Cummings, Redwood City, CA.

Bunge, M. A. (1977). *Ontology I: The Furniture of the World, Volume 3 of Treatise on Basic Philosophy*. D. Reidel Publishing Company, Dordrecht, Holland.

Bunge, M. A. (1979). *Ontology II: A World of Systems, Volume 4 of Treatise on Basic Philosophy*. D. Reidel Publishing Company, Dordrecht, Holland.

Coad, P. and Yourdon, E. (1990). *Object-Oriented Analysis*. Yourdon Press, Englewood Cliffs, NJ.

Evans, A., France, R., Lano, K., and Rumpe, B. (1999). The UML as a Formal Modeling Notation. In *The Unified Modeling Language UML'98: Beyond the notation, First International Workshop, Mulhouse, France, June 1998*.

Gemino, A. (1999). *Empirical Comparisons of Systems Analysis Modeling Techniques*. Ph.D. thesis, University of British Columbia, Canada.

Green, P. and Rosemann, M. (2000). Ontological Analysis of Integrated Process Modelling. *Information Systems*, **25**(2), 73–87.

Harel, D. (1988). On Visual Formalisms. *Communications of the ACM*, **31**(5), 514–530.

Harel, D. and Gery, E. (1996). Executable Object Modeling with Statecharts. In *Proceedings of the 18th Intarnational Conference on Software Engineering, 25-30 March 1996, TU Berlin, Germany (ICSE-18)*, pages 246–256.

Jacobson, I., Christerson, M., Jonsson, P., and Övergaard, G. (1992). *Object-Oriented Software Engineering: A Use Case Driven Approach*. Addison-Wesley, Wokingham.

Knapp, A. (1999). A Formal Semantics for UML Interactions. In *UML'99 The Unified Modeling Language - Beyond the Standard: Second International Workshop, Fort Collins, CO, October 28-30, 1999*, pages 116–130.

Lano, K. and Bicarregui, J. (1999). Semantics and Transformations for UML Models. In *The Unified Modeling Language UML'98: Beyond the notation, First International Workshop, Mulhouse, France, June 1998*, pages 107–119.

Lilius, J. and Paltor, I. (1999). Formalising UML State Machines for Model Checking. In *UML'99 The Unified Modeling Language - Beyond the Standard: Second International Workshop, Fort Collins, CO, October 28-30, 1999*, pages 430–445.

Mylopoulos, J. (1992). Conceptual Modeling and Telos. In P. Locuopoulos and R. Zicari, editors, *Conceptual Modeling, Databases and Cases*. John Wiley & Sons, Inc., New York et. al.

OMG (1999). *The Unified Modelling Language Specification. Version 1.3*. OMG.

OMG (2000). *UML 2.0 Superstructure RFP*. OMG.

Opdahl, A. and Henderson-Sellers, B. (1999). Evaluating and Improving OO Modelling Languages Using the BWW-Model. In *Proceedings of the Information Systems Foundation Workshop: Ontology, Semiotics and Practice 1999, Macquarie University, Sidney/Australia, 1999*. www.comp.mq.edu.au/isf99/Opdahl.htm.

Opdahl, A. and Sindre, G. (1993). Concepts for Real-World Modelling. In *Advanced Information Systems Engineering - 5th International Conference CAiSE'93, Paris/France, June 1993*, pages 309–327.

Opdahl, A., Henderson-Sellers, B., and Barbier, F. (1999). An Ontological Evaluation of the OML Metamodel. In E. D. Falkenberg and K. Lyytinen, editors, *Information System Concepts: An Integrated Discipline Emerging*. IFIP/Kluwer.

Övergaard, G. (1999). A Formal Approach to Collaborations in the Unified Modeling Language. In *UML'99 The Unified Modeling Language - Beyond the Standard: Second International Workshop, Fort Collins, CO, October 28-30, 1999*, pages 99–115.

Övergaard, G. and Palmkvist, K. (1999). A Formal Approach to Use Cases and Their Relationships. In *The Unified Modeling Language UML'98: Beyond the notation, First International Workshop, Mulhouse, France, June 1998*, pages 406–418.

Parsons, J. and Wand, Y. (1997). Using Objects for Systems Analysis. *Communications of the ACM*, 40(12), 104–110.

Rumbaugh, J. and Blaha, S. (1991). *Object Oriented Modeling and Design*. Prentice Hall, Englewood Cliffs, NJ.

Wand, Y. (1989). A Proposal for a Formal Model of Objects. In W. Kim and F. Lchovsky, editors, *Object-Oriented Concepts, Languages, Applications and Databases*, pages 537–559. ACM Press. Addison-Wesley.

Wand, Y. and Weber, R. (1989). An Ontological Evaluation of Systems Analysis and Design Methods. In E. Falkenberg and P. Lingreen, editors, *Information System Concepts: An In-Depth Analysis*. Elsevier Science Publishers B.V., North-Holland.

Wand, Y. and Weber, R. (1990). Mario Bunge's Ontology as a Formal Foundation for Information Systems Concepts. In P. Weingartner and G. Dorn, editors, *Studies on Mario Bunge's Treatise*. Rodopi, Atlanta.

Wand, Y. and Weber, R. (1993). On the Ontological Expressiveness of Information Systems Analysis and Design Grammars. *Journal of Information Systems*, (3), 217–237.

Wand, Y., Storey, V. C., and Weber, R. (1999). An Ontological Analysis of the Relationship Construct in Conceptual Modeling. *ACM Transactions on Database Systems*, 24(4), 494–528.

Weber, R. and Zhang, Y. (1996). An Analytical Evaluation of NIAM's Grammar for Conceptual Schema Diagrams. *Information Systems Journal*, 6(2), 147–170.

Developing Sequence Diagrams in UML

Il-Yeol Song

College of Information Science and Technology
Drexel University
Philadelphia, PA 19104
song@drexel.edu

Abstract. The UML (Unified Modeling Language) has been widely accepted as a standard language for object-oriented analysis and design. Among the UML diagrams, one of the most difficult and time-consuming diagrams to develop is the object interaction diagram (OID), which is rendered as either a sequence diagram or a collaboration diagram. Our experience shows that developers have significant trouble in understanding and developing OIDs. In this paper, we present an effective ten-step heuristic for developing sequence diagrams and illustrate the technique with a case study. In this technique, we show a proper use of control objects and boundary objects when developing sequence diagrams. In our heuristic the relationships among multiple sequence diagrams in a single use case are elegantly represented using control objects. We found that developers effectively developed sequence diagrams using this heuristic method.

1 Introduction

The UML (Unified Modeling Language) claims to be a language rather than a method. The UML provides a set of notations and concepts that are necessary for developing object-oriented software or systems. The UML includes nine inter-related diagrams which are used to model different aspects of the system being modeled. The relationships among the diagrams are shown in Fig. 1. Among the UML diagrams, one of the most difficult and time-consuming diagrams to develop is the object interaction diagram (OID), which is rendered as either a sequence diagram or a collaboration diagram. OIDs model dynamic behavior by showing how system components interact to complete core tasks defined in use case design [2]. While many novice designers put emphasis upon static models, they often fail to emphasize the use of dynamic models, which are very important for properly allocating responsibility among objects [8]. The purpose of interaction diagrams is to [6, 2; 14; 5, 8; 19, 3, 10, 15]:

- Model interactions between objects,
- Assist in understanding how a system (a use case) actually works,
- Verify that a use case description can be supported by the existing object classes,
- Identify responsibilities/operations and assign them to classes,
- Model synchronous/asynchronous message passing in real-time systems

While seemingly intuitive, methods for constructing an OID have not been described much in literature. Our experience shows that novice developers have significant trouble in understanding and developing OIDs. Most UML books simply explain the notations and semantics of OIDs and present pre-built sequence diagrams. Some authors provide simple guidelines for developing sequence diagrams. We found that those simple guidelines are not sufficient for many novice developers. Based on the author's several years of experience in teaching object-oriented analysis and design, we show an effective heuristic for developing interaction diagrams and illustrate the technique with a case study.

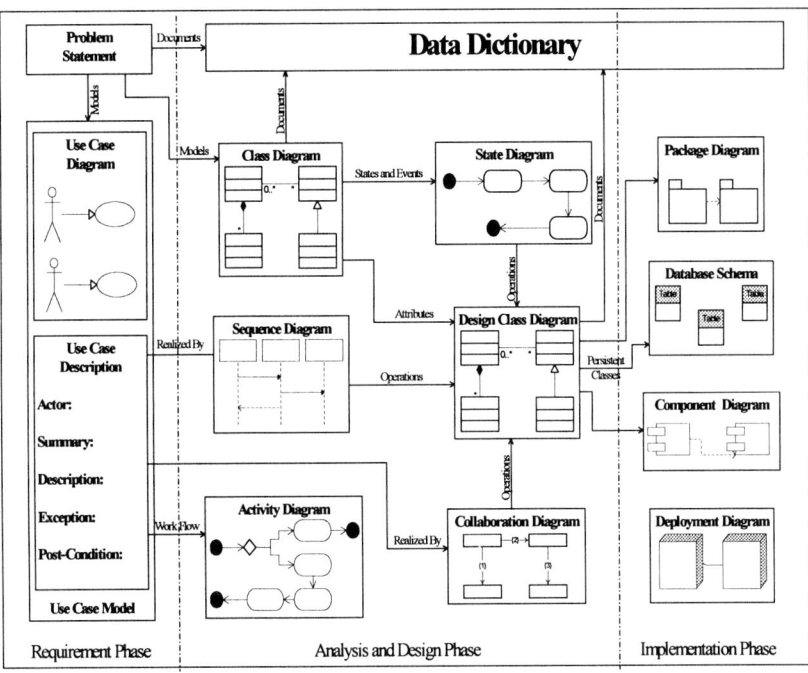

Fig. 1. Relationships among UML diagrams

Ideally, our heuristic assumes that the developer has already developed use case diagrams. use case descriptions and the class diagram. We develop interaction diagrams based on each primary use case. Our heuristic takes advantage of properties of stereotype objects – entity, boundary and control objects. We assume that an actor only directly communicates with a boundary object, but not with a control or an entity object. We create a control object for each primary, included or extended use case. This convention allows us to elegantly represent the relationships among multiple sequence diagrams in a single use case.

Since a sequence diagram can be easily converted into a collaboration diagram, our heuristic can be equally applied to developing collaboration diagrams.

For the rest of our paper, we use the terms *interaction diagram* and *sequence diagram* interchangeably.

The rest of the paper is organized as follows: Section 2 summarizes the notation and concepts of sequence diagrams. Section 3 reviews research activities in the areas of sequence diagrams and its development methods suggested by various authors. Section 4 describes the use of stereotype objects and their relationships. Section 5 presents the heuristics, and Section 6 illustrates the heuristics with a case study in a video rental system. Section 7 concludes our paper.

2 Sequence Diagrams

In this section, we define terminology and notation used in the sequence diagram in UML.

The popularity of the sequence diagram, originally called an object interaction diagram, is attributed to Jacobson et al. [6]. A sequence diagram focuses on time sequencing or time ordering of messages or the order in which messages are sent. The emphasis in these diagrams is what happens first, second, and so on. They represent the passage of time graphically. The schematic structure and notation of a typical sequence diagram is shown in Fig. 2.

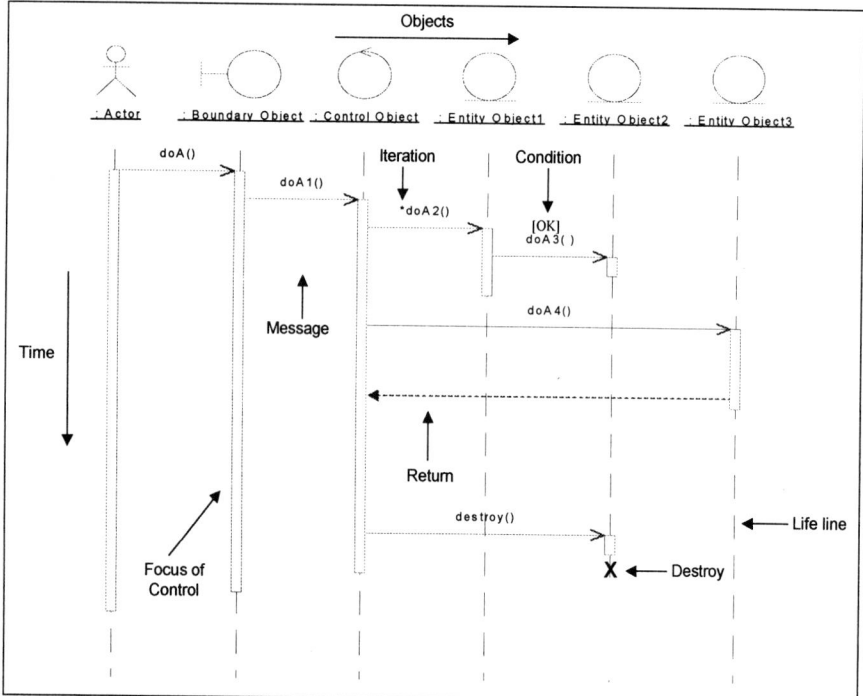

Fig. 2. A structure and notation of the sequence diagram

These diagrams have two axes: the horizontal axis displays the objects and the vertical axis shows time. In addition, sequence diagrams have two features not present in collaboration diagrams: an object's lifeline and the focus of control [2]. Object lifelines are used in the sequence diagram to represent the existence of the object during a scenario. While most objects will be in existence during the entire scenario, at times objects are created or deleted during the scenarios. For example, an order could be created and a reservation could be deleted.

The limitation of the sequence diagram is that it does not explicitly show the relationships or links between objects. These relationships are the primary emphasis of the collaboration diagram. One of the goals behind the development of the UML was to keep it as simple as possible while still being able to model the spectrum of systems that needed to be built [2]. However, it is more complicated than previously developed object-oriented methods, because it is intended to be more comprehensive. As a result, the UML diagrams are often difficult to develop. While developing the first draft of a sequence diagram, there are a lot of important design decisions to make. The sequence diagram may also be difficult to develop because the UML does not provide a process or specific steps that can be followed. It is up to the designer to choose or develop a method that will assist him or her in creating an effective diagram.

Booch et al [2] indicates that the sequence diagrams are a means to model some aspect of the dynamic behavior of the system and can be used in context of the whole system, a sub-system or they can be attached to a use case. Some indicate that a sequence diagram should be drawn, at least per use-case [6, 19, 5, 18]. When a sequence diagram is developed for a use case, the use case descriptions can be used to develop at least the initial draft of a sequence diagram. Throughout the design process the use case diagram can be revised based on the results of the sequence diagram, and vise versa, until both models are tuned appropriately [8, 10]. We identify operations from the use case description and represent them in sequence diagram (see Fig. 1).

Since a sequence diagram may be developed for each primary use case, *included* use case and *extended* use case, there will be a number of sequence diagrams developed. However, the UML does not define notations that connect these diagrams. Song et al proposes an idea for such a notation [17]. The suggestion is to insert a connector symbol on a sequence diagram that 'drills down' to a subordinate sequence diagram or 'rolls up' to a calling one. In this paper, we propose the use of control objects to connect multiple sequence diagrams.

3 Survey on the Sequence Diagram and Its Developments

In this section, we survey research activities on the sequence diagram and guidelines for developing the diagram suggested by various authors.

We found that most research activities on sequence diagrams have focused on real time systems [16, 9, 13, 4], simulation [7] or behavior-driven analysis and design [3].

Very few authors even mentioned possible methods, processes or steps that could be used to develop effective sequence diagrams.

Amber [1] outlines his suggestions for the steps for constructing a sequence diagram, as summarized in Table 1. His steps describe, in a very brief form, what needs to be done to put together the main parts of the diagram. However these steps do not give any type of detailed instruction on "how."

Table 1. Ambler's Steps for Constructing a Sequence Diagram [1, p.62]

1.	Identify the class in which the use-case scenario starts.
2.	Walk through the process logic of the scenario, identifying each message that needs to be sent and the object to which it is sent.
3.	Once an object is identified, draw its lifeline.
4.	Indicate the activity box on the object's lifeline where it sends a message or is expecting a return.

Rosenberg [14] discusses the development of sequence diagrams using robustness analysis, which was introduced by Jacobson et al. [6]. However, Rosenberg, does not include step-by-step guidelines for a developer to follow.

Booch et al [2] outlines separate steps for constructing the sequence diagram (See Table 2), as well as the collaboration diagram. While some of the steps overlap, there are different steps that represent the differences in the two diagrams. These steps are more detailed than Ambler's but still concentrate on what needs to be done rather than addressing "how" it can be done.

Booch et al [2] also outlines a number of characteristics for a well-structured interaction diagram (Table 3) and a number of tips for developing an interaction diagram (Table 4). While not specific, these are very helpful suggestions, especially for the novice and attention should be given to them.

Table 2. Steps for Constructing a Sequence diagram by Booch et al. [2, p. 251]

1.	Set the Context of the Interaction Diagram (System, Sub-system, Use Case).
2.	Identify the objects which play a role in the interaction and place the most important ones on the left.
3.	Set the lifeline of each of the objects.
4.	Starting with the message that initiates the interaction, layout each message from top to bottom between lifelines, showing each message's properties.
5.	Adorn to each lifeline the objects 'focus of control' or activation period, if this visualization is necessary.
6.	Adorn each message with time and space constraints, if needed.
7.	Adorn each message with pre- and post-conditions, if needed.

Developing Sequence Diagrams in UML 373

Table 3. A well-structured Interaction Diagram by Booch et al. [2, p. 256]

1.	Is focused on communicating one aspect of a system's dynamics.
2.	Contains only those elements that are essential to understanding that aspect.
3.	Provides detail consistent with its level of abstraction and should expose only those adornments that are essential to understanding.
4.	Is not so minimalist that it misinforms the reader about semantics that are important.

Table 4. Tips for drawing an Interaction Diagram by Booch et al. [2, p. 256]

1.	Give it a name that communicates its purpose.
2.	Lay out its elements to minimize lines that cross.
3.	Use notes and color as visual cues to draw attention to important features of your diagram.

Jacobson et al [6] categorizes sequence diagrams by structure. The *fork* or centralized sequence diagram contains one primary client operation that controls the flow of signals to multiple server operations. In contrast, the *stair* or decentralized sequence diagram uses delegation as the primary means for structuring communications among multiple objects. More specifically, Jacobson et al. describes a decentralized OID as one where "each object only knows a few of the other objects and knows which objects can help with a specific behavior. Here we have no 'central' object."

Jacobson recommends the more encapsulated stair configuration for situations where the communicating objects are connected to each other in some hierarchical fashion. On the other hand, a centralized fork structure is recommended for times when operations can change a sequence of operations and when new operations can be inserted into the sequence diagram. See Fig. 8.15 in [6] for the two structures.

When developing sequence diagrams, we found that these guidelines were not sufficient for many novice developers. Our experience shows that novice developers have significant trouble in understanding and developing sequence diagrams. Based on the author's experience in teaching object-oriented analysis and design, we have developed an effective ten-step heuristic for developing sequence diagrams. We illustrate the technique with a case study in Section 5.

4 Boundary Objects and Control Objects

Since our heuristic uses the notions of boundary objects and control objects, we briefly present their definitions and properties.

It was Jacobson et al [6] who first introduced entity, control and boundary objects for developing a robust system architecture. The idea was to distribute the behaviors specified in a use case description into those three object types. See Fig. 2 for the notations of the three object types. We adopt the definition and properties of these objects from [6, 19, 14].

Entity object classes represent real-life domain objects or concepts that are internal to the system. Examples are Customer, Rental and Video classes. External actors usually have no direct contact with entity objects. Instead they are accessed through boundary objects. *Boundary* object classes handle the communication with external actors, and they encapsulate environmental-dependent behavior, thereby protecting the integrity of the entity object. Examples are windows, screens and menus that are used for input and output. *Control* object classes are transaction classes that capture a sequence of operations. These objects capture business rules and policies. Jacobson et al [6] and Larman [8] use the control object to handle a use case. A control object is also frequently called a Handler or a Controller [8, 14].

As in [19, 14], the relationships among those three objects can be summarized as in Fig. 3. An actor communicates only with a boundary object. A control object bridges between a boundary object and an entity object. A boundary object is not recommended directly to communicate with an entity object. An entity object is not recommended to send a message directly to a boundary object as it increases coupling with specific interface of a system [8].

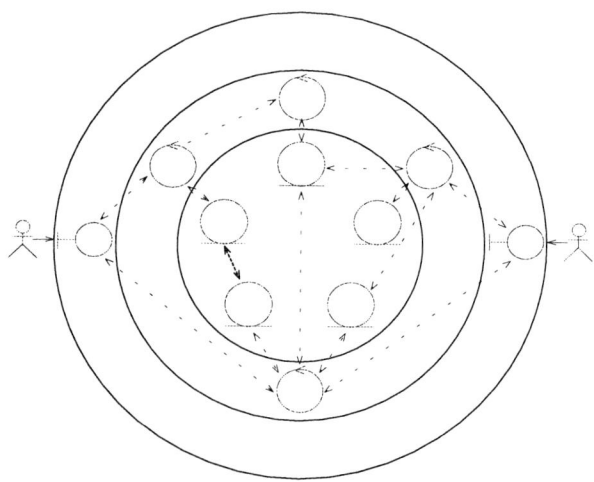

Fig. 3.. Relationships Among Boundary Objects, Control Objects, and Entity Objects.

The UML refers to these categories as *stereotypes* [2]. We note that entity object classes are eventually become persistent whereas controls and boundary objects classes do not usually become persistent. Entity, boundary, and control stereotypes will play a major role in Section 5 when the heuristic is described.

5 The Ten-Step Heuristic for Developing Sequence Diagrams

In this section, we present our heuristic for developing sequence diagrams.

Our methodology is based on the following ideas:
- An actor only directly communicates with a boundary object, but not with a control or entity object.
- We create a control object for each primary, included or extended use case.
- We create a boundary object for each pop-up screen in GUI.

For easy presentation of our paper, we have divided our method into two steps: pre-step and application step. The pre-step summarizes the necessary work that needs to be done to apply our heuristic. The application step shows the details of the heuristic.

Pre-Steps:
- Develop a problem statement.
- Develop a use case diagram.
- Develop use case descriptions for major primary use cases.
- Develop a class diagram for the problem.
- Develop pre-conditions and post-conditions for each primary use case.

We assume that post-conditions are developed in the form of contracts. We use Larman's categories to specify post-conditions as follows [8]:
- Instance creation and deletion.
- Attribute modification.
- Association formed and broken.

The ten-step heuristic for developing sequence diagrams is shown in Table 5. We note that association forming in Step 8.2 is done when an object is created. Thus, an association forming does not require a separate message passing. Steps 8.3.1-8.3.4 provide developers with tips for identifying various possible operations.

6 Case Study

In this section, we illustrate our ten-step heuristic. We apply the heuristics to a video rental system and develop sequence diagrams for the *rent items* use case.

6.1 The Problem Statement

This is about a small, local video rental store (VRS). The problem will be limited to rental, return, management of inventory (add/delete new tapes, change rental prices, etc.) and producing reports summarizing various business activities. The rental items of the store are limited to video tapes. Customer ID number (arbitrary number), phone

Table 5. The Ten-Step Heuristic on Sequence Diagram Development

1	Select the initiating actor and initiating event from the use case description.
2	Identify the primary display screen needed for implementing the use case. Call it the *Primary boundary object*.
3	Create a *use-case controller* (*primary control object*) to handle communication between the primary boundary object and domain objects.
4	If the use case involves any included or extended use case, create one *secondary control object* for each of them.
5	Identify the number of major screens necessary to implement the use case. Create one *secondary boundary object* for each of the major screens and create one *secondary control object* for each of them.
6	From the class diagram, list all *domain* classes participating in the use case by reviewing the use case description. If any class identified from the use case description does not exist in the class diagram, add it to the class diagram.
7	Use those classes just identified as block labels (Column names) in the sequence diagram. List classes in the following order: - The primary boundary stereotype - The primary use case controller - Domain classes (list in the order of access) - Secondary control objects and secondary boundary objects in the order of access

8	Identify all problem-solving operations based on the following classifications:
	  8.1 Instance creation and destruction
	  8.2 Association forming
	  8.3 Attribute modification:
	    8.3.1 Calculation
	    8.3.2 Change States
	    8.3.3 Display or reporting requirements
	    8.3.4 Interface with external objects or systems
	These problem-solving operations can be identified by:
	- Identify verbs from the use case description
	- Remove verbs used to *describe* the problem; select verbs used to solve the problem. We call these verbs *problem-solving verbs(PSVs)*.
	- From the problem-solving verbs, select verbs that represent an automatic operation. We call these PSVs *problem-solving operations(PSOs)* and use them in the sequence diagram.

9	Rearrange the sequence of messages among the object classes based on any pre-existing design patterns, when possible.
10	Name each message and supply it with optional parameters. This can be done at design stage as well.

number or the combination of first name and last name are entered to identify customer data and create an order. The bar code ID for each item is entered and video information from inventory is displayed. The video inventory file is decreased by one when an item is checked out. When all tape IDs are entered, the system computes the total rental fee, and payments are processed. The rental form is created, printed and stored. The customer signs the rental form, takes the tape(s) and leaves. A return is processed by reading the bar code of returned tapes. Any outstanding video rentals are displayed with the amount due on each tape and a total amount due. The past-due amount must be reduced to zero when new tapes are taken out. For new customers, the unique customer ID is generated and the customer information is entered into the system. Videos are stacked by their category such as Drama, Comedy, Action, etc. Any conflict between a customer and computer data is resolved by the store manager. Rental fees can be paid by either cash, check or a major credit card. Reporting requirements include viewing customer rental history, video rental history, titles by category, top ten rentals, items by status, overdue videos by customers and outstanding balances by customers.

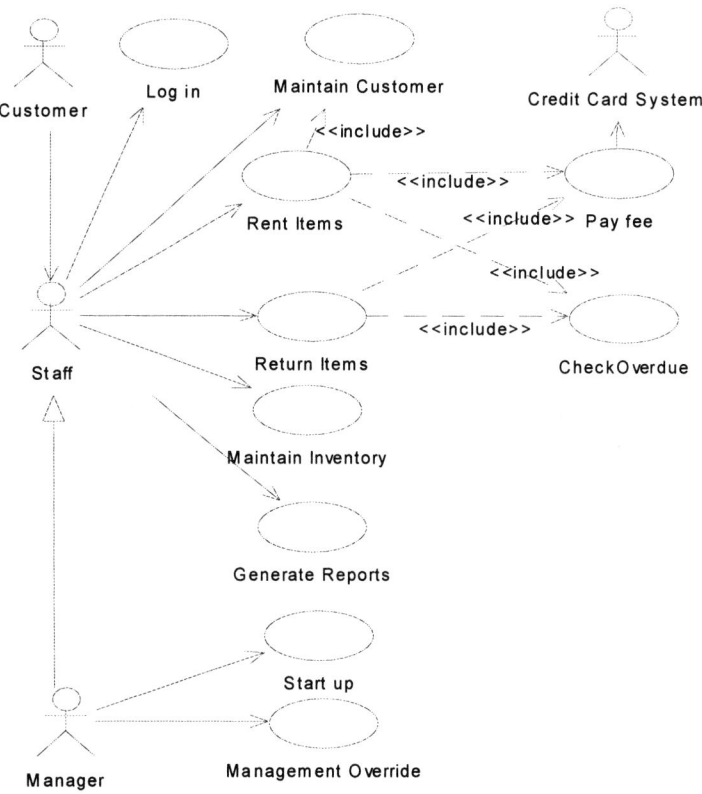

Fig. 4. Use case diagram for VRS

6.2 Use Case Diagram

A system-level use case diagram for the above VRS is shown in Fig. 4. In this use case diagram, we have identified four actors and eight primary use cases and two included use cases. Among them, *Customer* is an indirect actor who does not use the system. Only actors *Staff* and *Manager* use the system. Actor *Credit card system* is a supporting actor that receives a message and responds to the message.

6.3 Class Diagram

A class diagram for the above VRS is shown in Fig. 5. Note that we assumed that one *Item* can be associated with zero or more *RentalItem*s. This is because we wanted to keep all the rental data for six months before archival.

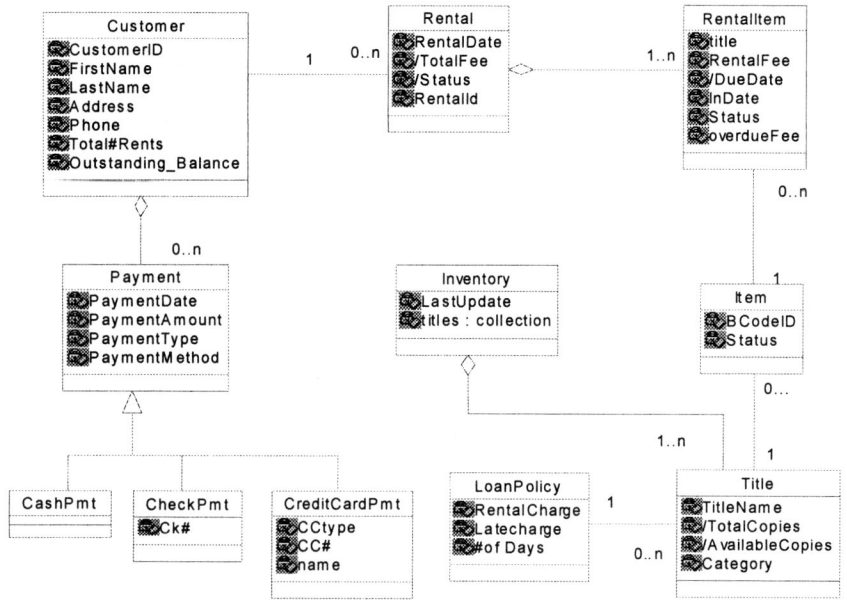

Fig. 5. The class diagram for VRS

6.4 Application of the Heuristic and the System Sequence Diagram

A sequence diagram can easily become complicated as the complexity of the problem domain increases. In order to reduce the complexity of the sequence diagram, we use the idea of a system sequence diagram used by Larman [8]. A system sequence diagram shows all the system events between the system actor and the system as a black box. A system event is an input that is generated by an actor to the system. Using this approach, an entire sequence diagram for a use case is decomposed into a set of system events allowing us to develop one sequence diagram for one or more system events. Fig. 6 shows the system sequence diagram of VRS having four system events.

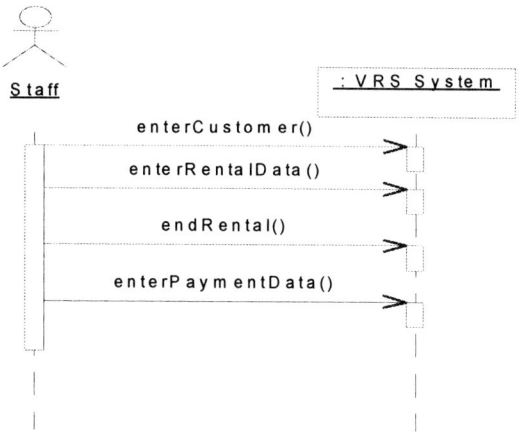

Fig. 6. The system sequence diagram for *Rent Items* use case

For lack of space, we only apply our heuristics for the second, third, and fourth system events: *enterRentalData()*, *endRental()* and *enterPaymentData()*. Note that customer data will be handled in the system event *enterCustomer()*, and payment object will be created and actual payment is processed in the included use case P*ayfee*. Thus, they will not be shown in our sequence diagram below.

1. Actor   Staff
2. *Primary boundary* object.   Rental window
3. *Use-case controller*   Rental handler
4. Secondary control object   Payfee
5. Secondary boundary object   None
6. Participating domain classes   Rental, Rental item, Item,
                                        Title, Payment, LoanPolicy
7. Block labels   Put Rental window object first,
                                        then Rental handler
                                        followed by domain classes
8. Major operations
    8.1 Instance creation: Rental handler, Rental, RentalItem
    8.2 Associate forming: Connect RentalItem to Item
                                        Connect RentalItem to Rental
                                        Connect Rental to Customer
    8.3 Attribute forming:
        8.3.1 Calculation: calculateDueDate(),
                                        calculateTax()
                                        calculateTotalRental(),
        8.3.2 Change States: updateItemStatus(),
                                        decreaseAvailableCopies(),
                                        setDueDate(),
                                        setRentaldate(),

8.3.3 Display/reporting requirements: getItem(),
getTitle(),
getRentalData(),
getlDuration(),
getFee(),
getRentalFee()
displayTotalFee(),
8.3.4 Interface with external objects or systems: None
9. Rearrange the sequence: None in this case
10. Name each message properly with obvious parameters: can add later during design stage

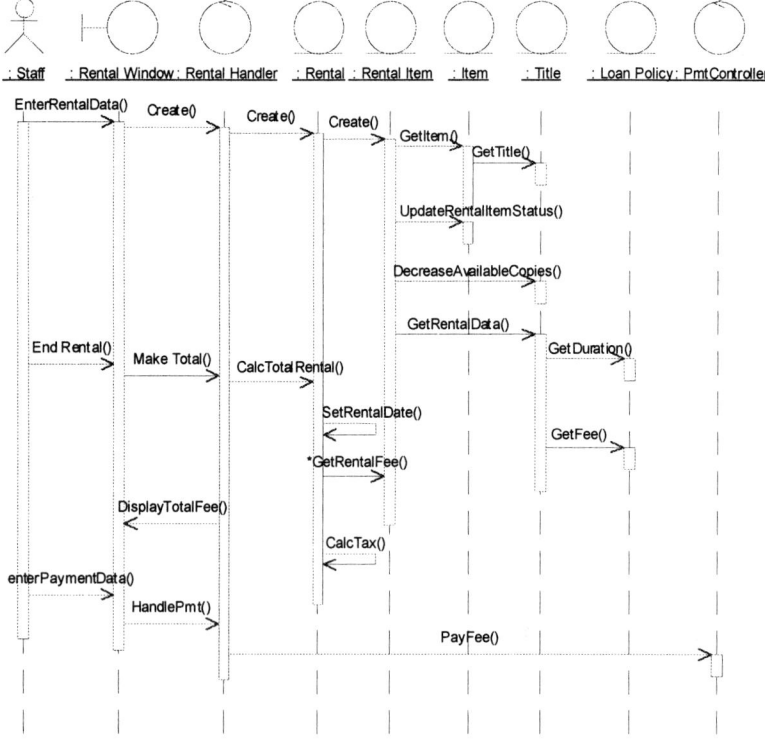

Fig. 7. The sequence diagram for System *Events enterRentalData(), endrental()* and *enterpaymentData()*

The constructed sequence diagram is shown in Fig. 7. Note that we develop a separate sequence diagram for each included or extended use case and represent each of included/extended use case by a secondary control object. Thus, we represented the included use case P*ayfee* (Fig. 4) by a secondary control object *PmtControlle*r. The primary control object *RentalHandler* calls the secondary control object

PmtController. In this way, connections among multiple included/extended use cases within a primary use case can be elegantly represented by message-passings between control objects. The sequence diagram for an included use case will begin with a secondary control object. For example, the sequence diagram for P*ayfee* will begin with the *PmtController*.

7 Conclusion

We notice that novice developers have significant trouble in understanding and developing sequence diagrams. Most UML books simply explain the notations and semantics of sequence diagrams and present pre-built sequence diagrams. Some authors provide simple guidelines for developing sequence diagrams. We found that those simple guidelines are not sufficient for many novice developers. In this paper, we have presented the ten-step heuristic for developing sequence diagrams. We do not claim that the ten-step heuristic presented in this paper always produces the best sequence diagram for all the situations. However, we believe that the technique is highly applicable regardless of problem domains. We also believe that the draft diagram produced by our heuristic can be easily customized and fine-tuned to the specific application. Our experience shows that students who used this method developed sequence diagrams easily and quickly. Even though we assumed that the developer had already developed use case modeling and descriptions, our heuristic can be easily applied without detailed use case modeling. We are currently developing fine-tuning techniques that can be applied after developing an initial sequence diagram using our heuristic.

References

[1] Ambler, S. *Building Object Applications That Work*, SIGS Books, 1998
[2] Booch, G., Rumbaugh, J., and Jacobson, I (1999). *The Unified Modeling Language: User Guide*. Addison Wesley.
[3] Delcambre, L.M.L. and Eckland, E., A Behaviorally driven Approach to Object-Oriented Analysis and Design with Object-Oriented Data Modeling, In *Advances in Object-Oriented Data Modeling*, MIT Press, 2000, pp. 21-40.
[4] Engels, G., Groenewegen, L., and Kappel, G. Coordinated Collaboration of Objects, In *Advances in Object-Oriented Data Modeling*, MIT Press, 2000, pp. 308-331.
[5] Eriksson, H. and Penker, M. (1998). *UML Toolkit*. New York: John Wiley, Inc.
[6] Jacobson, I., Christerson, M., Jonsson, P., and Overgaard, G. *Object-Oriented Software Engineering: A Use Case Driven Approach*. Addison-Wesley, 1992.
[7] Kabajunga, C and Pooley, R.. Simulating UML sequence diagrams. *UK Performance Engineering Workshop*, UK PEW 1998, pages 198—207, July 1998.
[8] Larman, C., *Applying UML and Patterns*, Prentice Hall, 1998.
[9] Li, X. and Lilius, J. Timing Analysis of UML Sequence Diagrams. *UML'99, The Unified Modeling Language. Beyond the Standard*. The Second International Conference, Fort Collins, CO, USA, October 28-30, 1999.
[10] Maciaszek, L. A., *Requirement Analysis and System Design: Developing Information Systems with UML*. Addison Wesley, 2001.

[11] Pooley, R. and Stevens, P., *Using UML: Software Engineering with Objects and Components*. Addison Wesley, 2000.
[12] Quantrani, T. *Visual Modeling with Rational Rose and UML*. Addison Wesley, 1998.
[13] Rudolph, E., Grabowski, J., and Graubmann, P. Towards a Harmonization of UML-Sequence Diagrams and MSC. *SDL'99 - The next Millenium*, Elsevier, June 1999.
[14] Rosenberg, D. (1999). *Use Case Driven Object Modeling with UML: A Practical Approach*, Addison Wesley.
[15] Siau, Keng (2001). *Unified Modeling Language: Systems Analysis, Design and Development Issues*. Idea Publishing Group.
[16] Seemann, J. and Wvg, J. (1998). Extension of UML Sequence Diagrams for Real-Time Systems, In Proc. *International UML Workshop*, Mulhouse, June 1988.
[17] Song, I.-Y., Watts, P., Hassell, L., and Wong, C. "Modeling Dynamic Behavior with Object Interaction Diagrams," *Proc. of 4th International Conference on Computer Science and Informatics (CSI '98)*, Oct. 23-28, 1998, pp. 408-412.
[18] Texel, P. and Williams C. *Use Cases Combined with Booch/OMT/UML: Process and Products*. Upper Saddle River: Prentice Hall PTR, 1997.
[19] Yourdon, E., Whitehead, K., Thomann, J., Oppel, K., and Nevermann, P. *Mainstream Objects: An Analysis and Design Approach for Business*. Upper Saddle River, NJ: Yourdon Press, 1995.

Translation of a High-Level Temporal Model into Lower Level Models:
Impact of Modelling at Different Description Levels

Peter Kraft and Jens Otto Sørensen

Department of Information Science, The Aarhus School of Business,
Fuglesangs Alle 4, DK-8210 Århus V, Denmark
{pkr, jos}@asb.dk

Abstract. The paper attempts theoretically to clarify the interrelation between various levels of descriptions used in the modelling and the programming of information systems. We suggest an analysis where we characterise the description levels with respect to how precisely they may handle information about given types of properties, and examine how descriptions on higher levels translate into descriptions on lower levels. Our example looks at temporal properties where the information is concerned with the existence in time. In a high level temporal model with information kept in a three-dimensional space the existences in time can be mapped precisely and consistently securing a consistent handling of the temporal properties. We translate the high level temporal model into an entity-relationship model, with the information in a two-dimensional graph, and finally we look at the translations into relational and other textual models. We also consider the aptness of models that include procedural mechanisms such as active and object databases.

1 Introduction

Using the properties of valid time, this paper discusses the problems that should be accounted for when specifying a system at different description levels. A desired quality of an information system is that the users can communicate with and reason about it using terms and concepts from their Universe of Discourses. To achieve this quality the developers use a number of different modelling and programming techniques. In order to implement the systems on computers the descriptions made by the various techniques are translated informally or formally from one description level into another ending up with binaries that can be executed on a particular computer with a particular brand of operation system and CPU. The theoretical differences between the levels of description are normally referred to as a question of abstraction mechanism whereby details on levels closer to the binary code are hidden. We take another approach. Our attention is on given property types in Universe of Discourses, how they are described using high level tools and how the descriptions translate from a high level to a lower level. By this way of analysis the focus will be on the complexity one should account for using lower level descriptions - and using lower lever descriptions, we argue, will normally be the case. When focusing on the abstraction mechanism one is tempted only to emphasise the virtue of the model in question.

We characterise the level of a model as how precisely and consistently it is able to describe given selected properties. If, for example, we focus only on the existence of entities and their mutual relationship, we may use a graph as a high level model. Each entity is modelled by one node only and every relationship is modelled by one edge only. The syntax of graphs, requiring edges to connect nodes, implies a consistent modelling of the property that relationships exist between entities. In a graph the property of existences is therefore always mapped completely and consistently.

In data models we classify the occurrences in the extensions as belonging to given types and describe the intentions of types in a schema. When any possible element in the extension is of a given type and each type is described precisely in the schema showing the possible properties of the elements, the schema with the intention is in close concordance with the extension. If we classify the entities and the relationships mapped in the graph, we can describe the corresponding types uniquely in the schema. If we use a diagram we can define symbols and syntax that show the possible relationship types the various types of entities may be involved in.

Having a precise and consistent mapping of properties in the Universe of Discourse to the extension and a close concordance between the extension and the schema, the symbols of the schema may immediately correspond to concepts applicable in the Universe of Discourse and visa versa. Moreover, we can use the symbols of the schema as variables for manipulating the extension generating derived information corresponding to derived concepts that are also immediately applicable in the Universe of Discourse.

Temporal data models are concerned with existence in time. This paper deals with valid time. A high-level temporal data model can be defined by extending the two-dimensional graph with a third continuous time dimension, and define symbols and syntax for a corresponding schema. Having the temporal data model on a high level, we can observe the requirement needed when translating it into a graphical data model that only models the pure existence on a high level.

In characterising textual data models, such as the relational model, we have difficulties recognising any properties from a Universe of Discourse that is modelled at a high level. Textual models have descriptions composed by one-dimensional sequence of symbols where you can apply meanings to a symbol, to the order in which given symbols are stated, and to the order in which given groups of symbols are stated. Thus, the most complex structures that map precisely and consistently into textual descriptions are hierarchical or nested structures. To accomplish descriptions of more complex structures one have to use recognisable marks at different places in the sequence so that partial descriptions positioned at different places can be tied together. Within the relational model, repeated use of attribute values serves this purpose.

As an aside, we may notice that the property of existence is a prerequisite for any ontology and thereby for the design of information systems [1]. The high level descriptions of existence and concepts in graphs and diagrams respectively can explain many of their intuitive usages for illustrations. We may also refer to the relational model where the natural join operation of the algebra and the rules of the normalization procedure indicate the importance of the existence in constructing proper models [2] and [3].

In the following we introduce a graph-oriented entity-relationship model in section two and a corresponding high level temporal model in section three based on the ideas outlined above. In section four a high level temporal model is translated into an entity-relationship model. Thereby the implication of modelling temporal properties on a lower level becomes clear. In section five discussing further translations into relational models and other textual models reinforces the implications. The models so far use declarative descriptions. In section six we touch upon dynamic updates of the information in a system and look at the correspondence between declarative and procedural styles of descriptions. Finally, section seven concludes the paper.

2 Symbols and Semantics of a Graph-Oriented ER-model

We refer to a version of the entity-relationship model called the Unified Entity-Relationship model [4] and [5]. It deviates in some respects from P. Chen's entity-relationship model from 1976 [6] and later versions, e.g. [7], [8] or [9]. We shall introduce only those aspects of the model that we need in the following.

The model can map the existence of entities and their mutual relationships precisely and consistently. Extensions are described in a binary graph. Corresponding to the property of existence, the derivation rules for the graph is defined as an equivalent class. In the schema, we only use two symbols: a "box" for entity types and a "craw foot" for what we call the basic relationship type which has a mandatory one-side and an optional many-side. All diagramming needs can be satisfied by these two symbols only. We will, however, introduce other symbols as convenient shorthand for some common special cases. For example, the well-known one-to-one relationship is a special case of the basic relationship type with a constraint specifying that the cardinality has a lower bound of one, and the upper bound is also one. The shorthand symbol for that is of course just a line without the craw foot.

The basic relationship type is the simplest possible. The argument is as follows: Assume that other more complex relationship types exist. Then replacing complex relationships with entities that are related to the entities of the relationships will eventually reach a symbol of a binary relationship with a mandatory one-side and an optional many-side.

The entities on the one-side are regular and the entities on the many-side are dependent on the existence of an entity on the one-side. We call the references along a basic relationship for a simple reference and a set reference respectively. Due to the derivation rules of the equivalent class, it is always possible to fit the concepts of the Universe of Discourse such that the concepts conform to the semantics of the symbols. I.e. complex relationships are conceptualised as entities.

Figure 1 a) shows a diagram with a basic relationship symbol and a sample of a corresponding graph of occurrences. Employees are always attached to one and only one department. Departments can have from zero to many employees. An entity also constitutes a relationship. At b) in the figure, jobs constitute conjunctions with one occurrence per relationship between an employee and a project. At c) departments constitute disjunctions with each occurrence relating a set of employees to a set of projects.

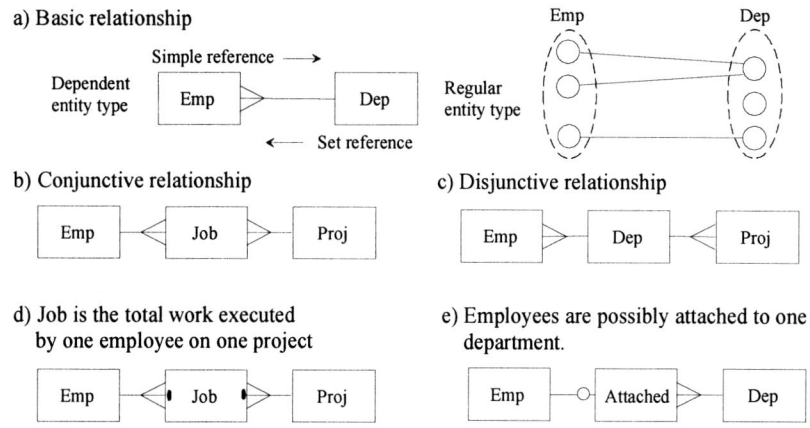

Fig. 1. Modelling relationships

We restrict the possible information captured in a model by constraining the sets of entities and interrelationships. At d) in the figure, the black marks indicate a composed key constraint. It restricts the set of jobs to at most one job per employee per project. The constraints add to the semantics of a model. At b) a job is any work executed by one employee on one project. At d) a job is the total work executed by one employee on one project.

A "circle" on the relationship symbol replacing the craw foot, shown at e), is used to indicate that a cardinality constraint is restricting the sets on the many-side to be zero or one. At e) we get an optional reference where an employee is attached to at most one department. Due to the implied one-to-one relationship the simple references from the attachment entities to employee entities constitute a non-composed key for the attachment entities. In the examples below, we show how more complex constraints are specified by first order logic statements, i.e. well formed formulas from the predicate calculus.

An attribute is a special case of an entity. Besides their existence, attributes have "visible values". We assume that for every attribute type all possible attribute values exist a priori and occur only once in the extension.

In figure 2 i) the attribute type, dep#, is diagrammed as an entity type referred to from Emp- and Proj-entities respectively. We have marked the attribute-entity type with a key-mark indicating that the values constitute the keys of the attributes. We also use the shorthand diagramming of attributes shown at ii). In any case, the diagramming of attributes corresponds to occurrences in the graph of the extensions as illustrated by the sample at iii).

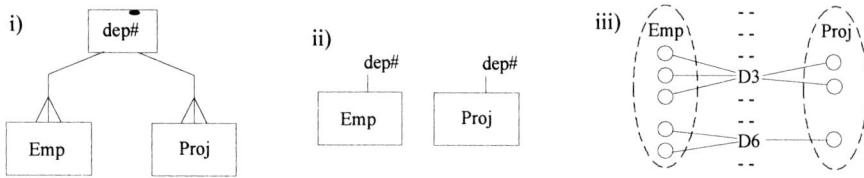

Fig. 2. Modelling of attributes

3 Symbols and Semantics of a Temporal High-Level Model

The high level temporal model expands the graph of the entity relationship model with a continuous time dimension such that the existence in time can be mapped. We assume that the corresponding concepts are stable over time and applicable on the Universe of Discourse at any one point in time. Thus, we may use a schema with the same set of symbols and constraints that apply to a non-temporal ER model.

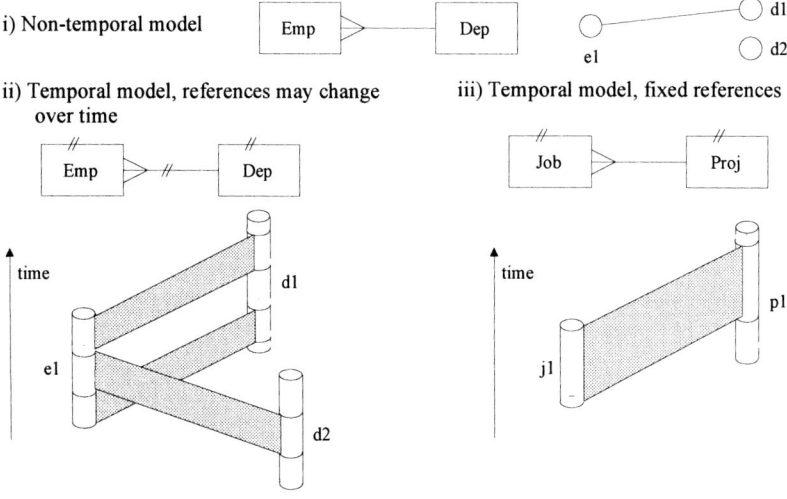

Fig. 3. Temporal symbols and their semantics

We define that an entity exists in an uninterrupted period and that a simple reference may vary between different entities during the life span of the corresponding dependent entity. To distinguish a temporal model from a non-temporal model we mark the entity and relationship symbols with a double stroke. Like restrictions on possible existences, we may put restriction on their expansions in time. If the entities exist from genesis to eternity, or simple references exist unchanged in the life span of the corresponding dependent entity then we remove the double stroke in the diagram. Attribute values exist a priori at all time.

Figure 3 at i) shows a non-temporal model and a sample of a graph with one employee and two departments. The following two models are temporal models illustrating the three-dimensional extensions. At ii) we have the unrestricted case. It illustrates the life span of one employee and two departments, where the employee is attached to one department at first, then to the other department and finally again to the first department. At iii) we constraint the simple references not to change during the life span of the jobs. The concept of a job is defined with respect to one project only.

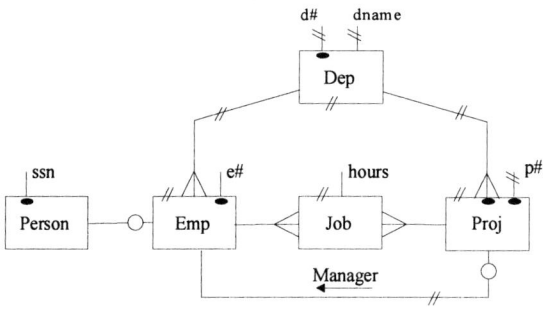

Fig. 4. Company case

In figure 4 we show a temporal model for a company. From the concepts described by the schema we read: A company may have several departments. The departments have at any time a unique d# and a not necessarily unique dname, where both d# and dname may vary during the life spans of the departments. An employee is at any time attached to one department and can be moved from one department to another. Employees have in their life span an unchangeable unique e# as key. An employee is a person. We are not concerned with the life span of persons, but we have modelled that a person can appear as different employees at different periods.

Projects can also move from one department to another. Projects have a changeable p# which at any time should be unique within the department that the project currently belongs to. Projects have for all times an employee as manager, but not necessarily the same employee in the whole lifetime of the projects. An employee can manage one project only at a given time. Jobs are arbitrary work executed by one employee on one project. A job runs over a limited time span and accounts for a number of hours.

4 High-Level Temporal Models Translated into ER-models

When we cannot directly model the continuous expansion in time, we must introduce some extra constructs. For use in ER models we introduce an abstract data type, say T, to capture expansions in time. For T we assume some functions, conditions, and constants. Among these:

Start time:	BeginT (T)
End time:	EndT (T)
T1 and T2 coincide:	T1 = T2
T1 included in T2:	T1 IN T2
T1 and T2 overlap:	T1 OVERLAP T2
Constant: now and forward:	NowT

The next two figures below show how different schema patterns of temporal models translate into the ER model.

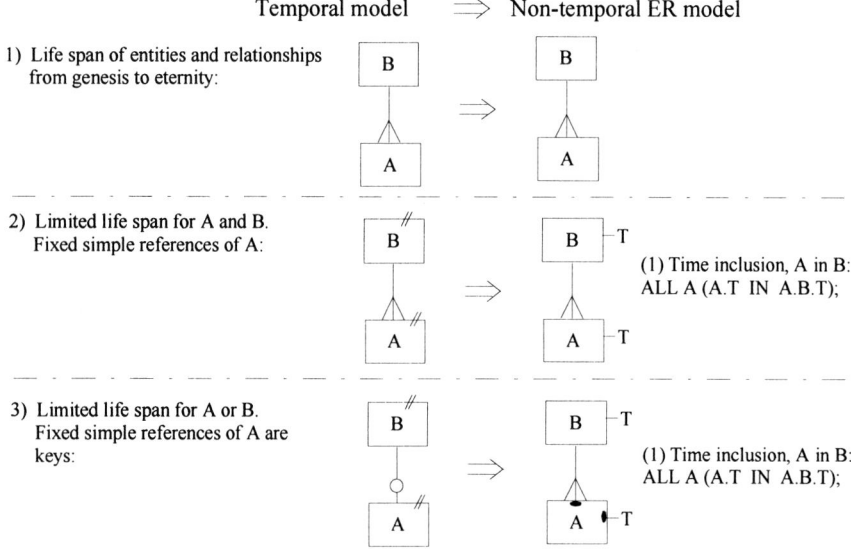

Fig. 5. Translation of patterns: Fixed simple references

Figure 5 shows patterns with non-varying simple references. At 1) the life spans of the entities are from genesis to eternity, and accordingly the relationships will have the same span of life. The translated model is equal to the non-translated model. At 2) the life spans of the entities are limited. In the translated model, we use the T-attribute to capture life spans. Further, we have to specify the time inclusion constraint (1) that guards that the life spans of the dependent A-entities are included in the life span of the entities referred to. Formally, we specify the constraint as a WFF of the predicate calculus and use path expressions to specify references via basic relationships. At 3) the simple reference from A to B is the key of A. At any time, only one A-entity should refer to a given B-entity. However, over time several A-entities could refer to the same B entity. In the translated model we get a non-restricted set reference from B to A and a key for A-entities composed of a simple reference to a B-entity and a T-attribute value. When a T-attribute is part in a key, comparison of two T-values should not overlap. Also here we need the time inclusion constraint (1).

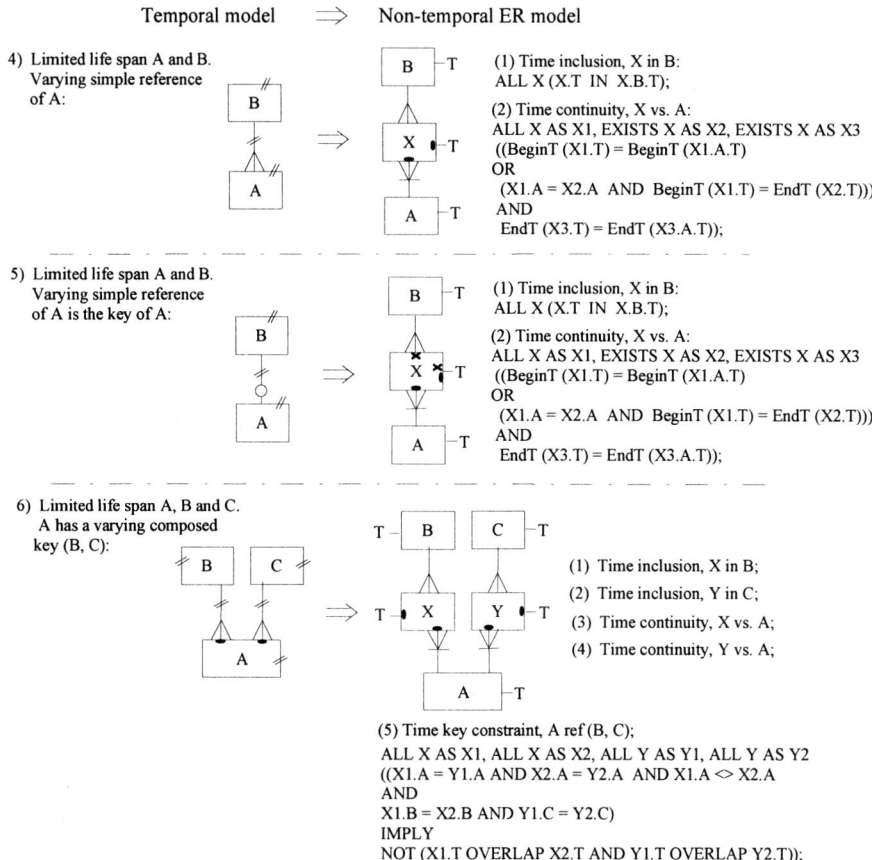

Fig. 6. Translation of patterns: Varying simple references

Figure 6 shows translation of a pattern where simple references may vary in time. The varying references imply that an extra entity type is added to the translated schema. At 4) in figure 6 the simple reference from A to B may vary. At different times an A-entity may refer to different B-entities such that, disregarding life spans, there is a many-to-many relationship between A- and B-entities. In the translated model we insert the X-entity type to capture these relationships. Further, we have to add a set of constraints: the bar on the relationship symbol is a cardinality constraint indicating that every A-entity should at least relate to one X-entity, and thereby to a B-entity. The time inclusion constraint (1) says that the life span of X-entities should be included in the life span of the B-entities referred to. The time continuity constraint (2) guaranties that during the total life span of an A-entity, X-entities referring to the A-entity exist, and the key constraint of the X-entities guaranties that no two different X-entities refer to the same A-entity at the same time.

At 5) the temporal model has a simple reference referring from A to B as the key of A. The translation is the same as for the pattern 4) except that there should not be two X-entities, which at the same time relates a B-entity with more than one A-entity and vice versa. This is secured by two candidate key constrains for the X-entity. One composed of T and the reference to A, and the other is T and the reference to B. In the figure we use different markings to distinguish between the two candidate keys.

At 6) we have a temporal model with a composed key for the A-entities where the corresponding simple references may vary in time. In the translated model, we should add the entity types, X and Y, for each of the simple references with corresponding constraints like in the pattern shown at 4). To guarantee the key property we specify the time key constraint (5). It says that for two different X-entities and for two different Y-entities when they all refer to the same A-entity, when the X-entities refer to the same B-entity, and when the Y-entities refer to the same C-entity, then the X-entities and the Y-entities should not both overlap in time.

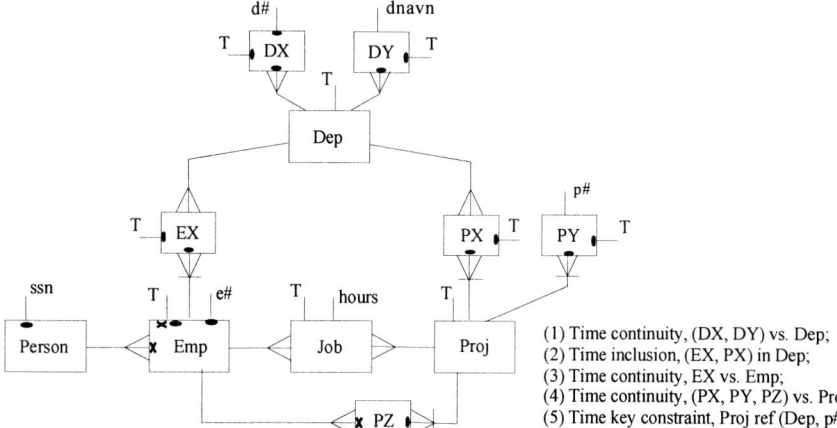

Fig. 7. Translation of the company case

Figure 7 shows the translation of the company case into a non-temporal ER model. We have stated the non-diagrammed constraints informally.

5 Translations into the Relational Model and Other Textual Models

An ER model translates into a relational model with one table per entity type. (We ignore that NULLs for attributes are allowed such that tables with the same primary key can be collapsed). Before the translation, a key must be defined for each entity type referred to by simple references. An added key could possibly be some kind of surrogate. The attributes of the tables are the attributes of the entities plus foreign key attributes. The foreign key attributes are inherited primary key attributes from the tables corresponding to entities referred to by simple references. If simple references are part of a key, a cascade of inheritances may occur.

Proper-modelled ER models normally translate into normalised relational models [5]. Primary key and foreign key integrity rules are in most cases maintained by the database management systems, where the former corresponds to the key constraint of the ER model, and the latter is needed to guard that relationships among tables correspond to simple references of the ER model. Other constraints of the ER model should also be accounted for, especially those that maintain the consistent handling of given properties, such as temporal properties.

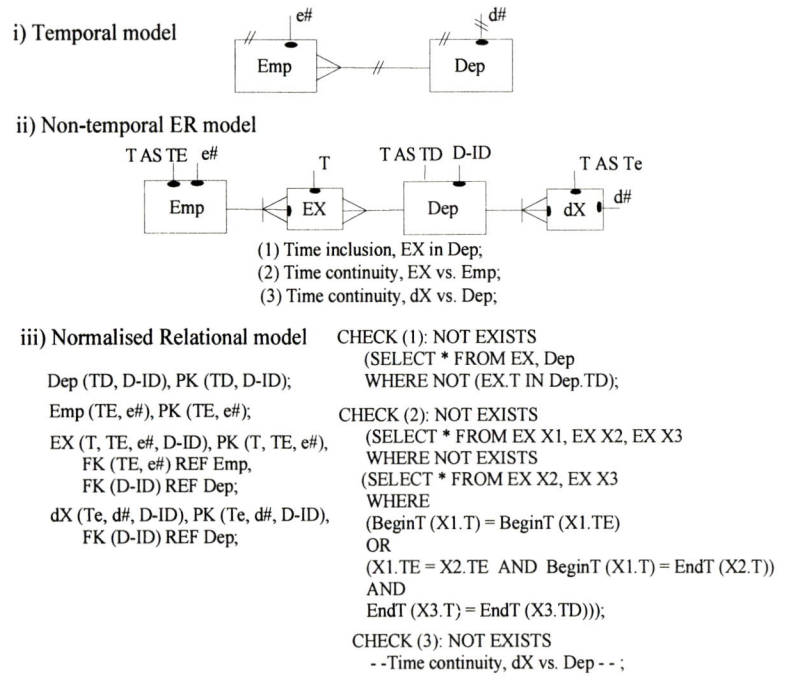

Fig. 8. Translation into a relational model

Figure 8 models a subset from the company case. At i) we show the temporal modelling. At ii) the translated ER model is shown. We have added a surrogate key-attribute, D-ID, to the Dep-entity type, since otherwise we cannot translate into a relational model. We have also renamed some of the T-attributes by an AS-clause partly because it is needed and partly for convenience in explanations. At iii) to the left is the set of tables translated from the ER model. We use a compact notation. The PK-clause specifies a primary key and the FK-REF-clause specifies a foreign key. To the right we use CHECK statements, available in some DBMS, to specify what corresponds to the time inclusion constraint (1) and the time continuity constraints (2) and (3) of the ER model.

We shall briefly refer to some proposed types of textual temporal models noticing their problems. A proposal for temporal normalisation results in sets of tables like the set we get by translations into the normalised relational model in figure 8 [10].

A crucial point normally not mentioned is the need for surrogate key attributes in cases where a component of a primary key may vary over time. However, in discussing a temporal model based on an entity-relationship model called the EER model, Navathe and Ahmed assume that each entity a priory has a non-visible surrogate key attribute [11]. In [12] Snodgrass considers time varying attributes modelled in SQL schemas. He recommends that time varying attributes are placed in their own table with foreign keys referring to the tables of the entity type in question, and that a table corresponding to an entity type with a time varying key is provided with a surrogate being a time-invariant key. This is like our translations via a non-temporal ER-model to a relational model, cf. figure 8.

Other types of textual models intend to map to a set of tables that correspond to a snapshot situation with normalized tables. Distinctions are made between models with 1NF tables and N1NF tables [13]. In the 1NF case the tables have a separate tupple for each variation in time of the attributes, e.g. [14]. This variant is also the base for TSQL2 [15]. In the N1NF case, the tupples have lists with time spans for each set of attributes that vary at the same time. In neither case, surrogate attributes are considered.

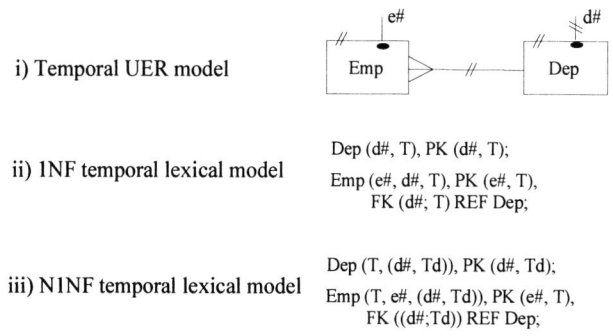

Fig. 9. Types of textual models

Figure 9 illustrates the implications of the two latter cases using the example shown by the temporal model i). Corresponding to a snapshot, we have two tables one for Dep and one for Emp. At ii) we show the 1NF tables. A department described in the Dep-table will have a new tuple for each time its d# changes. The time span attribute, T, delimits the life span in which a given d# is assigned to a given department. We have no means to distinguish whether two tuples with consecutive time span attributes correspond to the same department or to two different departments. Similarly, an employee described in the Emp-table will have a tuple for each time either a new department is referred to or the referenced department change its d#. The time span attribute, T, delimits the time when both the reference to a department and the d# of the referenced department are stable. When an e# for an employee, who has left the company, is reused afterwards by a new employee, we cannot distinguish between tupples corresponding to each employee.

At iii) we show the tables corresponding to a N1NF version of a temporal textual model. Each department and each employee has one tupple in the Dep and the Emp-tables respectively with the T attributes showing their life spans. In a Dep-tupple we have a list of the varying d# attributes together with their life spans, Td. Since a department is identified by the varying d#, there can be several keys identifying the same tuple. In the Emp-table we have a time-varying list of foreign keys. There will be a new member in the list each time an employee moves to a new department and each time the referenced department changes its d#.

We may notice that in both the 1NF and the N1NF cases a change of the key attribute d# for the Dep-table has an impact on the Emp-table as a new tuple should be added, or an adding to a list in a tuple should be made.

6 Dynamics

In connection with updating of information we will point out the dualism that exists between declarative descriptions such as those used above and procedural descriptions.

From e.g. C. A. R. Hoare's proof theories [16] and from formal methods like VDM [17] or Z [18] we know that we can specify the outcome of an algorithm in a declarative manner by asserting pre- and post-conditions accounting for invariant properties. We may equip the algorithm with a heading such as procedure or function headings or as statements in a procedural language like e.g. Pascal. The algorithm themselves - the implementation - are specified by a sequence of calls of other procedures and functions or by a sequence of statements in possibly another language. The proof theories or formal methods advice methods whereby it can be verified that the pre-, post- and invariant-conditions that are valid for the steps of the algorithm combine into the pre-, post- and invariant-conditions valid for the heading of the algorithm. From a descriptive point of view, a declaratively stated heading with implied semantics represents a higher level of descriptions than the procedural descriptions of the implementations. From an updating point of view the pre- and post-conditions correspond to the state of information kept by the system before and after an update, and the invariance to the specified constraints.

If we operate on a declaratively specified system, we should think of updating as if we directly manipulated the elements of the extensions. When the specification is on a high level, we can only manipulate the elements in a consistent way. When the specification is on a lower level, we may possibly have to manipulate several elements and should account for the constraints. We may also think of manipulations made with respect to partially high-level descriptions and of a translation into lower level procedural descriptions that manipulates the necessary set of elements accounting for the constraints. For example: when we have specified our temporal database by 1NF relations as in figure 9 we could state that a given department is now given a new d#. The update should then activate a procedure that adds the relevant row to both the Dep and the Emp table. We acknowledge specification tools where specifications of constraints are replaced by procedural specifications that activate an update, such as active databases and object databases.

7 Conclusion

As our starting point for our analysis we recognised the importance of property types as they occur in the Universe of Discourse. Our temporal example started with a three-dimensional high-level description. In general, information systems may have to account for many different types of properties, not just valid time as in our case, and there may not be a description for all the properties on a high level.

We looked at the distinction between description levels, where a high level description of given property types describes the property precisely and consistently. With temporal properties we examined how the properties are described through three levels of descriptions using three sorts of descriptions: a description with a continuous dimension describing the extensions in time, a description using a graph, and three descriptions using variations of textual descriptions.

When you have to describe elements of the extensions at a lower level we showed: 1) to specify continuous properties we need to introduce extra constructs stated as attribute values. 2) descriptions of given properties may be spread over several elements. And 3) the use of elements and attribute values will be restricted by given sets of constraints. We also showed that the dualism between declarative and procedural descriptions allows specifications of constraints to be compensated by algorithms activated at the time of the update.

As an overall conclusion from our study, which has shown the complications one should account for when specifying on lower levels, we suggest that it is valuable if similar analyses are made not only with respect to temporal properties but also with respect to various other types or categories of types of properties that can occur in information systems.

References

1. Sowa, J.F., *Knowledge Representation. Logical, Philosophical, and Computational Foundations.* 2000: Brooks/Cole.
2. Codd, E.F., *A relational model for large shared databanks.* Communication of the ACM, 1970. 13(6).
3. Codd, E.F., *Further normalization of the data base relational model*, in *Data Base System*, R. Rustin, Editor. 1972, Printice-Hall.
4. Kraft, P. and J.O. Sørensen. *Accessing Data Bases through Interface Views using a Unified Graph-Oriented Entity-Relationship Model.* in *Integrated Design & Process Technology (IDPT).* 1998. Berlin: Society for Design and Process Science.
5. Kraft, P. and J.O. Sørensen, *En Uniform Entity-Relationship Model.* 2001, Frederikshavn: Dafolo Forlag. 212.
6. Chen, P.P., *The Entity-Relationship Model - Toward a Unified View of Data.* ACM, Transaction on Database Systems, 1976. 1(1).
7. Teory, T.J., *Database Modelling and Design. The Entity-Relationship Approach.* 1990: Morgan Kaufmann.
8. Batini, C., S. Ceri, and S.B. Navathe, *Conceptual Database Design. An Entity-relationship Approach.* 1992: The Benjamin/Cummings Publishing Company, Inc.

9. Elmasri, R. and S.B. Navathe, *Fundamentals of Database Systems, Third Edition*. World Student Series. 2000: Addison-Wesley.
10. Navathe, S.B. and R. Ahmed, *Temporal Extension to the Relational Model and SQL*, in *Temporal Databases. Theory, Design, and Implementation*, A.U. Tansel, et al., Editors. 1993, The Benjamin/Cummings Publishing Company, Inc. p. 92 - 109.
11. Elmasri, R., G.T.J. Wuu, and V. Kouramajian, *A Temporal Model and Query Language for EER Databases*, in *Temporal Databases. Theory, Design, and Implementation*, A.U. Tansel, et al., Editors. 1993, The Benjamin/Cummings Publishing Company, Inc. p. 212-229.
12. Snodgrass, R.T., *Developing Time-Oriented Database Applications in SQL*. The Morgan Kaufmann Series in Data MAnagement Systems, ed. J. Gray. 2000, San Francisco: Morgan Kaufmann Publishers. 504.
13. Clifford, J., A. Croker, and A. Tuzhhilin, *On the Completeness of Query Languages for Grouped and Ungrouped Historical Data Models*, in *Temporal Databases. Theory, Design, and Implementation*, A.U. Tansel, et al., Editors. 1993, The Benjamin/Cummings Publishing Company, Inc. p. 497 - 533.
14. Date, C.J., *An Introduction to Database Systems. 7. ed.* 2000: Addison Wesley Longman, Inc.
15. Zaniolo, C., et al., *Advanced Database Systems*. 1997: Morgan Kaufmann Publishers, Inc.
16. Hoare, C.A.R., *An Axiomatic Basis for Computer Programming*. Communication of the ACM, 1969. 12(10): p. 576-583.
17. Jones, C.B., *Systematic Software Development Using VDM*. International Series in Computer Science, ed. C.A.R. Hoare. 1986, Hemel Hempstead: Prentice Hall.
18. Diller, A., *Z An Introduction to Formal Methods. 2. ed.* 1994: John Wiley & Sons.

Relationship Type Refinement in Conceptual Models with Multiple Classification

Dolors Costal, Antoni Olivé, Ernest Teniente

Universitat Politècnica de Catalunya
Dept. Llenguatges i Sistemes Informàtics
Jordi Girona 1-3, 08034 Barcelona (Catalonia)

[dolors | olive | teniente]@lsi.upc.es

Abstract. The definition of a relationship type includes its participant entity types and the cardinality constraints. Relationship type refinement is the specification of additional constraints when some of the participant entities are also instances of other entity types. The best known types of refinements are refinement of participants and refinement of cardinality constraints.

These refinements have been studied, up to now, only for conceptual models with single classification. In this paper we extend previous work by dealing with conceptual models with multiple classification. We characterize the refinements in this context, provide a graphical and textual notation for their specification, and give their formal definition in logical terms. Moreover, we provide a set of necessary conditions to guarantee that a given set of refinements is valid.

1 Introduction

Two kinds of integrity constraints are almost always defined for relationship types: referential integrity and cardinality constraints. Relationship type refinement is the specification of additional constraints that must hold when some of the entities that participate in a relationship type are also instances of other entity types. In principle, there may be several types of refinements but, in practice, two of them appear more frequently than the others: *refinement of participants* and *refinement of cardinality constraints*.

A classical example [BS85, MO95] of cardinality constraint refinement is the following. Assume that we have a relationship type that relates messages and the persons to whom messages are sent (i.e. their recipients). We know that, in general, a message may have any number of recipients. We may define a cardinality constraint refinement to restrict that a certain kind of messages (e.g. private messages, a subtype of message) can have at most one recipient. We may also define a refinement of participants to state that an officer message (a subtype of message) may be received only by officers (a subtype of person).

The identification and analysis of relationship type refinements is important for the same reason as any other kind of integrity constraints:

(1) to ease their use in conceptual schemas. It is easier to define a refinement graphically than to give its equivalent in some general-purpose language (OCL, FOL, etc.).
(2) to allow the development of specialized procedures for reasoning about them.
(3) to develop efficient patterns of implementation for their enforcement.

Relationship type refinements were already defined in [MBW80, BS85] and, during the last decade, they have been studied and used by many different authors and languages [BO92, CLF93, CD94, MO95, RJB99]. All these studies focus only on the case of refinements for conceptual models with single classification. That is, models where an entity may be a direct instance of only one entity type.

In this paper we extend previous work by dealing with conceptual models with multiple classification, in which an entity may be direct instance of one or more entity types at the same time [RJB99]. We characterize relationship refinements in this context and give their formal definition in logical terms.

Many authors have argued about the advantages of considering conceptual models with multiple classification. For instance, [BG95] argues that although multiple classification can be represented in a model with multiple specialization, the solution required to do this may lead to a lot of artificial subclasses. [MM92] discusses about the expressiveness gained when considering multiple classification. More recently, UML [RJB99, p. 54] states also that there is no logical necessity that an object have a direct entity type only, since we typically look at real-world objects from many angles simultaneously.

There have been several proposals of graphical notations to express relationship type refinements in single classification, but none of them is neither sufficiently clear nor general to express them. This could perhaps be the reason why UML does not provide a convincing graphical notation either. In this paper we suggest a graphical and textual notation that may be used in both single and multiple classification models.

On the other hand, we also state a number of necessary conditions to guarantee that a given set of refinements is valid. Roughly, a set of refinements is valid if there may be a non-empty population of the information base satisfying the constraints implied by the refinements. To the best of our knowledge, ours is the first study in this respect.

This paper is structured as follows. Next section reviews basic concepts for relationship refinement. Section 3 characterizes the refinements in the context of multiple classification, provides a notation for their specification and gives their formal definition. Section 4 is devoted to the problem of validating a set of refinements. Finally, section 5 presents our conclusions.

2 Basic Concepts for Relationship Refinement

In this section, we describe the main concepts involved in the refinement of relationships in conceptual models with single classification, and we introduce some basic notation we need to define them.

2.1 Basic Concepts

We assume that entities and relationships are instances of their types at particular time points [Bub77], which are expressed in a common base time unit such as second or day. We make this assumption for the sake of generality, but our work is also applicable when a temporal view is not needed.

We represent by $E(e,t)$ the fact entity e is instance of entity type E at time t. For instance, $Employee(Marta,D1)$ means that $Marta$ is an instance of $Employee$ at time $D1$ (day in this case). The population of E at t is defined as the set of entities that are instances of E at t.

A relationship type has a name and a set of n participants, with $n \geq 2$. A *participant* is an entity type that plays a certain role in the relationship type. $R(p_1:E_1,...,p_n:E_n)$ denotes a relationship type named R with entity type participants $E_1,...,E_n$ playing the roles $p_1,...,p_n$, respectively.

We say that $R(p_1:E_1,...,p_n:E_n)$ is the *schema* of the relationship type and that $p_1:E_1$, ..., $p_n:E_n$ are their participants. The order of the participants in the schema is irrelevant. Two different participants may be of the same entity type, but two different participants may not have the same role. When the role name is omitted, it is assumed to be the same as the corresponding entity type. In this paper we will only consider binary relationship types (i.e. with $n = 2$).

We represent by $R(e_1,...,e_n,t)$ the fact that entities $e_1,...,e_n$ participate in an instance of R at time t. The referential integrity constraints associated with R guarantee that e_1, ..., e_n are instance of their corresponding types $E_1,...,E_n$.

Given a binary relationship type $R(p_1:E_1, p_2:E_2)$, the cardinality constraint between p_1 and p_2 in R, that we denote by $Card(p_1; p_2; R)$, is a pair $Card(p_1; p_2; R) = (min, max)$ that indicates the minimum and maximum number of entities of type E_2 that may be related with any entity of type E_1 through R, at any time point [LEW93]. $Card(p_2; p_1; R)$ is defined in a similar way.

For instance, in the binary relationship type *Participates (Employee, Project)*, we would indicate that an employee may participate in any number of projects by $Card(employee; project; Participates) = (0, *)$.

Specialization and generalization are fundamental operations in conceptual modeling. Specialization consists in defining that an entity type (subtype) is a refinement of another one (supertype). Generalization is the converse operation. and it defines that an entity type is more general than a set of other entity types.

A specialization implies an inclusion constraint between the populations of the subtype and the supertype. Additional constraints on populations are usually defined in the context of generalizations, mainly the well-known union, disjointness and covering constraints [Len87].

A specialization is a relationship between two entity types E' and E, that we denote by E' *IsA* E. For instance, *JuniorEmp IsA Employee*. E' is said to be a subtype of E, and E a supertype of E'. In terms of the population of E' and E, this implies that all instances of E' at a certain time point are also instances of E at that time point. An entity type may be supertype of several entity types, and it may be a subtype of several entity types.

Generalization and specialization are two different viewpoints of the same IsA relationship, viewed from the supertype or from the subtype [RBP+91]. However, the term specialization tends to be used to mean a particular instance of the IsA relationship, while generalization uses to mean a set of IsA relationships with the same supertype.

We adopt here this meaning, and we denote by $E\ Gens\ E_1,...,E_n$ the generalization of entity types $E_1,...,E_n$ to E. Normally, the set of IsA included in a generalization are the result of some specialization criterion [SCG+95] or have the same classification principle [WJS95] or discriminator [RJB99].

A partition $E\ Partd\ E_1,...,E_n$ is a generalization $E\ Gens\ E_1,...,E_n$ in which every instance of E at t is both instance of at least one E_i at t and instance of at most one E_i at t. We write *Partd* as a shorthand for *Partitioned by*. Every generalization can be transformed into a partition, through the use of auxiliary entity types and generalizations. The transformation is information preserving in the sense that the information content of the schema is not changed [BCN92]. Thus, without loss of generality, we will assume that all generalizations are partitions.

2.2 Relationship Type Refinements in Conceptual Models with Single Classification

Refinement of participants of a relationship type R restricts the possible entity types that participate in R. For instance, consider the relationship type:
    Participates (Employee,Project)
and suppose that we have:
    Employee Partd JuniorEmp, SeniorEmp
    Project Partd Critical, NonCritical.
In this situation, we have a refinement of participants if we state that junior employees can only participate in non-critical projects.

To the best of our knowledge, even if refinement of participants have a long tradition in conceptual modeling [MBW80], none of the graphical notations proposed to express relationship type refinements (even in conceptual models with single classification) is sufficiently clear nor general to express them. The notation we propose, inspired in the one proposed by Syntropy [CD94], is aimed to overcome the limitations of previous proposals. According to our notation, the previous refinement is represented as shown in Figure 2.1.

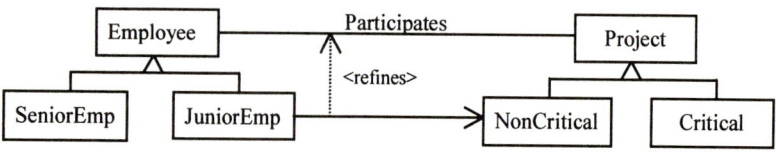

Figure 2.1

Note that a graphical notation to represent refinements of participants must explicitly define the direction of the refinement. For instance, the previous figure restricts junior employees to participate only in non-critical projects. However, it does not restrict the kind of employees that may participate in a non-critical project. Existing graphical notations do not explicitly define the direction of the refinement and, thus, it is impossible to determine the role of the relationship type to which the restriction defined by the refinement applies.

Refinement of cardinality constraints of a relationship type restricts the minimum and maximum number of entities of a certain participant of the relationship type that may be related with another participant entity type when one or both of them belong to a subtype of their corresponding entity type.

For instance, consider again the relationship type
   Participates (Employee, Project)
and assume also that we have
   Employee PartD JuniorEmp, SeniorEmp
In this situation, we have a refinement of cardinality constraints if employees may participate in any number of projects but junior employees can participate at most in five projects. This refinement is shown in the Figure 2.2.

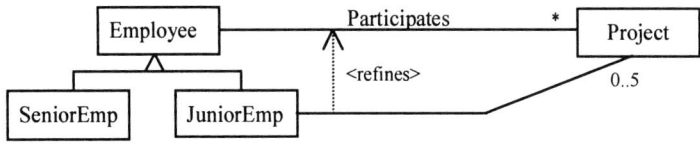

Figure 2.2

We do not need to define the direction of the refinement since the restricted multiplicity is already set on the side of the role for which the restriction applies.

3 Relationship Type Refinements in Conceptual Models with Multiple Classification

In this section we characterize the refinements in the context of conceptual models with multiple classification, provide a notation for their specification and give their formal definition in logical terms. We deal with refinement of participants and of cardinality constraints in sections 3.1 and 3.2, respectively.

3.1 Refinement of Participants

In the previous section, we have seen that refinement of participants constraint the possible entity types that participate in a relationship type R when some of the participant entities are instances of other entity types.

For the sake of simplicity, we will start by formalizing this type of refinement for a particular case. In this case, the restriction applies to entities that belong to a single subtype of the entity types participating in the relationship type.

Given a relationship type $R(p_1:E_1, p_2:E_2)$, a refinement of participants of R is represented by:

$$PRef = R(p_1:\{E_{1,i}\} \rightarrow p_2:\{E_{2,j}\})$$

The first argument, $p_1{:}E_{1,i}$, is the *antecedent* of the refinement, while the second, $p_2{:}E_{2,j}$, is the *consequent*. It means that when the participants p_1 in R belong to entity type $E_{1,i}$ then the participants p_2 must belong to $E_{2,j}$. Formally,

$$R(e_1,e_2,t) \wedge E_{1,i}(e_1,t) \rightarrow E_{2,j}(e_2,t)$$

In a similar way, we could define another refinement of participants $PRef' = R(p_2{:} \{E_{2,j}\} \rightarrow p_1{:} \{E_{1,i}\})$ in the opposite direction.

Using this notation, the refinement of Figure 2.1 would be defined as:

Participates (employee:{JuniorEmp} → project:{NonCritical}).

Sometimes the designer will need to define a refinement of participants where either the antecedent, the consequent or both are sets of entity types. Intuitively, the meaning of such a refinement is that when the participants p_1 are instance of *all* the entity types of the antecedent, then the participants p_2 must be instances of *some* of the entity types of the consequent. For instance, given

    Participates (Employee, Project)
    Employee Partd JuniorEmp, SeniorEmp
    Employee Partd Temporary, Permanent
    Project Partd ShortTerm, MediumTerm, LongTerm

we may want to express the constraint that employees that are junior and have a temporary position can only participate in short or medium term projects.

Now, the graphical notation we introduced in section 2 to express the refinements must be extended to allow refinements to consider more than one entity type. This is illustrated in Figure 3.1.

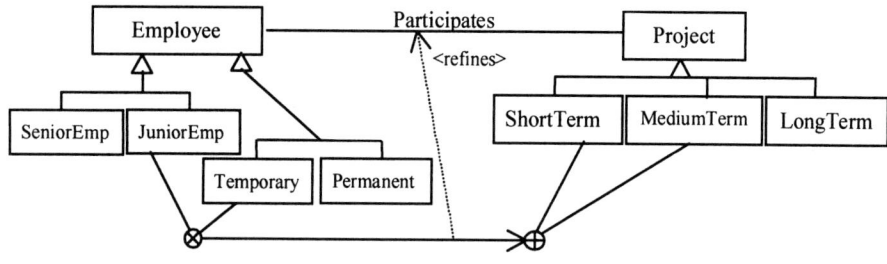

Figure 3.1

Definition 3.1: *Refinement of Participants*

Given a relationship type $R(p_1{:}E_1, p_2{:}E_2)$. A refinement of participants of R is defined as $PRef = R(p_1{:}\{E_{1,1},..., E_{1,n}\} \rightarrow p_2{:}\{E_{2,1},..., E_{2,m}\})$.

The meaning of PRef is that when participants p_1 are instances of all entity types $E_{1,1}$, ..., $E_{1,n}$ then participants p_2 must be instance of some of the entity types $E_{2,1}$, ..., $E_{2,m}$. Formally,

$$R(e_1,e_2,t) \wedge E_{1,1}(e_1,t) \wedge ... \wedge E_{1,n}(e_1,t) \rightarrow E_{2,1}(e_2,t) \vee ... \vee E_{2,m}(e_2,t)$$

Thus, the previous refinement would be defined as *Participates (employee: {JuniorEmp, Temporary} → project:{ShortTerm, MediumTerm}).*

There are two particular cases of refinement of participants that are noteworthy. The first is when the antecedent is empty: $R(\rightarrow p_2{:}\{E_{2,1},..., E_{2,m}\})$. The meaning, obvious, is that participants p_2 must necessarily be instance of some of the entity types $E_{2,1},..., E_{2,m}$, independently of the types of the other participants.

The second one is when the consequent is empty: $R(p_1:\{E_{1,1},..., E_{1,n}\} \to)$. The meaning now is that the entity types of the participants p_1 may not be instance of the entity types $E_{1,1},..., E_{1,n}$ at the same time.

3.2 Refinement of Cardinality Constraints

Refinement of cardinality constraints consists in constraining the minimum and maximum number of entities of a certain participant of the relationship type that may be related with another participant. For instance, given

    Participates (Employee, Project)
    Employee Partd JuniorEmp, SeniorEmp
    Employee Partd Temporary, Permanent
    Card(employee; project; Participates) = (0, *)

we may want to express a cardinality constraint refinement stating that employees that are junior and have a temporary position may participate at most in 3 projects, as shown in the following figure.

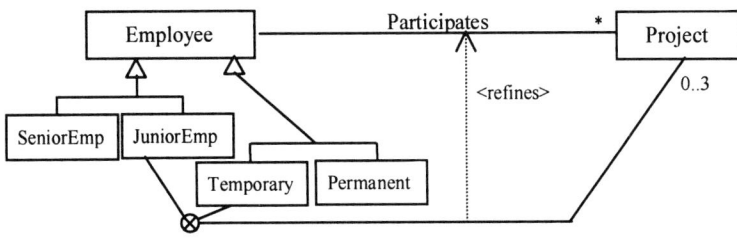

Figure 3.2

Definition 3.2: *Refinement of Cardinality Constraints*
Given a relationship type $R(p_i:E_i, p_j:E_j)$, with $i,j=1..2$. A refinement of cardinality constraints is specified as $CRef = Card(p_i:\{E_{i,1},..., E_{i,n}\}; p_j:\{E_{j,1}\}; R)=(min, max)$.

Formally, $Card(p_1:\{E_{1,1},..., E_{1,n}\}; p_2:\{E_{2,1}\}; R)=(min, max)$ if:
$E_1(e_1,t) \land E_{1,1}(e_1,t) \land ... \land E_{1,n}(e_1,t) \to min \leq |\{e_2 \mid R(e_1,e_2,t) \land E_{2,1}(e_2,t)\}| \geq max$
We omit the sets $\{E_{1,1},..., E_{1,n}\}$ or $\{E_{2,1}\}$ when they are just $\{E_1\}$ or $\{E_2\}$, resp.

The refinement of Figure 2.2 would be defined as *Card(employee: {JuniorEmp}; project; Participates) = (0,5)*, while that of Figure 3.2 would be defined as *Card(employee:{JuniorEmp, Temporary}; project; Participates) = (0,3)*.

To the best of our knowledge, cardinality refinements of the kind $(p_1:\{E_{1,1},..., E_{1,n}\}; p_2; R)$ are the only ones that have been considered by previous research. However, our formalization allows also refinements of the kind $(p_1; p_2:\{E_{2,1}\}; R)$ and $(p_1:\{E_{1,1},..., E_{1,n}\}; p_2:\{E_{2,1}\}; R)$.

For instance, given

    Participates(Employee, Project)
    Project Partd ShortTerm, MediumTerm, LongTerm
    Card(employee; project; Participates) = (0, *)

we may express that employees can participate at most in 3 long term projects by (see Figure 3.3):

Card(employee; project:{LongTerm}; Participates) = (0,3)

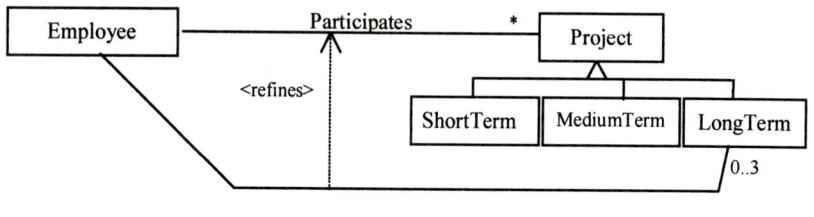

Figure 3.3

4 Relationship Type Refinement Validation

In the previous section, we have provided a characterization of relationship type refinements in conceptual models with multiple classification. The formalization we have presented is general enough to express all possible refinements of participants and of cardinality constraints. However, it may happen that a particular set of relationship refinements is not valid.

For instance, assume that we have:

Participates (Employee, Project)
Employee Partd JuniorEmp, SeniorEmp
Employee Partd Temporary, Permanent

with cardinality constraint refinements:

Card (employee:{JuniorEmp}; project; Participates) = (0, 3)
Card (employee:{Permanent}; project; Participates) = (5, *)

It is not difficult to see that these refinements are not valid if the domain we are modeling admits employees that are both junior and permanent.

Intuitively, we say that a set of refinements is valid if there may exist in the information base a set of entities satisfying them. In the rest of this section, we give a set of necessary conditions to guarantee that a given set of refinements is valid. We deal with refinements of participants and of cardinality constraints in sections 4.1 and 4.2, respectively.

Our notion of validity uses the concept of *valid type configuration (VTC)* [OCS99]. The type configuration of an entity is the set of entity types of which it is instance of at some time. A type configuration is valid if it satisfies all the constraints defined by specialization and generalization hierarchies.

A set of entity types $VTC = \{E_1,..., E_n\}$ is a valid type configuration if there may exist an entity e and a time t such that the type configuration of e at t is VTC.

For instance, the previous example allows the following valid type configurations (assuming that Employee and Project are disjoint):

VTC_1 = {Employee, JuniorEmp, Temporary}
VTC_2 = {Employee, JuniorEmp, Permanent}

VTC$_3$ = {Employee, SeniorEmp, Temporary}
VTC$_4$ = {Employee, SeniorEmp, Permanent}
VTC$_5$ = {Project}

[OCS99] shows how to obtain the set of all valid type configurations for a given conceptual schema in which all generalizations are partitions.

4.1 Refinement of Participants Validation

To simplify the presentation, we will start by considering refinements that have a single antecedent and a single consequent and defining validity in this case.

Assume that we have the conceptual schema of Figure 4.1 with refinements:

PRef$_1$ = Participates (employee:{JuniorEmp} → project:{ShortTerm})
PRef$_2$ = Participates (employee:{Permanent} → project:{LongTerm}).

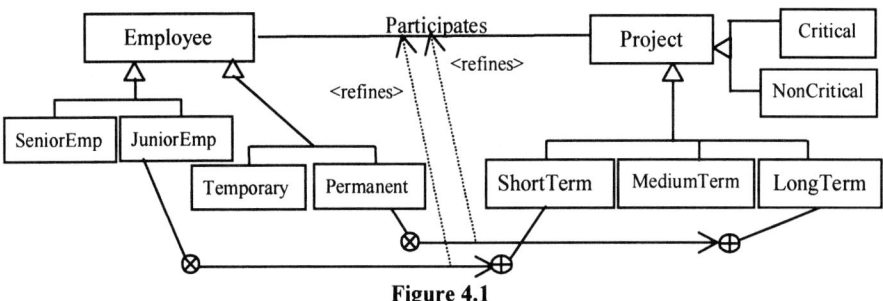

Figure 4.1

Therefore, employees that are junior and permanent should work in projects that are both short and long term. However, this is not possible since *Project Partd ShortTerm, MediumTerm, LongTerm*. Therefore, the set of refinements {PRef$_1$, PRef$_2$} is not valid.

A set of refinements of a relationship type $R(p_1:E_1, p_2:E_2)$ is valid if, for each VTC that includes E_1, there may exist a non-empty information base that contains an entity instance of the types in VTC and that satisfies those refinements.

Then, intuitively, to validate a set of refinements of participants, we have to consider the constraints that those refinements impose on each VTC (this is done by considering the refinements where the entity type of its antecedent belongs to VTC). Each such refinement, requires its consequent to belong to a certain entity type. Therefore, it must exist a VTC' that includes all the entity types required by those refinements.

This example allows four VTC for employees. The information base admits a non-empty population that satisfies VTC$_1$ because the only constraint applicable to it is *PRef$_1$* which requires junior employees to participate in short term projects and there exists a VTC' which includes {Project, ShortTerm}. In a similar way, VTC$_3$ and VTC$_4$ admit a non-empty population. However, this is not the case for VTC$_2$ since it does not exist any VTC including {Project, ShortTerm, LongTerm} (because of

Project PartD ShortTerm, MediumTerm, LongTerm). Therefore, the previous set of refinements is not valid.

In this example, if we had:

PRef'$_2$ = Participates (employee:{Permanent} → project:{Critical})

instead of *PRef$_2$*, then this new set of refinements would be valid since there exists a VTC'= {Project, ShortTerm, Critical}.

Formally, given a relationship type $R(p_1:E_1, p_2:E_2)$, and n refinements of participants $PRef_k = R(p_1:\{E_{1,k}\} \rightarrow p_2:\{E_{2,k}\})$, for $k=1..n$, we say that this set of refinements is valid with respect to a participant p_1 (and similarly for the other participant) if:

∀ VTC such that $E_1 \in$ VTC

Let $PRef_1, ..., PRef_s$ be all refinements of the form $PRef_t = R(p_1:\{E_{1,t}\} \rightarrow p_2:\{E_{2,t}\})$ such that $E_{1,t} \in$ VTC, for t=1..s.

Then ∃ VTC' such that $\{E_2\} \cup \{E_{2,1}\} \cup ... \cup \{E_{2,s}\} \subseteq$ VTC'

Once we have seen the particular case, it will be easier to understand the general one where both the antecedent and the consequent of the refinement may be sets of entity types. As usual, we start with an example and we provide the formalization afterwards.

Assume that we have the conceptual schema of Figure 4.2 with refinements:

PRef$_1$ = Participates (employee:{JuniorEmp, Temporary} → project:{ShortTerm, MediumTerm})

PRef$_2$ = Participates (employee:{Graduate} → project:{LongTerm}).

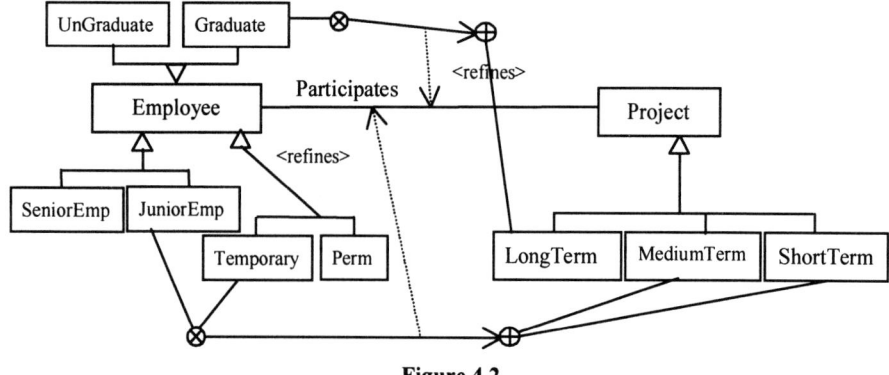

Figure 4.2

Therefore, employees that are junior, temporary and graduate, should work in projects that are either both long and medium term or both long and short term. However, this is not possible since *Project PartD ShortTerm, MediumTerm, LongTerm*. Therefore, the previous refinements are not valid.

The intuitive idea of the validation is similar to the previous case. The main difference is that now each refinement applicable to a certain VTC$_i$ requires its consequent to belong to one among several possible entity types. Therefore, it must exist a VTC' that includes one of the entity types required by each refinement applicable to VTC_i. Moreover, refinements applicable to VTC_i in this case are those refinements where all the entity types of its antecedent belong to VTC_i.

In the general case, validity of a set of refinements of participants is defined as follows:

Definition 4.1: *validity of a set of refinement of participants*

Given a conceptual schema with a relationship type $R(p_1: E_1, p_2: E_2)$, and n refinements of participants $PRef_k = R(p_1:\{E_{1,1},..., E_{1,i}\} \rightarrow p_2:\{E_{2,1},..., E_{2,j}\})$, for $k = 1...n$, we say that this set of refinements of participants is valid with respect to a participant p_1 (and similarly for the other participant) if:

$\forall$ VTC such that $E_1 \in$ VTC

Let $PRef_1, ..., PRef_s$ be all refinements of the form $PRef_t = R(p_1:Ant_t \rightarrow p_2:Cons_t)$ such that $Ant_t \subseteq$ VTC, for t=1..s, s ≤ n.

Then $\exists VTC'$ such that, for t=1..s, there exists an $E_{2,i}$ such that $E_{2,i} \in Cons_t$ and $E_{2,i} \in VTC'$.

In the previous example, we know that there is a VTC = {Employee, JuniorEmp, Temporary, Graduate}. $PRef_1$ is applicable to VTC and it requires projects to be either short or medium term. Moreover, $Pref_2$ is applicable to the same VTC and it requires projects to be long term. However, it does not exists a VTC' = {Project, ShortTerm, LongTerm} nor a VTC" = {Project, MediumTerm, LongTerm} and, therefore, this set of refinements is not valid.

4.2 Refinement of Cardinality Constraints Validation

We start by considering a particular case for refinement of cardinality constraints, where all refinements have the form $Card(p_1:\{E_{1,1},..., E_{1,n}\}; p_2; R)=(min,max)$.

Assume that we have the conceptual schema of Figure 4.3 with refinements:

CRef = Card (employee:{JuniorEmp}; project; Participates) = (0, 3)
CRef' = Card (employee:{Permanent}; project; Participates) = (5, *)

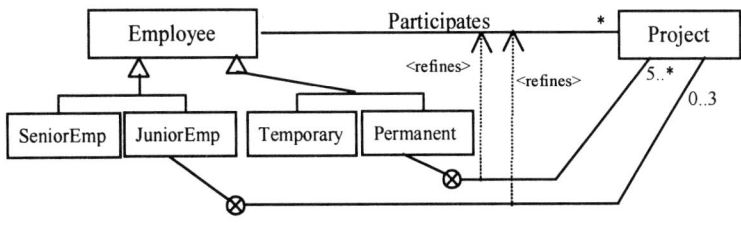

Figure 4.3

Note that since an employee may be junior and permanent, the two refinements are not valid because (0,3) and (5,*) do not have a non-empty intersection.

Given a relationship type $R(p_1:E_1, p_2:E_2)$, a cardinality constraint refinement $Card(p_1:Rest; p_2; R)$, where $Rest = \{E_{1,1},..., E_{1,n}\}$, constraints the minimum and maximum number of entities of type E_2 that may be related to entities of type E_1 when these entities are also instance of $E_{1,1}..., E_{1,n}$. Then, to validate a set of n cardinality constraint refinements $Card_i(p_1:Rest_i; p_2; R)$, $i = 1,..,n$, we have to check that, for each VTC that contains E_1, the intersection of the intervals (min_i, max_i) of the refinements such that $Rest_i \subseteq VTC$ is non-empty.

In the previous example, we have that CRef constraints junior employees to participate in between 0 and 3 projects, while CRef' constraints permanent employees to participate at least in 5 projects. Since there exists a VTC = {Employee, JuniorEmp, Permanent}, this set of refinements would be valid if there were a non-empty intersection of the intervals (0,3) and (5,*). However, this is not the case and we can conclude that the two previous cardinality constraint refinements are not valid.

Definition 4.2: Given a relationship type $R(p_1:E_1, p_2:E_2)$, and several cardinality constraint refinements $CRef_k = Card(p_1:Rest_k; p_2; R) = (min_k, max_k)$, k=1..n, we say that this set of refinements is valid if:

∀ VTC such that $E_1 \in$ VTC
Let $CRef_1, ..., CRef_s$ be all refinements of the form $CRef_t = Card(p_1:Rest_t; p_2; R) = (min_t, max_t)$, for t=1..s, such that $Rest_t \subseteq$ VTC
Then there exists a non-empty intersection of the intervals (min_t, max_t), t=1..s.

A second particular case appears when cardinality constraint refinements have the form $Card(p_1; p_2:\{E_{2,i}\}; R) = (min, max)$.

Assume that we have the conceptual schema of Figure 4.4 with refinements:
CRef = Card (employee; project:{Critical}; Participates)= (1,2)
CRef' = Card (employee; project:{NonCritical}; Participates) = (3,5).

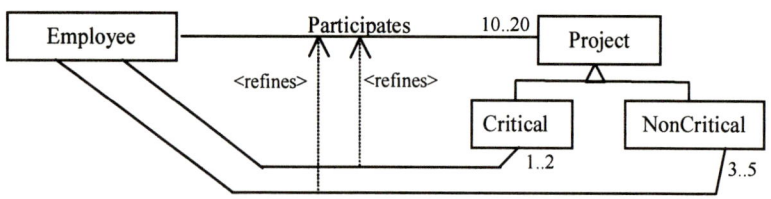

Figure 4.4

Note that $Card(employee; project; Participates) = (10,20)$. Moreover, CRef states that employees must participate at least in 1 and at most in 2 critical projects and CRef' establishes that they must participate at least in 3 and at most in 5 non-critical projects. On the other hand, since a project is either critical or non-critical, the above refinements constraint an employee to participate at least in 4 and at most in 7 projects. Therefore, this set of refinements is not valid since satisfying them is not compatible with satisfying the cardinality defined at the relationship type level, i.e. there is no intersection between (4,7) and (10,20).

To define validity in this case, we need to define also the concept of *entity type covering (ETC)*. Intuitively, an ETC of a certain entity type E, denoted by ETC(E), is a set of disjoint entity types (which may be direct or indirect subtypes of E) such that the union of their populations is equal to the population of E.

Definition 4.3: *Entity Type Covering (ETC)*
Let E be an entity class. An entity type covering of E, ETC(E), is defined as:
- ETC(E) = {E}
- ETC(E) = {$E_{1,1},...,E_{1,i}, ..., E_{n,1},...,E_{n,j}$} such that
  E Partd $E_1, ..., E_n$ and ETC(E_1) = {$E_{1,1},...,E_{1,i}$},..., ETC(E_n)={ $E_{n,1},...,E_{n,j}$}

In the example of Figure 4.4, we have two ETC for Project:
ETC$_1$ = {Project}
ETC$_2$ = {Critical, NonCritical}

The population of a certain ETC$_i$ (E) is equal to the population of E. Therefore, to validate a set of cardinality constraint refinements, we have to check that it is possible to populate the original relationship type, defined at the level of E, such that this population satisfies all the refinements defined at all different coverings of E. This is done by checking that there is a non-empty intersection among all the intervals required by the refinements applicable to all ETC$_i$(E) and the cardinality of the original relationship type. Note that, if there is no cardinality constraint refinement defined for some of the entity types belonging to ETC$_i$(E), then the maximum population allowed by this covering is ∞.

Definition 4.4: Given a relationship type $R(p_1:E_1, p_2:E_2)$, given *Card(p$_1$; p$_2$; R)= (min$_R$,max$_R$)* and *n* cardinality constraint refinements *Cref$_i$ = Card(p$_1$; p$_2$:{$E_{2,i}$}; R)= (min$_i$,max$_i$)*, for i=1..n.

For each ETC$_k$(E$_2$) we define (min$_k$, max$_k$) as follows:
- Let *CRef$_1$, ..., CRef$_s$* be all refinements of the form *CRef$_t$ = R(p$_1$; p$_2$:{$E_{2,t}$}) = (min$_t$, max$_t$)*, for t=1..s, such that $E_{2,t} \in$ ETC$_k$(E$_2$)
- Let min$_k$ = Σ min$_t$, for t=1..s if s > 0. Or, otherwise, min$_k$ = 0.
- Let max$_k$ = ∞ if $\exists$ $E_{2,y} \in$ ETC$_k$(E$_2$) such that $E_{2,y} \neq E_{2,t}$, for t=1..s.
  Or, otherwise, max$_k$ = Σ max$_t$, for t=1..s

We say that this set of refinements is valid if the k+1 intervals (min$_1$, max$_1$), ..., (min$_k$, max$_k$), (min$_R$, max$_R$) have a non-empty intersection.

In the example of figure 4.4, we have that (min$_R$, max$_R$) = (10,20). Moreover, there is a covering of Project, ETC$_2$(Project) = {Critical, NonCritical}, and we have that both cardinality constraint refinements apply to ETC$_2$(Project). In this case we have that min$_2$ = 1+ 3 = 4 and that max$_2$ = 2 + 5 = 7 and, since there is no intersection between (4,7) and (10,20), the previous set of refinements is not valid.

Note that, although it could seem the contrary at first glance, the refinements defined in Figure 4.5 (just a slight modification of the previous ones) are valid since they restrict an employee to participate at least in 4 and at most in 12 projects. Therefore, there is an intersection between (4,12) and (10,20) which allows a non-empty population of the entity types restricted by those refinements.

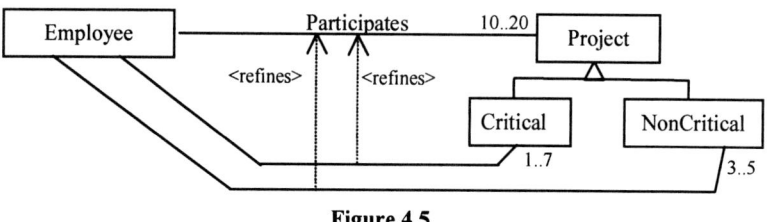

Figure 4.5

Validation of cardinality constraint refinements in the general case is defined by considering both particular cases together.

5 Conclusions and Further Work

We have characterized relationship type refinement in conceptual models with multiple classification. In this respect, we have extended previous work, which concerned only models with single classification.

We have provided also a textual and a graphical notation to express those refinements. Our notation is general, can be used in conceptual models with single or multiple classification, and can be adapted to any conceptual modeling language.

We have formalized in logic the integrity constraints implied by the refinements. In this way, we have given a clear semantics to them.

Finally, we have defined a number of conditions a set of refinements has to satisfy to be valid. The conditions can be implemented by the verification procedures included in conceptual modeling environments. Again, these conditions can be used for models with single and multiple classification.

One possible extension to this work is its application to relationship types of degree higher than two, since here we have dealt with binary ones only. Another interesting (and practical) extension could be to study how our refinements and notation can be used in conceptual schemas written in UML.

Acknowledgements

This work has been partially supported by the CICYT project TIC99-1048-C02-01.

References

[BCN92] C.Batini; S.Ceri; S.B.Navathe. "Conceptual Database Design: an Entity-Relationship Approach". The Benjamin/Cummings Pub. Co., 1992.

[BG95] E.Bertino; G.Guerrini. "Objects with Multiple Most Specific Classes". ECOOP 1995, pp. 102-126.

[BS95] R.J.Brachman; J.G.Schmolze. "An Overview of the KL-ONE Knowledge Representation System". Cognitive Science, Vol. 9, Num. 2, 1995, pp. 171-216.

[BO92]   S.E.Bratsberg; E.Odberg. "Relation Refinement in Object-Relation Data Models". Nordic Workshop on Programming and Software Development Research, Tampere (Finland), 1992.
[Bub77]   J.A.Bubenko. "The Temporal Dimension in Information Modelling". In *Architecture and Models in Data Base Management Systems*. North-Holland, 1977, pp. 93-113.
[CD94]   S.Cook; J.Daniels. "Designing Object Systems: Object-Oriented Modeling with Syntropy". Prentice-Hall, 1994.
[CLF93]   D.de Champeaux; D.Lea; P.Faure. "Object-Oriented System Development". Addison-Wesley, 1994.
[Len87]   M.Lenzerini. "Covering and Disjointness Constraints in Type Networks". Int. Conf. On Data Engineering, Los Angeles (California), 1987, pp. 386-393.
[LEW93]   S.W.Liddle, D.W.Embley, S.N.Woodfield. "Cardinality Constraints in Semantic Data Models".Data and Knowledge Engineering, Vol. 11, 1993, pp. 235-270.
[MBW80]   J.Mylopoulos, P.A.Bernstein, H.K.T.Wong. "A Language Facility for Designing Database-Intensive Applications". TODS, Vol. 5, Num. 2, 1980, pp. 185-207.
[MM92]   R.Motschnig-Pitrik; J.Mylopoulos. "Classes and Instances", Int. Journal of Intelligent and Cooperative Information Systems, Vol. 1, No. 1, 1992, pp. 61-92.
[MO95]   J.Martin; J.Odell. "Objects-Oriented Methods: a Foundation". Prentice-Hall, 1995.
[OCS99]   A.Olivé, D.Costal, M.R.Sancho. "Entity Evolution in ISA Hierarchies". Int. Conf. On Conceptual Modeling (ER'99), Paris (France), 1999, pp. 62-80.
[RBP+91] J.Rumbaugh; M.Blaha; W.Premerlani et al. "Object-Oriented Modelling and Design", Prentice-Hall, 1991.
[RJB99]   J.Rumbaugh; I.Jacobson and G.Booch. "The Unified Modeling Language Reference Manual", Addison-Wesley, 1999.
[SCG+]   F.Saltor; M.Castellanos; M.Garcia et al. "Modelling Specialization as BLOOM Semilattices". In *Information Modelling and Knowledge Bases*, IOS Press, Vol. VI, 1995.
[WJS95]   R.Wieringa; W. de Jong; P.Spruit. "Using Dynamic Classes and Role Classes to Model Object Migration". Theory and Practice of Object Systems (TAPOS), Vol. 1(1), pp. 61-83, 1995.

A Metamodel for Part – Whole Relationships for Reasoning on Missing Parts and Reconstruction

Martin Doerr, Dimitris Plexousakis, Chryssoyla Bekiari

Institute of Computer Science,
Foundation for Research and Technology – Hellas,
Science and Technology Park of Crete,
Vassilika Vouton, P.O. Box 1385, GR 711 10, Heraklion, Crete, Greece
{martin,dp,bekiari}@ics.forth.gr

Abstract: The ontological analysis of parts and wholes gathers recently increasing interest, and develops into a specific research area called *mereology*. So far, most research has focused on directions motivated by engineering examples and by linguistic analysis. In contrast to these, the related archeological problem is characterized by missing pieces and information, which cannot easily be recovered, and by reasoning and experimentation with multiple hypotheses. This aspect of mereology has not yet been formally analyzed. In this paper, we continue previous work by addressing the formalization of some of the reasoning needed to identify other parts of the same whole through knowledge about some parts, or to narrow down the category of wholes a part may have belonged to. We define a hierarchical and an associative *part-of* relation with conservative assumptions about dependency and sharing, and proceed to develop a metamodel and a novel reasoning methodology from factual to categorical knowledge. The ontological commitment and utility of this theory is discussed on the base of practical examples. This work is intended as a first step towards a more comprehensive theory covering the problem of reasoning about partially lost items.

1 Introduction

The ontological analysis of parts and wholes gathers recently increasing interest [15], and develops into a specific research area called *mereology* [29] [2] [13]. Implemented models for *part-of* relationships in (oo)DBMS [17], or in knowledge bases [27] have appeared in the literature. So far, most research work has been carried out in directions motivated by engineering examples and by linguistic analysis [14],[30],[24]. In this paper, we continue work presented in [7], towards a formalization of qualitative reasoning as needed for the implementation of reasoning algorithms about missing parts and reconstruction of wholes. For this purpose, we employ a model that generalizes specific attributes presented in [7] like *adjacent*, *element of* or *component of*. Consider the following example:
A porcelain piece **x1** is piece of a porcelain stand **x2**. In turn, **x2** is component of a table lamp **x3**. Obviously, **x1** is a part-of **x3**. This means that the implicit property

part-of, inherent in *component of* is transitive, even though *piece of* and *component of* do not imply each other (Fig. 1a).

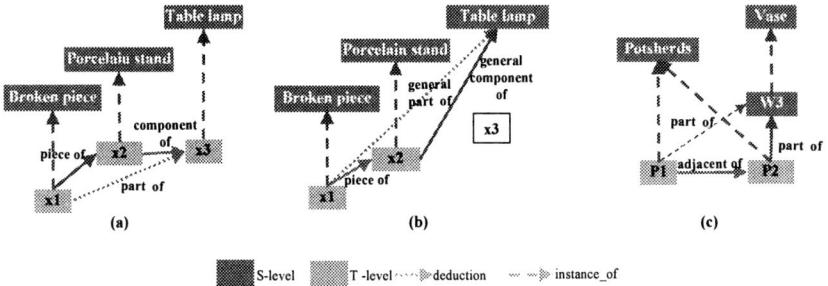

Fig. 1: Examples showing the inference based on associative knowledge about parts

Assume further that the lamp **x3** itself is lost, whereas **x2** exists, and that **x2** is characteristic enough to conclude, that it belongs to a table lamp. In our terms, **x2** is *general component of* "Table Lamp". Then, obviously, **x1** is a *general part of* "Table Lamp". This means that a path of type *part-of - general part of* can be replaced by an attribute of type *general part of* (Fig. 1b).

Regard further two potsherds **p1, p2**, which by their edges and decoration prove that they are adjacent pieces of a damaged whole. If we know that **p2** is a *part of* a known whole **W3**, then, obviously, **p1** is *part-of* **W3** (Fig. 1c). This means that under certain conditions which we investigate in this paper, one can conclude part-hood from associative knowledge about parts and vice versa, due to the intrinsic redundancy. Such conclusions become non-trivial if the whole under investigation is incomplete or lost. Pazzi in [22] argues that knowledge of association between parts is different from hierarchical part–whole knowledge and equally useful, even though this knowledge is redundant under simultaneous use of part–whole assignment. In this paper we observe, that this redundancy actually is useful in the case of incomplete knowledge. The presented kind of reasoning is characteristic for detective work of archeologists and museum curators, but it can be applied anywhere reconstruction is needed (e.g., in building restoration). This aspect of mereology has not yet been investigated in detail. The contribution of this paper is not only an application of knowledge representation theory to archeology, but also the presentation of a general ontological problem that can be learned from archeology. In particular, we aim at providing the building blocks for a generalization over the different kinds of part-hood introduced by [14] and others in a top-down approach. We use the archeological example for didactic purposes, because it is rich in examples and scientific reflection.

In this paper we formalize basic aspects of this kind of reasoning. For that purpose, we define a high-level model and a meta-model. We focus on the transition of reasoning between associative and hierarchical part-hood knowledge, and the transition from factual (token level) to categorical (class level) knowledge, an element so far hardly investigated, but very essential for the reasoning that narrows down search for candidate parts for reconstruction. The opposite type of inferencing, i.e., from attribute classes to instances, can be found in [1]. Such a mechanism is employed in sections 6.2 and 6.3. The remainder of this paper is structured as follows:

In section 2, we give a relatively narrow definition of *wholes*, sufficient for the museum case and the purpose of this paper, even though our reasoning may be applicable to more general applications. In section 3, we give a short account of our previous work related to this paper, and add a real archeological example for illustration in section 4. In section 5, we present the intuition for the basic model of this paper. In section 6 we describe the token-level and schema-level reasoning as well as their combination. The paper concludes in Section 7 with an outlook for further research.

2 What Is a Part

We propose here a definition of *part* and *whole* sufficient to support the world of archeological findings and our modeling objectives. As in [16] and [14], we consider only material parts and wholes with a definite mass. Parts are thought of as subsets of the physical extent of the whole. The latter need not be contiguous, as in the case of a set of chessmen. So what makes us regard an aggregate of molecules a whole?
Motschnig [19] observes that certain part-hood dependency constraints must be defined diachronically. In this line of argument, we regard the relative physical stability or a common physical life cycle over a relevant time span as the decisive feature that makes up a material whole. The actual size of the time-span depends on the context (consider sand-images from Himalayan monks, in contrast to dinosaur bones). The stability may be either given by physical contiguity - as with a pebble tumbling in a river bed - or enforced by people for functional reasons - as with chessmen etc. If functionality is lost due to loss of matter, we can fairly assume that the whole has stopped to exist. Simple loss of matter may not be crucial, as with a piece of chalk running over the blackboard. Clouds or fireworks plumes however are no wholes in our sense. Consequently, when we talk about potential wholes of the past, we refer to one arbitrary small time-span, when the configuration under investigation existed. Furthermore, we admit that different unity criteria (functional, physical contiguity of different kinds) give rise to different notions of wholes [13] (e.g., *mouse, keyboard, monitor* are justified by physical contiguity, *workstation* by functional unity). In this paper, we consider all respective predicates with respect to one criterion only.
For simplicity, we ignore wholes sharing parts during the same time span, even though this can happen with buildings or accessories. In practice, one may often define the union of those wholes as the actual whole. Parts belonging to different wholes at different time-spans make up a case that does not interfere with the reasoning presented here[1].

---

[1] In [12] and [25], a relational model with explicit temporal validity of part-hood relations for archaeology and museums is defined.

3 Previous Work

We have previously presented a model [7] motivated by problems of cultural heritage. This model was developed based on our experience and cooperation with cultural organizations [10], [4], [5], [6], [21] and closely related to the emerging standard of the CIDOC CRM [11], [9]. A basic feature of information in history, material cultural heritage preservation and study, is that information is incomplete and can in general not be completed. Therefore, reasoning concentrates on gathering evidence for missing parts and wholes, and drawing further conclusions from that knowledge. We regard part-hood as a relation. This is distinct from the fact, that many artificial objects are designed a priori to become parts, or that their current form is that of a part. In order to describe the different aspects of part-hood knowledge for museum objects [12], [8] and archeological findings, we based our model in [7] on groups of basic attribute categories and a set of basic classes. The attribute categories are:

- attributes for the part-hood role that one object can play with respect to another: *"piece of"*, *"component of"*, *"element of"*, *"adjacent"*
- modifiers to denote the instantiation level of the referred entity: *"specific"* / *"general"*. Attributes of type "*specific*" connect two particulars (tokens). Attributes of type "*general*" connect a particular with a universal (class) describing the *potential* referred-to particular.
- modifiers to denote the degree of evidence (rather than confidence!) for the reference: *"possible"*/ *"real"*

These three groups are combined into the actual 16 attributes. Each group might be refined or extended. These attributes are embedded into a complete logical structure of classes and metaclasses. This model has been related to the CIDOC CRM [9] as a specialization of the respective entities and has been implemented in the TELOS knowledge representation language [20]. Fig. 2 graphically depicts this model.

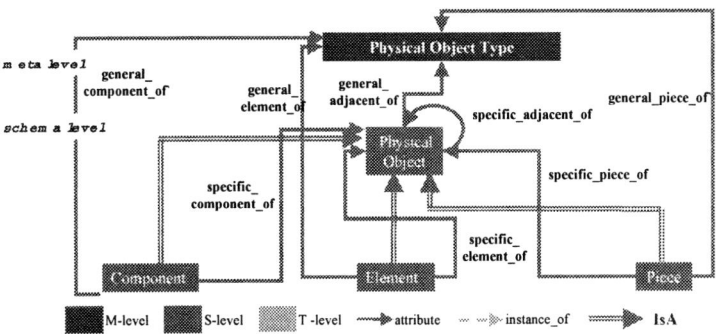

Fig 2: Graphical representation of the attributes in [7]

The attributes"*part_of*" and "*from_the_same_whole_as*" discussed in section 5 are regarded as generalizations (isA) of these more specific attributes. We shall leave the formalization of these isA relations to future work.

4 Application Example

This example has been published by the University of Leipzig [23], a story covering more than a hundred years:
58 potsherds of an ancient Greek vase, presumably parts from a single whole, were bought by the University of Leipzig in 1896 from Friedrich Hauser in Stuttgart (Fig. 3a). Careful drawings of this collection exist. The lost original was thought to be created by Phintias. In 1917, the famous Sir John Beazley recognized in them the style of Euphrinios, and declared them to be similar in form and decoration to *stamnoi* (a type of Greek vase) made by Smikros and kept in collections in Brussels, London and Paris. Some 20 years later, Beazley recognized, that a potsherd kept in Freiburg was adjacent to the Hauser collection. They were acquired in 1957 by the University of Leipzig. In 1942, another cluster of 4 pieces(Fig.3a) from the same whole was bought from a collection in Munich.

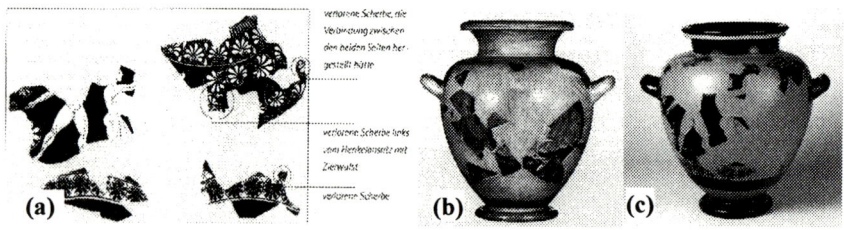

Fig. 3: Hauser's drawings, before 1897, after 1942, and in 1996

From the initial collection, four pieces were lost over the years, and one piece was recognized to belong to another whole. Two reconstructions were made, one after 1942, and another in 1996, which implied the pieces from Freiburg. The new reconstruction took into account the characteristics of the stamnoi of Smikros. One piece was repositioned after its adjacency to a specific part had been recognized. For reconstruction, the archeologists took the curvature, thickness, finger traces on the rotating pot, decoration and the general type of vase into account. Pieces are arranged in adjacent clusters, and then complemented to a new whole. (Fig. 3b, 3c)
This example demonstrates a complex intellectual and technical process including factual and categorical knowledge. It implies the hypothetical whole of the destroyed original, two constructed wholes and parts with individual history, taking part in multiple wholes. It demonstrates most of the theory we present here.

5 Super and Meta-attributes

In the following sections we formalize attributes of "part-hood" and of "unity" at three different levels. These will give us the means to argue **from a part about its whole**[2]. The fundamental question is, whether there had been any whole at all around

---

[2] We shall address at another time the reasoning from an incomplete whole to missing parts

that part. Obviously, if we hold only a part in our hands, usually nothing guarantees that there has ever been a whole it belonged to. Only broken pieces may prove by the shape of their fracture surface, that there has been "more around them". But even in the other cases, we have good reasons to assume that there had been a whole for a part, if those items are **usually used** to become parts of wholes. This hypothesis will enable us to produce criteria that may lead to the verification of the existence of the whole and to its determination by new findings. Therefore, without loss of generality, the following reasoning always begins with the assumption, that there has been a whole of the usual kind for that part.

Attribute metaclasses: The attribute metaclass *part_type_of* is instantiated by attribute classes specific to the hierarchical part structure of some class of physical objects: e.g., Table Leg *is_leg_of* Table, Piano Key Cover *is_cover_of* Piano Key, Piano Key *is_key_of* Piano , where Table, Table Leg etc. are instances of *Physical_Object_Type*, the metaclass of all classes of physical objects. Such an attribute class expresses that parts of the specified type are parts of the specified type of part or whole. Similarly, a model presented by [18] defines part-hood as an attribute metaclass. For simplicity, we assume that those types of parts are exclusive to the type of whole (i.e., cannot be used for other kinds of wholes [19]). This does not constrain the exchange of parts!

Attribute classes: The attribute class *part_of* is instantiated by attributes specific to the hierarchical part structure of some particular physical object: e.g., TL305 <*is_leg_of*> T257, where TL305 is instance of Table Leg, T257 instance of Table and <*is_leg_of*> instance of *is_leg_of* from the example above. *Physical_Object* is the associated superclass of *Physical_Object_Type,* and *part_of* the associated superclass of *part_type_of*, i.e., *part_of* attribute class and all its subclasses are regarded as instances of *part_type_of*. Therefore TL305, T257 are instances of *Physical_object*, and <*is_leg_of*> instance of *part_of*. We do however not exclude the direct instantiation of *Physical_object* and *part_of,* in the case of absence of any more detailed knowledge. The attribute is intended as a generalization over the attributes *specific_piece_of, specific_component_of, specific_element_of* [7].
The attribute class *from_the_same_whole_as* is a generalization over any knowledge that may connect two parts of a whole. This implies notions such as the fitting of broken pieces, identical traces of treatment or exposure from chemical analysis, clusters being found mounted in situ or adjacent at the place of destruction etc. For example, two splinters of car varnish can be proven to be from the same whole by tracing penetrated detergents and waxes, without conclusion on the model and their position on the car. Note that in detective work this knowledge often precedes knowledge about part-hood, but it is not very informative if we hold the complete object in our hands! This causes a major difference to reasoning in engineering examples. The attribute is intended as a generalization over the attributes *specific_adjacent_to, from_the_same_set_as* [7].

Attribute classes to the metalevel: The attribute class *general_part_of* is instantiated by attributes specific to the hierarchical part role a particular physical object has to a kind of whole or part: e.g.: TLS307 <*general_part_of*> Table Lamp, where TLS307 is instance of Table Lamp Stand, and Table Lamp instance of *Physical Object Type*. It means, that there exists an instance x of Table Lamp, such that TLS307 <*part_of*> x³.

---

[3] Together with the existence assumption above, we may also say: If there is an x with TLS307 <*part_of*> x, then x must be instance of Table Lamp

In practice, knowledge about the above relations can be acquired fairly independently. Many criteria lead to categorical knowledge about a missing whole. Take for instance a heap of components from several guns of the same type. They can be combined in various ways to the same type of whole. We are therefore interested here in all possible deductions from partial knowledge for those relations leading from parts to wholes, in order to (1) narrow down the kind of wholes for better understanding, (2) possibly find fitting objects in a reduced set of candidates, and (3) possibly reconstruct a whole from disparate pieces. The attribute is intended as a generalization over the attributes *general piece of, general component of, general element of* [7].

6 Reasoning about Parts and Wholes

We establish a logic-based model that supports reasoning at the token, class and meta-class level and follows closely the model of Telos [20]. It employs a number of axioms establishing the structural principles, as well as, the properties of the *part_of* relationship. A number of rules are employed in order to deduce new relationships from existing ones, at the token or class levels. We argue that the model is minimal and complete in the sense that no subset of it is sufficient for deducing the derived relationships and that all possible relationships are captured.

Our model employs a many-sorted 2nd-order structure $S = (T, C, P, X)$, where: T is a finite set of token-level objects, C is a finite set of class objects, P is a finite set of predicates and X is an enumerable set of variables. The set P includes the following predicates:

- instance_of (x,y) of sort $T \cup C \cup P \times C \cup P$
- Isa(x,y) of sort $C \cup P \times C \cup P$
- part_of$(x1,x2)$ of sort $T \times T$
- part_type_of $(c1,c2)$ of sort $C \times C$
- gpart_of$(t1,c1)$ of sort $T \times C$
- whole_of$(t2,t1)$ of sort $T \times T$
- fswa[4] $(x1,x2)$ of sort $T \times T$
- whole_type_of$(c2,c1)$ of sort $C \times C$
- type_conforming$(c1)$ of sort C

These predicates establish relationships between objects in our model. Specifically, the following properties are stated as axioms in the model, and are expressed in a many – sorted language:

A) The *IsA* relationship forms a partial order on C
- *IsA* is transitive : $\forall c1,c2,c3/C$ IsA$(c1,c2) \wedge$ IsA $(c2,c3) \Rightarrow$ Isa$(c1,c3)$
- *IsA* is reflexive : $\forall c/C$ IsA(c,c)
- *IsA* is antisymmetric: $\forall c1,c2 /C$ IsA$(c1,c2) \Rightarrow \neg$Isa$(c2,c1)$

B) The composition of *IsA* and *instance_of* permits the derivation of new *instance_of* relationships
- $\forall t/T, \forall c1,c2/C$ instance_of$(t,c1) \wedge$ IsA $(c1,c2) \Rightarrow$ instance_of$(t,c2)$

---

[4] *fswa* denotes the link *"from_the_same_whole_as"*

C) Classification constraint: any object is an instance of at least one class
- ∀t/T, ∃c/C instance_of(t,c)

This constraint permits the computation of class extents, i.e., for each c ∈ C, [[c]] = {t ∈ T | instance_of(t,c)}.
These axioms form the basis of our model and will be used in conjunction with the derivation rules.

6.1 Token Level

We first consider reasoning at the token level for complementing randomly missing knowledge about parts and the whole. The existing primary knowledge is either verifiable on the relict, or taken from the historical record.

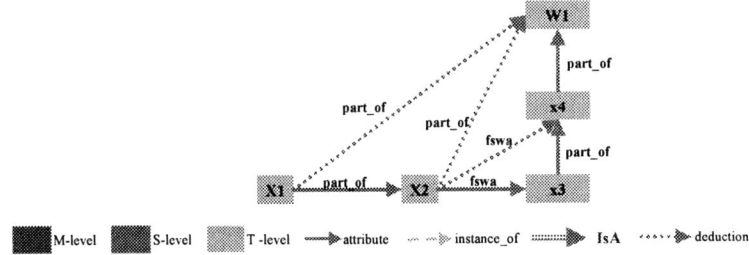

Fig. 4: Sample inference paths at token level

We begin by axiomatizing the *part_of* and *fswa* relationships[5]: *part_of* is transitive, reflexive and antisymmetric, hence a partial order

(A1) ∀ t1, t2, t3/T, part_of (t1,t2) ∧ part_of(t2,t3) ⇒ part_of(t1,t3)

(A2) ∀ t/T, part_of (t,t)

(A3) ∀ t1, t2/T, t1 ≠ t2, part_of (t1,t2) ⇒ ¬part_of(t2,t1)

Let us define a special part-of relationship: the whole (*whole_of*) of some item:

(D1) ∀ t1, t2/T, whole_of (t2,t1) ⇔ part_of(t1,t2) ∧¬(∃ t3/T, part_of(t2,t3) ∧ t2≠t3)

In other words, the whole contains this part and is not part of something else. This definition makes sense, as long as part-hood is seen under a specific unity criterion, (e.g., physical coherence). The complete Hauser Stamnos at its time of creation is such a whole. We do not adopt the abstract notion of wholes, where any set of items can be regarded to form a whole. Throughout the paper, and without loss of generality, we assume the existence of a whole for each part, i.e., we only refer to parts which belonged to a "normal" whole at the relevant historical time[6]. For instance, it is reasonable to assume that the complete Hauser Stamnos had existed.

---

[5] Where A# denotes an axiom, D# denotes a definition, C# denotes constraints, F#, PT#, G# denotes inferences
[6] See intraclass exclusiveness in [19]

A part is non-shared, if it only has a single whole which it belongs to:

(D2) $\forall$ t1/T, non shared (t1) $\Leftrightarrow$ ($\forall$t2,t3/T, whole_of (t2,t1) $\wedge$ whole_of (t3,t1) $\Rightarrow$ t2 = t3)

We define *fswa* as follows:

(D3) $\forall$t1, t2/T, fswa(t1,t2) $\Leftrightarrow$ $\exists$ t3/T, part_of(t1,t3) $\wedge$ part_of(t2,t3)

Note, that the archeological knowledge of an *fswa* relation does not necessarily imply the knowledge about any other part, i.e., it can be primary, as with adjacent broken pieces. This makes the following reasoning useful: Beasley recognized around 1930, that the potsherd from Freiburg continues the decoration of a piece of the Hauser collection. Hence both were from the same whole. Obviously, *fswa* is reflexive and symmetric (from D3, A2):

(F1) $\forall$ t/T, fswa (t,t)

(F2) $\forall$ t1, t2/T, fswa (t1,t2) $\Rightarrow$ fswa(t2,t1)

If parts are non-shared, as assumed here, "*fswa*" is also transitive (from D1,D2,D3,A1):

(F3) $\forall$ t1, t2, t3/T, fswa(t1,t2) $\wedge$ fswa(t2,t3) $\Rightarrow$ fswa(t1,t3)

For instance, the Freiburg potsherd fits to a cluster of Hauser potsherds, some of which fit to the Munich cluster. From that we conclude, that all these potsherds belong to one pot rather than to two overlapping pots. Actually sharing of parts under the relevant unity criteria seems to be a rare phenomenon for archeological objects. The relationship "*fswa*" subsumes the relationship "*part_of*" (from D3,A1,A2):

(F4) $\forall$ t1, t2/T part_of(t1,t2) $\Rightarrow$ fswa(t1,t2)

We now turn to the derivation rules that characterize the composition of "*part_of*" and "*from the same whole as*" relationships for non-shared parts: The first rule permits the derivation of *whole_of* relationships:

(F5) $\forall$ t1,t2,t3/T fswa (t1,t2) $\wedge$ part_of (t1,t3) $\Rightarrow$ $\exists$ t4/T, whole_of (t4,t2) $\wedge$ whole_of (t4,t3)

Note that t2,t1 are interchangeable. t4 may be identical with t3, in which case follows: whole_of (t3,t2). The next two rules permit the derivation of a "*fswa*" relationship:

(F6) $\forall$ t1,t2,t3/T part_of (t1,t2) $\wedge$ fswa (t1,t3) $\Rightarrow$ fswa (t2,t3)

(F7) $\forall$ t1,t2,t3/T part_of (t1,t2) $\wedge$ fswa (t2,t3) $\Rightarrow$ fswa (t1,t3)

An example of rule F7 consider the potsherds from Munich: let t2 be the Munich cluster, t1 be one piece of it, and t3 be the Hauser collection. Obviously, any piece t1 of the Munich cluster is from the same whole as the Hauser collection t3.

6.2 Schema Level

The Schema level describes how parts used to be combined. The recursive relationship *part_of* is specialized into typically non-recursive relationships specific to some technical, artistic model, or even biological species. This allows for reasoning as at the token level. *Isa* relations and inheritance however make things less conclusive. Also, the assumption that a part is non-shared has a far weaker equivalent: screws, nails etc. are used in many different models. We now formalize the analogous meta-relationships on the base of class-level relationships. We define *part_type_of* which means that:

(**D4**) ∀c1,c2/C part_type_of(c1,c2) ⇔ ∃ r/P, r(c1,c2) ∧ IsA(r, part_of)

Furthermore, we introduce a meta-relationship *whole_type_of*, the roots of *part_of* relationships at schema level:

(**D5**) ∀c1,c2/C whole_type_of(c1,c2) ⇔ part_type_of(c2,c1) ∧¬(∃ c3/C, part_type_of(c1,c3) ∧ c1≠c3).

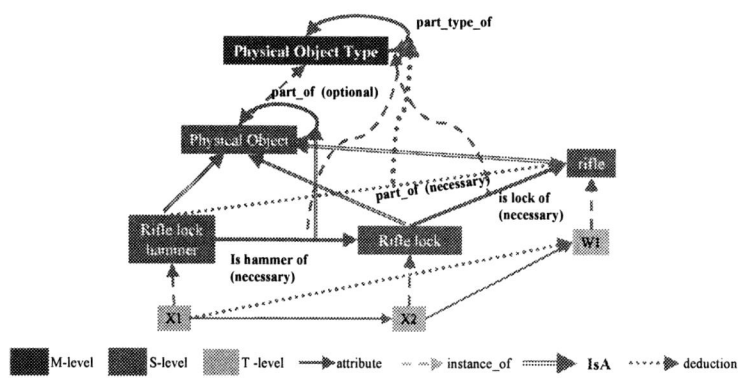

Fig. 5 : Example of schema level inference

Parts need not necessarily be embedded in the wholes that appear as roots of part-of relationships at schema level, either due to interrupted production or because the part-of relation is systematically optional. Such a behavior disrupts upwards reasoning. Therefore we regard a **necessary** *part_of* relationship:

Let Dc ⊂ C be the set of classes, for which the *part_of* relation is necessary:

(**C1**) ∀c1/Dc, ∀t1/T, instance_of(t1,c1) ⇒ (∃ c2/C, part_type_of(c1,c2) ⇒ ∃ t2/T, instance_of(t2,c2) ∧ part_of(t2,c2))

This constraint looks like the definition of dependent parts. We interpret it phenomenologically, during the historically relevant time interval, and not for the life-time of the part. This excludes all sorts of unfinished production stages, but also potential systematic cases, where the same kind of object may alternatively be used as a whole and as a part. (C1) allows us to infer from the transitivity of the *part_of* relationship the transitivity of *part_type_of*:

If *part_type_of(c1,c2)* and *part_type_of(c2,c3)* hold, then all instances of c1 are *part_of* an instance of c2, and those in turn are *part_of* an instance of c3. Hence, all instances of c1 are necessarily *part_of* an instance of c3. From that, we infer a necessary relationship of type *part_of* between c1 and c3, which satisfies D4 (see Fig. 5). The necessary *part_type_of* meta-relationship is transitive, reflexive and antisymmetric, hence a partial order:

(**PT1**) ∀ c1,c2,c3/Dc, part_type_of (c1,c2) ∧ part_type_of(c2,c3) ⇒ part_type_of(c1,c3)

(**PT2**) ∀ c/C, part_type_of(c,c)

(**PT3**) ∀ c1, c2/C, part_type_of (c1,c2) ⇒ ¬part_of(c2,c1)

As an example of (PT1) consider the following: If we find on a battlefield a firing pin, there should have been a gunlock for it, and for that in turn a gun. Normally, the type of the pin would be even characteristic for the model of the gun. As in this example, we often make the hypothesis, that an object of which we hold a part in our hands had been conforming with the *part_of* structure of the schema (we don't expect stone axes to have been used as table legs). This assumption allows for narrowing the search space for lost items, which may or may not confirm the assumption.

We therefore define the attribute *type_conforming* for the classes of parts, which had been parts of the foreseen type of whole at the historically relevant time-interval:

(D6) $\forall$ c1/C, type_conforming(c1) $\Leftrightarrow$ ($\forall$ t1/T, instance_of(t1,c1) $\Rightarrow$ ($\exists$ c2/C, t2/T, whole_type_of(c2,c1) $\wedge$ whole_of(t2,t1) $\wedge$ instance_of(t2,c2))

Finally, we could not find cases, where associative knowledge exists on the schema level without part-of knowledge. We assume therefore, that the relationship *from_the_same_whole_as* has no independent equivalent on the schema level that contributes to identifying information about wholes.

6.3 Token – Schema Level

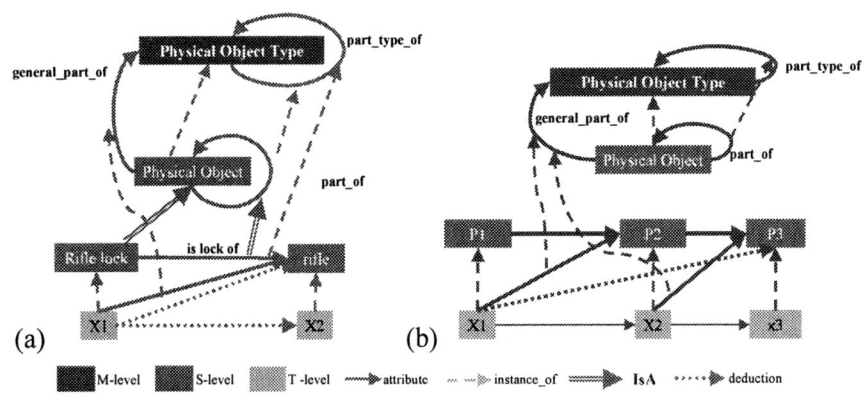

Fig. 6: Example of token to schema level inference

Let us now formalize the *general_part_of* relationship (*gpart_of*). It describes a situation, where evidence exists, that an object had been *part_of* something, but we only know a set of properties in order to determine the class it belongs to:

(D7) $\forall$t1/T,$\forall$c2/C, gpart_of(t1,c2) $\Leftrightarrow$ $\exists$ t2/T, instance_of(t2,c2) $\wedge$ part_of(t1,t2)

general_part_of is a very powerful concept, comprising a large class of reasoning on specific properties that can be formulated as classes for the missing object. The interest is of course to identify the smallest possible set or the most specific classes in an IsA hierarchy. We postpone this aspect for future work. An example is Beasley's recognition in 1917, that the Hauser collection are parts of a type of wholes like the stamnoi of Smirkos and parts of the set of stamnoi made by Euphrinius. In the sequence, we can infer the following rules for the basic transition from the token to the class level as indicated in Fig. 6a:

(G1) $\forall t1,t2/T, \forall c2/C$, part_of(t1,t2) $\land$ instance_of(t2,c2) $\Rightarrow$ gpart_of(t1,c2)

(G2) $\forall t1/T, \forall c1,c2/Dc$, instance_of(t1,c1) $\land$ part_type_of(c1,c2) $\Rightarrow$ gpart_of(t1,c2)

Note that G2 only holds for dependent parts or "complete" wholes. Finally, we analyze a kind of transitivity for gpart_of: any path from a token to a class following part_of, part_type_of relations and either one gpart_of or one instance_of relation can be reduced to a gpart_of relation (see Fig. 6b). As an example, consider those that imply one gpart_of relation:

(G3) $\forall t1,t2/T, \forall c3/Dc$, part_of(t1,t2) $\land$ gpart_of(t2,c3) $\Rightarrow$ gpart_of(t1,c3)

(G4) $\forall t1/T, \forall c2,c3/Dc$, gpart_of(t1,c2) $\land$ part_type_of(c2,c3) $\Rightarrow$ gpart_of(t1,c3)

The other paths follow trivially from G1,G2, P1, PT1.

For example, if we find on a battlefield a firing pin, there should have existed a gunlock and a gun of a model compatible with that pin. Finally, we describe the combination of associative information *fswa* with *gpart_of*.

(G5) $\forall\ t1,t2/T, \forall c3/C$, fswa(t1,t2) $\land$ gpart_of(t2,c3) $\land$ type_conforming(c3) $\Rightarrow$ $\exists\ c4/C$, whole_type_of(c4,c3) $\land$ gpart_of(t1,c4)

In other words, the whole type foreseen by the schema level for c3 is the type of whole of t1. If, in particular, c3=c4, the inference reads "*gpart_of(t1,c3)*". This inference is actually most interesting, as it describes the application of knowledge acquired about some part to an object associated to it.

7 Conclusions

In this paper, we presented basic inferences from parts to potential wholes characteristic for archeology and other detective work, based on the notion of *part_of* and *from_the_same_whole_as,* at the token level, the class level, and from the token to the class level. This work is the first formalization of the work presented in [7] and generalizes over more specific relationships presented there. Specific to the archeological or detective reasoning is the fact that knowledge is incomplete. So, otherwise redundant relationships allow for recovering part of the missing information. This knowledge is either useful by itself, or enables directed search to detect new facts either from different data sources or field studies. Until verified by new findings, most of the presented inferences remain hypothetical. These hypotheses appear as requirements for the existence of wholes, existence of part-of relations and non-shared parts at the token and class levels. Normally, such assumptions are reasonable, and can be supported by other contextual factors. For instance, we would not expect to find half-finished products in a grave. This is not the case if we excavate a stone-axe workshop. In the latter case, we expect to find half-finished products and by-products, and hence would not assume, that all parts belonged to the proper wholes. Further work is needed in order to refine this theory to cover the problem range laid out in [7]. We intend to formally connect the relationships presented in the latter to the work presented here, and to employ modal logic to describe the validity and validation of working hypotheses. Additionally, we are currently investigating the axiomatization of the other more specialized attributes of this model presented, as well as, the specification of the rules required for drawing other possibly interesting conclusions. A particular challenge seems to be the formalization of unity criteria, that allow for focusing reasoning on wholes within larger wholes, like carved blocks in buildings, metal fittings in wooden objects etc.

References

1. Analyti, A., Spyratos, N., Constantopoulos, P. : Deriving and Retrieving Contextual Categorical Information through Instance Inheritance, Fundamenta Informaticae 33, IOS Press, (1998) 1-37
2. Artale, A., Franconi, E., Guarino, N., Pazzi, L.: Part – Whole relations in Object – Centered Foralisms: An Overview, Data & Knowledge Engineering 20 (1996)
3. Artale, A., Franconi, E., Guarino, N.: Open Problems for Part-whole relations: International Workshop on Description Logics, Boston, MA (1996)
4. Bekiari, Ch., Constantopoulos, P., Bitzou, Th.: DELTOS - A Documentation Sytsem for the Antiquities and Preserved Buildings of Crete, Requirements Analysis. Technical Report FORTH-ICS/TR60 (1992)
5. Bekiari, Ch., Bitzou Th., Calomoirakis, D., Chronaki, D., Costantopoulos, P.: DELTOS - conservation documentation and administration of site monuments and preserved buildings. Proc. III Convegno Internazionale di Archeologia e Informatica, Roma (1995)
6. Bekiari, Ch., Gritzapi, Ch., Kalomoirakis, D.: POLEMON- A Federated Database Management System for the Documentation, Management and Promotion of Cultural Heritage. Proc. 26th Conference on Computer Applications in Archaeology, Barchelona, (1998)
7. Bekiari, Ch., Doerr, M. : Documentation and Reasoning on Parts and Potential Wholes. Computer Applications in Archaeology, Conference, Dublin Ireland (1999)
8. Constantopoulos, P.: Cultural Documentation- The CLIO System. Technical Report FORTH-ICS/TR-115 (1994)
9. Crofts, N., Dionissiadou, I., Doerr, M., Stiff, M. (eds): Definition of the CIDOC object-oriented Conceptual Reference Model (version 2.1). ICOM/CIDOC CRM Special Interest Group, http://cidoc.ics.forth.gr (1999)
10. Dionysiadou, I., Doerr, M.: Mapping of material culture to a semantic network. Proc. JOINT ANNUAL MEETING, International Council of Museums Documentation Committee and Computer Network, Washington USA (1994)
11. Doerr, M., Crofts, N.: Electronic Communication on Diverse Data - The Role of an Object-Oriented CIDOC Reference Model. CIDOC'98 Conference, Melbourne (1998)
12. Eaglestone, B., Holton, R., Rold, L.: GENREG- A historical data model based on event graphs. DEXA 96 Conference Proceedings, eds. Roland R. Wagner and Helmut Thoma, Lecture Notes in Computer Science vol.1134, Springer-Verlag, Berlin (1996)
13. Gangemi, A., Guarino, N., Masolo, C., Oltrami, A.: Understanding top-level ontological distinctions. LADSEB/CNR, Internal Report (2001)
14. Gerstl, P., Pribbenow, S.: A conceptual theory of part – whole relations and its applications. Data & Knowledge Engineering 20, North Holland- Elsevier (1996) 305-322
15. Guarino, N. , Pribbenow, S., Vieu L.: Modeling Parts & Wholes. Data & Knowledge Engineering vol. 20 no 3 (1996) 257-258
16. Habel, C., Pribbenow, S., Simmons, G.: Partonomies and Depictions - A Hybrid Approach. In J. Glasgow, H. Narayanan, B. Chandrasekaran (Eds.): Diagrammatic Reasoning: Computational and Cognitive Perspectives,AAAI/MIT Press (1995)
17. Halper, M, Geller, J., Perl J.: An OODB part-whole model: Semantics, notation and implementation. Data & Knowledge Engineering vol 27 no 1 (1998) 59-95

18. Motschnig – Pitrik, R. :The Semantics of Parts Versus Aggregates in Data/Knowledge Modelling. Proceedings of the CaiSE'93, Lecture Notes in Computer Science, No. 685, Springer 352-373 (1993)
19. Motschnig – Pitrik, R., Kaasboll, J.: Part – Whole Relationship Categories and Their Application in Object – Oriented Analysis. IEEE Transactions on Knowledge and Data Engineering, Vol. 11, No. 5, (1999)
20. Mylopoylos, J., Borgida, A., Jarke, M., Koubarakis, M. : Telos: Representing Knowledge about Information Systems. ACM Transactions on Information Systems 8(4) (1990)
21. Pantos, P., Bekiari, Ch.: POLEMON - A Project to Computerize the Monument Records at the Greek Ministry of Culture. Proc. Archaelogical Heritage: Inventory and Documentations Standards in Europe, Oxford (1995)
22. Pazzi, L.: Implicit versus Explicit characterization of complex Entities and Events. Data & Knowledge Engineering 31 (1999)
23. Pfisterer – Haas, S. : Wenn der Topf aber num ein Loch hat. Sonderausstellung im Antikenmuseum der Universitat Leipzig, vom 13. Mai bis (1998)
24. Polkowski, L. , Skowron, A.: Rough Mereology. Lecture notes in Computer Science vol. 869, (1994) 85-94
25. Rold, L. : GENREG: A simple and flexible system for object registration at the National Museum of Denmark. Selected papers from the 3rd International Conference on hypermedia and interactivity in Museums. San Diego, California.
26. Smith, B., Varzi, A.: Fiat and Bona Fide Boundaries: Towards on Ontology of Spatially Extended Objects. International Conference COSIT'97, Proceedings. Lecture Notes in Computer Science, Vol. 1329, Springer, (1997) 103-119
27. Uschold, M.: The use of the typed Lambda Calculus for guiding Naïve Users in the Representation and Acquisition of Part - Whole Knowledge. Data & Knowledge Engineering vol 20 no 3 (1996) 385-404
28. Vandenberg, Ph.: Nofrete. Eine archaeologische Biographie. Scherz Verlag Bern und (1975).
29. Varzi, A.: Parts, Wholes and part-whole relations- The prospects of mereotopology. Data & Knowledge Engineering 20, North Holland- Elsevier (1996) 259-286 .
30. Winston, M., Chaffin, R., Herrmann, D.: A Taxonomy of Part-Whole Relations. Cognitive Science 11(4), (1987) 417-444
31. Wolinski, F., Perrot, J. : Representation of Complex Objects: Multiple Facets with Part-Whole Hierarchies. Lecture Notes in Computer Science vol 512 (1991)
32. Zadrozny, W., Kim, M. : Computational Mereology - A Study of Part-of Relations for Multimedia Indexing. Annals of Mathematics and Artificial Intelligence, vol 15 (1995) 83-100

Developing XML Documents with Guaranteed "Good" Properties

David W. Embley[1] and Wai Y. Mok[2]

[1] Brigham Young University, Provo, Utah 84602, USA,
embley@cs.byu.edu
[2] University of Alabama at Huntsville, Huntsville, Alabama 35899, USA,
mokw@email.uah.edu

Abstract. Many XML documents are being produced, but there are no agreed-upon standards formally defining what it means for complying XML documents to have "good" properties. In this paper we present a formal definition for a proposed canonical normal form for XML documents called XNF. XNF guarantees that complying XML documents have maximally compact connectivity while simultaneously guaranteeing that the data in complying XML documents cannot be redundant. Further, we present a conceptual-model-based methodology that automatically generates XNF-compliant DTDs and prove that the algorithms, which are part of the methodology, produce DTDs to ensure that all complying XML documents satisfy the properties of XNF.

1 Introduction

Many DTDs (Document Type Definitions) for XML documents are being produced (e.g. see [XML]), and soon many XML-Schema specifications [XML00] for XML documents will be produced. With the emergence of these documents, we should be asking the question, "What constitutes a good DTD?"[1] Intuitively, this should ensure that complying XML documents are compactly connected in as few hierarchies as possible while simultaneously ensuring that no data value in any complying document can be removed without loss of information.

In this paper we formalize these ideas by defining XNF, a normal form for XML documents,[2] and we present a way to generate DTDs that are guaranteed to be in XNF. We assume that the DTDs produced are for XML documents representing some aspect of the real world—those for which conceptual modeling makes sense.[3] Under this assumption, we argue that to produce a "good" DTD

---

[1] Since we do not address issues beyond hierarchical structure in this document, we discuss the issues in terms of DTDs rather than XML-Schemas.
[2] The idea of XNF is based on nested normal form as defined in [MEN96] and is also related to other similar nested normal forms such as those surveyed in [Mok].
[3] The class of documents we are considering is certainly large, but also certainly not all-inclusive. We do not, for example, consider text documents where the order of textual elements is important.

for an application A, we should first produce a conceptual-model instance for A and then apply a transformation guaranteed to produce an XNF-compliant DTD.

Although we can guarantee XNF compliance, we cannot guarantee uniqueness. In general, several "good" DTDs, correspond to any given conceptual-model instance. Selecting the best depends on usage requirements and viewpoints that are "in the eye of the beholder." Sometimes these usage requirements or viewpoints should even cause the principles of XNF to be violated, but most of the time XNF-compliance should be compatible with usage requirements and viewpoints. Heuristic "rules of thumb" can go a long way toward resolving this problem of nonuniqueness and can often produce results that are highly satisfactory. We believe, however, that the ultimate resolution should be synergistic. Given heuristic rules and the principles of XNF, a system should work with a user to derive a suitable application DTD. The system can automatically derive reasonable XNF-compliant DTDs. The user may adjust, reject, or redo any of the generated suggestions. The system can check the revisions and report any violations of XNF so that the user is aware of the consequences of the revisions. Iterating until closure is reached, the user can further revise the DTD, and the system can evaluate and provide feedback.

We are aware of only one other research effort that closely parallels our work—namely [BGH00].[4] [BGH00] makes the same argument we make, namely (1) that graphical conceptual-modeling languages offer one of the best—if not the best—human-oriented way of describing an application, (2) that a model instance should be transformed automatically into an XML DTD (or XML schema), and (3) that the transformation should maximize connectivity among the XML components and should minimize the redundancy in complying XML documents. The authors of [BGH00] use Object Role Modeling [Hal99] as their conceptual model and give a set of twelve heuristics for generating the "best" XML schema. What is missing is the guarantee that their transformation achieves maximum connectivity and minimum redundancy. In this paper we use a more generic conceptual model and a simpler set of heuristics to achieve similar results, but the main contribution is the guarantee that complying XML documents satisfy the formal properties XNF.

We present our contribution as follows. Section 2 provides motivating examples and foundation definitions. Besides arguing that we can produce DTDs that yield only XNF-compliant XML documents, we also provide examples to show that even for simple applications, it is easy to produce (and thus nontrivial to avoid) DTDs that have redundancy and have more hierarchical clusters than necessary. In Section 3 we present straightforward algorithms that guarantee the properties of XNF for a large number of practical cases. We then show in Section 4, however, that these straightforward algorithms depend on the given

---

[4] Others, such as [BR00, CSF00], discuss a UML-to-XML transformations, but they do not investigate properties of conceptual-model generated XML documents. Similarly, OMG's XMI effort [XMI] also provides a way to represent UML in XML, but the effort is devoid of XNF-like guarantees for XML documents.

conceptual-model instance being in a particular canonical form. Although many practical model instances are naturally specified in the required canonical form, some are not. We therefore explain how to achieve this canonical form Section 4. We then prove that for a given conceptual-model instance in the canonical form, the algorithms in Section 3 yield XNF-compliant DTDs. In Sections 5 and 6 we generalize our approach and give algorithms for producing XNF-compliant DTDs for a more-inclusive set of conceptual-model instances. We conclude in Section 7 and present the status of our implementation.

2 Motivating Example

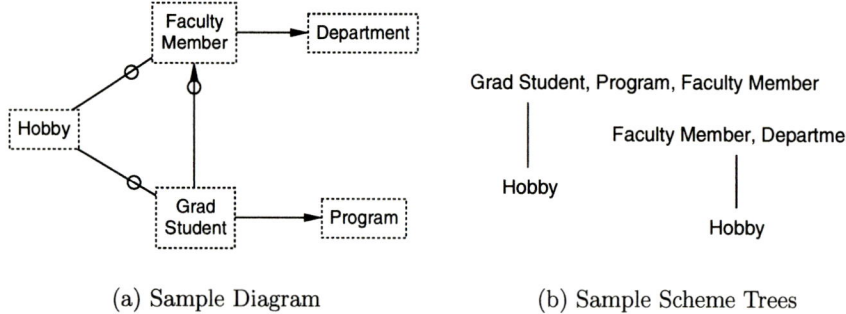

(a) Sample Diagram   (b) Sample Scheme Trees

Fig. 1. Simple Faculty-Student-Hobbies Diagram and Scheme Trees

As a motivating example, consider the conceptual-model diagram in Figure 1(a). Although based on [EKW92], the conceptual modeling approach we present here is generic. Users model the real world by constraint-augmented hypergraphs, which we call *CM hypergraphs* (conceptual-model hypergraphs). Vertices of CM hypergraphs are object sets denoted graphically as named rectangles. The object set *Hobby* in Figure 1(a), for example, may denote the set {*Chess, Hiking, Sailing*}. In the general conceptual model, edges have two or more connections to object sets, but we restrict ourselves until Section 5 to edges with just two connections. Edges representing functional relationships have arrowheads on the range side. In Figure 1(a), a graduate student enrolls in only one program (e.g. *PhD, MS*) and has only one faculty-member advisor. A connection between an object set and a relationship set may be optional or mandatory, denoted respectively by an "O" on the edge near the connection or the absence of an "O." A faculty member need not have hobbies and need not have advisees, but must be in a department. The inclusion constraints, which for Figure 1(a) are only simple referential integrity constraints, must all hold. For optional participation, the inclusion constraint allows a proper subset, but for mandatory participation, the subset can never be proper. Later in the paper, a triangle with its apex connected to a generalization object set and its base connected to one or more specialization object sets will denote an explicit inclusion constraint—the objects in any specialization object set must be a subset of the objects in the generalization object set.

An XML document has a hierarchical structure with a single root. The set of structures immediately below the single root constitutes a forest of hierarchical trees. It is this forest of trees we wish to derive from a conceptual-model instance. We abstractly represent each tree in this forest as a *scheme tree* [MEN96].

Example 1. The two scheme trees in Figure 1(b) cover the model instance in Figure 1(a). Textually written, the scheme trees in Figure 1(b) are *(Grad Student, Program, Faculty Member, (Hobby)*)** and *(Faculty Member, Department, (Hobby)*)*.* □

From a forest of scheme trees, we can derive a DTD for any model instance. There are several ways we can represent a scheme tree as a DTD (especially if we use XMI [XMI] or features such as ATTLIST, ID, and IDREF). We do not concern ourselves further with this issue, but rather concentrate on generating a forest of XNF-compliant scheme trees.

Example 2. As motivational examples, consider the following scheme-tree forests.

1. *(Department, (Faculty Member, (Hobby)*, (Grad Student, Program, (Hobby)*)*)*)**
2. *(Faculty Member, Department, (Hobby)*, (Grad Student, Program, (Hobby)*)*)**
3. *(Hobby, (Faculty Member)*, (Grad Student)*)*, (Grad Student, Program, Faculty Member)*, (Department, (Faculty Member)*)**
4. *(Hobby, (Faculty Member, Department)*, (Grad Student, Program, Faculty Member)*)**
5. *(Faculty Member, Department, (Hobby, (Grad Student)*)*)*, (Grad Student, Faculty Member, Program)** □

We claim (and will shortly give the formal basis for showing) that the first two sample scheme-tree forests in Example 2, which each consist of a single tree, can never have a redundant data value in any complying XML document. The third scheme-tree forest, as well as the scheme-tree forest in Figure 1(b), also never allow redundancy, but both have more than one scheme tree and thus neither is as compact as the first two sample scheme trees. The fourth sample scheme-tree forest allows redundancy—since faculty members and grad students are listed repeatedly for each additional *Hobby* in which they participate, department values for faculty members and program values as well as faculty advisors for grad students can be redundant. The first tree of the fifth scheme-tree forest also allows redundancy—whenever faculty members have the same hobbies, all the graduate students that also share these hobbies are listed.

Definition 1. *Let T be a scheme tree for a CM hypergraph M, and let t be a scheme-tree instance over T. A data value v in t is redundant with respect to a constraint C that holds for M if when v is replaced in t by some symbol, say $\bot$, where $\bot$ is not in t, C implies $\bot = v$.* □

Although many constraints are possible, we consider only functional constraints, multivalued constraints, and inclusion constraints. We further restrict this set to those that are conceptual-model compliant in the sense that they occur naturally within a conceptual-model instance as defined below. This set of constraints is a common standard set that is sufficient for many, if not most, practical cases.

Let T be a scheme tree. A *path* of T is a sequence of nodes from the root node of T to a leaf node of T. Thus, if T has n, $n \geq 1$, leaf nodes, T has n paths. A scheme tree T is *properly constructed* for a CM hypergraph M if every path of T embeds a sequence of some connected edges in M.

Definition 2. *Let T be a properly constructed scheme tree for a CM hypergraph M, and let t be a scheme-tree instance over T. Let $X \to Y$ be a functional edge in M that is contained in a path of T, and let s be a subtuple over XY in t. Let A be an attribute of Y,[5] and let a be the A value in s. Then t has redundancy with respect to the functional constraint $X \to Y$ if the a-value in s appears more than once in t. If such a scheme-tree instance t can exist, we say that T has potential redundancy with respect to the functional constraint $X \to Y$.* □

Example 3. Scheme-tree four in Example 2 has potential redundancy with respect to the functional edge *Faculty Member* → *Department* because faculty members appear once for each hobby and may participate in several hobbies. Similarly, since grad students also appear once for each hobby and may participate in several hobbies, there is potential redundancy with respect to both the functional constraints *Grad Student* → *Program* and *Grad Student* → *Faculty Member*.

Definition 3. *Let T be a properly constructed scheme tree for a CM hypergraph M, and let t be a scheme-tree instance over T. Let $X-Y$ be an edge in M that is contained in a path of T, and let s be a subtuple over XY in t. Let y be the Y subtuple in s.[6] Then t has redundancy with respect to the multivalued constraint $X-Y$ if the y-subtuple in s appears more than once in t. If such a scheme-tree instance t can exist, we say that T has potential redundancy with respect to the multivalued constraint $X-Y$.* □

Example 4. The first scheme tree in the fifth scheme-tree forest in Example 2 has potential redundancy with respect to the edge *Hobby — Grad Student*. Whenever faculty members have the same hobby, hobby values appear more than once.

Definition 4. *A scheme-tree forest F corresponds to a conceptual-model instance M if each tree of F is a properly constructed scheme tree and the union of the edges in all the scheme trees of F covers the edges in M.* □

---
[5] A is Y for the binary case, but in general, Y is a set of attributes.
[6] For the binary case y is a value, but in general, y is a subtuple.

Definition 5. *Let F be a scheme-tree forest corresponding to a conceptual-model instance M. Let T be a scheme tree in F with only a root node and only one object set G in the root node. If there exist object sets $S_1, ..., S_n$ within the nodes of F such that the S_i's ($1 \leq i \leq n$) are specializations of G in M and $G = \cup_{i=1}^{n} S_i$ for all scheme-tree-forest instances for F, the values in G are redundant and T has potential redundancy with respect to the inclusion constraint specifying that the S_i's are union specializations of G.* □

Example 5. To illustrate inclusion constraints and redundancy with respect to inclusion constraints, we present the CM hypergraphs in Figure 2. Figure 2(a) is the same as Figure 1(a) except that *Hobby* is optional for both *Faculty* and *Grad Student*. The diagram in Figure 2(a) allows all hobbies for both faculty and students to be listed, not just those shared jointly by at least one faculty member and grad student as is the case for the hobbies in the diagram in Figure 1(a). Using the application model instance in Figure 2(a), however, we cannot include all of the data values in scheme-tree instances for either the first or the second scheme tree in Example 2. This is because the model instance in Figure 2(a) allows hobbies to be listed that are neither faculty hobbies nor student hobbies; thus an "extra" scheme tree is necessary to accommodate these hobbies. If this is not what we want (it probably isn't), we should model our microworld as in Figure 2(b) where the union constraint[7] on the generalization/specialization ensures that *Hobby* contains only hobbies that are faculty hobbies (contained in *Faculty Hobby*) or student hobbies (contained in *Grad Student Hobby*). Since *Hobby = Faculty Hobby $\cup$ Grad Student Hobby*, *Hobby* is redundant and we should eliminate it as Figure 2(c) shows. For Figure 2(c), the first and second scheme tree in Example 2 apply, except that the *Hobby* element associated with *Faculty* should be *Faculty Hobby* and the *Hobby* element associated with *Grad Student* should be *Grad Student Hobby*. With this solution, we eliminate redundancy with respect to inclusion constraints, and we also have better names for XML tags. □

Definition 6. *Let M be a CM hypergraph. Let F be a scheme-tree forest corresponding to M. F is in XNF_C if each scheme tree in F has no potential redundancy with respect to a specified set of constraints C and F has as few, or fewer, scheme trees as any other scheme-tree forest corresponding to M in which each scheme tree has no potential redundancy with respect to C. When all constraints apply or when the specified set of constraints is clear from the context, we write XNF_C simply as XNF.* □

Example 6. We claim (and will later show) that only the first two scheme-tree forests in Example 2 are in XNF. □

---

[7] A union symbol inside a generalization/specialization triangle denotes that the generalization object set is a union of the specialization object sets.

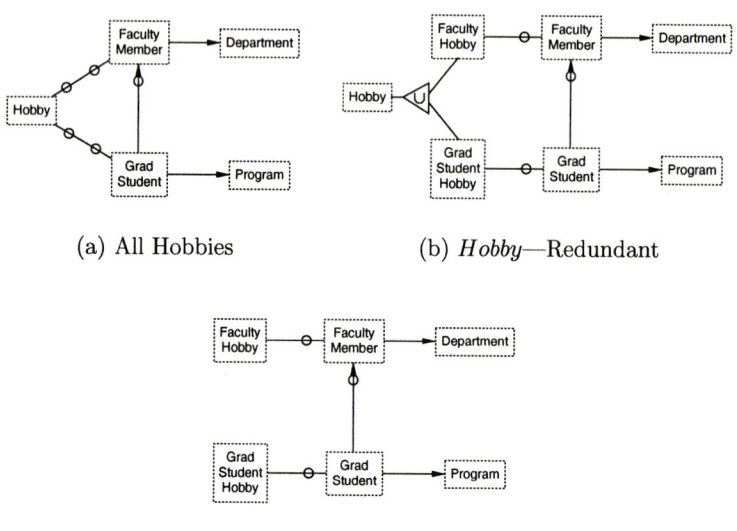

(a) All Hobbies (b) *Hobby*—Redundant

(c) No ID Redundancy

Fig. 2. Illustration for Inclusion Dependencies and ID Redundancy

3 Binary Algorithm

In Figure 3 We present our first algorithm to generate scheme-tree forests. This algorithm requires the input to be a conceptual-model instance with only binary edges connecting vertices and no explicit generalization/specialization.

Example 7. Consider the model instance in Figure 1(a) as the input to Algorithm 1. If we select *Department* as the root node, we make *Faculty Member* a child of *Department* and designate it as a continuation attribute and then make *Hobby* a child of *Faculty Member*; further since *Faculty Member* is a continuation attribute, we make *Grad Student* another child of *Faculty Member* and designate it as a continuation attribute and then add *Program* in the node with *Grad Student* and finally make *Hobby* a child node of the node containing *Grad Student*. The result is the first scheme tree in Example 2. If we select *Faculty Member* as the starting node, we can generate the second scheme tree in Example 2. If we select *Grad Student* as the starting node, proceed as far as we can, and then select *Faculty Member* from the remaining unmarked nodes and proceed, we can generate the scheme-tree forest in Figure 1(b). Similarly, we can generate the third scheme-tree forest in Example 2, by starting with *Hobby*, then *Grad Student*, and then *Department*. We cannot, however, generate either the fourth or the fifth scheme-tree forest in Example 2. □

Observe from our discussion of Examples 2, 3, 4, and 7 that Algorithm 1 disallows the sample scheme-tree forests that have potential redundancy. Indeed, we claim, and will prove in Section 4 that Algorithm 1 can be used to generate only scheme-tree forests that have no potential redundancy with respect to functional and multivalued constraints.

Input: a binary CM hypergraph H
  (with no explicit generalization/specialization).
Output: a scheme-tree forest.
Until all vertices and edges have been marked
    If one or more unmarked vertices remain
        Let V be a selected unmarked vertex in H;
        Mark V in H;
    Else
        Select an unmarked edge E;
        Let V be one of the two vertices of E;
        Make V the root node of a new scheme tree T;
        Designate V in T as a continuation attribute;
        While there is an unmarked edge $E = (A, B)$ in H
                such that A is a continuation attribute in T
            Mark E in H;
            If the B-E connection is mandatory, Mark B in H;
            If $A \leftrightarrow B$
                Add B to T in the node containing A;
                If the B-E connection is mandatory
                    Designate B in T as a continuation attribute;
            Elseif $A \rightarrow B$
                Add B to T in the node containing A;
            Elseif $B \rightarrow A$
                Add B to T in a new child node of the node containing A;
                If the B-E connection is mandatory
                    Designate B in T as a continuation attribute;
            Else Add B to T in the node containing A;

Fig. 3. Algorithm 1—Binary Algorithm

Although Algorithm 1 can guarantee no potential redundancy, it does not guarantee that the scheme trees are as compact as possible. To get XNF (no potential redundancy *and* maximum compactness), we can add the following to Algorithm 1:

- Before the *Until* statement, add the following statements:

    Compute the functional closure of each vertex using only fully functional edges
    (i.e. using only functional edges whose domain side is not optional);
    Order the vertices first on the number of closures in which the vertex appears (descending)
    then on the closure size (descending), and finally alphabetical (ascending);
    Discard from the tail-end of the ordered list, those vertices included in only a single closure;
    Order the discarded vertices on the number of incident edges (descending) and then
    alphabetical (ascending);
    Append this list of ordered "discarded" vertices to the tail-end of the first ordered list;

- Change the *If-Else* that selects the root of a new scheme tree to:

    From the ordered list of vertices, select the first unmarked vertex V in H to be
    the root node of a new scheme tree T.
    If there is no unmarked vertex left in the list, then select the marked vertex V such that V is
    in an unmarked edge and V comes before any other vertices in unmarked edges in the list.

We call Algorithm 1 with this modification *Algorithm 1.1*.

Example 8. For the CM hypergraph in Figure 1(a), fully functional closures are: $Department^+ = \{Department\}$, $Faculty\ Member^+ = \{Faculty\ Member, Department\}$, $Grad\ Student^+ = \{Grad\ Student, Faculty\ Member, Department, Program\}$, $Program^+ = \{Program\}$, $Hobby^+ = \{Hobby\}$. Thus, *Department* is included in three closures, *Faculty Member* is included in two, *Grad Student*, *Program*, and *Hobby* are included in one with *Grad Student* having the largest closure size. Since the last three vertices on the list are included in only a single closure, they are ordered according to their respective number of incident edges: *Grad Student* has 3, *Hobby* has 2, and *Program* has 1. Hence, the order is *Department, Faculty Member, Grad Student, Hobby, Program*. Observe that for Algorithm 1.1, we produce the first scheme tree in Example 2. □

An alternate way to select the starting node for a new scheme tree is:
Let V be the selected vertex in Algorithm 1.1.
If V has exactly one incident unmarked edge E and E is fully functional from W to V, select W;
Else Select V;

We call Algorithm 1 with this modification *Algorithm 1.2*.

Example 9. Observe that Algorithm 1.2 produces the second scheme tree in Example 2. □

As we shall prove in the next section, we can use Algorithm 1 to guarantee no potential redundancy for any starting vertex in Figure 1(a). Further, the algorithm can guarantee the fewest scheme trees if the starting vertices for scheme trees are chosen according to one of the two criteria presented. Thus, we can use Algorithm 1.1 or Algorithm 1.2 to produce scheme trees in XNF.

4 Assumptions, Requirements, and Guarantees

Unfortunately, Algorithms 1, 1.1, and 1.2 do not work for any CM hypergraph. Two conditions are required: (1) canonical and (2) binary. We discuss the canonical requirement in this section and show how to remove the binary requirement in the next section where we give a more general algorithm for producing scheme trees for XNF-compliant XML documents.

Definition 7. *A binary CM hypergraph H is* canonical *if (1) no edge of H is redundant; (2) no vertex of H is redundant; and (3) bidirectional edges represent bijections.* □

Example 10. Figure 4(a) shows a noncanonical CM hypergraph; Figure 4(b) shows its canonical counterpart. To illustrate the edge-redundancy requirement, consider the edge between *Grad Student* and *Department*. If it means the department of the student's faculty advisor, it is redundant.[8] Its removal preserves both information and constraints—we can recompute it as a join-project over the advisor and faculty/department relationship sets, and the constraints of these same two relationship sets imply both its functional and its mandatory and optional participation constraints. Similarly, if the edge between *Program* and *Department* represents the department that administers the student's program, it is redundant and can be removed. Assuming that the edge with optionals between *Grad Student* and *Program* represents a program a student has applied for, whereas the edge with no optionals represents the program in which the student is currently enrolled, neither edge is redundant. To illustrate the

---

[8] We make neither the universal-relation assumption nor the universal-relation-scheme assumption [FMU82, Ken81].

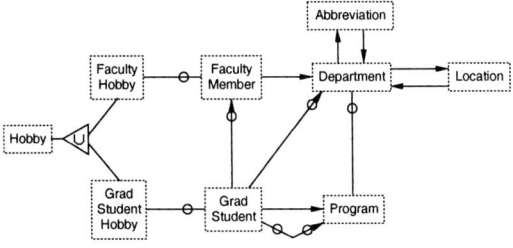

(a) Noncanonical

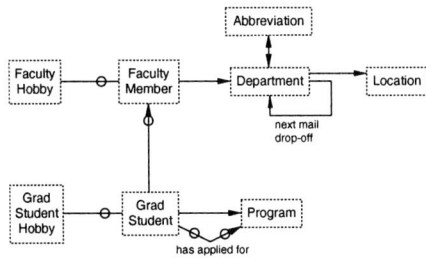

(b) Canonical

Fig. 4. Noncanonical and Canonical Model Instances

vertex-redundancy requirement, consider *Hobby*, which is a redundant object set as explained earlier in Example 5. To illustrate the bidirectional-edge requirement, consider the functional edges between *Department* and *Abbreviation* and between *Department* and *Location*. For the abbreviations, we have a bijection between departments and their abbreviations (e.g. *Computer Science* and *CS*), but for the locations we have a permutation—*Department* → *Location* gives the address of the department, whereas *Location* → *Department* gives the department for next mail drop for a mail carrier. Figure 4(b) shows a canonical CM hypergraph. No relationship set or object set is redundant, and the bidirectional edge[9] represents its only bijection. Since we have a permutation, we choose to model it as a permutation in a recursive relationship set Figure 4(b) shows.[10] □

Using the model instances in Figure 4(a), we can illustrate the redundancy problems that can arise from Algorithm 1 when a CM hypergraph is not canonical.

---

[9] Note that $A \leftrightarrow B$ is not the same as $A \rightarrow B$ and $A \leftarrow B$. The former indicates a bijection, whereas the latter simply means two functional relationships between A and B.

[10] This choice does not effect our XNF result, but it is a heuristic transformation that almost always produces a more pleasing result.

Example 11. Starting with *Department* in Figure 4(a), Algorithm 1 generates the scheme-tree forest with trees *(Hobby)** and *(Department, Abbreviation, (Abbreviation)*, Location, (Location)*, (Faculty Member, (Faculty Hobby)*, (Grad Student, (Grad Student Hobby)*, Program, Program)*)*, (Grad Student)*, (Program)*)**. First observe that *(Hobby)** is redundant as explained in Example 5. Next observe that *(Program)** is a list of programs for a department, but according to the model, these can all be computed by finding the programs of the grad students being advised by faculty members in the department. Similarly, *(Grad Student)** is a list of grad students in a department, but these can all be computed by finding the grad students being advised by faculty members in the department. Finally, observe that the constructions *Abbreviation, (Abbreviation)** and *Location, (Location)** are strange. For the departmental abbreviations which are in a one-to-one correspondence with the departments, we should drop the second mention in *(Abbreviation)** because it is redundant. For the locations, *(Location)** represents the address of the department whereas *Location* represents the address of the department next on the list in a mail route; thus, they should both be left as they are. As we shall see in the next example, however, we can fix this awkward construction by a heuristic modification. □

Example 12. By way of contrast to Example 11, starting with *Department* in Figure 4(b),[11] Algorithm 1 generates the scheme tree forest *(Department, Abbreviation, Location, Department of next mail drop-off, (Faculty Member, (Faculty Hobby)*, (Grad Student, (Grad Student Hobby)*, Program, Program applied for)*)*)**. Observe that the redundant lists of programs, grad students, and hobbies are not present and that the redundant abbreviations and awkward locations have disappeared. □

We now state our theorem proving that Algorithm's 1.1 and 1.2 generate XNF scheme trees.[12]

Theorem 1. *Let H be a canonical CM hypergraph with no explicit generalization/specialization whose edges are all binary. If F is a scheme-tree forest generated from H by Algorithm 1.1 or 1.2, then each tree in F is in* $\text{XNF}_{\{FC,MC\}}$.[13]
□

5 N-ary Algorithm

In this section we generalize Algorithm 1 for CM hypergraphs with n-ary edges. Three new problems arise in the generalization: (1) n-ary edges may be com-

---

[11] For clarity we make use of the names designating the meaning of some of the relationship sets. We suggest the use of clarifying information whenever there may be ambiguity, or even just whenever additional clarifying explanations are appropriate or desired.

[12] Proofs for this and all other theorems can be found in a technical report at http://osm.cs.byu.edu/Papers.html.

[13] In this notation, *FC* denotes a functional constraint, *MC* denotes a multivalued constraint, and *IC* denotes an inclusion constraint.

positions of edges with lesser arity, (2) connecting sets of attributes between relationship sets may have different meanings, and (3) there are more degrees of freedom for scheme-tree configurations. We discuss each of these problems in turn.

Edge Decomposition. As one example of edge decomposition, consider the edge connecting *Name*, *Address*, *Phone*, and *Major* in Figure 5(a). If the phone for the person identified by the *Name-Address* pair is the home phone at the address of the person (i.e. is not the cell phone, for example), the 4-ary edge can be reduced by making the phone dependent only on the address as Figure 5(b) shows. As another example of edge decomposition, consider the 5-ary edge in Figure 5(a). Assuming that the schedule depends only on the course itself (the normal assumption unless the course is an individual-instruction course), we can decompose the edge as Figure 5(b) shows. Whether we can split the day from the time depends on the scheduling policy; our choice in Figure 5(b) assumes that courses can be scheduled at different times on different days.

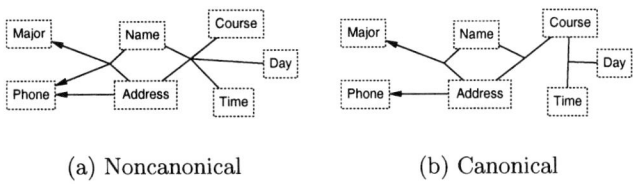

(a) Noncanonical   (b) Canonical

Fig. 5. *N*-ary Noncanonical and Canonical Model Instances

There are multiple ways an edge can be decomposed, but these are all found in the relational database literature. Thus, we only mention them here without redeveloping them. Included are reductions to satisfy the requirements of 3NF (head and tail reductions in [Emb98]), reductions to satisfy the stronger requirements of BCNF (embedded FD reductions [Emb98]), and reductions to satisfy the even stronger requirements of 4NF and 5NF (non-FD edge reductions [Emb98]). The sample reduction for home phones above is a head reduction, and the sample reduction for course schedules is a non-FD edge reduction.

To accommodate these requirements, we now augment our definition of what it means for a CM hypergraph to be canonical.

Definition 8. *A binary CM hypergraph H is* canonical *if (1) no edge of H is redundant; (2) no vertex of H is redundant; (3) bidirectional edges represent bijections; and (4) every n-ary edge is fully reduced.* □

Example 13. The CM hypergraph in Figure 5(a) is noncanonical—neither the 4-ary nor the 5-ary edge is fully reduced. Assuming, as stated earlier, that the *Course-Day-Time* relationship set cannot be further reduced, the CM hypergraph in Figure 5(b) is canonical. □

Different Meanings. Consider *Name-Address* pairs in Figure 5(b). Suppose there are two names n_1 and n_2 and two addresses a_1 and a_2. Further suppose that in the relationship set with *Major*, n_1 relates to a_1 and n_2 relates to a_2, but in the relationship set with *Course*, n_1 relates to a_2 and n_2 relates to a_1. Under these assumptions, we cannot have the scheme tree *(Major, (Name, Address, (Course)*)*)**, which we would expect should be permissible. We cannot have this scheme tree because under *Major* our scheme-tree instance would have the subtuples $\{(Name, n_1), (Address, a_1)\}$ and $\{(Name, n_2), (Address, a_2)\}$, but in order to nest courses under these tuples, we need $\{(Name, n_1), (Address, a_2)\}$ and $\{(Name, n_2), (Address, a_1)\}$.

In general, to provide for nesting, the projections on the intersecting attribute sets between two edges must be identical for every valid interpretation. This condition holds when the projections on the intersection object sets between two edges have the "*same meaning.*" Indeed, for the CM hypergraph in Figure 5(b), *Name-Address* pairs have the same meaning in both the *Major* relationship set and the *Course* relationship set—in both, the pair identifies an individual student.

Degrees of Freedom. Consider the ternary is-taking-course relationship set in the CM hypergraph in Figure 5(b). The scheme trees we may create for this relationship set include, for example, (a) *(Course, Name, Address)**, (b) *(Address, (Name, Course)*)**, and (c) *(Name, (Address, (Course)*)*)**. Whereas there are only three possible scheme trees for a nonfunctional binary relationship set, there are thirteen possible scheme trees for a nonfunctional ternary relationship set such as the is-taking-course relationship set in Figure 5(b). For an n-ary edge in general, we may have any of the $2^n - 1$ sets of vertices in the root node of its scheme tree, any of the $2^{n_1} - 1$ sets of vertices of the remaining n_1 vertices not chosen for the root in its first sublevel node, any of the $2^{n_2} - 1$ sets of vertices of the remaining n_2 vertices not chosen for the root or first sublevel node in its second sublevel node, and so forth.

The additional degrees of freedom make it more difficult to specify a scheme-tree generation algorithm, but the idea for the generalization of Algorithm 1 is straightforward—we are still searching for the largest hierarchical structures embedded within the CM hypergraph. Figure 6 shows Algorithm 2, which generalizes Algorithm 1 by allowing n-ary edges.

Example 14. Consider the model instance in Figure 5(b) as the input to Algorithm 2. We choose the initial single-path scheme tree to be *Major* as the root, with *Name* and *Address* together in a child node of the root. We mark all three attributes in the given hypergraph and designate all of them as continuation attributes in the scheme tree. Since the edge {*Name, Address, Course*} satisfies the five conditions of the while-loop, we add *Course* as a child of the node containing *Name* and *Address*. *Course* is then marked and designated as a continuation attribute. However, we can attach neither the edge {*Course, Day, Time*} nor the edge *Address* → *Phone* to the scheme tree since we cannot find the node N in Algorithm 2 that satisfies the five conditions for these two edges. In particular, Condition 4 cannot be satisfied. We thus create a scheme tree for each of these two edges. The resulting scheme-tree forest is: *(Major, (Name, Address, (Course)*)*)**, *(Course, (Day, Time)*)**, *(Address, Phone)**. □

Input: a canonical CM hypergraph H (with no explicit generalization/specialization).
Output: a scheme-tree forest.
Until all edges and vertices have been marked
    If one or more unmarked edges remain
        Select an unmarked edge E in H;
        Create a single-path scheme tree T from E such that
            the set of nodes in T is a partition of E, and
            either each vertex in the root node of T is mandatory for E,
            or there is at most one vertex in the root node of T;
        Mark E in H
        For each vertex V in E
            If the V-E connection is mandatory or V is the root node of T,
                Mark V in H and designate V in T as a continuation attribute;
        While there is an unmarked edge E in H such that
            (1) P is a path in T,
            (2) D is the maximal nonempty set of attributes in $E \cap P$ that
                has the "same meaning" in both E and P,
            (3) each of the attributes in D is designated as a continuation attribute in P,
            (4) there exists a node N in P such that $D \subseteq Ancestor(N)$ and
                $E \to Ancestor(N)$;
            (5) If there are more than one nodes that satisfy Condition 4,
                let N be the lowest one.
            Mark E in H;
            Create a single-path scheme tree T' from $E - D$ such that
                the set of nodes in T' is a partition of $E - D$;
            Make the root node of T' a child of N;
            For each vertex V in E
                If the V-E connection is mandatory,
                    Mark V in H and designate V in T as a continuation attribute;
    Else
        Select an unmarked vertex U;
        Make U the root node of a new scheme tree;
        Mark U in H;

Fig. 6. Algorithm 2—N-ary Algorithm

Although still an open question for future research, there appears to be no effective algorithm for guaranteeing the fewest possible scheme trees. The problem is that there are too many degrees of freedom—too many ways to add an n-ary edge to a scheme tree. Unfortunately, the choice makes a difference and the proper choice cannot always be determined until additional edges are added to a scheme tree. Thus, backtracking is required.

We can nevertheless apply variations to Algorithm 2 that are similar to the variations of Algorithm 1, as specified in Algorithm 1.1 and 1.2. For CM hypergraphs whose edges only intersect on single object sets or whose only multiple-object-set edge intersections follow a single path in the hypergraph, we can use variations similar to Algorithm 1.1 and 1.2 to guarantee minimality. Since real-world CM hypergraphs tend to have mostly binary edges or tend to satisfy these stricted constraints, there is usually an effective algorithm for generating XNF. Furthermore, when these conditions do not hold, the subgraphs over which non-deterministic backtracking must be applied is usually small enough to allow for an exhaustive search. We leave for future research precise characterizations of these claims.

In the meantime, for this paper, we let Algorithms 2.1 and 2.2 be similar in spirit to Algorithms 1.1 and 1.2,[14] and we let Algorithm 2.3 be Algorithm 2

---

[14] We do not specify these exactly since we cannot prove that they lead to XNF scheme-tree forests.

altered (1) to generate nondeterministic threads for all possible node configurations when an edge is added to a scheme tree and (2) to select a final minimal scheme-tree forest from the ones nondeterministically generated as a final step in the algorithm.

Theorem 2. *Let H be a canonical CM hypergraph with no explicit generalization/specialization. Let T be a scheme tree generated by Algorithm 2. T has neither redundancy with respect to a multivalued constraint nor redundancy with respect to a functional constraint. Further, if F is a scheme-tree forest generated from H by Algorithm 2.3, then each tree in F is in* $\text{XNF}_{\{FC,MC\}}$. □

6 General Algorithm

In this section we further generalize our algorithms to allow CM hypergraphs with explicit generalization/specialization denoted by *ISA* triangles in CM hypergraphs. This generalization causes two new problems: (1) object sets may be redundant, and (2) ISA constructs must be considered in scheme-tree generation algorithms. We discussed and illustrated object-set redundancy in Section 2: whenever we can compute the contents of an isolated root generalization object set as explained in Example 5, we eliminate it. To handle all other ISA constructs, we collapse them into roles and thus eliminate them too. Once all ISA constructs have been eliminated, we are left with CM hypergraphs that can be processed by Algorithm 2, or by Algorithm 1 if all relationship sets happen to be binary. We call this Algorithm 3.[15]

Theorem 3. *Let H be a canonical CM hypergraph. If F is a scheme-tree forest generated from H by Algorithm 3, then each tree in F is in* $\text{XNF}_{\{FC,MC,IC\}}$. □

7 Concluding Remarks

We have proposed and formally defined XNF (XML Normal Form). XNF guarantees that complying XML documents have no redundant data values and have maximally compact connectivity. We have also developed conceptual-model-based algorithms (Algorithms 1.1, 1.2, 2.3, and 3) to generate DTDs to ensure that complying documents are in XNF, and we have proved that these algorithms are correct (Theorems 1–3).

We have implemented a tool to work synergistically with a user to develop XNF-compliant DTDs. Currently our tool allows users to specify CM diagrams, to convert diagrams to CM hypergraphs, to apply either Algorithms 1.1 or 1.2, or to select root nodes for scheme trees and then apply Algorithm 1. In another tool, we have implemented, users can synergistically convert CM hypergraphs into canonical hypergraphs.

As for current and future work, we need to integrate these two tools so that we can have the synergistic system we desire. We also need to implement

---

[15] See http://osm.cs.byu.edu/Papers.html for examples and further details.

Algorithms 2 and 3 and their variations, and we need to formally characterize the restrictions to n-ary CM hypergraphs for which there exist effective scheme-tree generation algorithms. We also intend to investigate additional heuristic variations of scheme-tree generation algorithms and synergistic development of XNF-compliant DTDs.

Acknowledgements: This material is based upon work supported by the National Science Foundation under grant No. IIS-0083127. Kimball Hewett programmed the interface we used for our implementation, Eric Carter implemented the canonicalization procedures, and Troy Walker coded the implemented algorithms described in this paper.

References

[BGH00] L. Bird, A. Goodchild, and T. Halpin. Object role modelling and xml-schema. In *Proceedings of the Ninteenth International Conference on Conceptual Modeling (ER2000)*, pages 309–322, Salt Lake City, Utah, October 2000.

[BR00] V. Bisová and K. Richta. Transformation of uml models into xml. In *Proceedings the 2000 ADBIS-DASFAA Symposium on Advances in Databases and Information Systems*, pages 33–45, Prague, Czech Republic, September 2000.

[CSF00] R. Conrad, Deiter Scheffner, and J.C. Freytag. XML conceptual modeling using UML. In *Proceedings of the Ninteenth International Conference on Conceptual Modeling (ER2000)*, Salt Lake City, Utah, October 2000. 558–571.

[EKW92] D.W. Embley, B.D. Kurtz, and S.N. Woodfield. *Object-oriented Systems Analysis: A Model-Driven Approach*. Prentice Hall, Englewood Cliffs, New Jersey, 1992.

[Emb98] D.W. Embley. *Object Database Development: Concepts and Principles*. Addison-Wesley, Reading, Massachusetts, 1998.

[FMU82] R. Fagin, A.O. Mendelzon, and J.D. Ullman. A simplified universal relation assumption and its properties. *ACM Transactions on Database Systems*, 7(3):343–360, September 1982.

[Hal99] T. Halpin. *Conceptual Schema & Relational Database Design*. WytLytPub, revised 2nd edition, 1999.

[Ken81] W. Kent. Consequences of assuming a universal relation. *ACM Transactions on Database Systems*, 6(4):539–556, December 1981.

[MEN96] W.Y. Mok, D.W. Embley, and Y-K. Ng. A normal form for precisely characterizing redundancy in nested relations. *ACM Transactions on Database Systems*, 21(1):77–106, March 1996.

[Mok] W.Y. Mok. A comparative study of various nested normal forms. *IEEE Transactions on Knowledge and Data Engineering*. (to appear).

[XMI] Home Page for OASIS's XML Metadata Interchange (XMI). URL: http://www.oasis-open.org/cover/xmi.html.

[XML] Home Page for a listing of organizations producing industry-specific XML DTDs. URL: http://xml.org/xmlorg_registry/index.html.

[XML00] XML schema part 0: Primer: W3c working draft, 2000. URL: http://www.w3.org/TR/2000/WD-xmlschema-0-20000407/.

Dimension Hierarchies Design from UML Generalizations and Aggregations

Jacky Akoka[1], Isabelle Comyn-Wattiau[2], and Nicolas Prat[3]

[1]CEDRIC-CNAM & INT, 292 R St Martin, 75141 PARIS Cedex 03, France
akoka@cnam.fr
[2]Université de Cergy & ESSEC, 2 R A Chauvin, 95302 PONTOISE Cedex, France
isabelle.wattiau@dept-info.u-cergy.fr
[3]ESSEC, Av B Hirsch, BP 105, 95021 CERGY Cedex, France
prat@essec.fr

Abstract. Data for decision-making applications are based on dimensions, such as time, customer, and product. These dimensions are naturally related by hierarchies. Hierarchies are crucial to multidimensional modeling. Defining hierarchies using star or snowflake schemas can be misleading, since they are not explicitly well-modeled. However, deriving them from conceptual UML or ER schemas is a non-trivial task since they have no direct equivalent in conceptual models. This paper focuses on the definition of multidimensional hierarchies. We present and illustrate rules for defining multidimensional hierarchies from UML schemas, especially based on aggregation and generalization hierarchies. The definition of hierarchies is part of a data warehouse design method based on the three usual modeling levels : conceptual, logical, and physical. The conceptual schema is based on the UML notation. The logical schema is represented using a unified pivot multidimensional model. The physical schema depends on the target ROLAP or MOLAP tool.

1 Introduction

Characteristic features of MultiDimensional Data Base Systems (MDDBS) are fact and dimension. A fact consists of quantifying values stored in measures. Dimensions, called the axes of the data cube, represent different ways of analyzing the data. Typically, data in MDDBS have multiple dimensions such as product, region, customer, time, and vehicle. Each dimension is described by a set of attributes. Some attributes may be linked by a hierarchy. Dimension hierarchies are a distinctive feature of MDDBS. Multiple hierarchies can be defined on a single dimension. Most dimensions can have a complex structure that is generally hierarchical. Dimension hierarchies allow the designer to specify aggregation levels corresponding to different data granularities. In our view, dimensions determine the granularity for representing facts, whereas dimension hierarchies define the way to aggregate fact instances. Dimension hierarchies are usually classified into two types : a simple dimension hierarchy consisting of one linear aggregation path within a dimension, and a multiple dimension hierarchy containing two (or more) aggregation paths in a dimension.

Despite their central role in MDDBS, dimension hierarchies are often inadequately understood and poorly modeled. The standard way to model dimension hierarchies is with the star and snowflake schemas [3,4]. However, the star schema is not well suited for the natural and explicit representation of dimension hierarchies. It does not explicitly provide support for dimension hierarchies.

Snowflake schemas provide a refinement of star schemas, allowing us to represent dimension hierarchies explicitly, by normalizing the dimension tables. Each level of aggregation has its own dimension table. In other words, each level of a dimension hierarchy is represented in a separate table.

On the basis of the weaknesses inherent to star/snowflake schemas, it is necessary to provide alternative modeling approaches in order to reach a better understanding of dimension hierarchies. Two main approaches are used to tackle the problem of dimension hierarchies. The first one represents these hierarchies explicitly [1,4,12,16,19,20,23]. The second one uses some means such as functional dependencies [2,6,10,15,17]. The issue of reaching a consensus on the modeling aspect of dimension hierarchies is still open. Each of these models has its specific strengths. But none of them satisfies our requirement of deriving them from an UML-based conceptual model. This article provides a comprehensive introduction to dimension hierarchy design from generalizations and aggregations.

The rest of this paper is organized as follows. Section 2 is devoted to a synthetic presentation of our approach for designing a multidimensional database. Section 3 details the two meta-models, and some mapping rules used to derive the dimension hierarchies. The derivation of dimension hierarchies is discussed and illustrated through several cases of aggregation and generalization abstraction mechanisms. Finally, section 4 concludes and presents further research.

2 The Design Method

Starting from user requirements, our method is based on the three usual abstraction levels : conceptual, logical and physical (Figure 1). It is therefore decomposed into four phases :
- In the *conceptual phase*, the designer represents the universe of discourse using the UML notation [18] along with the associated approach of development [11] (step 1) ; the UML schema is then enriched and transformed to take into account the specific features of multidimensional modeling (step 2).
- In the *logical phase*, the enriched and transformed UML schema is mapped into our unified multidimensional model, using mapping rules.
- The *physical phase* allows the designer to convert the multidimensional schema into a physical schema, depending on the target multidimensional tool. A specific set of mapping rules from the logical to the physical model is defined for each type of tool.
- The *data confrontation phase* consists in mapping the physical schema data elements with the data sources. It leads to the definition of queries for extracting the data corresponding to each component in the physical schema.

Following our previous discussion, we concentrate only on the first two phases.

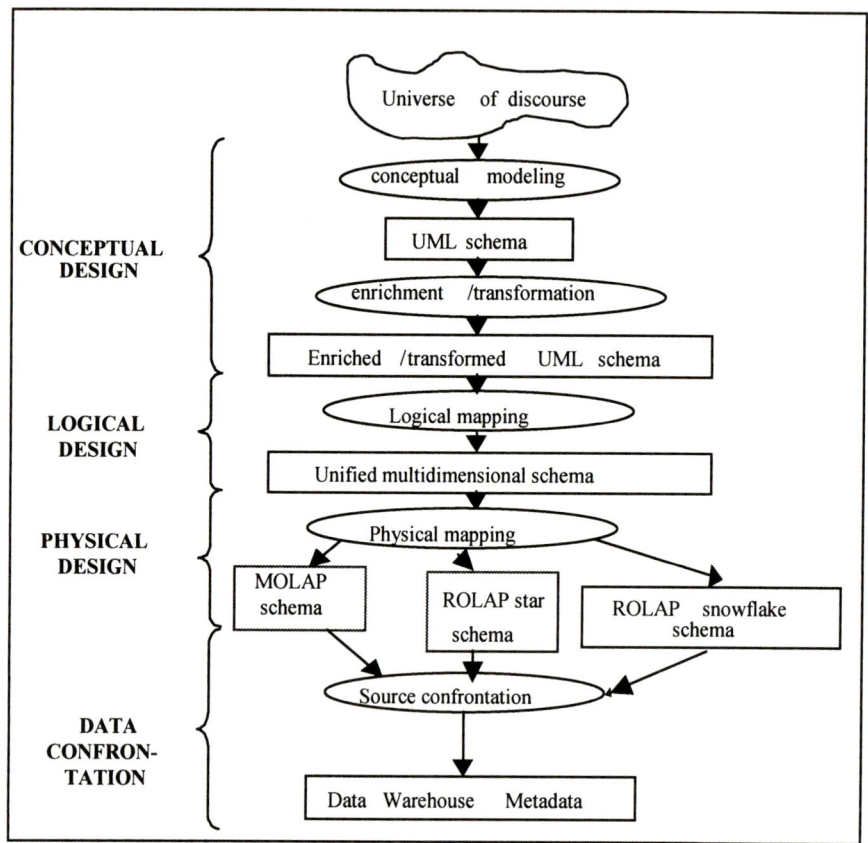

Fig. 1. The Four Phases of the Design Method

2.1 Conceptual Design

OLAP systems are emerging as the dominant approach in data warehousing. OLAP allows designers to model data in a multidimensional way as hyper-cubes. ROLAP snowflakes and stars as well as MOLAP cubes do not offer a visualization of data structures independently from implementation issues. Therefore, they do not ensure a sound data warehouse conceptual design.

Our design method uses the Unified Modeling Language (UML) at the conceptual level. This choice can be justified along at least three considerations :
- UML is now a well-known language for software engineers.
- It provides simple basic constructs to describe at a high level of abstraction the important concepts of the application domain.
- It can be easily mapped to relational as well as to multidimensional logical models.

Due to these considerations, many authors use the UML notation at the first step of the transactional database design. To the best of our knowledge, it has not been used in ROLAP or MOLAP system design.

Our design method consists of a two-step conceptual design :
- The first step leads to a UML schema, more precisely to a class diagram without operations.
- The second step enriches and transforms this schema in order to facilitate its automatic mapping to the multidimensional model. Four types of operations are conducted : the determination of identifying attributes, the determination of attributes representing measures, the migration of association attributes and the suppression of generalizations.

a) Determination of Identifying Attributes

In contrast to the ER model or to the relational model, the notion of identifying attribute is not defined in the standard UML notation; this notion is replaced by the concept of object identity. However, we need to determine the identifying attributes of classes in order to define the dimensions of the multidimensional model at the logical level. An association class is identified by the n-uple of the participating classes identifiers. Therefore, the determination of identifiers is necessary only for the other classes (called ordinary classes). For each ordinary class of the UML schema, the user and the data warehouse designer have to decide which attribute or combination of attributes identify the class. If necessary, a specific attribute is created in order to identify the class. Identifying attributes are specified using the UML construct of tagged value: the suffix {id} is added to each identifying attribute. This process can be synthesized by the following rule :
- *Rule R1: Each attribute of an ordinary class is either an identifying attribute or not.*

b) Determination of Attributes Representing Measures

We differentiate between attributes representing measures, and attributes which can be defined as qualitative values. This distinction is not strictly based on data types, even if measures are generally represented as numerical data, whereas qualitative attributes are based on non-numerical data. Therefore this differentiation cannot be performed automatically. The user and the data warehouse designer have to decide which attributes must be considered as measures. Note that this is not necessary for the identifying attributes determined previously, since an identifying attribute cannot be a measure. In the UML schema, attributes representing measures are specified by the tagged value {meas}. This process can be synthesized by the following rule :
- *Rule R2: Each attribute is either a measure or not.*

c) Migration of Association Attributes

This step is concerned with 1-1 and 1-N associations having specific attributes (these associations are actually association classes, since an ordinary association cannot bear attributes in UML). Let us mention that this case is rarely encountered. If specific attributes are present in these associations, the designer has first to check the validity of this representation. Even if their presence cannot be questioned, they cannot be

mapped into multidimensional models by using hierarchies. The reason is that, in multidimensional models, these hierarchies do not contain information. Therefore, they must migrate from the association to the participating class on the N side. In case of 1-1 association, they can indifferently migrate into one of the two classes. After migrating the attributes of a 1-N or 1-1 association, the latter is transformed into an ordinary association unless it is connected to other associations or classes. The rules for migrating association attributes are expressed as follows :
- *Rule R3 : Each attribute belonging to a 1-1 association is transferred to one of the classes involved in the association.*
- *Rule R4 : Each attribute belonging to a 1-N association is transferred to the N-class, i.e. the class involved several times in the association.*

	RULES	R1	R2	R3	R4	R5
CONCEPTUAL	Attribute	X	X			
	1-1 association attribute			X		
	1-N association attribute				X	
	Generalization					X
CONCEPTUAL	Identifying attribute	X				
	Attribute - measure		X			
	Attribute - not a measure		X			
	Class attribute			X	X	
	Class					X
	N-1 aggregation					X

Fig. 2. Transformation of the UML Schema

d) Suppression of Generalizations

The inheritance links of the UML notation cannot be mapped directly to hierarchies in the multidimensional model, since the semantics of hierarchies in object-oriented models and multidimensional model differ. However, we want to preserve the information contained in UML generalizations and transform these hierarchies to enable their correct mapping to multidimensional hierarchies in the logical phase. To this end, we transform the generalizations into aggregations and classes following the proposal of [17] for ER models. We have adapted this rule to UML and extended it to consider the different cases of partial specialization and/or overlapping specialization. The corresponding rule is informally described below :
- *Rule R5 : For each level i of specialization of a class C, a class named Type-C-i is created. The occurrences of these classes define all the specializations of C. An additional special value is created for each case of overlapping between two or*

more sub-classes. In case of partial specialization, the special value "others" is added. A N-1 aggregation is created between the classes C and Type-C-i.

These rules are sketched in Figure 2. Thanks to these transformations, the resulting UML schema can then be automatically mapped into a logical multidimensional schema, as described in the following section.

2.2 Logical Design

In this section, we first describe our logical model, called Unified Multidimensional Model. Then we describe how a unified multidimensional schema can be generated from an enriched UML schema.

a) The Unified Multidimensional Model

In contrast with the relational model, there is no standard multidimensional database model. More precisely, there is no commonly accepted formal multidimensional data model. As a consequence, many multidimensional models have been proposed in the literature [1,3,4,5,7,8,9,13,16,19,23]. The concepts used vary depending on the authors and some concepts, e.g. the notion of "fact", are employed with various meanings. Furthermore, there is no consensus concerning the level of the multidimensional model (physical, logical or conceptual). The star and snowflake models presented in [13] have often been considered to be at the physical level, since the choice between stars and snowflakes is based on performance considerations (trade-off between query performance and optimization of disk space). More recent publications have placed the multidimensional model at the logical level [22] or even at the conceptual level [7,10].

Our strong belief is that the multidimensional model belongs to the logical level. Even though there is no consensus on this model, it clearly exists independently of physical implementations. However, the multidimensional model should not be considered at the conceptual level since the concepts of this model (e.g. the concept of dimension) are not as close to reality as concepts like the concept of object (used in conceptual object models such as UML [18] for example). There is indeed a strong parallel between the relational model and the multidimensional model - e.g. the definitions or attempts to define an associated query language and a normalization theory. This is the reason why we argue that both models should be considered as belonging to the same level, i.e., the logical level.

In our unified multidimensional model, data are organized in (hyper)cubes and its semantics is based on the notions of *measure, dimension, hierarchy* and *attribute*. It is generic and can be easily mapped into the usual multidimensional models that can be found in the literature and/or in multidimensional tools. This model is used as a pivot model in our design method.

b) Mapping the Enriched UML Conceptual Schema to the Unified Multidimensional Model

To perform such a mapping allowing us to derive dimension hierarchies, we use two meta-models : a UML meta-model and a Multidimensional meta-model. In the meta-models, we concentrate on the dimension hierarchies aspects, since they are the major subject of this paper. They are described in the section below.

3 The Derivation of Dimension Hierarchies

Dimension hierarchies are derived from several abstraction mechanisms. More especially, dimension hierarchies can be generated both from generalization and aggregation mechanisms as defined in [21]. To the best of our knowledge, very few papers deal with the multidimensional translation of generalization/ specialization hierarchies. Intuitively, a specialization of a class can be expressed naturally as a dimension hierarchy, as explained above (Rule R5). In order to facilitate the mapping from the UML conceptual schema to the multidimensional schema, we transform each generalization hierarchy into a UML aggregation. As an example, professors can be either assistant professors or full professors. This is materialized by an aggregation from Professor to Type-professor. Type-professor will have {assistant, full} as a set of values.

It is rather natural to map a 1-N aggregation into a dimension hierarchy. However, other associations may be mapped to dimension hierarchies. We present production rules to transform several types of aggregations into dimension hierarchies. The confrontation of these rules with others which transform associations into measures must be ensured by meta-rules or heuristics analyzing the properties of such associations. This is beyond the scope of this paper. We concentrate here on the relationship between conceptual aggregation hierarchies and logical dimension hierarchies.

In this section, we first describe the two meta-models, used to define in a structured way the mapping from the UML conceptual schema to the unified multidimensional logical schema. Then we describe and illustrate the main rules enabling this mapping, and dealing with the generalization and aggregation hierarchies.

3.1 The Meta-models

Two meta-models have been defined to capture the concepts used on the one hand at the conceptual level and on the other hand at the logical level. They are formalized using UML notation. The first meta-model is briefly sketched at Figure 5. It represents the main UML concepts, especially those which are supposed to be transformed into dimension hierarchies. It is enriched with several notions which are necessary to perform the mapping toward the multidimensional model.

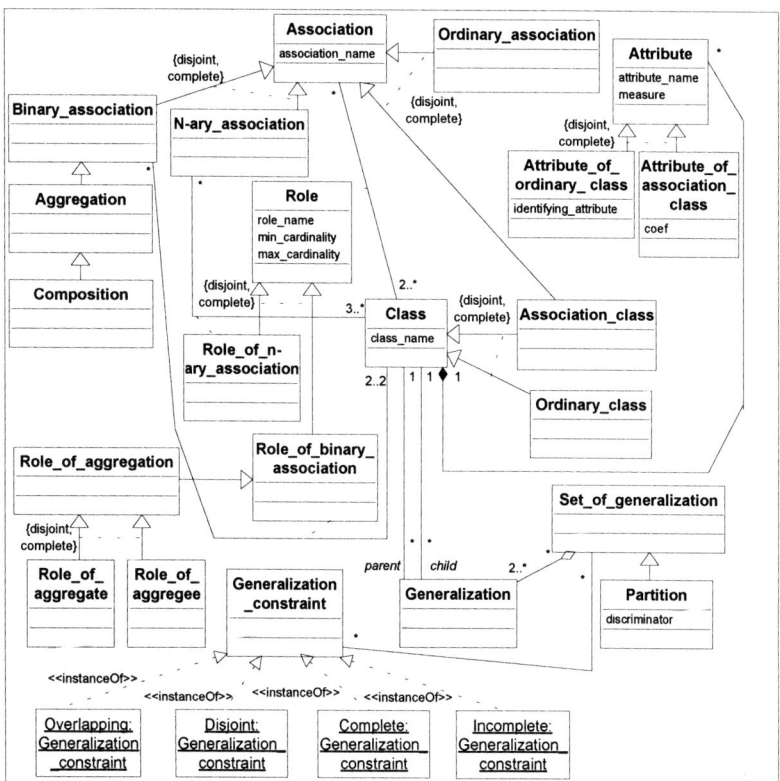

Fig. 5. The Enriched UML Meta-Model

The main concepts are the classes possibly linked by ordinary, binary or N-ary associations. Classes may be ordinary classes or association classes. Classes are composed of attributes. Each attribute is either a measure or not. Each attribute of ordinary class is either an identifying attribute or not. A coefficient measuring the participation of a class in an association is carried by an attribute of an association class. Compositions and aggregations are specific classes of binary associations. The role of classes inside associations is very important. It is described by a name, a minimum, and a maximum cardinality. More particularly, for aggregations, we need to distinguish between the role of aggregate and the role of aggregated. Classes may be linked by generalizations. There are different ways to define partitions of a class. Each partition is said to be a set of generalizations. The discriminator of a partition is an element allowing the designer to distinguish between the different specific classes of the partition. For each set of generalizations, we can define two generalization constraints representing the four generalization types :
- complete disjoint (mathematical partition),
- incomplete disjoint,
- complete overlapping,
- incomplete overlapping.

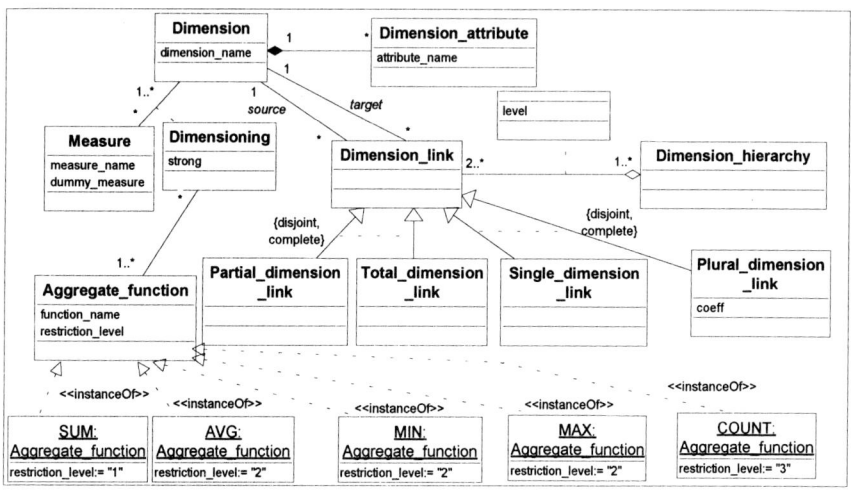

Fig. 6. The Multidimensional Meta-Model

The multidimensional meta-model is represented at Figure 6. It describes the main concepts of our unified multi-dimensional model. Dimensions are composed of dimension attributes. Measures, either regular or dummy, are defined upon one or several dimensions. Dimensions are linked together to constitute dimension hierarchies. These dimension links may be partial or total. A dimension link is partial if all the instances of the dimension are not aggregated in the other dimension. Otherwise, it is total. The dimension link between Doctors and Research Laboratory is partial if at least one doctor is not a member of a laboratory. A dimension link is single if instances of the dimension can be aggregated only once in the other dimension. For example, if we define a dimension link between the dimension doctor and the dimension laboratory and if a doctor may belong to several laboratories, then the dimension link is said to be plural. The different links between a given doctor and each laboratory are characterized by a coefficient measuring the membership of this doctor to this laboratory. Finally, the link between a measure and a dimension is characterized by a set of aggregate functions. These aggregate functions are characterized by a restriction level as suggested by [10]. A sum aggregate function is less restrictive than a count aggregate function in the sense that it allows more analysis.

The two meta-models are used to express the mapping rules. They structure the definition of this mapping and allow us to derive new rules in a more systematic way.

3.2 The Mapping Rules between the Two Meta-models

We describe below two sets of mapping rules. The first set is concerned with the enrichment of the initial UML schema, thus enabling a mapping of concepts at the same conceptual level. This step facilitates the multidimensional derivation process. The second set of rules is concerned with the mapping from the conceptual to the logical level.

		R6	R7	R8	R9	R10	R11	R12
C O N C E P T U A L	Set of generalization	X	X	X	X			
	Overlapping generalization constraint		X	X				
	Disjonction generalization constraint	X			X			
	Completeness generalization constraint	X		X				
	Incompleteness generalization constraint		X		X			
	Generalization G1					X	X	
	Generalization G2					X	X	
	Class C child of G1 and G2					X		
	Class C child of G1 and parent of G2						X	
	Aggregation							X
	Max card = N for aggregate role							X
C O N C E P T U A L	Class	X	X	X	X	X	X	X
	Aggregation	X	X	X	X		X	X
	Coeff		X	X				X
	Min card = 0 for aggregate role		X		X			
	Min card = 1 for aggregate role	X		X				
	Max card = 1 for aggregate role	X			X			
	Max card = N for aggregate role		X	X				
	Generalization G'1						X	
	Generalization G'2						X	

Fig.7. Mapping Rules from UML to Enriched UML Schema

The first six rules refine the R5 rule, dealing with the different cases of generalization hierarchies. We describe them informally below and synthesize them into a decision table at Figure 7. The rules R6 to R9 deal with the different cases of generalization constraints :

- *Rule R6 : If a set of generalizations is characterized by both a disjunction and a completeness constraint, then it is transformed into an aggregation between the parent class C and a class named Type-C. The aggregate role is characterized by a minimum and a maximum cardinality equal to 1.*
- *Rule R7 : If a set of generalizations is characterized by both an overlapping and an incompleteness constraints, then it is transformed into an aggregation between the parent class C and a class named Type-C. The aggregate role is characterized by a minimum cardinality equal to 0 and a maximum cardinality equal to N.*
- *Rule R8 : If a set of generalizations is characterized by both an overlapping and a completeness constraints, then it is transformed into an aggregation between the parent class C and a class named Type-C. The aggregate role is characterized by a minimum cardinality equal to 1 and a maximum cardinality equal to N.*
- *Rule R9 : If a set of generalizations is characterized by both a disjunction and an incompleteness constraints, then it is transformed into an aggregation between the parent class C and a class named Type-C. The aggregate role is characterized by a minimum cardinality equal to 0 and a maximum cardinality equal to 1.*

The rule R10 tackles the multiple inheritance case :
- *Rule R10 : If a class C is a child of both G1 and G2 generalizations, and if the generic classes do not have an identical super-class, then this super-class is created. Thus, the multiple inheritance case will be managed like a multilevel generalization hierarchy, as performed by the rule R11.*

The rule R11 deals with the problem of multilevel generalization hierarchies :
- *Rule R11 : If a class C is a child of a generalization G1 and parent of a generalization G2, a second aggregation level and a second class are created.*

The rule R12 deals with the M-N aggregation case. This aggregation is specific to UML since, generally, aggregation is considered to be a 1-N link. UML allows aggregations describing situations like, for example, professors aggregated into departments but some professors may belong to several departments. To deal with such an aggregation, we propose to transform this aggregation into an association-class with an attribute called Coeff measuring the degree of participation of a class in the other, for example of a professor in one department.

The second set of rules is concerned with the mapping from the enriched UML schema to the logical multidimensional schema (Figure 8). The first four rules (R13 to R16) deal with the four cases of generalization constraints transformed into cardinality constraints in the previous phase. As an example, R13 maps an aggregation with both minimum and maximum cardinalities equal to 1 into a total single dimension link. R14 maps an aggregation with a minimum cardinality equal to 0 and a maximum cardinality equal to N into a partial plural dimension link. R15 maps an aggregation with a minimum cardinality equal to 1 and a maximum cardinality equal to N into a total plural dimension link. Finally, R16 maps an aggregation with a minimum cardinality equal to 0 and a maximum cardinality equal to 1 into a partial single link. In case of plural dimension link, the coefficient defined at the conceptual level is transferred as an attribute of this link.

The remaining rules are concerned with the other associations, namely associations which are aggregations according to [21] but which are represented as binary or N-ary associations with UML notation. More precisely, rules R17 to R19 map 1-1 binary associations into dimension hierarchies. Depending on the minimum cardinalities, we distinguish three cases. Rule R17 deals with different minimum cardinalities : one is equal to 0 and the other is equal to 1. In this case, we consider that the dimension whose role has a minimum cardinality equal to 0 (role R1) is the source of the dimension link. In the two other cases, when minimum cardinalities are identical (both equal to 0 in R18 or both equal to 1 in R19), the rules build the dimension links but the orientation of the link (definition of a source dimension and a target dimension) is conducted by heuristics or specified by the designer. Rule R20 transforms the M-N aggregations into a plural dimension link. Finally, rule R21 deals with the most classical case of aggregation, i.e. the 1-N aggregation transformed into a single dimension link between two dimensions.

		R13	R14	R15	R16	R17	R18	R19	R20	R21
C O N C E P T U A L	Aggregation	X	X	X	X				X	X
	Coeff		X	X					X	
	Aggregate Min card=0		X		X					
	Aggregate Min card=1	X			X					
	Aggregate Max card=1	X			X					
	Aggregate Max card=N			X	X					
	Binary association					X	X	X		
	Role R1 Max card = 1					X	X	X		X
	Role R2 Max card = 1					X	X	X		
	Role R1 Min card = 0					X	X			
	Role R2 Min card = 1					X		X		
	Role R2 Min card = 0						X			
	Role R1 Min card = 1						X			
	Role R1 Max card = N								X	
	Role R2 Max card = N								X	X
L O G I C A L	Partial dimension link			X		X		X		
	Total dimension link	X		X		X		X		
	Single dimension link	X				X	X	X		X
	Plural dimension link		X	X					X	
	Coeff		X	X					X	
	Dimension	X	X	X	X					
	Dimension R1					X	X	X	X	X
	Dimension R2					X	X	X	X	X
	Dimension R1 source						X			X

Fig. 8. Mapping Rules from UML to Multidimensional Schema

These rules illustrate several ways to derive dimension hierarchies from generalization and aggregation hierarchies. The following cases were considered :
- a partial vs. a total specialization hierarchy,
- an overlapping vs. a disjoint specialization hierarchy,
- a multiple inheritance hierarchy,
- a multi-level generalization hierarchy,
- a 1-N aggregation,
- a 1-N aggregation path,
- a 1-1 aggregation,
- a M-N aggregation.

For each case, we proposed one or several possible mappings. Others can be added. Moreover, heuristics to choose between different mappings must be defined. Very specific sub-cases need still to be explored, such as a non-balanced multi-level generalization hierarchy for example. We have also to examine what can be deduced from an aggregation path containing several types of aggregations (association, aggregation, composition for example).

Figure 9 illustrates the successive application of our rules to map two UML generalizations into the multidimensional model. In the UML schema, the two generalizations are overlapping (a site may be both a factory and a warehouse) and incomplete (not all types of sites are specified); therefore, the generalizations are mapped in the enriched UML schema into an aggregation using rule R7. The attribute coeff in the aggregation is used to indicate what percentage of the surface of a given site is devoted to production and to warehousing respectively. The cardinalities for the role of the aggregate (i.e. Site) are deduced from the generalization constraints. Based on these cardinalities, the aggregation is mapped into a partial plural dimension link in the multidimensional model.

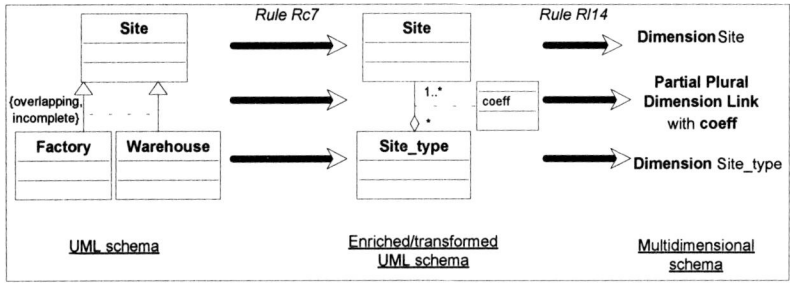

Fig. 9. Mapping Example

4 Conclusion and Further Research

In this article, we have introduced the concept of dimension hierarchy in MDDBS, examining its actual usage and its varieties. We pointed out that there is no consensus on a single model of dimension hierarchies in MDDBS. In order to derive such dimension hierarchies, we proposed a design method based on an UML schema at the conceptual level and a unified multidimensional model at the logical level. The mapping between the two levels is performed using two associated meta-models and production rules. These mapping rules allow us to derive dimension hierarchies from generalizations and aggregations embedded in the UML schema. Several examples illustrate this mapping.

Several questions remain open and need more study :
- the issue of reaching a consensus on the modeling issues at the logical level,
- the relationship between dimension hierarchies and their equivalence at the conceptual level (aggregations and generalizations),
- an efficient implementation of our design method and some experimentation on some large real life problems,
- a fair number of mapping rules has been defined. However, we need to develop more rules in order to solve combined problems and heuristics for facilitating the choice between candidate mapping rules.

References

1. Agrawal, R., Gupta, A., Sarawagi, S. : Modeling multidimensional databases. 13th International Conference on Data Engineering (ICDE '97), Birmingham, UK, April.
2. Baralis, E., Paraboschi, S., Teniente, E.: Materialized view selection in a multidimensional database. Proceedings of the International Conference on Very Large Databases (1997)
3. Blaschka, M.,Sapia, C., Höfling, G., Dinter, B. : Finding your way through multidimensional data models. DEXA Workshop on Data Warehouse Design and OLAP Technology (DWDOT '98), Vienna, Austria.
4. Cabibbo, L.,.Torlone, R. : A Logical Approach to Multidimensional Databases. Proceedings of 6th International Workshop on Extending Database Technology (EDBT'1998), Valencia (Spain), March.
5. Chaudhuri, S., Dayal, U.: An overview of data warehousing and OLAP Technology. SIGMOD Record, 26(1) (1997)
6. Gebhardt, M., Jarke, M., Jacobs, S. : A Toolkit for Negotiation Support Interfaces to Multidimensional Data. Proceedings of ACM SIGMOD Conf, Arizona, USA (1997)
7. Golfarelli, M., .Maio, D., .Rizzi, S. : Conceptual design of data warehouses from E/R schemes. 31st Hawaii International Conference on System Sciences, Hawaii, USA (1998)
8. Golfarelli, M., Rizzi, S. : A methodological framework for data warehousing design. ACM workshop on data warehousing and OLAP (1998)
9. Gyssens, M., Lakshmanan, L.V.S. : A foundation for multi-dimensional databases. 23rd VLDB Conference, Athens, Greece (1997)
10. Hüsemann, B., Lechtenbörger, J., Vossen, G. : Conceptual data warehouse design. 2nd International Workshop on Design and Management of Data Warehouses (DMDW 2000), Stockholm, Sweden, June
11. Jacobson, I., Booch, G., Rumbaugh, J.: The Unified Software Development Process. Addison Wesley Publishing Company
12. Jagadish, H.V., Lakshmanan, L.V.S., Srivastava, D. : What can Hierarchies do for Data Warehouses ? Proceedings of the 25th VLDB Conference, Edinburgh, Scotland (1999)
13. Kimball, R. : The data warehouse toolkit. John Wiley & Sons
14. Kimball, R. : A Dimensional Modeling Manifesto. DBMS on-line. http://dbmsmag.com/
15. Lehner, W., Albrecht, J., Wedekind, H.: Normal Forms for Multidimensional Databases. Proceedings 10th SSDBM conference, Italy, July (1998)
16. Li, C., Wang, X.S. : A data model for supporting on-line analytical processing", Proceedings Conference on Information and Knowledge Management (CIKM'1996), Baltimore, USA
17. Moody, D.L., Kortink, M.A.R. : From Enterprise Models to Dimensional Models : A Methodology for Data Warehouse and Data Mart Design. 2nd International Workshop on Design and Management of Data Warehouses (DMDW 2000), Stockholm, Sweden (2000)
18. Unified Modeling Language, http://www.omg.org/technology/documents/formal
19. Pedersen, T.B., Jensen, C.S. : Multidimensional data modeling for complex data. 15th International Conference on Data Engineering (ICDE '99), Sydney, Australia (1999)
20. Sapia, C., Blaschka, M., Höfling, G., Dinter, B. : Extending the E/R Model for the Multidimensional Paradigm. International Workshop on Data Warehousing and Data Mining in conjunction with ER98, Singapore (1998)
21. Smith, JM., Smith, DCP "Database Abstractions: Aggregations and Generalizations". ACM TODS, 2(2) (1977)
22. Vassiliadis, P. : Gulliver in the land of data warehousing : practical experiences and observations of a researcher. Proceedings of the International Workshop on Design and Management of Data Warehouses (DMDW'2000), Stockholm, June (1999)
23. Vassiliadis, P., Sellis, T. : A survey of logical models for OLAP databases. SIGMOD Record, 28(4) December (1999)

Minimize Mark-Up !
Natural Writing Should Guide the Design of Textual Modeling Frontends

Markus Lepper, Baltasar Trancón y Widemann, and Jacob Wieland

Technische Universität Berlin, Fakultät IV, ÜBB, Sekr. FR 5–13,
Franklinstr. 28/29, D–10587 Berlin,
{lepper,bt,ugh}@cs.tu-berlin.de

Abstract Designing and implementing modeling frontends for domains in which *text* is predominant (it may be informal, semi-formal or formal) can and should benefit from using the evolving standard mark-up languages (**SMGML** and **XML**), since standardization of interfaces, transmission and storage protocols as well as many valuable tools „come for free".

But the idiosyncratics of the existing mark-up concepts neither provide a structure clean enough to serve as foundation for syntax and semantics of exact modeling frontends, nor do they offer an *input format* feasible for text-based data maintanance.

Direct Document Denotation (DDD) as presented in this paper tries to remedy these defects: (1) it abstracts from the rough edges of XML, (2) it realizes a practical frontend processor for denotation of structured documents with special considerations to disabled users and voice controlled input, – and (3) is described completely and mathematically precise as a small system of transformation relations.

The theoretical basics and practical issues of DDD are discussed and a case study is reported.

Keywords: Data Acquisition, Semi-Formal Data, Accesibility, *inter language working*, XML, *Document Object Model*, DOM, *data binding*, SCHEMA

1 Introduction and Related Work

In the field of design and implemention of modeling tools there are three rôles in which XML will become more and more important:

- As underlying data exchange medium:
  „Invisibly" to the user XML will be a coding standard for interchanging structured information in a relocatable format between different tools and different locations.
- As input format :
  Using *screen mask editors* which are configured by DTD or SCHEMA, XML structured data can be directly acquisited and maintained by domain experts or less qualified personal.

– As mark-up language :
   For shorter texts (e.g. configuration files) XML frontend syntax can be typed directly.

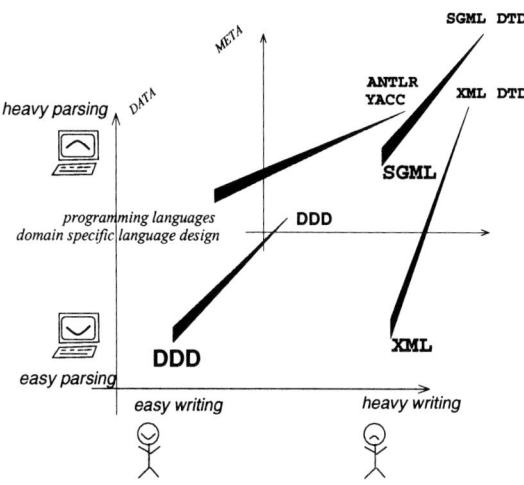

But the last kind of application guarantees a maximum of inconvenience, even if supported by a syntax controled editor. This is somehow amazing, since the original SGML is intended to be a mark-up language for authoring purposes. The downgrading derivation of XML but aimed solely at simplificating the *computer's* task of parsing, not the human task of writing (see figure 1). While it was easily possible to write SGML-DTDs which were *not parsable at all*, XML takes the other extreme making the instances of all structure definitions parsable in LL(1), with the intention to enable the silliest browsers to display cool web pages with minimum knowledge of modern parsing techniques.

Fig. 1. Efforts needed for authoring vs. for parsing

This requirement must lead to the opposite of an elaborated user-friendly textual input frontend.

The approach presented in this paper is called *Direct Document Denotation* (DDD) and tries to close this gap, thus realizing a fourth rôle of XML:

– XML is used as underlying Structure Definition generating a convenient *textual* input frontend automatically.

DDD is intendend to be useful in at least two cases: (1) There exists legacy data which is semi-formally textually coded and shall now be lifted to an exact and computer processible format with minimum effort, and (2) a textual modeling frontend for a given domain problem has to be created from scratch, and the designers and developers want to concentrate on semantic issues and get an input frontend for free.

We estimate DDD to be superiour to mask editors in those cases where (1) the kind of text data requires more flexibility, e.g. if recursive structure definitions are dominant, and (2) where the domain experts are strongly used to express themselves by authoring and are used to the comforts of „their" text editing tool.

In both these cases a *minimal* mark-up syntax is beneficial, which follows the style of *natural writing* as established by the text gender or domain experts' tradition as close as possible.

DDD comes with a small definition language which *in parallel* defines content models and input syntax. Thus being a further schema definition language – which would be among the things needed least at the moment, cf. [6] – the focus of its design and of this paper lies on the frontend generating aspect.

As an authoring tool the design of the DDD is inspired by the frontend behavior of TEX[5], m4 [1], curl [7] and Lout [3], [4], concerning the means of recognizing the structure of input, e.g. the borders between parameter values, with minimal typing efforts and minimal „visual noise"[1].

It is an interesting fact that the most flexible frontend feature of TEX which allows the free definiton of LL(1) parsers for macro parameters is only used by very experienced „TEXhackers" and hardly by „users", even not by computer experts which do extensive programming on LaTEX-level. So we decided to limit the degree of freedom for defining the input parsers, intending to make the definition of input patterns as well as their usage more transparent.

As a schema definition language DDD is restricted to a required minimum. It will be part of future work (see section 3 below) to correlate its expressiveness with other approaches. This should be done using a formal framework as in [8]. That paper of MAKOTO MURATA et.al. is as far as we know the first approach applying formal methods (i.e. mathematics) to XML. Since it is mainly about *validation* of given XML structures it cannot be compared with our work, because the parser approach of DDD only deals with documents which are „correct by construction". Nevertheless [8] is an important and inspiring paper in our context.

2 Description and Specification of DDD

2.1 DDD Principles

DDD is a meta-language for defining and performing transformations of a document given as sequence of characters into a tree-like „Document Object Model" (= DOM).

DDD stands for *Direct Document Denotation*, as the user can directly describe the tree structure of the document with a minimal count of keystrokes. It closely follows some fundamental paradigms found in SGML/XML, so that the resulting DOM is processable by eg. XSLT or other tools built on these standards, but DDD tries to abstract from all idiosyncratic distinctions made there. The tree constructed by DDD consists of *nodes*, which (under certain conditions of usage, see 8) can represent XML „ELEMENTs" as well as their character data contents as well as „ATTRIBUTE" values.

---

[1] The generated output of these tools are DVI, Postscript, HTML or pure ASCII text resp., therefore the backends are not comparable.

property	EL	ATT
Can contain structure.	YES	no
Can be permutated arbitrarily in frontend syntax	no	YES
Can be assigned attribute values	YES	no
Are **implicitly** typed by their „name"; these types are totally unrelated	YES	no
Can be typed explicitely	no	YES
Must be typed explicitely	no	YES
Can have a default value	no	YES
Class names are unique w.r.t. a „module"	YES	no

Table 1. Properties of ELEMENTs and ATTRIBUTEs in SGML/XML

A concrete DDD system is a collection of parametrized definition modules[2]. A module primely defines node classes by declaring their structure (attribute list and content model) *together* with a convenient input representation. In addition a module can provide auxiliary objects like enumerations (used for ATTRIBUTEs of the appropriate type), macros, character sets etc. Each such definition is referred to by an identifier which is unique in the scope of the module.

A module can be defined by referring to other modules via `import` statements; node classes are defined by recurring to other (maybe imported) node definitions or to predefined parser types.

The basic operation of a DDD system is to apply the definition of one single „toplevel" node to a text file. If the text file conforms to this definition, a Document Object Model is created, which can then be further processed, either by accessing it directly via an API or by writing it into a standard XML file[3].

2.2 Central Features of DDD

The basic principles of DDD seem to be rather trivial and aim solely at increasing the orthogonality of XML based object structures, trying to make exact reasoning and mathematical analysis feasible. But since the definitions try to cover all of the variants in XML usage, the consequences are not trivial at all.

These principles can be summarized:

- Unification of ELEMENT and ATTRIBUTE.
  We assume that the dichotomy ELEMENT and ATTRIBUTE come from an original intention to represent „object level" text data and „meta level" annotations. The design flaw is that belonging to the object- or the meta-level is decided when *interpreting* data structures, and should not happen on representation level: E.g. a table definition in – say – microsoft „ACCESS" is „meta" w.r.t. one window and at the same time „object" in another window.
  This dichotomy led to a somehow „random" conjunction of properties which from the abstract point of view should be freely combinable, see table 1.

---
[2] The current implementation does not yet support parametrization
[3] In the current prototypical implementation a Xerces DOM is constructed[9], supporting the W3C DOM API.

The (uncessarily) arising complexity is depicted nicely by figures 4 and 5 of [2], which still are simplified as in native XML „cardinality" is not a property of an element type, but of the referring context.
- Inference of almost all *closing* tags.
  The original SGML approach of declaring tags as omittable has turned out to be unfeasible since the construction of parsers and the parsing itself can easily become NP-complete. The flaw was that „omissibility" is a property of the *context* and can in general not be verified statically.
- Syntax directed automized tagging.
- Partial parsing of incomplete, intermediate text versions.
  When constructing a text in the „flow of authoring", i.e. writing from the beginning to the end, many people prefer to work with *partially incomplete* texts, which are completed in later iterations. The DDD semantics support this method, – text structures not conformant to their corresponding structure definition, but to a *prefix* thereof, are accepted and tagged accordingly, either im- or explicitly.

Basically the DDD approach realizes a *two-staged* transformation :

On **top level**, with coarse granularity, there is an *explicit* tagging. For the sake of **accessibility** by the handicapped user – as one of the authors is – this level (1) uses only *one single* escape character, which (2) can be *redefined* for sake of maximal convenience in typing, and (3) can easily be mapped to *voice input*. The character data between (or „below") these top-level tags will mostly be copied *opaquely* into the contents of a leaf node of the node tree under construction.

Alternatively there can be a further, „finer" processing by a simple user-defined, token-based parser , generating at the **lower level** an *implicit*, syntax directed tagging.

The parser definition facility is intentionally rather limited. Its purpose is to define the analysing of *small* syntactic phaenomena appearing in everyday applications, as calendar dates, personal names and adresses, bible citations, short formulae etc. If parsing is required in a larger scale a different approach as in [11] is appropriate.

This two-staged approach leads to the fact, that in practice much expressive power is reached by the cooperation of *rather small* structures from both levels. This yields several advantages:

- Implementation can be done straight-forward. Since the structures tend to be rather small, all non-determinism/backtracking is strictly localized, thus performance is not really an issue.
- All interpretation of user input is exactly localized; error diagnosis and recovery is much less difficult to automize.
- Research on compositionality, reusability, refinement and extendability becomes feasible in practice.

In the following we give (1) an operational description of the semantics of the tagging level and (2) a function based denotation of the semantics of both levels in DDD. The former is more suited to the user, the latter allowing reasoning and supporting correct implementation.

2.3 DDD Case Study

A first DDD case study was performed in 2000 ([12]). Exctracts from the sources are given in appendix A to illustrate the following descriptions. They construct an XML page as service for protestant sacral musicians, listing all sundays and observances of the year 2000 of the German Protestant Church (= EKD) together with the related bible texts, which again are related to cantatas and motets, which on their part have been set to notes by different composers, requiring different ensembles of choir and solo voices[4]. The reader is asked to refer to these examples when reading the following specifications. We assume these sources – while based on German terms – nevertheless to be self-explanatory.

The data type definition modules (last example in appendix A) had of course been created by the developers, together with one prototypical data file for each toplevel node.

But the completion and maintenance of all DDD data file sources had successfully been done by total *laymen/laywomen* in the field of programming or even data acquisition.

2.4 Operational Semantics of the Explicit Tagging Level

When explaining the semantics of DDD to such a layman, who is e.g. a typist used to construct textual documents „from left to right", an operational model of semantics seems adequate, which analyzes the text in the same direction. In future such an interpreter could be implemented as integral part of a syntax driven editor.

Roughly spoken: Whenever this interpreter starts its basic evaluation cylce, the name of a (currently visible) node class must be found at its current input pointer[5]. Then a *new node of the given class* is constructed and inserted into the tree built so far at the *lowest possible position* (as seen from the point of the last preceding insertion). Only if no such position exists, an error is thrown and the input is rejected.

This implements the feature of „inference of closing tags", which is central for supporting Natural Writing.

All currently growing nodes the contents of which are „complete" w.r.t. their contents' spefication are closed implicitly, – all those with *incomplete* content are marked as such and closed as well, iff the interpreter runs in a mode permitting incomplete documents. Otherwise an error is thrown.

This behavior allows handling of temporarily incomplete documents, and is also of main importance for Natural Writing.

If the contents' definition of the new node requests *text data*, then all input characters up to (but excluding) the next *escape character* are copied into the

---

[4] These special pages have by now disappeared from the webside for business reasons, but all other informative pages there are instances of DDD as well.
[5] Additionally there are a few built-in commands for controlling the interpreters behavior, which can also appear at these positions and can be considered as removed from the text after their successful execution.

$$\text{Node} : (\text{Ident} \times \text{seq Nodes}) \cup (\{\$text\} \times \text{seq CHAR}) \to \text{Nodes}$$
$$P \in \text{Parsers}$$
$$i, i_N, i_P, i_E \in \text{Ident}$$
$$\text{UPCDATA} = \text{seq CHAR}$$
$$\kappa \in \text{UPCDATA}$$
$$j, k, m \in \mathcal{N}$$
$$e_N = i_N \mid i_P$$
$$\mid e_N\ e_N \mid e_N\text{"|"}\ e_N \mid e_N\text{ "?"} \mid e_N\text{ "+"} \mid e_N\text{ "*"} \mid e_N\ j\text{ "..*"} \mid e_N\ j\text{ ".."}k \mid \text{"("}\ e_N\ \text{")"}$$
$$e_P = \text{"\#ident"} \mid \text{"\#numeric"} \mid \text{"\#string"}\ c \mid \ldots \mid \text{\#like}\ i_P \mid i_P \mid \text{"["}\ i\ e_P\ \text{"]"}$$
$$\mid e_P\ e_P \mid e_P\text{"|"}\ e_P \mid e_P\text{ "?"} \mid e_P\text{ "+"} \mid e_P\text{ "*"} \mid e_P\ j\text{ "..*"} \mid e_P\ j\text{ ".."}k \mid \text{"("}\ e_P\ \text{")"}$$
$$[\![\,\_\,]\!]^N, [\![\,\_\,]\!]^{N+}, [\![\,\_\,]\!]^{N-} : e_N \to (\text{UPCDATA} \to \text{seq Nodes})$$
$$[\![\,\_\,]\!]^P : e_P \to (\text{UPCDATA} \to \text{seq (Nodes} \cup \text{CHAR)})$$
$$[\![\,\_\,]\!]^X : (e_P \cup e_N) \to (\text{UPCDATA} \to \text{seq Nodes})$$

Fig. 2. Basic Types and Notations

$$[\![\ '"'\ const\ '"'\ ]\!]^P = \{\langle\text{"const"}\rangle \mapsto \langle\text{"const"}\rangle\}$$
$$[\![\ \text{\#numeric}\ ]\!]^P = \{\text{"0"} \mapsto \text{"0"}, \text{"1"} \mapsto \text{"1"}, \ldots\}$$
$$[\![\ \text{\#ident}\ ]\!]^P = \{\text{"a"} \mapsto \text{"a"}, \text{"aa"} \mapsto \text{"aa"}, \ldots\}$$
$$[\![\ \text{\#string}\ c\ ]\!]^P = \{\kappa \frown \langle c\rangle \mapsto \kappa \mid \kappa \in \text{seq (CHAR} \setminus \{c\})\}$$
$$[\![\ \text{\#escape}\ ]\!]^P = \{\text{"\#"} \mapsto \text{"\#"}\}$$
$$[\![\ \text{\#select from}\ i_E\ ]\!]^P = \{ident0a \mapsto \text{"0"}, ident0b \mapsto \text{"0"}, ident1a \mapsto \text{"1"}, \ldots\}$$
$$\ldots$$

$$\square \in \{N, P, X\}$$
$$[\![\ e_1\ e_2\ ]\!]^\square = [\![\ e_1\ ]\!]^\square\ \widehat{\times}\ [\![\ e_2\ ]\!]^\square$$
$$A\ \widehat{\times}\ B = \lambda((a,b),(c,d)) \bullet a\frown c \mapsto b\frown d\quad (\!|A \times B|\!)$$
$$[\![\ e_1\ \text{"|"}e_2\ ]\!]^\square = [\![\ e_1\ ]\!]^\square\ \cup\ [\![\ e_2\ ]\!]^\square$$
$$[\![\ e\ \text{"?"}\ ]\!]^\square = [\![\ e\ ]\!]^\square\ \cup\ \{\langle\rangle \mapsto \langle\rangle\}$$
$$[\![\ e\ \text{"*"}\ ]\!]^\square = [\![\ e\ 0..*\ ]\!]^\square$$
$$[\![\ e\ \text{"+"}\ ]\!]^\square = [\![\ e\ 1..*\ ]\!]^\square$$
$$[\![\ e\ j\text{".."}\text{"*"}\ ]\!]^\square = [\![\,\_\,]\!]^\square (\!|\{\langle e_1, \ldots, e_m\rangle \mid j \leq m, e_\_ = e\}|\!)$$
$$[\![\ e\ j\text{".."}\ k\ ]\!]^\square = [\![\,\_\,]\!]^\square (\!|\{\langle e_1, \ldots, e_m\rangle \mid j \leq m \leq k, e_\_ = e\}|\!)$$

$$[\![\ \text{"("}\ e_1\ \text{"|"}\ \ldots\ \text{"|"}\ e_m\ \text{")"}\ \text{"!"}\ ]\!]^N = [\![\,\_\,]\!]^N (\!|\text{permutations}\ \{e_1, \ldots, e_m\}|\!)$$

Fig. 3. Extended Regular Expressions, generic for both Levels of Parsing

contents of this node. This text is typed as normal plain text, as the person doing the acquisition is used to do. After discarding the escape character the basic cycle is entered again.

Furthermore explicit closing tags are supported, too, in which case the automized closing inference is carried out up to the lowest node of the class requested for closing. A variant of the closing tag called „break tag" permits the user to mark a node's content as incomplete explicitly.

$[\![\ "\sim"\ ]\!]^N = \langle\rangle \mapsto \langle\rangle$
def node i as parser : e_P "."
$\Longrightarrow [\![\ i\ ]\!]^N = \lambda(a,b) \bullet \langle i\rangle^\frown a \mapsto (\text{Node}(i, \text{filter } b)) \ (\![\ e_P\ ]\!]^P)$
$\wedge\ [\![\ i\ ]\!]^P = [\![\ [\ i\ e\ ]\ ]\!]^P$
$\wedge\ [\![\ \#\text{like } i\ ]\!]^P = [\![\ e\ ]\!]^P$
$[\![\ "["\ i\ e\ "]"\ ]\!]^P = \lambda(a,b) \bullet a \mapsto (\text{Node}(i, \text{filter } b)) \ (\![\ e\ ]\!]^P)$
$\text{filter } \alpha = \begin{cases} \alpha & \text{if } \text{ran } \alpha \cap \text{Nodes} = \{\} \\ \text{squash } (\alpha \triangleright \text{Nodes}) & \text{otherwise} \end{cases}$

def node i as empty "."
$\Longrightarrow [\![\ i\ ]\!]^N = \langle i\rangle \mapsto \langle\text{Node}(i, \langle\rangle)\rangle$
def node i as plain text "."
$\Longrightarrow [\![\ i\ ]\!]^N = \lambda(a,b) \bullet \langle i\rangle^\frown a \mapsto \langle\text{Node}(i, b)\rangle \ (\![\ \#\text{string "\#"}\ ]\!]^P)$
def node i as grammar : e_N "."
$\Longrightarrow [\![\ i\ ]\!]^N = \lambda(a,b) \bullet \langle i\rangle^\frown a \mapsto \langle\text{Node}(i, b)\rangle \ (\![\ e_N\ ]\!]^N)$
def node i as mixed : $i_1, \ldots, i_k$ "."
$\Longrightarrow [\![\ i\ ]\!]^N = \lambda(a,b) \bullet \langle i\rangle^\frown a \mapsto \langle\text{Node}(i, b)\rangle$
$(\ [\![\ [\$text \#\text{string "\#"}]\ (\ "\sim"\ [\$text \#\text{string "\#"}] \mid i_1 \mid \ldots \mid i_k\ ) *\ ]\!]^X)$

$\text{mixembed}(a, b, i) = \{a \mapsto b\} \cup \{\ a^\frown \kappa^\frown \langle"\#"\rangle \mapsto b^\frown \langle\text{Node}(\$text, \kappa)\rangle$
$\mid \neg\exists \kappa', \kappa'' \bullet \kappa = \kappa'^\frown \kappa'' \wedge \kappa^\frown \kappa' \in \text{dom}[\![\ i\ ]\!]$
$\wedge\ a.(\#a) \neq "\#"\ \wedge\ "\#" \notin \kappa\ \}$
$[\![\ i\ ]\!]^X = \lambda(a,b) \bullet \text{mixembed}(a, b, i) \ (\![\ i\ ]\!]^N \cup [\![\ i\ ]\!]^P)$

$[\![\ i\ ]\!]^{N+} = [\![\ i\ ]\!]^N \cup \lambda((a,b),c,d) \bullet a^\frown c^\frown d \mapsto b \ (\![\ i\ ]\!]^N \times \{\langle"/", i\rangle, \langle\rangle\} \times \text{seq } \{"\#"\})$

Fig. 4. Semantics of the Node and Parser Definition Statements

$\text{parse}^{+/-} : \text{Ident} \times \text{UPCDATA} \to \text{Nodes}$
$\text{parse}^{+/-} (i, \kappa) = \mu\ (\ (\langle i\rangle^\frown \kappa)\ \triangleleft\ [\![\ i\ ]\!]^{N+/-}\ )$

Fig. 5. Applying the top-level parsing function to a text

2.5 Denotational Semantics

The semantics of a mark-up language like DDD can be seen as a *syntactic transformation*. For this it is not too hard to give an exact specification, which can be found in figures 2 to 7. As notation we use a weak variant of a small subset of the Z notation, since the Z toolkit [10] provides exact definitions and handy conventions for a kind of „common sense" set based mathematics, which in most parts is readable without further explanation. Some notations special to Z are explained in appendix B[6].

---

[6] Furthermore we use some self explaining slight extensions to the original Z notation, eg. using mere juxtaposition of elements for building singleton lists and concatenations : $[\![\ i\ \alpha\ x\ ]\!]$ is an abbreviated notation for $[\![\ \langle i\rangle\ ^\frown\ \alpha\ ^\frown\ \langle x\rangle\ ]\!]$.

The Document Object Model is defined as a **Node**, which is a free type either with an identifier as constructor and a sequence of **Nodes** as data, or with the special reserved identifier *$text* as constructor and a character sequence as data.

Basic paradigm is to define *parsing functions* of type seq CHAR $\rightarrow$ Node. The semantic function $[\![\_]\!]^P$ assigns such a parsing function to the predefined primitive parsers as well as to the names of user defined parsers, $[\![\_]\!]^{N+}$ and $[\![\_]\!]^{N-}$ do the same on the upper level of node class names, the former forbidding, the latter allowing incomplete documents.

The semi-formal notation in figure 4 using „$\Longrightarrow$" shows how a syntactic construct in a definition module defining a new node or parser induces the semantic function $[\![\_]\!]^{P/N+/N-}$ for the newly defined identifier by combining other parsing functions.

Aim of the game is to define a parsing function for the top-level node of the document, which is applied to the text as a whole as seen in figure 5[7].

The reader who considers these definitions somewhat complicated may be assured that the given formulae *completely* describe the DDD transformation framework, and that they can easily be lifted to a fully formal specification.

Please compare this *specification* to the 200 pages of plain english *description* of XML.

2.6 Additional Information in Definition Modules

The grammar of DDD definition modules is (of course ;-) a self-application and provides firstly the basic defining statements for node classes, the semantics of which are depicted in figure 4 and have been discussed above. Furthermore there are additional *modifiers* which can be applied to each single node class definition[8].

The most important of these is the modification attribute xmlrep, which determines the encoding when writing out the internal document tree to an external XML file or when masquerading as W3C DOM. Hairy context conditions are checked by the existing implementation to ensure feasibility: a node declared as ATTRIBUTE must not appear more than once in the language of the grammar of *any* node, a node used for plain prefix in a complex definition must be of flavour parser or plain text, and so must be each node with xmlrep equal to CDATA, etc.

To minimize the count of required constructs there is no special means for defining abstract grammars. Instead there is a „#like *Ident*" construct which makes the pure grammar definition of a node class accessible, – speaking with [8] it shortens a production in P to its corresponding content model, which is a production in P2.

---

[7] Function application is written as finding the only element (by using „μ") of a domain restriction.
[8] The modifier grammar is meant as user-extendable. There are modifiers foreseen to support connection to a type system, to configure a syntax controlled editor etc.

$\kappa \in$ UPCDATA
def node i_0 as plain text .
def parser p ... .
$q = p \quad \vee \quad q = \langle \text{\#like, } p\rangle$

---

def node i as complex :
  plain prefix : i_0 ";"
  grammar : e_N ";"
$\Longrightarrow [\![i]\!]^N = \lambda(a,b) \bullet \langle i\rangle^\frown \kappa^\frown \langle "\#"\rangle^\frown a \mapsto \mathsf{Node}(i, \mathsf{Node}(i_0, \kappa)^\frown b) \quad (\![e_N]\!]^N [\!)$

def node i as complex :
  plain prefix : \#content ";"
  grammar : e_N ";"
$\Longrightarrow [\![i]\!]^N = \lambda(a,b) \bullet \langle i\rangle^\frown \kappa^\frown \langle "\#"\rangle^\frown a \mapsto \mathsf{Node}(i, \mathsf{Node}(\$text, \kappa)^\frown b) \quad (\![e_N]\!]^N [\!)$

def node i as complex :
  plain prefix : q ";"
  grammar : e_N ";"
$\Longrightarrow [\![i]\!]^N = \lambda((a,b),(c,d)) \bullet \langle i\rangle^\frown a^\frown c \mapsto \mathsf{Node}(i, b^\frown d) \quad (\![q]\!]^N \times [\![e_N]\!][\!)$

def node i as complex :
  grammar : e_N ";"
  mixed with chars : i_1 "," ... "," i_k ";"
$\Longrightarrow \ [\![i]\!]^N = \lambda((a,b),(c,d) \bullet \langle i\rangle^\frown a^\frown c \mapsto \langle \mathsf{Node}(i, b^\frown d)\rangle$
$(\![e_N]\!]^N \times [\![[\$text\ \text{\#string}\ "\#"]\ ("\sim"\ [\$text\ \text{\#string}\ "\#"] \mid i_1 \mid ... \mid i_k) *]\!]^X [\!)$

def i as complex :
  β_1
  once: a_1 ,..., a_k;
  optional: b_1 ,..., b_l;
  grammar: γ ;
  β_2
	==	def i as complex :
		  β_1
		  grammar : ($a_1 \mid ... \mid a_k \mid b_1? \mid ... \mid b_l?$) ! γ ;
		  β_2

Fig. 6. Semantics of „Complex" Node Definitions

2.7 Extendability and Refinement

The seperation into two layers of transformation yields localization and thereby supports stepwise refinement of transformation definitions.

In a project where a new text format is defined from scratch, new node classes can be defined and alternatives can *incrementally* be added to some contents grammar, as soon as necessity arises (see future work below, 3).

In a project of tagging existing legacy semi-formal text data in a first approach only the explicit, coarse tagging can be defined and inserted into the text. As soon as a more structured access turns out to be necessary, parser definitions can be added, requiring re-editing only of these parts which do not yet confirm to the new grammar.

In our case study (appendix A) there was no parser provided for the „plain text header" of "psalm", "lesung" etc., which was stored as plain text in a node

$$A_{i,\kappa} = \{\alpha \mid \exists \kappa' \bullet [\![i]\!]^N (\langle i \rangle^\frown \kappa^\frown \kappa') = \alpha\}$$

pretrees : seq Nodes $\to$ $\mathcal{P}$ seq Nodes

pretrees(Node($\$text, \kappa$)) = { Node($\$text, \kappa$) }
pretrees(Node(i, α)) = { Node(i, α) }
$\cup$ { Node(i, α') | $l = \# \alpha' \wedge \forall k \in 1\ldots(l-1) \bullet \alpha.k = \alpha'.k$
$\wedge \alpha'.l \in$ pretrees $\alpha.l$ }

markinc : Nodes $\times$ Ident $\to$ Nodes

markinc(Node($i, \alpha^\frown\langle n\rangle), j$) = Node($i, \alpha^\frown\langle$markinc$(n,j)\rangle^\frown\langle$Node($\$incomplete, j$)$\rangle$)

$\alpha_{i,\kappa} = \mu$ ($\bigcap$ pretrees$(\!|A_{i,\kappa}|\!)$)

$[\![i]\!]^{N-} = [\![i]\!]^{N+}$ $\cup$ $\{\forall \kappa | \kappa \notin [\![i]\!] \wedge A_{i,\kappa} \neq \{\} \bullet \langle i \rangle^\frown \kappa \mapsto$ markinc$(\alpha_{i,\kappa}, i)$ }
$\cup$ $\{\forall \kappa | A_{i,\kappa} \neq \{\} \bullet \langle i \rangle^\frown \kappa^\frown \langle "///", i\rangle \mapsto$ markinc$(\alpha_{i,\kappa}, i)$ }

Fig. 7. Semantics of Incomplete Node Denotations

class element "`quelle`". To give *finer control* of correctness of the input we can add ...

```
def public enum books   mos = 0,    mosis = 0,
                        gen = 1,    genesis = 1,
                        ex  = 2,    exodus = 2,
                        lev = 3,    leviticus = 3,
                        ....
                        apoc = 666 .
def enum subverse   a,b,c,d,e,f,g,h .

def public parser cites    cite (";" cite) * .
def public parser cite     #numeric ?   #select from books
                           pericope  ( "," pericope )* .
def parser pericope        #numeric ?
                           #numeric (#select from subverse)?
                           ( "-" #numeric (#select from subverse)? )? .
```

"`cites`" now accepts input like
        2 mos 1 14- 16, 18, 2 1 ; apoc 1 12 - 14
which is linked to the existing definition by
        `def quelle like cites` .
"`cites`" delivers all correctly parsed character substrings as a whole simply as plain text. If one wants a structured node representation the names of the subnodes have to be provided in brackets "`[]`" :

```
def public parser cite     [booknumber #numeric]? [book #select from books]
                           pericope
                           ( "," pericope )* .
def parser pericope        [chapter #numeric] ?
                           [firstverse #numeric (#select from subverse)?]
                           ( "-" [lastverse #numeric (#select from subverse)?] )? .
```

3 Conclusion and Future Work

Direct Document Denotation, DDD, a modular system for generic definition of transformations from a slightly mark-uped text document into an XML conformant document object model has been presented. Its semantics are described formally, – with some weakening for sake of readability.

A prototypical implementation has been successfully applied to enable non-professionals doing data acquisition and maintanance of text oriented, semi-structured data.

While this seems a promising start (with much work still to do on the engineering side) there are still open questions on the research side: How can DDD *parser* definitions be converted into into sensible XML schema definitions automatically? – How far can a DDD frontend definition be derived from an XML schema automatically? – How can a given XML document be converted into DDD format? – Of what practical use would it be to introduce „offside rule" in the input format? – And how can this be formalized? –

The most interesting research concerns „evolving schemata": Since, as explained above, DDD is intended for gradual refinement of tagging and parsing of legacy data „on demand", the rules ensuring compositionality of definition modules have to be explored, thereby bringing together established and new results in parser theory and data base theory.

4 Acknowledgements

We owe special thanks and respect to our dear colleagues WOLFGANG GRIESKAMP (now at microsoft research), MICHAEL CEBULLA and PETER PEPPER, the head of the ÜBB team. Without the intensive and exciting discussions on their results, our problems and the common visions this paper could not have been written.

References

[1] Free Software Foundation, http://www.seindal.dk/rene/gnu/man/. m4 *Manual*.
[2] Gerti Kappel, Elisabeth Kapsammer, Stefan Rausch-Schott, and Werner Retschitzegger. X-ray – toward integrating xml and realational database systems. In *Conceptual Modeling – ER 2000*. Springer LNCS 1920, 2000.
[3] Jeffrey H. Kingston. *A New Approach in Document Formatting*.
http://snark.ptc.spbu.ru/~uwe/lout/overview.ps.gz, 1992.
[4] Jeffrey H. Kingston. *The Lout Homepage*.
http://snark.ptc.spbu.ru/~uwe/lout/lout.html, 2000.
[5] Donald E. Knuth. *The TEXbook*. Addison-Wesley, 1987.
[6] Dongwon Lee and Wesley W.Chu. Comparative analysis of six xml schema languages. *ACM SIGMOD record*, 29(3), 2000.
[7] MIT Laboratory for Computer Science,
http://curl.lcs.mit.edu/curl/wwwpaper.html. *curl*.

[8] Makoto Murata, Dongwon Lee, and Murali Mani. Taxonomy of xml schema languages using formal language theory. In *Extreme Markup Languages*, http://www.cobase.cs.ucla.edu/tech-docs/dongwon/mura0619.ps, august 2001.
[9] Apache XML Project. *Xerces Java Parser.* Apache Software Foundation, http://xml.apache.org/xerces-j.
[10] J. M. Spivey. *The Z Notation: A Reference Manual.* Prentice Hall International Series in Computer Science, 2nd edition, 1992.
[11] Baltasar Trancon y Wideman, Markus Lepper, Jacob Wieland, and Peter Pepper. Automized generation of abstract syntax trees represented as typed dom xml. In *Proceedings of the ICSE 2001 First International Workshop on XML Technologies and Software Engineering (XSE'01)*, 2001.
[12] Zacharias Musikversand, http://www.kirchennoten.de. *DDD Generated Web Pages*, 2000.

A Examples Extracted from the Case Study Sources

────────────────────── Source Text 1 ──────────────────────
```
1... #d2d text using musicaSacra : annusLiturgicus_EKD ;
2...
3...    tag Karfreitag #datum 21. April 2000 #
4...
5...       wochenspruch Joh 3,16 #~
6...          Also hat Gott ## die Welt geliebt, #nl
7...          daß er seinen eingeborenen Sohn gab, #nl
8...          damit alle, die an ihn glauben, nicht verloren werden, #nl
9...          sondern das ewige Leben haben.#
10..
11..       werk  Motette "Also hat Gott die Welt geliebt"#
12..          vertonung Schütz      #vox 5 #
13..          vertonung Hufschmidt  #vox Soli S+T + 4 #
14..
15..       psalm  LV I Phil 2, 8; LV II Phil 2, 10, 8b  #
16..       werk    Motette "Ecce homo" #
17..          vertonung Reda     #vox 4
18..             #bemerkung Frühes Werk, nicht einfach,
19..             #spitzenton T = a', #spitzenton S = a''
20..       #
21.. eof
Ende of Source
```

────────────────────── Source Text 2 ──────────────────────
```
1... <?xml version="1.0" encoding="ISO-8859-1"?>
2... <celebrationdays>
3...   <tag datum=" 21. April 2000 " name=" Karfreitag ">
4...     <wochenspruch quelle="  Joh 3,16"> Also hat Gott # die Welt
5...        geliebt, <nl/>   daß er seinen eingeborenen Sohn gab,<nl/>
6...        damit alle, die an ihn glauben, nicht verloren werden,<nl/>
```

```
 7...            sondern das ewige Leben haben.
 8...               <werk> Motette &quot;Also hat Gott die Welt geliebt&quot;
 9...                  <vertonung composer="Schütz"    " voices=" 5 "/>
10..                   <vertonung composer="Hufschmidt" voices=" Soli S+T+4"/>
11..                </werk>
12..             </wochenspruch>
13..             <psalm>  LV I Phil 2, 8; LV II Phil 2, 10, 8b;
14..                <werk>   Motette &quot;Ecce homo&quot;
15..                   <vertonung composer=" Reda       " voices=" 4 ">
16..                      <bemerkung> Früher Reda, nicht einfach,
17..                         <spitzenton voice="T" pitch=" a' "/>,
18..                         <spitzenton voice="S" pitch=" a'' "/>
19..                      </bemerkung>
20..                   </vertonung>
21..                </werk></psalm></tag>
22..</celebrationdays>
Ende of Source
```

───────────────── *Source Text 3* ─────────────────

```
 1...#d2d module musicaSacra ; import  richtext ;
 2...def public node annusLiturgicus_EKD   as list of tag+ ;
                                       xmlrep = el celebrationDays .
 3...def node tag   as complex :
 4...          plain prefix : (def name; xmlrep att) ;
 5...          once :       (def datum; xmlrep att),
 6...                       wochenspruch ;
 7...          optional :   psalm, graduale, lesung, epistel, halleluja,
 8...                       evangelium, predigt .
 9...def node wochenspruch as complex :
10..          plain prefix        : quelle ;
11..          mixed with chars    : #from richtext:rtf copy #all .
12..def node psalm as complex :
13..          plain prefix        : quelle ;
14..          grammar             : werk * .
15..use type of psalm for graduale, lesung, epistel, halleluja,
16..                   evangelium, predigt .
17..def node werk   as complex : plain prefix   : #content ;
18..                             grammar        : vertonung + .
19..def node vertonung as complex :
20..          plain prefix        : (def composer ; xmlrep = att) ;
21..          once                : (def vox ; xmlrep = att voices) ;
22..          optional            : (def bemerkung as mixed with chars :
23..                                 #from richtext:rtf copy #all ,
24..                                 spitzenton, (def schwer as empty)).
25..def node spitzenton as parser  [voice #ident] "=" [pitch #ident] .
26..eof
Ende of Source
```

B Some Special Symbols and Constructs in Z

$R \,(\!\lvert\, A \,\rvert\!)$	= the set containing the results of applying relation R to all elements of the set A.
$A \vartriangleleft R$	= „domain restriction" = the relation identical to R, but containing only those pairs the left element of which is in the set A.
$R \vartriangleright B$	= „range restriction" = the relation identical to R, but containing only those pairs the right element of which is in the set B.
$\mu\, A$	= the only element contained in the set A. If A does not contain exactly one element, this expression is *undefined*.
$\#\, A$	= the cardinality of any set A.
$a \mapsto b$	= just syntactic sugar for (a, b).
seq A	= the set of all sequences of elements of A. Each $S \in \mathsf{seq} A$ is a finite mapping $\mathcal{N}^+ \rightarrow A$, where there are no „holes" in the domain, i.e. S is defined for all n with $1 < n < \#\, S$.
$S_1 \frown S_2$	= the concatenation of two sequences.
$S.k$	= the kth element of S. Only defined if $1 < k < \#S$.
squash S	= if S is of type $\mathcal{N}^+ \rightarrow A$, then squash A is the sequence made by „compactifying" S by „shifting left" all elements right to a „hole".

An Approach for Method Reengineering

Jolita Ralyté *, Colette Rolland **

* CUI, Université de Genève, 24 rue du Gén. Dufour, CH-1211 Genève 4, Switzerland
ralyte@cui.unige.ch
** CRI, Université de Paris 1, 90 rue de Tolbiac, 75013 Paris, France
rolland@univ-paris1.fr

Abstract. The increasing complexity of the Information Systems (IS) asks for new IS development methods constructed 'on the fly' to be adapted to the specific situations of the projects at hand. Situational Method Engineering responds to this need by offering techniques to construct methods by assembling reusable method fragments stored in some method repository. For method engineering to be performed it is necessary to build method bases. In this paper we propose an approach supporting the reengineering of existing methods. The reengineering process leads to the representation of an existing method in a modular fashion i.e. as a set of reusable method chunks, easy to retrieve and to assemble one the others. Once the method chunks are stored in a method repository they can be assembled in different manners to construct new methods. The emphasis of this paper is on the guidance provided by the method reengineering process model. The approach is exemplified with the OOSE reengineering case study.

1. Introduction

More and more real world activities are supported by *Information Systems* (IS). Besides, the complexity of these IS increases whereas the development time reduces. As a consequence, the traditional rigid IS engineering methods are inadequate to provide the necessary support in new IS developments. New methods, more flexible and better adaptable to the situation of every IS development project, must be constructed.

To take this problem into account, *Situational Method Engineering* (SME) proposes to support 'on the fly' construction of methods based on a reuse strategy. By assembling reusable method fragments originating from different methods, a new method can be tailored to the project situation at hand. Works performed in the SME area introduce the notions of *method fragment* [3], [16], [13] and *method chunk* [14], [10] as the basic blocks for constructing 'on the fly' methods. Reusable method fragments/chunks are stored in some method repository [16], [4], [14], [10]. In addition there are a number of proposals for approaches to assemble these fragments/chunks [18], [2], [8], [9], [11]. New methods can thus be constructed by selecting the fragments/chunks that are the most appropriate to a given situation [2], [8] from the method repository. As it can be seen, SME favours the construction of modular methods that can be modified and augmented to meet the requirements of a given situation [3], [17].

Whether attention has been paid to the language for describing method chunks, the question of how to support the method fragments/chunks retrieval and assembly process is not well tackled in the literature. Besides, the prerequisite for modular method construction is a method repository containing a large collection of method chunks. This requires reengineering existing methods to produce the method chunks that populate the method repository. *Method Reengineering* is our concern in this paper.

This paper is organised as follows: section 2 provides an overview of our method reengineering approach. In section 3, we sum up the notion of a method chunk whereas in section 4 we describe the method reengineering process model. Section 5 illustrates the approach with an example demonstrating the reengineering process step by step. Section 6 draws some conclusions and discussions around our future work.

2. Overview of the Approach

The work presented in this paper is a part of our assembly-based method engineering approach summarised in Figure 1. As shown in this figure, the process starts with the reconstruction of the existing IS engineering methods in a modular way. The result is a collection of reusable method chunks, which are stored in the method base. Once the method base is populated with a number of chunks, the construction of a new method is possible through the retrieval of those chunks that match the characteristics of the project situation at hand and their assembly to form the new method.

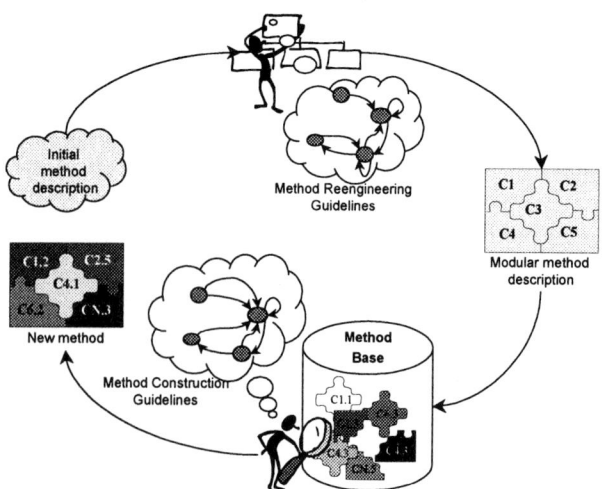

Fig. 1. Assembly based method engineering

In previous papers [14], [10] we presented a *modular method meta-model* allowing to represent any method as an assembly of method chunks. We also proposed a structure for a method chunks repository that we called a method base. Furthermore in

[12], we presented an *assembly process model* to guide the construction of new methods by selecting and assembling method chunks. In this paper we bridge the gap between existing methods and their modular representation. We complete our approach by defining a *method reengineering process model* providing guidelines to reengineer an existing IS development method into reusable method chunks. Figure 2 summarises our method reengineering approach.

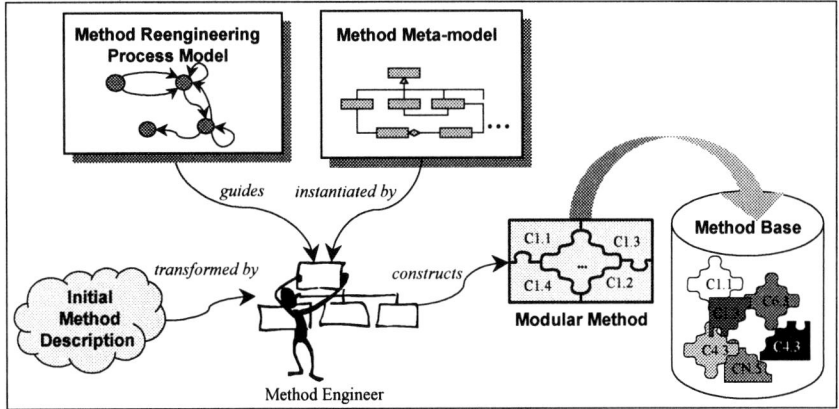

Fig. 2. The approach for method reengineering

As shown in this figure, the central element of our approach is the *method reengineering process model*, which guides the method engineer in the reconstruction of every method into an assembly of method chunks. While guided by this process model, the method engineer instantiates the method meta-model to describe the identified method chunks. In the next section we describe the method meta-model and in section 4 we present the reengineering process in detail.

3. The Notion of a Method Chunk

Situational method engineering proposes to assemble fragments of existing methods to construct a new method. Based on the observation that any method has two interrelated aspects, product and process, several authors propose two types of method fragments: process fragments and product fragments [4], [2]. In our approach we integrate these two aspects in the same fragment that we call a *method chunk*.

A method chunk ensures a tight coupling of some process part and its related product part. It is a coherent module and any method is viewed as a set of loosely coupled method chunks expressed at different levels of granularity [10]. Our modular view of methods favours their adaptation and extension. Moreover, this view permits to reuse chunks of a given method in the construction of new ones. Figure 3 shows the method meta-model (using UML notations [19]). According to this meta-model a method is also viewed as a method chunk of the highest level of granularity. The definition of the method chunk is 'process-driven' in the sense that a chunk is based on the decomposition of the method process model into reusable *guidelines*. Thus, the core of a method chunk is its guideline to which are attached the associated *product parts* needed to perform the process encapsulated in this guideline.

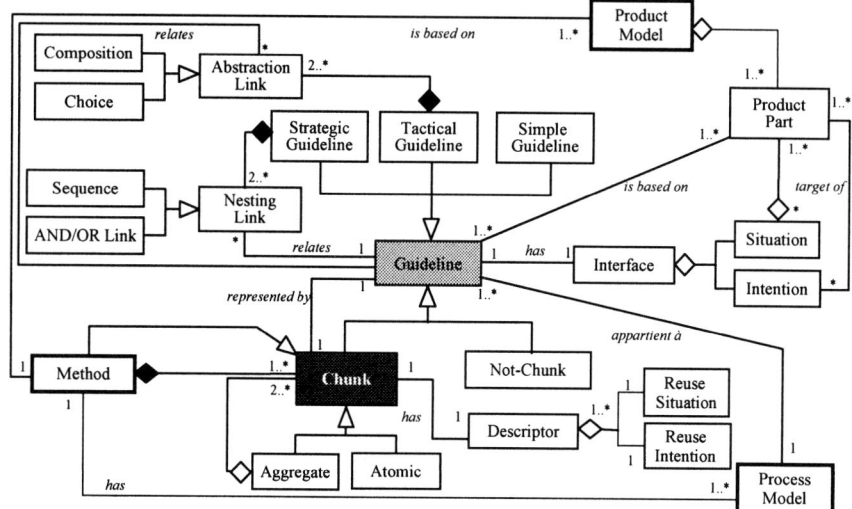

Fig. 3. The method meta-model

A guideline is defined [7] as 'a set of indications on how to proceed to achieve an objective or perform an activity'. For us, a guideline embodies *method knowledge* to guide the application engineer in achieving an intention in a given situation. Therefore, the guideline has an *interface*, which describes the conditions of its applicability (the situation) and a *body* providing guidance to achieve the intention, i.e. to proceed in the construction of the target product. The interface is a couple <*situation, intention*>, which characterises the situation that is the input of the chunk process and the intention (the goal) that the chunk achieves. The body of the guideline details how to apply the chunk to achieve the intention. The interface of the guideline is also the interface of the corresponding method chunk. Guidelines in different methods have different contents, formality, granularity, etc. In order to capture this variety, we identify three types of guidelines: simple, tactical and strategic.

A *simple guideline* may have an informal content advising on how to proceed to handle the situation in a narrative form. It can be more structured comprising an *executable* plan of actions leading to some transformation of the product under construction.

A *tactical guideline* is a complex guideline, which uses a tree structure to relate its sub-guidelines one with the others. This guideline follows the *NATURE* process modelling formalism [6], which proposes two different structures: the *choice* and the *plan*. Each of its sub-guidelines belongs to one these types of guideline.

A *strategic guideline* is a complex guideline called a *map* [15], [1], which uses a graph structure to relate its sub-guidelines. Each sub-guideline belongs to one of the three types of guidelines. A *strategic guideline* provides a strategic view of the development process telling which *intention* can be achieved following which *strategy*. Thus, a map is a labelled directed graph in which the nodes are the intentions and the edges between intentions are strategies. The map permits to represent a process allowing several different ways to develop the product. A set of guidelines is associated to the map. They help the application engineer to progress in the map and to achieve the intentions following selected strategies. More exactly, a map is a composition of a set of sections where a section is a triplet <*source intention, target intention, strategy*>. An *Intention Achievement Guideline* (IAG) is associated to every section and defines how to realise the target intention from the source intention following the selected strategy. Two other types of guidelines, *Intention Selection Guideline* (ISG) and *Strategy Selection Guideline* (SSG), help to progress in the map i.e. to select the next intention and to select next section respectively.

A *descriptor* is associated to every method chunk. It extends the contextual view captured in the chunk interface to define the context in which the chunk can be reused. The two key elements of the descriptor are the *reuse situation* and the *reuse intention*. Every chunk can be applied in one or several system engineering domains and can support one or more activities in the system design process. The *reuse situation* captures this information in the *Application domain* and *Design activity* attributes. The *reuse intention* expresses the objective that the method chunk helps to satisfy in the corresponding design activity. The descriptor also contains a narrative description of the objective of the chunk and specifies its type (i.e. atomic or aggregate) and identifies the *origin* of the chunk (i.e. the originator method of the chunk). See [10], [11], [14] for more information on the method chunk structure.

4. The Reengineering Process

The process of method reengineering that we propose in this paper makes the assumption that it is worth representing the process model of every method as a map with its associated guidelines. Consequently, method reengineering in our approach consists in redefining the existing method process model in the form of a map and its associated guidelines. The required product parts and descriptors are associated to the each of these guidelines to define them as complete method chunks.

As shown in Figure 4, our method reengineering process model is an instance of the strategic process meta-model (a map) introduced in the previous section and consists in satisfying reengineering intentions using appropriated strategies. We comment the intentions of this map and their associated strategies in turn.

4.1 Map Intentions

As shown in Figure 4, the process model is based on the achievement of four main intentions: *Define a section, Define a guideline, Identify a method chunk* and *Define a method chunk*.

The first two intentions allow the method engineer to restructure the initial method process model (if existing) or to define it (if the method does not have any formalised process model) as a map. As mentioned in the previous section, a map is made of sections with associated guidelines. Thus, the intention *Define a section* aims at section identification whereas the intention *Define a guideline* refers to the definition of the guidelines associated to these sections.

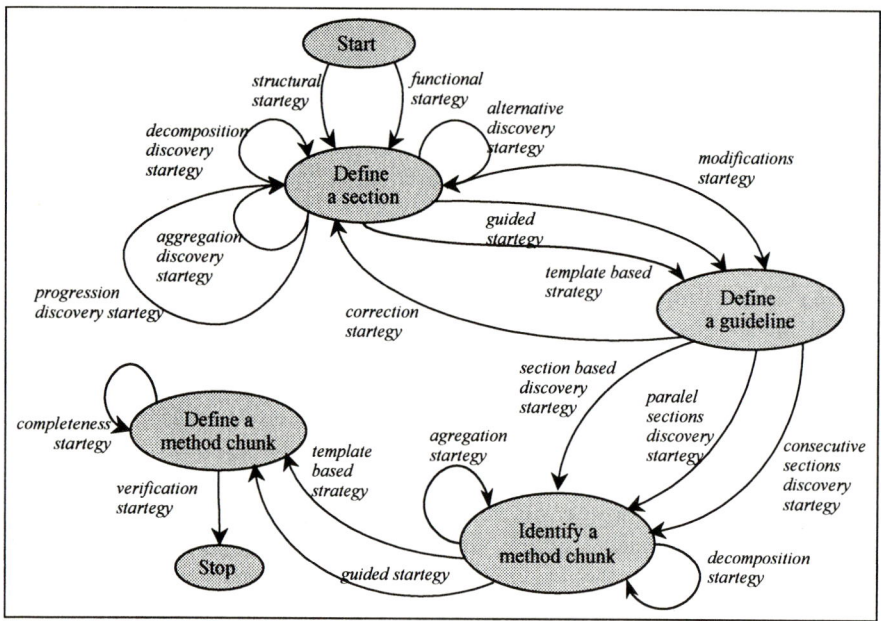

Fig. 4. Method reengineering process model

The two next intentions correspond to the identification and definition of method chunks. This is based on sections and their grouping. Indeed, according to our method chunk concept, every section in the method map is candidate to be defined as a method chunk. The chunk is legitimate if the intention achievement guideline associated to the section identifies an autonomous and reusable methodological procedure. Some aggregations of sections can also form reusable chunks. This reengineering work is supported by the fulfilment of the intention *Identify a method chunk* in Figure 4. The intention *Define a method chunk* supports the definition of the identified method chunks. This includes the completion of the guidelines and the definition of their descriptors.

4.2 Map Strategies

The method reengineering process map presented in Figure 4 proposes a set of strategies to satisfy the four intentions of the map. For example, there are two strategies *structural* and *functional* to achieve the intention *Identify a section*. The *structural strategy* is recommended when the reengineered method does not provide the method engineer with a process model formally defined but rather simply with a description of the product to construct. This strategy uses a glossary of generic process intentions to support the discovery of method intentions. In the contrary, the *functional strategy* should be preferred if the method has a defined process model taking the form of some steps and recommended actions. This strategy helps to identify the method map sections from these actions, and steps.

When the section definition is completed, the method engineer can either define the guidelines associated to these sections (to progress to the intention *Define a guideline*) or to define new sections (to repeat the intention *Define a section*).

The definition of the section guidelines consists in describing the IAG associated to each section, the ISG associated to a set of sections having the same source intention and different target intentions and the SSG associated to every set of parallel sections. The definition of these guidelines is supported by two strategies: the *template based strategy* and the *guided strategy*. The former provides a template for every type of guideline and is advised to experts whereas the latter helps novices by providing more detailed recommendations.

The definition of new sections based on the existing ones may be achieved in four different manners: the *decomposition discovery strategy* helps decomposing an existing section in several ones, the *aggregation discovery strategy* advises how to combine a set of sections into a new one, the *alternative discovery strategy* helps to identify a new section having an alternative strategy or an alternative source or target intention to the existing one, and the *progression discovery strategy* helps to define a new section allowing to progress in the method map from the existing one.

Analysing the already defined guidelines may imply the definition of new sections or the modification of the existing ones. For example, if an intention achievement guideline needs to be decomposed into several sub-guidelines, the corresponding section must also be decomposed. In a similar manner, the modifications (decomposition, aggregation) realised on sections imply modifications on the associated guidelines. The *modification strategy* guides the method engineer to accomplish these transformations.

The identification of method chunks is supported by three strategies: the *section based discovery strategy*, the *parallel sections discovery strategy* and the *consecutive sections discovery strategy*. The first strategy is based on the assumption that every section in the method map may be considered as a method chunk. More exactly, the IAG associated to this section is a basis for a method chunk if it is reusable outside its originator method. According to our method meta-model, the aggregation of the IAG associated to the parallel map sections may be considered as an aggregate chunk too. The *parallel section discovery strategy* helps to identify the IAG associated to parallel sections and to aggregate them into a new guideline. In the same manner, the *consecutive sections discovery strategy* helps to identify the IAG associated to the consecutive map sections and to integrate them with the objective to obtain the guideline of a new aggregate chunk.

Finally, every guideline declared as a reusable one is defined as a method chunk. This is supported by the *template based* and the *guided* strategies that help the method engineer to attach the necessary product parts to the guideline and to define the chunk descriptor. The method reengineering process ends with the *verification strategy*. This strategy helps to verify if all guidelines associated to the map sections have been defined, if all possible combinations of the guidelines have been analysed to identify the method chunks and if all identified chunks have been described. Due to space limitation we cannot present all these guidelines. However some of them will be further explained when used in the case study presented in Section 5. See also [11] for more details.

5. Case Study

In this section we illustrate the method reengineering process model presented in the previous section to reengineer the OOSE method as described in [5]. This method proposes five different models: use case, analysis, design, implementation and test. We restrict our case study to reengineering the use case model construction.

Step 1: Starting the reengineering process. The OOSE description is an informal text describing the structure of the use case model and providing some heuristics " to construct this model". As a consequence, we select the *structural strategy* of Figure 4 to start the reengineering process.

Step 2: Defining the OOSE map sections. The selected strategy recommends first to identify the method map interface, then to identify the intentions and the associated strategies and finally to order them in the map.

The source document makes clear the method goal (the map interface intention) that is *to construct the use case model* of the system under construction starting with the initial *description of the corresponding problem* (the interface situation). The interface of the OOSE method map is therefore as follows:

<(Problem description), Construct the use case model following the OOSE strategy>

To identify the map intentions the guideline suggests to couple the key product parts of the method product model with some of the generic intentions provided in our method base glossary. The use case model includes the following product parts: *actor, basic scenario, exception scenario* and *use case*. The generic intentions selected from the glossary that seem suitable to those products parts are shown in the table below.

Product part	Intention verb
Actor	Identify, Define
Basic scenario	Write, Validate
Exception scenario	Write, Validate
Use case	Identify, Discover, Conceptualise

Combining intentions and product parts (verb + target) leads to candidate OOSE map intentions. Based on the OOSE documentation, the final choice of the relevant intentions is made. For example, as the structure of the concept *actor* is very simple (it contains only two attributes: *name* and *informal description*), the intention *Define an actor* can be merged with the intention *Identify an actor*. The OOSE process does not provide any mean to validate the *basic scenario* and the *exception scenario*. Thus, we eliminate the intentions *Validate a basic scenario* and *Validate an exceptional scenario* from the list of candidate OOSE map intentions. The intentions *Identify a use case* and *Discover a use case* are equivalent because the verbs identify and discover are synonyms in the method base glossary. Finally, we select the following list of intentions:

- Identify an actor
- Write a basic scenario
- Write an exemption scenario
- Discover a use case
- Conceptualise a use case

An Approach for Method Reengineering   479

The next sub-step is to identify the potential strategies to realise these intentions. For this, we need to find the different manners to satisfy these intentions out of the OOSE description. Every identified manner may be considered as a strategy or a tactics. The following table summarises the strategies' identification process.

Intention	Manner (extracted from the OOSE book)	Strategy
Identify an actor	Ask the questions: • Which persons will use one or several functions of the system? • Which persons will handle and maintain the system? • Which external systems will interact with the system ?	*Questions driven strategy*
Write a basic scenario	Write a scenario describing the best understood case of system use.	*Normal case strategy*
Write an exception scenario	Write scenarios describing variations in the basic scenario that correspond to an exceptional system functioning.	*Exception case strategy*
Discover a use case	Ask the questions: • What are the main tasks of each actor? • Does the actor need to read, write or modify the information stored in the system? • Does the actor need to inform the system of external changes?	*Actor based discovery strategy*
Conceptualise a use case	Group the basic scenario with the exception scenarios concerning the same use case.	*Integration strategy*
	Extend the complete use case by other use cases with the objective to represent: • the optional parts of the use case, • the complex and unusual scenarios, • the possibility to introduce new use cases , etc.	*Extension strategy*
	Identify and extract the descriptions, which are common to several use cases, and define them as abstract use cases.	*Abstraction strategy*
	Verify the completeness of the use case model.	*Completeness strategy*

Finally, the guideline suggests to identify the precedence links between the selected intentions. For every intention and one associated strategy we must identify the situation in which the intention may be applied following this strategy. That is, we need to identify the product part necessary to achieve this intention and then to identify the intention constructing this product part. For example, the product necessary to achieve the intention *Identify an actor* following the *question driven strategy* is the *initial description of the problem*. This product part exists when the analysis process starts; therefore the *Identify an actor* intention follows the *Start* intention. The achievement of the intention *Write a basic scenario* is possible only if the corresponding *use case* has been identified. Thus, the intention *Write a basic scenario* follows the intention *Discover a use case*. According to the source description, the *basic scenario* must always be written before the *exception scenarios* are produced. We also know that the use cases discovery is based on actors. Then, the intention *Discover a use case* follows the intention *Identify an actor*. Use case extension and abstraction is a mean to conceptualise new use cases from already conceptualised ones. This means that the *extension* and *abstraction* strategies are reflexive strategies. Figure 5(a) illustrates the result of the initial identification of the OOSE map sections.

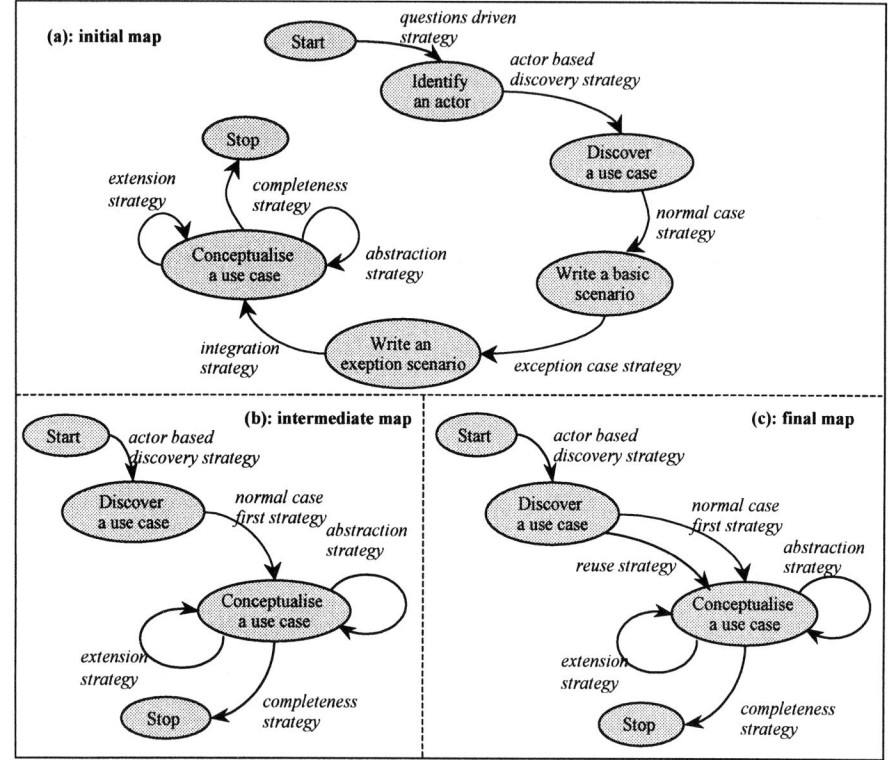

Fig. 5. The construction of the OOSE method map

Step3: Revising the defined sections. The current candidate OOSE map (Figure 5(a)) exhibits an entirely linear use case construction process that suggests some adjustments. Let us use the *aggregation strategy* (Figure 4) to help us combining sections. In the chain of intentions *Start, Discover an actor, Discover a use case*, only one strategy supports the achievement of every of these intentions. It can be noticed that even defined as a full step in the OOSE method, the identification of actors is not useful as such but only as a mean to identify use cases. For a better reusability of the OOSE approach it is worth transforming the actor identification as a strategy to identify use cases. Thus, we replace the sequence of these sections by the section <*Start, Discover a use case, actor based discovery strategy*> (Figure 5(b)).

In a similar manner we replace the chain of intentions *Write a basic scenario, Write an exception scenario* and *Conceptualise a use case* by the section <*Discover a use case, Conceptualise a use case, normal case first strategy*>. This is justified by the fact that only very basic guidelines are provided by the OOSE method for scenario writing, scenario variation discovery and scenario integration in a single use case. This leads us to Figure 5(b). The analysis of this map allows us to notice that *abstract use cases* are generated (following the *abstraction strategy*) but not used. The OOSE method advises to reuse them in the conceptualisation of new use cases but does not say when and how to do it. The *alternative discovery strategy* in the reengineering map (Figure 4) gives us the idea to introduce a *reuse strategy* as a means to achieve the intention *Conceptualise a use case*. This new strategy guides the reuse of abstract use cases in the description of concrete use cases. Thus, by adding the section <*Discover a use case, Conceptualise a use case, reuse strategy*> we obtain the OOSE map shown in Figure 5(c).

Step 4: Defining guidelines. We can now move on in the reengineering map (Figure 4) to the definition of guidelines. We follow the *guided strategy* to associate an IAG to every section of the OOSE map. Let us consider the IAG associated to the section <*Start, Discover a use case, actor based discovery strategy*>. The definition of an IAG consists in defining its interface and its body. The interface situation refers to the product, which is the target of the source intention, the *Start* intention in our case. The product part is the *"problem description"* and, the interface of the IAG is <*(Problem description), Discover a use case with the actor based discovery strategy*>. The definition of its body depends on its type (simple, tactical or strategic). We identify the IAG under construction as a tactical guideline, which can be represented by a plan including two steps: the definition of actors and the definition of use cases. These two steps are defined as sub-guidelines as shown in Figure 6.

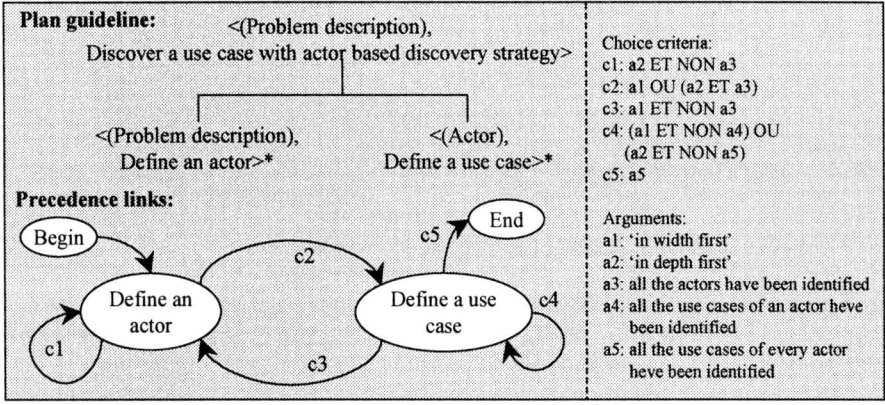

Fig. 6. The IAG associated to the section < Start, Discover a use case, actor based discovery strategy>

Next, we need to define the precedence links between these sub-guidelines. According to the initial method description, the definition of the use cases always follows the identification of the actors. However, one can proceed in different manners, we can identify all the actors first and then define the corresponding use cases or define the corresponding use cases after the identification of every actor. These two ways of proceeding are integrated in the guideline definition through the arguments called *"in width first"* and *"in depth first"* in Figure 6. Moreover, the plan must help verifying if all actors have been identified, if all use cases have been defined for an actor and if all use cases have been defined for all actors. The different combinations of these arguments allow us to define choice criteria of every precedence link of the IAG plan presented in Figure 6. It shall be noticed that the chunk concept contributes to a substantial improvement of the method guideline initially provided by the OOSE description. Following similar approach the two sub-guidelines can be defined.

Step 5: Identifying method chunks. To illustrate the identification of the method chunks in the reengineering process, let us apply the *section based discovery strategy* of the reengineering map (Figure 4) to the OOSE map. This strategy draws the method engineer attention to the fact that a method chunk must satisfy some reusability criteria to be inserted in the method base. This leads to verify if every IAG may be reused as an independent method unit. For example, the IAG associated to the section *<Start, Discover a use case, actor based discovery strategy>* has been transformed enough from its initial version in the OOSE map to be applicable in many different but similar situations requiring to identify the services that an information system must provide to its users. Therefore, we confirm that a method chunk can be based on this IAG.

Let us consider another example to illustrate the *sequence discovery strategy* (Figure 4). Following this strategy we select two consecutive sections *<Start, Discover a use case, actor based discovery strategy>*, *<Discover a use case, Conceptualise a use case, normal case first strategy>* to construct a new guideline embedding the two IAG associated to these two sections of the OOSE map. This guideline is a tactical plan guideline introducing an ordering of the plan elements of the two initial IAG (see Figure 7).

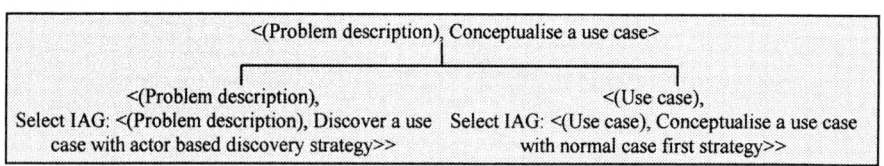

Fig. 7. Example of method chunk

Step 6: Defining method chunks. Finally, we illustrate the definition of a method chunk using the *guided strategy* of the reengineering map (Figure 4). We apply this strategy to the guideline defined in the previous step and presented in Figure 6. The strategy recommends to define first the product parts used by the guideline and then, to define the chunk descriptor. The product parts used in the use case discovery process are the two concepts: *actor* and *use case*. According to the method meta-model presented in Section 3, the definition of the chunk descriptor consists first in determining in which domain and for which design activity the chunk is applicable. This information may be explicitly stated in the method description or inferred from it or from the chunk descriptions. The method base includes a catalogue of predefined domains and design activities that can be selected to characterise a given chunk in the reengineering process. In the example at hand, the chunk may be applied in the following domains: *information systems, interactive systems* or *business process reengineering* to support the *discovering of system requirements*. Second, the descriptor intention shall be formulated. It specifies the objective of the chunk and the manner used to attain this objective. In our case, we propose the following: *Discover functional system requirements following a use case discovery strategy*. Third, in order to facilitate the retrieval of the method chunk from the method base it is recommended to complete this information by the informal description of the chunk objective. In our case, the chunk objective is to help the requirements engineer to identify the users of the system and the services that the system must provide. Finally it is recommended to provide the links to the aggregate chunks that include this one as well as the components of this chunk. The chunk of our example is an atomic one, but it is used in other aggregate chunks that we designate by their interfaces: <*(Problem description), Construct a use case model following the OOSE strategy*> (the whole use case model) and <*(Problem description), Conceptualise a use case*> (the chunk identified in Figure 7). Figure 8 shows the completed method chunk.

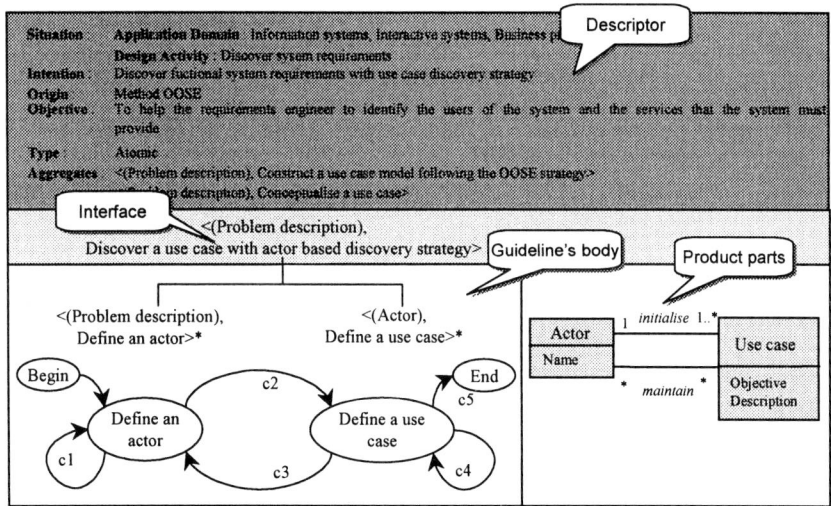

Fig. 8. Example of a completed OOSE method chunk

6. Conclusion

In this paper we look at situational method engineering from the reuse perspective. This method engineering discipline promotes the 'on the fly' method construction by reusing the existing methods' chunks. To enable such method construction we need to build repositories containing different reusable method chunks. Therefore, the existing methods are not presented in a modular way and are not ready to be stored in a method repository. As a solution we propose a process model supporting reengineering of the existing methods in a modular fashion. A method, reconstructed following our reengineering process, is represented by a set of reusable method chunks easy to store in a method repository, to retrieve and to assemble in different manners with the aim to construct new methods.

The reengineering process model is represented as a map with associated guidelines. This allows us to offer flexibility to the method engineer for carrying out the reengineering activity. Besides, guidelines provide a methodological support based on the method meta-model. This meta-model allows to represent any method as a collection of the chunks of different granularity levels where the highest level corresponds to the overall method represented by a strategic guideline i.e. a map with associated guidelines.

Our reengineering process has been evaluated on different methods. The obtained results are encouraging and the experience is positive. In this paper we illustrate the application of this process on the OOSE method. A software environment to support our reengineering process and to improve its effectiveness is our current preoccupation.

References

1. Benjamen A., *Une Approche Multi-démarches pour la modélisation des démarches méthodologiques*. Thèse de doctorat en informatique de l'Université Paris 1, 1999.
2. Brinkkemper S., M. Saeki, F. Harmsen, *Assembly Techniques for Method Engineering*. 10th Conference on Advanced Information Systems Engineering, CAiSE'98. Pisa Italy, 1998.
3. Harmsen A.F., S. Brinkkemper, H. Oei, *Situational Method Engineering for Information System Projects*. In Olle T.W. and A.A. Verrijn Stuart (Eds.), Mathods and Associated Tools for the Information Systems Life Cycle, Proc. of the IFIP WG8.1 Working Conference CRIS'94, pp. 169-194, North-Holland, Amsterdam, 1994.
4. Harmsen A.F., *Situational Method Engineering*. Moret Ernst & Young, 1997.
5. Jacobson I., M. Christenson, P. Jonsson, G. Oevergaard, *Object Oriented Software Engineering: a Use Case Driven Approach*. Addison-Wesley, 1992.
6. Jarke M., C. Rolland, A. Sutcliffe, R. Domges, *The NATURE requirements Engineering*. Shaker Verlag, Aachen 1999.
7. Le Petit Robert, French Dictionary, Dictionnaires LE ROBERT, France,1995.
8. Plihon V., J. Ralyté, A. Benjamen, N.A.M. Maiden, A. Sutcliffe, E. Dubois, P. Heymans, *A Reuse-Oriented Approach for the Construction of Scenario Based Methods*. 5th International Conference on Software Process (ICSP'98), Chicago, Illinois, USA, 1998.
9. Ralyté J., C. Rolland, V. Plihon, *Method Enhancement by Scenario Based Techniques*. 11th Conference on Advanced Information Systems Engineering CAiSE'99, Germany, 1999.
10. Ralyté J., *Reusing Scenario Based Approaches in Requirement Engineering Methods: CREWS Method Base*. Proc. of the 10th Int. Workshop on Database and Expert Systems Applications (DEXA'99), 1st Int. REP'99 Workshop, Florence, Italy, 1999.
11. Ralyté J., *Ingénierie des méthodes par assemblage de composants*. Thèse de doctorat en informatique de l'Université Paris 1. Janvier, 2001.
12. Ralyté J. C. Rolland, *An Assembly Process Model for Method Engineering*. 13th Conf. on Advanced Information Systems Engineering, CAISE'01 Interlaken, Switzerland, 2001.
13. Rolland C., N. Prakash, *A proposal for context-specific method engineering*, IFIP WG 8.1 Conf. on Method Engineering, pp 191-208, Atlanta, Gerorgie, USA, 1996.
14. Rolland C., V. Plihon, J. Ralyté, *Specifying the reuse context of scenario method chunks*. 10th Conf. on Advanced Information Systems Engineering, CAiSE'98. Pisa Italy, 1998.
15. Rolland C., N. Prakash, A. Benjamen, *A multi-model view of process modelling*. Requirements Engineering Journal, p. 169-187,1999.
16. Saeki M., K. Iguchi, K Wen-yin, M Shinohara, *A meta-model for representing software specification & design methods*. Proc. of the IFIP¨WG8.1 Conference on Information Systems Development Process, Come, pp 149-166, 1993.
17. van Slooten K., S. Brinkkemper, *A Method Engineering Approach to Information Systems Development*. In Information Systems Development process, N. Prakash, C. Rolland, B. Pernici (Eds.), Elsevier Science Publishers B.V. (North-Holand), 1993.
18. Song X., *A Framework for Understanding the Integration of Design Methodologies*. In: ACM SIGSOFT Software Engineering Notes, 20 (1), pp. 46-54, 1995.
19. Rational Software Corporation, *Unified Modelling Language version 1.3*. Available at http://www.rational.com/uml/resources/documentation/, 2000.

Modeling and Structuring Multiple Perspective Video for Browsing

Yoshihiro Nakanishi[1], Tatsuo Hirose[1]*, and Katsumi Tanaka[2]

[1] Graduate School of Science and Technology, Kobe University
{nakanisi, hirose}@db.cs.kobe-u.ac.jp
[2] Graduate School of Informatics, Kyoto University
ktanaka@i.kyoto-u.ac.jp

Abstract. Recently, MPV(multiple perspective video) has become popular because of recent advancement in digital video technologies. Actually, video surveillance is currently a big application of MPV. In the case of the usage of a lot of video cameras, human's keyword annotation is a tedious task, and automatic image recognition techniques takes an expensive cost to find what are taken in the MPV. Therefore, we need an effective way of capturing camare metadata and sharing annotation information among MPV data. In this paper, we propose a way of modeling and structuring MPV data based on several semantic relationships for browsing and retrieval.

1 Introduction

Multiple perspective video (abbreviated by MPV) data is a collection of mutually-synchronized video data taken by multiple cameras. There have been many applications of MPV databases, such as *video surveillance systems* and *TV programs containing sport/music events*. Furthermore, it is possible to integrate and construct a MPV database containing footage taken by the general public from several distinct events.

One of the major problems in searching and browsing MPV data is organizing lots of mutually-synchronized video data and retrieving and/or browsing the vast volume of data. For this purpose, we need an appropriate modeling framework which considers the characteristics of the MPV data. The important characteristics of MPV data are summarized as follows:

- **Continuous media**
  Video data is a continuous-media data. This leads to the fact that any portion of a video data can become a unit for indexing and retrieval.
- **Synchronized media**
  MPV data is a collection of multiple video data which takes the same target or place simultaneously. The number of video cameras vary depending on applications. For example, in TV programs containing sport/music events,

---

* Currently, Tatsuo Hirose is with Matsushita Electric Industrial Co., Ltd.

usually, 10 or more cameras are used. In video surveillance systems, more cameras have been used in building surveilance systems or highway surveillance systems. The increase of the number of cameras for MPV makes their indexing task more difficult.
- **Treatment of un-identified anonymous cameras**
  Recently, rapid progress has been made in digital video (DV) camera technology for the usage of the general public. Whenever an open event is held, many DV cameras are used by members of the general public. In this case, various individuals are unaware of what event is being captured by every camera. Therefore, if we wish to integrate those MPV data, we need to cope with the anonymous property.

In the present paper, we introduce a data model for MPV data. Our data model incorporates a camera's physical metadata (such as focused object area, zoom, tilt information) as well as annotation information. Then, we define four kinds of semantic relationships (synchronized relationship, interval-inclusion relationship, FOA-inclusion relationship and better-capturedness relationship) to interrelate the MPV data with each other. Based on these semantic relationships, we propose a method to inherit annotation information from MPV data. Finally, based on the proposed data model, we describe a way of structuring MPV fragments for overviewing the entire data or for viewing query results in an effective manner.

2 Related Works

Because of the rapid progress in broadband Internet technology, there is now growing interest in querying the large resources of digital video data and delivering them in the high-speed Internet.

There have been several pioneering frameworks for modeling and structuring video data. Allen's work on temporal intervals [1] laid the foundation for many researches concerned with time intervals [6] [5]. He showed that there are 13 distinct temporal relationships that can exist between two arbitrary time intervals. Some researches on video databases have thus been greatly influenced by Allen's temporal model. In [5], temporal-interval-based models have been presented for time-dependent multimedia data such as video.

Over the past few years, researchers around the world have developed systems which are capable of providing database support to video data [7] [4] [11]. Object Video Database (OVID) [7], which was introduced by one of the authors' of the present paper, is an instance-based video data model. In OVID, an arbitrary set of contiguous intervals can be defined as a meaningful entity, which they call a video object. Inheritable and non-inheritable attributes can be assigned to those video objects. Inheritable attributes are shared between objects on the basis of interval-inclusion relationship between them. The basic idea is to let video objects share inheritable attributes with their parent video object and relieve some burden of the manual annotation process. Our recent work, which will appear in [8,9,10] differs from OVID. We introduced *glue* operation to dynamicaly synthesize all the video intervals that contain all the specified keywords from fragmentarily index video.

Algebraic video data model [11] is based on the stratification approach. Unlike simple stratification, however, in the algebraic video model, it is possible to define the hierarchical relationship between descriptions that are associated with the same video data. Parent nodes in the hierarchy represent the context of their child nodes. Therefore, by using this hierarchy, it is possoble to attach multiple views with different context to the same video data.

VideoSTAR [3] is another video database project developed at Norwegian Institute of Technology. A generic model to support both the structural indexing and contents indexing has been proposed. Various interval-based and set-based operations have been defined as well. Three different kinds of descriptions — basic, primary and secondary — based on the context in which they appear can be associated with a video data. Video documents can be composed from various sources of video data and only those descriptions that are contextually related will be inherited by the newly composed documents. Their work also focussed more on building a perfect annotation model for indexing which makes the system even more complex.

Yeung et al [12] proposed a way of summarizing video by extracting story units from a video. They use a way to discover a story structure from the video and its metadata.

All of the above works do not focus on characteristics of MPV data. Recently, R. Jain [13] et al introduced a *semiorder* data model for MPV data. They especially focused on the temporal aspects of MPV data.

Recently, we introduced a new query formulation method, called *Query by Camera* for retrieving MPV data[2]. A cameraman takes video scenes with a video camera while looking for some focused objects through a finder, defining composition, focusing a camera, and pushing a record button. Such camera operations are very familiar with the general public. In our *Query by Camera* approach, each query for MPV data is formulated by focusing some object and push start and end bottons by a certain camera. Then, the system searches for video scenes from MPV data such that each scene takes the same object which is *better* than the original query camera. In this approach, we assume that each captured video data is associated with a time series of its focusing areas and fragmentarily-annotated keywords[1]. In order to obtain video scenes with *better-capturedness*, our system compares a video's focusing-area sequence with that of the query camera. The *better-capturedness* measurement is described in Section 4.

Suppose that we are watching a basketball game as an application example for querying MPV data by *Query By Camera* metaphor. (see Figure 1) After a user has finished taking video of the game, she/he requires video intervals taken by the other people. The query information is given by the video intervals

---

[1] In our prototype system, the distance of the focused object, camera position, and several camera information are automatically captured together with the taken video data.

taken by herself/himself. Video intervals containing the focused objects from various viewpoints are retrieved. She/he specifies how the objects are captured interactively and selects the preferable video scenes. On the other hand, she/he may require a reconstructed video containing the objects closest at each moment.

Fig. 1. Concept

3 Modeling MPV Data

3.1 Basic Model

The basic constructs of our MPV data model are *video objects* which convey video data and its metadata (focused area information and annotation information) and several *semantic relationships* among video objects. These are summarized as follows:

- **Video objects**
    - Video frame sequence
    - Focused area information (for short, FOA)
    - Annotation
- **Semantic Relationships**
    - Synchronized relationship
    - Interval-inclusion relationship
    - FOA-inclusion relationship
    - Better-Capturedness relationship

A *video object* is intuitively a video scene taken by a certain camera togethter with its metadata. The video object is a basic entity in our model. Formally, a *video object* O_i is represented by a triple $O_i = (F_i, A_i, K_i)$ consisting of the followings:

- **A video frame sequence**
  $F_i = f_{i_1} f_{i_2} \cdots f_{i_p}$
  Here, each f is a video frame taken by a certain camera. We assume the timecode function (denoted by $timecode(f)$) and the camera number function (denoted by $camera(f)$) are defined for each frame f. For example, $timecode(f) =' 19:05:35'$ denotes that the frame f was taken at time '19:05:35'. Also, $camera(f) =' 3'$ denotes that the frame f was taken by the camera with camera number '3'.
- **Focused area information** (for short, FOA)
  $A_i = a_{i_1} a_{i_2} \cdots a_{i_p}$
  Here, each a is a focused object area information of the corresponding frame f. A focused object area information basically consists of the position coordinates of the target and the radius of the focused area (circle).
- **Annotation information** (a keyword set)
  $K_i = \{k_{i_1}, k_{i_2}, \ldots, k_{i_q}\}$
  Here, K_{i_r} denotes a keyword, and each keyword is assumed to describe the content of the whole scene S_i.

Suppose that we have two video objects O_i and O_j as follows:
$O_i = (F_i, A_i, K_i)$ and $O_j = (F_j, A_j, K_j)$
Here,

$F_i = f_{i_1} f_{i_2} \cdots f_{i_p}$, $A_i = a_{i_1} a_{i_2} \cdots a_{i_p}$, $K_i = \{k_{i_1}, k_{i_2}, \ldots, k_{i_q}\}$, and
$F_j = f_{j_1} f_{j_2} \cdots f_{j_{p'}}$, $A_j = a_{j_1} a_{j_2} \cdots a_{j_{p'}}$, $K_j = \{k_{j_1}, k_{j_2}, \ldots, k_{j_{q'}}\}$.

Synchronized relationship
In the MPV environment, many cameras are used to take video simultaneously. So, some target objects or events may be captured by more than one camera at the same time. Intuitively, if two videos are taken during the same time period, then, we say these videos are synchronized. Formally, if $p = p'$ and $timecode(f_{i_r}) = timecode(f_{j_r})$ holds for each $r \in \{1, 2, \ldots, p\}$, then the two video objects are defined to be *synchronized*. That is, when the above condition holds, then the *synchronized relationship*, denoted by $synchronized(O_i, O_j)$, is said to hold.

Inclusion relationship
If one video scene is completely included by the other video scene, then we intuitively say that one is included by the other one. We extend the notion of the inclusionship into MPV environment. Formally, if $p > p'$ and F_j is a subsequence of F_i, then F_j is said to be *included by* F_i. That is, the scene F_j is a subscene of F_i. We denote the *inclusion relationship* by $include(O_i, O_j)$.

FOA-inclusion relationship
In the MPV environment, one camera captures a wider area than the other camera during a time period. Then, intuitively, we say the camera captures a spatially wider area than the other camera. This notion is formalized as follows. If $synchronized(O_i, O_j)$ holds and $a_{i_r} \supseteq a_{j_r}$ holds for each $r \in \{1, 2, \ldots, p\}$, then we say the two video objects are defined to have an *FOA-inclusion relationship*, denoted by $FOA - include(O_i, O_j)$.

Better-Capturedness relationship
In the MPV environment, the same target object or event may be taken by more than two cameras. One camera may have captured the target *better* than another camera during a certain time period. The relationship is formalized by the following. If $synchronized(O_i, O_j)$ holds and the video object O_i is considered to *capture better* than the video object O_j, then we say there is a *better-capturedness relationship* between O_i and O_j, and it is denoted by $captureBetter(O_i, O_j)$. The next section describes how to determine which video object has been captured better.

It should be noted that the definitions of several semantic relationships among video objects above are not always limited to a sequence of video frames from the same camera. One of the goals of our framework is to provide a conceptual model which can be applied to video scenes which are composed from more than one camera's video scenes.

3.2 Annotation Inheritance

One of the major problems of MPV data is determining a way to annotate information for multiple video streams. In our previous work OVID[7], we have introduced a mechanism to cope with this problem. We introduced an interval-inclusion inheritance mechanism which automatically inherits some annotation information from a video interval to its subinterval. However, in OVID we considered such a mechanisim for sharing annotation information only within a single video stream data. By extending the idea of OVID and by using the above semantic relationships, we introduce a new inheritance mechanism for sharing annotation information among MPV data.

- **Interval-inclusion inheritance**
  When one video object *includes* another video object($include(O_i, O_j)$ holds), then annotation K_i can be inherited to K_j. That is, the new K_j becomes $K_j \cup K_i$. Indeed, this seems to be the interval-inclusion inheritance of OVID. However, it should be noted that the interval-inclusion inheritance is applied not ony for a single video stream, but also to MPV data.
- **FOA-inclusion inheritance**
  The FOA-inclusion inheritance is a *bottom-up inheritance* for annotation. When two video objects O_i and O_j have the relationship $FOA-include(O_i, O_j)$ (O_i takes a wider area than O_j), then the annotation information K_j is inherited to K_i. It should be noted that this occurs usually in MPV environments. In other words, some cameras capture a close-up while others capture a perspective view during the same time period.
- **Inheritance through better-capturedness relationship**
  This inheritance occurs among video objects which have the *better-capturedness* relationships. The inheritance is bi-directional. Since both video objects are considered to capture the same targets, the annotation information of the one camera can be inherited to the other and vice versa.

4 Computing Better-Capturedness

The MPV data is searched spatio-temporally by comparing the focused object areas of video objects. The comparison is based on a measure that indicates how well the focused object is captured in the video interval. Then, video intervals that capture the objects "better" are retrieved. "Better" indicates, for example, that the object is captured much closer than or from a reverse angle to a user's viewpoint.

Suppose that we have two video obejcts $O_i = (F_i, A_i, K_i)$ and $O_j = (F_j, A_j, K_j)$ such that O_i and O_j are *synchronized*. Then, in order to compute the *better-capturedness* relationship, we introduce a measure called the *capture condition measure*.

The calculations of the *capture condition measure* implemented in our prototype consists of two steps.

First, a similarity degree between two sequences A_i and A_j of focused object areas is calculated. We compute the similarity by comparing focused object areas of two corresponding video frames for each time, t. In the current implementation, if the center of one's focused object area is included in the other's focused object area and/or the center of the one's focused object area is included in the other's focused object area, then two frames are considered to capture the same targets.

Next, the capture condition measure, which indicates how well a focused object is captured is calculated. There are three kinds of constructs in the capture condition measure.

- Capture size
  An object size on a video frame changes according to the position and the focus of a camera. A user may require a video scene capturing the object bigger or a video scene capturing a wider area.
- Capture direction
  A camera angle for the object changes according to the position and the direction of a camera. A user may require a video scene capturing the object from the opposite angle or a set of video scenes capturing the object from various angles.
- Capture duration
  A user may want to see a collection of short video intervals as highlight scenes or a video scene that continues to capture the object for a long time.
  A user specifies the above capture condition according to her/his preference when the query result is displayed. Video intervals with the higher capture condition measures are selected and replayed synchronously, or they are restructured and displayed as a single stream.

A *capture condition measure* at time t is defined as follows.

1. Capture size
   The capture condition measure, s for each kind of requirements about capture size are defined as follows.

- An object is taken bigger
$$s = min(rr)/rr \text{ if } rr > 1, \text{ otherwise } 0$$
- An object is taken as the same size
$$s = rr \text{ if } rr \leq 1, \text{ otherwise } 1/rr$$
- An object is taken smaller
$$s = 0 \text{ if } rr \leq 1, \text{ otherwise } rr/max(rr)$$

Here, rr is a radius ratio between one camera's focused object area to another focused object area. $min(rr)$ and $max(rr)$ are respectively the minimum and the maximum radius ratios among the video intervals that have been retrieved.

2. Capture direction

A capture condition measure, a for a required direction is as follows:

$$a = |cos(\theta - \theta_r)/2|$$

θ is a camera angle and θ_r is the requested camera angle as shown in Figure 2.

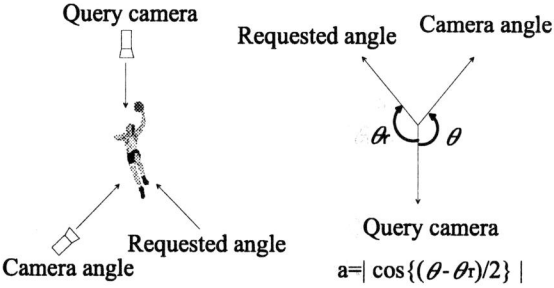

Fig. 2. Capture Condition Measure for Direction

As the value of a approaches 1, the video frame is said to better satisfy the requested angle.

Next, the capture condition measures S and A for the video interval are calculated by averaging the capture condition measures $s(t)$ and $a(t)$ at time t over the video interval as follows:

$$S = (\int s(t)dt)/tv, A = (\int a(t)dt)/tv$$

Here, tv is the video object's interval duration. Supposing some other video objects duration is tq, the capture condition measure for captured duration T is defined as follows:

$$T = tv/tq$$

Figure 3 shows a prototype that considers an offline application. In this figure, a user specifies a video interval as a query. The system then searches other synchronized video which captures *better* than the original query video.

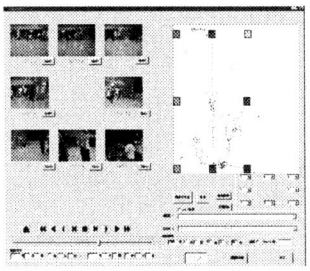
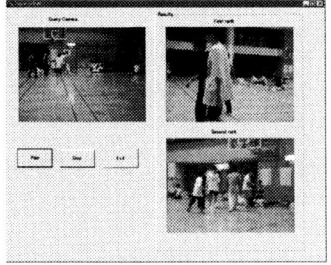

Query Screen   Result Screen

Fig. 3. Better Caputured Video

5 Summarization and Serialization of MPV Data

In this section, we propose a way to summarize MPV data in order to browse MPV data effectively. We also propose a way to serialize video objects with consideration to both the better-capturedness relationship and camera switching.

MPV Summarization

As shown in Figure 4, a *catalog* is composed of video segments taken from MPV data and it shows a summary of the data. A desirable image diplays all of the important contents from the entire MPV data of a certain video object. One way to acheive this is by making a single video object which contains all the keywords *somewhere* within the MPV data.

The general flow of the summarization is as follows:

1. A user specifies a set of keywords of interest to query an MPV database.
2. The system searches candidate sets of video objects such that *somewhere* within each set, *all* the specified keywords are contained. For example, consider the query $\{k_1, k_2, k_3\}$. When the video object O_1's annotation contains keywords $\{k_1, k_2\}$, and another video object O_2's annotation contains keywords $\{k_2, k_3\}$, then the set $\{O_1, O_2\}$ becomes a candidate answer for the query.
3. For each candidate set of video objects, the system sorts all the video objects by time-order for each camera. For example, let $\{O_{11}, O_{12}\}, \{O_{21}, O_{25}\}$ be sorted video objects for Camera 1 and Camera 2, respectively. At this stage, it should be noted that some video objects may be temporally overlapped. For example, suppose that the time periods of $O_{11}, O_{12}, O_{21}, O_{25}$ are [10,300], [500,800], [200,400], and [700,1000], respectively. Then, the time periods of O_{11} and O_{21} and the time periods of O_{12} and O_{25} overlap.
4. The system partitions a video object into smaller video objects such that whenever two objects overlappe they remain synchronized. For example, the above video objects are partitioned into the following set of smaller video objects:

$O_{111} : [10, 200], O_{112} : [200, 300], O_{211} : [200, 300], O_{212} : [300, 400],$
$O_{121} : [500, 700], O_{122} : [700, 800], O_{251} : [700, 800], O_{252} : [800, 1000]$

Here, O_{112} and O_{211} are synchronized. O_{122} and O_{251} are also synchronized.
5. The system serializes some of the video objects in time-order. For example, one possible solution for the above is $O_{111}O_{211}O_{212}O_{121}O_{122}O_{252}$. Another solution is $O_{111}O_{112}O_{212}O_{121}O_{251}O_{252}$.

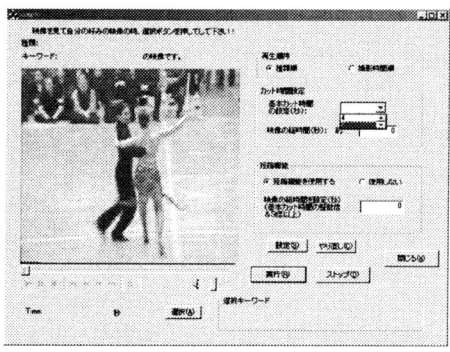

Fig. 4. Video Catalog

Serializing retrieved video fragments

When a retrieval request by keywords is issued to an MPV database, a set of video objects satsifying the specified keywords are returned from the MPV data. Since each video object is a fragment of a certain video stream, it is not easy for the user to see each resulting video object. We propose a way to serialize retrieval results and display it.

The general flow of the serialization is as follows:

1. A user specifies a set of keywords to query to an MPV database.
2. The system searches for video objects which contain annotation of *all* the specified keywords.
3. The system sorts all the video objects by time-order for each camera.
4. The system partitions video obeject into smaller synchronized video objects such that every two overlapping objects are synchronized.
5. The system serializes some of the video objects in time-order.

As seen in the final steps of the summarization and serialization procedures, there may be more than one possible solution. In order to obtain a better solution, we need to consider the following two factors:

- Better-Capturedness Relationship
- Camera switching

As for the better-capturedness relationship, it seems to be feasible to select a better-captured video. In the above example, the video objects O_{112} and O_{211} are synchronized. If these two objects represent the same target, it would be preferrable to select the better-captured video object as a component of the final answer. However, if we use the better-capturedness relationship as the only criteria to select from a set of synchronized video objects, the final solution may become a video which is difficult for users to view. This is due to the frequent change of camera positions since the final answer is composed of video fragments taken by multiple cameras. Sudden changes which may occur when cameras are switched may make it visually unsuitable for viewing. For example, a video that shows a person's feet when switched to a video that shows a person's face will cause visual confusion. According to the *grammer of movie*, in order to avoid such visual confusion, the scene agreement rule must be followed. This rule avoids visual jumps by making use of the position and movement of the object onscreen and the viewer's eye line. However, it is impossible to figure out the viewer's eye line by only using the objects area information. Since, the user will have difficulty in viewing onscreen objects that change in size suddenly, we should take the object's size into account too.

In order to cope with the switching problem mentioned above, we calculate the *level of switching* between cameras. The degree of switching shows appropriateness to change a camera and it consists of the position, movement, and size of the object. A degree of switching is calculated for every synchronized video object which is a candidate for the present video object.

- Agreement of position
  As shown in Figure 5, the videos before and after the cameras are switched are compared and the target with the closest onscreen position to the position of the onscreen target before the cameras are switched is considered to be proper. The angle between the target being captured and the cameras central axis is considered. The angle which is closest to the video before it is switched is considered to be proper.
  A degree of switching $p_{1,2}$ by the agreement of the position between camera 1 before switching and camera 2 after switching is represented by the following formula:

  $$p_{1,2} = |\ \theta_2/f_2 - \theta_1/f_1\ |$$

  θ_1, θ_2 represent the angle between the object being captured and the camera's central axis before and after switching respectively. f_1, f_2 represent the field angle of the cameras before and after switching respectively.
- Agreement of movement
  As shown in Figure 6, the videos before and after the cameras are switched are compared and the target with the closest onscreen movement to the movement of the onscreen target before the cameras are switched is considered proper. The positions of the target before and after the cameras are switched are connected by a straight line. If the cameras are located on the same side of the line, the degree of switching becomes higher. If a target is

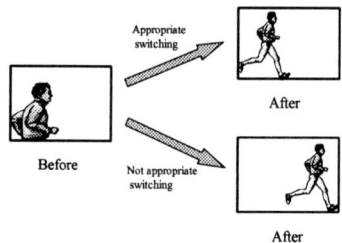

Fig. 5. Agreement of position

standing still, the degree of switching is the same for all cameras. The degree of switching $d_{1,2}$ by the agreement of the movement between camera 1 before switching and camera 2 after switching is shown as follows:

if $\quad ax_1 + by_1 \leq k$

$$d_{1,2} = \begin{cases} 0, & ax_2 + by_2 \leq k \\ 1, & ax_2 + by_2 > k \end{cases}$$

if $\quad ax_1 + by_1 \geq k$

$$d_{1,2} = \begin{cases} 0, & ax_2 + by_2 \geq k \\ 1, & ax_2 + by_2 < k \end{cases}$$

Here (x_1, y_1) is the position of camera 1, (x_2, y_2) is the position of camera 2.

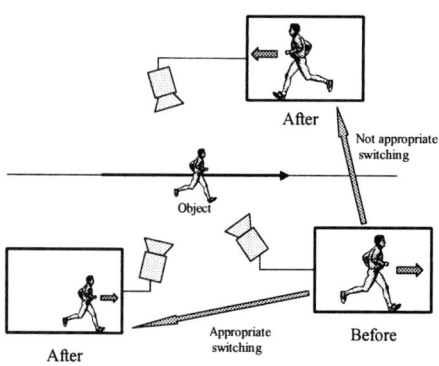

Fig. 6. Agreement of movement

- Agreement of size
  The actual onscreen size of the target being captured can be calculated using the distance between the target and the camera and the camera's field angle. The ratio in size before and after the cameras are switched is compared. The cameras with the smaller ratio have a higher degree of switching. The degree of switching $s_{1,2}$ by the agreement of size between camera 1 before switching and camera 2 after switching is shown as follows:

$$s_{1,2} = \begin{cases} \frac{l_2 \cdot \tan(f_2)}{l_1 \cdot \tan(f_1)}, & \frac{l_2 \cdot \tan(f_2)}{l_1 \cdot \tan(f_1)} \leq 0 \\ \frac{l_1 \cdot \tan(f_1)}{l_2 \cdot \tan(f_2)}, & \frac{l_1 \cdot \tan(f_1)}{l_2 \cdot \tan(f_2)} > 0 \end{cases}$$

Finally, the degree of switching between camera 1 and camera 2 is calculated using the three parameters expressed by the following formula:

$$R_{1,2} = \alpha p_{1,2} + \beta d_{1,2} + \gamma s_{1,2}$$

α, β, γ are the weight coefficients for each parameter. The total sum of these weight coefficients is 1.

Figure 7 shows an implementation of the process mentioned above.

Fig. 7. Serialized Video

6 Conclusion

In the present paper, we introduced a data model for MPV data. Our data model incorporates camera's physical metadata (such as focused object area, zoom, tilt information) as well as annotation information. We defined four kinds of semantic relationships (synchronized relationship, interval-inclusion relationship, FOA-inclusion relationship and better-capturedness relationship) to interrelate MPV data with each other. Based on the proposed semantic relationships, we proposed a method to inherit annotated information for MPV data. Finally, based on the proposed data model, we described a way of structuring MPV fragments to be overviewed the whole MPV data or to view query results in an effective manner.

Acknowlegement

This research was partly supported by Research for the Future Program of Japan Society for the Promotion of Science under the project "Researches on Advanced Multimedia Contents Processing," (project no. JSPS-RFTF97P00501).

References

1. J.F. Allen. "Maintaining Knowledge about Temporal Intervals". *Communications of the ACM*, 26(11):832–843, 1983.
2. T. Hata, T. Hirose, Y. Nakanishi, K. Tanaka. "Querying Multiple Perspective Video by Camera Metaphor". *Proc. of 7th International Conference on Database Systems for Advanced Applications (DASFAA*, Hong Kong, April 18-20, 2001.
3. R. Hjelsvold, R. Midtstraum, and O. Sandst. "Searching and Browsing a Shared Video Database". Multimedia Database Systems. Design and Implementation Strategies. chapter 4. Kluwer Academic Publishers, 1996.
4. E.J. Hwang and V.S. Subrahmanian. "Querying Video Libraries". *Journal of Visual Communications and Image Representation*, 7(1):44–60, March 1996.
5. T.D.C. Little and A. Ghafoor. "Interval-Based Conceptual Models for Time-Dependent Multimedia Data". *IEEE Transactions on Knowledge and Data Engineering*, 5(4):551–563, August 1993.
6. N.A. Lorentzos and Y.G. Mitsopoulos. "SQL Extension for Intervals Data". *IEEE Transactions on Knowledge and Data Engineering*, 9(3):480–499, May/June 1997.
7. E. Oomoto and K. Tanaka. "OVID: Design and Implementation of a Video-Object Database System". *IEEE Transactions on Knowledge and Data Engineering*, 5(4):629–643, August 1993.
8. S. Pradhan, K. Tajima, and K. Tanaka. "Interval Glue Operations and Answer Filtering for Video Retrieval". *IPSJ Transactions on Databases*, vol.40, no.SIG3:80–90, February 1999.
9. S. Pradhan, K. Tajima, and K. Tanaka. "A Query Model to Synthesize Answer Intervals from Indexed Video Units". to appear in *IEEE Transactions on Knowledge and Database Systems*. Vol. 13, No. 6, Nov/Dec 2001.
10. K. Tanaka, K. Tajima, T. Sogo, S. Pradhan. "Algebraic Retrieval of Fragmentarity Index Video". *New Generation Computing*, pp.359-374, 18(2000).
11. R. Weiss, A. Duda, and D. Gifford. "Composition and Search with a Video Algebra". *IEEE MultiMedia*, 2(1):12–25, Spring 1995.
12. M. Yeung, B. Yeo, and B. Liu. "Extracting Story Units from Long Programs for Video Browsing and Navigation". In *International Conference on Multimedia Computing and Systems*, pages 296–305, June 1996.
13. S.K. Bhonsle, A. Gupta, S. Santini, R. Jain. "Semiorder Database for Complex Activity Recognition in Multi-Sensory Environment" *Proc. ICDE2000*, pp.689-691, March 2000.

Modeling Dynamic Objects in Video Databases: A Logic Based Approach

Biswajit Acharya, Arun K. Majumdar, and Jayanta Mukherjee

Department of Computer Science and Engineering
Indian Institute of Technology, Kharagpur, INDIA
{bach, akmj, jay}@cse.iitkgp.ernet.in

Abstract. In this work we propose a state-based approach to model video data so that the semantics of the video is specified by the properties (static and dynamic) of the objects present in the video. The object dynamics is captured by the states and state transitions. The video database is then segmented and indexed based on these information. Finally, examples have been given to show how state-based queries can be used to retrieve information from the video database.

1 Introduction

With the advances in multimedia technologies and its usage, video modeling, creation and measurement of video databases have received considerable attention. In video modeling different approaches have been advocated to capture semantics of video segments[1][2][3][4][5]. A detailed survey of existing works can be found in [2]. In this context, object oriented models often treat video segments as first class entities and support operations such as concatenation, segmentation (projection), etc. to create new segments. However, the existing models do not give adequate importance to the behaviour of objects present in the video. This is specially important when a video is used as a tool to analyze the dynamic behaviour of a system. For example, an echocardiogram video, which is a very important tool for diagnosis and monitoring of cardiac diseases, depicts the dynamics of the heart chambers and valves. The segments of an echocardiogram should therefore be more intimately related to the dynamics of the heart, such as systolic and diastolic phases of heart. Again, Colour Doppler echocardiogram images are also used to study the condition of the heart. In medical diagnosis, it will be immensely useful if parallel composition of ordinary echocardiogram video and Colour Doppler echocardiogram video are shown in different windows with proper synchronization. The semantics of synchronization should be guided by the behavioural semantics of the underlying objects. Thus, a cardiologist can look into the video segments corresponding to systolic or diastolic phase of the cardiac cycle of a patient as obtained from the ordinary echocardiogram and Colour Doppler echocardiogram recordings, in two different windows on the screen.

In this paper, we introduce a video data model where besides defining the algebra of video segments, the dynamics of the objects present in a video segment is used to define the semantics of the segment. With this in view, the paper is organized as follows. In section 2, we introduce the concepts of objects, states, state transition. In section 3, we describe video and its components with relation to the objects and states. In section 4, the syntax and semantics of the algebra for the proposed model has been described. In section 5, several operators for video segments and temporal relationships are defined and illustrated with suitable examples. Finally in section 6, topics related to video indexing and retrieval have been discussed.

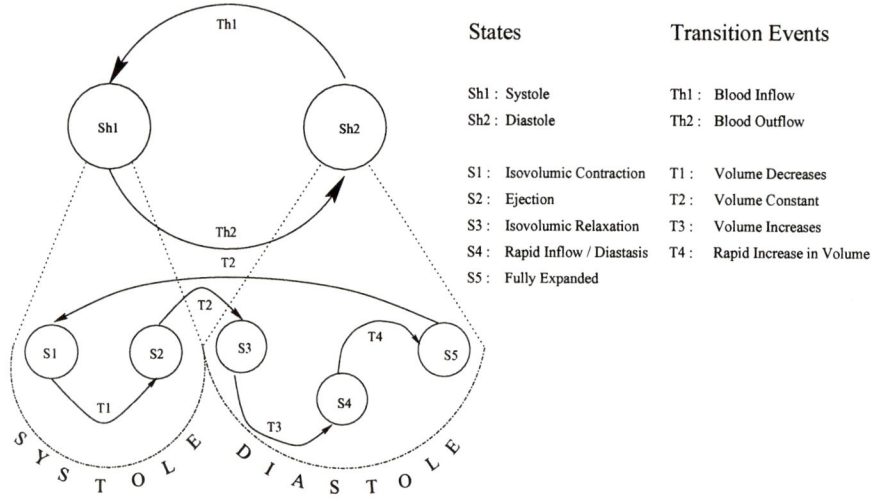

Fig. 1. State transition diagram of left ventricle

2 Objects, States, and State Transition

An object is a real-life or a conceptual entity. An object is described and identified by its properties, such as, its name, object-id, etc. If an object contains other objects then it is called a *composite* object. A video is assumed to depict the behaviour of a set of objects. The information about the objects present in a video is captured following object oriented (OO) paradigm. In the proposed scheme, the objects can be static or dynamic. The state-chart approach adopted in UML [6] is used to capture the dynamic behaviour of the objects. A schematic diagram of the state transition of left ventricle, a component object of the object *heart*, that appears in an echocardiogram video has been shown in Fig. 1. In the next subsection we define some of the terms and concepts of state-chart diagrams.

Following the UML paradigm, dynamic aspects of a system can be described by state machines which are visualized by state-chart diagrams. A *state machine* specifies the sequence of states of an object during its lifetime in response to events. It also specifies the responses of the object to those events. A *state* is a situation within the lifetime of an object during which it satisfies some conditions, performs some activity, or waits for some event. An object remains in a state for a finite amount of time. A *sub-state* is a state that is nested inside another state. A state that has sub-states is called a *composite state*. A composite state may contain either concurrent(orthogonal) or sequential(disjoint) sub-states. An *event* is the specification of a significant occurrence that has a location in time and space. So, an event is an occurrence of a stimulus that can trigger a state transition. A *transition* is a relationship between two states indicating that an object in the first state performs certain actions and enters into a second state. A transition can be autonomous or can occur as a consequence of a specific event. The firing of a transition may also depend on the satisfiability of some conditions.

3 Video, Video Frame, and Video Segment

The term *video frame* is used to describe nothing but a picture captured by a camera snap and doesn't carry any temporal information as such. The temporal aspect comes only in the context of a video which is a dense sequence of video frames. Each video frame depicts pictures of some objects. Similarly, each object appears in some or all of the video frames. Mathematically speaking, let $\mathbb{O}$ be the set of all objects present in the database. Let $\mathbb{V}$ be the set of all video frames. The set of objects associated with a frame $f \in \mathbb{V}$ is identified by a mapping

$$\alpha : \mathbb{V} \mapsto \wp(\mathbb{O}) \qquad (1)$$

where $\wp(\mathbb{O})$ is the power set of $\mathbb{O}$ and hence, $\alpha(f) \in \wp(\mathbb{O})$. Similarly, the set of frames in which an object $O \in \mathbb{O}$ is present is determined by a mapping

$$\beta : \mathbb{O} \mapsto \wp(\mathbb{V}) \qquad (2)$$

where $\beta(O) \in \wp(\mathbb{V})$ and $\wp(\mathbb{V})$ is the power set of $\mathbb{V}$

In the proposed model, the objects present in a video may have static or dynamic behaviour. The structural description of an object is specified by UML like class and object diagram. The behavioural description is specified by methods and state-chart diagrams. The object attributes may be *intrinsic* such as, name, type, object components, states, etc. The object behaviour is described by its methods and state transitions. In addition to that, the depiction of an object in a video frame is associated with some *presentation* attributes, such as,

- Visual properties: colour, texture, shape, size, etc.
- Perspective views: top-view, front-view,etc.
- Camera dependent properties: close-shot, long-shot, pan, zoom, etc.
- Positional and Topological properties - left-of, right-of, inside, occluded etc.

The intrinsic properties of objects are inherent properties and do not change throughout the video database. For example, an object heart has four chambers (its components)– *left atrium, left ventricle, right atrium, right ventricle* and two states – *systole, diastole*. On the other hand, presentation properties of an object may vary from video to video containing the same object. Some of these presentation properties are related to video segments and hence all the frames in those segments have same presentation property. That is, depending on the camera operations during recording a video, a set of objects may be seen in a segment through close-shot followed by another segment where the same objects are seen in through the long-shot of camera. Such situations are often observed in sports video. Even, these properties of an object may vary from frame to frame of a particular video containing the same object. For example, an object heart may be seen with all its four chambers in one view of echocardiogram and may also be seen with only two chambers in another view, depending upon the transducer location. Nevertheless, the heart is described by its intrinsic properties in both the views as its components and states remain same irrespective of the views. With the ideas discussed above, we now formally define video as follows.

Definition 1 (Video). *A video is a dense sequence of frames. The attributes of a video are as given below:*

- **Attributes :**
    - *vid:* to identify the video uniquely, e.g. **video1**
    - *pid:* to identify the id of the parent video from which it has been created.
    - *name:* to describe briefly the type of the video, e.g. **news video, soccer, movie**, etc.
    - *duration:* to describe the length of the video in terms of number of frames present, where the first frame is defined by $start(vid) = 1$ and the last frame in the sequence of frames by $end(vid)$
- **methods :**
    - *start*(vid)*:* to retrieve the first frame number with respect to the parent video.
    - *end*(vid)*:* to retrieve the last frame number with respect to the parent video.
    - *select_frame*(int *i*)*:* to extract the *i*th frame of the video.

A video object is uniquely identified in the video database by its *vid*. A part of a video can also be extracted and can either be used temporarily (*transient*) or be stored in the database (*persistent*). A *transient* video object's *pid* is the *vid* of the video from which it is derived. A *persistent* video object's *pid* is set to NULL to distinguish from a *transient* video object. The term "duration" or "video interval" is denoted by I or $[i, j]$. $I = [i, j] \in \mathbb{N} \times \mathbb{N}$ where $\mathbb{N}$ is the set of natural numbers and $i \leq j$. Moreover, the term "dense sequence" means that $\forall\ k \in [i, j-1]$, the consecutive frames $v.select\_frame(k)$ and $v.select\_frame(k+1)$ are present in video v.

In many applications, videos recorded from multiple cameras are often shown simultaneously in different windows. This is necessary for better understanding of the recorded event and also is required for video editing. For example, in the recording of a cricket match several cameras are used: one camera may focus on the batsman, one camera on the bowler, and one attached to the stamp (known as stamp camera) may track closely the motion of the ball and the action taken by the batsmen. Such concurrent depiction of videos necessitated the definition of *complex video* object.

Definition 2 (Complex Video). *A complex video object is a "synchronized" collection of a set of existing video objects. The videos from which the complex video is created are termed as component video objects.*

Here, the term "synchronized" means that all the videos are captured at same frame rate and synchronization may be done on any arbitrary frame numbers (within the respective durations of the videos) of the component videos. Henceforth, we use the term video or simple video to mean a non-complex video. A video frame of a complex video contains synchronized frames of its component videos. In other words, a complex video is a logical representation for viewing two or more synchronized video objects.

Definition 3 (Video Frame). *A video frame is an atomic part of video data. A video frame may be a simple video frame or a complex video frame. Number of frames present in a video data describes the duration of a video. A video frame is designated by its sequence number with respect to the beginning of the video. Start frame number is, in general, taken as 1. The kth video frame of a video v is expressed as $v[k]$.*

Definition 4 (Video Segment). *A video segment $v_s[i,j]$ of a video v is a video which is a dense subsequence of the set of frames from the ith frame to the jth frame of v.*

In OO parlance, a video segment is a class derived from a video class and an instance of it has *pid* equal to *vid* of the video from which it is extracted. Thus, the duration of the segment $v_s[i,j]$ is $j - i + 1$ and its initial frame is $v_s.pid.select\_frame(i)$ and its last frame $v_s.pid.select\_frame(j)$, where $v_s.pid$ identifies video from which this segment is created. The start frame number and the end frame number of a video segment can be retrieved by the methods $start(v_s.vid)$ and $end(v_s.vid)$ respectively. The objects present in a video segment $v_s[i,j]$ are given by

$$\alpha(v_s[i,j]) = \bigcup_{k=i}^{j} \alpha(v_s.select\_frame(k))$$

Again, for a set of objects $O' \subseteq \mathbb{O}$, the set of frames that contains these objects can be written as

$$\beta(O') = \bigcup_{k=1}^{n} \beta(O'_k)$$

where $|O'| = n$, $k \in [1,n]$ and O'_k is the kth element of the set $O' = \{O'_1, O'_2, \ldots, O'_k, \ldots, O'_n\}$.

In the discussion that follows, start and end frame of a video v will be denoted by $v.start$ and $v.end$ respectively.

In order to capture the semantics of a video segment, we associate a first order predicate called *guard condition(predicate)* with it. The following section deals with the algebra of video segments and the associated guard predicates.

4 Video Algebra

The guard predicate for a video segment $v_s[i,j]$ is defined as follows:

1. Let Σ be a set of constant symbols. This set is a union of five disjoint sets:
   - Σ_1: a set of atomic values; these values may be of types *int, float, char, string, video interval (duration)*, etc. e.g. 1, 2, 3, 3.4, "systole", [23, 87].
   - Σ_2: a set of object instances; these objects are the instances of the classes defined in the schema. e.g. v, v', O, O_1, s_1, s_2.
   - Σ_3: a set of video segments. e.g. v'_s, v''_s.
   - Σ_4: a set of constant functions defined on the sets $\Sigma_1, \Sigma_2, \Sigma_3$, e.g. α, β, *select_frame, start, end* etc.
2. A set $\widehat{V}$ of variables;
3. Connectives: $\wedge$(and), $\vee$(or), $\neg$(not)
4. Operators: := (assignment), [ ] (interval), $\Rightarrow$ (implication), $\equiv$ (equivalence)
5. Quantifiers: $\forall$ (universal quantifier), $\exists$(existential quantifier)

We also use the following notations:

- Parenthesis: ( )
- Separator: ,
- Predicate Symbol: $\bar{p}, \bar{q}$, etc. are denoted by lowercase letter with bar over it.
- Function Symbol: $\tilde{f}, \tilde{g}$, etc. are denoted by lowercase letter with tilde over it.

In the following, the attribute A of an object X is denoted by $X.A$. Thus, for a video segment v, it's attributes will be denoted by $v.x$. Also, the implication operator $X \Rightarrow Y$ means that $\neg X \vee Y$. Again, $X \equiv Y$ is equivalent to $(X \Rightarrow Y) \wedge (Y \Rightarrow X)$.

Definition 5 (Term). *Terms are defined inductively as follows:*

1. *Every variable or constant (elements of Σ) is a term*
2. *If f is an n-ary function and $t_1, \ldots, t_n$ are terms, then $f(t_1 \ldots t_n)$ is a term.*

Definition 6 (Atomic Formula). *If $\bar{p}$ is an n-ary predicate and $t_1, \ldots, t_n$ are terms, then $\bar{p}(t_1 \ldots t_n)$ is an atomic formula.*

Let $X, Y \in \widehat{\mathcal{V}}$ be object variables with attributes A and B having atomic values. Let $c \in \Sigma_1$ be a constant and let θ be a binary predicate. Then, $X.A\,\theta\,c$ and $X.A\,\theta\,Y.B$ are atomic formulae. Here, it is assumed that $X.A$, $Y.B$ and c are of same data type (*int,float,string*, etc.) and the binary predicate θ is defined for that data type.

If $X.A$ and $Y.B$ represent attributes A and B (of same data type) of objects X and Y respectively and if the binary predicate θ (e.g., $=, <, \leq, >, \geq, +, -$, etc.) is defined over such type, then $\theta(X.A, Y.B)$ (which may also be written as $X.A\,\theta\,Y.B$) is an atomic formula.

For a video frame f and an object $X \in \Sigma_2$, $X \in \alpha(f)$ is an atomic formula. Again, for an interval $I = [i, j]$, $k \in I$ is an atomic formula.

Similarly, with videos v_1 and v_2 having an attribute A and binary predicate θ defined over the domain of A $v_1.A\,\theta\,v_2.A$ is an atomic formula, where $v_1, v_2 \in \Sigma_3 \cup \widehat{\mathcal{V}}$.

Example: With an echocardiogram video, let X be the object *left_ventricle* and let A be the attribute *state* and let *systole* be a constant symbol for state. Then, the statement *left_ventricle.state* = "systole" is an atom. Similarly, with two video segments *left_ventricle_Systole* and *left_ventricle_Diastole* created from an echocardiogram video, that the duration of these two segments are equal correspond to an atomic formula

$$left\_ventricle\_Systole.duration = left\_ventricle\_Diastole.duration$$

Definition 7 (Formula). *A formula, also called well-formed formula (wff) is defined as follows.*

1. *An atomic formula is a formula.*
2. *If F and G are two formulae, then so are $(F \vee G), (F \wedge G)$ and $\neg F$.*
3. *If F is a formula and x is a variable, then $\forall x F$ and $\exists x F$ are formulae.*

As mentioned earlier, we intend to capture the semantics of a video segment by associating a guard predicate with it. A guard predicate is a well-formed formula specified according to the Definition 7. A guard predicate may consist of following types of formulae.

Relational: Here, the guard condition is specified by a formula involving attributes of the video segment. For example,

$$\bar{p}(v_s) : v_s.duration = 30 \wedge v_s.name = \text{``soccer''},$$

to mean that the segment v_s corresponds to a soccer match and consists of 30 frames.

Compositional: The segment specification depends on the properties of the objects present in the frames. For example, the predicate

$$\bar{p}(v_s) : \forall k \in [v_s.start, v_s.end] \, \exists O \in \alpha(v_s.select\_frame(k))$$
$$(O.player\_name = \text{``Pele''})$$

implies that each frame of the video segment v_s contains the player "Pele" in it.
State-based: A special type of compositional guard condition, which is of interest to us, involves states of the objects present in the video segment. The state-based guard predicates can be specified as follows.

$$\bar{p}(v_s) : \forall k \in [v_s.start, v_s.end] \, (\exists O \in \alpha(v_s.select\_frame(k))$$
$$\wedge \, O.name = \text{``left\_ventricle''} \wedge O.state = \text{``systole''})$$

to mean that there is an object O (left ventricle) in the segment v_s such that the state of the object O is state *systole*.

5 Operations on Segments

In this section we describe the operations on video segments. Let v_s, v_s' and v_s'' be video segments and let $i, j, k \dots$ denote frame numbers of videos. Then operations on video segments are defined as follows.

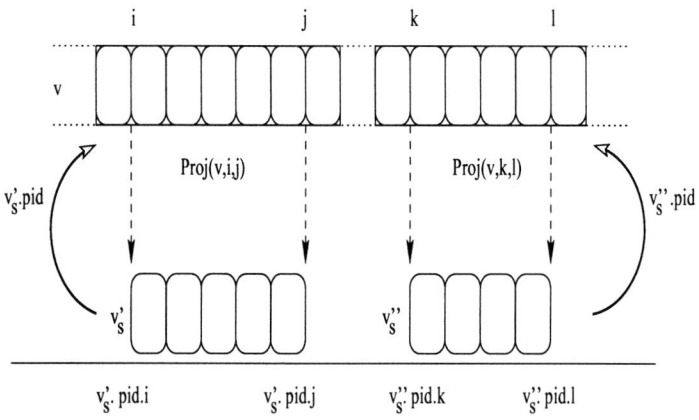

Fig. 2. Projection from a video

Definition 8 (Projection). *A projection operation of a segment v_s on an interval $[i, j]$ is defined as $Proj(v_s, i, j) = v_s'$ For the projected segment v_s', $v_s'.pid = v_s.pid$. Since, $end(v_s') - start(v_s') \leq end(v_s) - start(v_s)$, $duration(v_s') \leq duration(v_s)$*

The projection operation defines an inheritance hierarchy among the video segments, where the projected segment inherits the frames of its parent segment. The parent-child relationship in this hierarchy is determined by the pid attribute. Since, frames of the projected video segment are identified with respect to the parent video segment, a frame $v'_s[k]$ of video segment v'_s corresponds to the $v_s[i + k - 1]$th frame of the segment v_s from which it has been projected. The projection operation is illustrated in Fig. 2.

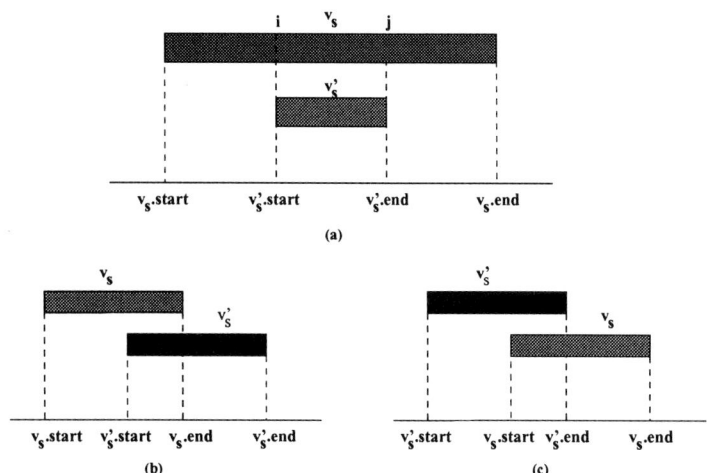

Fig. 3. Operations on video segments: (a) v'_s **contained-in** v_s, v_s **contain** v'_s, and (a),(b),(c) v_s **overlap** v'_s

Lemma 1. *Consider a video segment v_s with guard predicate $\bar{p}(v_s)$. Let $v'_s = Proj(v_s, i, j)$ be a projection of v_s. Suppose that $\bar{p}(v_s)$ involves an existentially quantified variable k over $[v_s.start, v_s.end]$ such that*

$$\bar{p}(v_s) \equiv \exists k \in [v_s.start, v_s.end]\ \bar{p}'(v_s, k) \wedge \bar{p}''(v_s)$$

where $\bar{p}''(v_s)$ does not contain any existentially quantified variable over $[v_s.start, v_s.end]$. Then the guard predicate $\bar{p}(v'_s)$ is given by $\bar{p}(v'_s) = \bar{p}''(v'_s)$, where $\bar{p}''(v'_s)$ is obtained from $\bar{p}''(v_s)$ by replacing all occurrences of v_s by v'_s.

Definition 9 (Concatenation). *Concatenation operation is a binary operation $\oplus : \wp(\mathbb{V}) \times \wp(\mathbb{V}) \rightarrow \wp(\mathbb{V})$ of two video segments v'_s and v''_s. A video segment v_s is defined to be a concatenation of video segments v'_s and v''_s, denoted by $v_s = v'_s \oplus v''_s$, if*

- *$v'_s \oplus v''_s$ is a dense sequence of video frames*
- *$v'_s.pid = v''_s.pid = v_s.pid$*
- *$v'_s.end = v''_s.start$*
- *$v_s.start = v'_s.start$ and $v_s.end = v''_s.end$*

Note that, the concatenation operation is non-commutative, i.e., $v'_s \oplus v''_s \neq v''_s \oplus v'_s$. In other words, concatenation operation is a special case of sequential composition of video segments defined later.

Definition 10 (Contained-in). *Contained-in is a binary predicate* $\sqsubseteq \; : \wp(\mathbb{V}) \times \wp(\mathbb{V}) \to \{0,1\}$ *on video segments. A video segment v_s is contained-in a video segment v'_s, denoted by $v_s \sqsubseteq v'_s$, if and only if*

- $v_s.pid = v'_s.pid$
- $start(v'_s) \leq start(v_s) \leq end(v_s) \leq end(v'_s)$

Similarly, we define the **Contains** as the inverse operator of **Contained-in** and is denoted by $v_s \sqsupseteq v'_s$. The negation of contained-in and contains operation are denoted by, $v_s \not\sqsubseteq v'_s$ and $v_s \not\sqsupseteq v'_s$

Definition 11 (Overlap). *Overlap is a binary predicate* $\sqsubseteq\sqsupseteq \; : \wp(\mathbb{V}) \times \wp(\mathbb{V}) \to \{0,1\}$ *over video segments. A video segment v_s overlaps another video segment v'_s, denoted by $v_s \sqsubseteq\sqsupseteq v'_s$, if*

- $v_s.pid = v'_s.pid$
- either $start(v_s) \leq start(v'_s) \leq end(v_s) \leq end(v'_s)$
- or, $start(v'_s) \leq start(v_s) \leq end(v'_s) \leq end(v_s)$
- or, $v_s \sqsubseteq v'_s$
- or, $v_s \sqsupseteq v'_s$

Two segments v_s and v'_s strictly overlap if $v_s \sqsubseteq\sqsupseteq v'_s$ and neither $v_s \sqsubseteq v'_s$, nor $v_s \sqsupseteq v'_s$. It is written as $v_s \sqsubset\sqsupset v'_s$

The **containement** and **overlapping** operations are illustrated in Fig. 3

5.1 Temporal Relationships

Definition 12 (Follow). *The relation follow between video segments is denoted by $\succ$ and is defined as follows. Then $v_s \succ v'_s$ if*

- $v_s.pid = v'_s.pid$
- $start(v_s) \geq end(v'_s)$

Likewise, we introduce the relation **Followed-by** as an inverse relation of **Follow** and denote it as $v_s \prec v'_s$.

Definition 13 (Follows-immediate). *The relation follows-immediate between two video segments v_s and v'_s, denoted by $v_s \succ\succ v'_s$, and is defined if*

- $v_s \succ v'_s$
- $v_s.start = v'_s.end$

Similarly, we can define the relation **Followed-by-immediate** between two video segments v_s and v'_s, denoted by $v_s \prec\prec v'_s$, as the inverse relation of the relation **Follows-immediate**.

Lemma 2 (Reachability). *Let the video segments v_s and v'_s have following state-based guard predicates $\bar{p}(v_s)$ and $\bar{p}'(v'_s)$ respectively as follows:*

$$\bar{p}(v_s) : \forall k \in [v_s.start, v_s.end] \quad v_s[k].O.state = s_i$$

$$\bar{p}'(v'_s) : \forall k \in [v'_s.start, v'_s.end] \quad v'_s[l].O.state = s_j$$

Let $v_s \prec v'_s$. Then the state s_i must be reachable from the state s_j ($s_j \leadsto s_i$).

The formal definition of the term *reachable* is given in next section. Thus the guard predicates with state-based conditions can be linked to the state transition model of the underlying objects.

Definition 14 (Sequential Composition). *A sequential composition of two video segments v'_s and v''_s is denoted by $v_s = v'_s \star v''_s$, and is defined as follows. If $v'_s.pid = v''_s.pid$ and $v''_s \rightarrowtail v'_s$ then*

- $v_s.pid = v'_s.pid = v''_s.pid$
- $v_s.start = v'_s.start$
- $v_s.end = v''_s.end$

Otherwise, a new video is formed by this operation with

- *a new vid*
- $v_s.pid = NULL$
- $v_s.duration = v'_s.duration + v''_s.duration$

Obviously, for a video segment created by sequential composition of two segments, the set of objects in the new segment contains all objects present in the component video segments. Thus we make the following observation. Let v'_s and v''_s be two video segments and let the video segment $v_s = v'_s \star v''_s$ be the sequential composition of v'_s and v''_s. Then

$$\alpha(v_s) = \alpha(v'_s) \cup \alpha(v''_s)$$

Theorem 1. *Let v'_s and v''_s be two video segments with guard predicates $\bar{p}'(v'_s)$ and $\bar{p}''(v''_s)$ such that*

$$\bar{p}'(v'_s) \equiv \exists k_1 \in [v'_s.start, v'_s.end] \; \phi_1(k_1)$$

$$\bar{p}''(v''_s) \equiv \exists k_2 \in [v''_s.start, v''_s.end] \; \phi_2(k_2)$$

where ϕ_1 and ϕ_2 are wff involving bound variables k_1 and k_2 respectively. Then the guard predicate $\bar{p}(v_s)$ for the video segment $v_s = v'_s \star v''_s$ is given by

$$\bar{p}(v_s) \equiv \exists k_1, k_2 \in [v_s.start, v_s.end] \; (\phi_1(k_1) \wedge \phi_2(k_2))$$

However, for component segments with guard predicates having universally quantifiable variables, the guard predicate for resulting segment can be obtained as follows.

Theorem 2. *Let v'_s and v''_s be two video segments with guard predicates $\bar{p}'(v'_s)$ and $\bar{p}''(v''_s)$ such that*

$$\bar{p}'(v'_s) \equiv \forall\, k_1 \in [v'_s.start, v''_s.end]\; \phi_1(k_1)$$

$$\bar{p}''(v''_s) \equiv \forall\, k_2 \in [v''_s.start, v''_s.end]\; \phi_2(k_2)$$

where ϕ_1 and ϕ_2 are wff involving bound variables k_1 and k_2 respectively. Then guard predicate $\bar{p}(v_s)$ of the video segment $v_s = v'_s \star v''_s$ is given by

$$\bar{p}(v_s) \equiv \forall\, k \in [v_s.start, v_s.end]\; (\phi_1(k) \lor \phi_2(k))$$

We now introduce the parallel composition operator of two video segments. The motivation behind this idea was that if required user can view two segments of two different videos on the same screen but in two different windows. However, to compose two videos parallelly we need to ensure the synchronization of the component video segments. This means, the component segments must have been captured at same frame rate (number of frames captured per unit time).

For example, the "diastole" state of heart can be seen in both the Color Doppler echocardiogram and the ordinary echocardiogram video. Now, to see the heart in that state from these two videos in two different windows, we first segment the videos on the basis of a guard predicate related to "diastole" state and then do the parallel composition of these segments. Note that, the fact that the heart is in "diastole" state can be expressed uniquely by a predicate irrespective of mode of capturing video. Hence, a state-based guard predicate $\bar{p}$ for "diastole" segment is true for such segments of ordinary echocardiogram as well as Color Doppler echocardiogram.

Definition 15 (Parallel Composition). *Parallel composition of two video segments v'_s and v''_s is written as $v_s = v'_s \amalg v''_s$ and is defined as*

- *v_s is a complex video with component videos v'_s and v''_s*
- *$v'_s.duration = v''_s.duration = v_s.duration$*
- *$\alpha(v_s) = \alpha(v'_s) \cup \alpha(v''_s)$*

The guard condition of a complex video segment created by parallel composition of two simple video segments is obtained as follows.

Theorem 3. *Let v'_s and v''_s be two video segments with guard predicates $\bar{p}'(v'_s)$ and $\bar{p}''(v''_s)$ respectively. Let $v_s = v'_s \amalg v''_s$. Then*

$$\bar{p}(v_s) = \bar{p}'(v'_s) \land \bar{p}''(v''_s)$$

6 State-Based Retrieval

In the above sections we have introduced the syntax and semantics of the algebra for video. In the proposed model we incorporate the temporal information of video in terms of the states and state transition of the objects. The states and

the state-transitions of the objects are defined by appropriate guard predicates. Thus the state-transition mapping can be considered as an extensional database (EDB) which enables us to capture the temporal relationships among objects. To proceed further, we define the relation *reachable* with respect to the states of objects.
Let s_1 and s_2 be two states of an object O such that there exists a transition from state s_1 to state s_2 as described in the corresponding state transition diagram. The EDB predicate $next\_state(O.s_1, O.s_2)$ corresponds to the state transition table of O, where the state s_2 is reached as a consequence of a one-step transition from the state s_1. Thus,

Definition 16 (Reachable). *The relation* reachable, *denoted by* $s_1 \leadsto s_2$, *is defined recursively as follows*

- $reachable(O.s_1, O.s_2) \Leftarrow next\_state(O.s_1, O.s_2)$
- $rechable(O.s_1, O.s_2) \Leftarrow next\_state(O.s_1, O.s_3) \land reachable(O.s_3, O.s_2)$

Consider the relation *follow* ($\succ$) between two video segments v'_s and v''_s with guard predicates $\bar{p}'(v'_s)$ and $\bar{p}''(v''_s)$ respectively, where

$$\bar{p}'(v'_s) \equiv \forall k_1 \in [v'_s.start, v'_s.end](\exists O \in \alpha(v'_s.select\_frame(k_1)) \land O.state = \text{'}s_1\text{'}$$

$$\bar{p}''(v''_s) \equiv \forall k_2 \in [v''_s.start, v''_s.end](\exists O \in \alpha(v''_s.select\_frame(k_2)) \land O.state = \text{'}s_2\text{'}$$

The observation in lemma 2 of last section can now formally be expressed as given below.

$$v'_s \succ v''_s \land \bar{p}'(v'_s) \land \bar{p}''(v''_s) \Rightarrow reachable(O.s_1, O.s_2)$$

Also,

$$\bar{p}(v'_s) \land \bar{p}(v''_s) \land reachable(O.s_1, O.s_2) \Rightarrow v'_s \succ v''_s$$

Similar rules can be specified for other temporal relations such as *precede*, etc. These observations indicate that the proposed state-based video data model can be used to support associative retrieval of video segments depicting specific dynamic behaviour of the underlying objects. With this in view, we now briefly describe the echocardiogram video database.

The proposed echocardiogram video database (*Vdb*) contains following tables: (i) a Video table containing unique *vids*, *name* of video, *duration*, *camera-view*, etc. and any other information as required to the application domain; (ii) a State table containing unique *state-id*, *vid* (in which video it appears), *start-frame*, *end-frame* and *object-contained*; (iii) a set of Object tables containing *object-id*, *object-pid* (to describe the object containment) and a list of *attributes*, such as, *size*, *colour*, etc.; (iv) a Synchronization table containing *vid-1*, *vid-2*, *frame-1* and *frame-2* (the table keeps information about video objects that are synchronized and the respective frame numbers where the synchronization is valid). Depending on the application domain of video database there may be more than one object tables, e.g., Heart, Patient tables in echocardiogram video, Player table, Team table, etc. in a sports video database. Thus, to retrieve state-based information, the video is first indexed on *state-id* and then on *start-frame*. Hence, all video segments related to a particular state can be extracted from the (*start-frame, end-frame*) pair of the State table. The associated object properties can be obtained by joining the State table and the Object table(s). For parallel composition, the Synchronization table is used.

Therefore, a query to retrieve the segments v of echocardiogram video where an object, say *left_ventricle*, is in state, say *expanding* is written as,
select v **from** Vdb
where
$\qquad O$ in v **and** $O.name = $ '*left_ventricle*' **and** $O.state = $ '*expanding*'

Again, suppose we want to find the video segments v that precede a given video segment v' such that for an object O present in both the segments v and v', the state of O in v' is reachable from the state of O in v. Such a query can be expressed as follows.
select v **from** Vdb
where
$\qquad O$ in v **and** $O.state = s_1$
and
$\qquad O'$ **in** (**select** v' **from** Vdb
$\qquad\qquad$ **where** $O'.state = s_2$ **and** $O = O'$ **and** $reachable(O.s_1, O.s_2)$

7 Conclusion

In this paper, we have proposed a state-based approach to model video database. An algebra for the model has been introduced. The syntax and semantics of the video algebra have been discussed. Also, examples are given to illustrate how state-based queries can be formulated and appropriate information can be retrieved from the database. Further details in this direction will be discussed in our future works.

References

[1] Oomoto, E., Tanaka, K.: OVID: Design and implementation of a video-object database system. IEEE Transaction on Knowledge and Data Engg. **5** (1993) 629–643
[2] Hacid, M.S., Decleir, C., Kouloumdjian, J.: A database approach for modeling and querying video data. IEEE Transaction on Knowledge and Data Engg. **12** (2000) 729–750
[3] Marcus, S., V.S.Subrahmanian: Foundations of multimedia database systems. J. ACM **43** (1996) 474–523
[4] T.-S.Chua, Ruan, L.Q.: A video retrieval and sequencing system. ACM Trans. Information Processing **13** (1995) 373–407
[5] Yoshitaka, A., Hosoda, Y., Yoshimitsu, M., Hirakawa, M., Ichikawa, T.: VIOLONE: Video retrieval by motion example. J. Visual Languages and Computing **7** (1996) 423–443
[6] Booch, G., Rumbaugh, J., Jacobson, I., eds.: The Unified Modeling Language User Guide. 1 ISE edn. Addison-Wesley (1999)

Pockets of Flexibility in Workflow Specification

Shazia Sadiq, Wasim Sadiq*[1], Maria Orlowska[2]

School of Computer Science and Electrical Engineering
{shazia,maria}@csee.uq.edu.au
*Distributed Systems Technology Center
The University of Queensland
QLD 4072 Australia
wasim@dstc.edu.au

Abstract: Workflow technology is currently being deployed in quite diverse domains. However, the element of change is present in some degree and form in almost all domains. A workflow implementation that does not support the process of change will not benefit the organization in the long run. Change can be manifested in different forms in workflow processes. In this paper, we first present a categorization of workflow change characteristics and divide workflow processes into dynamic, adaptive and flexible processes. We define flexibility as the ability of the workflow process to execute on the basis of a loosely, or partially specified model, where the full specification of the model is made at runtime, and may be unique to each instance. To provide a modeling framework that offers true flexibility, we need to consider the factors, which influence the paths of (unique) instances together with the process definition. We advocate an approach that aims at making the process of change part of the workflow process itself. We introduce the notion of an open instance that consists of a core process and several pockets of flexibility, and present a framework based on this notion, which makes use of special build activities that provide the functionality to integrate the process of defining a change, into the open workflow instance.

1 Introduction

Workflows have emerged as a powerful technology for automating the coordinative and collaborative aspects of business processes. Workflow technology is being applied in quite diverse areas. This diversity has had a strong impact on workflow research. We can find in the literature [11], several categories of workflow types, such as production, collaborative, ad-hoc etc. To determine suitability of workflow technology, process characteristics such as functional complexity, predictability and repetitiveness are often considered, especially in the general class of *production*

---

[1] The work reported in this paper has been funded in part by the Cooperative Research Centres Program through the Department of the Prime Minister and Cabinet of the Commonwealth Government of Australia.
[2] Prof. Maria Orlowska is currently a visiting professor at the Department of Computer Science, Hong Kong University of Science and Technology.

workflows. However, the predictability and repetitiveness of production workflows cannot be counted upon, in the dynamic business environments of today, where processes are being continually changed in response to advances in technology, new methods and practices, and changes in laws and policies. Furthermore, these processes are often confronted by exceptional cases, and need to deviate from prescribed procedures without loosing control. These exceptional cases may or may not be foreseen. At the same time, proponents of CSCW [8] often speak of *adhoc* workflows, where the process cannot be completely defined prior to execution. Although we do not advocate ad-hocism in workflow processes to the extent of a complete relaxation of coordination constraints, it is obvious that ad-hocism is meant to promote flexibility of execution. There is sufficient evidence that process models that are too prescriptive introduce a rigidity that compromises the individualism and competitive edge of the underlying business procedures.

The necessity for the support of change in workflow systems is well recognized. Providing support for changing processes in workflow systems is, and has been for a few years, an active area of research [2], [3], [4], [15]. In the following sections, we will first provide a categorization of change characteristics in workflow processes, dividing them into dynamic, adaptive and flexible workflows.

This paper primarily deals with the last. In the subsequent sections, we will present a unique, generic and practical approach for the handling of flexible workflows. Our approach is based on the principle of recognizing change as an ongoing process, and integrating the process of change into the workflow process itself. The framework presented in this paper introduces the concept of a flexible workflow comprising of a core process and one or more pockets of flexibility within the core process. These pockets are concretized at runtime using special build activities. Building defines a template for a particular instance to follow and as such provides a means of flexible process definition, which as we shall demonstrate, would not be possible in a typical production-style workflow modeling framework.

2 Dimensions of Change in Workflows

We first introduce basic terminology for the sake of clarity. By a workflow **Model** we mean a definition of the tasks, ordering, data, resources, and other aspects of the process. Most, if not all, workflow models are represented as graphs which depict the flow of the process tasks, together with a description of other task properties. A workflow **Instance** is a particular occurrence of the process. An **Instance Type** is a set of instances that follow the same execution path within a given process model.

2.1 Dynamism

The first dimension represents dynamism - which is the ability of the workflow process to change when the business process evolves. This evolution may be slight as for process improvements, or drastic as for process innovation or process reengineering. In any case, the assumption is that the workflow processes have pre-defined models, and business process change, causes these models to be changed.

Pockets of Flexibility in Workflow Specification 515

The biggest problem here is the handling of active workflow instances, which were initiated in the old model, but need to comply now with the new specification. The issue of compliance is rather a serious issue, since potentially thousands of active instances may be affected by a given process change. Achieving compliance for these affected instances may involve loss of work and therefore has to be carefully planned [18].

A typical example of dynamic workflows can be found in university admissions. Consider a scenario of a large tertiary institute that processes thousands of admission applications every year. The procedure for application, review and acceptance is generally well defined and understood. Suppose that the office of postgraduate studies revises the admission procedure for postgraduate students, requiring all applicants to submit a statement of purpose together with their application for admission. To implement this change, there can be two options available; one is to *flush* all existing applications, and apply the change to new applications only. Thus all existing applications will continue to be processed according to the old process model. This requires the underlying workflow system to at least provide some version management support [7]. The second option to implement the change is to *migrate* to the new process. It may be decided that all applicants, existing and new, will be affected by the change. Thus all admission applications, which were initiated under the old rules, now have to migrate to the new process. This migration may involve addition of some transition workflow activities as well as rollback activities. Defining the migration strategy is a complex problem and has been the target of extensive research in this area [5], [9], [10], [13].

2.2 Adaptability

The second dimension of change is adaptability - which is the ability of the workflow processes to react to exceptional circumstances. These exceptional circumstances may or may not be foreseen, and generally would effect one or a few instances. Of course the handling of exceptions, which cannot be anticipated, is more complex. However, a large majority of exceptions can be anticipated [6], [17], and by capturing these exceptions, the adaptability of the workflow is promoted. In fact, unless these exceptions are captured within the workflow model, their handling will continue to be done outside of the system, in the form of "system workarounds", the consequences of which may come in conflict with process goals. However the complete set of exceptions for a given process can never be captured, thus dealing with unanticipated (true) exceptions will always be an issue [12], [14].

Using the same example as before, we can consider dealing with an admission application for a student with a multi-disciplinary background. For example, a student with a background in microbiology may be applying for a degree in IT. The review of this application may require the services of an academic outside the offering department. This may be rare but, if captured within the process model, could be handled within the workflow system.

Another example, which represents a true (unanticipated) exception, can be found in the employment workflow. An employment instance may have reached a stage where even the letter of intent has been issued. If at that time the organization issues a spending freeze, the active instances of the employment workflow will have to be dealt with, requiring rollback and/or compensation activities, even though the original employment workflow remains unchanged.

2.3 Flexibility

The third dimension is flexibility - which is the ability of the workflow process to execute on the basis of a loosely, or partially specified model, where the full specification of the model is made at runtime, and may be unique to each instance. Processes which depend on the presence of such flexibility for the satisfactory attainment of process goals can be found in many applications:
- A typical example of flexibility is healthcare, where patient admission procedures are predictable and repetitive, however, in-patient treatments are prescribed uniquely for each case, but none-the-less have to be coordinated and controlled.
- Another application is higher education, where students with diverse learning needs and styles are working towards a common goal (degree). Study paths taken by each student need to remain flexible to a large extent, at the same time providing study guidelines and enforcing course level constraints is necessary to ensure a certain quality of learning.
- Web content management is also characterized by flexible processes, where especially in large projects, every development suggests the need for an overall plan to provide the objectives, approvals, and strategy, as well as a flexible means of coordinating the combined efforts of the theme designers, graphic experts, programmers, and project planners.
- Effective Customer Relationship Management (CRM), a critical component in enterprise solutions, also signifies the need to provide a flexible means of composing call center activities according to the available resources and data, by integrating CRM systems with core organizational workflow processes and underlying applications.

The key issue in flexible workflows is the modeling of the loose or partial workflow. Thus rather than enforcing control through a rigid, or highly prescriptive model that attempts to capture every step and every option within the process, the model is defined in a more relaxed or "flexible" manner, that allows individual instances to determine their own (unique) processes. How to achieve such an approach to modeling is the main focus of this paper.

3 Framework for Flexible Workflows

Several workflow products and research prototypes exist. Most, if not all, provide process modeling tools that follow some variation of the workflow modeling language introduced by the workflow coalition [21]. In Figure 1, we briefly introduce the basic structures of a generic workflow modeling language [19], also based on the coalition standards to a large extent. This language will be used in later sections to illustrate various examples.

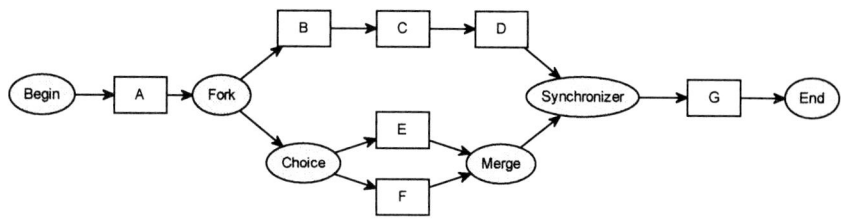

Fig 1. Workflow Modeling Language

In terms of a prescriptive language as above, one can say that the degree of flexibility is indicated by the number of instance types that can be generated from the process model. Number of instance types have a direct correlation with the number of choice constructs found within the process model [20]. For example in the above figure, a choice-merge construct encapsulates two activities, E and F. In any given execution of this process, only one of E or F will be executed. Thus the process has two instance types. This is a straightforward and well-understood concept.

However, consider a scenario where a process generates a very large number of instance types, that is, demands a high degree of flexibility. Suppose that a large number, say k number of paths are present within a choice-merge construct. Each of these paths potentially represents a complex sub-process. There can be several such constructs within the process model, which may include nesting also. One can see that a typical workflow language may not provide a very elegant means of representing such a process. In order to seek some alternative way of modeling, let us start first with some simple approaches.

- Flexibility by Definition: Flexibility may be built into the model through choice merge constructs. Limitations of this approach have already been discussed. This would result in a highly complex model, which in some cases may still be incomplete.
- Flexibility by Granularity: Flexibility may be achieved by encapsulating activity details within workflow tasks, and keeping sub-activities 'internal' (and flexible), or outside the direct control of the workflow [16]. This approach can be applied to a limited extent, but it cannot be used at a generic level without compromising the purpose of deploying workflow technology, namely to coordinate and control the flow of process activities.
- Flexibility by Templates: Flexibility may be achieved by providing separate templates for a given (set of) instance type. This slightly improves the readability and consequently maintainability of the model. However, choosing an instance type from a set of templates rather than one model with many choices will have advantages only if the number of templates can be restricted to a reasonably small number.

A common disadvantage of the above approaches is that they still rely on a prescriptive model. Thus, not only is it cumbersome to model all choices in flexible processes, there may be choices which cannot be anticipated. Flexibility as we defined it earlier, is the ability of the workflow process to execute on the basis of a partial model, where the full specification is made at *runtime*. To provide a modeling framework that offers true flexibility, we need to consider the factors, which influence the paths of (unique) instances together with the process definition. In the following section, we present our approach to defining the flexible workflow, which aims at achieving the above.

3.1 Defining the Flexible Workflow

Almost all workflow enactment systems differentiate between the two aspects of workflow specification, namely, the workflow process and the workflow execution (control) data. Traditionally, the process model defines the process logic that provides the schema for particular instances. Workflow execution data on the other hand, consists of *work items*, where each work item relates to a particular execution of an activity. The work item thus stores all execution parameters of a particular activity such as client assigned, relevant data, and temporal values. In view of the specific requirements for modeling and enacting flexible workflows, we present a variant of the typical specification framework. Since flexible workflows need to consider the factors that dictate the individual instance paths, our approach aims at bridging these two aspects. The fundamental feature of our approach is:

- To introduce a layer between the definition and execution data. This represents an *open* copy of the workflow model, for a particular instance, and
- To have a workflow model which in itself constitutes only the *partial* definition.

Model Specification

The specification of the partial, which we now call the *flexible* workflow consists of:
- A defined *core process* containing
    - Identifiable (pre-defined) workflow activities
    - *Pockets of flexibility* within the process with an associated
        - Set of *workflow fragments*, where a workflow fragment may consist of a single activity, or a sub-process
        - Special workflow activity called the *build activity* that provides the rules for concretizing the pocket with a valid composition of workflow fragments.

The assumption is that the control flow between the fragments is not completely defined in the core process. The concept of pockets of flexibility aims at compensating for this inability to completely specify the process. The concept as such, is thus not limited to the workflow modeling language used to demonstrate the examples in this paper. As shown in figure 2, the pocket can simply be seen as a special BUILD activity within the workflow model, together with the set of workflow fragments from which the build activity will form a valid composition.

Current workflow products and projects have introduced an assortment of workflow modeling languages that support several variants of the typical (Sequence, Choice, Fork and Iteration) modeling constructs [1]. Introducing flexibility of specification by introducing more constructs within the modeling language has many drawbacks. There is often a semantic overlap in many of these constructs, making it difficult to define and verify. Furthermore, their enactment introduces unnecessary complexity in the workflow engine, limiting its scope and interoperability. However, the pocket concept provides the means for flexible definition without compromising the genericity or simplicity of the modeling language. We shall demonstrate this further in subsequent sections.

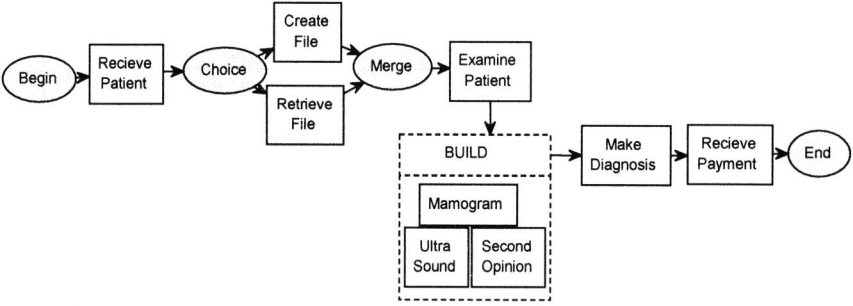

Fig 2. Specifying the Flexible Workflow

In figure 2, we give an example of a flexible workflow representing a typical diagnostic process for investigation of breast cancer. A new patient coming into the center will first be entered into the system, or the file of an old patient will be retrieved. All patients then consult with an attending physician, who will determine what tests need to be performed, on a case-by-case basis. This forms the pocket of flexibility for the process. After the tests, the patient is called again by the attending physician who explains the results of the tests and makes a diagnosis. The patient is then required to report to accounts to make the required payments before leaving the center.

Instance Specification

The instance specification initially consists of a copy of the core process. As a particular instance proceeds with execution, the build activities provide the means of customizing the core process for that particular instance. The instance specification prior to building, we call an *open instance*. The instance specification after building we call an *instance template*. Thus the instance template is a particular composition of the fragments within the flexible workflow. The instance templates in turn have a schema-instance relationship with the underlying execution data. In traditional terms, the instance template acts as the process model for a particular instance. Execution takes place with full enforcement of all coordination and temporal constraints, as in a typical production workflow. However, template building is progressive. The core process may contain several pockets of flexibility which will be concretized through the associated build activities as they are encountered. As such, the template remains *open* until the last built activity has completed.

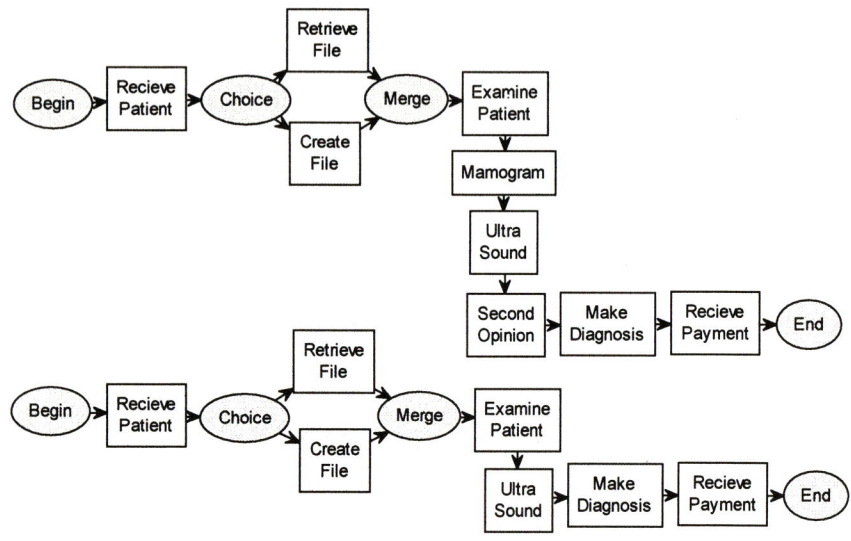

Fig 3. Instance Templates

In figure 3, we give example instance templates for the flexible workflow given in figure 4. Execution will commence with the initial activity of the core process, which establishes the creation of the instance and necessary data. After successful completion[3] of the initial activity and subsequent activities, a pocket of flexibility is encountered, and the associated build activity is activated. The execution of the build activity replaces the open instance with the instance template, which in turn serves as a process model for that instance.

A critical question however is, why is the instance template in figure 4 a valid composition. Where, validity relates to the semantic correctness of the composition in relation to the process under consideration. Valid instance templates must be ensured through the build rules captured within the build activities. Building may be constrained by several factors, including at least the data relating to that instance, the stage of execution of the instance, temporal constraints, and the business rules of the particular application for which the template is being defined. For example, in education, it will be constrained by the progress of the student, such that at any given stage of the study process, the student can build the template from a specified set of study activities. A student, for example, cannot take up a study activity whose prerequisites have not been met.

3.2 Building Instance Templates

The functionality of the build activity is fundamental to this approach. In this section we will discuss and identify the set of parameters that are essential to define a build activity at a generic level.

---

[3] We ignore failure of workflow activities at this time

First of all there is no reason why the build activity should allow building from existing fragments only. There are several examples of processes, where entirely new (unprecedented and hence not pre-defined) activities have to be performed for a given instance, and perhaps subsequently used for other instances. By extending the functionality of the build activity, processes with such a high level of flexibility can also be catered for. We see the build activity providing one of the following:

- Fully Automated Support: The Build activity automatically builds the instance template from the given set of workflow fragments based on the instance data and given constraints.
- Partially Automated Support: The Build activity invokes an application program that allows a workflow client, to build the instance template from the given set of workflow fragments, but within given constraints.
- Manual Control: The Build activity allows a workflow client to define new fragments, and then build the instance template from the new as well as existing fragments.

Secondly, there will be constraints on the *extent* of building. For example, a student may be allowed to take not more than 4 subjects consecutively. Extents may also be defined on the basis of other factors such as temporal properties. For example, a doctor may prescribe tests to be performed in the next 3 days. Thus building will be restricted by both the pool of workflow activities (fragments) that are available for selection, as well as the extent of selection.

Lastly, there is the question of composing the selected fragments. From an engineering point of view, the workflow client may not (rather should not) be given an interface to compose the fragments using a complex workflow modeling language. Instead, we see the build activity as another application within the process, since making an assumption about the user's knowledge of process models and workflow languages is unrealistic. This is a strong justification of the argument that our approach integrates the process of change within the workflow process. Behind the build application, an instance template will be composed, and made available to the workflow engine. In the following sections, we will discuss the ways of composing selected workflow fragments, explaining how each of these compositions provide a means of capturing flexible specifications without compromising the simplicity of the modeling language.

Sequence

The build activity allows workflow fragments to be arranged in sequence. However, the choice of order remains flexible and is determined by the user during the build activity. Figure 4 gives an example composition using the sequence construct.

It is interesting to note that this flexibility of composition contradicts conventional sequential constraints, where "A is followed by B" indicates a control flow dependency between A and B. This dependency cannot be established in the above scenario. However, such a flexible sequential composition is required to fulfill constraints such as "Do all of A, B and C, but one at a time".

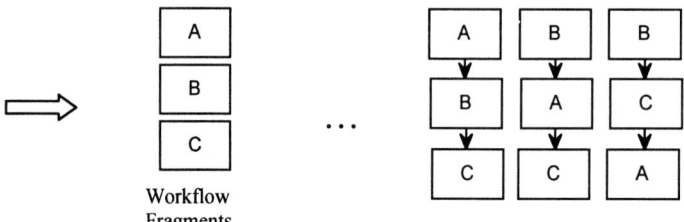

Fig 4. Building Sequential Constructs

Fork

The build activity introduces a fork coordinator and arranges selected workflow fragments in a fork structure. Flexibility of definition is especially required when the fork can be built from any number of fragments. A typical constraint for the above can be "Do any 3 of A, B, C or D". Figure 5 shows the various templates that the build activity can compose using a fork construct.

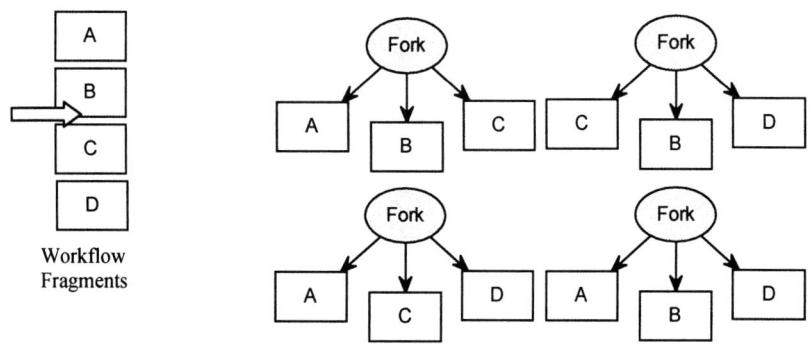

Fig 5. Building Fork Constructs

Synchronize

Instance templates that contain the fork construct, will require the fragments constituting the fork to be synchronized at some point. Synchronization can be achieved in one of two ways:

1. Immediate Synchronization: A synchronizer is added as part of the build activity that introduces the fork. This is a simple option as illustrated in Figure 6 (a). Providing synchronization within the pocket preserves its boundary, and provides a clean connection to the core process.
2. Deferred Synchronization: Synchronizing may be premature at this stage for some applications, and may unnecessarily hold up the progress of the instance. For

example Figure 6(b) shows a template built against the constraint, "Do all of A, B and C, but do not wait for A to complete. In this case it has to be ensured that eventually all multiple branches will be synchronized, or at least completed before the core process completes.

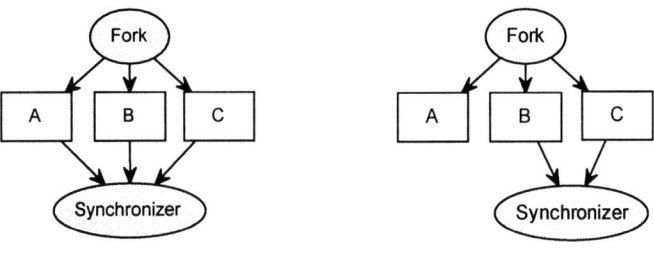

a. Immediate Synchronization   b. Deferred Synchronization

Fig 6. Building Synchronizing Constructs

Choice and Merge

While choice and merge constructs may be present within workflow fragments, we propose that these constructs not be used to build the instance template. Since an instance template represents a particular occurrence of the workflow process, the choices should be made during the execution of the build activity. For example, the constraint "Do any one of A, B or C" will be built as either A or B or C, and not all within a choice-merge construct. The elimination of the choice-merge construct from the instance template, further has the advantage of simplifying the model, and removing the chance of deadlocks or lack of synchronization [19].

Iteration

Iteration and/or multiple executions may take many forms [1]. The build activity can provide these constructs with significant convenience as compared to pre-defined models.

1. Arbitrary Cycles: A fragment may be encapsulated in a typical do-while/repeat-until construct, with a given condition for iteration.
2. Multiple Executions: The case of multiple executions is more interesting. A fragment may be required to be executed any k number of times, for example to fulfill the constraint " Do A k number of times" where k is instance dependent. Figure 7 illustrates the possibilities for multiple execution of A, which can be (a) multiple executions in sequence, or (b) multiple executions in a fork.

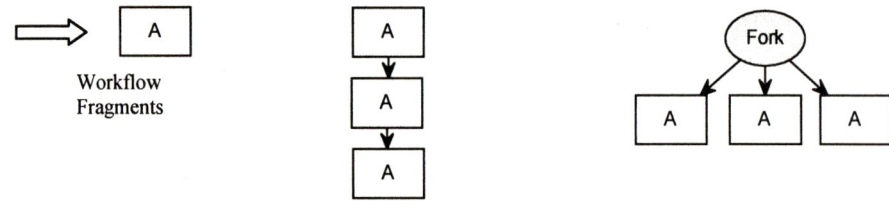

a. Multiple Executions in Sequence **b.** Multiple Executions in a Fork

Fig 7. Building Multiple Executions

The above discussion reveals the fact that the build activity is a fundamental object of constraint specification in this framework. These constraints represent the process logic of the application under consideration. The challenge is to identify a generic set of parameters, which would allow the customization of the build activity. We identify the following three factors, which *at least* need to be specified, in order to customize a build activity for a given application:

- Type: Whether the selection of the workflow fragments will be (fully/ partially) automated or manually controlled. This determines the available pool of workflow fragments.
- Extent: How many fragments can be selected from the available pool.
- Structure: What modeling construct will be used to compose the selected fragments.

The design of an appropriate language which facilitates the specification of build rules and constraints is a whole new, interesting and challenging research issue. The functionality of the process definition tool must be extended with the ability to define the pockets of flexibility. Also, the build activities must have the ability to access and change open instances as they execute. There are several interesting architectural implications of this framework. Currently, we are working on extending the functionality of a process modeling and verification tool FlowMake [http://www.dstc.edu.au/praxis], to incorporate the concept of pockets of flexibility.

4 Conclusions

Difficulties in dealing with change in workflow systems has been one of the major factors limiting the deployment of workflow technology. At the same time, it is apparent that change is an inherent characteristic of today's business processes. This paper provides a comprehensive categorization of change characteristics in workflow processes, based on which we present an approach that recognizes the presence of change, and attempts to integrate the process of defining a change into the workflow process itself. Our basic idea is to provide a powerful means of capturing the logic of highly flexible processes without compromising the simplicity and genericity of the workflow specification language. This we accomplish through pockets of flexibility in workflow specifications, which allow workflow processes to be tailored to individual instances at runtime.

Acknowledgements

The authors would like to acknowledge the comments and feedback provided by Karsten Schulz at the Distributed Systems Technology Center, Brisbane, Australia.

References

1. W.M.P. van der Aalst, A.P. Barros, A.H.M. ter Hofstede, and B. Kiepuszewski. Advanced Workflow Patterns. O. Etzion and P. Scheuremann, editors, Proceedings Seventh IFCIS International Conference on Cooperative Information Systems, CoopIS 2000, Volume 1901 of Lecture Notes in Computer Science, pages 18-29, Eilat, Israel. Springer-Verlag. September (2000).
2. W.M.P. van der Aalst and S. Jablonski. Dealing with Workflow Change: Identification of issues and solutions International Journal of Computer Systems, Science, and Engineering, 15(5):267-276, (2000).
3. S. Ellis, K. Keddara , G. Rozenberg. Dynamic Changes within Workflow Systems. Proceedings of ACM Conference on Organizational Computing Systems COOCS 95 (1995).
4. J Eder, W. Liebhart. The workflow activity model WAMO. Proceedings of the 3rd international conference on Cooperative Information Systems (CoopIs), Vienna, Austria, May (1995).
5. Fabio Casati, S. Ceri, B. Pernici, G. Pozzi. Workflow Evolution. In Proceedings of the 15th International Conference on Conceptual Modeling, ER'96, Cottbus, Germany. Springer Verlag, Lecture Notes in Computer Science (1996).
6. Fabio Casati, Giuseppe Pozzi. Modeling Exception Behaviors in Commercial Workflow Management Systems. Proceedings of the Fourth IFCIS International Conference on Cooperative Information Systems (CoopIS99). Edinburgh, Scotland. Sep 2-4, (1999).
7. Gregor Joeris, Otthein Herzog. Managing Evolving Workflow Specifications. Proceedings of the third IFCIS International Conference on Cooperative Information Systems (CoopIS 98). NewYork, USA. Aug (1998).
8. Mark Klein, Chrysanthos Dellarocas, Abraham Bernstein (eds.) Workshop on Adaptive Workflow Systems. Conference on Computer Supported Cooperative Work (CSCW), Seattle, USA. November (1998).
9. Markus Kradolfer, Andreas Geppert. Dynamic Workflow Schema Evolution based on Workflow Type Versioning and Workflow Migration. Proccedings of the Fourth IFCIS International Conference on Cooperative Information Systems (CoopIS99). Edinburgh, Scotland. Sep 2-4, (1999).
10. Chengfei Liu, Maria Orlowska, Hui Li. Automating Handover in Dynamic Workflow Environments. Proceedings of 10th International Conference on Advances in Information System Engineering (CAiSE 98), Pisa, Italy, June (1998).
11. Mohan C. Tutorial: State of the Art in Workflow Management System Research and Products, 5th International Conference on Extending Database Technology, Avignon, France, March (1996).

12. Manfred Reichert, Peter Dadam. ADEPTflex - Supporting Dynamic Changes of Workflow without loosing control. Journal of Intelligent Information Systems (JIIS), Special Issue on Workflow and Process Management (1998).
13. Shazia Sadiq. Handling Dynamic Schema Change in Process Models. Australian Database Conference, Canberra, Australia. Jan 27 - Feb 02, (2000).
14. Shazia Sadiq. On Capturing Exceptions in Workflow Process Models. Proceedings of the 4th International Conference on Business Information Systems. Poznan, Poland. April 12 - 13 (2000).
15. Amit Sheth. From Contemporary Workflow Process Automation to Adaptive and Dynamic Work Activity Coordination and Collaboration. Siggroup Bulletin, 18(3):17-20, (1997).
16. Keith D. Swensen, Kent Irwin. Workflow Technology: Tradeoffs for Business Process Re-engineering. Proceedings of ACM Conference on Organizational Computing Systems (COOCS 95), Milpitas, CA. USA, Nov (1995).
17. Diane M. Strong, Steven M. Miller. Exceptions and Exception Handling in Computerized Information Processes, ACM Transactions on Information Systems, Vol. 13, No 2, Pages 206-233, April (1995).
18. Shazia Sadiq, Olivera Marjanovic, Maria E. Orlowska. Managing Change and Time in Dynamic Workflow Processes. International Journal of Cooperative Information Systems. Vol. 9, Nos. 1 & 2. March -June (2000).
19. Wasim Sadiq, Maria E. Orlowska. On Correctness Issues in Conceptual Modeling of Workflows. In Proceedings of the 5th European Conference on Information Systems (ECIS '97), Cork, Ireland, June 19-21, (1997).
20. Wasim Sadiq, Maria E. Orlowska. Analyzing Process Models using Graph Reduction Techniques. Information Systems, Vol. 25, No. 2, pp. 117-134, 2000. Elsevier Science. June (2000).
21. Workflow Management Coalition. Interface 1: Process Definition Interchange, Process Model, Document Number WfMC TC-1016-p. (1998).

Agent-Oriented Enterprise Modeling Based on Business Rules

Kuldar Taveter[1] and Gerd Wagner[2]

[1] VTT Information Technology (Technical Research Centre of Finland),
P.O.Box 1201, FIN-02044 VTT, Finland,
kuldar.taveter@vtt.fi
[2] Eindhoven University of Technology, Faculty of Technology Management,
P.O. Box 513, 5600 MB Eindhoven, The Netherlands,
G.Wagner@tm.tue.nl
http://tmitwww.tm.tue.nl/staff/gwagner

Abstract. Business rules are statements that express (certain parts of) a business policy, defining business terms and defining or constraining the operations of an enterprise, in a declarative manner. Since these rules define and constrain the interaction among business agents in the course of business processes, they have to refer to the components of their mental state, such as the knowledge/information and the commitments of an organization. We propose an agent-oriented approach to business rules and show how to represent and visualize business rules and business processes in Agent-Object-Relationship modeling.

1 Introduction

Agent-Orientation is emerging as a new paradigm in software and information systems engineering. It offers a range of high-level abstractions that facilitate the conceptual and technical integration of communication and interaction with established information system technology. Agent-Orientation is highly significant for business information systems since business processes are driven by and directed towards agents (or *actors*), and hence have to comply with the physical and social dynamics of interacting individuals and institutions.

While today's enterprise information system technology is largely based on the metaphors of *data management* and *data flow*, and is under pressure to adopt concepts and techniques from the highly successful object-oriented programming paradigm, Agent-Orientation emphasizes the fundamental role of actors/agents[1] and their mental state, and of communication and interaction, for analyzing and designing organizations and organizational information systems. This turns out to be crucial for a proper understanding of business rules. Since these rules define and constrain the interactions among business agents, they have to refer to the components of their mental state, such as the knowledge/information and the commitments of an organization.

---
[1] We use the terms 'actor' and 'agent' as synonyms.

We attempt to show that our agent-oriented approach, that is based on the Agent-Object-Relationship (AOR) metamodel proposed in [Wag01a, Wag01b], allows to capture more of the dynamic and deontic semantics of enterprise modeling than object-oriented modeling approaches, such as the UML, do. Taking into account that the main motivation for object-oriented modeling stems from software engineering and not from enterprise modeling, or cognitive modeling, this should not be surprising.

The rest of the paper is organized as follows. In Section 2, we review the relevant literature on business rules, and present our own definitions of business rules and business processes. In Section 3, we review the Agent-Object-Relationship (AOR) metamodel which we use as the basis of our agent-oriented business rule modeling. Finally, in Section 4, we discuss the formalization and visualization of business rules on the basis of the AOR metamodel.

2 Business Rules and Business Processes

According to Martin and Odell [MO98], business rules allow user experts to specify policies in *small, stand-alone units* using explicit statements. The term *business rule* can be understood both at the level of a business domain and at the operational level of an information system. The more fundamental concept are business rules at the level of a business domain. In certain cases, they can be automated by implementing them in an information system, preferably in the form of an executable specification. It should be the goal of advanced information system technology to provide more support for business rules in the form of high-level machine-executable declarative specifications, similar to the SQL concepts of *assertions* and *triggers*.

2.1 Business Rules at the Business Level

At the business level, a business rule is defined as

- a statement about how the business is done, i.e., about guidelines and restrictions with respect to states and processes in an organization [Her97];
- a law or custom that guides the behaviour or actions of the actors connected to the organization [Ass88];
- a declaration of policy or condition that must be satisfied [OMG, 1992].

Business rules can be enforced on the business from the outside environment by regulations or laws, or they can be defined within the business to achieve the goals of the business. A business rule is based on a *business policy*. An example of a business policy in a car rental company is "only cars in legal, roadworthy condition can be rented to customers" [HH00]. Business rules are *declarative* statements: they describe *what* has to be done or *what* has to hold, but not *how*.

Our definition of business rules is based on [HH00], [Ass88], [KK92], and [BBS]: ***Business rules are statements that express*** (certain parts of) ***a*** *business policy, such as defining business terms, defining deontic assignments (of powers, rights and duties), and defining or constraining the operations of an enterprise, in a declarative manner* (not describing/prescribing every detail of their implementation).

According to [HH00] and [MDC99], business rules can be divided into 'structural assertions' (or 'term rules' and 'fact rules'), 'action rules', and 'derivation rules'.[2] Similarly, Bubenko et al [BBS] categorize business rules into 'constraint rules', 'event-action rules', and 'derivation rules', while Martin and Odell [MO98] group rules into two broad classes, 'constraint rules' and 'derivation rules' (remarkably, they subsume 'stimulus response rules' – which we call *reaction rules* – under 'constraint rules'). [Her97] distinguishes between 'integrity rules' (that are further divided into static and dynamic integrity constraints) and 'automation rules'.

In [HH00], a further class of business rules, *authorizations*, is proposed. Authorizations represent a particular type of *deontic assignments*. Synonyms for authorizations are *rights* and *permissions*. They define the privileges of an agent (type) with respect to certain (types of) actions. Complementary to rights, we also consider *duties*.

In summary, three basic types of business rules have been identified in the literature: *integrity constraints* (also called 'constraint rules' or 'integrity rules'), *derivation rules*, and *reaction rules* (also called 'stimulus response rules', 'action rules', 'event-action rules', or 'automation rules'). A fourth type, *deontic assignments*, has only been partially identified (in the proposal of considering 'authorizations' as business rules).

An ***integrity constraint*** is a an assertion that must be satisfied in all evolving states and state transition histories of an enterprise viewed as a discrete dynamic system. There are state constraints and process constraints. *State constraints* must hold at any point in time. An example of a state constraint is: "a customer of the car rental company EU-Rent must be at least 25 years old". *Process constraints* refer to the dynamic integrity of a system; they restrict the admissible transitions from one state of the system to another. A process constraint may, for example, declare that the admissible state changes of a `RentalOrder` object are defined by the following transition path: *reserved → allocated → effective → dropped-off*.

A ***derivation rule*** is a statement of knowledge that is derived from other knowledge by an inference or a mathematical calculation. Derivation rules capture terminological and heuristic domain knowledge that need not to be stored explicitly because it can be derived from existing or other derived information on demand. An example of a derivation rules is: "the rental rate of a rental is inferred from the rental rate of the group of the car assigned to the rental".

---

[2] 'Structural assertions' introduce the definitions of business entities and describe the connections between them. Since they can be captured by a conceptual model of the problem domain, e.g. by an Entity-Relationship (ER) or a UML class model, we do not consider them as business *rules* but rather as forming the business *vocabulary* (or *ontology*).

Reaction rules are concerned with the invocation of actions in response to events. They state the conditions under which actions must be taken; this includes triggering event conditions, pre-conditions, and post-conditions (effects). An example of a reaction rule from the domain of car rental is: "when receiving from a customer the request to reserve a car of some specified car group, the branch checks with the headquarter to make sure that the customer is not blacklisted".

Deontic assignments of powers, rights and duties to (types of) internal agents define the deontic structure of an organization, guiding and constraining the actions of internal agents. An example of a deontic assignment statement is: "only the branch manager has the right to grant special discounts to customers".

The triggering event conditions in the definitions of reaction rules in [HH00], [Her97], [BBS], and [MDC99] are either explicitly or implicitly bound to update events in databases. Depending on some condition on the database state, they may lead to an update action and to system-specific procedure calls. In contrast to this, we choose the more general concept of a reaction rule as proposed in [Wag98]. Reaction rules define the behaviour of an agent in response to environment events (perceived by the agent), and to communication events (created by communication acts of other agents).

2.2 Business Rules at the Level of an Information System

In certain cases, business rules expressed at the business level can be automated by mapping them to executable code at the information system level as shown in Table 1.

Concept	*Implementation*
Constraints	if-then statements in programming languages; `DOMAIN`, `CHECK` and `CONSTRAINT` clauses in SQL table definitions; `CREATE ASSERTION` statements in SQL database schema definitions
Derivation Rules	deductive database (or Prolog) rules; SQL `CREATE VIEW` statements
Reaction Rules	if-then statements in programming languages; `CREATE TRIGGER` statements in SQL; production rules in 'expert systems';

Table 1. Mapping of business rules from the business level to the information system level using currently available technology.

This mapping is, however, not one-to-one, since programming languages and database management systems offer only limited support for it. While general purpose programming languages do not support any of the three types of expressions (with the exception of the object-oriented language Eiffel that supports integrity constraints in the form of 'invariants' for object classes), SQL has some built-in support for constraints, derivation rules (views), and limited forms of reaction rules (triggers).

2.3 Business Processes

Business rules define and control *business processes*. A widely accepted definition of a business process is [Dav92]: "A business process can be defined as a collection of activities that takes one or more kinds of input, and creates an output that is of value to the customer". In [HC93] this definition is paraphrased by stating: "A [business] process is simply a structured set of activities designed to produce a specified output for a particular customer or market". A business process describes from start to finish the sequence of events required to produce the product or service [YWT$^+$96]. A business process is assumed to consume input in terms of information and/or material and produce output of information and/or material [BBS]. Business processes typically involve several different functional organization units. Often business processes also cross organizational boundaries.

We prefer to adopt a more general perspective and consider a business process as a special kind of a *social interaction process*. Unlike physical or chemical processes, social interaction processes are based on communication acts that may create commitments and are governed by norms. We distinguish between an interaction process type and a concrete interaction process (instance), while in the literature the term 'business process' is ambiguously used both at the type and the instance level.

We thus refine and extend the definitions of [YWT$^+$96], [HC93], and [Dav92]: *A business process is a social interaction process for the purpose of doing business.* According to [Wag01b], a *social interaction process* is a temporally ordered, coherent set of events and actions, involving one or more communication acts, perceived and performed by agents, and following a set of rules, or protocol, that is governed by norms, and that specifies the type of the interaction process. Notice that we did not choose *activities* as the basic elements of a process. While an *action* happens at a time point (i.e., it is immediate), an *activity* is being performed during a time interval (i.e., it has duration), and consists of a set of actions.

We propose to model both business rules and business processes in the framework of the *Agent-Object-Relationship* metamodel reviewed in Section 3.

3 Principles of Agent-Object-Relationship Modeling

Agent-Object-Relationship (AOR) diagrams were proposed in [Wag01a, Wag01b] as an agent-oriented extension of Entity-Relationship diagrams, or UML-style class diagrams. In order to capture more semantics of the dynamic and deontic aspects of organizations and organizational information systems, such as the events and actions related to the ongoing business processes of an enterprise, it is proposed to make an ontological distinction between active and passive entities, that is, between *agents* and *ordinary objects*. AOR modeling suggests that the semantics of business transactions can be more adequately captured if the specific **business agents** associated with the involved events and actions are explicitly represented in organizational information systems in addition to passive **business objects**.

In AOR modeling, an entity is either an *agent*, an *event*, an *action*, a *claim*, a *commitment*, or an *ordinary object*. An organization is viewed as a complex **institutional agent** defining the rights and duties of its internal agents that act on behalf of it, and being involved in a number of interactions with external agents. **Internal agents** may be humans, artificial agents (such as software agents, agentified information systems, robots or agentified embedded systems), or institutional agents (such as organizational units).

As usual, entity types are visually represented by rectangles while relationship types are represented by connection lines (possibly with crows feet endings in order to indicate multiplicity). While an *object type* is visualized as an ordinary rectangle, an *agent type* is graphically rendered as a rectangle with rounded corners. An internal agent type is visualized by such a rectangle with a dashed line drawn within the institutional agent rectangle it belongs to (like Branch in Fig. 1). An instance of an agent type is distinguished from an agent type by underlining its name (like the EU-Rent in Fig. 1).

3.1 Actions and Events

In a business domain, there are various types of actions performed by agents, and there are various types of state changes, including the progression of time, that occur in the environment of the agents. For an external observer, both actions and environmental state changes constitute events. In the internal perspective of an agent that acts in the business domain, only the actions of other agents count as events.

Actions create events, but not all events are created by actions. Those events that are created by actions, such as delivering a product to a customer, are called **action events**. Examples of business events that are not created by actions are the fall of a particular stock value below a certain threshold, the sinking of a ship in a storm, or a timeout in an auction.

We make a distinction between *communicative* and *non-communicative* actions and events. Many typical business events, such as receiving a purchase order or a sales quotation, are communication events. Business communication may be viewed as asynchronous point-to-point message passing. The expressions *receiving a message* and *sending a message* may be considered to be synonyms of *perceiving a communication event* and *performing a communication act*.

As opposed to the low-level (and rather technical) concept of messages in object-oriented programming, AOR modeling assumes the high-level semantics of speech-act-based *Agent Communication Language (ACL)* messages (see [KQM, FIP]).

3.2 Commitments and Claims

Commitments are fundamental components of business interaction processes. This is acknowledged by the ebXML standardization initiative in the statement

"The business semantics of each commercial transaction are defined in terms of the Business Objects affected, and the *commitment(s)* formed or agreed."[3]

Representing and processing commitments and claims in information systems explicitly helps to achieve coherent behavior in interaction processes. In [Sin99], the social dimension of coherent behavior is emphasized, and commitments are treated as ternary relationships between two agents and a 'context group' they both belong to. For simplicity, we treat commitments as binary relationships between two agents.

Commitments to perform certain actions, or to see to it that certain conditions hold, typically arise from certain communication acts. For instance, sending a sales quotation to a customer commits the vendor to reserve adequate stocks of the quoted item for some time. Likewise, acknowledging a sales order implies the creation of a commitment to deliver the ordered items on or before the specified delivery date.

Some of these modeling concepts are *indexical*, that is, they depend on the perspective chosen: in the perspective of a particular agent, **actions** of other agents are viewed as **events**, and **commitments** of other agents are viewed as **claims** against them.

In the internal perspective of an agent, a commitment refers to a specific action to be performed in due time, while a claim refers to a specific event that is created by an action of another agent, and has to occur in due time.

3.3 External AOR Models

In an external AOR model, we adopt the view of an external observer who is observing the (prototypical) agents and their interactions in the problem domain under consideration. Typically, an external AOR model will have a *focus*, that is an agent, or a group of agents, for which we would like to develop a state and behavior model. We do not consider internal AOR models (taking the internal/subjective perspective of a particular agent/system to be modeled) in this paper.

An **Agent Diagram** depicts the focus agent (or agents) and the agent types it is (or they are) interacting with. If another agent (type) is to be represented by a focus agent (type) with 'proprietary' attributes (that have only meaning for the representer), such as when `Customer` is to be represented by `Headquarter` with the proprietary Boolean attribute `isBlacklisted`, then a corresponding agent rectangle with a dot-dashed line is drawn as a representation of the 'real' agent (type) within the focus agent (type), as in Fig. 1. Such an explicit representational duplication of an entity type is only necessary if proprietary attributes are to be included in the agent diagram. Otherwise, it is tacitly assumed that the focus agent has a representation of all agents it deals with in terms of 'standard' attributes.

In the view of an external observer, actions are also events, and commitments are also claims, exactly like two sides of the same coin. Therefore, an external

---
[3] From the *ebXML Technical Architecture Specification* v0.9.

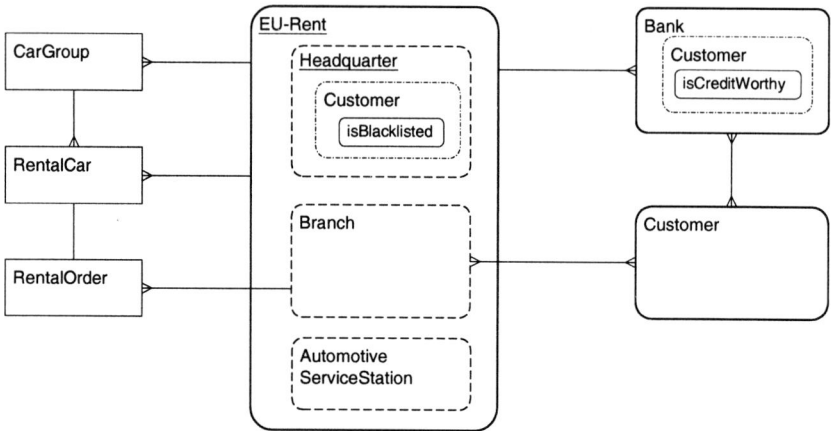

Fig. 1. An *Agent Diagram*: The car rental company **EU-Rent** is the focus agent. It consists of an internal agent **Headquarter** and (instances of) the internal agent types **Branch** and **AutomotiveServiceStation**. The headquarter classifies customers by means of the proprietary attribute **isBlacklisted**. Similarly, banks classify customers by means of the proprietary attribute **isCreditWorthy**. In both cases, a rectangle with a dot-dashed line is used to graphically render the internal representation entity type **Customer**.

AOR model contains, besides the agent and object types of interest, the action event types and commitment/claim types that are needed to describe the interactions between the focus agent(s) and the other types of agents. They are visualized in an *Interaction Frame Diagram*.

In an external AOR model, a *commitment* of agent a_1 towards agent a_2 to perform an action of a certain type (such as a commitment to return a car) can also be viewed as a *claim* of a_2 against a_1 that an action of that kind will be performed. Commitments/claims are conceptually coupled with the type of action event they refer to (such as *returnCar* action events). This is graphically rendered by an arrow rectangle with a dotted line on top of the action event rectangle it refers to, as depicted in Fig. 2.

Action event types, and commitment/claim types are graphically rendered like in Fig. 2 which depicts the *interaction frames* between **Customer** and **Branch**, and between **Branch** and **Headquarter**. Notice that not for all action event types there is a corresponding commitment/claim type. For instance, there are no commitments of (or claims against) customers to pick up a car, whereas there are commitments and claims to return a car. An interaction frame between two agent types consists of those action event types and commitment/claim types that form the basis of the interaction processes in which these two agent types are involved. Unlike a UML sequence diagram, it does not model any sequential process but provides a static picture of the possible interactions including commitment/claim types.

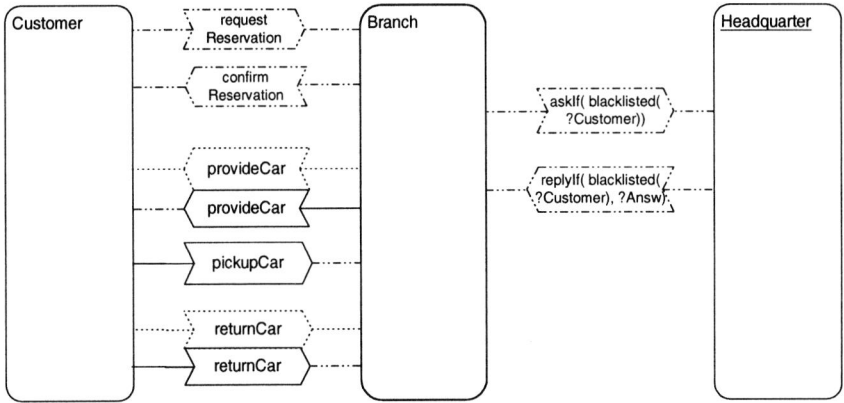

Fig. 2. An *Interaction Frame Diagram*: The interaction frame between the agent types Customer and Branch consists of the communicative action event (or ACL message) types requestReservation and confirmReservation, the action event type pickupCar, and the commitment/claim types provideCar and returnCar coupled with the corresponding action event types. The interaction frame between the agent type Branch and the agent Headquarter consists of the ACL message types askIf(blacklisted(?Customer)) and replyIf(blacklisted(?Customer), ?Answer)).

An external AOR model should not include any software artifacts. It should rather represent a conceptual analysis view of the problem domain, similarly to the function of a UML *use case* model.

4 Business Rules as Reaction Rules

We propose to formalize business rules as integrity constraints, as derivation rules, as reaction rules, or as deontic assignments in the semantic framework of *knowledge-perception-memory-commitment (KPMC)* agents. The concept of KPMC agents is an extension of the *knowledge- and perception-based (KP)* agent model proposed in [Wag96, Wag98]. We can only sketch this logical framework here.

A KPMC agent consists of five components: a knowledge base KB, an event queue EQ (representing the perception state), a memory base MB (recording past events and actions), a commitment/claim base CB, and a set of reaction rules RR (encoding the behavior of the agent). The schema of a KPMC agent is composed by a knowledge system (in the sense of [Wag98]), an agent communication language (ACL), an action language, and an environment event language. Integrity constraints and derivation rules are expressible on the basis of a knowledge system (and the query and input language defined by it). For expressing reaction rules one needs, in addition to the query and input language of a knowledge system, languages for expressing events and actions.

In this paper, for space limitations, we restrict our considerations to *reaction rules* that are visualized in **Interaction Pattern Diagrams**. In [TW01], we discuss *deontic assignments*.

Business rules that define the interactive behavior of business agents are best formalized as reaction rules. Business interactions are influenced by commitments and claims. So, reaction rules are those business rules where an agent-oriented approach is most promising. At the same time, they seem to be the most important type of business rules.

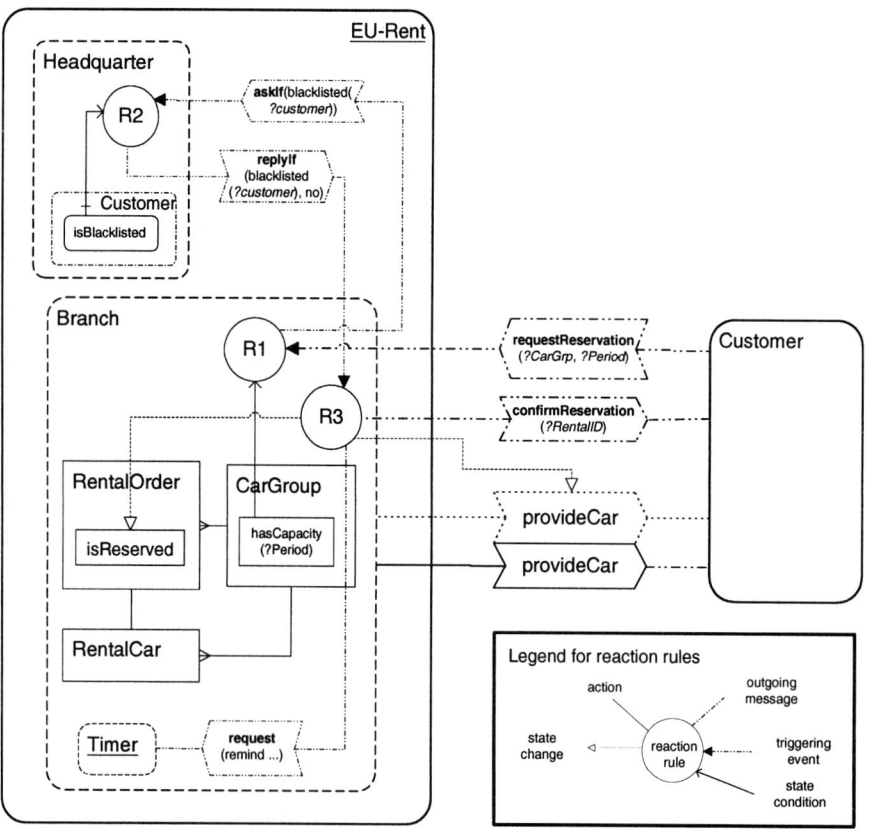

Fig. 3. An *Interaction Pattern Diagram*: Visualizing a process fragment defined by the reaction rules R1, R2 and R3.

In Fig. 3, the business process type of rental reservation is modeled on the basis of three reaction rules, R1, R2 and R3. Variables in the parameter list of a message type or predicate are prefixed with a question mark.

R1: Upon receiving from a `Customer` the request to reserve a car of some `?CarGroup` for a certain rental `?Period`, if that car group has sufficient capacity during the period requested – determined by evaluating the intensional predicate hasCapacity(?Period) of the corresponding instance of CarGroup – the Branch sends a query to the Headquarter to make sure that the customer is not blacklisted.

R2: Upon receiving from a Branch a query if some customer is blacklisted, the headquarter checks if the concerned customer is blacklisted, and if he is not, replies with 'no'.

R3: Upon receiving from the Headquarter a reply telling that the Customer is not blacklisted, the Branch creates the corresponding rental reservation (i.e. an instance of RentalOrder with the status isReserved), commits towards the customer to provide a car, sends a request to the Timer software agent to remind about the allocation time of a car for the given rental order (a car is allocated for the rental reservation 12 hours before the pickup-time), and sends a confirmation to the customer.

A reaction rule is visualized as a circle with incoming and outgoing arrows. Each reaction rule has exactly one incoming arrow that is solid: it represents the triggering event condition which is also responsible for instantiating the reaction rule. In addition, there may be ordinary incoming arrows representing state conditions (referring to corresponding instances of other entity types). There are two kinds of outgoing arrows. An outgoing arrow of the form –▷ denotes a mental effect referring to a change of beliefs and/or commitments. An outgoing connector to an action type denotes the performance of an action of that type.

Reaction rules may also be represented in textual form. For instance, R1 could be expressed as

```
ON RECEIVE requestReservation(?CarGrp, ?Period) FROM ?Customer
IF ?CarGrp.hasCapacity(?Period)
THEN
    SEND askIf( blacklisted(?Customer)) TO headquarter
```

and R3 could be expressed as

```
ON RECEIVE replyIf( blacklisted(?Customer), no) FROM headquarter
THEN
    COMPUTE ?RentalNo = getNewRentalNo();
    CREATE BELIEF RentalOrder(?RentalNo, ?Customer, isReserved, ... )
    CREATE COMMITMENT TOWARDS ?Customer TO provideCar(... ) BY ...
    SEND request( remind(?RentalNo, ... )) TO timer
    SEND confirmReservation(?RentalNo,... ) TO ?Customer
```

5 Related Work

We restrict our discussion of related work to those approaches in enterprise modeling where business rules play an essential role.

In object-oriented approaches, rules are frequently implemented within the methods of a business object class. In many cases, however, this binding of a business rule to a specific object class is not adequate. Typically, a rule refers to more than one type of business object. Therefore, business rules should be defined on top of the business object definitions (classes) in a separate module.

In [EP99], Eriksson and Penker propose an approach to business modeling with UML based on four primary concepts: resources, processes, goals, and rules. In this proposal, there is no specific treatment of agents. They are subsumed, together with "material, information, and products" under the concept of *resources*. This unfortunate subsumption of human agents under the traditional 'resource' metaphor prevents a proper treatment of many agent-related concepts such as commitments, deontic assignments, and communication/interaction.

Ross [Ros97] has proposed one of the most comprehensive methodologies for modeling business rules. The Ross Notation is, however, largely a database-oriented methodology, and does therefore not allow to model events and actions. Neither does it support to model business processes. E.g., [Hur98] remarks that the primary deficiency of the Ross Notation is its inability to model process aspects, due to its fundamental restriction of only considering persistent data as a basis for business rules.

The Enterprise Knowledge Development (EKD) approach described in [BBS] also addresses the modeling of business rules, business processes, and actors. The EKD approach does not, however, bring these notions straightforwardly to the operational level like we do in our approach. Also, visualization of business rules and processes in EKD is quite simplistic (by boxes).

Recently, in [OvDPB00], an agent-oriented extension of UML, called *AUML*, mainly concerning the expressivity of sequence diagrams and activity diagrams, has been proposed. However, AUML does not distinguish between agents and objects. In fact, UML class diagrams are not modified at all in AUML. Neither does it provide any support for (business) rules.

6 Conclusion

Business rules have traditionally been modeled and implemented in the narrow context of (active) databases. We have adopted a broader view, and a more cognitive stance, by proposing to model and implement business rules as the "rules of behaviour" of business agents. We have also shown how to visualize business rules in Agent-Object-Relationship models. We did not say anything about a suitable modeling process/method associated with the AOR modeling language. This is a topic for further research.

In addition to the case study of a car rental company, the methodology described in this paper has been used in designing an information system in support of inter-enterprise business processes of electronic advertising in newspapers, and in designing the scheduling information system for a ceramic factory, see [Tav01].

We are aware that, by introducing new concepts for enterprise modeling, we have also created new problems and research challenges. Some of the new questions that arise from our approach are:

- How can commitments/claims be used in real systems? What is their operational semantics?
- How can we relate our formalization of business rules with goals and goal-oriented behavior based on planning and plan execution?
- How can we handle exceptions to standard processes (for instance, when a customer does not appear to pick up a car as agreed, or when the automotive service station fails to return a car on time)? Possibly as violations of commitments?

These and many more questions will guide our future work.

Acknowledgements We are grateful to the anonymous referees for their valuable hints and suggestions.

References

[Ass88]   F. Van Assche. Information systems development: a rule-based approach. *Knowledge-Based Systems*, 1(4):227–234, 1988.

[BBS]   J. A. Bubenko, D. Brash, and J. Stirna. EKD user guide. Technical report, Kista, Dept. of Computer and Systems Science, Royal Institute of Technology (KTH) and Stockholm University, Stockholm, Sweden. http://www.dsv.su.se/~js/ekd_user_guide.html.

[Dav92]   T. H. Davenport. *Process Innovation: Reengineering Work through Information Technology*. Harvard Business School Press, 1992.

[EP99]   H.E. Eriksson and M. Penker. *Business Modeling with UML: Business Patterns at Work*. John Wiley & Sons, 1999.

[FIP]   Foundation for intelligent physical agents (FIPA). http://www.fipa.org.

[GLC99]   B.N. Grosof, Y. Labrou, and Hoi Y. Chan. A declarative approach to business rules in contracts: Courteous logic programs in XML. In *Proc. 1st ACM Conference on Electronic Commerce (EC99)*, Denver, Colorado, USA, November 1999.

[HC93]   M. Hammer and J. Champy. *Reengineering the Corporation*. Harper Collins, New York, 1993.

[Her97]   H. Herbst. *Business Rule-Oriented Conceptual Modeling*. Contributions to Management Science. Springer-Verlag, 1997.

[HH00]   D. Hay and K. A. Healy. Defining business rules - what are they really? Technical Report 1.3, The Business Rules Group, July 2000. http://businessrulesgroup.org/first_paper/br01c0.htm.

[Hur98]   Russ Hurlbut. *Managing Domain Architecture Evolution Through Adaptive Use Case and Business Rule Models*. PhD thesis, Illinois Institute of Technology, 1998.

[KK92]   A. Kieser and H. Kubicek. *Organisation*. De Gruyter, Berling/New York, 3rd edition edition, 1992.

[KQM]   Knowledge query and manipulation language (KQML). http://www.cs.umbc.edu/kqml/.

[MDC99] Meta data coalition open information model, business engineering model, business rules. review draft, Kista, Dept. of Computer and Systems Science, Royal Institute of Technology (KTH) and Stockholm University, July 1999. http://www.mdcinfo.com/OIM/models/BRM.html.

[MO98] James Martin and James Odell. *Object-Oriented Methods: A Foundation (UML Edition)*. Prentice-Hall, 1998.

[OvDPB00] J. Odell, H. van Dyke Parunak, and B. Bauer. Extending UML for agents. In G. Wagner, Y. Lesperance, and E. Yu, editors, *Proc. of the 2nd Int. Workshop on Agent-Oriented Information Systems*, Berlin, 2000. iCue Publishing.

[Ros97] R. G. Ross. *The Business Rule Book: Classifying, Defining and Modeling Rules*. Database Research Group, Inc., Boston (MA), 2nd edition edition, 1997.

[Sin99] M.P. Singh. An ontology for commitments in multiagent systems. *Artificial Intelligence and Law*, 7:97–113, 1999.

[Tav01] Kuldar Taveter. *Agent-Oriented Business Modelling and Simulation*. PhD thesis, Tallinn Technical University, 2001.

[TW01] K. Taveter and G. Wagner. Agent-oriented business rules: Deontic assignments. In *Proc. of Int. Workshop on Open Enterprise Solutions: Systems, Experiences, and Organizations (OES-SEO2001)*, Rome, Italy, September 2001.

[Wag96] G. Wagner. A logical and operational model of scalable knowledge- and perception-based agents. In W. Van de Velde and J.W. Perram, editors, *Agents Breaking Away*, volume 1038 of *Lecture Notes in Artificial Intelligence*, pages 26–41. Springer-Verlag, 1996.

[Wag98] G. Wagner. *Foundations of Knowledge Systems – with Applications to Databases and Agents*, volume 13 of *Advances in Database Systems*. Kluwer Academic Publishers, 1998. See http://www.inf.fu-berlin.de/~wagnerg/ks.html.

[Wag01a] G. Wagner. Agent-oriented analysis and design of organizational information systems. In J. Barzdins and A. Caplinskas, editors, *Databases and Information Systems. Fourth International Baltic Workshop, Vilnius, Lithuania, May 2000*, Vilnius, Lithuania, 2001. Kluwer Academic Publishers.

[Wag01b] Gerd Wagner. The Agent-Object-Relationship meta-model: Towards a unified conceptual view of state and dynamics. Technical report, Eindhoven Univ. of Technology, Fac. of Technology Management, **http://tmitwww.tm.tue.nl/staff/gwagner/AOR.pdf**, May 2001. Submitted.

[YWT+96] E. Yourdon, K. Whitehead, J. Thomann, K. Oppel, and P. Nevermann. *Mainstream Objects: An Analysis and Design Approach for Business*. Yourdon Press, 1996.

A Three-Layer Model for Workflow Semantic Recovery in an Object-Oriented Environment

Dickson K.W. Chiu

Dickson Computer Systems, 7A Victory Avenue, 4th floor, Homantin,
Kowloon, Hong Kong
kwchiu@ieee.org

Abstract. There have been numerous attempts to provide semantic recovery workflow support in order to maintain atomicity and consistency. However, they concentrate on compensation activities for individual tasks. This paper propose a three-layer model to provide comprehensive recovery support in an advanced object-oriented workflow environment, which take cares many other properties and aspects of a workflow management system (WFMS). At the workflow layer, the workflow composition hierarchy, workflow semantics and workflow commitment determines recovery requirement and data objects affected. At the data object layer, object class properties, data dependencies determines data recovery requirement. At the recovery primitive layer, users can define different types of reusable primitives to address the above recovery requirements. Based on this model with respect to ADOME-WFMS, this paper illustrates how the problem of workflow recovery can be adequately addressed, especially from an exception-handling viewpoint. In particular, a novel web-based support for cooperative workflow semantic recovery is highlighted.

1 Introduction

Workflow is automation of a business process. A Workflow Management System (WFMS) is a system that assists in defining, managing and executing workflows. Since it is not possible to specify all possible outcomes and alternatives (especially with various special cases and unanticipated possibilities), exceptions can occur frequently during the execution of a business process. A comprehensive WFMS should be able to automate exception handling by supporting the users to reallocate resources (data / object update) or to amend workflow such as adding alternatives (*workflow evolution*). Further, frequent occurrences of similar exceptions have to be incorporated into workflows as *expected exceptions*. Such workflow evolutions can help avoid unnecessary exceptions by eliminating error-prone activities, adding alternatives or by enhancing the operation environment. This can lead to a WFMS that supports workflow adaptation through exceptions.

On the other hand, various advanced transaction models have been developed to cope with advanced applications. A detailed classification can be found in [20]. The concepts of transactions provide useful properties such as failure atomicity, concurrency control and recovery to workflow. Thus, some researchers view workflow as an extension of advanced transaction models. However, because of the rich semantics and requirements of advanced workflow applications, semantic aspects should also be addressed adequately, in addition to transactional aspect for workflow and their exception handling.

When an exception occurs, a WFMS often needs to undo the effects of failed tasks and backtrack consistently, before re-executing the failed task or pursuing another path. As such, the workflow at a higher level can maintain progress on the whole, despite exceptions occurring in constituting tasks. This is referred as *workflow semantic recovery*. While most research in advanced transactional models and transaction workflow are at a low-level or with a strong theoretical basis, this paper concentrates on workflow recovery issues at semantic level (not on transactional aspects), which has not been addressed comprehensively by fellow researchers. In particular, this paper attempts to provide a high-level perspective on how workflow semantic recovery can be applied to WFMSs for exception handling.

The objectives and contributions of this paper include: (i) a high-level perspective on workflow exceptions, handlers and semantic recovery; (ii) a comprehensive three-layer model for workflow semantic recovery in an object-oriented workflow environment; (iii) demonstration of the feasibility of ADOME-WFMS for effective support of workflow semantic recovery; (iv) reuse issues for specification of workflow semantic recovery, and (v) a novel web-based support for cooperative workflow semantic recovery.

The rest of our paper is organized as follows. Section 2 discusses an overview of workflow exception and recovery requirements. Section 3 presents a three-layer model for workflow semantic recovery in an object-oriented environment. Section 4 illustrates the architecture of ADOME-WFMS, with focus on the mechanism of the *Recovery Manager*. Section 5 compares related work. Finally, the paper concludes with our plans for further research in Section 6.

2 Workflow Exceptions and Recovery Requirement

This section gives an overview of the requirement of workflow semantic recovery to support exception handling in an advanced contemporary object-oriented WFMS (with respect to ADOME-WFMS). This motivates the design of the three-layer workflow semantic recovery model in this paper.

In this paper, we model a business process as a workflow executed by a set of problem solving agents. A *Problem Solving Agent* (PSA) is a hardware/software system or a human being, with an ability to execute a finite set of tasks in an application domain. Typically a workflow is recursively decomposed into *sub-workflows* and eventually down to the unit level called *tasks*. A task is usually handled by a *single* PSA. The WFMS schedules and selects the PSAs for executing the tasks. We match the tasks with PSAs by using a capability-based *token/role* approach [4], where the main criterion is that the set of capability tokens of a chosen PSA should be matched to the requirement of the task. A *token* embodies certain capabilities of a PSA to execute certain functions / procedures /tasks, e.g., programming, database-administration, Japanese-speaking, while a *role* represents a set of responsibilities, which usually correspond to a job-function in an organization, e.g., project-leader, project-member, programmer, analyst, etc. Each PSA can play a set of PSA-roles and hold a set of extra capabilities. For example, John is a Japanese analyst-programmer who is leading a small project; thus he may play all the above-mentioned roles (project-leader, project-member, programmer, analyst, etc.), and in addition holds an extra capability (token) of Japanese-speaking.

Our overall objective of effective support of exception handling is to reduce, as much as possible, human intervention and increase reuse of workflow and exception definitions. We use an integrated, event-driven approach for execution, coordination, and exception handling in our WFMS. Events (such as database events / exceptions, or external inputs) trigger the WFMS *Execution Manager* to start a workflow. The WFMS *Execution Manager* uses events to trigger execution of tasks, while finished tasks will inform the *Execution Manager* with new events. Upon an exception, exception events will trigger the WFMS *Exception Manager* to take control of resolutions.

The workflow composition hierarchy specifies and records the activities and their constituting sub-workflows recursively down to the task level. Tasks are atomic activities with no sub-workflows. Sub-workflows are made up of tasks. The workflow composition hierarchy matches the nested transaction model. The nested transaction model is an important extension to the traditional transaction model where a multi-level structure is allowed. A nested transaction is a set of sub-transactions that may recursively contain other sub-transactions to form a transaction tree. A parent transaction may terminate only after all its children terminate. If a parent transaction is aborted, all its children are aborted. However, when a child fails, the parent may choose its own way of recovery, such as by executing a compensation transaction. This exactly corresponds to the composition hierarchy of a workflow. Starting a workflow corresponds to starting a nested transaction, with the sub-activities being sub-transactions. The process continues down to a task level, corresponding to a leaf transaction. However, transactional aspects apply to systems level but many other workflow-level semantics need to be addressed during recovery. This situation motivates the development of a comprehensive model for semantic workflow recovery.

When an exception occurs, it does not necessarily mean a failure if a suitable exception handler can remedy the situation and allow continuation of execution. An exception handler can be considered as a sub-workflow executing another sub-transaction. From a recovery point of view, exception handlers may have different levels of achievement:

Total remedy - to fix the problem so that execution is resumed as normal and other transactions / tasks are not affected. For example, when a purchase is slightly out of budget, the WFMS automatically increase the budget (with notification to the management) and continue.

Sacrificing remedy - to fix the problem with actions affecting other activities so that execution of the current workflow is resumed as normal. This may cause exceptions to other activities and aborting other transactions. For example, purchases for less important projects are canceled or put on hold so that there can be enough funding for purchases needed for a vital project.

Backtracking - the effect of the current problematic sub-workflow is undone (say, in the form of compensating task) so that the WFMS can execute an alternate path or re-execute the current sub-workflow in a consistent manner. (This issue is to be further elaborated and discussed in the following sections.)

Failure determination - unable to find other viable remedies or alternate execution paths, thus the current sub-workflow has to abort, which causes an exception to its parent workflow. The partial result of the failed task has to be undone.

3 A Three-Layer Semantic Workflow Recovery Model

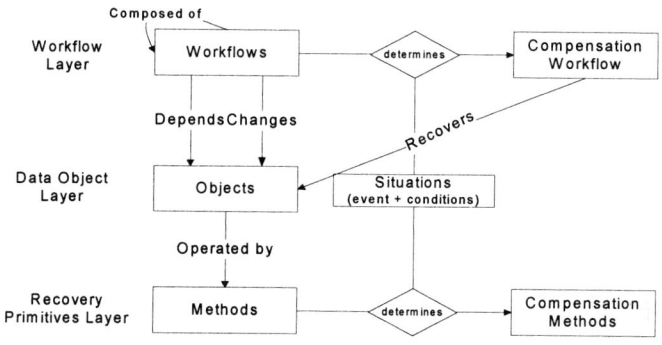

Fig. 1. Three-layer Semantic Workflow Recovery Model

The previous section has presented the requirement of workflow semantic recovery in an advanced contemporary WFMS (with respect to ADOME-WFMS). However, there have only been scattered attempts in workflow recovery at a semantic level, while most other work contributes in the transaction level. Therefore, we develop a three-layer semantic workflow recovery model to address this problem, as depicted in Fig. 1. At the workflow layer, the workflow composition hierarchy, workflow commitment, and workflow semantics determine recovery requirement and data objects affected. At the data object layer, object class properties, data dependencies determines data recovery requirement. At the recovery primitive layer, users can define different types of reusable primitives to address the above recovery requirements.

3.1 Semantic Recovery at the Workflow Layer

At the workflow layer, the basic approach of semantic recovery is to associate each task/sub-workflow with a compensation sub-workflow for backtracking. In this model, with respect to ADOME-WFMS, association of compensation sub-workflows to target workflows is very flexible due to the workflow composition hierarchy, event-condition-action (ECA) rule mechanisms and meta-modeling. Moreover, workflow recovery performance and semantic expressiveness can be improved with the workflow semantic commit mechanism.

3.1.1 Flexible Association of Compensation Sub-workflows to Workflows

First, we generalize the notion of compensation task to compensation sub-workflow because the compensation process may be a complicated one involving many steps. For example, an airline reservation sub-workflow has to be undone by a corresponding cancellation sub-workflow. According to standard terminologies, the cancellation process is a sub-workflow instead of a task because it consists of a number of steps (or tasks), such as authorization from the supervisor, application to the travel agency, refund procedures, etc. However, in case that no compensation sub-workflow has been specified for a target sub-workflow, we need to undo individual component tasks/sub-workflows recursively down the composition hierarchy.

Second, in addition the association of compensation sub-workflow at task level, the workflow hierarchical composition provides a choice of granularity for compensation sub-workflows, depending on workflow semantics. For example, the airline reservation sub-workflow is undone by a corresponding cancellation sub-workflow as a whole, i.e., we can associate a compensation sub-workflow to a target sub-workflow instead of to individual tasks, which are to be undone. Similarly, we should cancel travel packages (hotel plus air-ticket) as a whole, rather than their components one by one. As such, the workflow recovery semantics is much better maintained than associating compensation tasks/sub-workflows with individual target tasks.

Third, in ADOME-WFMS, users may specify different compensation sub-workflows under the scope of different workflow classes, or under different situations (event plus condition), from the default one associated with the target sub-workflow for compensation. Moreover, ECA-rules can be used to specify compensation sub-workflows other than defaults, like specifying exception handlers. For example, the cancellation sub-workflow associated with the airline reservation sub-workflow is fine for most workflow classes in the organization, but the marketing department may want another process because they most likely want to change an air-ticket for another trip instead of canceling it. The ECA rule to specify this looks like: (E: airline_reservation(a).compensation, C:a.dept="Marketing", A: change_flight (a)). Similarly, if air-tickets from regional offices to the head office are reusable, we can specify similar ECA rules to override the default. More details about how to specify ECA rules with scoping can be found in [4][7].

Finally, because ADOME-WFMS employs a meta-modeling approach in specifying workflows [4], generic compensation sub-workflows can be defined (or generalized from specific ones) for maximized reuse. For example, service cancellation sub-workflow templates can be defined so that specific service cancellation (e.g., air-ticket, hotel) can be instantiated for execution. Note that human intervention (cooperative workflow semantic recovery) may also be specified as a compensation sub-workflow (cf. Section 4.4).

3.1.2 Task States and Workflow Semantic Commit

To improve recovery performance and to enhance semantic support, we introduce the mechanism of workflow semantic commit support. Fig. 2 illustrates the various states of a task, which are related to workflow recovery as follows:

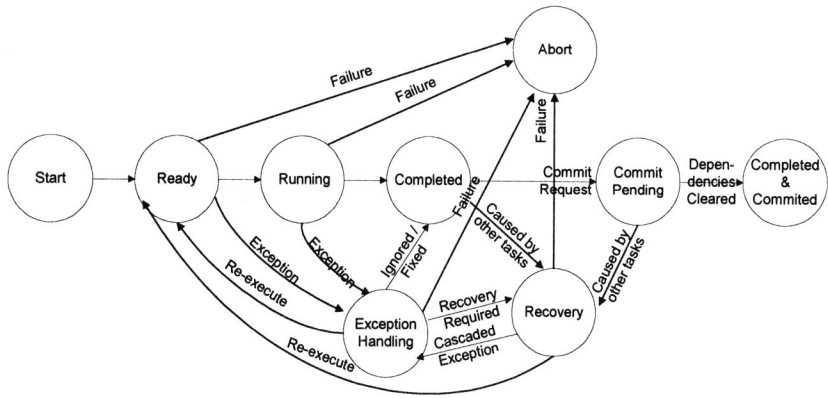

Fig. 2. State Diagram for a Task

1. *Start*: A task instance is created with a *start* state, where the WFMS carries out various house-keeping actions, such as preparing ECA-rules of event-driven execution and exception handling. This corresponds to the start of a workflow sub-transaction at database system transaction level.
2. *Ready*: The WFMS will then allocate resources and find a capable PSA for the task. If workflow exceptions occur, such as no resources, out of budget, no PSA, the *Exception Manager* takes over.
3. *Running*: If everything proceeds well and the PSA acknowledges the assignment, the task will then be in a *running* state. After working on the task, the PSA will report the result, either successful completion or exception.
4. *Exception Handling*: Should exceptions occur in the *ready* or *running* state, the *Exception Manager* takes over to execute exception resolution in the *exception handling* state.
5. *Recovery*: If the *Exception Manager* decides to backtrack, it invokes the *Recovery Manager* to perform semantic workflow recovery in the *recovery* state. After that, the task can then be ready again for re-execution.
6. *Abort*: Failure in any state may cause the task to *abort*. This propagates the exception to the parent workflow level.
7. *Completed*: A successful task will finish in a *completed* state.
8. *Commit Pending*: Before committing a task, all the objects and states referred by the task should be from committed tasks; otherwise waiting is required.
9. *Completed and Committed*: At certain checkpoints, the user may decide to commit the previous successfully completed tasks, so that the changes are permanent. This corresponds to the end of a workflow sub-transaction at database system transaction level.

Note that we distinguish between *completed* and *committed* states in order to allow the *Exception Manager*, or human intervention to backtrack a *completed* (but not *committed*) task subsequent *inter-dependent* tasks as needed. Committed task need not be undone and therefore recovery performance is improved.

3.2 Semantic Recovery at the Data Object Layer

In the absence of compensation sub-workflow for a target task, we may tackle the problem of semantic recovery with another approach, by considering the update log of the task, and try to undo the changes to the affected objects. In an object-oriented environment, different methods encapsulate richer semantics behind that traditional database updates. Since different methods have different semantics, they need different compensation methods or recovery primitives.

With semantic recovery support at data object layer, compensation sub-workflows at the workflow semantic layer can concentrate on specific items or situations that need special attention. After finishing the main logic, they may invoke the *Recovery Manager* to clean up other data objects modified and apply default semantic recovery at the data object layer, in order to maximize reuse and improve the ease of programming.

Moreover, should any other workflows depend on the data objects that are changed during semantic recovery, there is a potential problem of inconsistency. Therefore, the *Recovery Manager* will raise events (exceptions) to alert those dependent workflows, so that they can take proper actions. Thus, there is a possibility for cascaded backtracking and exceptions in general (cf. Section 4.5).

3.3 Recovery Primitives Layer

As explained above, different methods have different semantics, they need different compensation methods or recovery primitives. However, there are some general compensation methods, such as:

Simple rollback - the previous value or state of the object is restored. This is typical for handling traditional database update in workflow when the item is locked.

Do nothing – some information should simply be kept whatever happens afterwards. For example, application level logs should be kept instead of being destroyed. Time wasted cannot be recovered, and many resources or budget used up cannot be recovered in general. Partial work done, such as design and working documents, should be kept for reference, because they are probably helpful in decreasing the cost of subsequent work. On the other hand, unimportant effects (e.g., duplicated supplier acknowledgement) can just be ignored while beneficial information and effects should be kept (e.g. correct product information obtained).

Mark void - useful documents, though now ineffective, should be kept, but marked void for records, such as invoice and purchase orders.

Human intervention – unanticipated or critical situations may require human intervention to clear up. However, the user can define rules for subsequent backtrack action to automate handling of further occurrences of this situation.

Similar to the process of specifying compensation sub-workflows for target sub-workflow, we can use ECA-rules to associate different *compensation methods / sub-workflows* (which can be considered as a part of an exception handler) to undo object methods under different situations. Thus, complicated conditions and variations in compensation methods can be programmed with lots of opportunities for reuse. On the other hand, general compensation methods can be attached to objects and reused through the class hierarchy.

4 Implementation Issues

This section presents some implementation issues for the three-layer model for workflow semantic recovery, with reference to the ADOME-WFMS.

4.1 Architecture

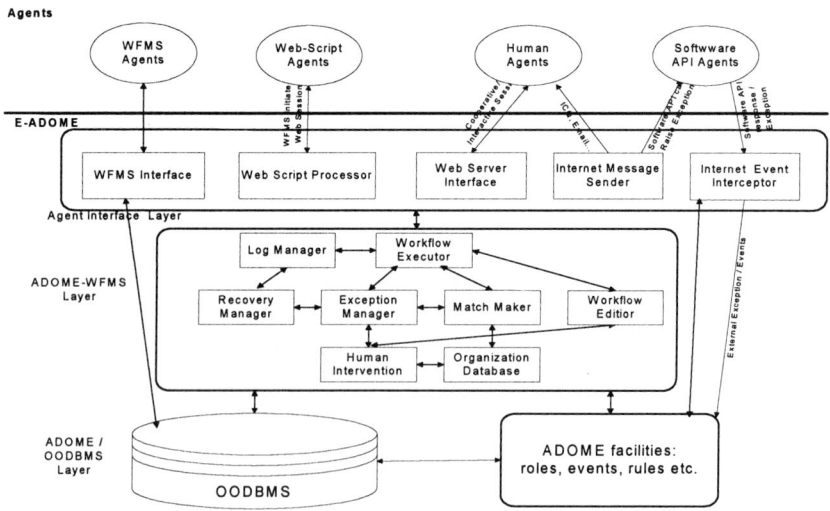

Fig. 3. Architecture of ADOME Workflow Management System

The ADOME system was developed to enhance the knowledge-level modeling capabilities of OODBMS models [18], to allow them to more adequately deal with data and knowledge management requirements of advanced information management applications. The ADOME prototype has been built by integrating an OODBMS (ITASCA [13]) and production inference engine (CLIPS [8]), with support of advanced ECA-rules. Therefore, a WFMS can be implemented on top of it with relative ease. The architecture and functional aspects of the resultant ADOME-WFMS (as depicted in Fig. 3) are as follows: *ADOME active expert OODBMS* provides a unified enabling technology for the WFMS, viz., object and role database, event specification and execution, rule / constraint specification and processing. *Workflow Editor* facilitates the decomposition of activities into tasks. The user provides the knowledge and related data to decompose activities into tasks by a user interface. *Organizational Database* manages data objects for the organization, as well as PSA classes, instances and their capability token (role) specifications. Besides maintaining user-specified extensional tokens / roles systematically, intensional token/role derivation for a PSA is also supported. *Workflow Executor* coordinates execution by user-raised and database generated events. *Recovery Manager* keeps track of task workflow transactions, execution states, results and dependencies. *Match Maker* selects PSAs for executing tasks of a workflow according to some selection criteria. *Exception Manager* handles various exceptions by re-executing failed tasks or their alternatives (either resolved by the WFMS or determined by the user) while maintaining forward progress.

Recently, we have added an E-ADOME *Agent Interface Layer* to enable ADOME-WFMS to interact with agents through the Internet. It supports effective management of agents, cooperative exception handling, cooperative semantic recovery, user-driven computer supported resolution of unexpected exceptions / workflow evolution and inter-organization workflow in an E-commerce / E-service environment [6].

4.2 Features of ADOME-WFMS Facilitating Workflow Recovery

The workflow decomposition hierarchy of ADOME-WFMS [4] facilitates the application of a nested transaction model described in Section 2. ADOME-WFMS has rich features to avoid task failures during exception handling and therefore sub-transaction aborts. These include adaptive human resource management in PSA modeling, capability matching and reasoning, and extensive features in reuse of exception handlers.

Compensation sub-workflows are considered as part of the exception handling procedure and modeled as sub-workflows of the exception handlers. We allow the execution and definition of compensation sub-workflows as ECA rules, which corresponds to the integrated framework of event-driven workflow execution in ADOME-WFMS. This allows different compensation sub-workflows/methods to be executed according to the exception type and general conditions under execution. As such, our environment provides many opportunities for reuse, as explained in the previous section.

4.3 The ADOME-WFMS Recovery Manager

The function of the ADOME-WMFS *Recovery Manager* can mainly be divided into housekeeping functions and backtrack functions.

House-keeping functions of the ADOME-WFMS *Recovery Manager* includes the following: (i) upon starting of a task or sub-workflow, a sub-transaction starts; (ii) keep track of the sequence of executing tasks and sub-activities for backtracking; (iii) maintain the states of all executing tasks; (iv) for every task, keep track of all updates (methods) until it commits; (v) for uncommitted tasks, keep track of all references to uncommitted results, and (vi) make sure before committing a task, all the objects and states referred should be from committed tasks; otherwise waiting is required.

```
Method Workflow.Backtrack (t, restart_point: Workflow)
    /* backtrack from t to restart_point of in a workflow transition graph */

    FOREACH s IN Traceback(t, restore_point) DO /* trace back the execution path */
        /* do wf level compensation, if defined */
        c = ECA_first_match(s, Workflow.Compensation);
        IF exist(c)
            c.Start;        /* execute compensation wf of the scope */
        ELSIF exist(s.Compensation)
            s.Compensation.Start;       /* Execute default compensation */
        ELSIF is_composite(s)           /* s is composite sub-workflow */
            Backtrack(s.End, s.Start);  /* backtrack its components */
        ELSE        /* no wf level compensation, do object layer compensations */
            Object.Backtrack(s.method_log);
        ENDIF
    ENDDO
END

Method Object.Backtrack (s: Set of MethodLog)
    FOREACH m IN REVERSE s DO
        /* execute different recovery primitives according to methods */
        CASE m.Recovery_Primitive IN
            Simple_rollback: m.Database_simple_rollback;
            Mark_void: m.Void := TRUE;
            Do_nothing: {};
            Compensation: /* execute relevant ECA rule bounded to object */
                c = ECA_first_match(m, Method.Compensation);
                execute c;
            Human_intervention:  Human_recover(t, restart_point, m);
        ENDCASE
    ENDDO
    /* find out other tasks referring to rollback objects */
    task_affected := {}
    FOREACH m IN REVERSE s DO
        IF m.Recovery_Primitive IN {Simple_rollback, Mark_void}
            task_affected := task_affected UNION m.Object.Refer
        ENDIF
        IF m.Recovery_Primitive IN {Compensation, Human_intervention}
            AND o.Object.Old <> o.Object.New  /* object really changed */
            task_affected := task_affected UNION m.Object.Refer
        ENDIF
    ENDDO
    /* these (sub)activities are inconsistent */
    FOREACH a IN activities_affected DO
        Raise(a.Inconsistent_refer)
    ENDDO
END
```

Fig. 4. Main Algorithm of ADOME-WFMS *Recovery Manager*

With the above housekeeping functions, the three-layer model for workflow semantic recovery described in the previous section can be implemented. The algorithm is depicted in Fig. 4. In summary, the recovery logic includes the following. When the *Exception Manager* determines to re-execute a task or to execute an alternate task, backtrack (to one or more steps backward) is necessary to ensure that re-execution can be performed in a consistent manner. Then, the *Recovery Manager* will be invoked to undo the effect of tasks/sub-workflows backward along the execution path and down the workflow composition hierarchy if necessary. If there are no workflow compensation sub-activities defined for individual tasks, data object layer semantic recovery will be executed by tracing back the method execution log. For all objects that have been recovered successfully, the *Recovery Manager* will look for other tasks that are *data-dependent* on them. Since these tasks are not consistent any more, the *Recovery Manager* thus raises inconsistency exceptions to all of them. As such, cascaded exceptions and backtrack will happen. Note that the data object layer semantic recovery method (entry point) is also serviceable to compensation sub-workflows, which can pass over a sub-log to recover some objects by default actions.

4.4 Cooperative Semantic Recovery

Recently, we have designed a web-based interface for cooperative semantic recovery in ADOME-WFMS, as illustrated by Fig. 5, in addition to other web-based cooperative features as detailed in [7]. For example, if a project is cancelled, should the requisition department cancel the related order from the supplier? This may depend on: (i) whether other customers or potential customers need this item, (ii) whether there is enough money to keep this stock, (iii) if the order is not cancelled, extra funding and space for storage are required, which may or may not be justified, (iv) time required for delivery, (v) the cost of canceling the order. This example also illustrates that both *forward* and *backward* semantic recovery should be supported in a unified manner, depending on business situations.

Under unanticipated, complicated, or critical situations, human intervention (or a cooperative mode) may be necessary for workflow recovery. When cooperative semantic recovery is required, the target user is alerted (by ICQ, and if not available, by email) with the URL of the page generated by the E-ADOME interface layer. After logging in, the web page presents a list of relevant objects for decision and a list of options. In addition, the user may browse the decision history for reference. Therefore, ADOME-WFMS supports *automatic* (ECA-rule based) and *cooperative* semantic recovery in both *forward* and *backward* direction.

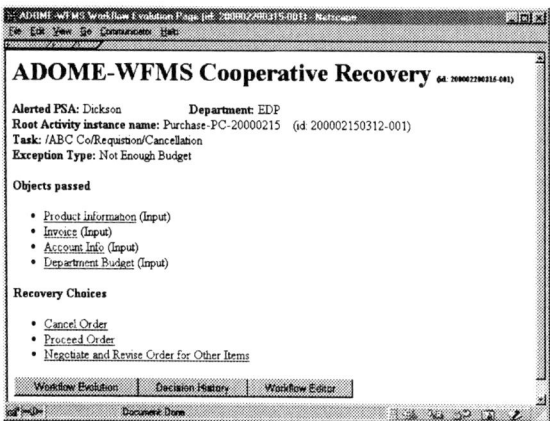

Fig. 5. Sample Screen of ADOME-WFMS Cooperative Semantic Recovery

4.5 Handling Cascaded Exceptions, Loops, and Backtrack

Since workflow transactions are long running, a higher degree of concurrency is desired. In order to employ an optimistic approach, results of completed (but not committed) tasks should normally be released for use by other activities. However, this dependency must be tracked for consistency enforcement. Exceptions will occur to all tasks depending on the items, which are changed or deleted upon backtrack and thus cascaded exceptions and backtrack may occur. Thus, compensation actions may be designed to keep the result of a failed sub-workflow if possible and justified. Secondly, compensation actions themselves are sub-workflows, and thus may cause exceptions, which in turn may cause cascaded exceptions and backtrack.

In order to handle cascaded exceptions effectively and avoid infinite generation of cascaded exceptions, the following *safeness* measures are employed in ADOME-WFMS: (i) Notification within the exception handling workflow to the human deciding on the handler for an unexpected exception (e.g., to report even expected exceptions upon cascaded exceptions). (ii) If cascaded exceptions occur, the same PSA should be notified for better management and decisions. (iii) Tighter constraints, such as deadline and budget, can be introduced to avoid exception handling sub-activities to run indefinitely, and let the control pass back for human decisions. (iv) When a human decides a jump back to a certain point for re-execution (including simple retry of the currently failed task), there may be a potential danger of looping and the human will be provided with a warning. (v) The *Execution Manager* will keep track of the sequence of executed tasks. If a task or sequence of tasks are repeatedly executed due to occurrence of same exceptions, then a warning or an exception will be raised for human intervention or alternate actions. (vi) Cooperative workflow recovery enables the human expert to undo some of the decisions taken (if possible) and finalize on the resolution once all different aspects of exception handling are taken care of.

5 Related Work

[20] presented a detailed survey in transactional workflow and recovery. WAMO [9] uses Sagas and flexible transactions for workflow exception handling. ConTract [19] focuses on workflow control and execution but not on organization modeling and workflow specification. OPERA [12] incorporates primitives based on exception handling concepts developed for programming languages coupled with ideas from advanced transaction models. Similarly, other works like [11] focus on lower level issues, such as transactional aspects. Recent efforts on semantic recoveries include: CREW [14] supports opportunistic compensation and re-execution to reduce recovery overhead; Flowback [16] provides backward recovery for Flowmark [1].

A classical paper on exception handling is [2], which focused on database aspects of exception and handling techniques instead of workflow systems. TriGSflow [14] is perhaps the closest system to ours in that it adopts an OO design, and utilizes rules and roles, but it has little support for handling exceptions. [17] described a framework of using roles, event-based execution model and exception handling rules in a WFMS. However, they did not address a variety of exception conditions or support workflow decomposition to facilitate workflow definition and execution. WIDE [3] used object and rule modeling techniques and suggested some measures in handling exceptions. They addressed reuse and management of exception handlers with implementation details, but not adequately considered high level semantics, especially inter-relationship among entities in a WFMS.

In summary, other WFMS either do not address problems in exception handling comprehensively or concentrate only on extended transaction models in relational paradigms. For current works in object-oriented WFMS, few particularly address the problem of workflow semantic recovery. Our previous work [4][7] focused on exceptions and handlers, modeling and meta-modeling issues for WFMS, but do not address the problem of workflow semantic recovery. Though we have some preliminary work [5], this paper is a major enhancement on workflow semantic recovery for handling exceptions because a proper model with new extensions has been developed.

6 Conclusion

This paper has presented a three-layer model for workflow semantic recovery high-level in a flexible WFMS (viz. ADOME-WFMS) based on an active OODBMS extended with role and rule facilities. At the workflow layer, association of compensation sub-workflows to target workflows is very flexible due to the workflow composition hierarchy, ECA-rule mechanisms and meta-modeling. Moreover, workflow recovery performance and semantic expressiveness can be improved with the workflow semantic commit mechanism. At the data object layer, semantic recovery is convenient and highly reusable. At the recovery primitive layer, general primitives have been identified to augment specific compensation methods, which may also be flexibly defined with ECA-rules. ADOME-WFMS supports a rich taxonomy of exception types and their handling approaches, and a novel augmented solution for exception handling based on workflow evolution. As such, workflow failures can be avoided. This paper has also described how workflow recovery is actually handled with the ADOME-WFMS *Recovery Manager* in a high-level manner, with a detailed algorithm. ADOME-WFMS is currently being built on top of the ADOME prototype system. Furthermore, a novel web-based cooperative workflow semantic recovery is supported. Further research issues include further measures to avoid cascaded exceptions, loops and rollback, full-range transactional workflow capabilities, and impact of workflow evolution on recovery. On the other hand, we are investigating workflow recovery in an inter-organization workflow E-commerce / E-service environment (E-ADOME [6]).

7 References

1. Alonso, G., et al.: Exotica/FMDC: a workflow management system for mobile and disconnected clients. *Distributed & Parallel Databases*, vol. 4(3), 229-247, (1996)
2. Borgida, A.: Language Features for Flexible Handling of Exceptions, *ACM Trans. on Database Systems* (1985).
3. Casati, F., Fugini, M.G., and Mirbel, I: An Environment for Designing Exceptions in Workflows. Proceedings of CAiSE 98, LNCS Springer Verlag, Pisa, June (1998).
4. Chiu, D.K.W., Li, Q., and Karlapalem, K.: A Meta Modeling Approach for Workflow Management Systems Supporting Exception Handling, *Information Systems*, Elsevier Science, vol 24(2), (1999) 159-184

5. Chiu, D.K.W., Li, Q., and Karlapalem, K.: Facilitating Exception Handling with Recovery Techniques in ADOME Workflow Management System. *Journal of Applied Systems Studies*, Cambridge International Science Publishing, 1(3), (2000) 467-488
6. Chiu, D.K.W., Li, Q., and Karlapalem, K.: Views for Inter-Organization Workflow in an E-Commerce Environment, 9th IFIP 2.6 Working Conference on Database Semantics (DS-9), Hong Kong, April (2001) 151-167
7. Chiu, D.K.W., Li, Q., and Karlapalem, K.: Web Interface-Driven Cooperative Exception Handling in ADOME Workflow Management System. Information Systems, Pergamon Press, Elservier Science, 26(2), (2001) 93-120
8. Clips: http://www.ghg.net/clips/CLIPS.html
9. Eder, J., Liebhart, W.: The Workflow Activity Model WAMO. In *Proceeding of CoopIS-95*, 97-98, (1995) 87-98
10. Ellis, S., et al.: Dynamic Change within Workflow Systems, *Proceedings of the Conference on Organizational Computing Systems* (1995) 10-21
11. Georgakopoulos, D., Hornick, M. F., and Manola, F.: Customizing Transaction Models and Mechanisms in a Programmable Envioronment Supporting Reliable Workflow Automation. *IEEE Transactions on Knowledge and Data Engineering*, 8(4), (1996) 630-649
12. Hagen, C. and Alonso G., Flexible Exception Handling in the OPERA Process Support System, *18th International Conference on Distributed Computing Systems* (ICDCS 98), Amsterdam, The Netherlands, (1998)
13. Ibex Corporation. *http://www.ibex.ch/*
14. Kamath, M., Ramamritham, K.: Failure Handling and Coordinated Execution of Concurrent Workflows, Proceedings of 14th International Conference on Data Engineering, Orlando, Florida, February (1998) 334-341
15. Kappel, G., Rausch-Schott, S., Retschitzegger W.: Coordination in Workflow Management Systems - A Rule-Based Approach, *Coordination Technology for Collaborative Applications - Organizations, Processes, and Agents*, Springer LNCS 1364, (1988) 99-120
16. Kiepuszewski, B., Muhlberger R., Orlowska, M.: FlowBack: providing backward recovery for workflow management systems; Proceedings of ACM SIGMOD international conference on Management of data, (1998) 555-557
17. Kumar, A., et.al. A framework for dynamic routing and operational integrity controls in a workflow management system. In *Proceedings of the Twenty-Ninth Hawaii International Conference on System Sciences*, vol 3, (1996) 492-501
18. Li, Q. and Lochovsky, F. H. ADOME: an Advanced Object Modeling Environment. *IEEE Transactions on Knowledge and Data Engineering*, 10(2), (1998) 255-276
19. Reuter, A. and Schwenkreis, F. ConTacts - A Low-Level Mechanism for Building General-Purpose Workflow Management Systems. *IEEE Bulletin of the Technical Committee on Data Engineering*, 18 (1), (1995) 4-10
20. Worah, D. and Sheth, A. Transactions in Transactional Workflows in Advanced Transaction Models and Architectures, S. Jojodia and L. Kerschberg, Eds., Kluwer Academic Publishers, (1997) 3-35

Recognizing Ontology-Applicable Multiple-Record Web Documents

David W. Embley, Yiu-Kai Ng, and Li Xu

Dept. of Computer Science, Brigham Young University, Provo, Utah 84602, USA
{embley,ng,lx}@cs.byu.edu

Abstract. Automatically recognizing which Web documents are "of interest" for some specified application is non-trivial. As a step toward solving this problem, we propose a technique for recognizing which multiple-record Web documents apply to an ontologically specified application. Given the values and kinds of values recognized by an ontological specification in an unstructured Web document, we apply three heuristics: (1) a density heuristic that measures the percent of the document that appears to apply to an application ontology, (2) an expected-value heuristic that compares the number and kind of values found in a document to the number and kind expected by the application ontology, and (3) a grouping heuristic that considers whether the values of the document appear to be grouped as application-ontology records. Then, based on machine-learned rules over these heuristic measurements, we determine whether a Web document is applicable for a given ontology. Our experimental results show that we have been able to achieve over 90% for both recall and precision, with an F-measure of about 95%.

1 Introduction

The World Wide Web contains abundant repositories of information in Web documents—indeed, it contains so much, that locating information "of interest" for an application becomes a huge challenge. Even sorting through a tiny subset of Web documents is overwhelming. How can we automatically select just those documents that have the needed information for an application? When we construct automated processes to recognize which documents apply to a user's information needs, we must be careful not to discard relevant documents and not to accept irrelevant documents. A process that discards too many relevant documents has poor *recall*—ratio of the number of relevant documents accepted to the total number of relevant documents. A process that accepts too many irrelevant documents has poor *precision*—ratio of the number of relevant documents accepted to the total number of documents accepted. The harmonic mean[1] of the precision and recall, which is called the *F-measure* [BYRN99], is a standard way to combine precision and recall. We wish to have an automated recognition process that has a good F-measure so that it has both high recall and high precision.

---

[1] $F = \dfrac{2}{\frac{1}{recall} + \frac{1}{precision}}$

In this paper we propose an approach for recognizing whether a Web document is relevant for a chosen application of interest. We base our approach on application ontologies [ECJ+99], which are conceptual-model snippets of standard ontologies [Bun77], and we apply techniques from information retrieval [BYRN99] and machine learning [Qui93].

Our work reported here is also partly motivated by our success in using application ontologies to extract information from unstructured multiple-record Web documents and structure the information so that it can be queried using a standard query language [ECJ+99]. For several applications we have tried—automobile want-ads, obituaries, jobs, real estate, stocks, musical instruments, precious gems, games, personals, and computer monitors—we have achieved fact-extraction recall rates mostly around 90% and fact-extraction precision rates mostly better than 90%, and we have achieved robustness over a wide range of pages and pages that change in format, content, and style [ECJ+99]. In these experiments, however, we have assumed (and have made sure by human inspection) that the Web pages were multiple-record documents appropriate for the application we were using. Thus, in the context of our larger project, the purpose of this work is to automate applicability checking. If we can locate documents applicable to an ontology, we can apply techniques we have already developed, to extract, structure, query, and archive in databases, information found in data-rich, application-specific Web documents. Hence, the contributions of this work have the potential to be more far-reaching than just the salient contribution of increasing recall and precision in recognizing targeted Web documents.

Our approach to document recognition is related to text classification[BB63]—each application ontology can be a class—but our work fundamentally differs from other text-classification work. Text classification systems usually attempt to place articles such as newspaper articles in predefined classes according to the subject matter of the article, whereas our approach seeks to do "high-precision" text classification (with similarities to [RL94]) in which we not only determine whether a listing of ads such as the classified ads in a newspaper contain ads of interest for a predefined application ontology, but we also determine whether particular elements of interest are also present in each ad. We further assume that a subsequent process can extract the information and create a database record for each ad.

Despite this basic differences, we nevertheless compare our work with the work in text classification (e.g. [BM98]) in order to highlight some advantages and disadvantages of the approaches that have been taken. Most text classification systems are based on machine learning. In typical machine-learning approaches, each document is transformed into a feature vector. Usually, each element of a feature vector represents a word from a corpus. The feature values may be binary, indicating presence or absence of the word in the document, or they may be integers or real numbers indicating some measure of frequency of the word's appearance in the text. This text representation is referred to as a "bag of words," which is used in most text-classifiers. A major difficulty for this bag-of-words approach is the high dimensionality of the feature space. Thus, it is highly desirable to reduce dimensionality of the space without sacrificing classification accuracy. Since our approach uses a predefined application ontology whose object sets constitute the features of interest, we immediately identify a space with comparatively small dimensionality and thus avoid this high-dimensionality problem. Further, our predefined application ontology also overcomes many of the limitations imposed by word-based techniques. There is no need to find object relevancy with respect to a corpus because the application ontology already defines the relationships among the conceptual objects. Moreover, our approach is sensitive to context and domain knowledge and can thus more effectively retrieve the relevant information from a document and use it to classify a document with respect to an application. For example, the basic idea of McCallum's Naive Bayes classifier [BM98], which is one of the most successful systems used in text classification applications and which is implemented in Rainbow [McC96], is to use the joint probabilities of words and categories, which are computed based on labeled training documents, to estimate the probability of categories given a document. However, the naive part of the approach is the assumption of word independence, which makes the classifier less appropriate for "high-precision" classifiers like ours. In compensation for these disadvantages, typical machine-learning approaches may take less user effort to produce—the effort being mainly the work to provide and label a set of training documents. Our experience in teaching others to use our system suggests that an application ontology of the kind we use can be created in a few dozen person-hours, which is roughly comparable to the time and effort it may take to label a set of training documents. Furthermore, the application ontology produced can also serve as an information extractor (see [ECJ+99]); and hence, little, if any, additional work is required to also create a classifier.

Although our work differs fundamentally from most text classifiers, as just discussed, the work reported in [RL94] takes an approach similar to ours in that it also attempts to do "high-precision" classification for information extraction. Like most text classifiers, [RL94] uses machine learning, but to obtain the desired high precision, considerably more effort must be expended to establish the basis for machine learning. Not only must documents be marked as relevant and non-relevant, but each individual relevant element plus the context for each individual relevant element must also be marked. In addition, an application-domain-specific dictionary must be created. The basic trade-off in human effort between our approach and the approach in [RL94] is the effort to tag the elements in the document and create the domain-specific dictionary versus the effort to create the application ontology.

Some recent work has been reported that uses machine learning with less human effort for doing "high-precision" classification for domain-specific search engines [MNRS99] and focused crawling [CvdBD99]. By mostly using unsupervised learning, human effort can be greatly reduced. The challenge, however, is to reach high accuracy, and it may not be possible to achieve the accuracy that can be obtained with an ontology-based approach. Ultimately, some combination of the approaches may be best. In the meantime, we pursue our goal of high-precision binary classification based on ontological specifications.

We outline the rest of our paper as follows. Section 2 briefly describes the model we use for specifying application ontologies and provides an example to which we refer throughout the paper to illustrate our ideas. Given an application ontology and a set of Web documents, we automatically obtain statistics for three heuristics for each document: (1) a density heuristic, (2) an expected-values heuristic, and (3) a grouping heuristic. Section 3 describes these heuristics and the statistical measures we obtain for each, as well as the machine-learned decision-tree rules we obtain for judging document applicability. In Section 4 we discuss our experimental results—which, for the two applications we tried (car advertisements and obituaries), are in the 90% range for both recall and precision. In Section 5, we give concluding remarks.

2 Application Ontology

For our work in data extraction, we define an *application ontology* to be a conceptual-model instance that describes a real-world application in a narrow, data-rich domain of interest (e.g. car advertisements, obituaries, job advertisements) [ECJ+99]. Each of our application ontologies consists of two components: (1) an *object/relationship-model instance* that describes sets of objects, sets of relationships among objects, and constraints over object and relationship sets, and (2) for each object set, a *data frame* that defines the potential contents of the object set. A data frame for an object set defines the lexical appearance of constant objects for the object set and establishes appropriate keywords that are likely to appear in a document when objects in the object set are mentioned. Figure 1 shows part of our car-ads application ontology, including object and relationship sets and cardinality constraints (Lines 1-8) and a few lines of the data frames (Lines 9-18).[2]

An object set in an application ontology represents a set of objects which may either be lexical or nonlexical. Data frames with declarations for constants that can potentially populate the object set represent lexical object sets, and data frames without constant declarations represent nonlexical object sets. *Year* (Line 9) and *Mileage* (Line 14) are lexical object sets whose character representations have a maximum length of 4 characters and 8 characters respectively. *Make*, *Model*, *Price*, *Feature*, and *PhoneNr* are the remaining lexical object sets in our car-ads application; *Car* is the only nonlexical object set.

We describe the constant lexical objects and the keywords for an object set by regular expressions using Perl syntax. When applied to a textual document, the **extract** clause (e.g. Line 10) in a data frame causes a string matching a regular expression to be extracted, but only if the **context** clause (e.g. Line 11) also matches the string and its surrounding characters. A **substitute** clause (e.g. Line 12) lets us alter the extracted string before we store it in an intermediate file,

---

[2] The full ontology for car ads is about 600 lines in length. Our obituary ontology, which is the other application ontology we discuss in this paper is about 500 lines in length, but it references both a first-name lexicon and a last-name lexicon, which each contain several thousand names.

1. Car [-> object];
2. Car [0:0.975:1] has Year [1:*];
3. Car [0:0.925:1] has Make [1:*];
4. Car [0:0.908:1] has Model [1:*];
5. Car [0:0.45:1] has Mileage [1:*];
6. Car [0:2.1:*] has Feature [1:*];
7. Car [0:0.8:1] has Price [1:*];
8. PhoneNr [1:*] is for Car [0:1.15:*];

9. Year matches [4]
10. constant {extract "\d{2}";
11. context "\b'[4-9]\d\b";
12. substitute "^" -> "19"
13. ...
14. Mileage matches [8]
15. ...
16. keyword "\bmiles\b", "\bmi\.",
17. "\bmi\b", "\bmileage\b";
18. ...

Fig. 1. Car-Ads Application Ontology (Partial)

in which we also store the string's position in the document and its associated object set name. One of the nonlexical object sets is designated as the *object set of interest*—*Car* for the car-ads ontology. The notation "[-> object]" in Line 1 designates the object set of interest.

We denote a relationship set by a name that includes its object-set names (e.g. *Car has Year* in Line 2 and *PhoneNr is for Car* in Line 8). The *min:max* pairs and *min:ave:max* triples in the relationship-set name are *participation constraints*: *min* designates the minimum number of times an object in the object set can participate in the relationship set; *ave* designates the average number of times an object is expected to participate in the relationship set; and *max* designates the maximum number of times an object can participate, with * designating an unknown maximum number of times. The participation constraint on *Car* for *Car has Feature* in Line 6, for example, specifies that a car need not have any listed features, that a car has 2.1 features on the average, and that there is no specified maximum for the number of features listed for a car.

For our car-ads and obituary application ontologies, which we use for illustration in this paper, we obtained participation constraints as follows. To make our constraints broadly representative, we selected ten different regions covering the United States and found one car-ads page and one obituary page from each of these regions. From each of these pages we selected twelve individual car-ads/obituaries by taking every $n/12$-th car-ad/obituary, where n was the total number of car-ads/obituaries on the page. We then simply counted by hand and obtained minimum, average, and maximum values for each object set in each relationship set and normalized the values for a single car ad or obituary.

3 Recognition Heuristics

We are interested in determining whether a given document D is suitable for an application ontology O. In our document-recognition approach, we consider three different heuristics: (H_1) *density*, (H_2) *expected values*, and (H_3) *grouping*. H_1 measures the density of constants and keywords defined in O that appear in D. H_2 uses the Vector Space Model (VSM) [SM83], a common information-retrieval measure of document relevance, to compare the number of constants expected for each object set, as declared in O, to the number of constants found in D for each object set. H_3 measures the occurrence of groups of lexical values found in D with respect to expected groupings of lexical values implicitly specified in O.

The next three subsections define these three heuristics, explain the details about how we provide a measure for each heuristic, and give examples to show how they work. The fourth subsection explains how we use machine learning to combine these heuristics into a single document-recognition rule. When reading these subsections, bear in mind that in creating these heuristics, we favored simplicity. More sophisticated measures can be obtained. For example, for H_1 we could account for uncertainty in constant and keyword matches [EFKR99]. For H_2, we could more accurately match object sets with recognized values by using our more sophisticated downstream heuristics [EX00]. For H_3, we could first compute record boundaries [EJN99] and appropriately rearrange record values [EX00]. However, more sophisticated measures are more costly. We have chosen to experiment with less costly heuristics, and, as will be shown, our results bear out the seeming correctness of this choice.

3.1 H_1: Density Heuristic

A Web document D that is relevant to a particular application ontology A should include many constants and keywords defined in the ontology. Based on this observation, we define a *density heuristics*. We compute the density of D with respect to O as follows:

$$Density(D, O) = \text{total number of matched characters / total number of characters}$$

where *total number of matched characters* is the number of characters of the constants and keywords recognized by O in D, and *total number of characters* is the total number of characters in D.

We must be careful, of course, not to count characters more than once. For example, in the phrase "asking only 18K" a car-ads application ontology might recognize "18K" as potentially both a price and a mileage. Nevertheless, we should only count the number of characters as three, not six. Document position information for recognized strings tells us which strings overlap.

Consider the Web document D_a in Figure 2(a). Recall that the lexical object sets of the car-ads application ontology are *Year*, *Make*, *Model*, *Mileage*, *Price*, *Feature*, and *PhoneNr*. Some of the lexical values found in D_a include 1989 (Year), $1900 (Price), 100K (Mileage), Auto (Feature), Cruise (Feature), (336)835-8579 (PhoneNr), Subaru (Make), and SW (Model). Only the keywords, "miles" and "mileage" appear in D_a. The total number of characters in D_a is 2048, whereas the number of matched characters is 626. Hence, the density of D_a is $0.3056 = 626/2048$.

When we apply the density heuristic for the car-ads application ontology to the Web document D_b in Figure 2(b), the density is much lower. Although no makes, models, or car features appear, there are years, prices, and phone numbers

Last Updated
Monday, January 24, 2000 12:19pm Cars for Sale

DEPENDABLE CAR
1989 Subaru SW. Auto, AC, $1900 OBO. Call (336)835-8579.

FACTORY WARRANTY
1998 Elantra. Black 4 door w/ tinted windows. Auto, pb, ps, cruise, am/fm cassette stereo, a/c. Excellent condition pay off OBO. Call (336)526-5444 anytime & leave message.

1994 HONDA ACCORD EX
Auto, power everything, jade green w/gold package. Under 100K miles. Call (336)526-1081 after 7pm.

1999 GRAND AM
27,000 miles, silver, auto, still under warranty. $14,000 OBO. Call (336)366-4996 anytime.

'53 Chevy Bel Aire. All original, looks like new. Serious inquiries only. $8500. Call (336)468-8924 after 4 pm.

TWO GREAT CARS
1973 MGB convertible. British racing green. Mags, new tires, 4-speed, 1 owner, excellent running condition. $4500.
1977 Olds Cutlass Supreme. New white paint job w/ 1/2 red Landau top, original mags & new tires. Auto., 1 owner, low mileage, loaded. Call (336)984-2843.
-----
95 FORD CONTOUR
5-speed, great condition, one owner, $5300. Call (336)526-8853 & leave message if no answer.

SEIZED CARS FROM $500
Sports, luxury & economy cars, trucks, 4x4's utility and more. For current listings, call 1-800-311-5048 ext. 10012.

1996 VW JETTA GL
26,000 miles. 4 door, 5-speed, AC, sunroof, 1 owner. $11,000. Call (336)874-7317 anytime.

'85 Buick Park Avenue. $500. Head may be cracked. Will run. Body good condition. Call (336)526-2768.

'95 Ford Thunderbird. Loaded, V-8, 45K, $6995. Call S&J Motors at (336)874-3403.

'96 Mercury Tracer. 4 door, 5 speed, 34K, $4995. Call S&J Motors at (336)874-3403.

'88 Firebird. V8, 5.0, fuel injected, T-tops, 109,000 miles, red, runs great. $1880. Call (336)526-1164 anytime.

1990 CONVERSION VAN
350 motor, auto, new tires, TV, VCR, captain chairs, front & rear AC. $4,995. Call (336)320-2658 anytime.

COMMERCIAL WORK VAN
'95 Chevy Astro, V6, w/ac & fully equipped utility shelves. $9400. Call (336)526-2675 & leave message.

Last update: Wednesday, December 22, 1999

Select a category

Apartment For Rent For Sale or Rent Lost or Found
For Rent Help Wanted
For Sale House For Rent

Apartment For Rent
ONE EFFICIENCY, 2 & 3 bdrm, all utilities paid. Call 281-2051 -
-----
For Rent
HOUSING SOLUTIONS - Free TV cable furn. $60/wk - $210/mo. 281-4060. -
-----
For Sale
1998 JD 455 mower, 60' deck. Call for price. Also, homemade Go-Cart. Call after 5:30 pm 218-281-1128. -
-----
For Sale or Rent
10,000 SQ. FT. office building. Handicap accessible. Call 281-3631. -
-----
Help Wanted
NOW HIRING full time and part time customer service representatives. Advancement possible and weekly pay. Must be able to work weekends and holidays. Apply at Superamerica, 411 N Main St., Crookston, MN EOE -
-----
PART-TIME AND weekend help working with developmentally disabled adults. Call Melissa or Karen at 281-3872. -
-----
REM-NORTHWEST Services, Inc. has a full time Program Coordinator/Coordinator position open in Crookston working with four developmentally disabled adults. Duties include hiring, staff supervision, scheduling, oversight of most areas of the home's operation. Applicant must be 18 years of age or older. Must have a high school diploma or equivalent. One year experience serving people with developmental disabilities preferred. Must have a valid driver's license and driving record that meets REM's insurability requirements. Insurance and benefits available. If interested call for application at 218-281-5113. E.O.E. -
-----
REM-NORTHWEST Services, Inc. has full and part time Coordinator positions available in Crookston, MN, working with citizens who are developmentally disabled. Excellent benefits are offered including health, dental, life, 401K and profit sharing for full and part time employees working 20 hours a week or more. Exceptional training is provided. Applicants must be 18, have a valid driver's license and high school diploma or GED. Apply by calling for application at 218-281-5113 or 1-800-532-7655. E.O.E. -
-----
House For Rent
3 BDRM HOUSE $450/mo. 281-1970. 22 STEEL BUILDINGS, NEW, must sell. 40x60x14 was $17,500 now $10,971; 50x100x16 was $27,850 now $19,990; 80x135x16 was $79,850 now $42,990; 100x175x20 was $129,650 now $78,850. 1-800-406-5126. -
-----
Lost or Found
FOUND: Golden retriever about 4 months old. Found 7 miles south of Crookston. Call after 5:30 pm 281-1128. -
-----

(a) Car advertisements retrieved from http:// www.elkintribune.com/.

(b) Items for sale advertisements retrieved from http://www.crookstontimes.com.

Fig. 2. A car advertisement Web document and a non-car advertisement Web document.

and the ontology (mistakenly) recognizes "10,000" (in "10,000 SQ. FT.") and "401K" (the retirement plan) as potential mileages. Altogether 196 characters of 2671 are recognized by the car-ads ontology. Thus, the density is 0.0734.

3.2 H_2: Expected-Values Heuristic

We apply the VSM model to measure whether a multiple-record Web document D has the number of values expected for each lexical object set of an application ontology O. Based on the lexical object sets and the participation constraints in O, we construct an ontology vector OV. Based on the same lexical object sets and the number of constants recognized for these object sets by O in D, we construct a document vector DV. We measure the relevance of D to O with respect to our expected-values heuristic by observing the cosine of the angle between DV and OV.

To construct the ontology vector OV, we (1) identify the lexical object-set names—these become the names of the coefficients of OV, and (2) determine the average participation (i.e. the expected frequency of occurrence) for each lexical object set with respect to the object set of interest specified in O—these become the values of the coefficients of OV. Since we do not in general know, indeed do not care, how many records we will find in documents given to us, we normalize these values for a single record. For example, the ontology vector for the car-ads application ontology is < Year:0.975, Make:0.925, Model:0.908, Mileage:0.45, Price:0.8, Feature:2.1, PhoneNr:1.15 >, where these values are obtained as explained in Section 2. Thus, for a typical single car ad we would expect to almost always find a year, make, and model, but we only expect to find the mileage about 45% of the time, the price about 80% of the time. Further, we expect to see a list of features that on the average has a couple of items in it, and we expect to see a phone number and sometimes more than one phone number[3].

The names of the coefficients of DV are the same as the names of the coefficients of OV. We obtain the value of each coefficient of DV by automatically counting the number of appearances of constant values in D that belong to each lexical object set. Table 1 shows the values of the coefficients of the document vector for the car-ads document in Figure 2(a), and Table 2 shows the values of the coefficients of the document vector for the non-car-ads document in Figure 2(b). Observe that for document vectors we use the actual number of constants found in a document. To get the average (normalized for a single record), we would have to divide by the number of records—a number we do not know with certainty[4]. Therefore, we do not normalize, but instead merely

---

[3] It is easy to see that the variance might be useful, as well, but we found that the expected numbers were sufficient to get good results for the examples we tried.

[4] We can estimate the number of records by dividing the length of the document vector by the length of the ontology vector. Indeed, we use this information downstream, but here we are still trying to determine whether the given document applies to the ontology. If it does, the length-division estimate for the number of records makes sense; otherwise, the estimate may be nonsense.

Name of Lexical Object Set	Corresponding Lexical Values Found in the Document	Number of Lexical Values Found
Year	1989, 1998, 1994, 1999, '53, 1973, 1977, 95, 1996, ...	16
Make	Subaru, HONDA, Chevy, Olds, FORD, VW, Buick, Mercury, ...	10
Model	SW, Elantra, ACCORD, GRAND AM, Cutlass, CONTOUR, JETTA, ...	12
Mileage	100K, 27000, 26000, 45K, 34K, 109000	6
Price	$1900, $14,000, $8500, $4500, $5300, $11,000, $6995, $4995, $1880, ...	11
Feature	Auto, Black, 4 door, pb, ps, cruise, am/fm, cassette, stereo, green, ...	29
PhoneNr	(336)835-8579, (336)526-5444, (336)526-1081, (336)366-4996, ...	15

Table 1. Lexical values found in the multiple-record car advertisements in Figure 2(a).

Name of Lexical Object Set	Corresponding Lexical Values Found in the Document	Number of Lexical Values Found
Year	1999, 1998, 60, 401K, 50, 80	6
Make		0
Model		0
Mileage	10,000, 401K	2
Price	$17,500, $10,971, $27,850, $19,990, $79,850, $42,990, $129,650, $78,850	8
Feature		0
PhoneNr	281-2051, 281-4060, 218-281-1128, 281-3631, 281-3872, 218-281-5113, 218-281-5113, 800-532-7655, 281-1970, 800-406-5126, 281-1128	11

Table 2. Lexical values found in the multiple-record *Items for Sale* document in Figure 2(b).

compare the cosine of the angles between the vectors to get a measure for our expected-values heuristic.

We have discussed the creation of a document vector as if correctly detecting and classifying the lexical values in a document is easy—but it is not easy. We identify potential lexical values for an object set as explained in Section 2; this can be error-prone, but we can adjust the regular expressions to improve this initial identification and achieve good results [ECJ[+]99]. After initial identification, we must decide which of these potential object-set/constant pairs to accept. In our downstream processes, we use sophisticated heuristic based on keyword proximity, application-ontology cardinalities, record boundaries, and missing-value defaults to best match object sets with potential constants. For upstream ontology/document matching we use techniques that are far less sophisticated and thus also far less costly. In our simple upstream procedures we consider only, two cases: (1) a recognized string has no overlap either partially or completely with any other recognized string, and (2) a recognized string does overlap in some way with at least one other recognized string. For Case 1, we accept the recognized string for an object set even if the sophisticated downstream processes would reject it. For Case 2, we resolve the overlap simplistically, as follows. There are three subcases: (1) exact match, (2) subsumption, and (3) partial overlap. (1) If a lexical value v is recognized as potentially belonging to more than one lexical object set, we use the closest keyword that appears before or after v to determine which object set to choose; if no applicable keyword is found, we choose one of the object sets arbitrarily. (2) If a lexical value v is a proper substring of lexical value w, we retain w and discard v. (3) If lexical value v and lexical value w appear in a Web document, such that a suffix of v is a prefix of w, we retain v and discard w.

As mentioned, we measure the similarity between an ontology vector OV and a document vector DV by measuring the cosine of the angle between them. In particular, use use the *Similarity Cosine Function* defined in [SM83], which calculates the acute angle $SIM(D, O) \cos \theta = P/N$, where P is the inner product of the two vectors, and N is the product of the lengths of the two vectors. When the distribution of values among the object sets in DV closely matches the expected distribution specified in OV, the angle θ will be close to zero, and $\cos \theta$ will be close to one.

Consider the car-ads application ontology O as shown in Figure 1 and the Web document D_a as shown in Figure 2(a). The coefficients of OV for O are 0.975, 0.925, 0.908, 0.45, 0.8, 2.1, and 1.15, which are the expected frequency values of lexical object sets *Year, Make, Model, Mileage, Price, Feature*, and *PhoneNr*, respectively for a single ad in the car-ads application ontology. The coefficients of DV for D_a are 16, 10, 12, 6, 11, 29, and 15 (see the last column of Table 1), which are the actual number of appearances of the lexical values in D_a. We thus compute $SIM(D_a, O)$ to be 0.9956. Now consider the car-ads application ontology O again and the Web document D_b as shown in Figure 2(b). The coefficients of OV are always the same, but the coefficients of DV for D_b are 6, 0, 0, 2, 8, 0, and 11 (see the last column of Table 2). We thus compute $SIM(D_b, O)$ to be 0.5669.

3.3 H_3: Grouping Heuristic

A document D may have a high density measure for an ontology O, may also have a high expected-values measure for O, and still not be considered as a multiple-record document for O. This is because the values must also form groups that can be recognized as records for O. As a simple heuristic to determine whether the recognized values are interleaved in a way that could be considered consistent with potential records of O, we consider the sequence of values in D that should appear at most once in each record and measure how well they are grouped.

We refer to an object set whose values should appear at most once in a record as a *1-max lexical object set*. Maximum participation constraints in an

Year: 2000 Year: 1989 Make: Subaru Model: SW -- Nr of Distinct "One Max" Object Sets: 3	Year: 1999 Year: 1998 Year: 1960 Mileage: 10000 -- Nr of Distinct "One Max" Object Sets: 2
Price: 1900 Year: 1998 Model: Elantra Year: 1994 -- Nr of Distinct "One Max" Object Sets: 3	Mileage: 401000 Year: 1940 Price: 17500 Price: 10971 -- Nr of Distinct "One Max" Object Sets: 3
Make: HONDA Model: ACCORD Mileage: 100000 Year: 1999 -- Nr of Distinct "One Max" Object Sets: 4	Year: 1950 Price: 27850 Price: 19990 Year: 1980 -- Nr of Distinct "One Max" Object Sets: 2
Model: GRAND AM Mileage: 27000 Price: 14000 Year: 1953 -- Nr of Distinct "One Max" Object Sets: 4	Price: 79850 Price: 42990 Price: 129650 Price: 78850 -- Nr of Distinct "One Max" Object Sets: 1
(a) First four groups of 1-max lexical values extracted from Figure 2(a).	(b) First four groups of 1-max lexical values extracted from Figure 2(b).

Fig. 3. Groups of 1-max lexical values extracted from advertisement Web documents.

ontology constrain the values of the 1-max object sets to appear at most once in a record. For example, in the car-ads application ontology, the 1-maximum on *Car* in the relationship set *Car [0:0.975:1] has Year [1:*]* specifies that *Year* is a 1-max object set. Other 1-max lexical objects in the car-ads ontology are *Make*, *Model*, *Mileage*, and *Price*.

Instead of counting the number of 1-max lexical objects in an application ontology O, a more adequate counting approach is to sum the average values expected for the 1-max objects in O. Since the average values expected for *Year*, *Make*, *Model*, *Mileage*, and *Price* in the car-ads ontology are 0.975, 0.925, 0.908, 0.45, and 0.8, respectively, the anticipated number of lexical values from these object sets in a car advertisement is 4.058. We truncate the decimal value of the anticipated number to obtain the expected group size.

The expected group size n is an estimate of the number of 1-max object-set values we should encounter in a document within a single record. On the average, each record should have n 1-max object sets. Thus, if we list all recognized 1-max object-set values in the order they occur in a document D and divide this sequence into groups of n, each group should have n values from n different object sets. The closer a document comes to this expectation, the better the grouping measure should be. For the multiple-record car-ads Web document in Figure 2(a), Figure 3(a) shows the first four groups of 1-max lexical object-set values extracted from the document, and Figure 3(b) shows the first four groups of 1-max lexical object-set values extracted from the document in Figure 2(b).

We measure how well the groups match the expectations with a grouping factor (denoted G_{factor}), which is calculated as follows:

$$G_{factor}(D, O) = \frac{\text{Sum of Distinct Lexical Values in Each Group}}{\text{Number of Groups} \times \text{Expected Number of Values in a Group}}$$

For example, the number of extracted groups from the Web document D_a in Figure 2(a) is 13 (1 group of 2, 5 groups of 3, and 7 groups of 4). Since the number of anticipated lexical values in each group is four, G_{factor} of D_a is 0.8653. Comparatively, the number of extracted groups from the Web document D_b in Figure 2(b) is 4 (1 group of 1, 2 groups of 2, and 1 group of 3). Since the number of anticipated lexical values in each group is four, G_{factor} of D_b is 0.5.

3.4 Combining Heuristics

The result we obtain when we run the heuristics on a Web document for an application ontology is a triple of heuristic measures: (H_1, H_2, H_3). For example, when O is the car-ads application ontology and the Web document is the one in Figure 2(a), the heuristic-measure triple, which we derived in the previous three subsections, is (0.3056, 0.9956, 0.8653). For the Web document in Figure 2(b), the triple we derived is (0.0734, 0.5669, 0.5).

Since we did not know exactly how these three heuristics should be combined to best match application ontologies with documents, we decided to use machine learning. We did not know, for example, whether we should use all the heuristics or just one or two of them, and we did not know what threshold values to apply. Since the popular machine-learning algorithm C4.5 [Qui93] answers these questions, we decided to use it to combine the three heuristics into a single decision rule. C4.5 is a rule post-pruning decision tree algorithm. The learning task is to judge the suitability of a Web document for a given application ontology (i.e. to do binary classification by returning "YES" when a document is suitable, and returning "NO" otherwise). The performance measure is the percent of documents correctly classified when using a generated rule (i.e. the accuracy). The bias favors the shortest rule, so that if several rules are equally accurate, a decision tree with the fewest branches is chosen. The training data is a set of Web documents classified by a human expert in the application domain.

We represent every instance of a Web-document/application-ontology pair in both training and test sets as a triple (H_1, H_2, H_3) composed of the measures returned by the three heuristics. We trained C4.5 with 20 positive examples and 30 negative examples for each of our two application ontologies—car ads and obituaries. The positive examples included in the training sets came from 20 different sites, two each selected arbitrarily from 10 different geographical regions in the United States. To select 20 of the 30 negative examples, we first chose 20 document subjects and then found a Web page for each subject. Because we wanted to be able to make fine distinctions when recognizing documents, we chose most of the subjects based on a perceived similarity between the subject and either car-ads or obituaries. To make sure that gross distinctions were also recognized properly, we also chose a few documents "arbitrarily." In addition to

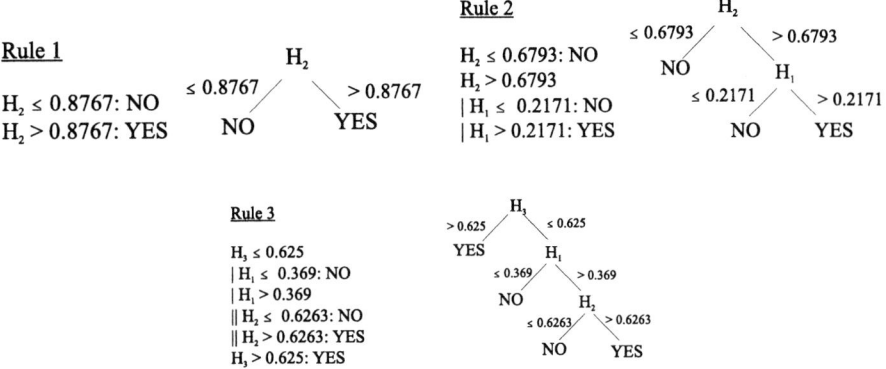

Fig. 4. Rules generated by machine-learning algorithm C4.5.

the negative examples, we also used 10 car-ads documents (one from each region) to play the role of 10 negative obituary examples and 10 obituary documents (one from each region) to play the role of 10 negative car-ad examples.

Based on the 50 training examples for our car-ads application ontology, C4.5 generated Rule 1. Thus, our document-recognition technique selects a document as a car ad if its expected-values measure is greater than 0.8767 (i.e. if the cosine between the car-ads ontology vector and the document vector is greater than 0.8767). C4.5 also generated Rule 2, which indicates that our technique selects a document as an obituaries document only if its expected-values measure is greater then 0.6793 and its density measure is greater than 0.2171. Searching for a potential universal rule over both ontologies, we combined the 50 training triples for car ads and the 50 training triples for obituaries, and applied the C4.5 algorithm to produce Rule 3. To use Rule 3 for an application ontology A for a Web document W, we would obtain the heuristic triple (H_1, H_2, H_3) for W with respect to A and apply Rule 3. Our document-recognition technique would classify W as suitable for A if the grouping measure (H_3) is greater than 0.625 or if the grouping measure (H_3) is less than 0.625, the density measure (H_1) is greater than 0.369, and the expected-values measure (H_2) is greater than 0.6263.

4 Results and Discussion

To test the machine-learned rules, we chose 30 test documents—10 positive documents for car ads, 10 positive documents for obituaries, and 10 negative examples. We chose the 10 positive examples for car ads and the 10 positive examples for obituaries from sites located in the ten US geographical regions we had previously designated for training sets. The test sites, of course, were different from the training sites even though they were located in the same geographical regions. For the negative test documents, we selected documents whose subjects were fairly close to either car ads or obituaries. Indeed, the page selected for antique cars turned out to be "too close" to car ads (even a human expert could not tell the difference), and we later classified it as a positive example for car ads. We also used the 10 car-ads positive documents in the test set as 10 negative obituary documents and vice versa.

4.1 Experimental Results

Generated Rules 1 and 2 successfully recognized the test set for both the car-ads application ontology and the obituary application ontology with the same F-measure, 95.3%. The precision for the car-ads application ontology was 100%, and the recall was 91%. One document containing car ads was improperly labeled as a document not containing car ads. The precision for the obituary ontology application was 91%, and the recall was 100%. One document that did not contain obituaries was incorrectly labeled as a document that contained obituaries. We also applied Rule 3, the generated universal rule, to the test set. The F-measure for Rule 3 was 91.3%, the precision was 84%, and the recall was 100%.

4.2 Discussion

Incorrect Negative Response. The car-ads document for which Rule 1 gave an incorrect negative response was "quite different." The last "ad" was not a single car ad; instead it was a dealer ad for several dozen cars. This, by itself, was not a problem, but there were three complications that did cause problems. (1) The "Year" and the "Price" were concatenated, with no space between them. Our *Year* data frame in Figure 1 did not anticipate this concatenation, and thus the years were not recognized. (2) These ads contained neither mileage information nor feature information about the cars. Missing mileage and feature information is generally not a problem, but since there were more cars mentioned in the "last" ad than in all the rest of the car ads together, missing mileage and feature information made more difference that it otherwise would have. (3) The phone number was factored out of each individual ad within the "last" ad because it is the same for all dealership cars. As a result of these three problems, most of the cars in these three documents have only a *Make*, *Model*, and *Price*. Even so, the 0.7958 measure for the expected-values heuristic is almost high enough to be acceptable (see Rule 1).

Incorrect Positive Response. One negative example, "Missing People," was misjudged. The document consisted of a list of descriptions for missing persons. Each description typically contained several lexical objects that were defined in our obituary ontology—name, birth date, and age. Although other special lexical objects exist only in obituaries (e.g. interment, funeral, relative-name list), the precision for these lexical objects is much lower than the precision of the lexical objects such as date and age. Hence, "thinking" that it is working on an obituary, the obituaries application ontology extracts places and times in the missing-people document that it "thinks" are lexical objects for interment and funeral places and times, and it extracts names it "thinks" are relative names. Thus, all the heuristic measurements are artificially inflated and the document is judged incorrectly.

Universal Rule. Test results for Rule 3 show that the F-measure and recall of this "universal rule" remain high, above 90%, but that the precision drops to 84%. Since this rule spans application ontologies, it may be useful to apply Rule 3 for a new application ontology. However, since both the extraction precision and the three heuristic measures have some differences for different ontology applications, we suggest using application-dependent rules, such as Rule 1 for car ads and Rule 2 for obituaries, to recognize suitable documents.

5 Concluding Remarks

We presented an approach for recognizing which multiple-record Web documents apply to an ontology. Once an application ontology is created, we can train a machine-learning algorithm over a triple of heuristics (density, expected-values, grouping) to produce a decision tree that accurately recognizes multiple-record documents for the ontology. Results for the tests we conducted showed that the F-measures were above 95% with recall and precision above 90% for both of our applications.

Acknowledgements: This material is based upon work supported by the National Science Foundation under grant No. IIS-0083127.

References

[BB63] H. Borko and M. Bernick. Automatic document classification. *Journal of the ACM*, 10(2):151–162, 1963.

[BM98] L.D. Baker and A.K. McCallum. Distributional clustering of words for text classification. In *Proceedings of the 21th ACM SIGIR*, pages 96–103, 1998.

[Bun77] M.A. Bunge. *Treatise on Basic Philosophy: Vol. 3: Ontology I: The Furniture of the World*. Reidel, Boston, 1977.

[BYRN99] R. Baeza-Yates and B. Ribeiro-Neto. *Modern Information Retrieval*. Addison Wesley, Menlo Park, California, 1999.

[CvdBD99] S. Chakrabarti, M. van den Berg, and B.E. Dom. Focused crawling: A new approach for topic-specific resource discovery. *Computer Networks*, 31:1623–1640, 1999.

[ECJ+99] D. Embley, D. Campbell, Y. Jiang, S. Liddle, D. Lonsdale, Y.-K. Ng, and R. Smith. Conceptual-model-based data extraction from multiple-record web pages. *Data & Knowledge Engineering*, 31(3):227–251, November 1999.

[EFKR99] D.W. Embley, N. Fuhr, C.-P. Klas, and T. Roelleke. Ontology suitability for uncertain extraction of information from multi-record web documents. In *Proceedings of the Workshop on Agenten, Datenbanken und Information Retrieval (ADI'99)*, Rostock-Warnemuende, Germany, 1999.

[EJN99] D.W. Embley, Y.S. Jiang, and Y.-K. Ng. Record-boundary discovery in Web documents. In *Proceedings of the 1999 ACM SIGMOD*, pages 467–478, Philadelphia, Pennsylvania, 31 May - 3 June 1999.

[EX00] D.W. Embley and L. Xu. Record location and reconfiguration in unstructured multiple-record web documents. In *Proceedings of the 3rd Intl. Workshop on the Web and Databases*, pages 123–128, Dallas, Texas, May 2000.

[McC96] Andrew Kachites McCallum. Bow: A toolkit for statistical language modeling, text retrieval, classification and clustering. http://www.cs.cmu.edu/ mccallum/bow, 1996.

[MNRS99] A. McCallum, K. Nigam, J. Rennie, and K. Seymore. Building domain-specific search engines with machine learning techniques. In *Proceedings of the AAAI Spring Sym. on Intelligent Agents in Cyberspace*, March 1999.

[Qui93] J.R. Quinlan. *C4.5: Programs for Machine Learning*. Morgan Kaufmann, San Mateo, California, 1993.

[RL94] E. Riloff and W. Lehnert. Information extraction as a basis for high-precision text classification. *ACM TOIS*, 12(3):296–333, 1994.

[SM83] G. Salton and M. J. McGill. *Introduction to Modern Information Retrieval*. McGraw-Hill, New York, 1983.

Querying Web Information Systems

Klaus-Dieter Schewe

Massey University, Department of Information Systems,
Private Bag 11 222, Palmerston North, New Zealand
k.d.schewe@massey.ac.nz

Abstract. The concept of *media object* is known as a view-centered approach to enable the development of maintainable web-based information systems. It allows tight linkages between databases, dialogues, processes and flexible representations at the user interface. The problem is to extend this approach by adequate query facilities.

In order to solve this problem a *query algebra* will be defined by operations induced from a type system that are complemented by a simple generalized join-operation. It is shown that such an algebra is able to capture basic operations as known from relational algebra, aggregate operations as known from SQL and restructuring operations such as nesting and unnesting. Furthermore, the creation of URLs is supported.

The focus of the paper is on the content of media objects. For the presentation of query results via web pages the metaphor of *information container* is exploited.

Keywords. media object, query algebra, web-based system

1 Introduction

A database-backed information systems that is realized and distributed over the web user access via web browsers is a *web information system*. Information is made available via pages including a navigation structure between them and to sites outside the system. Furthermore, there should also be operations to retrieve data from the system or to update the underlying database(s).

Web information systems are all around. However, the web still appears to be a huge, unordered collection of pages. In many cases most of the effort for designing these pages has been spent on nice (or not so nice) presentations with the consequence that maintenance consumes a vast amount of time and money.

On the other hand, it is argued that the design of reasonable web applications should be based on the mature methods of conceptual modelling [3]. This implicitly implies a concentration on data-intensive web-applications. Various approaches to develop design methods for data-intensive web-sites have been proposed so far, e.g. ARANEUS [1], Embley [4], HDM [8], WebComposition [9], Gehrke [10], FLASH [11] and OOHDM [20]. The work in [12] considers active web-based system emphasizing dynamic changes.

We believe that conceptual modelling for web information system is indispensible. Our work is based on the central notion of *media object* which was introduced in [7], further investigated in [16,17] and embedded in a complete methodology for conceptual web site modelling in [15]. Media objects are a decisive conceptual means for the description of content, operational functionality, navigational functionality, and usage of web pages. This exceeds work in [3,13] focussing primarily on the navigation aspect. Furthermore, the approach adapts known abstraction principles in order to support the conceptual design with *media types*.

In this paper we extend the concept of media types by an algebraic query language. The language will be defined in a generic way in order to allow it to be used for various underlying types of databases. This language completes the picture of a web information system.

In Section 2 we present the concepts of media object and media type in its current advanced form. Then in Section 3 we outline our algebraic approach to querying web information systems. In Section 4 we briefly sketch the problem of how how to present the result of a query. We finish with a few conclusions in Section 5.

2 Media Objects Revisited

Let us look again at the media objects from [15]. They were introduced as a means to formalize descriptive means for web sites. The major intention was to abstract completely from presentational issues, but nevertheless to keep in mind the capability for presentation. Thus, according to the outline in the introduction media objects should combine descriptions of content, functionality and usage.

- As to the content media objects provide abstract structural descriptions based on type systems including navigation structures. They also support database connections via views. The data provided by a media object may include hidden data, e.g., links, as well as context and escort information. In addition, there are also specific media objects called *session objects* to support rhetoric figures / metaphors such as shopping cart, wishlists, notepads, etc. In order to support different presentations to end-users and various end-devices media objects allow different granularity and density of content.
- As to functionality this is achieved by adding functions. These can be internal functions such as database processes, internal search and navigation, or external connections such as general search, links to other sites, etc., or support functions such as marking, extraction in connection with the session objects.
- As to usage we introduce user dimensions with scales and user profiles. These can be taken as the basis to define user types.

Figure 1 illustrates the general idea underlying the concept of media object. On the lowest level we find main data and escort data stored in databases. In particular, the quality criteria for database design apply to this level. The next level is built by raw media objects. These are extracted from the database using views. In addition, the functions that are required to model active functionality are added at this level. The third level is the one of the media objects that result from the raw media objects by tailoring their content (and hence also functionality) by various forms of controlled loss of information. Finally, we have to pay attention to the level of users. On one side the profiling of users determines the tailoring of the media objects. On the other side the information provided by the media objects is wrapped and presented to the users.

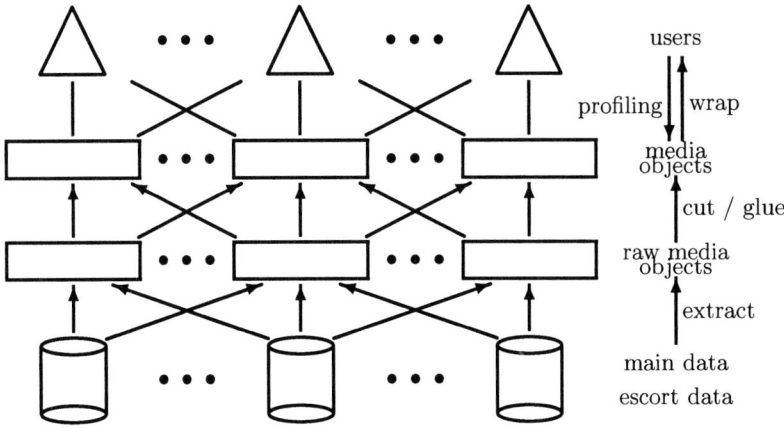

Fig. 1. Media Objects: The General Picture

2.1 Database Types

We assume that we have an underlying database. In principle, it is not important what kind of database we have as long as there exists a sufficiently powerful query mechanism that allows to define views. For the purpose of our presentation here, however, we focus on a conceptual description of such databases using a datamodel close to the higher-order Entity-Relationship model (HERM) [24].

Thus, we shall distinguish between *data types* as means for the conceptual description of values and *database types* for describing database objects. For both of these we obtain schemata, i.e. a type system (with set semantics), and a database schema with databases as instances.

Let the underlying type system be defined as $t = b \mid (a_1 : t_1, \ldots, a_n : t_n) \mid \{t\} \mid [t]$. Here b represents an arbitrary collection of *base types*, e.g., *BOOL* for boolean values **T** and **F**, *OK* for a single value *ok*, *TEXT* for text, *PIC* for images, *MPIC* for video data, *CARD* and *INT* for numbers, *DATE* for dates, *URL* for URL-addresses, *MAIL* for e-mail-addresses, etc. The constructors $(\cdot)$, $\{\cdot\}$ and $[\cdot]$ are used for records, finite sets and finite lists.

Definition 2.1. A *database type of level* k has a name E and consists of a set $comp(E) = \{r_1 : E_1, \ldots, r_n : E_n\}$ of components with pairwise different role names r_i and database types (or clusters) E_i on levels lower than k with at least one database type of level exactly $k - 1$, a set $attr(E) = \{a_1, \ldots, a_m\}$ of attributes, each associated with a data type $dom(a_i)$ as its domain, and a key $id(E) \subseteq comp(E) \cup attr(E)$. We shall write $E = (comp(E), attr(E), id(E))$.

A *cluster of level k* has a name E and consists of a set $frag(E) = \{f_1 : E_1, \ldots, f_n : E_n\}$ of fragments with pairwise different fragment names r_i and database types (or clusters) E_i on levels at most k with at least one of the E_i of level exactly k.

A *database schema* is a finite set $\mathcal{S}$ of database types and clusters such that for all $E \in \mathcal{S}$ and all $(r_i : E_i) \in comp(E)$ or $(f_i : E_i) \in frag(E)$, respectively, we also have $E_i \in \mathcal{S}$. □

Following [24] the definition of *databases* over a given database schema $\mathcal{S}$ is straightforward. Furthermore, we can easily define a graphical representation for a database schema.

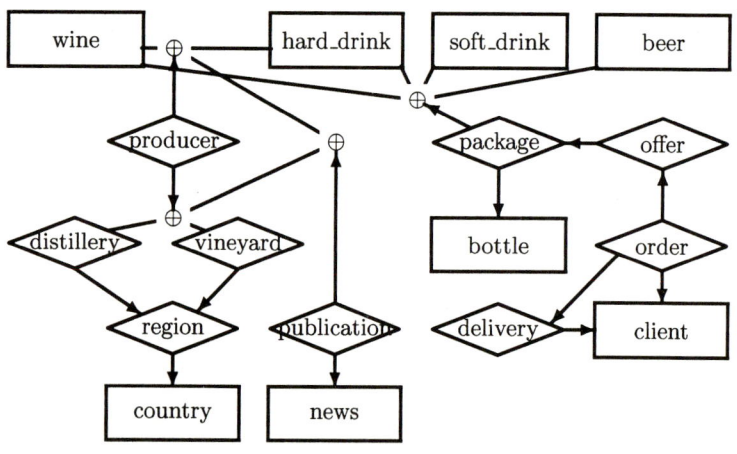

Fig. 2. Graphical Representation of a Database Schema

Example 2.1. We choose an e-commerce application as a running example. A bottleshop is going to deliver wines, champaigns, beers, juices, soft drinks and hard alcoholics drinks (esp. Cognac, Grappa, Scotch and Irish Whiskey) via the internet. There shall be a catalogue containing the offered products as well as occasional special offers. Additional information about wines, grapes, vineyards (also for Cognac, Grappa, Calvados and Whiskey) shall be provided as well. There shall be information about the shop itself, historical and actual information about certain grapes, wine producers, etc. There shall be special information about best sellers, new products, etc.

Figure 2 provides a graphical representation of a database for this application. According to the common convention in Entity-Relationship diagrams we represented types on level 0 by rectangles and types on higher levels by diamonds. Attributes and role names have been omitted in the schema. Clusters are represented by the ⊕ symbol, but we omitted cluster names as well as fragment names. □

2.2 Raw Media Types

The core of a raw media object is defined by a view, which, roughly speaking, is itself defined by a stored query. We leave details of suitable query languages to the next section.

Definition 2.2. A *view* V on a database schema $\mathcal{S}$ consists of a view schema $\mathcal{S}_V$ and a defining query q_V, which transforms databases over $\mathcal{S}$ into databases over $\mathcal{S}_V$. □

The defining query may be expressed in any suitable query language, e.g. query algebra, logic or an SQL-variant. We shall outline a general algebraic approach in the next section following the observation made in [18]. For our purposes, however, this is yet not sufficient, since in all these cases the query result will be a set of values. One key concept that is missing in the views is the one of *link*.

In order to introduce links, we we must create URLs in the rsult of a query. This can be done by the following operations:

- create_urls transforms a set $\{v_1, \ldots, v_m\}$ of values into a set $\{(u_1, v_1), \ldots, (u_m, v_m)\}$ of pairs with new created URLs u_i of type URL;
- create_urls also transforms a list $[v_1, \ldots, v_m]$ of values into a list $[(u_1, v_1), \ldots, (u_m, v_m)]$ of pairs with new created URLs u_i of type URL;
- create_url transforms a value v of any type into a pair (u, v) with a new URL u.

We shall talk of *query languages with create-facility*. As a second extension we may want to provide also escort information, which can be realized by a super-typing mechanism. This leads to the definition of *raw media type*.

Definition 2.3. A *raw media type* has a name M and consists of a content data type $cont(M)$ with the extension that the place of a base type may be occupied by a pair $\ell : M'$ with a label ℓ and the name M' of a raw media type, a finite set $sup(M)$ of raw media type names M_i, each of which will be called a supertype of M, and a defining query q_M with create-facility such that $(\{t_M\}, q_M)$ defines a view. Here t_M is the type arising from $cont(M)$ by substitution of URL for all pairs $\ell : M'$. □

Finite closed sets $\mathcal{C}$ of raw media types define *content schemata*. Then a database $\mathcal{D}$ over the underlying database schema $\mathcal{S}$ and the defining queries determine finite sets $\mathcal{D}(M)$ of pairs (u, v) with URLs u and values v of type t_M for each $M \in \mathcal{C}$. We use the notion *pre-site* for the extension of $\mathcal{D}$ to $\mathcal{C}$.

Finally, we collect all raw media types $M_1, \ldots, M_k$ with $(u, v_i) \in \mathcal{D}(M_i)$ for a given URL u. The pair $(u, (M_1 : v_1, \ldots, M_k : v_k))$ will be called a *raw media object* in the pre-site $\mathcal{D}$.

Example 2.2. Let us extend the previous example. We want to have a view decsribing New Zealand red wines from 1995 on with at least 30% Cabernet Sauvignon on plus vineyards, regions, orders, offers, packages, average price per litre and year, and consumed litres. Then Figure 3 describes the content type of such a raw media type. □

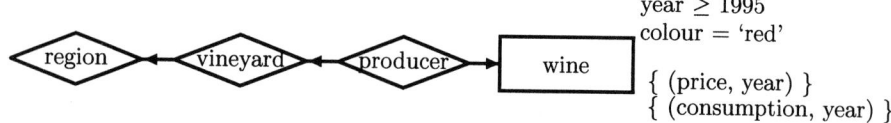

Fig. 3. Content Type of a Raw Media Type

The introduction of supertypes in raw media types allows repeated parts to be modelled. In particular, it is possible to associate general functionality or escort information with supertypes.

In order to model the required functionality we add operations to raw media types. This is completely analogous to the d-operations on dialogue types [14].

Definition 2.4. An *operation* on a raw media type M consists of an operation signature, i.e., name, input-parameters and output-parameters, a selection type which is a supertype of $cont(M)$, and a body which is defined via operations accessing the underlying database. □

The discussion in [5] listed several standard operations that are of particular interest in web information systems.

2.3 Media Types

Raw media objects are not yet sufficient for modelling web information systems. In order to allow the information content to be tailored to specific user needs and presentation restrictions, we must extend raw media types.

For many of the values we have to provide not only the type, but also the *measure unit*, e.g. Joule or kcal, PS or kW, cm, mm or m, etc. There exist fixed means for the calculation between the different units. Formally, each base type b should come along with a set $unit(b)$ of possible measure units. Each occurrence of b in the database or the raw media types has to accompanied by one element from $unit(b)$. This lead to an implicit extension of the defining queries q_M. We shall talk of a *unit-extended* raw media type.

Since the raw media types are used to model the content of the information service, order is important. Therefore, we claim that the set constructor should no longer appear in content expressions. Then we need an *ordering-operator* $ord_\leq$ which depends on a total order $\leq$ defined on a type t and is applicable to values v of type $\{t\}$. The result $ord_\leq(v)$ has the type $[t]$. We shall tacitly assume that ordering operators are used in the defining queries q_M. In this case we talk of an *order-extended* raw media type.

Adhesion introduces a controlled form of information loss. Formally, we define a partial order $\leq$ on content data types, which extends subtyping in a straightforward way such that references and superclasses are taken into consideration.

Definition 2.5. If $cont(M)$ is the content data type of a raw media type M and $sup(cont(M))$ is the set of all content expressions exp with $cont(M) \leq exp$, then a preorder $\preceq_M$ on $sup(cont(M))$ extending the order $\leq$ on content expressions is called an *adhesion preorder*. Clearly, $cont(M)$ is minimal with respect to $\preceq_M$. □

Small elements in $sup(cont(M))$ with respect to $\preceq_M$ define information to be kept together, if possible.

Example 2.3. In our bottleshop system we may consider name, year and grapes for a wine more 'important' than vineyard or region or additional information. Thus, we define an adhesion preorder in such a way that this information is kep together. □

An alternative to adhesion preorders is to use *proximity values*.

Definition 2.6. Let $exp_1, \ldots, exp_n$ be an antichain with respect to $\preceq$. A symmetric $(n \times n)$-matrix $\{p_{ij}\}_{1 \leq i,j \leq n}$ with $0 \leq p_{ij} \leq 1$ is called a *set of proximity values*. □

The antichain in the definition represents a possible split of the information content. The higher the proximity value, the more do we wish to keep the components together.

Example 2.4. A promimity value of 0.2 for (*consumption*) to all other expressions in an antichain indicates that we are likely to separate this part. □

Another possibility to tailor the information content of raw media types is to consider dimension hierarchies as in OLAP systems. Flattening of dimensions results in information growth, its converse in information loss. Such a hierarchy is already implicitly defined by the component or link structures, repectively.

Formally, flattening can be defined by operators $flat_r$. If E' is a component of E corresponding to the role r, we may replace E by $flat_r(E)$ defined as by $comp(flat_r(E)) = comp(E) - \{r : E'\} \cup comp(E')$ and $attr(flat_r(E)) = attr(E) \cup attr(E')$. The new key is $id(E) - \{r : E'\} \cup id(E')$ in the case $(r : E') \in id(E)$; it is $id(E)$ otherwise. We may extend this definition and flatten occurrences of links $\ell : M'$ in content data types $cont(M)$. We simply substitute $cont(M')$ for $\ell : M'$. The resulting raw media type will be denoted as $flat_\ell(M)$.

The converse operator $raise_P$ for $P \subseteq comp(E) \cup attr(E)$ is defined analogously. Again, this may be generalized to $raise_{exp}(M)$ for a content expression occurring within $cont(M)$. This will introduce a new link expression replacing exp.

For a raw media type M let $\bar{H}(M)$ be the set of all raw media types arising from M by applying a sequence of flat-operations or their converses to raw media types or underlying database types. A *set of hierarchical versions* of M is a finite subset $H(M)$ of $\bar{H}(M)$ with $M \in H(M)$. Each adhesion order $\preceq_M$ on M induces an adhesion order $\preceq_{M'}$ on each element $M' \in H(M)$.

Definition 2.7. A *media type* is a unit-extended, order-extended raw media type M together with an adhesion order $\preceq_M$ (or a set of promimity values) and a set of hierarchical versions $H(M)$. □

A *media schema* is defined in the same way as a content schema replacing raw media types by media types. A database $\mathcal{D}$ over the underlying database schema $\mathcal{S}$ extends to a unique pre-site. Furthermore, we may extend $\mathcal{D}$ to all hierarchical versions $M' \in H(M)$ and all $M'' \succ_{M'} M'$ defined by the adhesion orders. This wide extension of $\mathcal{D}$ will be called a *site*.

Finally, we collect all media types $M_1, \ldots, M_k$ together with their hierarchical versions and types defined by the adhesion order such that $(u, v_i) \in \mathcal{D}(M_i)$ holds for a given URL u. The pair $(u, (M_1 : v_1, \ldots, M_k : v_k))$ will be called a *media object* in the site $\mathcal{D}$.

3 Queries on Media Objects

As described in the introduction we want to extend the conceptual model of web information systems by querying facilities. As the core of the content description for media objects is defined via views over an underlying database, thus already depends on a query language, we simply have to make this query language explicit. We have to make sure that we can handle the creation of URLs and that this fits smoothly into the other operations of a query language. Furthermore, the approach to querying must be general enough to cope with all possible underlying databases, as we did not want to fix one particular underlying datamodel.

Therefore, we follow the algebraic approach described in [18]. There it has been shown that any query algebra can be defined by operations defined from the underlying type system plus one generalized join-operation. This extends to rational tree types, hence is suitable for our case, as we may expand the links defined via values of type URL to obtain rational trees. On the other hand, it can be shown that the create-facility which we assumed for our query language is equivalent to such a language working on rational trees.

Roughly speaking, a rational tree in our case would correspond to a page of infinite size which results from replacing all links by copies of the referenced page. As the navigation structure may contain cycles, the resulting page would be infinite.

3.1 The General Approach to Query Algebra

We claimed that for any query algebra a single "general join-operation" is enough: all other operations are induced by the underlying type system. For this we have to clarify what we mean by induction from the underlying type system and "general join-operation".

Let us first look at the easiest example which is given by relational algebra. Abstracting from relational algebra gives the motivation for our claim.

The constants are just the relation names R given by a schema $\mathcal{S}$ and unary relations $\{(A : a)\}$ with a single tuple. The operations comprise *projection*, *selection*, *renaming*, (natural) *join*, *union* and *difference*, denoted by π, σ, δ, $\bowtie$, $\cup$ and $-$, respectively.

Renaming only concerns syntax. Union and difference are standard set operations, i.e. they are defined by the set type constructor, which is implicitly around in the underlying type system. The same applies to selection, which always filters out a subset of those elements which meet the selection condition φ. This condition can be expressed by a boolean-valued function. Finally, projection is an operation inherent to tuple types. The projection operation in relational algebra, is an operation on sets of tuples; projection (on tuples) is applied to each element of the set.

In this sense all operations of relational algebra except $\bowtie$ are induced from the underlying type system. Now let us look at other types and type constructors that may occur in a type system.

In particular, we consider a trivial type denoted $\mathbb{1}$ and a boolean type $BOOL$. Values of these types are $\mathbf{1}$ and $\mathbf{T}, \mathbf{F}$, respectively. There is no operation on $\mathbb{1}$, but for $BOOL$ we may consider the operations $\wedge : BOOL \times BOOL \to BOOL$ (conjunction), $\neg : BOOL \to BOOL$ (negation) and $\Rightarrow : BOOL \times BOOL \to BOOL$ (Implication). Furthermore, we consider two constants $\texttt{true} : \mathbb{1} \to BOOL$ and $\texttt{false} : \mathbb{1} \to BOOL$.

For tuple types we consider $\textit{projection } \pi_i : t_1 \times \cdots \times t_n \to t_i$ and $\textit{product }$ $o_1 \times \cdots \times o_n : t \to t_1 \times \cdots \times t_n$ for given operations $o_i : t \to t_i$.

For set types me may consider $\cup$ (union), $-$ (difference), the constant $\texttt{empty} : \mathbb{1} \to \{t\}$ and the $\textit{singleton}$ operation $\texttt{single} : t \to \{t\}$ with well known semantics. In addition, we consider structural recursion, which will be discussed in detail in the next subsection. We dispense with a discussion of the similar situation for list and multiset types.

For function types we consider $\textit{composition } \circ : (t_2 \to t_3) \times (t_1 \to t_2) \to (t_1 \to t_3)$, $\textit{evaluation } \texttt{ev} : (t_1 \to t_2) \times t_1 \to t_2$, and $\textit{abstraction } \texttt{abstr} : (t_1 \times t_2 \to t_3) \to (t_1 \to (t_2 \to t_3))$. All these operations are standard.

For completeness assume an equality predicate $=_t : t \times t \to BOOL$ for all types t except function types and a membership predicate $\in : t \times \{t\} \to BOOL$. We shall also use a unique "forget"-operation $\texttt{triv} : t \to \mathbb{1}$ for each type t. Combining all the operations for all types of the type system gives all operations induced from the type system.

Let us now take a closer look at a powerful class of operations defined by the method of structural recursion [24]. Here, we will define and apply this method only for set types, but it works as well for lists, multisets, binary trees, etc.

For set types there are three natural constructors: the constant $\texttt{empty}$, the singleton operation and the union operation. In order to define an operation on a set type, say $\texttt{op} : \{t\} \to t'$ it is therefore sufficient to define it on the empty set, on singleton sets and on unions.

Formally, we define $\texttt{op} = \texttt{src}[e, g, \sqcup]$ with a value e of type t', a function $g : t \to t'$ and a function $\sqcup : t' \times t' \to t'$. Then $\texttt{src}[e, g, \sqcup]$ is defined by $\texttt{src}[e, g, \sqcup](\emptyset) = e$, $\texttt{src}[e, g, \sqcup](\{x\}) = g(x)$ and $\texttt{src}[e, g, \sqcup](X \cup Y) = \texttt{src}[e, g, \sqcup](X) \sqcup \texttt{src}[e, g, \sqcup](Y)$ for each x of type t, and each X, Y of type $\{t\}$. Sometimes it is necessary to consider only disjoint unions. In this case we use the notation $\texttt{srcd}[e, g, \sqcup]$.

Let us illustrate structural recursion by some more or less standard examples. First consider a function $f : t \to t'$ for arbitrary types t and t'. We want to "raise" f to a function $\mathtt{map}(f) : \{t\} \to \{t'\}$ by applying f to each element of a set. Obviously, we have $\mathtt{map}(f) = \mathtt{src}[\emptyset, \mathtt{single} \circ f, \cup]$. Recall that projection in relational algebra can be defined by $\mathtt{map}$.

Next consider a function $\varphi : t \to BOOL$. We want to define an operation $\mathtt{filter}(\varphi) : \{t\} \to \{t\}$, which associates with a given set the subset of all elements "satisfying the predicate" φ, i.e. elements that are mapped to $\mathbf{T}$. Then we may write $\mathtt{filter}(\varphi) = \mathtt{src}[\emptyset, \mathtt{if} \circ (\varphi \times \mathtt{single} \times (\mathtt{empty} \circ \mathtt{triv})), \cup]$ with the function $\mathtt{if} : BOOL \times t \times t \to t$ with $(\mathbf{T}, x, y) \mapsto x$ and $(\mathbf{F}, x, y) \mapsto y$.

As a third example assume that t is a "number type", on which addition $+ : t \times t \to t$ is defined. Then $\mathtt{srcd}[0, id, +]$ with the identity function id on t defines the sum of the elements in a set. In this way all the known aggregate functions of SQL (and more) can be defined by structural recursion.

In [18] it has been shown that the operations defined so far are sufficient to express operations such as nest and unnest.

3.2 The Join Operation

Let us now look at the the generalized join-operation, for which relational algebra again is the motivating example fromn which we abstract to the more general case.

Suppose we want to build the natural join of two relations R_1 and R_2. According to our definition these are finite sets of values of type t_1 and t_2, respectively. Of course, t_1 and t_2 are tuple types. The common components give rise to another tuple type t and we get natural projections $\pi_t^i : t_i \to t$.

The tuple type used for $R_1 \bowtie R_2$ – we shall denote this type by $t_1 \bowtie_t t_2$ – now has the following nice properties:

- There are canonical projections $\pi_{t_i} : t_1 \bowtie_t t_2 \to t_i$ such that $\pi_t^1 \circ \pi_{t_1} = \pi_t^2 \circ \pi_{t_2}$ holds.
- For any other tuple type t' with projections $\pi'_{t_i} : t' \to t_i$ with $\pi_t^1 \circ \pi'_{t_1} = \pi_t^2 \circ \pi'_{t_2}$ there is a unique projection $\pi : t' \to t_1 \bowtie_t t_2$ with $\pi_{t_i} \circ \pi = \pi'_{t_i}$.

With this observation, the (natural) join is easily defined as $R_1 \bowtie R_2 = \{z : t_1 \bowtie_t t_2 \mid \exists z_1 \in R_1. \exists z_2 \in R_2. \pi_{t_1}(z) = z_1 \wedge \pi_{t_2}(z) = z_2\}$.

This can be taken as the guideline for the generalization, provided we are able to obtain the type $t_1 \bowtie_t t_2$ and the corresponding functions π_{t_i} for the general case, too. The first natural idea is to exploit subtyping on the type system. This is a preorder $\leq$ on the types defined in the standard way.

Then each subtype relation $t \leq t'$ defines an associated subtype function $\pi_{t'} : t \to t'$. Note that the projections in relational algebra are just such subtype functions. Indeed, t is the least common supertype of t_1 and t_2; $t_1 \bowtie_t t_2$ is a common subtype. The following theorem is central for the definition of the general join.

Theorem 3.1. *Consider a type system with the trivial type $\mathbb{1}$ as one of its base types and with constructors among the tuple, set, list and multiset constructors. If t is a common supertype of t_1 and t_2 with associated subtype functions $\pi_t^i : t_i \to t$, then there exists a common subtype $t_1 \bowtie_t t_2$ together with subtype functions $\pi_{t_i} : t_1 \bowtie_t t_2 \to t_i$ such that $\pi_t^1 \circ \pi_{t_1} = \pi_t^2 \circ \pi_{t_2}$ holds. Furthermore, for any other common subtype t' with subtype functions $\pi'_{t_i} : t' \to t_i$ with $\pi_t^1 \circ \pi'_{t_1} = \pi_t^2 \circ \pi'_{t_2}$ there is a unique subtype function $\pi : t' \to t_1 \bowtie_t t_2$ with $\pi_{t_i} \circ \pi = \pi'_{t_i}$.* □

With the existence of the *join types* $t_1 \bowtie_t t_2$ the join over t can be defined as in the relational case. For this let C_1 and C_2 be classes. We define $C_1 \bowtie_t C_2 = \{z : T_{C_1} \bowtie_t T_{C_2} \mid \exists z_1 \in C_1.\exists z_2 \in C_2.\pi_{t_1}(z) = z_1 \wedge \pi_{t_2}(z) = z_2\}$.

Example 3.1. Consider $t_1 = \{b_1 \times \{b_2 \times b_3\} \times b_4\}$ and $t_2 = \{b_1 \times \{b_5 \times b_3\} \times b_6\}$ with the common supertype $t = \{b_1 \times \{b_3\}\}$. Then we obtain the join type $t_1 \bowtie_t t_2 = \{b_1 \times \{b_2 \times b_5 \times b_3\} \times b_4 \times b_6\}$. □

3.3 Handling URLs

The structures allowed by the definition of databases in the previous section are all finite. In fact, values can be represented as finite trees. A slight generalization would be to allow infinite trees, but of course only such infinite trees that can be represented in a finite way. For this we introduce *labels* ℓ. We extend any given type system in such a way allowing types to be adorned with labels and labels themselves to be treated in the same way as base types. Thus, our type system extends to $t = b \mid \ell \mid t_1 \times \cdots \times t_n \mid \{t\} \mid [t] \mid \ell : t$.

Furthermore, we have to restrict ourselves to *well-defined* types. For this we require that for each label ℓ occurring within a type t—in a place, where we could have a base type instead—some decorated type $\ell : t'$ must occur in t, too. Values of such types with labels can be written as an infinite tree. Figure 4 a) shows such a tree.

We call a tree *rational* iff the number of different subtrees is finite. Then only rational trees will be allowed as values of well-defined types with labels. This means to restrict to values of the form $(n_1, a_1, (n_2, a_2, (\ldots, (n_k, a_k, (\ldots)))))$, such that $n_i = n_j$ and $a_i = a_j$ holds for some i and j. In addition, we would like to add a constraint and require $i = 1$, $j = 3$, but this constraint must be added explicitly; it is not captured by the type system. Figure 4 b) illustrates such a rational tree.

Since we restrict ourselves to well-defined types with labels, which can be written as rational trees, and allow only rational trees as values, we shall talk of *rational tree types*.

One important feature of rational tree types is that the query algebra outlined in the previous subsection extends naturally to rational tree types. Furthermore, as the representation with URLs can be regarded as a means to finitely represent rational trees, it can also be shown that we can replace the rational trees by the URLs, iff the query language is extended by a create-facility.

Theorem 3.2. *Let S be a database schema, where the types of classes are rational tree types and let S' be an equivalent schema that uses the type URL, but no rational tree types. Then the result of an algebra query on S' with schema create-facily is the URL-based representation of the result of the same query applied to S and vice versa.* □

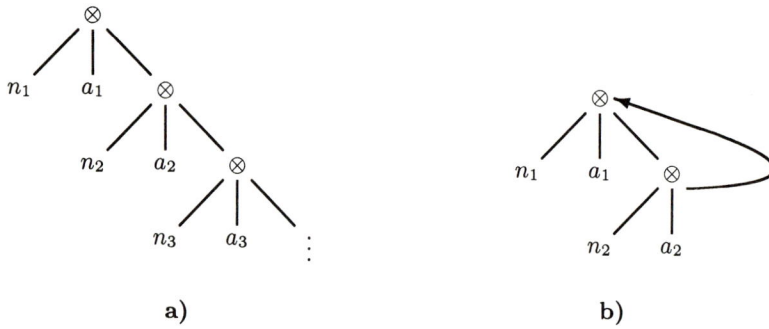

Fig. 4. Rational Tree

4 Presentation of Query Results

As media objects abstract completely from presentational issues, the remaining problem is to clarify how query results are to be presented. For this we exploit the container metaphor introduced in [5].

The underlying idea is as follows. Selected information will be wrapped, loaded into a (generic) container, shipped to the user and then unloaded with the help of a browser. So the goal is to provide predefined containers that are able to capture the expected results of queries.

Ideally, containers should be usable for different contents, but nevertheless the design of container is heavily influenced by the usage of media objects in the scenarios, the user profile and the technical constraint arising from size and presentation facilities of the supported presentation devices.

For instance, we may assume a scale for the size of the devices ranging from tiny (as for WAP handies) over small (for videotext screens) to normal, large and huge (for different kinds of screens). It might be the case that not all sizes are to be supported. Formally, such a scale is a totally ordered set analogous to the scales for user dimensions.

Other technical constraints may be the unability to present images or video/audio information or channel bandwidth (e.g., for mobile devices).

Basically, the possible content of a container can be described by a content data type same as for media types. Any actual content must fit into this type, i.e. it must give rise to a supertype. Furthermore, the content data type must be accompanied by some presentation layout matching the technical constraints. This layout may include constants such as recurring pictures, background, etc. It may be realized by a parameterized HTML document. Formally, a *container* has a name C and consists of a content $cont(C)$ and a presentation layout $lay(C)$.

Loadability of a media object $(u, (M_1 : v_1, \ldots, M_k : v_k))$ into a container C holds, if the content data type $cont(M_i)$ is a supertype of $cont(C)$ for at least one i. Since M_i arises from a media type including versions originating from adhesion or hierarchy, this implies that v_i matches the content description of the container C.

The *wrapping* of the media object $(u, (M_1 : v_1, \ldots, M_k : v_k))$ into the container C then means the identification of the suitable M_i in order to load a maximum amount of information. Formally, this means to choose $cont(M_i)$ minimal, so that loadability can be guaranteed.

Finally, the *loading* of the container consists in the generation of the page replacing the parameters by the loaded information.

5 Conclusion

In recent work [6,7,16,17] the notion of media object has ben introduced as a conceptual means to model web information systems. In this paper we extended this work by adding a reasonable query language to this concept. The query language is based on the generalized algebraic approach in [18] according to which a query algebra can always be defined by operations of an underlying type system plus a generalized join operation. This approach is powerful enough to handle the cycles in web site navigation structures. It is easy to extend such an algebra in a way that even fixpoint queries can be handled, but this issue has not been discussed in this paper.

With the approach at hand it is possible to design integrated web sites and to offer query facilities for them. As we assume database technology to be used in such web sites, the maintainance is much easier than in hand-knitted sytems. The project in [23] with around 20,000 mainly generated web pages has realized the idea of media objects. In fact, the ideas realized in this project [2,19,21,22,23] have also contributed to the development of this concept, which may now be applied to other projects as well.

References

1. P. Atzeni, A. Gupta, S. Sarawagi. Design and Maintenance of Data-Intensive Web-Sites. *Proc. EDBT '98*: 436-450. Springer LNCS 1377, 1998.
2. W. Clauß and J. Lewerenz, Abstract interaction specification for information services. Proc. IRMA Int. Conf., Hershey (Pennsylvania) 1999.
3. O. De Troyer. Designing Well-Structured Websites: Lessons Learned from Database Schema Methodology. In T.W. Ling, S. Ram, M.L. Lee (Eds.). *Conceptual Modeling – ER'98*: 51-64. Springer LNCS 1507, 1998.
4. D. Embley et al. A Conceptual-Modeling Approach to Extracting Data from the Web. In T.W. Ling, S. Ram, M.L. Lee (Eds.). *Conceptual Modeling – ER'98*: 78-91. Springer LNCS 1507, 1998.

5. T. Feyer, K.-D. Schewe, B. Thalheim. Conceptual Modelling and Development of Information Services. in T.W. Ling, S. Ram (Eds.). *Conceptual Modeling – ER '98*. Springer LNCS 1507, 7-20.
6. T. Feyer and B. Thalheim. E/R based scenario modeling for rapid prototyping of web information services. In P.P. Chen et al. (Eds.), Advances in Conceptual Modeling, Springer LNCS 1727, 1999, 253-263.
7. T. Feyer, O. Kao, K.-D. Schewe, B. Thalheim. Design of Data-Intensive Web-Based Information Services. In *Proc. 1st International Conference on Web Information Systems Engineering*. Hong Kong (China) 2000.
8. P. Fraternali, P. Paolini. A Conceptual Model and a Tool Environment for Developing more Scalable, Dynamic and Customizable Web Applications. *Proc. EDBT '98*: 422-435. Springer LNCS 1377, 1998.
9. M. Gaedtke et al. Object-Oriented Web Engineering for Large-Scale Web Service Management. *Proc. HICSS '99*. Hawaii 1999.
10. D. Gehrke and E. Turban, Determinants of successful website design – Relative importance and recommendations for effectiveness. Proc. HICSS '99, Hawaii 1999.
11. D.M. Germán, D.D. Cowan. Formalizing the Specification of Web Applications. In P.P. Chen et al. (Eds.). *Advances in Conceptual Modeling*: 281-292. Springer LNCS 1727, 1999.
12. B. Ludäscher and A. Gupta, Modeling interactive web sources for information mediation. In P.P. Chen et al. (Eds.) Advances in Conceptual Modeling, Springer LNCS 1727, 1999, 225-238.
13. G. Rossi, D. Schwabe, F. Lyardet. Web Application Models are more than Conceptual Models. In P.P. Chen et al. (Eds.). *Advances in Conceptual Modeling*: 239-252. Springer LNCS 1727, 1999.
14. K.-D. Schewe, B. Schewe. Integrating Database and Dialogue Design. *Knowledge and Information Systems* vol. 2 (1), 2000, 1-32.
15. K.-D. Schewe, B. Thalheim. *Conceptual Modelling of Internet Sites*. Tutorial Notes. ER'2000.
16. K.-D. Schewe, B. Thalheim. Modeling Interaction and Media Objects. In E. Métais (Ed.). *Proc. 5th Int. Conf. on Applications of Natural Language to Information Systems* (NLDB 2000). Versailles (France) 2000. to appear in Springer LNCS.
17. K.-D. Schewe, B. Thalheim. *Die Theorie der Medienobjekte im Entwurf von Informationsdiensten* (in German). Leipziger Informatik-Tage 2000 (invited talk).
18. K.-D. Schewe. On the Unification of Query Algebras and their Extension to Rational Tree Structures. In M. Orlowska, J. Roddick (Eds.). *Proc. Australasian Database Conference* (ADC 2001).
19. T. Schmidt, Konzepte, Betrachtungen und Lösungen für die Basistechnologie eines Informationssystems – Clientseite. M.Sc. Thesis. BTU Cottbus 1998.
20. D. Schwabe, G. Rossi. An Object Oriented Approach to Web-Based Application Design. *TAPOS*. vol. 4 (4): 207-225. 1998.
21. R. Schwietzke, Konzepte, Betrachtungen und Lösungen für die Basistechnologie eines Informationssystems – Serverseite. M.Sc. Thesis. BTU Cottbus 1998.
22. B. Thalheim, Codesign of structures, functions and interfaces in database applications. Preprint I-05-1997, 22. 2. 1997, Institut für Informatik, BTU Cottbus, 1997, 80p.
23. B. Thalheim, Development of database-backed information services for Cottbus-Net. Report CS-20-97, BTU Cottbus 1997.
24. B. Thalheim, Entity-Relationship Modeling – Foundations of Database Technology. Springer 2000.

A Conceptual Modelling Framework for Standards-Driven Web-Based Distance Learning

Luis Anido, Martín Llamas, Manuel J. Fernández, Judith Rodríguez,
Juan Santos, and Manuel Caeiro

ETSI Telecomunicaciones, Universidad de Vigo
Campus Universitario, s/n
E36200-Vigo, Spain
{lanido,martin,manolo,jestevez,jsgago,mcaeiro}@ait.uvigo.es

Abstract. Internet-based learning environments have proliferated over the last years. Many institutions, both public and private, benefit from them and offer on-line courses and training programs. In most cases, educational resources or software-supported learning services cannot be reused among heterogeneous systems. Additionally, although they share many common features, most e-learning systems are developed from the scratch. In this situation, a need for a standardized conceptual model becomes apparent.
Institutions like the IEEE, the US Department of Defense or the Aviation Industry are currently specifying standards to support information models used in e-learning environments. From these works we present a framework for e-learning. Our proposal includes the application of an OO methodology to derive a reference architecture and design model from those conceptual entities identified by the learning technology standardization process. We have used UML, the Unified Software Development process, object-oriented methodologies for the model definition, and eventually, CORBA technology to provide a final implementation.

1 Introduction

Advances in Information and Communication technologies and specifically in Multimedia, Networking, and Software Engineering, promote the apparition of a new generation of computer-based training systems. Internet is today a ubiquitous supporting environment for virtual and distributed learning environments. As a consequence, many institutions, both public and private, take advantage of new technologies to offer training products and services at all levels using the World Wide Web.

The use of multimedia material including text, audio, video and simulations offers an attractive environment to learners. In addition, networked training systems have played an important role because of its economical advantages, both for trainees and instructors and for the institutions that are responsible for carrying out the training process. Internet/Intranet-based environments are a practical and suitable platform for delivering courses and other training material.

As a consequence, e-learning systems proliferate and a need for standardization becomes apparent: new systems are usually developed ad-hoc from the scratch to meet the requirements of a particular institution, with no interoperability mechanism with external systems. Therefore, courses developed for a particular system cannot be delivered by a different one, student records and profiles cannot be easily transferred and there is no predefined procedure to share learning services at runtime.

This paper addresses interoperability issues among large-scale distributed e-learning systems. We propose a standards-driven object-oriented framework to develop such systems. Underlying information models are based on current work on learning technology standardization (c.f. section 2) by institutions like the US Department of Defense, the IEEE or the Aviation Industry, which are important consumers of educational software. They propose standards that define specifications for learning metadata, content structure, trainee records and profiles, etc. Thus enabling easy training resources reuse and transfer among institutions or internal departments. We have used CORBA [1] to develop a learning application using the framework. CORBA, and its object-oriented distributed computing capabilities, allowed us to add software interoperability and a reduction of the time-to-market factor for new developed training systems.

The paper is organized as follows: Section 2 introduces current works in the e-learning standardization area. Section 3 presents the methodology used to derive the framework. The process is explained through sections 4 (use case model), 5 (analysis model), 6 (reference model), 7 (reference architecture) and 8 (design model and IDL specifications). We end with some conclusions and proposals for the future.

2 E-learning Standardization

The learning technology standardization process is taking the lead role in the research efforts into distributed e-learning. Like in other standard-driven initiatives, standardization applied to learning technologies will enable reuse and interoperation among heterogeneous systems. Thus, institutional users of educational software are joining their efforts to achieve standards and recommendations to support the interoperation of heterogeneous learning systems. This is an active, continuously evolving process that will last for years to come, until a clear, precise and generally accepted set of standards for educational-related systems is developed. Organizations like the IEEE's LTSC [2], IMS project [3], Aviation Industry's AICC [4], US DoD's ADL initiative [5], ARIADNE [6], GESTALT project [7], PROMETEUS [8], CEN/ISSS/LT [9], GEM project [10], and many others are contributing to this standardization process. The IEEE LTSC is the institution that is actually gathering recommendations from other standardization institutions and projects. ISO/IEC JTC1 created in November 1999 the Standards Committee for Learning Technologies SC36 [11], to develop ANSI or ISO standards. Next paragraphs introduce the main areas of concern.

A key aspect in networked educational systems is to define, as precisely as possible, the educational contents offered to potential users. The trend seems to describe this information using learning metadata. The most outstanding contribution so far is the Learning Object Metadata (LOM) specification, proposed by the IEEE LTSC, which is becoming a de-facto standard. LOM defines the attributes required to fully and adequately describe learning resources. The latest draft document dates from February 2001. IMS, ADL, ARIADNE, GESTALT, GEM and EdNA have their own metadata proposals, which are based on LOM.

Description of learner's profiles and records has also been studied. They describe information that characterizes learners and their knowledge. This information is used to maintain records of learners. The IEEE LTSC Public and Private Information (PAPI) specification describes implementation independent learner records. Another important specification is the IMS Enterprise Data Model aimed at e-learning administration including group and enrolment management. Very recently, the IMS also delivered its first specification on learner profiles: IMS Learner Information Packaging Specification.

Other basic aspect subject to standardization is educational content organization, that is, data models to describe static and dynamic course structure. Static course structure defines the a priori relations among course contents (lessons, sections, exercises, etc.), whereas course dynamics determines the particular vision that users have depending on their attributes and previous interactions. In a similar way, learning environments need to understand the course structure to schedule the next student activity. The AICC guidelines for interoperability of Computer-Managed Instruction (CMI) systems, and the ADL's SCORM, based on the AICC specification, deal with this problem. They propose a Web-based Runtime environment scheme based on the division between the learning contents and the Web-based management system. This allows different learning resources to be managed by heterogeneous systems.

Other standards address to content packaging to facilitate course transfer among institutions (IMS Content Packaging Specification), question and test interoperability (IMS QTI specification), student tracking, competency definitions, and many others that are still in their definition process.

The more mature results are centered on the definition of information models to exchange learning resources. In most cases, XML [12] is used to define supporting information models enabling easy interoperability in WWW settings. Neither open reference architecture nor service definitions have been proposed so far. The work we present in this paper is a proposal towards such open architecture. Over standardized information models, a set of services is offered to the domain community of distributed e-learning systems developers.

3 Methodology

The framework's design process has been guided by the Unified Software Development Process [13] and modeled using the Unified Modeling Language (UML)

[14]. We combined the Unified Software Development Process with the recommendations by Bass et al. [15] to derive our software architecture.

The Unified Process identifies a set of iterations in the software development process: requirements, analysis, design, implementation and test. Designers begin by capturing customer requirements as use cases in the use case model. Then, they analyze and design the system to meet the use cases, thus creating first an analysis model, then a design and deployment model; and they implement the system in an implementation model. Finally, the developers prepare a test model that enables them to verify that the system provides the functionality described in the use cases.

On the other hand, Bass states that a reference model and a reference architecture are previous steps toward an eventual software architecture. The reference model is a division of the functionality, together with the corresponding data flow between the identified components. Whereas a reference model divides the functionality, a reference architecture is the mapping of that functionality onto a system decomposition.

Through next sections we show how these methodologies are related with each other, and how they were applied to the design of a conceptual modeling framework for e-training.

4 Use Case Model

We took into account the whole functionality that a computer-based training system provides. No pedagogical methodology assumption was made. Use cases identified has been derived from the authors' experience in the e-learning domain and the documentation provided by institutions involved in the learning technology standardization (specially the guidelines set by the IEEE's Learning Technology System Architecture (LTSA)) [16].

Our use case model was derived using a refinement process. At the most abstract level, generic use cases let us derive the first components (c.f. UML diagram in Figure 1). Three actors are involved: the trainee, who looks for expertise; the manager, who looks for experts; and the supervisor, who is responsible for the correct operation of the whole system. From them, we may derive the existence of an Educational System.

As the use cases mature and are refined and specified in more detail, more of the functional requirements are discovered. This, in turn, leads to the maturation of more use cases and, even new actors may show up. Use cases are not selected in isolation, they drive the system architecture and the system architecture influences the selection of the use cases. Therefore, both the system architecture and the actual use cases mature together.

As an example of this process, we show in Figure 2 the refinement of the Get Expertise use case. In this step, we identify the need for possible extensions to the base use case (Get Expertise). We need to provide access to the competency definitions of an expertise area, and the location of the defined courses. From here, we derive the need for a learning *Broker* that helps trainees to find courses

A Conceptual Framework for Web-Based Distance Learning

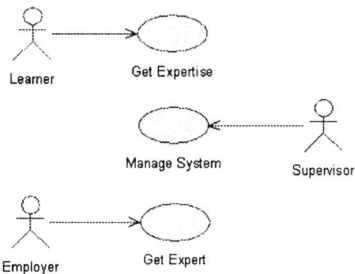

Fig. 1. Highest-Level Use Cases.

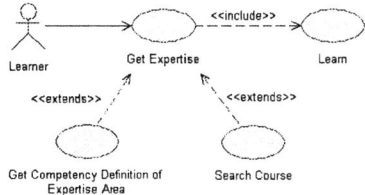

Fig. 2. Get Expertise Use Case Refinement.

provided by *Educational Service Providers*, which can belong to the trainee organization or to an external training company. These use cases were refined until the complete set of requirement was specified in the eventual use case model.

5 Analysis Model

Use cases are realized by class collaborations. The goal is to realize the use cases cost-effectively so that the system offers suitable performance and can evolve in the future. The analysis model grows incrementally as more and more use cases are analyzed. For each iteration we selected a set of use cases that we realize in the analysis model. The system is built as a structure of classifiers (analysis classes) and relationships between them. Collaborations describe realization of use cases.

We used three different stereotypes on classes: <<boundary>> (to model interaction between the system and its actors), <<control>> (to represent coordination, sequencing, transactions, etc.) and <<entity>> (to model information). For example, Figure 3 shows the analysis class diagram to realize those use cases related to training contents searching and location. There is a unique control class that implements the search logic. Searcher classes use entity classes that encapsulate training courses metadata, trainee preferences and course providers' data. Clients access search services through a boundary class.

Use cases related to access to learning resources are realized by the classes depicted in Figure 4. Three entity classes model metadata, content structures and

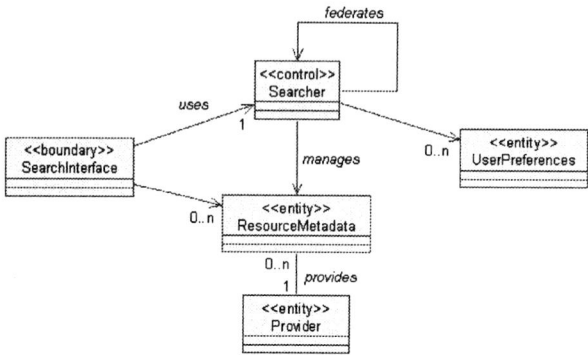

Fig. 3. Search course class diagram.

educational resources. Underlying information models are directly derived from the standards presented in section 2. The Repository boundary class manages access to them. Repository capabilities can be enhanced by a IMS Packaging specification-compliant control class.

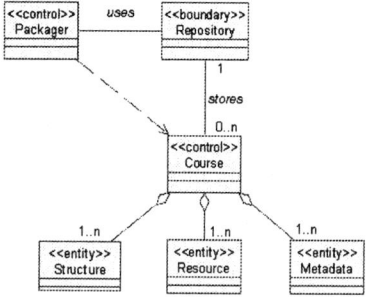

Fig. 4. Repository class diagram.

Learning runtime environments are responsible for content delivery and learner tracking. The corresponding analysis class diagram is shown in Figure 5. Course structure and learner's traces format specifications are used respectively by a Navigation and Tracking Manager control classes.

6 The Reference Model

Like the analysis model, the reference model is derived from the use cases and the functional needs identified from them. A further insight into the analysis model may let us abstract higher level functional elements. Specially, for large-scale systems, architects should study the analysis model to abstract a reference model.

A Conceptual Framework for Web-Based Distance Learning   591

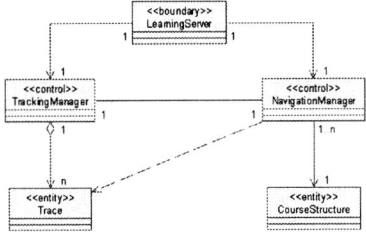

Fig. 5. Learning runtime environment class diagram.

We identified three functional modules (c.f. Figure 6) for the reference model. *Educational Content Providers* (ECP) are responsible for developing educational contents and offering them, maybe under payment, to the *Educational Service Providers* (ESP). Authors, multimedia and pedagogical experts are the main actors who interact with the ECP. Standardized course structure formats and metadata to describe contents are used at the ECP.

Learners interact with ESP modules through their learning process, from course enrolment to graduation. These modules are responsible for providing: structured storage and management of learning objects; an on-line environment for the delivery of learning content; and administration facilities to handle the registering and course progress of educational sessions. Developers of ESP must use existing information models for course structures, learner records, tracking data, and ADL/AICC-like Runtime environments.

Brokers help learners and ESP to find suitable courses to achieve a specific skill. *Brokers* must maintain metadata information about courses offered by associated ESP. *Brokers* also help ESP to find contents offered by ECP. Course transfer should be done using existing course packaging mechanisms.

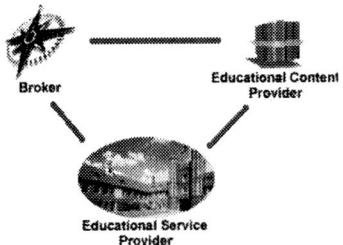

Fig. 6. Reference Model for E-learning.

Finally, employers look for experts into the *Profile Repository* (PR), which maintain learner high-level performance data and student overall records. ESP feed PR as their students acquire new expertise.

7 The Reference Architecture

Mature domains are supposed to have reference architectures that guide software developers to build new systems. Analysis model classes should be grouped into subsystems, especially for large systems. A subsystem is a semantically useful grouping of classes or other subsystems. It should be possible to install a subsystem in a customer system only in its entirety. Subsystems are also used to model groups of classes that tend to change together. In our case, changes in information models from learning technology standards should affect to the less number of subsystems as possible. Subsystems identified from the analysis model form the reference architecture (c.f. Figure 7), which is also implementation independent.

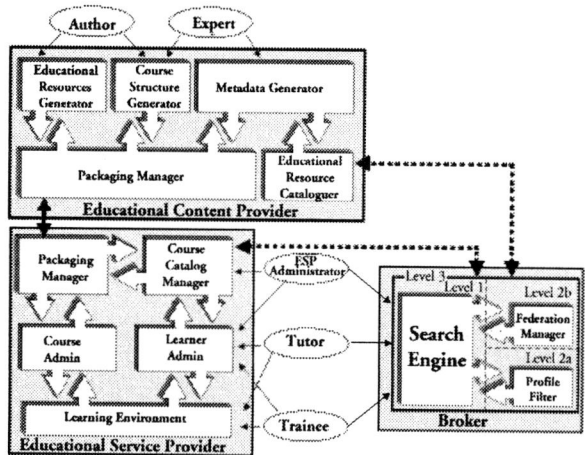

Fig. 7. Reference Architecture.

7.1 Broker Reference Architecture

The *Broker* architecture is composed of three different software subsystems: *Search Engine* (SE), *Federation Manager* (FM) and *Profile Filter* (PF). SE deals with the metadata repository to search for a learning object. No particular metadata scheme is imposed. In fact, the interface offered to external modules should be the same regardless of the underlying metadata model used to describe learning objects. At the same time, there must exist a mechanism to report supported metadata schemes to client modules. The design model should explicitly define this introspection procedure.

Search results may be filtered according to user preferences. Customers provide the brokerage subsystem with their preference profile (or a reference to it)

A Conceptual Framework for Web-Based Distance Learning   593

that is used to fit further searches to the predefined preferences. The PF is responsible for this. No particular learner information model is imposed. Reflective methods must offer information about the data models that are supported by the component implementation.

While at the reference model the *Broker* is a single module, at the reference architecture its functionality may have to be implemented by the collaboration of a group of federated brokers. The FM software subsystem manages federations according to the topology they are configured with. Searches sent through the *Federation Manager* are forwarded to external *Search Engines* and, possibly, to external *Federation Managers*.

To be compliant with this architecture, only the *Search Engine* component must be implemented. The Brokerage architecture defines several service levels. According to the level the *Broker* is compliant with, *Profile Filters* and/or *Federation Managers* have to be implemented. Table 1 shows the service levels defined for a *Broker* and the components needed for each of them.

Table 1. Broker Levels of Service

	Single Search	Search Filtered using Preference Data	Search Forwarding to Federated Brokers
Level 1	X		
Level 2a	X	X	
Level 2b	X		X
Level 3	X	X	X

This architecture should be fully scalable, a single SE-broker might add PF or FM subsystems in the future. The standardized information model that each component deals with drove our design criteria. A change or update in the data model that defines learning metadata or user preference profile information would only affect the SE or PF component respectively. Thus, we keep information models changes in the scope of a local reference architecture subsystem.

7.2 ESP Reference Architecture

Educational Service Provider (ESP) reference architecture is composed of five software subsystems (c.f. Figure 7): *Learning Environment* (LE), *Learner Admin* (LA), *Course Admin* (CA), *Packaging Manager* (PM) and *Course Catalogue Manager* (CCM). The LE subsystem is responsible for student routing through a course, learning content delivery in a networked environment and student tracking. *Learner Admin* manages course enrolment, user authentication and student curricula records and profiles. *Course Admin* manages the actual learning resources courses are composed of. It delivers contents to the LE and receives new resources from content providers through the *Packaging Manager*. CCM maintains up-to-date information about the actual courses being offered by the institution and publishing them through educational *Brokers*.

7.3 ECP Reference Architecture Educational

Content Provider (ECP) reference architecture is composed of five software subsystems (c.f. Figure 4): *Educational Resources Generator* (ERG), *Course Structure Generator* (CSG), *Metadata Generator* (MG), *Packaging Manager* (PM) and *Educational Resource Cataloguer* (ERC). The first three subsystems deal with the development, structure and cataloguing of new learning objects. ERC publicizes available resources through the *Brokers* in order to allow *Educational Service Providers* to find them. Eventually, courses are packaged by the PM and sent to an ESP, where ESP's PM unpacks them.

8 The Design Model: CORBAlearn

CORBAlearn software architecture is modeled using the design model of the Unified Process. The design model of the Unified Process is created using the analysis model as the primary input, but it is adapted to the selected implementation environment, such as an object request broker, a GUI construction kit, or a database management system. Similarly to the analysis model, the design model also defines classes, relationships among them, and collaborations that materialize the use cases. However, the elements defined in the design model are the design counterparts of the more conceptual elements defined in the analysis model, in the sense that the former are adapted to the implementation environment, whereas the latter (analysis) elements are not. In other words, the design model is more physical in nature, whereas the analysis model is more conceptual.

The design process that leads to this software architecture is driven by the reference architecture and available standardized information models: Changes in these information models should imply only local changes affecting the less number of objects as possible. Inclusion of new components from the reference architecture should be straightforward and not affect objects already running in the system.

CORBAlearn covers all those aspects of a distributed e-learning system identified by the reference architecture. For the sake of brevity, we just present here part of the static and dynamic view of the architecture elements. We encourage the reader to request the whole set of specifications to the authors.

8.1 Broker Services

Three brokerage service levels have been defined (c.f. Figure 7 and Table 1): Level 1 addresses basic searching in the metadata repository maintained by the Search Engine. Level 2a considers predefined user preference data to filter search results. Level 2b includes search federation where requests are forwarded to other *Brokers* in a distributed federation network. Level 3 supports both user

A Conceptual Framework for Web-Based Distance Learning   595

preference filtering and federation. In any case, access to a broker component is done through a *BrokerComponent* object that maintains references to the available service interfaces.

Upgrading of the service level provided by a broker can be made at run time. New objects implementing a higher service look for the *BrokerComponent* in the Naming Service [17] to update its references to new available service interfaces. Further client accesses to the *BrokerComponent* allow them to navigate to the recently deployed services.

Level 1-compliant brokers must implement the *BrokerManager* interface, to feed the broker metadata repository and the Searcher interface, which defines search and browse services. This allows developers of educational brokers implement a push-like feeding policy: *Educational Service/Content Provider* subsystems introduce metadata description into the broker. CORBAlearn specifications for these subsystems also define metadata access services. Therefore, a pull-like feeding policy is also possible: brokers subsystems get metadata descriptions from the providers.

Level 2a-compliant brokers need *ProfileSearcher* and *ProfileManager* interfaces. The former is used to deal with preference filtering and the latter to access or update those preferences. User preference data may be obtained directly from an ESP or PM, or a new preference profile can be created (i.e. data can be obtained by reference or value).

Level 2b compliance requires the implementation of the *FederatedSearch* interface. This interface defines as one of its attributes a reference to a *FederationManager* object that actually maintains the federation topology information. Finally, Level 3 requires the implementation of all the interfaces presented above.

ResourceRepository offers access to complete learning objects metadata descriptions. Finally, Provider Searcher and *ProviderManager* objects define services to locate the actual *Educational Service Provider* or *Educational Content Provider* where the learning object can be accessed. These three objects are used in the learning objects location phase [18].

Federated Brokerage Example Figure 8 exemplifies an interaction to perform a search through a federation network. Objects involved in that search may be distributed into four different computers, as shown in the deployment diagram shown in Figure 9. In that case, we assumed that the federation topology is maintained in a different computer (situated on the left). However, it is also possible that the same component that implements the *FederatedSearch* implemented the *FederationManager* interface. Thus, the level 2b compliant Broker would keep topology information.

As introduced in the reference architecture description, scalability between different service levels is straightforward: new objects implementing level 2a or 2b would look for the *BrokerComponent* in the Naming Service and update its interface references. Support for communication among objects distributed in different computers over a WWW/Internet environment is provided by the CORBA IIOP protocol.

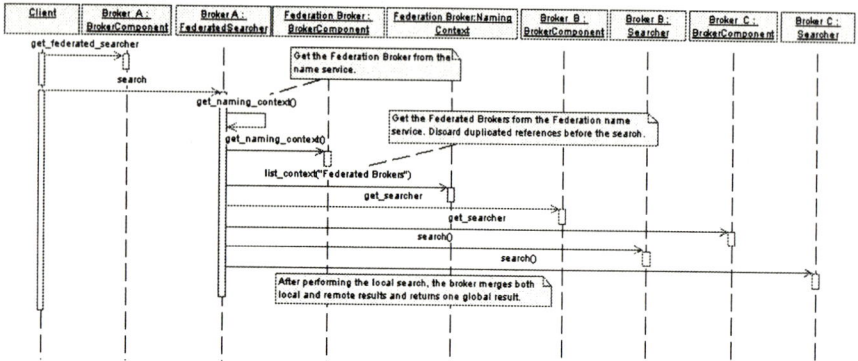

Fig. 8. Federated Brokerage Service Sequence Diagram.

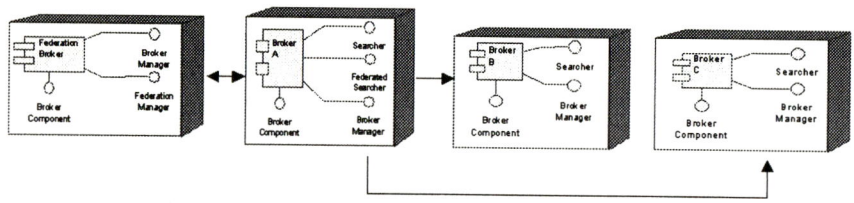

Fig. 9. Component Distribution for a Federated Search Example.

8.2 Learning Environment Services

CORBAlearn defines the UML class diagram depicted in Figure 5 to model the Learning Environment subsystem. Responsibilities are mainly divided into a *TrackingManager* object that follows student performance during a learning session, and a *NavigationManager* object that performs course routing according to a particular course structure format and student previous actions. These two objects work together to perform basic course routing and trading Learning Server Factory creates a Learning Server object to manage each student that access a different course.

Example of Applicability Defined services include common functionality for Learning Runtime environments. Developers of particular Web-based learning systems benefit from the offered services and their reuse. Thus, time to market is reduced. As an example of applicability, we developed a Web-based courseware system that conforms to the US Department of Defense ADL runtime model [19]. This model is bound to be accepted by the learning technology standards community as the common way for launching and getting lesson information in a Web-based distance learning environment. For this, we just needed to develop a thin layer between the Web browser and the CORBAlearn server objects.

The API defined by the ADL model can be easily implemented using the CORBAlearn objects. 16 hours of a junior Java software developer were needed to implement the ADL-compliant Web-based learning objects deliverer using the services offered by CORBAlearn.

9 Conclusions

Web-based software development is one of the most growing areas in the software industry. Several application domains have benefited from the new means of access and visualization of information supported by the World Wide Web. As a consequence, multiple and heterogeneous Web-based applications proliferate. However, although domain applications follow common eventual objectives, they are developed from the scratch with few or no interoperability mechanisms among them. Conceptual modeling provides a suitable environment where it is possible to build frameworks for domain specific applications. These users are, at the same time, developers of their own domain software products. On the other hand, those applications developed from them rely on clearly identified services. These specifications are a step further toward the standardization of the domain allowing interoperability among different and heterogeneous applications.

In this paper, we have presented a proposal for a conceptual modeling framework for technology learning systems. In this field great efforts are being done towards its standardization. Service definition was based on recommendations from the institutions involved in this process and the authors experience in the e-learning area. A reference model and reference architecture were identified as previous steps towards the software architecture that supports the conceptual modeling framework.

Acknowledgements

We want to thank Fundación Caixa Galicia-Claudio San Martín, Xunta de Galicia (grant PGIDT00TIC3220PR "Arquitecturas Distribuidas para Teleservicios") and University of Vigo (grant "Infraestructura CORBA para Sistemas de Teleformación").

We also want to thank engineers Diego Conde, Fernando Gómez, Jorge Domínguez and Juan Aguiar for their contribution to the implementation of CORBAlearn.

References

[1] Siegel, J.: CORBA 3 Fundamentals and Programming. Wiley and Sons (1999)
[2] LTSC: Learning Technologies Standardization Committee (2001) WWW site. http://ltsc.ieee.org. Last access July 2th, 2001.
[3] IMS: IMS Global Learning Consortium (2001) WWW site. http://www.imsproject.org. Last access July 2th, 2001.

[4] AICC: Aviation Industry Computer Based Training Committee (2001) WWW site. http://www.aicc.org. Last access July 2th, 2001.
[5] ADL: US Department of Defense, Advanced Distributed Learning (ADL) initiative (2001) WWW site. http://www.adlnet.org. Last access July 2th, 2001.
[6] ARIADNE: The Alliance of Remote Instructional Authoring and Distribution Networks for Europe (2001) WWW site. http://ariadne.unil.ch. Last access July 2th, 2001.
[7] GESTALT: Getting Educational System Talk Across Leading edge Technologies project (2001) WWW site. http://www.fdgroup.co.uk/gestalt. Last access July 2th, 2001.
[8] PROMETEUS: PROmoting Multimedia access to Education and Training in EUropean Society (2001) WWW site. http://prometeus.org. Last access July 2th, 2001.
[9] CEN/ISSS/LT: European Committee for Standardization (CEN), Information Society Standardization Systems (ISSS), Learning Technologies Workshop (LT) (2001) WWW site. http://www.cenorm.be/isss/Workshop/lt/.
[10] GEM: Gateway to Educational Materials (2001) WWW site. http://www.geminfo.org. Last access July 2th, 2001.
[11] ISO/IEC: International Standardization Organization/Institute Electrotechnical Commision Committee for Learning Technologies (ISO/IEC JTC1 SC36) (2001) WWW site. http://www.jtc1sc36.org. Last access July 2th, 2001.
[12] Bray, T., Paoli, J., Maler, E.: Extensible Markup Language. Technical report, W3C (2001) [on-line] http://www.w3.org/TR/2000/REC-xml-20001006.
[13] Jacobson, I., G.Booch, J.Rumbaugh: The Unified Software Development Process. Addison-Wesley (1999)
[14] Jacobson, I., Booch, G., Rumbaugh, J.: The Unified Modelling Language User Guide. Addison Wesley Longman (1999)
[15] Bass, L., Clements, P., Kazman, R.: Software Architecture in Practice. Addison-Wesley (1999)
[16] Tyler, J., Cheikes, B., Farance, F., Tonkel, J.: Draft Standard for Learning Technologies. Learning Technology Systems Architecture (LTSA), Draft 8. Technical report, IEEE Inc. (2001) [on-line]
http://ltsc.ieee.org/doc/wg1/IEEE_1484_01_D08_LTSA.pdf.
[17] OMG: Interoperable Naming Service Specification (2000) [on-line] ftp://ftp.omg.org/pub/docs/formal/00-11-01.pdf.
[18] ACTS: GAIA, Generic Architecture for Information Availability. Technical report, Fretwell-Downing (2000) [on-line]
http://www.infowing.org/ACTS/RUS/PROJECTS/FINAL-REPORTS/fr-221.pdf.
[19] Dodds, P.: ADL Shareable Courseware Object Reference Model (SCORM). Version 1.1. Technical report, Advanced Distributed Learning Initiative (2001) [on-line] http://www.adlnet.org/Scorm/docs/SCORM1.1.zip.

XML-schema Dynamic Mapped Multimedia Content Description Tool

Takayuki Kunieda and Yuki Wakita

Software Research Center, Ricoh Company
Koishikawa 1-1-17 Bunkyo-ku, Tokyo 112-0002, Japan
{kunieda, yuki}@src.ricoh.co.jp

Abstract. MovieTool is a Description tool for multimedia content with XML oriented representation. MovieTool can generate a content description file in the format defined MPEG-7, which is known as the multimedia content description interface. We adopted XML-Schema dynamic mapping mechanisms for the multimedia content description schemes. As a result, MovieTool can provide the flexibility and general versatility for various meta-data standards not only MPEG-7 but also B-XML etc.

1 Introduction

The cumulation of multimedia data has created a strong demand for multimedia archiving systems. Content-based retrieval schemes are being standardized using several different approaches. Progress in storage technology and CPU power enable easy browsing of such multimedia content. However, only a few ways enable searching and selecting contents easily using user-friendly interfaces. Along with the progress in web- and XML-technology, several structure description languages have been proposed (e.g., SMIL, MPEG-7, BXML). MPEG-7 [1], a multimedia-content description interface, was starting to be standardized. We focus on contributing to the standardization process and started to develop the description tool.

2 MovieTool

We have started developing a multimedia-content description tool named MovieTool. MovieTool can read and write MPEG-7 formatted content-description files. First, this tool is used to either manually or automatically construct a structure. It can apply automatic segmentation methods using a content-based analysis. Then, a key frame is selected, content-based features are extracted, and a syntactic structure is generated. After that, attribute values can be input into each segment as well as into the overall content. MovieTool provides many attributes that are defined in MPEG-7 description schemes. It is one component of a multimedia content retrieval system we are developing. In this system, a content description value is registered to a database in an MPEG-7 file. In the easy web interface, attribute values are set as a condition, and then the required scenes or contents are displayed. They can be selected and played in specified order. To develop this system, we adopted XML-Schema dynamic mapping mechanisms for MovieTool.

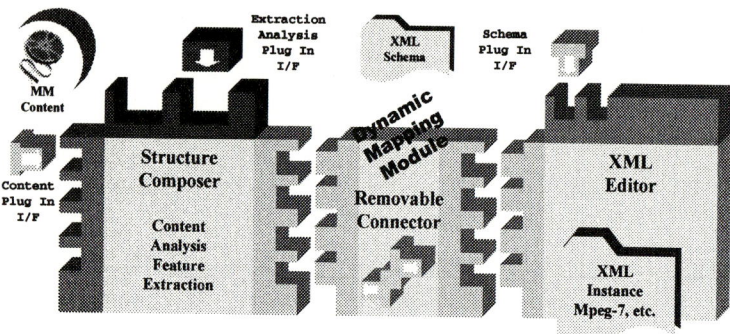

Fig. 1. MovieTool module structure

In MPEG-7 description, the description content is conceptually classified into two parts: syntactic, which is generated automatically or semi-automatically using existing extraction and analysis methods, and semantic, which demands human thought processes. To develop the description tool, the latter must be considered sufficiently. Taking this into account, we strictly separated the functionality of the modules. Figure 1 is a perspective representation of the module structure of MovieTool.

2.1 The Structure Composer

This module builds an audiovisual structure. It can be used manually or automatically, and it can apply some automatic segmentation methods using content-based analysis. A key frame is selected, content-based features are extracted, and a syntactic structure is generated. All data are represented using the package-segment model (PS-Model) [2], [3]. The PS-Model is a data model that principally composed by package and segment nodes. A segment represents a cut, scene, or a logical duration in the content stream. A package plays a role in generalizing a segment set. The PS-Model structure resembles a tree structure. Each node can have an attribute node, which consists of some attributes of the parent node as well as user-defined supplemental information. This module also provides two plug-in interfaces: a content plug-in and an extraction-and-analysis plug-in. Therefore, the user can easily adapt various formatted media and develop a new extraction plug-in module. These functions enable a flexible application.

2.2 The Removable Connector

This module corresponds to meaning of XML-Schema. It provides bridging functions between the XML element and the PS-Model node. This module provides the dynamic mapping mechanism mentioned in the next paragraph for each XML-Schema definition.

2.3 The XML Editor

This module can input and edit body and attribute values in each segment as well as in the overall content. MovieTool provides all elements defined in MPEG-7 description schemes. This editor provides the basic functions for XML editing.

3 Dynamic Mapping

The removable-connector module plays a key role in the dynamic-mapping function. Here, we focus on the dynamic-mapping mechanism between the element defined by the XML-Schema and the node used in the structure-composer module. Figure 2 shows the mapping relations between the MPEG-7 and PS-Model spaces. The temporal decomposition element in MPEG-7 corresponds to the package node in the PS-model and the audio-visual segment corresponds to the segment node. Because these relations can be modularized as a removable connector, the tool can be easily adapted to various schemata.

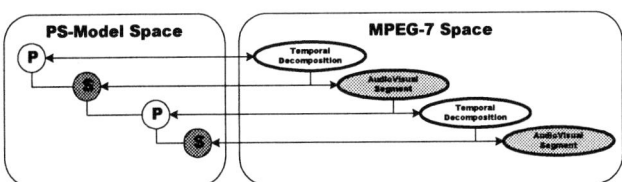

Fig. 2. Sample mapping relation

4 Conclusion

The following window images are real-world tool interfaces. The left window shows the structure composer and the right one the XML editor. In reality, the removable connector is located between them, so the user can seamlessly change from applying automatic analysis to human annotation to describe the content. With the dynamic mapping mechanism, MovieTool provides flexibility and general versatility for use with various meta-data standards, not only in MPEG-7 but also in B-XML, and others. We plan to test these characteristics in the future.

References

1. The MPEG Home Page: http://www.cselt.it/mpeg/
2. Kunieda T. and Wakita Y., "Package-Segment Model for Movie Retrieval System and Adaptable Applications," IEEE International Conference on Multimedia Computing Systems Proceedings," Volume.2, Florence, Italy, June 1999, pages 944-948.
3. Wakita Y., Kunieda T., Takahashi N., Hashimoto T., and Kuboki J., "Extended Package-Segment Model and Adaptable Applications," 6th international Workshop IDMS'99 Proceedings. Toulouse, France, October 1999, pages 163-176.

Constructing a Data Map of Korea Telecom

Eunsook Jin, Jungmin Seo, Kwangjoon Lee, Ju-won Song

Multimedia Research Lab., Korea Telecom,
17 Woomyeon-dong, Seocho-gu, Seoul 137-792, Korea
{ejin, jmseo, kjoon, jwsong}@kt.co.kr

Abstract. Successful business marketing depends on how the information to be maintained, integrated, and extracted from the large scale of data systems. Though CRM, SCM, and ERP are the representative efforts to make relationship between marketing and data, they show low success rates. One of the main reasons is the impetuous processing without enough analysis on the data in order to show the result promptly. Korea Telecom has about 200 information systems that are constructed and maintained separately. Now these independent systems should be integrated as the basis of CRM, SCM, or ERP for the customer-oriented marketing. Constructing a data map that describes the metadata of all information systems and the relationship between systems is the first step of data integration project. We explain the details of the data map and related tool, and describe their effectiveness in this paper.

1. Introduction

Korea Telecom (KT), the leading telecommunication company of Korea, has about 200 information systems. But each system has been developed and maintained separately, so anyone doesn't know exactly which data they have or which information is processed by the other departments. So, systems were integrated one by one whenever they have to be integrated and the integration process was very complex and difficult as well as they were constructed without considering common rules. AS the goal of business is moving more into customers and the amount of data increases rapidly, KT needs to analyze systematically which data it owns, who manages them, their detail characteristics, the relationship with other systems, and so on. Without these kinds of detail and precise analysis, the high-level data integration projects like CRM, ERP, or SCM could not constructed successfully. For too many data systems that are very large, complex, and developed separately, we want to construct a data map that describes the relationship of information systems we own, and provide the detail, precise, and current information of data hidden in each information system for the continual integration process of information systems.

2. Enterprise Data Map (EDM) and Data Map Tool (DMT)

EDM is a kind of roadmap which describes the purpose, functions, architecture, the details of data, and relationships with other systems for each information system in the company. EDM shows information systems using hierarchical layer. At the top layer, EDM shows all the information systems KT has, and inter-relationship (or data flow) between systems using a specific diagramming notation. At the second layer, EDM refines the information provided at the top level both horizontally and vertically. The vertical refinement shows the detail metadata for each system, for example, the objectives, functionality, related staff and departments, description of HW or SW configuration, and so on. In the other hand, the horizontal refinement provides more detail data flow information between two systems. That is, horizontal refinement provides detail description of data that should be transferred, formats and method of transferred data, and a period of data transfer. With these kinds of information, user can analyze side effects of a schema evolution of a specific system. Finally, at the third level, EDM describes the detail schema of system including the type of fields, constraints, index, keys as well as the relationship between entities in a system. In fact, contents of the third layer are included in the logical database design specification that is generated during the system development. But, as we mentioned earlier, each system of KT has been developed by different departments and staff without considering standard, so documents that describes data schema don't provide the reader with common depth of explanation nor common interface. Even, some systems don't have any documentation about data at all. So, it's very important and useful to rearrange the logical database design specification for all the systems with common concept.

All things described above should be retrieved and updated in efficient way. So, we constructed a metadata repository using DMP(Data Map Tool) plays a role in the management of EDM by providing a web-based graphical interface. Any authorized user can view and retrieve any information on EDM from the top layer to the third layer as well as he/she can update the content of EDM whenever the target system is changed. Followings are the main functions of DMP.

- retrieve/update/insert/maintenance of metadata (metadata repository)
- represent/manipulate relationships between systems and entity relationships for each systems
- automatically populate schema related metadata from the schema dump file of source systems, export metadata to Enterprise Data Warehouse of KT
- generate report, provide statistic analysis, analyze side effects of a system component

3. Conclusion

We mentioned the EDM and DMT in this paper. The construction of EDM is very important for KT to promote data oriented business, and we're sure that EDM could be a necessary basis of CRM, ERP, and other projects that need data integration. Our next version of DMT would include version control mechanism.

Competency of Set Analysis in CRM Closed Loop Marketing

Tatsuo Oba

Beacon IT Inc.
Ebisu MF Bldg. #14, 1-6-10 Ebisu Minami, Shibuya-ku, Tokyo150-0022
oba@beacon-it.co.jp

Abstract. Diversification of customer tastes has brought an end to Mass Marketing. In order to increase profits, corporations must urgently put into practice new techniques for CRM (Customer Relationship Management) that improve customer loyalty by strengthening customer relationships. This paper proposes a customer management Data Warehouse model design based on TimeCube and the application of Set Theory technology to develop a new technique for closed loop marketing (Hypotheses and Verification).

1 Customer Management Model in CRM

The goal of Customer Relationship Management (CRM) is to establish an ongoing relationship between a corporation and its customers. In order to have a good relationship with its customers, a corporation must first understand its customers. This can be achieved by gathering customer data and storing it in a Data Warehouse. Generally data is stored in a customer attribute table and a purchase transaction table (2-dimensional tables) within a relational database and queries are made using SQL. The customer attribute table is usually updated to store the last value, while data is simply appended to the purchase transaction table.

In order to achieve real CRM and create long lasting relationships with customers, it is necessary for a company to observe and act according to how the customer's attributes and buying habits are changing over time. Faux pas, such as sending a credit card upgrade offer to a customer who recently upgraded or sending discount coupons to a customer who recently paid full price, should not occur. It is critical that the customer's attribute history and past purchase characteristics are analyzed in assessing his current status.

2 TimeCube Data Model

Within the TimeCube system, developed by Beacon IT, Japan, customer data is stored in 3-dimensional cubes. The 2-dimensional table from relational databases is augmented with a time axis to create a logical 3-dimensional model for storing data. For each unique customer, data is stored along the time axis for all attributes. Whenever there is a change to an attribute, a history record is created of the previous attribute value and so on all the way from the first value. Similarly customers purchase transaction data is also stored as records along a time axis. For each of these record types timestamps are very important.

In addition to storing data sequentially along the time axis, TimeCube also creates specialized indices. Consider customer attributes such as rank and preferred shopping location. These not only indicate a fact at a point of time but also a state of being that exists for a period of time. This type of data with continuous states is stored and indexed by the TimeCube system in a 3-dimensional Profile Cube. Now, queries like *"Find all customers with rank A for more than 6 months?"* or *"Find all customers that have changed address within the last two weeks?"* can be easily created and executed. Purchase transaction records, which reflect facts at a point of time, are stored by customer in a 3-Dimensional Transaction Cube. This functionality of storing transaction data is called "Cubed Transac-tion."

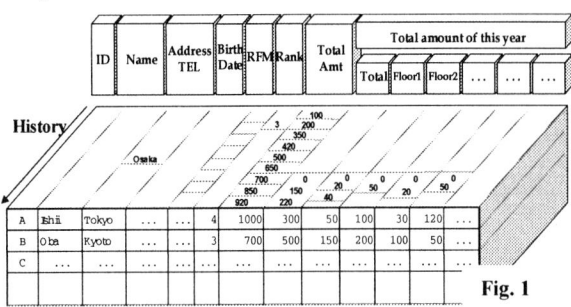

Fig. 1

Each cube can store between several hundred thousand to ten million customers. Customer attribute data does not change frequently and usually has only an average of a dozen histories while customers' purchase behavior data such as click-through data on an e-commerce site can be more than thousands of records for each customer. Several million customer records are thus stored physically in two cubes, although users can access it as if from one cube using a combined view. While the "join" method is applied to combine cubes using, say, Customer ID, a unique method named "connect" is available to combine cubes using the timestamp and Customer ID.

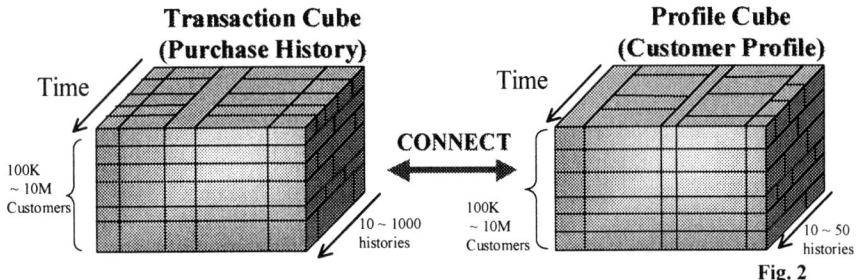

Fig. 2

3 CRM Closed Loop Marketing (Hypotheses and Verification) and Set Theory

A customer information Data Warehouse is built, as shown in Fig.2, to explain CRM using TimeCube. Firstly, it is necessary to clearly identify, *"Who are the current good customers?," "Who were the good customers in the past?," "Who are the target for our newly released product?"* and so on. In the present day, where everything changes so rapidly, sales revenues do not increase by conducting only a single sales promotion and it does not lead to a deep relationship with customers at all. To develop an effective sales promotion plan, it is necessary to find customers who can be the target for the plan from the Data Warehouse, and make a "hypothesis" such as *"These customers will purchase the product if we approach in a particular way"* and quickly take action. Once the action is taken, we "verify" the results of the action and establish a cycle of taking account of the verification results for our next hypothesis. Fig.3 shows an example of this "Closed Loop Marketing" for a wine sales promotion.

For example, when we send an email to customers, we need to think about the timing, to whom, and the contents of the mail. These issues form the "hypotheses" in the closed loop marketing. It is possible to identify "What kind of customers" and "the timing" only if the attributes and purchase histories of customers are stored along the time axis. TimeCube uses Set Theory concepts to identifying customers and users can easily find their target customers with set operations. It also enables users to save the so obtained customer groups as sets and use them for the results verification of the sales promotion activities to customers

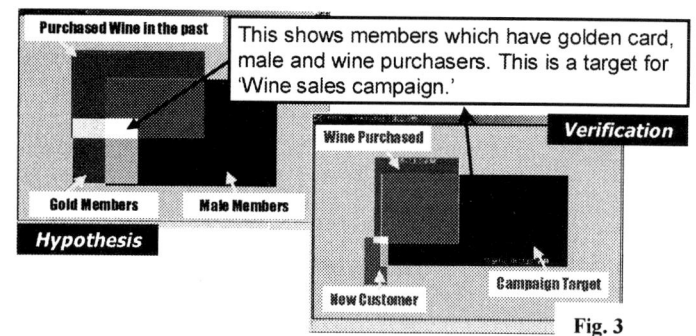

Fig. 3

As compared to an SQL statement that returns only one result set for each search condition, the Set Operation shown here is much more suitable to One-to-One marketing. For example, when we create and display three sets, "Age," "City" and "Purchase Amount," we see eight sets from the overlapping Sets. Refer to Fig.4. We obtain eight customer groups at one time and can realize One-to-One marketing by changing the approach to each customer group. With SQL, eight different statements would need to be written and executed.

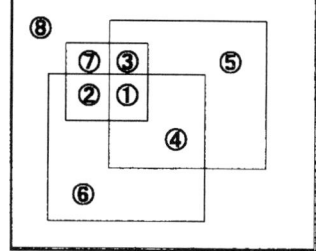

4 Conclusion

Fig. 4

In the customer management model using TimeCube system, data of customer attributes and purchase behaviors are stored respectively in different cubes. Queries related to time are executed at a very high speed due to the Time Index and adopting a new method, "connect" instead of "join". Furthermore, concepts of Set Theory are employed; using which each customer is regarded as an element of a Set and Set operations are conducted to segment customers for One-to-One marketing. In comparison to relational databases, these are the benefits of TimeCube. However, the TimeCube system does not support SQL Extension or TSQL and is not a standard approach.

A dozen corporations in Japan are using the TimeCube system. In Company A, salesmen make hypotheses utilizing Set Operations on their customer information, and use them for their sales activities in order to find target customers. In Company B, data on their customer corporations are managed as an ASP and they have started to provide an application to use this customer information via internet.

XML-based E2E Test Report Management

Ray Paul

Department of Defense, Washington, DC 20016

Wei-Tek Tsai, Bing Li, Xiaoying Bai

Department of Computer Science and Engineering
Arizona State University, Tempe, AZ 85287

Abstract. This paper presents an XML-based test report management system for end-to-end (E2E) integration testing. This system allows test engineers at different sites using different platforms to collaborate and exchange testing effort by using XML-based communication. The system also supports report creation, storage, search, version management, and project management.

1 Introduction

Testing especially integration testing has been a serious challenge for system development. To address this problem, the U.S. Department of Defense (DoD) recently proposed an End-to-End (E2E) testing process to test an integrated system [DoD 2001, Tsai 2001a, Tsai 2001b]. This E2E testing and addresses test specifications, test case generation, risk analysis, regression testing [Tsai 2001b], ripple effect analysis, test schedules, test planning, and test result analysis. We developed a web-based system to support the E2E testing [Bai 2001]. This paper focuses on test report management in the testing tool using XML. Test data include test specifications, design, results, and reports.

The class diagram of test assets in the E2E tool can be interchanged through XML. Using XML, engineers can share and exchange test assets independent of any machine platforms. Tools and repositories that need to exchange metadata do not need to implement a new API, which can be expensive, or to re-host to a new repository, which can be costly too. They need to provide only an XML export and import facility.

2 XML-based Reporting Subsystem

Figure 1 shows the architecture of the test report subsystem. On the client side, Report Format Customizer and Report Query Customizer accept users' requests, and Report Specification Generator generates specifications of the requests. On the server side, Report Generator, in Application Server, accepts requests from clients, and generates reports based on data stored in the test asset database, Web Server publishes reports and enables users to remote access reports through web-browsers; Report Builder periodically generating reports to ensure that reports are current, Report Analyzer compares different reports and generates analysis reports.

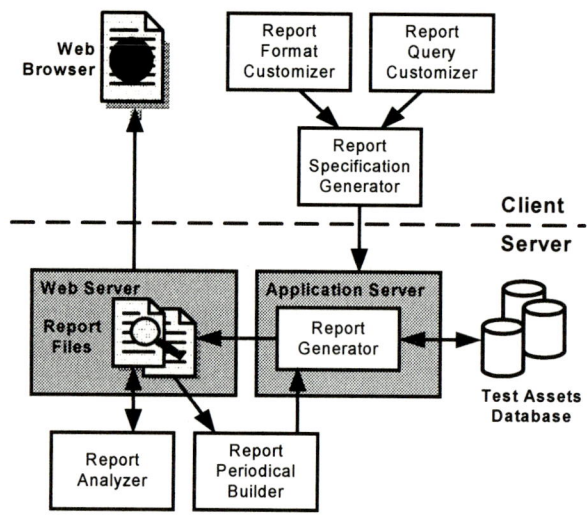

Figure 1 Structure of Test Report Subsystem

The main issue in test report management is that report definitions are highly dynamic and change often. Users may define different report structures by selecting various combinations of assets and asset attributes. They may also define different report representations. Traditionally, each test report must be coded individually. In this way, one must repeat work such as designing database structures and storage. This is costly. Our test report subsystem avoids this problem. When one needs a new test report, the only thing to do is to describe the new report's model in DTDs and submit the DTDs into the subsystem. No additional programming is needed, and all the relevant design work such as creation, searching and storage management can be reused.

References

1. [Bai 2001] X. Bai, W. T. Tsai, Ray Paul, Ke Feng, and Lian Yu, "Distributed End-To-End Test Management", to appear in Proc. of IEEE EDOC, 2001.
2. [DOD 2001] DoD OASD C3I Investment and Acquisition, "End-to-End Integration Testing Guidebook", 2001.
3. [Tsai 2001a] W.T. Tsai, X. Bai, R. Paul, W. Shao, V. Agarwal, T. Sheng, and B. Li, "End-to-End Integration Testing Design", to appear in Proc. of IEEE COMPSAC, 2001.
4. [Tsai 2001b] W.T. Tsai, X. Bai, R. Paul, and L. Yu, "Scenario-Based Functional Regression Testing", to appear in Proc. of IEEE COMPSAC, 2001.
5. [Tsai 2000] W.T. Tsai, X. Bai, B. Huang, G. Devaraj, and R. Paul, "Automatic Test Case Generation for GUI Navigation", in The Thirteenth International Software & Internet Quality Week, 2000.

A Framework for Reusing Business Objects by Multilevel Object Patterns

Hajime Horiuchi[1], Masaharu Obayashi[2], and Yoshihide Nagase[3]

[1] Tokyo International University
1-13-1 Matobakita, kawagoe, Saitama, 350-1197 Japan
hori@tiu.ac.jp, http://www.cbop.gr.jp

[2] Kanrikougaku Kenkyusho Co., ltd.
Meguro Suda Bldg., 3-9-1 Meguro, Meguro-ku, Tokyo 153-0063, Japan
obayashi@kthree.co.jp, http://www.kthree.co.jp

[3] Technologic Arts Co., Ltd.
4-1-4 Hongou, Bunkyou-ku, Tokyo, 113-0033 Japan
yoshi@tech-arts.co.jp, http://www.tech-arts.co.jp

Abstract. This paper deals with the multilayered object pattern technologies (BFOP) for sharing business objects among different organizations that were standardized by a consortium named *"Consortium for Business Object Promotion (CBOP)"* in Japan.

1 Introduction

CBOP (Consortium for Business Object Promotion) was formulated on December 1, 1997, by 27 companies, to standardize common bases for the sharing and exchanging of Business Objects. As a product of activities, a set of object patterns, named *BFOP (Business Function Object Patterns)*, were standardized and provided to the development of object models in various business areas domains.

2 BFOP Pattern Principle

To improve the share-ability of domain-specific object models, there must be common bases, which consist of normative objects and patterns to be applied when it is necessary for some business semantics to be represented. Following are the design principles which were considered during the BFOP development.
- The model must be defined using predefined normative modeling constructs.
- Predefined modeling constructs should include common atomic objects, such as, Date, Currency, Country-code, which are needless to be discussed when they are used

- Common aggregated objects, such as Customer, Company, or Order, which represent business entities, also should be predefined as normative modeling constructs. They should be defined using the normative atomic objects.
- Business concepts, such as, Trade or Invoice, which are represented by relationships, should be defined as aggregations of common elementary objects and/or aggregated objects. They must be predefined as normative modeling constructs.
- The aggregations could be defined as object patterns, which can be predefined using basic and elementary patterns as the base.
- Patterns can represent business concepts with the aggregation of elementary patterns. Therefore, the aggregation mechanism of patterns must be provided.
- Business rules should be represented as constraints to be encapsulated in patterns. Therefore, the mechanism for constraint inheritance among patterns must be provided.

3 Pattern Hierarchy in BFOP

The BFOP consists of more than three layers of object patterns. At the lowest layer, elementary patterns are specified to be used in materialization of upper layer patterns. The elementary patterns, such as "Role" provide a facility to keep consistency among modeling constructs by requiring that an object should be defined using pre-existing normative objects. This implies that nobody can ignore pre-existing objects. The multilayered patterns could bring the effectiveness in reusing constraints or rules to be applied to a composite object pattern. Elementary object patterns also provide means to examine the commonalities among composite patterns when they are compared.

4 BFOP and UML Tools

In representing an aggregation (synthesis) of object patterns, *the parametric collaboration notation,* which was proposed to UML1.4, was used. In August 1998, CBOP submitted a proposal on BFOP to OMG to cope with their RFP "UML profile for EDOC". At the end of March 2001, a project in CBOP finished the development of a tool which enables the BFOP manipulation, such as integration and unfolding of patterns through the graphical interface. This tool is expected to improve share-ability of object models by the guiding use of BFOP and by the automated inheriting mechanism of business constraints embedded in patterns. CBOP is now preparing a common registry which enables the registering and exchanging of business domain models and domain specific object patterns to accumulate through the experiences of BFOP applications.

A Mediation System Based on Universal Relation Modeling

Takashi Honishi, Gengo Suzuki, Nobuyuki Kobayashi, and Kazuya Konishi

NTT Cyber Space Laboratories, NTT Corporation
1-1 Hikari-no-oka, Yokosuka-Shi, Kanagawa, 239-0847 Japan
{honishi, gsuzuki, kobayasi, koni}@dq.isl.ntt.co.jp

Abstract. The explosive spread of the Internet in recent years has made it possible to access a huge number of information sources. These sources include web home pages, relational databases, image databases and so on. To enable these information sources to be utilized to the fullest extent, it is necessary to integrate these into identical data structures and user interfaces. This paper proposes the information integration system called MediPresto/M, which was designed based on a mediation architecture and universal relation model. Using some real applications, we demonstrate the advantages of this system.

1 Introduction

Various methods of integrating information sources have been tried to efficiently access sources in open network environments. Two typical methods of integrating information sources have been tried so far. One is the federated database architecture [1] based on an integrated schema (or global schema), and the other is the mediation architecture [2]. The former enables users to access many kinds of information sources through an identical schema, but making the integrated schema is extremely difficult.

As a means of enabling huge information sources in the Internet environment to be searched efficiently and usefully, we have developed an information source integration system based on the mediation architecture, which does not need integrated schema.

2 Proposed Method and System Outline

To integrate many kinds of information sources, it is necessary to resolve the schema and value differences between them. Typical differences are as follows.

(1) Differences in schema structures. In information sources, schema structures must be defined in terms of relation (RDB) or as a tree structure (XML, HTML).

(2) Differences in schema definition names. Information sources normally have structured items, and item names are different in each individual system.

(3) Data range differences. Information source data items may have different values even for items with identical meaning. For example, the price of an item may be given as "1000 yen", "59.48 F", or "$ 8.05"; all represent the same notional value.

As a means of addressing the problems created by differences among information sources, we have developed the mediation system called "MediPresto/M". The primary feature of our system is that it is designed around a mediator architecture [2] and has a universal relation as the user interface [3]. The universal relation can treat the structure of information sources as one relation that constructs a set of data items. Users can treat many different information sources having complicated structures as one relation. This enables them to obtain results through simple queries to the universal relation. This system can execute queries over heterogeneous information sources by making use of rules. The rules are mapped between each source, RDB, Web, XML, Image Database, and so on, and the universal relation. Even though the mapping rules are prepared by system designers in advance, they consist of just the definitions needed to retrieve data items relevant to the universal relation.

3 Application

We evaluated the efficacy of our system through the use of a prototype that integrated a number of databases. The original information sources consisted of five types of databases with a total of 25 tables and 627 items. We found that by using our system, the man hours needed to create integrated schemas were reduced to about 1/8 [3] of those needed when the system was not used. Our system was used for a number of actual integrated information retrieval services. For example, it was applied in one of the information retrieval services of the Integrated Multi-Archiving Service (IMAS) in the Waseda University Library [4]. In this application, users were able to execute retrieval across 10 integrated information sources on a network in real time (on the order of several seconds) [5]. In addition, our system is being used in a number of actual integrated information retrieval services such as hospital information services, public information services and so on.

In many cases, users wanted to use our mediator system to request updates via the universal relation interface. Regrettably we have not yet formulated a good approach to answering such requests, and a primary objective in future work will be to develop a suitable method for doing so through the use of the mediator architecture system.

References

1. A.P.Sheth, J.A.Larson: Federated Database Systems for Managing Distributed, Heterogeneous, and Autonomous Database. ACM Computing Surveys, Vol.22. No.3. (1990) 183-236
2. G.Wiederhold: Mediators in the Architecture of Future Information Systems. IEEE Computer, Vol.25. No3. (1992) 38-49
3. T. Ikeda, G. Suzuki, H. Machihara, H. Yasuda: An Approach to Schema Construction in Federated Database Systems. IPSJ, Vol.40. No.SIG8 (TOD4). (1999) 29-40 (in Japanese).
4. http://www.wul.waseda.ac.jp/index.html
5. http://sena.wul.waseda.ac.jp

Author Index

Acharya, Biswajit, 499
Akoka, Jacky, 442
Anido, Luis, 585

Bai, Xiaoying, 607
Behr, Thomas, 56
Bekiari, Chryssoyla, 412
Berti-Equille, Laure, 256
Bussler, Christoph, 26

Caeiro, Manuel, 585
Calì, Andrea, 270
Calvanese, Diego, 270
Chen, Qiming, 1
Chiu, Dickson K.W., 541
Comyn-Wattiau, Isabelle, 442
Costal, Dolors, 397

Dalamagas, Theodore, 325
Dani, Ajay R., 193
Dayal, Umeshwar, 1
De Giacomo, Giuseppe, 270
Detienne, Virginie, 208
Doerr, Martin, 412
Düsterhöft, Antje, 179

Embley, David W., 426, 555
Enoki, Kei-ichi, 17
Evermann, Joerg, 354

Fernandes, Alvaro A.A., 84
Fernández, Manuel J., 585
Fiddian, Nicholas J., 225

Gray, William A., 225
Griffiths, Tony, 84

Hainaut, Jean-Luc, 208
Hartmann, Sven, 241
Heuser, Carlos Alberto, 133
Hirose, Tatsuo, 485
Hong, Seokjin, 299
Honishi, Takashi, 611
Horiuchi, Hajime, 609
Hsu, Meichun, 1

Huang, Bo, 84
Hwang, Yousub, 70

Ishikawa, Yoshiharu, 41

Jensen, Christian S., 27
Jin, Eunsook, 602

Kambayashi, Yahiko, 285
Karlapalem, Kamalakar, 193
Khatri, Vijay, 70
Kitagawa, Hiroyuki, 41
Kobayashi, Nobuyuki, 611
Konishi, Kazuya, 611
Kraft, Peter, 383
Krishna, P. Radha, 193
Kunieda, Takayuki, 599

Lbath, Ahmed, 339
Lee, Dongwon, 149
Lee, Kwangjoon, 602
Lee, Sukho, 299
Lenzerini, Maurizio, 270
Lepper, Markus, 456
Li, Bing, 607
Li, Ying, 164
Liu, Lin, 164
Llamas, Martín, 585

Majumdar, Arun K., 499
Mani, Murali, 149
Mason, Keith T., 84
Mello, Ronaldo dos Santos, 133
Mok, Wai Y., 426
Mukherjee, Jayanta, 499
Muntz, Richard. R., 149
Mylopoulos, John, 117

Nagase, Yoshihide, 609
Nakanishi, Yoshihiro, 485
Ng, Yiu-Kai, 555

Oba, Tatsuo, 604
Obayashi, Masaharu, 609
Olivé, Antoni, 397
Orlowska, Maria, 513

Paton, Norman W., 84
Paul, Ray, 607
Peng, Zhiyong, 285
Pernul, Günther, 311
Pinet, François, 339
Plexousakis, Dimitris, 412
Prat, Nicolas, 442
Price, Rosanne, 27
Priebe, Torsten, 311

Ralyté, Jolita, 471
Ram, Sudha, 70
Rodríguez, Judith, 585
Rodríguez-Gianolli, Patricia, 117
Rolland, Colette, 471

Sadiq, Shazia, 513
Sadiq, Wasim, 513
Santos, Juan, 585
Schewe, Klaus-Dieter, 571
Schneider, Markus, 56, 103
Seo, Jungmin, 602
Simitsis, Alkis, 325
Snodgrass, Richard T., 70
Song, Byoungho, 299
Song, Il-Yeol, 368

Song, Ju-won, 602
Sørensen, Jens Otto, 383
Stavropoulos, Manos, 325
Suzuki, Gengo, 611

Tanaka, Katsumi, 485
Taveter, Kuldar, 527
Tawil, Abdel-Rahman H., 225
Teniente, Ernest, 397
Thalheim, Bernhard, 179
Theodoratos, Dimitri, 325
Trancón y Widemann, Baltasar, 456
Tryfona, Nectaria, 27
Tsai, Wei-Tek, 607
Tsichritzis, Dennis, 19

Wagner, Gerd, 527
Wakita, Yuki, 599
Wand, Yair, 354
Wieland, Jacob, 456
Worboys, Michael, 84

Xu, Li, 555

Yu, Eric, 164

Lecture Notes in Computer Science

For information about Vols. 1–2144
please contact your bookseller or Springer-Verlag

Vol. 2122: H. Alt (Ed.), Computational Discrete Mathematics. VII, 173 pages. 2001.

Vol. 2145: M. Leyton, A Generative Theory of Shape. XVI, 554 pages. 2001.

Vol. 2146: J.H. Silverman (Eds.), Cryptography and Lattices. Proceedings, 2001. VII, 219 pages. 2001.

Vol. 2147: G. Brebner, R. Woods (Eds.), Field-Programmable Logic and Applications. Proceedings, 2001. XV, 665 pages. 2001.

Vol. 2149: O. Gascuel, B.M.E. Moret (Eds.), Algorithms in Bioinformatics. Proceedings, 2001. X, 307 pages. 2001.

Vol. 2150: R. Sakellariou, J. Keane, J. Gurd, L. Freeman (Eds.), Euro-Par 2001 Parallel Processing. Proceedings, 2001. XXX, 943 pages. 2001.

Vol. 2151: A. Caplinskas, J. Eder (Eds.), Advances in Databases and Information Systems. Proceedings, 2001. XIII, 381 pages. 2001.

Vol. 2152: R.J. Boulton, P.B. Jackson (Eds.), Theorem Proving in Higher Order Logics. Proceedings, 2001. X, 395 pages. 2001.

Vol. 2153: A.L. Buchsbaum, J. Snoeyink (Eds.), Algorithm Engineering and Experimentation. Proceedings, 2001. VIII, 231 pages. 2001.

Vol. 2154: K.G. Larsen, M. Nielsen (Eds.), CONCUR 2001 – Concurrency Theory. Proceedings, 2001. XI, 583 pages. 2001.

Vol. 2155: H. Bunt, R.-J. Beun (Eds.), Cooperative Multimodal Communication. Proceedings, 1998. VIII, 251 pages. 2001. (Subseries LNAI).

Vol. 2156: M.I. Smirnov, J. Crowcroft, J. Roberts, F.Boavida (Eds.), Quality of Future Internet Services. Proceedings, 2001. XI, 333 pages. 2001.

Vol. 2157: C. Rouveirol, M. Sebag (Eds.), Inductive Logic Programming. Proceedings, 2001. X, 261 pages. 2001. (Subseries LNAI).

Vol. 2158: D. Shepherd, J. Finney, L. Mathy, N. Race (Eds.), Interactive Distributed Multimedia Systems. Proceedings, 2001. XIII, 258 pages. 2001.

Vol. 2159: J. Kelemen, P. Sosík (Eds.), Advances in Artificial Life. Proceedings, 2001. XIX, 724 pages. 2001. (Subseries LNAI).

Vol. 2161: F. Meyer auf der Heide (Ed.), Algorithms – ESA 2001. Proceedings, 2001. XII, 538 pages. 2001.

Vol. 2162: Ç. K. Koç, D. Naccache, C. Paar (Eds.), Cryptographic Hardware and Embedded Systems – CHES 2001. Proceedings, 2001. XIV, 411 pages. 2001.

Vol. 2163: P. Constantopoulos, I.T. Sølvberg (Eds.), Research and Advanced Technology for Digital Libraries. Proceedings, 2001. XII, 462 pages. 2001.

Vol. 2164: S. Pierre, R. Glitho (Eds.), Mobile Agents for Telecommunication Applications. Proceedings, 2001. XI, 292 pages. 2001.

Vol. 2165: L. de Alfaro, S. Gilmore (Eds.), Process Algebra and Probabilistic Methods. Proceedings, 2001. XII, 217 pages. 2001.

Vol. 2166: V. Matoušek, P. Mautner, R. Mouček, K. Tauser (Eds.), Text, Speech and Dialogue. Proceedings, 2001. XIII, 452 pages. 2001. (Subseries LNAI).

Vol. 2167: L. De Raedt, P. Flach (Eds.), Machine Learning: ECML 2001. Proceedings, 2001. XVII, 618 pages. 2001. (Subseries LNAI).

Vol. 2168: L. De Raedt, A. Siebes (Eds.), Principles of Data Mining and Knowledge Discovery. Proceedings, 2001. XVII, 510 pages. 2001. (Subseries LNAI).

Vol. 2169: M. Jaedicke, New Concepts for Parallel Object-Relational Query Processing. XI, 161 pages. 2001.

Vol. 2170: S. Palazzo (Ed.), Evolutionary Trends of the Internet. Proceedings, 2001. XIII, 722 pages. 2001.

Vol. 2171: R. Focardi, R. Gorrieri (Eds.), Foundations of Security Analysis and Design. VII, 397 pages. 2001.

Vol. 2172: C. Batini, F. Giunchiglia, P. Giorgini, M. Mecella (Eds.), Cooperative Information Systems. Proceedings, 2001. XI, 450 pages. 2001.

Vol. 2173: T. Eiter, W. Faber, M. Truszczynski (Eds.), Logic Programming and Nonmonotonic Reasoning. Proceedings, 2001. XI, 444 pages. 2001. (Subseries LNAI).

Vol. 2174: F. Baader, G. Brewka, T. Eiter (Eds.), KI 2001: Advances in Artificial Intelligence. Proceedings, 2001. XIII, 471 pages. 2001. (Subseries LNAI).

Vol. 2175: F. Esposito (Ed.), AI*IA 2001: Advances in Artificial Intelligence. Proceedings, 2001. XII, 396 pages. 2001. (Subseries LNAI).

Vol. 2176: K.-D. Althoff, R.L. Feldmann, W. Müller (Eds.), Advances in Learning Software Organizations. Proceedings, 2001. XI, 241 pages. 2001.

Vol. 2177: G. Butler, S. Jarzabek (Eds.), Generative and Component-Based Software Engineering. Proceedings, 2001. X, 203 pages. 2001.

Vol. 2180: J. Welch (Ed.), Distributed Computing. Proceedings, 2001. X, 343 pages. 2001.

Vol. 2181: C. Y. Westort (Ed.), Digital Earth Moving. Proceedings, 2001. XII, 117 pages. 2001.

Vol. 2182: M. Klusch, F. Zambonelli (Eds.), Cooperative Information Agents V. Proceedings, 2001. XII, 288 pages. 2001. (Subseries LNAI).

Vol. 2183: R. Kahle, P. Schroeder-Heister, R. Stärk (Eds.), Proof Theory in Computer Science. Proceedings, 2001. IX, 239 pages. 2001.

Vol. 2184: M. Tucci (Ed.), Multimedia Databases and Image Communication. Proceedings, 2001. X, 225 pages. 2001.

Vol. 2185: M. Gogolla, C. Kobryn (Eds.), «UML» 2001 – The Unified Modeling Language. Proceedings, 2001. XIV, 510 pages. 2001.

Vol. 2186: J. Bosch (Ed.), Generative and Component-Based Software Engineering. Proceedings, 2001. VIII, 177 pages. 2001.

Vol. 2187: U. Voges (Ed.), Computer Safety, Reliability and Security. Proceedings, 2001. XVI, 249 pages. 2001.

Vol. 2188: F. Bomarius, S. Komi-Sirviö (Eds.), Product Focused Software Process Improvement. Proceedings, 2001. XI, 382 pages. 2001.

Vol. 2189: F. Hoffmann, D.J. Hand, N. Adams, D. Fisher, G. Guimaraes (Eds.), Advances in Intelligent Data Analysis. Proceedings, 2001. XII, 384 pages. 2001.

Vol. 2190: A. de Antonio, R. Aylett, D. Ballin (Eds.), Intelligent Virtual Agents. Proceedings, 2001. VIII, 245 pages. 2001. (Subseries LNAI).

Vol. 2191: B. Radig, S. Florczyk (Eds.), Pattern Recognition. Proceedings, 2001. XVI, 452 pages. 2001.

Vol. 2192: A. Yonezawa, S. Matsuoka (Eds.), Metalevel Architectures and Separation of Crosscutting Concerns. Proceedings, 2001. XI, 283 pages. 2001.

Vol. 2193: F. Casati, D. Georgakopoulos, M.-C. Shan (Eds.), Technologies for E-Services. Proceedings, 2001. X, 213 pages. 2001.

Vol. 2194: A.K. Datta, T. Herman (Eds.), Self-Stabilizing Systems. Proceedings, 2001. VII, 229 pages. 2001.

Vol. 2195: H.-Y. Shum, M. Liao, S.-F. Chang (Eds.), Advances in Multimedia Information Processing – PCM 2001. Proceedings, 2001. XX, 1149 pages. 2001.

Vol. 2196: W. Taha (Ed.), Semantics, Applications, and Implementation of Program Generation. Proceedings, 2001. X, 219 pages. 2001.

Vol. 2197: O. Balet, G. Subsol, P. Torguet (Eds.), Virtual Storytelling. Proceedings, 2001. XI, 213 pages. 2001.

Vol. 2198: N. Zhong, Y. Yao, J. Liu, S. Ohsuga (Eds.), Web Intelligence: Research and Development. Proceedings, 2001. XVI, 615 pages. 2001. (Subseries LNAI).

Vol. 2199: J. Crespo, V. Maojo, F. Martin (Eds.), Medical Data Analysis. Proceedings, 2001. X, 311 pages. 2001.

Vol. 2200: G.I. Davida, Y. Frankel (Eds.), Information Security. Proceedings, 2001. XIII, 554 pages. 2001.

Vol. 2201: G.D. Abowd, B. Brumitt, S. Shafer (Eds.), Ubicomp 2001: Ubiquitous Computing. Proceedings, 2001. XIII, 372 pages. 2001.

Vol. 2202: A. Restivo, S. Ronchi Della Rocca, L. Roversi (Eds.), Theoretical Computer Science. Proceedings, 2001. XI, 440 pages. 2001.

Vol. 2204: A. Brandstädt, V.B. Le (Eds.), Graph-Theoretic Concepts in Computer Science. Proceedings, 2001. X, 329 pages. 2001.

Vol. 2205: D.R. Montello (Ed.), Spatial Information Theory. Proceedings, 2001. XIV, 503 pages. 2001.

Vol. 2206: B. Reusch (Ed.), Computational Intelligence. Proceedings, 2001. XVII, 1003 pages. 2001.

Vol. 2207: I.W. Marshall, S. Nettles, N. Wakamiya (Eds.), Active Networks. Proceedings, 2001. IX, 165 pages. 2001.

Vol. 2208: W.J. Niessen, M.A. Viergever (Eds.), Medical Image Computing and Computer-Assisted Intervention – MICCAI 2001. Proceedings, 2001. XXXV, 1446 pages. 2001.

Vol. 2209: W. Jonker (Ed.), Databases in Telecommunications II. Proceedings, 2001. VII, 179 pages. 2001.

Vol. 2210: Y. Liu, K. Tanaka, M. Iwata, T. Higuchi, M. Yasunaga (Eds.), Evolvable Systems: From Biology to Hardware. Proceedings, 2001. XI, 341 pages. 2001.

Vol. 2211: T.A. Henzinger, C.M. Kirsch (Eds.), Embedded Software. Proceedings, 2001. IX, 504 pages. 2001.

Vol. 2212: W. Lee, L. Mé, A. Wespi (Eds.), Recent Advances in Intrusion Detection. Proceedings, 2001. X, 205 pages. 2001.

Vol. 2213: M.J. van Sinderen, L.J.M. Nieuwenhuis (Eds.), Protocols for Multimedia Systems. Proceedings, 2001. XII, 239 pages. 2001.

Vol. 2214: O. Boldt, H. Jürgensen (Eds.), Automata Implementation. Proceedings, 1999. VIII, 183 pages. 2001.

Vol. 2215: N. Kobayashi, B.C. Pierce (Eds.), Theoretical Aspects of Computer Software. Proceedings, 2001. XV, 561 pages. 2001.

Vol. 2216: E.S. Al-Shaer, G. Pacifici (Eds.), Management of Multimedia on the Internet. Proceedings, 2001. XIV, 373 pages. 2001.

Vol. 2217: T. Gomi (Ed.), Evolutionary Robotics. Proceedings, 2001. XI, 139 pages. 2001.

Vol. 2218: R. Guerraoui (Ed.), Middleware 2001. Proceedings, 2001. XIII, 395 pages. 2001.

Vol. 2220: C. Johnson (Ed.), Interactive Systems. Proceedings, 2001. XII, 219 pages. 2001.

Vol. 2221: D.G. Feitelson, L. Rudolph (Eds.), Job Scheduling Strategies for Parallel Processing. Proceedings, 2001. VII, 207 pages. 2001.

Vol. 2224: H.S. Kunii, S. Jajodia, A. Sølvberg (Eds.), Conceptual Modeling – ER 2001. Proceedings, 2001. XIX, 614 pages. 2001.

Vol. 2225: N. Abe, R. Khardon, T. Zeugmann (Eds.), Algorithmic Learning Theory. Proceedings, 2001. XI, 379 pages. 2001. (Subseries LNAI).

Vol. 2229: S. Qing, T. Okamoto, J. Zhou (Eds.), Information and Communications Security. Proceedings, 2001. XIV, 504 pages. 2001.

Vol. 2230: T. Katila, I.E. Magnin, P. Clarysse, J. Montagnat, J. Nenonen (Eds.), Functional Imaging and Modeling of the Heart. Proceedings, 2001. XI, 158 pages. 2001.

Vol. 2232: L. Fiege, G. Mühl, U. Wilhelm (Eds.), Electronic Commerce. Proceedings, 2001. X, 233 pages. 2001.

Vol. 2233: J. Crowcroft, M. Hofmann (Eds.), Networked Group Communication. Proceedings, 2001. X, 205 pages. 2001.

Vol. 2239: T. Walsh (Ed.), Principles and Practice of Constraint Programming – CP 2001. Proceedings, 2001. XIV, 788 pages. 2001.

Vol. 2241: M. Jünger, D. Naddef (Eds.), Computational Combinatorial Optimization. IX, 305 pages. 2001.

Lecture Notes in Computer Science 2224
Edited by G. Goos, J. Hartmanis, and J. van Leeuwen

Springer
*Berlin
Heidelberg
New York
Barcelona
Hong Kong
London
Milan
Paris
Tokyo*